SHURLEY ENGLISH

English Made Easy

Student Textbook Level 5

06-07
ISBN 978-1-58561-101-0 (Level 5 Student Textbook)

For additional information or to place an order, write to: Shurley Instructional Materials, Inc.
366 SIM Drive
Cabot, AR 72023

1 07

Table of Contents

SHURLEY ENGLISH

Student Textbook

Level 5

CHAPTER 1

CHAPTER 2

Table of Contents

CHAPTER 4

Table of Contents

CHAPTER 6

CHAPTER 7

CHAPTER 8

CHAPTER 9

CHAPTER 10

Table of Contents

CHAPTER 11

CHAPTER 12

CHAPTER 13

Table of Contents

CHAPTER 18

CHAPTER 19

Table of Contents

PRETEST TIME

As you begin a new year, it is important for you to evaluate what you know about grammar, mechanics, usage, editing, and writing by taking a pretest. Later in the school year, you will take a posttest. Then, you will be able to compare the pretest and posttest to tell how much you have learned in English.

Lesson 1

You will
- take pretest.
- write goals.
- do a Goal Book activity.

GOALS

Learn It: SETTING GOALS

In order to make the most of your time, setting goals is important. Goals will keep you pointed in the direction you want to go, will focus your efforts, and will keep you on track. With a list of goals, you can check your progress. Long-term goals are what you want to accomplish in life, usually focused on your education and your career. Short-term goals will help you plan for a week or a month at a time. Getting organized and setting aside study time are always important short-term goals because they help you achieve your long-term goals.

Examples of Goals for a Fifth-Grade Student

Long-Term Goals:

1. Make good grades in fifth grade.
2. Graduate from high school.
3. Go to college or to a technical school.
4. Get a good job.

Short-Term Goals:

1. Make a daily schedule to plan my time.
2. Keep my schoolwork and supplies organized.
3. Make good grades each day.
4. Schedule study time each night.

Apply It: SETTING GOALS

Make a Goal Booklet of your long-term and short-term goals. The information in Reference 1 will guide you.

Reference 1 **Activity for Goal Booklets**

Directions for your Goal Booklet:

1. Write the title **Long-Term Goals** on a sheet of white paper.
2. Write your long-term goals on another sheet of white paper.
3. Write the title **Short-Term Goals** on a sheet of white paper.
4. Write your short-term goals on another sheet of white paper.
5. Make goal-evaluation pages that will be used throughout the year.
   Write **Evaluation 1**, **Evaluation 2**, **Evaluation 3**, **Evaluation 4** on four separate sheets.
   Put them at the back of the booklet.
6. Use a folder or two sheets of construction paper as the cover of your booklet.
   Write the title **My Goal Booklet** and your name on the front cover.
7. Put the pages in order. Staple them on the left side or use a folder with brads.
8. Illustrate the cover page. (*Suggestions: clock, books, pencils, diploma, school building, etc.*)

START LESSON 2

Lesson 2

You will

- recite new jingle (Study Skills).
- listen and respond to the Quigley stories.
- assess study skills.

LISTENING AND SPEAKING:

Recite the new jingle.

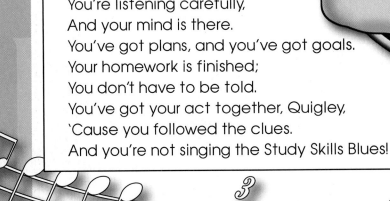

| ♪ | Jingle 1 | **The Study Skills Jingle** |

Un-Quigley, Un-Quigley,
What are you going to do?
You've got a frown on your face,
And you're singing the blues!
You're not organized, Quigley;
You are not prepared.
You're not listening,
And your mind's not there.
You don't have plans, and you don't have goals.
Your homework's unfinished,
And you've been told.
You need to get your act together
'Cause you don't have a clue.
You've got the Study Skills Blues!

O-Quigley, O-Quigley,
Now, you see what to do.
You've got a smile on your face,
And you're lookin' cool!
You're so organized, Quigley;
You are so prepared.
You're listening carefully,
And your mind is there.
You've got plans, and you've got goals.
Your homework is finished;
You don't have to be told.
You've got your act together, Quigley,
'Cause you followed the clues.
And you're not singing the Study Skills Blues!

QUIGLEY AND STUDY SKILLS

Read It: **QUIGLEY AND STUDY SKILLS**

All through school, Quigley had a big problem with organization. He had no organizational plan at all, and it affected everything he did. He was a bright student, but he had not been able to keep up with his work at home or school. He would get sidetracked easily, and he would forget books and assignments and other responsibilities.

When Quigley was unorganized and unprepared, he was stressed and felt terrible. This resulted in Quigley having **Un-Quigley** days because he was "**Un**-organized." But when Quigley was organized and prepared, he felt in control and had confidence in himself. This resulted in Quigley having **O-Quigley** days because he was "**SO**-organized."

The type of day Quigley had affected how he felt about school. In the past, Quigley's mom and all his teachers had tried to help him get organized, but somehow it never clicked. Quigley did not realize that good study habits and good work habits were the keys to making his life easier and happier.

The Un-Quigley Story:
When Quigley Was Not Organized

When Quigley woke from his latest daydream, his classmates were busily working on math problems. Quigley didn't mind math, but first he would have to find his math book and pencil. Mrs. Rainwater frowned as Quigley noisily rummaged through his desk. He found his scissors that had been missing since Halloween. He found lots of odds and ends that he couldn't remember putting in his desk, but he couldn't find his pencil or his math book. Finally, in the back of his desk, he spied an unsharpened pencil he could use. But where was his math book? Oh! Quigley remembered now. He had left it in his backpack. Grabbing his pencil, he headed for the back of the room to get his math book and to sharpen his pencil.

"Quigley," Mrs. Rainwater scolded, "you have already wasted fifteen minutes of working time. Settle down and get busy!"

Quigley hurried back to his seat. Lucky for him that Mrs. Rainwater had written the assignment on the board. Now all he had to do was get it down on paper. Oh, no! Quigley had a sinking feeling in his stomach. He had forgotten to tell Mom that he needed paper!

Discuss It:

1. In what ways did Quigley show that he was not organized?
2. Why did Quigley's teacher scold him?
3. What should Quigley have done to be better organized?

Learn It: **GETTING ORGANIZED**

📖 | **Reference 2** | **Study Skills for Getting Organized**

GET ORGANIZED...

1. **Be prepared!** Have pencils sharpened and supplies handy before you begin the day. Keep an assignment notebook to record assignments, page numbers, and due dates.
2. **Organize your desk!** Each time you put something in it, know exactly where it goes. Avoid "stuffing." Start today by having a complete clean-out and fix-up. Put all folders and notebooks on one side of your desk, and put all textbooks on the other side. Small items should be kept in the front in a zippered bag.
3. **Everything has a place!** Keep each subject in a separate folder so that you can find papers easily.
4. **Directions are important!** Take time to read carefully and understand each direction even if you know what to do. Look at your teacher and concentrate on what your teacher is saying.
5. **Proofread your work!** Check it over. Read everything you have written. Do your answers make sense? Have you skipped any items?

The Un-Quigley Story:
When Quigley Did Not Listen

Quigley wasn't even trying to concentrate while Mrs. Rainwater was explaining that BORING history lesson. He tapped his pencil and swung his legs back and forth to the tune of "Space Walk," a song he had learned at space camp. His mind relived the exciting special on space exploration last night. What a show!

"Quigley," Mrs. Rainwater interrupted his thoughts. "Can you explain what important event changed American education during the Eisenhower administration?"

As Quigley stammered and stuttered, Mrs. Rainwater continued impatiently, "Well, you may look up the answer that we have just discussed in your book! Write your answer in complete sentences and make sure you have covered the topic thoroughly! The rest of the class will be in the library. We have a guest speaker from the space program today."

A speaker from the space program! How could he have messed up so badly? Angry at himself, Quigley opened his history book to Chapter 10. He couldn't believe his eyes! This chapter was about space. The answer to his question was right in front of him, and it wasn't boring at all! If only he had been listening during the history lesson! Then he could be listening to the guest speaker from the space program with the rest of the class.

Discuss It:

1. In what ways did Quigley show that he was not listening?

2. Why was Quigley's teacher impatient with him?

3. What should Quigley have done to be a better listener?

Learn It: LISTENING

 Reference 3 **Study Skills for Listening**

LISTEN...

1. **Listen with your whole body!** Turn your body toward the speaker and look directly at him. Keep your legs and hands still. Try to be interested in what the speaker is saying. You will learn more, and you will show him that he is important.

2. **Ask questions!** Try to understand what the speaker is saying. When the speaker says something you don't understand, raise your hand and wait to be acknowledged. Remember to ask your question before the speaker moves on to something else.

3. **Write it down!** Write down anything that you think you might forget.

4. **Concentrate!** Think about what the speaker is saying. Listen with your brain as well as your ears.

5. **Listen to directions!** Listen to understand each step. Ask questions if you do not understand the directions.

 Student Tip...

For additional information and activities on following directions, refer to the Resource Tools Section on pages 514-515.

The Un-Quigley Story:
When Quigley Did Not Plan His Time

Quigley couldn't believe his ears! Mrs. Rainwater was reminding the class that a book report, a science project, and a math assignment were all due on Monday. Quigley hadn't even started reading his book yet. As for his science project, Mrs. Rainwater had assigned it so long ago that he couldn't even remember what kind of project it was supposed to be!

He stuffed his math book in his desk and rushed out the door to ask Lisa about the science project. Then he began collecting leaves for his science project on his way home from school. He found seven different kinds - only thirteen more to go! Then he would look them up and label them over the weekend. This was going to be a snap after all!

Once home, Quigley laid his leaves on his dresser. He would finish them later. After all, he had until Monday. He went downstairs and found out that his cousins from out of town were coming for a visit.

The weekend was a full one for Quigley. He went on a wonderful fishing trip with his uncle. He worked on his tree house with his cousins, and he watched a couple of specials on space travel. It wasn't until Sunday afternoon when his Mom started fussing about the curled-up leaves on his dresser that Quigley even thought of all the work that was due tomorrow.

Oh, gosh! It was hopeless! The leaves he had collected on Friday were ruined, and he would have to start over. Besides that, he still hadn't read a book for his book report. The clincher for Quigley came when he realized that he had left his math book at school and could not do his math homework. Mrs. Rainwater was going to be furious with him. Quigley was so discouraged! Why did school have to be so hard?

SCHOOL:
☑ Follow Daily Schedule
☑ Check Assignment Folder
☐ Prepare for Homework

HOME:
☐ Eat Snack
☐ Do Chores
☐ Do Homework
☐ Free time
☐ Eat Dinner

Discuss It:

1. In what ways did Quigley show that he did not plan his time wisely?
2. Why did Quigley think his teacher would be furious with him on Monday?
3. What should Quigley have done to plan his time better?

Learn It: PLANNING YOUR TIME

Reference 4	**Study Skills for Planning Your Time**

PLAN YOUR TIME...

1. **Set goals for yourself!** Choose one study skill at a time that you need to improve. Think of reasons why you need help in this area. Make a list of the things you can do to improve. Then, stick to it.
2. **Plan your day!** Make an assignment folder and check it every day. Know what you need to do and plan time to work on it. Check off completed assignments.
3. **Do what is important first!** Assignments that are due first should be completed first.
4. **Make each minute count!** Concentrate on the job at hand. If you don't waste time, you will have more time to do the things you like to do. Keep your eyes on your work and keep your pencil moving. Don't give yourself a chance to stop working by breaking your concentration.
5. **Reward yourself!** When you complete a goal, allow yourself to feel proud for a job well done.

English Made Easy

The Un-Quigley Story:
When Quigley Did Not Do His Homework

Quigley knew he had homework tonight because Mrs. Rainwater made him take all his unfinished class work home. Before he started on his homework, he decided to do some of the chores that Mom had written down for him to do over a week ago. First, he mowed the grass, and then he trimmed the bushes. Feeling very proud of himself, Quigley headed for his room to start on his spelling and math homework. He could read his science lesson on the bus.

As he entered his room, his eyes fell on the half-built model rocket that Dad had gotten him for his birthday. It was going to be gorgeous when he got through with it! All thoughts of schoolwork left him as he walked over to the model. Soon, he was gluing pieces and putting on stickers. He lost all track of time until Mom knocked on his door. Surely, it wasn't bedtime already! He had tons of homework to do, and he hadn't even started! But Mom insisted he go to bed, saying he should have done his homework first.

Quigley closed his eyes and swallowed hard. How was he going to explain this to Mrs. Rainwater? It didn't look good, even to him. Why did everything have to happen to him?

Discuss It:

1. What were some of the problems that Quigley had with his homework?
2. What would Quigley's teacher think about his excuse for not doing his homework?
3. What should Quigley have done to make sure his homework was completed?

Learn It: DOING HOMEWORK

 Reference 5 | **Study Skills for Doing Homework**

DO YOUR HOMEWORK...

1. **Think before you leave school!** Check your assignment folder and decide what you need to take home. Put books and folders you will need in your book bag.
2. **Schedule a time to study!** Think about your family's routine and decide on a good study time. Stick to your schedule.
3. **Study where you can concentrate!** You can get homework done in a very short time if you do it away from TV, conversations, or other distractions. Have all the supplies you will need at your study area.
4. **Set a time limit to study!** See how long you can concentrate. You might use a timer to set a time for a focused study period and then give yourself a break or a reward at the end of that time.
5. **Have a special place to keep homework!** When your homework is finished, put it in your book bag, and you will always have it ready to take to school.

The 0-Quigley Story:
When Quigley Had Good Study Habits

Quigley walked happily into the classroom. This was the first day of school in fifth grade, and Quigley was anxious to meet his friends and his new fifth-grade teacher. He immediately liked his teacher, Mrs. Rainwater. She was a good teacher who expected a lot from her students, but that meant that her students would also learn a lot. Knowing that he would be expected to pull his own load, Quigley quickly prepared himself.

First, he organized his desk and materials so he would not waste time and energy looking for things. Next, he listened very carefully to everything Mrs. Rainwater said because she gave a lot of extra information and shared inside jokes if her students were listening. Then, Quigley quietly made a study chart so he could get the most done in the scheduled time. Finally, Quigley made sure he had his homework assignments written down and the books and supplies he would need in his book bag.

As he waited for the final bell, Quigley smiled in contentment. He loved school and couldn't wait to come back! He was prepared for everything that fifth grade had to offer.

Discuss It:

1. What do you think about the new Quigley?
2. How does the organized Quigley differ from the unorganized Quigley?
3. Do you think good study skills helped Quigley become a better student?
4. Do you think good study skills could help you become a better student?
5. What study habits would you like to improve?

Apply It: EVALUATING INDIVIDUAL STUDY HABITS

Do you enjoy learning new things at school? Do you work hard to improve your study skills? Do you use good study habits? Most of you know the answers to these questions by the time you are in fifth grade.

Being a good student involves more than how fast you learn. Most students who do well in school know how to get organized, how to listen, how to plan their time, and how to get their homework finished.

You will now assess your personal study habits. This assessment is a tool to help you evaluate your study habits as you begin fifth grade. As you read each section, you should mark whether you think your study skills are excellent, average, or poor. This assessment will not be graded. It is designed to help you discover your weak areas so that you can improve them.

>>>>>>>>>>>> Student Tip...

Ask your parents to help you practice these study skills until they become good habits. Make posters of the study skills for your room to remind you what to do.

Study Skills Assessment

Name:_____ Date:_____

Directions: Rate your skills in each category by marking the appropriate column with an **X**.

GET ORGANIZED: Reference 2	Excellent	Average	Needs Improvement
1. Being prepared	☐	☐	☐
2. Organizing your desk	☐	☐	☐
3. Putting everything in its place	☐	☐	☐
4. Realizing the importance of directions	☐	☐	☐
5. Proofreading your work	☐	☐	☐

LISTEN: Reference 3	Excellent	Average	Needs Improvement
1. Listening with your whole body	☐	☐	☐
2. Asking questions	☐	☐	☐
3. Taking notes	☐	☐	☐
4. Concentrating	☐	☐	☐
5. Listening to directions	☐	☐	☐

PLAN YOUR TIME: Reference 4	Excellent	Average	Needs Improvement
1. Setting goals for yourself	☐	☐	☐
2. Planning your day	☐	☐	☐
3. Doing what is important first	☐	☐	☐
4. Making each minute count	☐	☐	☐
5. Rewarding yourself	☐	☐	☐

DO YOUR HOMEWORK: Reference 5	Excellent	Average	Needs Improvement
1. Collecting assignments before you leave school	☐	☐	☐
2. Scheduling a time to study	☐	☐	☐
3. Studying where you can concentrate	☐	☐	☐
4. Setting a time limit to study	☐	☐	☐
5. Having a special place to keep homework	☐	☐	☐

If you marked any areas as "Average" or "Needs Improvement," look back at the references in those areas to help you find ways to improve. Find a study skills partner to check your progress, to encourage you, and to give you advice and help.

Chapter 1

START LESSON 3

Lesson 3

You will

- practice Jingle 1.
- implement study plans for school and home.
- read, listen, and implement journal writing.
- write in your journal.

LISTENING AND SPEAKING:

 Jingle Time

Recite It: Practice Jingle 1 in the Jingle Section on page 498.

STUDY PLANS

Learn It: **A STUDY PLAN TO ORGANIZE SCHOOLWORK**

You have learned that goals are important because they are a constant reminder of what you want to happen in your future. Remember that goals are your destination. A schedule is your road map. You may take a few detours, but you still know the general direction in which you are headed and how to get there.

The first step in good organization is to make and follow a plan of action.

 Reference 6   **Study Plan to Organize Schoolwork**

You should use this plan to keep things in order!

1. Keep all necessary school supplies in a handy, heavy-duty plastic bag or a pencil bag that zips shut.

2. Make a folder labeled **Unfinished Work**. Put all unfinished work for every subject in this folder so that any unfinished work is easy to find. *(Keep this folder on the top left side of your desk so that it is available to you and your teacher at all times.)*

3. Make a folder labeled **Finished Work** for each school subject. (Finished Work for Math, Finished Work for English, etc.) Place only the finished papers for a subject in the left pocket of the appropriate folder immediately after finishing the work. Put notes to study, graded tests, and study guides in the brads so that you will have them to study for scheduled tests. *(Choose a different-colored folder for each subject to make it easier to find a specific subject.)*

4. Make a folder labeled **Progress** for all graded work that will be sent home for parents to view.

5. Make a folder labeled **Paper** to store two kinds of paper: unused paper and papers to throw away. Place clean sheets of unused paper in the right pocket and keep it full at all times. In the left pocket, place papers that need to be thrown away. Check this pocket and empty it at the end of every day. Make sure you do not stuff trash papers in your subject folders or your desk!

6. Make a folder labeled **Assignments** and review it every day. Ideas for your Assignment folder are listed below.

   A. Keep a monthly calendar of assignments, test dates, report-due dates, project-due dates, extra activities, important dates and times, review dates, etc.

   B. Keep a grade sheet to record the grades received in each subject. *(You might also consider keeping your grades on the inside cover of each subject folder. However you keep track of your grades, just remember to record them accurately. Your grades are your business, so keep up with them! Grades help you know which subject areas need attention.)*

   C. Make a list every day of the things you want to do. Mark off tasks as you complete them and move the unfinished items to a new list the next day. *(Making this list takes time, but it's your road map to success. You will always know at a glance what you set out to accomplish and what still needs to be done.)*

Learn It: A STUDY PLAN FOR SCHOOL

A study plan for school gives you a daily routine to follow.

 Reference 7 **Study Plan for School**

You should check this plan every day!

1. Eat a nutritious breakfast to start your day.

2. Attend class regularly.

3. Develop the "I'm-willing-to-do-what-it-takes-to-get-the-job-done-right" attitude. Schoolwork is your job; so, make it an important part of your daily life.

4. Work with your teachers and parents to correct any attitudes or habits that keep you from learning.

5. Make the effort to listen. Ask questions if you don't understand and answer questions if you are asked.

6. Write it down! Write it down! Write it down! Make a habit of taking notes in class. Put the notes in the correct subject folder.

7. Write down your assignments. Then, check your assignment folder every day. Know what is on your calendar. Remember to record everything on your calendar so you won't forget things.

8. Do what is important first! Assignments that are due first should be completed first. Turn your daily assignments in on time. If you are absent, ask about make-up work and turn it in on time.

9. Concentrate on the job at hand. If you don't waste time, you will get more work finished. Keep your eyes on your work and keep your pencil moving. Don't break your concentration; just keep working. Every time your eyes leave your paper to look around, you lose working time!

10. Think before you leave school! Check your assignment folder and decide what you need to take home. Put the books and folders you will need in a book bag so you won't forget them.

Learn It: A STUDY PLAN FOR HOME

A study plan for home gives you a checklist of important things to consider when studying at home.

 Reference 8 **Study Plan for Home**

Stick to this plan every evening!

1. Schedule a time to study. Think about your family's routine and decide on a good study time. Stick to your schedule.

2. Study where you can concentrate. Complete your homework and studying before watching TV, playing computer games, or talking on the telephone.

3. Make a personal decision to concentrate 100 percent on completing your homework assignments. By doing this, you can accomplish more in less time.

4. Check your assignment folder every day. This puts you in charge!

5. Have a special place to keep homework. When your homework is finished, put it in your book bag or another designated place immediately. You will always have it ready to take to school, no matter how rushed you are the next morning.

6. Use your home study time to complete your assignments and/or to review for a test. Don't wait until the last minute to study for a test. Study a little every night so that you won't overload the night before the test. (You might have something unexpected come up the night before the big test!)

7. If possible, set a weekly meeting time to discuss your progress and problems with your parents. If this is not possible, evaluate your own progress. You need to decide which study skills you did not follow. Figure out how to "fix" the problem and try again! You will get better with practice.

Write It: JOURNAL WRITING

Reference 9   Journal Writing

What is journal writing? **Journal Writing** is a written record of your personal thoughts and feelings about people, things, or events that are important to you. Recording your thoughts in a journal is a good way to remember how you felt about what was happening in your life at a particular time. You can record your dreams, memories, feelings, and experiences. You can ask questions. You can answer questions. A journal can also be a place to look for future writing topics, creative stories, poems, etc. Keeping a journal should develop into a lifelong habit. Later, you will enjoy looking back at what you have written because it shows how you have matured and the changes that have taken place in your life.

WHAT DO I WRITE ABOUT?

Journals are personal, but sometimes it helps to have ideas to get you started. Remember, in a journal, you do not have to stick to one topic. Write about someone or something you like. Write about what you did last weekend or on vacation. Write about what you hope to do this week or on your next vacation. Write about home, school, friends, hobbies, special talents (yours or someone else's), or the hopes and fears you have about things now and in the future. Looking at what's wrong with your world, what would you do to "fix" it? Write about the good things in your world and how you feel about them.

A journal can also be an excellent record of events. You can record details about past or present events. You could write opinions of past, present, or future events that have changed or could change the way you think about things. If something bothers you, record it in your journal. If something interests you, write about it in your journal. If you just want to write about something that does not seem important at all, record it in your journal. After all, it is *your* journal!

HOW DO I GET STARTED?

Use a spiral notebook or folder for your journal writing. Write the title, **My Personal Journal for the Year 20—**, on the front cover of your notebook or folder. Ask your teacher if you should write with a pen or pencil in your journal. On the first line of the journal entry, put the journal entry number and the date. Example: **Journal Entry 1 for September ____, 20—**. Skip the next line and begin your entry. You might write one or two sentences, a paragraph, a whole page, or several pages. If you have several entries on one page, skip three lines between each entry.

Except for the journal entry number and date, no particular organizational style is required for journal writing unless you are given instructions for a special assignment. You decide how best to organize and express your thoughts. Feel free to include sketches, diagrams, lists, etc., if these will help you remember your thoughts about a topic or an event. You will need a quiet place and at least 5-10 minutes of unin-terrupted writing time. If you do not finish your journal entry during the assigned time, finish it during a study period. If you need to review what to do during Journal Writing, refer to this page.

Possible Topics:

My best friend	I am thankful for...	I feel strongly about...	My family
A person I admire	Things I do well	Things I would like to do well	What I do when I am bored

JOURNAL WRITING [1]

Write an entry in your journal.
Use Reference 9 above.

English Made Easy

LISTENING AND SPEAKING:

Recite It: Practice Jingle 1 in the Jingle Section on page 498.

Learn It: THE IMPORTANCE OF CAPITALIZATION AND PUNCTUATION

It is important for you to know how to capitalize and punctuate any type of writing correctly.

START LESSON 4

Lesson 4

You will

- practice Jingle 1.
- read and discuss the importance of capitalization and punctuation.
- read and discuss capitalization rules.
- do Classroom Practice 1.
- write in your journal.

 Reference 10 **The Importance of Capitalization and Punctuation**

Can you imagine trying to read something with no capitalization or punctuation? How would you know when a writer's thought was complete? How would you know when to pause and when to take a breath? Read this short paragraph aloud and see if it makes sense to you. Read it with no pauses and without expression because there are no punctuation marks to tell you what to do.

the kids in my neighborhood gather for a space battle at my house once a year they bring water guns beach towels soap bubbles and a change of clothes for the space wars i provide a bubble machine and lots of water as the kids use their water guns to fight the invading bubble forces everyone gets wet has a great time and develops new strategies for next year

Learn It: CAPITALIZATION RULES

The capitalization rules are organized into sections of similar rules. Read the titles of each section.

 Reference 11 **Capitalization Rules**

SECTION 1: **CAPITALIZE THE FIRST WORD**

1. The first word of a sentence. *(He likes to take a nap.)*
2. The first word in the greeting and closing of letters. *(Dear, Yours truly, Sincerely, etc.)*
3. The first, last, and important words in titles of literary works.
   (books, songs, short stories, poems, articles, movie titles, magazines, newspapers, etc.) (Note: Conjunctions, articles, and prepositions with fewer than five letters are not capitalized unless they are the first or last words.)
4. The first word of a direct quotation. *(Dad said, "We are going home.")*
5. The first word in the topics, subtopics, and details of an outline.

SECTION 2: **CAPITALIZE NAMES, INITIALS, AND TITLES OF PEOPLE**

6. The pronoun I. *(May I go with you?)*
7. The names and nicknames of people. *(Sam, Joe, Jones, Slim, Junior, etc.)*
8. Family names when used in place of or with a person's name.
   (Grandmother, Auntie, Uncle Joe, etc.) (Note: Do not capitalize family names when a possessive noun or pronoun is used with it: My mom, Kim's mom, Jim's father, His aunt, etc.)
9. Titles used with, or in place of, people's names. *(Mr., Ms., Prime Minister, Dr. Lin, Captain, President, Sir, etc.)*
10. People's initials. *(J. D., C. Smith, K. C. Jones, etc.)*

Continued on next page. >>>

SHURLEY ENGLISH

Reference 11 continued from previous page.

SECTION 3: CAPITALIZE DESIGNATIONS OF TIME

11. The days of the week and months of the year. *(Monday, Wednesday, July, February, etc.)*
12. The names of holidays. *(Christmas, Thanksgiving, New Year's Day, etc.)*
13. The names of historical events, periods, laws, documents, conflicts, and distinguished awards.
    (Civil War, Middle Ages, Bill of Rights, Medal of Honor, etc.)

SECTION 4: CAPITALIZE NAMES OF PLACES

14. The names and abbreviations of cities, towns, counties, states, countries, nations, and continents.
    (Dallas, Texas, Fulton County, Africa, America, USA, CA, TX, etc.)
15. The names of avenues, streets, roads, highways, routes, and post office boxes.
    (Main Street, Jones Road, Highway 89, Rt. 1, Box 2, P.O. Box 45, etc.)
16. The names of lakes, rivers, oceans, other bodies of water, mountain ranges, deserts, parks, stars, planets, and constellations. *(Beaver Lake, New York Harbor, Rocky Mountains, Glacier National Park, Sahara Desert, etc.)*
17. The names of schools and specific school courses that are either numbered or name a language.
    (Walker Elementary School, Mathematics II, French, English, etc.)
18. North, South, East, and West when they refer to geographical regions of the country.
    (up North, lives in the East, traveled out West, Southern gentleman, etc.)
    (Note: Do not capitalize directional words: Go south two miles.)

SECTION 5: CAPITALIZE NAMES OF OTHER NOUNS AND PROPER ADJECTIVES

19. The names of pets. *(Spot, Tweety Bird, Muffin, etc.)*
20. The names of products. *(Dixie cups, Dove soap, Ford automobiles, etc.)*
21. The names, abbreviations, or acronyms of companies, buildings, stores, monuments, ships, airplanes, spaceships. *(Empire State Building, Titanic, IBM, The Big Tire Co., Statue of Liberty, Challenger, etc.)*
22. Proper adjectives. *(the English language, Italian restaurant, French test, etc.)*
23. The names of clubs, organizations, groups, or teams. *(Lion's Club, Jaycees, Beatles, Dallas Cowboys, etc.)*
24. The names of political parties, religious preferences, nationalities, and races.
    (Democratic party, Republican, Jewish synagogue, American flag, etc.)

Learn It: CAPITALIZATION RULES AND CORRECTIONS

Look at Sentence 1 in Reference 12. The capitalization rule numbers have been written above the corrections to verify the reasons for the corrections.

Reference 12 — Using Capitalization Rules

For the first sentence, write the capitalization rule numbers for each correction in **blue** type to verify the reason for the correction. Use Reference 11 to look up the capitalization rule numbers.

   1   6   14   14   11

1. Yes, I'll go to Topeka, Kansas, in June for our national sales meeting.

For the second sentence, find each capitalization mistake and write the correction above it.

  m c   c   p   c   p   p m

2. mr. chang, when did the chinese students leave pueblo, colorado, on their way to pikes peak mountain?

English Made Easy

Classroom Practice 1

It is time to practice the skills you are learning. You will use the classroom practice on the next page to apply these skills.

Student Tip...

If you need a more in-depth study of how to use the dictionary, refer to the Resource Tools Section on page 523.

JOURNAL WRITING [2]

Write an entry in your journal. Use Reference 9 on page 12 for ideas.

Classroom Practice 1

Name:_____ Date:_____

SKILLS

▶ **Exercise 1:** Using Reference 11 on page 13, write the capitalization rule number in column A and the letter that best illustrates each rule in column B.

A	B		
		1. Capitalize the names and nicknames of people.	A. Spot, Tweety Bird
		2. Capitalize titles used with, or in place of, people's names.	B. J. D., C. Smith
		3. Capitalize the days of the week and months of the year.	C. Christmas, New Year's
		4. Capitalize proper adjectives.	D. Atlantic Ocean
		5. Capitalize the names of pets.	E. Dear,
		6. Capitalize the names of products.	F. Monday, July, October
		7. Capitalize the names of holidays.	G. Ivory soap
		8. Capitalize people's initials.	H. Mr., Mrs., Dr., Sir
		9. Capitalize the first word in the greeting of letters.	I. Dallas, Texas
		10. Capitalize the names of cities, towns, and states.	J. English test, Asian food
		11. Capitalize the pronoun I.	K. Sam's Grocery Store
		12. Capitalize the first word of a direct quotation.	L. I walked to town.
		13. Capitalize the names of clubs, groups, or teams.	M. Sam, Joe, Slim, Junior
		14. Capitalize the names of rivers, oceans, and mountains.	N. "Go home!" he yelled.
		15. Capitalize the names of companies, stores, and ships.	O. The Trolley Dance Team

EDITING

▶ **Exercise 2:** Write the capitalization rule numbers for each correction in **bold**.
Use Reference 11 on page 13 to look up the capitalization rule numbers.

Was **M**r. **D**. **J**. **H**unter transferred to **S**pokane, **W**ashington, on **F**riday, **A**pril 12, 2005?

▶ **Exercise 3:** Find each capitalization mistake and write the correction above it.

yes, i'll be on vacation in london, england, in june, july, and august.

English Made Easy

LISTENING AND SPEAKING:

Recite It: Practice Jingle 1 in the Jingle Section on page 498.

Learn It: **Punctuation Rules**

The punctuation rules are also organized into sections of similar rules. Read the titles of each section.

START LESSON 5

Lesson 5

You will
- practice Jingle 1.
- read and discuss punctuation rules and the editing guide.
- do Classroom Practice 2.
- write in your journal.

 Reference 13 | **Punctuation Rules**

SECTION 1: END-MARK PUNCTUATION

1. Use a period (**.**) for the end punctuation of a sentence that makes a statement. *(Mom baked us a cake.)*
2. Use a question mark (**?**) for the end punctuation of a sentence that asks a question. *(Are you going to town?)*
3. Use an exclamation point (**!**) for the end punctuation of a sentence that expresses strong feeling. *(That bee stung me!)*
4. Use a period (**.**) for the end punctuation of a sentence that gives a command or makes a request. *(Close the door.)*

SECTION 2: COMMAS TO SEPARATE TIME WORDS

5. Use a comma between the day of the week and the month and day. *(Friday, July 23)* Use a comma between the day and year. *(July 23, 2009)*
6. Use a comma after the year when the complete date is used in the middle of the sentence. *(We spent July 23, 2004, with Grandmother.)* **Note:** When just the month and the year appear in a sentence, no comma is required. *(We leave in May 2006 for our first vacation.)*

SECTION 3: COMMAS TO SEPARATE LOCATION WORDS

7. Use a comma to separate the city from the state (or country) or route numbers from the street address (or box number). *(I will go to Dallas, Texas.   He is from Paris, France.   Rt. 2, Box 55   Rt. 4, Smokey Lane)*
8. Use a comma to separate the state or country from the rest of the sentence when the name of the state or country follows the name of a city. *(We flew to Dallas, Texas, in June.   We flew to Paris, France, in July.)*

SECTION 4: COMMAS TO MAKE MEANINGS CLEAR

9. Use a comma to separate words or phrases in a series. *(We had soup, crackers, and milk.)*

Continued on next page. >>>

Reference 13 continued from previous page.

10. Use a comma **after** an introductory word, an introductory prepositional phrase, or an introductory clause. (*Oh, I see. In the morning, the ship will dock. If you go, I will go.*) (Other introductory words: *well, today, now, yes, no, so*) Use a comma **before** the conjunction in a compound sentence and before *too* when it means "also." (*Jim mowed the yard, and Larry raked the leaves. I want a brownie, too.*)

11. Use commas to set off most appositives. An appositive is a word, phrase, title, or degree used directly after another word to explain or rename it. (*Sue, my friend, likes to draw. My brother, Tim, is working today.*)

12. Use commas to separate a noun of direct address (the name of a person directly spoken to) from the rest of the sentence. (*Mom, do you want some tea?*)

SECTION 5: PUNCTUATION IN GREETINGS AND CLOSINGS OF LETTERS

13. Use a comma (**,**) after the salutation (greeting) of a friendly letter. (*Dear Sam,*)

14. Use a comma (**,**) after the closing of any letter. (*Yours truly,*)

15. Use a colon (**:**) after the salutation (greeting) of a business letter. (*Dear Madam:*)

Reference 14 **Punctuation Rules**

SECTION 6: **PERIODS**

16. Use a period after most abbreviations or titles that are accepted in formal writing. (*Mr., Ms., Dr., Capt., St., Ave., St. Louis, etc.*)
(*Note: These abbreviations should not be used alone. They should be used with a proper noun.*)
In the abbreviations or acronyms of many well-known organizations or words, periods are not required. (*USA, GM, TWA, GTE, AT&T, TV, AM, FM, GI, etc.*)
Use only one period after an abbreviation at the end of a statement. Do not put an extra period for the end-mark punctuation.

17. Use a period after initials. (*C. Smith, D. J. Brewton, Thomas A. Jones, etc.*)

18. Place a period after Roman numerals, Arabic numbers, and letters of the alphabet in an outline. (*II., IV., 5., 25., A., B., etc.*)

SECTION 7: **APOSTROPHES**

19. Form a contraction by using an apostrophe in place of a letter or letters that have been left out. (*I'll, he's, isn't, wasn't, can't, etc.*)

20. Form the possessive of singular and plural nouns by using an apostrophe. (*boy's football, boys' football, child's football, children's football, etc.*)

21. Form the plurals of letters, symbols, numbers, and signs with an apostrophe and *s* (*'s*). (*9's, B's, b's, etc.*)

Continued on next page. >>>

Reference 14 continued from previous page.

SECTION 8: UNDERLINING

22. Use underlining for writing the titles of ships, books, magazines, newspapers, motion pictures, full-length plays, works of art, and long musical compositions. (Our newspaper is the <u>Gazette</u>.) (<u>Titanic</u>, <u>Charlotte's Web</u>, <u>Reader's Digest</u>, <u>Macbeth</u>, etc.) These titles may also be italicized instead of underlined. (Our newspaper is the *Gazette*.) (*Titanic, Charlotte's Web, Reader's Digest, Macbeth*, etc.)

SECTION 9: QUOTATIONS

23. Use quotation marks around titles of book chapters, magazine articles, short stories and plays, essays, single poems, television and radio programs, songs, and short pieces of music.
    (Do you like to sing the song "America" in music class?)

24. Use quotation marks at the beginning and end of the speaker's words to separate what the speaker said from the rest of the sentence. Since the quotation tells what is being said, it should always have quotation marks around it.

25. Do not use quotation marks to set off explanatory words, the words that tell who is speaking.
    *(Fred said, "I'm here.") (**Fred said** is explanatory and should not be set off with quotation marks.)*

26. Use a new paragraph to indicate a change of speaker.

27. When a speaker's speech is longer than one paragraph, use quotation marks at the beginning of each paragraph and at the end of the last paragraph of that speaker's speech.

28. Use single quotation marks to enclose a quotation within a quotation.
    ("My bear says 'I love you' four different ways," said little Amy.)

29. Use a period at the end of explanatory words that come at the end of a sentence.

30. Use a comma to separate a direct quotation from the explanatory words.

Learn It: CAPITALIZATON AND PUNCTUATION
RULES AND CORRECTIONS

Look at Sentence 1 in Reference 15. The capitalization rule numbers have been written above the corrections to verify the reasons for the corrections. The punctuation rule numbers have been written below the corrections to verify the reasons for the corrections. When you are required to write rule numbers, it is helpful to work with capitalization rules first and then work with punctuation rules.

Reference 15 — Capitalization & Punctuation Rules and the Editing Guide

For the first sentence, write the capitalization and punctuation rule numbers for each correction in **blue** print to verify the reason for the correction. Use References 11, 13, and 14 to look up the capitalization and punctuation rule numbers.

```
     1   6        14    14        11
1. Yes, I'll go to Topeka, Kansas, in June for our national sales meeting.
     10 19            7        8                                    1
```

Checking a sentence or a paragraph for mistakes is called **proofreading**. Correcting these mistakes is called **editing**. You will have an **Editing Guide** that will tell you how many mistakes of each kind you will find in the sentence or paragraph to be edited.

For the second sentence, put punctuation corrections within the sentence. Write all other corrections above the sentence.

Editing Guide: Capitals: 8   Periods: 1   Commas: 3   Misspelled Words: 1   End Marks: 1

```
   M  C              C              P    C                      P   P   Mountain
2. mr. Chang, when did the chinese students leave pueblo, colorado, on their way to pikes peak mountin?
```

Learn It: THE EDITING GUIDE

Look at Sentence 2. An **Editing Guide** shows how many mistakes of each kind you will correct in an editing sentence or paragraph. As a capitalization mistake or misspelled word is found, the correction is written above it. As a punctuation mistake is found, the correction is written within the sentence.

The second sentence has an Editing Guide that tells how many capitalization, punctuation, and spelling mistakes are in the sentence. The number 8 after the word **Capitals** means that there are eight capitalization mistakes to correct. A number after the word **Periods** refers to periods used after abbreviations and initials *within* the sentence. The number 3 written after the word **Commas** means that there are three comma mistakes. The number 1 after **Misspelled Words** means that there is one spelling mistake to correct. A number after **End Marks** refers to any period, question mark, or exclamation point at the *end* of a sentence.

After you have made the corrections listed in the Editing Guide, you must always double-check your work by counting each type of correction you made to make sure the total matches the Editing Guide.

>>>>>>>>>>>>>> Student Tip...

If you need a more in-depth study of how to use the dictionary, refer to the Resource Tools Section on page 523.

JOURNAL WRITING [3]

Write an entry in your journal. Use Reference 9 on page 12 for ideas.

Classroom Practice 2

It is time to practice the skills you are learning. You will use the classroom practice on the next page to apply these skills.

Classroom Practice 2

Name:_____ Date:_____

SKILLS

▶ **Exercise 1:** Using References 13–14 on pages 17–18, write the punctuation rule number in column A and the letter that best illustrates each rule in column B.

A	B		
		1. Use an apostrophe to form a contraction.	A. D. J. Brewton
		2. Use a comma between the day and the year.	B. boy's basketball
		3. Use a comma to separate words or phrases in a series.	C. Memphis, Tennessee
		4. Use a colon after the salutation of a business letter.	D. I'll, he's, can't
		5. Use an apostrophe to make a noun possessive.	E. B's, b's
		6. Use underlining for titles of books and magazines.	F. soup, crackers, and milk
		7. Use a comma to separate the city from the state.	G. Dear Sam,
		8. Use an apostrophe to form the plural of letters.	H. Charlotte's Web
		9. Use a period after initials.	I. Dear Madam:
		10. Use a comma after the salutation of a friendly letter.	J. July 23, 2009

▶ **Exercise 2:** Using Reference 11 on page 13, write the capitalization rule number in column A and the letter that best illustrates each rule in column B.

A	B		
		1. Capitalize the names of pets.	
		2. Capitalize the names of products.	A. Friday, May, February
		3. Capitalize the names of clubs, organizations, and teams.	B. Elm Street, Mill Road
			C. Gulf War, D-Day
		4. Capitalize the names of holidays.	D. YMCA, Houston Astros
		5. Capitalize people's initials.	E. Whiskers, Spot, Fido
		6. Capitalize titles used with, or in place of, people's names.	F. Mr., Mrs., Dr., Sir
			G. Lansing, Michigan
		7. Capitalize the names of historical events.	H. Kraft mayonnaise
		8. Capitalize the days of the week and months of the year.	I. J. T., C. J. Manning
			J. Independence Day
		9. Capitalize the names of avenues, streets, and roads.	
		10. Capitalize the names of cities and states.	

EDITING

▶ **Exercise 3:** Write the capitalization and punctuation rule numbers for each correction in **bold**. Use References 11, 13, and 14 on pages 13, 17–18 to look up the capitalization and punctuation rule numbers.

Were **M**rs**.** **B**rown**'**s triplets**,** **J**erry**,** **B**arry**,** and **L**arry**,** born on **T**uesday**,** **A**ugust 7**,** 2001**?**

▶ **Exercise 4:** Put punctuation corrections within the sentence. Write all other corrections above the sentence.
Editing Guide: Capitals: 8   Commas: 2   Periods: 1   Underlining: 1   Misspelled Words: 1   End Marks: 1

ms dean our amerian literature teacher wants us to read moby dick by herman melville

START LESSON 6

Lesson 6

You will

- practice Jingle 1: recite new jingle (Sentence).
- analyze synonyms/antonyms.
- learn new vocabulary word.
- study new vocabulary: make Card 1: write own sentence using the vocabulary word.
- do Classroom Practice 3.

LISTENING AND SPEAKING:

Recite It: 1. Practice Jingle 1 in the Jingle Section on page 498.
2. Recite the new jingle.

♪	Jingle 2	**The Sentence Jingle**

A sentence, sentence, sentence
Is complete, complete, complete
When five simple rules
It meets, meets, meets.

It has a subject, subject, subject
And a verb, verb, verb.
And it makes sense, sense, sense
With every word, word, word.

Add a capital letter
And a punctuation mark.
And now our sentence has all its parts!

But REMEMBER—
Subject and **verb** and **complete sense**,
With a **capital letter** and an **end mark**, too.
Our sentence is complete,
And now we're through!

Learn It: SYNONYMS AND ANTONYMS

You are able to communicate more effectively when you do not use the same words over and over again. That is why it is necessary to add a wide variety of synonyms and antonyms to your vocabulary.

📖*	Reference 16	**Synonyms and Antonyms**

Synonyms are words that have similar, or almost the same, meanings.
Antonyms are words that have opposite meanings.

1. honesty, integrity	2. plan, design	3. myth, fact
<u>Synonyms</u> or Antonyms	<u>Synonyms</u> or Antonyms	Synonyms or <u>Antonyms</u>

>>>>>>>>>>>>> Student Tip...

> You will learn new synonyms and antonyms during Vocabulary and Analogy Time. Use the dictionary for a more in-depth study of any synonym or antonym presented. Refer to the Resource Tools Section on page 523 for more information on using the dictionary.

Vocabulary & Analogy Time

Learn It: VOCABULARY WORDS

Notice how the vocabulary section is arranged. For each vocabulary word, there is a definition of the word, a synonym and antonym for the word, and a sentence that helps you understand the word and remember how it is used.

Reference 17	**Vocabulary Words**

Word: prior (prī'ər)
> **Definition:** earlier in time or order
> **Synonym:** before   **Antonym:** after
> **Sentence:** A practice will be held **prior** to the race

Vocabulary Card 1: Record the vocabulary information above and write your own sentence, using the new word.

Apply It: MAKING CARDS FOR VOCABULARY WORDS

Making cards for vocabulary words will help you remember them.

Reference 18	**Making Cards for Vocabulary Words**

TO MAKE A VOCABULARY CARD

Use a 4x6 index card with lines to record vocabulary information. Write the vocabulary word on the blank side of the card, and write the other information about the vocabulary word on the side with lines. At the bottom of the card, write your own sentence, using the new vocabulary word.

Use the index cards as flash cards to study vocabulary words with a study partner at home or at school. Keep the vocabulary cards in plastic zip bags or recipe boxes.

Classroom Practice 3

It is time to practice the skills you are learning. You will use the classroom practice on the next page to apply these skills.

Classroom Practice 3

Name:_____ Date:_____

SKILLS

▶ **Exercise 1:** Match the definitions by writing the correct letter beside each number.

_____ 1. periods, commas, apostrophes, end marks   A. study skills

_____ 2. words with similar meanings   B. antonyms

_____ 3. words with opposite meanings   C. editing

_____ 4. correcting mistakes in a sentence or paragraph   D. punctuation

_____ 5. organizing, listening, planning, doing homework   E. synonyms

▶ **Exercise 2:** Identify each pair of words as synonyms or antonyms by underlining the correct answer.

1. error, mistake   2. annoy, bother   3. petite, large

Synonyms or Antonyms   Synonyms or Antonyms   Synonyms or Antonyms

▶ **Exercise 3:** Using References 13–14 on pages 17–18, write the correct rule number beside each **punctuation** rule.

_____ 1. Use a period after most abbreviations or titles that are accepted in formal writing.

_____ 2. Form a contraction by using an apostrophe in place of the letter(s) that has (have) been left out.

_____ 3. Use a comma after the closing of both a friendly and business letter.

_____ 4. Use a comma to separate the city from the state.

_____ 5. Use underlining or italics for titles of books, magazines, works of art, ships, and newspapers.

_____ 6. Use a comma after the year when the complete date is used in the middle of the sentence.

_____ 7. Use a comma between the day of the week and the month and between the day and year.

▶ **Exercise 4:** Using Reference 11 on page 13, write the correct rule number beside each **capitalization** rule.

_____ 1. Capitalize proper adjectives.

_____ 2. Capitalize family names when used in place of or with the person's name.

_____ 3. Capitalize the names and abbreviations of cities, towns, counties, states, and countries.

_____ 4. Capitalize the pronoun I.

_____ 5. Capitalize North, South, East, and West when they refer to geographical regions of the country.

EDITING

▶ **Exercise 5:** Write the capitalization and punctuation rule numbers for each correction in **bold**.
Use References 11, 13, and 14 on pages 13, 17–18 to look up the capitalization and punctuation rule numbers.

Was **C**raig**'**s **TCA** flight from **B**oston to **N**ew **Y**ork delayed on **W**ednesday**?**

▶ **Exercise 6:** Put punctuation corrections within the sentence. Write all other corrections above the sentence.
Editing Guide: Capitals: 8   Commas: 5   Apostrophes: 1   Misspelled Words: 1   End Marks: 1

are ray dave and jay going to timothys gratuation in juneau alaska on june 2 2007

LISTENING AND SPEAKING:

START LESSON 7

Lesson 7

You will
- practice Jingles 1–2.
- learn new analogy.
- respond to oral analogy exercise.
- analyze new analogy; make Card 1; write own analogy.
- do Classroom Practice 4.

Recite It: Practice Jingles 1–2 in the Jingle Section on page 498.

Vocabulary & Analogy Time

Today, analogies will be added to Vocabulary and Analogy Time. First, look at Reference 19 to review the vocabulary word **prior** that you learned in the last lesson.

Reference 19	Vocabulary & Analogy Words

Word: prior (prīˈər)
   Definition: earlier in time or order
   Synonym: before   **Antonym:** after
   Sentence: A practice will be held **prior** to the race.

Analogy: afraid : brave :: shallow : deep
   Antonym relationship: Just as **afraid** is the opposite of **brave**, **shallow** is the opposite of **deep**.

   Analogy Card 1: Record the analogy information and write your own analogy, using the same relationship as the analogy above.

Before you learn the new analogy in Reference 19, look at Reference 20 for information about analogies.

Learn It: **WORD ANALOGIES**

Reference 20	Word Analogies

An **analogy** is a way of looking at pairs of words to find out what they have in common or how they are related. An analogy usually has one word missing. An analogy has symbols that must be read a certain way. Notice how the colons are placed in the analogy below.

This is an analogy statement: **leaf : tree :: petal :** _flower_

This is the proper reading of the analogy: leaf is to tree as petal is to _flower_.

To solve an analogy, you must divide it into two parts. In one part, you are given two words. You must decide how these two words relate to each other. Some ways that words can be related are listed below.

Common Relationships	Analogy	How the Words Are Related
1. Synonym	see : view	**See** means nearly the same as **view**.
2. Antonym	heavy : light	**Heavy** is the opposite of **light**.
3. Part-to-whole	petal : flower	A **petal** is part of a **flower**.
4. Purpose or use	broom : sweep	A **broom** is used to **sweep**.
5. Type or kind	banana : fruit	A **banana** is a kind of **fruit**.
6. Descriptive or characteristic	yellow : sun	**Yellow** describes the **sun**.
7. Rhyming	team : beam	**Team** rhymes with **beam**.
8. Homonym	peace : piece	**Peace** and **piece** sound alike but have different meanings and spellings.

Continued on next page. >>>

Reference 20 continued from previous page.

In the other part of the analogy, you are given only one of the two words. Since you must supply the missing word, you must think about how the first pair of words is related. Then, choose the word that makes the second pair relate in the same way.

1. **see : view :: hear : _____**   (Read as: See is to view as hear is to __.)
   Thinking process: **Synonym** - Just as see means nearly the same as view, hear means nearly the same as <u>listen</u>.

2. **heavy : light :: problem : _____**   (Read as: Heavy is to light as problem is to __.)
   Thinking process: **Antonym** - Just as heavy is the opposite of light, problem is the opposite of <u>solution</u>.

3. **petal : flower :: toe : _____**   (Read as: Petal is to flower as toe is to __.)
   Thinking process: **Part-to-whole** - Just as a petal is a part of a flower, a toe is a part of a <u>foot</u>.

4. **broom : sweep :: _____ : paint**   (Read as: Broom is to sweep as __ is to paint.)
   Thinking process: **Purpose or use** - Just as a broom is used to sweep, a <u>brush</u> is used to paint.

5. **banana : fruit :: _____ : vegetable**   (Read as: Banana is to fruit as __ is to vegetable.)
   Thinking process: **Type or kind** - Just as a banana is a kind of fruit, <u>corn</u> is a kind of vegetable.

6. **yellow : sun :: _____ : lime**   (Read as: Yellow is to sun as __ is to lime.)
   Thinking process: **Descriptive or characteristic** - Just as yellow describes sun, <u>green</u> describes lime.

7. **team : beam :: _____ : block**   (Read as: Team is to beam as __ is to block.)
   Thinking process: **Rhyming** - Just as team rhymes with beam, <u>clock</u> rhymes with block.

8. **peace : piece :: _____ : main**   (Read as: Peace is to piece as __ is to main.)
   Thinking process: **Homonym** - Just as peace is a homonym of piece, <u>mane</u> is a homonym of main.

Review: Step 1: Decide how one pair of words is related.

Step 2: Think how the other pair of words relates in the same way.

Step 3: Choose a word that makes both pairs relate that way.

Word Analogy Exercise: Choose the correct missing word and put the letter in the blank.

1. thorns : cactus :: quills : <u>b</u>   a. bush   b. porcupine   c. fish   d. desert
2. mare : horse :: <u>c</u> : sheep   a. lamb   b. wool   c. ewe   d. flock
3. woods : <u>d</u> :: lake : swimmers   a. fish   b. water   c. snakes   d. hikers
4. engine : caboose :: <u>c</u>   a. head : hair   b. head : red   c. head : feet   d. head : eyes

Apply It: **MAKING CARDS FOR ANALOGY WORDS**
Making cards for analogies will help you remember them.

Reference 21   Making Cards for Analogies

TO MAKE AN ANALOGY CARD:

Use a 4x6 or a 3x5 index card with lines. Write all the analogy information on the side with lines. At the bottom of the card, write your own analogy, using the same relationship as the analogy in the reference.

Use the index cards to study analogies with a study partner at home or at school. Keep the analogy cards in plastic zip bags or recipe boxes.

Classroom Practice 4

It is time to practice the skills you are learning. You will use the classroom practice on the next page to apply these skills.

Classroom Practice 4

Name:_____ Date:_____

SKILLS

▶ **Exercise 1:** Match the definitions by writing the correct letter beside each number.

_____ 1. periods, commas, apostrophes, end marks   A. analogies

_____ 2. words with similar meanings   B. antonyms

_____ 3. words with opposite meanings   C. editing

_____ 4. correcting mistakes in a sentence or paragraph   D. punctuation

_____ 5. organizing, listening, planning, doing homework   E. synonyms

_____ 6. comparisons of words with similar relationships   F. study skills

▶ **Exercise 2:** Identify each pair of words as synonyms or antonyms by underlining the correct answer.

1. rip, mend   2. expired, ended   3. finish, begin
   Synonyms or Antonyms   Synonyms or Antonyms   Synonyms or Antonyms

▶ **Exercise 3:** Choose the correct missing word and put the letter in the blank.

1. zipper : coat :: button : ___   a. hat   b. shirt   c. scarf   d. white

2. green : leaves :: ___ : sky   a. pie   b. clouds   c. sun   d. blue

3. shade : ___ :: light : sight   a. sunny   b. lamp   c. fade   d. night

4. gift : present :: ___   a. wash : cleanse   b. boat : motor   c. hen : egg   d. stop : go

EDITING

▶ **Exercise 4:** Write the capitalization and punctuation rule numbers for each correction in **bold**.
Use References 11, 13, and 14 on pages 13, 17–18 to look up the capitalization and punctuation rule numbers.

Yesterday, I watched the movie, Hoosiers, with my friends, Freddie, Nicholas, and Walter.

▶ **Exercise 5:** Put punctuation corrections within the sentence. Write all other corrections above the sentence.
Editing Guide: Capitals: 9 Underlining: 1 Misspelled Words: 1 End Marks: 1

sir arthur conan doyle published his storey about sherlock holmes in the strand magazine

START LESSON 8

Lesson 8

You will

- practice Jingles 1-2.
- respond to oral review questions.
- take Chapter 1 Test.

CHAPTER TEST

It is time to evaluate your knowledge of the skills you have learned in this chapter. Your teacher will give you the Chapter 1 Test to help you assess your progress.

LISTENING AND SPEAKING:

Recite It: Practice Jingles 1–2 in the Jingle Section on page 498.

Oral Review Questions

Discuss It:

1. What are words with opposite meanings?
2. What are words with similar meanings?
3. What is the relationship between the words meal and feel?
4. What is the relationship between the words green and grass?
5. What is the relationship between the words key and lock?
6. What is proofreading?
7. When you correct mistakes in a sentence or paragraph, what are you doing?
8. What does an editing guide tell you?
9. True or False. Except for the journal entry number and date, no particular organizational style is required for journal writing.
10. True or False. As a student in the fifth grade, short-term goals should include your plans for college and career.
11. What punctuation would you use to separate words in a series?

>>>>>>>>>>>>>>>>>>>>>> **Student Tip...**

For information about test-taking strategies, refer to the Resource Tools Section on page 520.

English Made Easy

LISTENING AND SPEAKING:

Jingle Time

Recite It: 1. Practice Jingles 1–2 in the Jingle Section on page 498.
2. Recite the new jingles.

Lesson 1

You will

- practice Jingles 1–2; recite new jingles (Noun and Verb).
- identify nouns, subject nouns, and verbs.
- learn how to classify sentences.
- classify Introductory Sentences.
- identify a Pattern 1 sentence.
- identify the five parts of a sentence.
- use **SN V** to write a Practice Sentence.
- do Classroom Practice 5.

♪ **Jingle 3** — **The Noun Jingle**

This is a noun jingle, my friend,
A noun jingle, my friend.
You can shake it to the left
And shake it to the right.
Find yourself a noun,
And then recite:

A noun names a person.
A noun names a thing.
A noun names a person,
Place, or thing,
And sometimes an idea.

Person, place, thing, idea!
Person, place, thing, idea!

So, shake it to the left,
And shake it to the right.
Find yourself a noun,
And feel just right!

♪ **Jingle 4** — **The Verb Jingle**

A verb, a verb.
What is a verb?
Haven't you heard?
There are two kinds of verbs:
The **action verb**
And the **linking verb**.

The action verb
Shows a state of action,
Like **stand** and **sit** and **smile**.
The action verb is always in motion
Because it tells what the subject does.
*We **stand**! We **sit**! We **smile**!*

The linking verb shows a state of being,
Like **am**, **is**, **are**, **was**, and **were**,
Looks, **becomes**, **grows**, and **feels**.
The linking verb shows no action
Because it tells what the subject is.
*He **is** a clown. He **looks** funny.*

 Grammar Time

Learn It: NOUN, SUBJECT NOUN, AND VERB

📖 Reference 22	Noun, Subject Noun, and Verb

NOUN AND SUBJECT NOUN

1. A **noun** names a person, place, thing, or idea. A noun is a naming word. Words like *teacher* and *Amanda* name people. Words like *library* and *river* name places. Words like *cat* and *truck* name things. Animals are grouped in the category of things. Words like *freedom* and *beauty* name ideas.

2. The **subject** of a sentence tells who or what a sentence is about. Every sentence has a subject. Since a noun names a person, place, thing, or idea, a *subject noun* tells who or what a sentence is about.

3. A **subject noun** is labeled with the abbreviation **SN**.

VERB

4. A **verb** tells what the subject does or what the subject is. Every sentence has a verb. **Verbs** that tell what people or things do are called **action verbs**. Girls *walk*. Girls *play*. Puppies *walk*. Puppies *play*.

5. A **verb** is labeled with the abbreviation **V**.

Learn It: THE QUESTION AND ANSWER FLOW

📖 Reference 23	The Question & Answer Flow

1. The **Question and Answer Flow** is a series of questions and answers used to identify the parts of a sentence.

2. **Classifying** is naming or identifying each word in a sentence by using the Question and Answer Flow. As you classify the words of a sentence, you will label each word with an abbreviation to identify its function.

3. To classify a subject noun in the Question and Answer Flow, ask a subject question to find the noun that serves as the subject of the sentence. The subject questions are **who** or **what**. Ask *who* if the sentence is *about people*. Ask *what* if the sentence is **not about people**, but about places, things, or ideas. Then, label the subject noun with the abbreviation **SN**.

4. To classify a verb in the Question and Answer Flow, ask the verb question *what is being said about* _____ *(the subject)* since the verb tells what the subject does. Then, label the verb with the abbreviation **V**.

The Question and Answer Flow for the Subject Noun and Verb

Practice Sentence: Pilots flew.

1. Who flew? **pilots - subject noun (SN)**
2. What is being said about pilots? **pilots flew - verb (V)**

```
  SN      V
Pilots flew.
```

Learn It: PATTERN 1

Reference 24 — Pattern 1

1. The **pattern**, or core, of a sentence identifies the **order of its main parts**.
2. A **Pattern 1** has only two main parts as its core: a subject noun (**SN**) and a verb (**V**).
3. A Pattern 1 sentence is identified with the abbreviations of its main parts and pattern number: **SN V P1**. It is also known as a noun-verb (**N V**) core.
4. In the Question and Answer Flow, the pattern of a sentence is identified after all the words in a sentence have been classified.
5. To identify a Pattern 1 sentence, say "Subject Noun, Verb, Pattern 1" and write **SN V P1** on the line in front of a Pattern 1 sentence.

Adding Pattern 1 to the Question and Answer Flow

Practice Sentence: Pilots flew.

1. Who flew? **pilots - subject noun (SN)**
2. What is being said about pilots? **pilots flew - verb (V)**
3. **Subject Noun, Verb, Pattern 1 (SN V P1)**

SN V
_____   Pilots flew.
P1

Apply It: These Introductory Sentences are used to apply the new grammar concepts taught. Classify these sentences orally with your teacher. You will say the **questions** and **answers** with your teacher. The Question and Answer Flow should have a lively rhythm and should be recited in unison.

Introductory Sentences — Chapter 2: Lesson 1

1. _____ Fans applauded.
2. _____ Geese honked.
3. _____ Spaceships docked.

Skill Time

Learn It: THE FIVE PARTS OF A COMPLETE SENTENCE

A **complete sentence** is a group of words that has a subject and a verb and states a complete idea. A complete sentence should also begin with a capital letter and end with a punctuation mark. The five parts of a sentence are identified in the Sentence Jingle.

GRAMMAR & WRITING CONNECTION:
Practice Sentence

Learn It: **THE PRACTICE SENTENCE FOR** *SN V*

A **Practice Sentence** is a sentence you write from the grammar labels that you are learning, like **SN** and **V**. To write a Practice Sentence, you must follow the labels and think of words that fit the labels and that make sense.

Reference 25	Practice Sentence for Sn V
Labels:	SN V
Practice:	Astronauts waited.

Look at the labels **SN** and **V** in Reference 25. First, think of a noun that you want to use as the subject noun. The example uses the word *astronauts* as the subject noun. Notice that the word *astronauts* is written *under* the label **SN** to identify it as the subject noun.

Next, think of a verb that tells what the subject does. You must make sure that the verb makes sense with the subject noun. The example uses the word *waited* as the verb. The word *waited* is written *under* the label **V** to identify it as the verb.

Apply It: **WRITE A PRACTICE SENTENCE, USING THE LABELS** *SN V*

Write a Practice Sentence, using a subject noun and a verb. On the top line of a sheet of notebook paper, write the title ***Practice Sentence***. After you write your title, skip down two lines. On the third line, write the sentence labels **SN V**. Be sure to leave plenty of writing space between each label.

1. Go to the **SN** label for the subject noun. Think of a noun that tells who or what you want to use as the subject of your sentence (*person, place, thing, or idea*). Write the noun you have chosen on the line *under* the **SN** label.

2. Go to the **V** label for the verb. Ask the verb question, "*what is being said about _____ (the subject)?*" to help you think of a verb that tells what your subject does. Make sure that your verb makes sense with the subject noun. Write the verb you have chosen on the line *under* the **V** label.

Practice It:

Write four more sentences, using the same steps that you used to write the first Practice Sentence. Remember to check each Practice Sentence for the five parts of a correct sentence. Each sentence must have a subject and a verb, it must make sense, it must start with a capital letter, and it must end with an end mark.

 Classroom Practice 5

It is time to practice the skills you are learning. You will use the classroom practice on the next page to apply these skills.

Classroom Practice 5

Name:_____ Date:_____

GRAMMAR

▶ **Exercise 1:** Fill in the blanks below for this sentence: **Travelers arrived.**

1. Who arrived?..................................... _____ Subject Noun _____

2. What is being said about travelers? .... _____ _____ Verb _____

3. Subject Noun, Verb, Pattern 1.................. _____

Classify this sentence: _____ Travelers arrived.

▶ **Exercise 2:** Match the definitions by writing the correct letter beside each number.

_____ 1. verb question

_____ 2. subject-noun question (thing)

_____ 3. parts of a complete sentence

_____ 4. subject-noun question (person)

_____ 5. sentences should begin with

_____ 6. tells what the subject does

_____ 7. person, place, thing, idea

A. what

B. a capital letter

C. action verb

D. noun

E. subject, verb, complete sense

F. who

G. what is being said about

SKILLS

▶ **Exercise 3:** Identify each pair of words as synonyms or antonyms by underlining the correct answer.

1. cheap, costly
   Synonyms or Antonyms

2. solitary, alone
   Synonyms or Antonyms

3. single, plural
   Synonyms or Antonyms

▶ **Exercise 4:** Choose the correct missing word and put the letter in the blank.

1. tulip : flower :: apple : ___   a. carrot   b. garden   c. fruit   d. tree

2. food : body :: ___ : light bulb   a. electricity   b. human   c. water   d. steam

3. nest : ___ :: ocean : octopus   a. eight   b. bird   c. best   d. near

4. house : mouse :: ___   a. leaves : tree   b. in: out   c. host : most   d. diamond : gem

EDITING

▶ **Exercise 5:** Write the capitalization and punctuation rule numbers for each correction in **bold**.
Use References 11, 13, and 14 on pages 13, 17–18 to look up the capitalization and punctuation rule numbers.

Was **C**ol**. W**atson able to get a direct flight from **C**hicago**, I**llinois**,** to **P**ortland**, O**regon**?**

▶ **Exercise 6:** Put punctuation corrections within the sentence. Write all other corrections above the sentence.
Editing Guide: Capitals: 7   Commas: 2   Periods: 2   End Marks: 1

savannah takes her dog muffin on walks near the lincoln memorial in washington dc every day

START LESSON 2

Lesson 2

You will

- practice Jingles 3-4; recite new jingles (Adverb and Adjective).
- identify adverbs and adjectives.
- classify Introductory Sentences.
- use **Adj SN V Adv** to write a Practice Sentence.
- do Classroom Practice 6.

LISTENING AND SPEAKING:

Recite It: 1. Practice Jingles 3–4 in the Jingle Section on page 499.
2. Recite the new jingles.

♪	Jingle 5	**The Adverb Jingle**

An adverb modifies a verb, adjective, or another adverb.
An adverb asks, "HOW? WHEN? WHERE?"
To find an adverb: **Go,** *(snap)* **Ask,** *(snap)* **Get.** *(snap)*
But where do I **go**? *To a verb, adjective, or another adverb.*
What do I **ask**? *HOW? WHEN? WHERE?*
What do I **get**? An adverb, man. Cool!

♪	Jingle 6	**The Adjective Jingle**

An adjective modifies a noun or a pronoun.
An adjective asks, "WHAT KIND?"
An adjective asks, "WHICH ONE?"
An adjective asks, "HOW MANY?"
To identify an adjective: **Go!** *(stomp, stomp)* **Ask!** *(clap, clap)* **Get!** *(snap)*
Where do I **go**? *(stomp, stomp)* To a noun or a pronoun.
What do I **ask**? *(clap, clap)* WHAT KIND? WHICH ONE? or HOW MANY?
What do I **get**? *(snap, snap)* An Adjective!

Apply It: These Introductory Sentences are used to apply the new grammar concepts taught. Classify these sentences orally with your teacher.

Introductory Sentences	Chapter 2: Lesson 2

1. _____ Muskrats swim gracefully around sometimes.

2. _____ Students studied rather late tonight.

3. _____ Three loaded cargo ships arrived rather early.

English Made Easy

Learn It: ADVERBS

 Reference 26 | **Adverbs**

There are several things you should know about adverbs.

1. The Adverb Jingle gives a lot of information about an adverb quickly and easily.

2. The adverb definition says that an adverb modifies a verb, an adjective, or another adverb.

3. The adverb questions are *How? When? Where?*

4. The adverb definition uses the word *modifies.* The word **modify** means to describe. When the adverb definition says that an adverb modifies a verb, an adjective, or another adverb, it means that an adverb **describes** a verb, an adjective, or another adverb.

5. An *adverb* is labeled with the abbreviation **Adv**.

6. An adverb is not part of a sentence pattern because it is not considered a core part. Always identify the core parts of a sentence, the subject noun and verb, before identifying other parts of the sentence.

Adding Adverbs to the Question and Answer Flow

Practice Sentence: Pilots flew skillfully around yesterday.

1. Who flew skillfully around yesterday? **pilots – subject noun (SN)**

2. What is being said about pilots? **pilots flew – verb (V)**

3. Flew how? **skillfully – adverb (Adv)**

4. Flew where? **around – adverb (Adv)**

5. Flew when? **yesterday – adverb (Adv)**

6. **Subject Noun, Verb, Pattern 1 (SN V P1)**

	SN	V	Adv	Adv	Adv

$\underline{\text{SN V}}$ Pilots flew skillfully around yesterday.
$\overline{\text{P1}}$

Discuss It:

1. Where do you go to find an adverb?

2. Where do you go **first** to find an adverb?

3. What is the verb in the practice sentence?

4. What do you ask after you go to the verb *flew*?

5. How do you know which adverb question to ask?

6. Which adverb question would you use to find the first adverb in this sentence?

7. Which adverb question would you use to find the second adverb in this sentence?

8. Which adverb question would you use to find the third adverb in this sentence?

Learn It: ADJECTIVES

| 📖 | **Reference 27** | **Adjectives** |

There are several things you should know about adjectives.

1. The Adjective Jingle gives a lot of information about an adjective quickly and easily.
2. The adjective definition says that an adjective modifies a noun or pronoun.
3. The adjective questions are *What kind? Which one? How many?*
4. The adjective definition uses the word *modifies*. The word **modify** means to describe. When the adjective definition says that an adjective modifies a noun or pronoun, it means that an adjective **describes** a noun or pronoun.
5. An *adjective* is labeled with the abbreviation **Adj.**
6. An adjective is not part of a sentence pattern because it is not considered a core part. Always identify the core parts of a sentence, the subject noun and verb, before identifying other parts of the sentence.

Adding Adjectives to the Question and Answer Flow

Practice Sentence: Three trained pilots flew skillfully around yesterday.

1. Who flew skillfully around yesterday? **pilots – subject noun (SN)**
2. What is being said about pilots? **pilots flew – verb (V)**
3. Flew how? **skillfully – adverb (Adv)**
4. Flew where? **around – adverb (Adv)**
5. Flew when? **yesterday – adverb (Adv)**
6. What kind of pilots? **trained – adjective (Adj)**
7. How many pilots? **three – adjective (Adj)**
8. **Subject Noun, Verb, Pattern 1 (SN V P1)**

```
         Adj   Adj   SN    V   Adv     Adv    Adv
SN  V  _____ Three trained pilots flew skillfully around yesterday.
P1
```

Discuss It:

1. Where do you go to find an adjective?
2. Where do you go **first** to find an adjective?
3. What is the subject noun in the practice sentence?
4. What do you ask after you go to the subject noun pilots?
5. How do you know which adjective question to ask?
6. Which adjective questions would you use to find the adjectives in this sentence?

GRAMMAR & WRITING CONNECTION:
Practice Sentence

Learn It: **THE PRACTICE SENTENCE FOR *ADJ, SN, V, ADV***

Add adjectives and adverbs to the **Practice Sentence**.

✐*	Reference 28	Practice Sentence for Adj Adj SN V Adv Adv

Labels:	Adj	Adj	SN	V	Adv	Adv
Practice:	Seven	older	astronauts	waited	eagerly	today.

The Practice Sentence in Reference 28 uses six labels: **Adj, Adj, SN, V, Adv,** and **Adv**. The word *astronauts* is the subject noun, and the word *waited* is the verb. The words *astronauts* and *waited* are written *under* the labels **SN** and **V** to identify them as the subject noun and verb.

Adverbs and adjectives are used to expand the sentence. The words *eagerly* and *today* are written *under* the labels **Adv** to identify them as the two adverbs in the sentence. The adverb *eagerly* tells *how* the astronauts waited, and the adverb *today* tells *when* the astronauts waited. You may add more adverbs to a Practice Sentence, but the adverbs must make sense.

The words *seven* and *older* are written *under* the labels **Adj** to identify them as the two adjectives in the sentence. The adjective *older* tells *what kind* of astronauts, and the adjective *seven* tells *how many* astronauts. You may add more adjectives to a Practice Sentence, but the adjectives must make sense.

Apply It: **WRITE A PRACTICE SENTENCE,**
 USING THE LABELS *ADJ, ADJ, SN, V, ADV, ADV*

Write a Practice Sentence, adding adjectives and adverbs. On the top line of a sheet of notebook paper, write the title **Practice Sentence**. After you write your title, skip down two lines. On the third line, write the sentence labels **Adj Adj SN V Adv Adv**. Be sure to leave plenty of writing space between each label.

1. Go to the **SN** label for the subject noun. Think of a noun that tells who or what you want to use as the subject of your sentence *(person, place, thing, or idea)*. Write the noun you have chosen on the line *under* the **SN** label.

2. Go to the **V** label for the verb. Ask the verb question, "*What is being said about _____ (the subject)?*" to help you think of a verb that tells what your subject does. Make sure that your verb makes sense with the subject noun. Write the verb you have chosen on the line *under* the **V** label.

3. Go to the first **Adv** label for the first adverb. Go to the verb in your sentence and ask an adverb question. What are the adverb questions? *(How? When? Where?)* Choose one adverb question to ask and write your adverb answer *under* the first **Adv** label.

4. Go to the second **Adv** label for another adverb. Go to the verb again and ask another adverb question. You can ask the same question or a different question. *(How? When? Where?)* After choosing an adverb question, write your adverb answer *under* the second **Adv** label.

5. Go to the second **Adj** label for the adjective that is closest to the subject noun. Go to the subject noun of your sentence and ask an adjective question. What are the adjective questions? *(What kind? Which one? How many?)* Choose one adjective question to ask and write your adjective answer *under* the **Adj** label next to the subject noun.

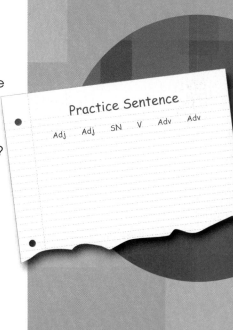

Practice Sentence

Adj   Adj   SN   V   Adv   Adv

Continued on next page. >>>

6. Go to the subject noun of your sentence again and ask another adjective question for the first **Adj** label. You can ask the same question or a different question. *(What kind? Which one? How many?)* After choosing an adjective question to ask, write your adjective answer *under* the first **Adj** label.

7. Always check to make sure your word choices make sense in the sentence.

Practice It:

Write one more sentence, using the same steps that you used to write the first Practice Sentence. Remember to check your Practice Sentence for the five parts of a complete sentence. Your sentence must have a subject and a verb, it must make sense, it must start with a capital letter, and it must end with an end mark.

Classroom Practice 6

It is time to practice the skills you are learning. You will use the classroom practice on the next page to apply these skills.

Classroom Practice 6

Name:_____ Date:_____

GRAMMAR

▶ **Exercise 1:** Fill in the blanks below for this sentence: **Some energetic little chipmunks darted playfully around.**

1. What darted playfully around? . . . . _____ Subject Noun _____

2. What is being said about chipmunks? . . . . _____ _____ Verb _____

3. Darted how? . . . . _____ Adverb _____

4. Darted where? . . . . _____ Adverb _____

5. What kind of chipmunks? . . . . _____ Adjective _____

6. What kind of chipmunks? . . . . _____ Adjective _____

7. How many chipmunks? . . . . _____ Adjective _____

8. Subject Noun, Verb, Pattern 1. . . . . _____

Classify this sentence: _____ Some energetic little chipmunks darted playfully around.

▶ **Exercise 2:** Write a Practice Sentence, using the following labels. **Adj Adj SN V Adv Adv**

_____

▶ **Exercise 3:** Write the correct answer.

1. What does an adverb modify? . . . . _____

2. What does an adjective modify? . . . . _____

3. What does a noun name? . . . . _____

4. What are the adverb questions? . . . . _____

5. What are the adjective questions? . . . . _____

EDITING

▶ **Exercise 4:** Write the capitalization and punctuation rule numbers for each correction in **bold**.
Use References 11, 13, and 14 on pages 13, 17–18 to look up the capitalization and punctuation rule numbers.

Harry Pickford, my best friend, lives at 137 Oak Avenue in Gulfport, Mississippi.

▶ **Exercise 5:** Put punctuation corrections within the sentence. Write all other corrections above the sentence.
Editing Guide: Capitals: 6   Commas: 2   Misspelled Words: 1   End Marks: 1

uncle joe aunt carla and my cousins travled from the northeast to the southeast on vacation

START LESSON 3

Lesson 3

You will

- practice Jingles 3–6; recite new jingle (Article Adjective).
- identify article adjectives.
- classify Introductory Sentences.
- use **A Adj SN V Adv** to write a Practice Sentence.
- do Classroom Practice 7.

LISTENING AND SPEAKING:

Recite It: 1. Practice Jingles 3–6 in the Jingle Section on page 499.
2. Recite the new jingle.

♪	Jingle 7	**The Article Adjective Jingle**

We are the article adjectives,
Teeny, tiny adjectives.
A, AN, THE—A, AN, THE

We are called article adjectives and noun markers.
We are memorized and used every day.
So, if you spot us, you can mark us
With a capital A.

We are the article adjectives,
Teeny, tiny adjectives.
A, AN, THE—A, AN, THE

Apply It: These Introductory Sentences are used to apply the new grammar concepts taught. Classify these sentences orally with your teacher.

Introductory Sentences	Chapter 2: Lesson 3
1. _____	The big, ugly mosquito buzzed annoyingly around.
2. _____	A fierce lion roamed hungrily around tonight.
3. _____	An excited marathon runner leaned eagerly forward.

Learn It: **ARTICLE ADJECTIVES**

📖	Reference 29	**Article Adjectives**

There are several things you should know about article adjectives.

1. The Article Adjective Jingle gives a lot of information about an article adjective quickly and easily.
2. Only three adjectives are called articles. They are **a, an, the**. They are also known as noun markers.
3. Article adjectives must be memorized because you do not ask questions to find them.
4. Use the article **a** before singular words that begin with a consonant sound. Use the article **an** before singular words that begin with a vowel sound. The articles **a** and **an** are called *indefinite* articles, meaning *one* of several. (**a** book, meaning one of several books; **an** answer, meaning one of several answers)
5. Use the article **the** before words that begin with either a consonant or a vowel sound. Use the article **the** before either singular or plural words. The article **the** is called a *definite* article, meaning "a specific person, place, thing, or idea." (**the** book, meaning a specific book; **the** five books, meaning five specific books)

Continued on next page. >>>

Reference 29 continued from previous page.

6. The article **the** has two pronunciations:
   a. A long **e** (used when the article comes before a word that begins with a vowel sound: the egg, the igloo)
   b. A short **u** (used when the article comes before a word that begins with a consonant sound: the mop, the store)
7. An *article adjective* is labeled with the abbreviation **A**.
8. An article adjective is not part of a sentence pattern because it is not part of the core. Always identify the core parts of a sentence, the subject noun and verb, before identifying other parts of the sentence.

Adding an Article Adjective to the Question and Answer Flow

Practice Sentence: The three trained pilots flew skillfully around yesterday.

1. Who flew skillfully around yesterday?
   pilots - subject noun (SN)
2. What is being said about pilots?
   pilots flew - verb (V)
3. Flew how? **skillfully - adverb (Adv)**
4. Flew where? **around - adverb (Adv)**

5. Flew when? **yesterday - adverb (Adv)**
6. What kind of pilots?
   trained - adjective (Adj)
7. How many pilots? **three - adjective (Adj)**
8. **The - article adjective (A)**
9. **Subject Noun, Verb, Pattern 1 (SN V P1)**

$$\underline{\underset{P1}{SN\ V}} \quad \overset{A}{The}\ \overset{Adj}{three}\ \overset{Adj}{trained}\ \overset{SN}{pilots}\ \overset{V}{flew}\ \overset{Adv}{skillfully}\ \overset{Adv}{around}\ \overset{Adv}{yesterday.}$$

Discuss It:

1. What are the three article adjectives?
2. How do you find article adjectives?
3. What are article adjectives sometimes called?

GRAMMAR & WRITING CONNECTION:
Practice Sentence

Learn It: **A PRACTICE SENTENCE FOR A, ADJ, ADJ, SN, V, ADV, ADV**

Add an article adjective to the **Practice Sentence**.

Reference 30	Practice Sentence for A Adj Adj SN V Adv Adv
Labels:	A Adj Adj SN V Adv Adv
Practice:	**The seven older astronauts waited eagerly today.**

The Practice Sentence in Reference 30 uses seven labels: **A, Adj, Adj, SN, V, Adv,** and **Adv**. The words *astronauts* and *waited* are written *under* the labels **SN** and **V** to identify them as the subject noun and verb. The words *eagerly* and *today* are written *under* the labels **Adv** to identify them as the two adverbs in the sentence. The words *seven* and *older* are written *under* the labels **Adj** to identify them as the two adjectives in the sentence.

The word *the* is written *under* the label **A** to identify it as an article adjective. Of the three articles, only the article adjective *the* can be used before the plural noun, *astronauts*.

Apply It: **WRITE A PRACTICE SENTENCE,**
USING THE LABELS A, *ADJ, ADJ, SN, V, ADV, ADV*

Write a Practice Sentence, adding an article adjective. On the top line of a sheet of notebook paper, write the title ***Practice Sentence***. After you write your title, skip down two lines. On the third line, write the sentence labels **A Adj Adj SN V Adv Adv**. Be sure to leave plenty of writing space between each label.

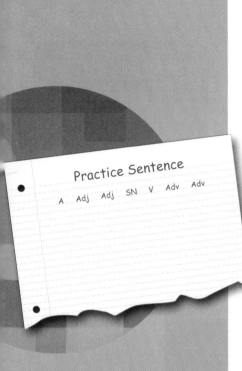

1. Go to the **SN** label for the subject noun. Think of a noun that tells who or what you want to use as the subject of your sentence *(person, place, thing, or idea)*. Write the noun you have chosen on the line *under* the **SN** label.

2. Go to the **V** label for the verb. Ask the verb question, "*What is being said about _____ (the subject)?*" to help you think of a verb that tells what your subject does. Make sure that your verb makes sense with the subject noun. Write the verb you have chosen on the line *under* the **V** label.

3. Go to the first **Adv** label for the first adverb. Go to the verb in your sentence and ask an adverb question. What are the adverb questions? *(How? When? Where?)* Choose one adverb question to ask and write your adverb answer *under* the first **Adv** label.

4. Go to the second **Adv** label for another adverb. Go to the verb again and ask another adverb question. You can ask the same question or a different question. *(How? When? Where?)* After choosing an adverb question to ask, write your adverb answer *under* the second **Adv** label.

5. Go to the second **Adj** label for the adjective that is closest to the subject noun. Go to the subject noun of your sentence and ask an adjective question. What are the adjective questions? *(What kind? Which one? How many?)* Choose one adjective question to ask and write your adjective answer *under* the **Adj** label next to the subject noun.

6. Go to the subject noun of your sentence again and ask an adjective question for the first **Adj** label. You can ask the same question or a different question. *(What kind? Which one? How many?)* After choosing an adjective question to ask, write your adjective answer *under* the first **Adj** label.

7. Go to the **A** label for the article adjective. What are the three article adjectives? *(a, an, and the)* You will choose the article adjective that makes the best sense in the sentence. After choosing the article adjective, write it *under* the **A** label.

8. Always check to make sure your word choices make sense in the sentence.

Practice It:

Write one more sentence, using the same steps that you used to write the first Practice Sentence. Remember to check your Practice Sentence for the five parts of a complete sentence. Your sentence must have a subject and a verb, it must make sense, it must start with a capital letter, and it must end with an end mark.

Classroom Practice 7

It is time to practice the skills you are learning. You will use the classroom practice on the next page to apply these skills.

Classroom Practice 7

Name:_____ Date:_____

GRAMMAR

▶ **Exercise 1:** Fill in the blanks below for this sentence: **The tardy student ran incredibly fast.**

1. Who ran incredibly fast? .... _____ Subject Noun _____

2. What is being said about student?............ _____ _____ Verb _____

3. Ran how?.. _____ Adverb _____

4. How fast? .... _____ Adverb _____

5. What kind of student?........................... _____ Adjective _____

6. _____ Article Adjective _____

7. Subject Noun, Verb, Pattern 1................... _____

Classify this sentence: _____ The tardy student ran incredibly fast.

▶ **Exercise 2:** Write a Practice Sentence, using the following labels. **A Adj Adj SN V Adv Adv**

_____

▶ **Exercise 3:** Write the correct answer in each blank.

1. What are the article adjectives? .... _____

2. What does an adverb modify?................. _____

3. What are the adverb questions?.............. _____

4. What does an adjective modify?.............. _____

5. What are the adjective questions?........... _____

6. What does a noun name?...................... _____

EDITING

▶ **Exercise 4:** Write the capitalization and punctuation rule numbers for each correction in **bold**. Use References 11, 13, and 14 on pages 13, 17–18 to look up the capitalization and punctuation rule numbers.

Mom, I'll make reservations for you at the Italian restaurant on Vine Street on Friday, June 10.

▶ **Exercise 5:** Put punctuation corrections within the sentence. Write all other corrections above the sentence.
Editing Guide: Capitals: 6 Commas: 2 Apostrophes: 1 Misspelled Words: 1 Periods: 1 Underlining: 1 End Marks: 1

mrs jameson the libarian showed mary an unusual article in this weeks florida star herald

START LESSON 4

Lesson 4

You will

- practice Jingles 2–7.
- identify four kinds of sentences and recite the End Mark Flow.
- identify skill check, complete subject, and complete predicate.
- classify Introductory Sentences.
- recognize nouns, verbs, adjectives, and adverbs as parts of speech.
- do Classroom Practice 8.

LISTENING AND SPEAKING:

Recite It: Practice Jingles 2–7 in the Jingle Section on pages 498–499.

Apply It: These Introductory Sentences are used to apply the new grammar concepts. Classify these sentences orally with your teacher.

Introductory Sentences	Chapter 2: Lesson 4
1. _____ The very determined young doctor spoke confidently today.	
2. _____ An unusually talented musician played especially well tonight.	
3. _____ All the terrified animals bolted fearfully away!	

Learn It: **THE FOUR KINDS OF SENTENCES AND THE END MARK FLOW**

The top part of Reference 31 tells about the four kinds of sentences, and the bottom part tells about the End Mark Flow.

📖 Reference 31   The Four Kinds of Sentences and the End Mark Flow

1. A **declarative** sentence makes a statement. It is labeled with a **D**.
   Example: We are going to the game tonight.
   (Period, statement, declarative sentence)

2. An **imperative** sentence gives a command. It is labeled with an **Imp**.
   Example: Watch for the school bus.
   (Period, command, imperative sentence)

3. An **interrogative** sentence asks a question. It is labeled with an **Int**.
   Example: Did you swim in the city pool?
   (Question mark, question, interrogative sentence)

4. An **exclamatory** sentence expresses strong feeling. It is labeled with an **E**.
   Example: A huge tree fell in the middle of the road!
   (Exclamation point, strong feeling, exclamatory sentence)

END MARK FLOW

The **End Mark Flow** identifies the end mark, gives the definition, and names the kind of sentence.
(Example: period, statement, declarative sentence.)

Directions: Read each sentence, recite the End Mark Flow in parentheses, and put the end mark and the abbreviation for the kind of sentence in the blank at the end of each sentence.

1. We ate at the new restaurant today **.** D
   (Period, statement, declarative sentence)

2. Listen quietly to the storyteller **.** Imp
   (Period, command, imperative sentence)

3. Did you wash the dishes **?** Int
   (Question mark, question, interrogative sentence)

4. That snake crawled across my foot **!** E
   (Exclamation point, strong feeling, exclamatory sentence)

>>>> **Student Tip...**

> Develop hand signals for the End Mark Flow. Suggestions: Make a fist in your palm as you say "period, statement, declarative sentence." Slap two fingers in your palm as you say "period, command, imperative sentence." Arch both arms high in the air with fingertips touching as you say "question mark, question, interrogative sentence." Make both hands into fists, bend your arms back to your chest, straighten your arms quickly, and point your index fingers as you say "exclamation point, strong feeling, exclamatory sentence."

Learn It: SKILL CHECK, END MARK FLOW, COMPLETE SUBJECT, AND COMPLETE PREDICATE

Reference 32	**Skill Check, End Mark Flow, Complete Subject, & Complete Predicate**

After a sentence has been classified and the pattern identified, a **Skill Check** will be added to the Question and Answer Flow to identify specific skills. The Skill Check will identify the End Mark Flow, the complete subject, and the complete predicate. Other skills will be added to the Skill Check later.

A REVIEW OF THE END MARK FLOW FOR THE FOUR KINDS OF SENTENCES
When you say the End Mark Flow *(such as period, statement, declarative sentence)*, you are identifying the end mark, giving the definition, and naming the kind of sentence. As you write the abbreviation at the end of the sentence, you are verifying that you have gone through the End Mark Flow and have identified the kind of sentence.
1. Period, statement, declarative sentence (**D**)
2. Period, command, imperative sentence (**Imp**)
3. Question mark, question, interrogative sentence (**Int**)
4. Exclamation point, strong feeling, exclamatory sentence (**E**)

COMPLETE SUBJECT AND COMPLETE PREDICATE
The **complete subject** is the subject and all the words that modify it. The complete subject usually starts at the beginning of the sentence and includes every word up to the verb of the sentence. A vertical line in front of the verb shows where the <u>subject parts end</u>.

The **complete predicate** is the verb and all the words that modify it. The complete predicate usually starts with the verb and includes every word after the verb. A vertical line in front of the verb shows where the <u>predicate parts begin</u>.

To identify the complete subject and predicate in the Question and Answer Flow, say, "Go back to the verb. Divide the complete subject from the complete predicate." Draw a vertical line in front of the verb to divide the subject parts on the left from the predicate parts on the right.

Note: At this time, the Question and Answer Flow for the Practice Sentence below will use abbreviations to identify the sentence parts. You will continue saying the words for which the abbreviations stand.
(Example: For the abbreviation **SN**, you will continue to say the words *subject noun*.)

Adding a Skill Check to the Question and Answer Flow

Practice Sentence: The three trained pilots flew skillfully around yesterday.

1. Who flew skillfully around yesterday? **pilots - SN**
2. What is being said about pilots? **pilots flew - V**
3. Flew how? **skillfully - Adv**
4. Flew where? **around - Adv**
5. Flew when? **yesterday - Adv**
6. What kind of pilots? **trained - Adj**
7. How many pilots? **three - Adj**

8. **The - A**
9. **SN V P1**
10. Skill Check
11. **Period, statement, declarative sentence**
    *(Write **D** at the end of the sentence.)*
12. Go back to the verb. Divide the complete subject from the complete predicate.
    (As you say <u>divide</u>, draw a vertical line before the verb.)

```
        A    Adj    Adj    SN    V    Adv    Adv    Adv
SN V ____ The  three trained pilots / flew skillfully around yesterday.  D
P1
```

SHURLEY ENGLISH

Learn It: PARTS OF SPEECH

Do you know that all words in the English language have been put into eight groups called the **Parts of Speech**? How a word is used in a sentence determines its part of speech. The sentences you have been classifying are made from four parts of speech. Do you know the names of these four parts of speech?

Classroom Practice 8

It is time to practice the skills you are learning. You will use the classroom practice on the next page to apply these skills.

Classroom Practice 8

Name:_____ Date:_____

GRAMMAR

▶ **Exercise 1:** Fill in the blanks below for this sentence:
Nasty computer viruses appear very unexpectedly.

1. What appear very unexpectedly?............. _____ Subject Noun _____

2. What is being said about viruses?............. _____ _____ Verb _____

3. Appear how?................................. _____ Adverb _____

4. How unexpectedly?........................ _____ Adverb _____

5. What kind of viruses? .... _____ Adjective _____

6. What kind of viruses? .... _____ Adjective _____

7. Subject Noun, Verb, Pattern 1............... _____

8. Skill Check

9. Period, statement, declarative sentence...... _____

10. Go back to the verb. Divide the complete subject from the complete predicate. _____

Classify this sentence: _____ Nasty computer viruses appear very unexpectedly.

▶ **Exercise 2:** Name the four parts of speech that you have studied so far.

1._____   2._____   3._____   4._____

SKILLS

▶ **Exercise 3:** Put the end mark and the End Mark Flow for each kind of sentence in the blanks.
Use these words in your answers: *declarative, exclamatory, imperative, interrogative.*

1. Sit down for dinner___.................. _____

2. Did you do well on your exam___....... _____

3. The fire is out of control___ .... _____

4. I'm leaving on my trip tomorrow___ ... _____

EDITING

▶ **Exercise 4:** Write the capitalization and punctuation rule numbers for each correction in **bold**.
Use References 11, 13, and 14 on pages 13, 17–18 to look up the capitalization and punctuation rule numbers.

Gen. A. J. Patton returned to Miami, Florida, in March after four years in Cairo, Egypt.

▶ **Exercise 5:** Put punctuation corrections within the sentence. Write all other corrections above the sentence.
Editing Guide: Capitals: 7   Commas: 3   Misspelled Words: 1   Apostrophes: 1   Underlining: 1   End Marks: 1

leslie ill take you lori and melanie to the productsion of cats on broadway in july

START LESSON 5

Lesson 5

You will

- study new vocabulary; make Card 2; write own sentence using the vocabulary word.
- analyze new analogy; make Card 2; write own analogy.
- practice Jingle 2.
- do Classroom Practice 9.
- create and label a sentence in a group activity.
- write in your journal.

LISTENING AND SPEAKING:

Vocabulary & Analogy Time

Learn It: Recite the new vocabulary and analogy words.

📖 Reference 33	Vocabulary & Analogy Words

Word: abolish (ə bŏl'ĭsh)
   Definition: to do away with
   Synonym: eliminate   **Antonym:** establish
   Sentence: Egyptian kings **abolished** statues of former kings.

Analogy: sail : sale :: sent : cent
   Homonym relationship: Just as a **sail** is a homonym of **sale**,
               sent is a homonym of **cent**.

    Vocabulary Card 2: Record the vocabulary information above and write your own sentence, using the new word.
    Analogy Card 2: Record the analogy information and write your own analogy, using the same relationship as the analogy above.

Jingle Time

Recite It: Practice Jingle 2 in the Jingle Section on page 498.

GRAMMAR & WRITING CONNECTION:
Practice and Revised Sentences

Learn It: **A REVISED SENTENCE**

You have been writing Practice Sentences, using all the parts of speech that you have studied. Now, you must learn how to improve your Practice Sentence by writing a Revised Sentence. A **Revised Sentence** is a sentence made from the Practice Sentence, which is changed and improved through the use of synonyms, antonyms, complete-word changes, and/or by adding or deleting words. Writing Revised Sentences helps you learn to make better word choices as you revise the content of your Practice Sentence.

Reference 34	Independent Practice and Revised Sentences

1. Write a Practice Sentence according to the labels you choose. Use the **SN V** labels once. You may use the other labels in any order and as many times as you wish in order to make a Practice Sentence. Chapter 2 labels for a Practice Sentence: (**SN, V,** Adj, Adv, A)

2. Write a Revised Sentence. Use the following revision strategies: *synonym (**syn**), antonym (**ant**), word change (**wc**), added word (**add**), deleted word (**delete**)*, or *no change (**nc**)*. Under each word, write the abbreviation of the revision strategy you use.

3. As you go through each word of your Practice Sentence, think about the changes and improvements you want to make. Think about what you really want to say. After a Practice Sentence is written, it is easier to look more critically at each word in the sentence to see if you can think of a better word to express your thought.

4. As you write a Revised Sentence, you may make several changes or only a few. Antonym changes and complete-word changes will alter the meaning and direction of your sentence. Knowing different ways to revise sentences gives you more flexibility as you work to improve your sentences.

5. When you have finished, your Practice and Revised Sentences should resemble the examples below.

Labels:	A	Adj	Adj	SN	V	Adv	Adv
Practice:	**The**	**seven**	**older**	**astronauts**	**waited**	**eagerly**	**today.**
Revised:		**Seven**	**experienced**	**astronauts**	**stepped**	**enthusiastically**	**forward.**
Strategies:	(delete)	(nc)	(syn)	(nc)	(wc)	(syn)	(wc)

Apply It:

You will write a Practice Sentence and a Revised Sentence for Classroom Practice 9. Since the directions for a Practice Sentence and a Revised Sentence are very important, they are listed and explained below.

1. Write a Practice Sentence according to the labels you choose. <u>Use the **SN V** labels once</u>. You may use the <u>other</u> labels in any order and as many times as you wish in order to make a Practice Sentence. Chapter 2 labels for Practice Sentence: **SN**, **V**, Adj, Adv, A

2. Write a Revised Sentence. Use the following revision strategies: synonym (*syn*), antonym (*ant*), word change (*wc*), added word (*add*), deleted word (*delete*), or no change (*nc*). Under each word, write the abbreviation of the revision strategy you use.

In each chapter, new labels will be added. You must make your Practice Sentence only from the labels that are listed. The pattern labels, or core parts, are listed first in bold letters. The other labels are not pattern indicators, and they are not in bold type.

First, you will write the labels for your Practice Sentence. You will use your pattern label, **SN V**, only one time. You can use the other labels that are not in bold type (Adj, Adv, A) as many times as you want. For example, you can use the adjective label five times if you want your Practice Sentence to have five adjectives.

Next, you will write your Practice Sentence, following the label guides you have chosen. If you need to rearrange your labels, do it while you are writing the Practice Sentence. Then, you should look carefully at your Practice Sentence to find ways to improve and revise it. You will use the revision strategies listed on your page to help you write a Revised Sentence. Finally, you will write the abbreviation of the revision strategy you used under each word.

Use the information in Reference 35 to help you build and expand your Practice and Revised Sentences.

Reference 35 | **A Guide for Using Nouns, Verbs, Adjectives, and Adverbs to Build and Expand Sentences**

1. **SN (subject noun)** Think of a noun that tells who or what *(person, place, thing, or idea)* will be the subject of your sentence. The subject is very important because it determines your choice of words for the rest of the sentence. Write the noun you have chosen for the subject of your sentence.

2. **V (verb)** Ask the verb question, "*what is being said about _____ (the subject)*?O" to help you think of a verb that tells what your subject does. Make sure that the verb makes sense with the subject noun. Write the verb you have chosen for your sentence.

3. **Adv (adverb)** Go to the verb and ask an adverb question *(How? When? or Where?)* to help you think of an adverb. Write the adverb in your sentence. Repeat this step for each adverb you add to the sentence.

4. **Adj (adjective)** Go to a noun and ask an adjective question *(What kind? Which one? or How many?)* to help you think of an adjective. Write the adjective in your sentence. Repeat this step for each adjective you add to the sentence.

5. **A (article adjective)** Choose the article adjective *(a, an, or the)* that makes the best sense and write it in your sentence. Repeat this step for each article adjective you add to the sentence.

6. Always check to make sure all your word choices make sense in the sentence.

✏ Classroom Practice 9

It is time to practice the skills you are learning. You will use the classroom practice on the next page to apply these skills.

Student Activity

Create a sentence with other students. Divide into small groups. Each group will complete three jobs.

Job 1. Write each of these sentence labels on separate sheets of construction paper: **SN, V, A, Adj, Adj, Adj, Adv, Adv**

Job 2. Write a period (.) and an exclamation point (!) on separate sheets of construction paper. Write the words **capital letter** on another sheet of construction paper.

Job 3. Write 3 to 6 words on separate sheets of construction paper for each label below.

SN words: (3 to 6 nouns)   **Adj** words: (3 to 6 adjectives)

V words: (3 to 6 verbs)   **Adv** words: (3 to 6 adverbs)

A words: (3 article adjectives)

Now, each group exchanges its words with another group. Following the directions below, each group must create a sentence with the other group's words. The teacher will select enough class members to help each group construct its sentence.

1. **Group:** Decide the order of the sentence labels.
   Helpers: Hold up the labels in the selected sentence order.

2. **Group:** Select the words to fit each label.
   Helpers: Kneel in front of the appropriate labels, holding the selected words.

3. **Group:** Decide where the capital letter and the period or exclamation point should be placed.
   Helpers: Stand at the beginning and end of the sentence with the appropriate signs.

4. **Group:** Read the sentence aloud to the class.
   Class: Check to make sure the sentence has all its parts.

The subject and verb are the main parts of a sentence. Notice that the subject and verb determine the choice of words for the rest of the sentence.

JOURNAL WRITING 4

Write an entry in your journal. Use Reference 9 on page 12 for ideas.

Classroom Practice 9

Name: _____

Date: _____

PRACTICE & REVISED SENTENCES

1. Write a Practice Sentence according to the labels you choose.
Use the **SN V** labels once. You may use the other labels in any order and as many times as you wish in order to make a Practice Sentence.
Chapter 2 labels for a Practice Sentence: **SN, V,** Adj, Adv, A

2. Write a Revised Sentence. Use the following revision strategies: *synonym (syn), antonym (ant), word change (wc), added word (add), deleted word (delete),* or *no change (nc).* Under each word, write the abbreviation of the revision strategy you use.

Labels:

Practice:

Revised:

Strategies:

Labels:

Practice:

Revised:

Strategies:

Labels:

Practice:

Revised:

Strategies:

START LESSON 6

Lesson 6

You will

- study new vocabulary; make Card 3; write own sentence using the vocabulary word.
- analyze new analogy; make Card 3; write own analogy.
- identify topics.
- identify supporting/ nonsupporting ideas and sentences.
- do Classroom Practice 10.

LISTENING AND SPEAKING:

Learn It: Recite the new vocabulary and analogy words.

📖 Reference 36	Vocabulary & Analogy Words

Word: integrity (ĭn tĕg'rĭ tē)
    Definition: honorable character
    Synonym: honesty   **Antonym:** deceit
    Sentence: We never questioned our neighbor's **integrity**.

Analogy: new : few :: minor : diner
    Rhyming relationship: Just as **new** rhymes with **few**,
                  minor rhymes with **diner**.

  Vocabulary Card 3: Record the vocabulary information above and write your own sentence, using the new word.

    Analogy Card 3: Record the analogy information and write your own analogy, using the same relationship as the analogy above.

Learn It: TOPICS AND PARAGRAPHS

✏️ Reference 37	Topics and Paragraphs

A **topic** can tell what a paragraph or what a group of words is about. A **paragraph** is a group of sentences that tells about one topic. The topic is also called the **subject** of a paragraph.

Directions for finding the topic: Write the name of the topic that best describes what each group of words is about.

Choose from these topics: **Grains**   **Animals**   **State Capitals**   **Insects**

(1) State Capitals	(2) Insects	(3) Grains
Des Moines	beetle	rye
Salem	wasp	wheat
Austin	ant	rice
Phoenix	butterfly	corn

Learn It: SUPPORTING AND NONSUPPORTING IDEAS AND SENTENCES

When a topic has been selected, all sentences and ideas should tell about that topic. A sentence or idea that tells about the topic is called **supporting** and can be used to develop the topic. A sentence or idea that does not support the topic is called **nonsupporting** and should not be used.

Reference 38	Supporting and NonSupporting Ideas and Sentences

In each column, cross out the one idea that does not support the underlined topic.

(1) Southern States	(2) Presidents	(3) Oceans
Georgia	Zachary Taylor	Atlantic
Alabama	James Polk	~~Mediterranean~~
Texas	~~Edward Kennedy~~	Pacific
Florida	James Buchanan	Indian
~~Colorado~~	Rutherford Hayes	Arctic

Cross out the sentence below that does not support the topic.

Topic: Freshwater Sharks

Although most people think that sharks only live in the ocean, quite a few species actually live in freshwater. There are forty-three species that actually survive in freshwater lakes and rivers. ~~**An ingredient found in the liver oil of deep-sea sharks is used in some medicines**~~. These freshwater sharks are found in Australia, Southeast Asia, Africa, South America, Central America, and Southeastern parts of North America.

Classroom Practice 10

It is time to practice the skills you are learning. You will use the classroom practice on the next page to apply these skills.

Classroom Practice 10

Name:_____ Date:_____

GRAMMAR

▶ **Exercise 1:** Classify each sentence.

1. _____ The stormy weather stopped quite abruptly.

2. _____ The covered wooden wagons climbed steadily uphill.

3. _____ The totally exhausted veterinarian drove wearily home tonight.

SKILLS

▶ **Exercise 2:** In each column, cross out the word that does not support the underlined topic at the top.

1. **Reptiles**	2. **Eye**	3. **Fruits**
crocodiles	iris	strawberry
lizards	pupil	watermelon
giraffe	lashes	pear
salamander	calendar	orange
python	lens	rose

▶ **Exercise 3:** Write the name of the topic that best describes what each column of words is about. Choose from these topics. **Weather   Spices   Electronics   Seasons   Solar System   Holidays**

1._____	2._____	3._____
salt	rain	sun
pepper	snow	planets
nutmeg	sleet	asteroids
ginger	fog	comets

▶ **Exercise 4:** Cross out the sentence in the paragraph that does not support the topic.

Topic: Tropical Birds

The Tropics are home to some of the world's most beautiful birds. Parrots and cockatoos are popular birds from the Tropics. Toucans are fun to watch as they eat fruit with their big, colorful beaks. Penguins can easily survive the frigid temperatures of the arctic. The flamingo brightens the Tropics with its beautiful pink feathers.

EDITING

▶ **Exercise 5:** Put punctuation corrections within the sentence. Write all other corrections above the sentence.
   Editing Guide: Capitals: 6   Commas: 2   Misspelled Words: 1   Apostrophes: 2   End Marks: 1

the worlds first artificial satellite the ussrs sputnik 1 was lawnched in 1957

Chapter 2 Checkup 11

Name:_____ Date:_____

GRAMMAR

▶ **Exercise 1:** Classify each sentence.

1. _____ The dangerous germs spread incredibly fast!

2. _____ The dry, thin twigs snapped loudly nearby.

3. _____ The tiny gray mole dug tirelessly.

▶ **Exercise 2:** Name the four parts of speech that you have studied so far.

1._____ 2._____ 3._____ 4._____

SKILLS

▶ **Exercise 3:** Read the topic and paragraph. Cross out the sentence that does not support the topic.

Topic: **President Roosevelt**

　　Franklin D. Roosevelt became the thirty-second President of the United States in 1933 at the age of fifty-one. Abe Lincoln was elected the sixteenth President in 1860. Roosevelt was stricken with polio at the age of 39. President Roosevelt started the Warm Springs Foundation to help other people who suffered from polio.

▶ **Exercise 4:** Put the end mark and the End Mark Flow for each kind of sentence in the blanks.
Use these words in your answers: *declarative, exclamatory, imperative, interrogative.*

1. That bee stung me___................. _____

2. Raccoons are clever___.............. _____

3. Follow that car ___ .... _____

4. Where is your coat___................ _____

EDITING

▶ **Exercise 5:** Write the capitalization and punctuation rule numbers for each correction in **bold**.
Use References 11, 13, and 14 on pages 13, 17–18 to look up the capitalization and punctuation rule numbers.

Jonathan will you water **M**others **A**frican violets on **S**aturday

▶ **Exercise 6:** Put punctuation corrections within the sentence. Write all other corrections above the sentence.
Editing Guide: Capitals: 7　Commas: 2　Quotation Marks: 2　Misspelled Words: 1　End Marks: 1

kay graham my neice sang the star spangled banner at our baseball game on friday

START LESSON 8

Lesson 8

You will
- read and discuss a three-point expository paragraph.

Writing Time

Discuss It:

1. What is a topic?
2. What is a paragraph?
3. What is another word for topic?
4. How is a subject like a topic?

Learn It: **EXPOSITORY WRITING AND THE THREE-POINT FORMAT**

Reference 41	Expository Writing and the Three-Point Format

Expository writing is the sharing of ideas. Its purpose is to inform, to give facts, to give directions, to explain, or to define something. Since expository writing is informational, it provides some type of information to the reader.

Since expository writing deals with information of some kind, it is very important to focus on making the meaning clear. The reader must be able to understand exactly what the writer means. So, first you will learn to organize your writing.

Expository writing may be organized in different ways. One of the most common ways to write an expository paragraph is by using a three-point format. A **three-point format** presents three points, or main ideas, and develops these main ideas with supporting sentences. The three-point format makes your writing understandable.

Before you begin writing a three-point paragraph, you must do two things. First, select a topic. Then, list the three main points about the topic that you will develop.

WRITING TOPIC: My Favorite Foods

LIST THE THREE POINTS ABOUT THE TOPIC

- Select three points to list about the topic. **1.** pizza **2.** hamburger **3.** ice cream

Learn It: **WRITING THE INTRODUCTION FOR A THREE-POINT EXPOSITORY PARAGRAPH**

The sentences in a paragraph can be divided into three basic parts: the **Introduction**, the **Body**, and the **Conclusion**.

Reference 42	Writing the Introduction for a Three-Point Expository Paragraph

THE INTRODUCTION

TOPIC AND NUMBER SENTENCE
The topic and number sentence will be the **first** sentence in the paragraph because it tells what the paragraph is about. A topic sentence is very important because it tells the main idea of the paragraph. Sometimes, the topic sentence is not the first sentence, but, for now, it is important to write it as the first sentence in a three-point paragraph.

Continued on next page. >>>

Reference 42 continued from previous page.

The topic sentence should not say, "I am going to tell you about my three favorite foods." You do not need to tell the reader you are going to tell him something; you simply do it. To say, "I am going to tell you about" is called *writing about your writing*. You should never begin a paragraph with "I am going to tell you about" because **good writers do not write about their writing**.

To write the Topic and Number Sentence, use some or all of the words in your topic and add a general or specific number word that tells the number of points that will be discussed.

> **General number words:** *several, many, some,* etc.
> **Specific number words:** *two, three, four,* etc.

In the sample sentence below, words from the topic *(favorite foods)* are used, and the specific number word *(three)* is used instead of a general number word.

Sentence 1 – **Topic and Number Sentence:**

> **Of all the foods I like, my three favorites are the ones I eat the most.**

THREE-POINT SENTENCE

Now that the topic sentence has been written, the next sentence will be the three-point sentence. The three-point sentence lists or names the three points to be discussed in the order that you will present them in the body of your paper.

To write the Three-Point Sentence, list the exact three points in the order you will develop them in the body of the paragraph. You should also repeat words from the topic that connect this sentence to the topic sentence.

In the sample sentence below, the specific points, *pizza, hamburger, and ice cream,* are named, and the topic word *foods* is repeated. Repetition is a good device for making your paragraph flow smoothly.

Sentence 2 – **Three-Point Sentence:**

> **My favorite foods are pizza, hamburger, and ice cream.**

Learn It: **WRITING THE BODY**
FOR A THREE-POINT EXPOSITORY PARAGRAPH

The body of a three-point paragraph contains six sentences. Notice that the body lists each of the three points, and each of the three main points has at least one supporting sentence.

 Reference 43 | **Writing the Body for a Three-Point Expository Paragraph**

THE BODY

After the topic sentence and the three-point sentence have been written, you will present and support each point in the body. The three points will be developed, one at a time. Do not forget that the three points should be presented in the same order in which they were listed in the three-point sentence.

The third sentence states the first listed point. Next, a **supporting sentence** is written about the first point. The details in this sentence must **support** the first point. This is why it is called a **supporting sentence**. The supporting sentence can explain or describe, but it must be about the first point. Next, Sentence 5 is written to state the second point, and Sentence 6 supports it. Then, Sentence 7 is written to state the third point, and Sentence 8 supports it.

Sentence 3 – **First Point:** Write a sentence stating your first point.

> **Pizza is, without a doubt, at the top of my list.**

Sentence 4 – **Supporting Sentence:** Write a sentence that gives more information about the first point.

> **I especially love the great Italian taste of pizza with crunchy pepperoni, mozzarella cheese, and lots of spicy tomato sauce on a thick crust.**

Continued on next page. >>>

Reference 43 continued from previous page.

Sentence 5 – Second Point: Write a sentence stating your second point.

Another favorite food of mine is a juicy grilled hamburger on a toasted bun.

Sentence 6 – Supporting Sentence: Write a sentence that gives more information about the second point.

To me, the best hamburgers should be loaded with all the trimmings, including bacon.

Sentence 7 – Third Point: Write a sentence stating your third point.

Ice cream is yet another favorite of mine.

Sentence 8 – Supporting Sentence: Write a sentence that gives more information about the third point.

Although I like chocolate the best, ice cream in any flavor can't be beat

When you keep your writing focused on the topic, your paragraph will have what is called **unity**; it will be a **unified** paragraph. In a unified paragraph, all sentences work together to focus on one topic. Use only ideas that support your topic. Discard all nonsupporting ideas.

Learn It: **WRITING THE CONCLUSION**
FOR A THREE-POINT EXPOSITORY PARAGRAPH

The conclusion forms the last part of a three-point paragraph. It consists of only one sentence called the **concluding general sentence**.

Reference 44

Writing the Conclusion for a Three-Point Expository Paragraph

THE CONCLUSION

CONCLUDING GENERAL SENTENCE

Now that the three points have been made and supported, you need to complete the paragraph, leaving the reader with the impression that he/she has read a finished product. In order to complete the paragraph, you need a conclusion, or final sentence. The concluding general sentence should tie all the important points together with a restatement of the main idea and your final comments on it.

To write the Concluding General Sentence, read the topic sentence again and then rewrite it, using some of the same words. The Concluding General Sentence is meant to be general in nature and restates the topic sentence. In the sample sentence, the general word, *foods*, is used instead of the particular points, *pizza*, *hamburger*, and *ice cream*.

Sentence 9 – Concluding General Sentence:

I like foods of all kinds, but I especially enjoy my three favorites.

Learn It: WRITING THE TITLE

The title forms the fourth part of a three-point paragraph.

Reference 45 | **Writing the Title for a Three-Point Expository Paragraph**

WRITING THE TITLE

Most paragraphs and longer pieces of writing have a title. A title will be the first item appearing at the top of a paragraph. The title not only tells what you are writing about, but it grabs the reader's attention. Since there are many possibilities for titles, the writer usually finds it easier to think of a title after the paragraph has been completed. In effect, the title will become the fourth and last part of a paragraph.

To write the title, look at the topic and the three points listed about the topic. You may use the topic as your title or choose another word or phrase that is interesting and that tells what your writing is about. Your title can be long or short. In your title, capitalize the first word, the last word, and all of the important words between them. Unless they are first or last words, prepositions, conjunctions, and articles are not normally capitalized.

In the sample title, nothing has been added to the topic to express accurately what the paragraph is about.

Title: My Favorite Foods

Sample Three-Point Paragraph

My Favorite Foods

Of all the foods I like, my three favorites are the ones I eat the most. My favorite foods are pizza, hamburger, and ice cream. Pizza is, without a doubt, at the top of my list. I especially love the great Italian taste of pizza with crunchy pepperoni, mozzarella cheese, and lots of spicy tomato sauce on a thick crust. Another favorite food of mine is a juicy grilled hamburger on a toasted bun. To me, the best hamburgers should be loaded with all the trimmings, including bacon. Ice cream is yet another favorite of mine. Although I like chocolate the best, ice cream in any flavor can't be beat. I like foods of all kinds, but I especially enjoy my three favorites.

Discuss It:

1. What does the **Introduction** contain?

2. What does the **Body** contain?

3. What does the **Conclusion** contain?

Reference 46 | **Main Parts of an Expository Paragraph**

Topic:	My Favorite Foods
Three points about the topic:	pizza, hamburger, ice cream
Introduction:	**Sentence 1:** Topic and number sentence
	Sentence 2: A three-point sentence
Body:	**Sentence 3:** A first-point sentence
	Sentence 4: A supporting sentence for the first point
	Sentence 5: A second-point sentence
	Sentence 6: A supporting sentence for the second point
	Sentence 7: A third-point sentence
	Sentence 8: A supporting sentence for the third point
Conclusion:	**Sentence 9:** A concluding general sentence
Title:	My Favorite Foods

START LESSON 9

Lesson 9

You will

- read and discuss prewriting (Step 1 in the writing process).
- plan and write sentences on sentence outline form from prewriting map for WA 1, Part 1 (expository).

Writing Time

Learn It: **PREWRITING, THE FIRST STEP IN THE WRITING PROCESS**

Reference 47	**Prewriting Checklist for Step 1 in the Writing Process**

The first step in the writing process is called prewriting. In the prewriting stage, you plan and organize your ideas and thoughts for writing. A graphic organizer, which is a visual aid, can help you organize your prewriting ideas. Lists, maps, outlines, and Venn diagrams are some of the graphic organizers you will use this year. Use the prewriting steps below as you begin the writing process.

1. **Know the purpose.** Before you begin writing, you should know the purpose of your writing. Knowing the purpose will help you focus on your topic. The purpose of your writing determines the type of writing you will do. The different types of writing and their purposes are listed below.

   Expository: to explain or inform

   Persuasive: to win over or convince

   Descriptive: to describe

   Narrative: to tell a story

   Creative: to entertain through different forms, or genres: stories, poems, plays, etc.

   Compare/Contrast: to tell how things are alike and/or how things are different

2. **Know the audience.** Who will read your writing? Is this writing intended for you, your classmates, friends, family, teacher, principal, or someone else?

3. **Choose a topic.** Sometimes your teacher will assign a topic. Other times, you will select your own topic. If you select your own topic, you should list several topic ideas from which to choose. You should consider all of your topic choices and then select the one that you can best develop with main points and details from your experience and/or knowledge.

4. **Narrow the topic.** If the topic is too broad for you to cover well, it must be narrowed. A narrowed topic makes it easier to develop the main points you want to make. Decide if you need to narrow the topic.

5. **Collect ideas and details.** Think about your topic. **Brainstorm** for ideas and details that can be used to develop the topic. This is the time you will broaden your original ideas and elaborate on existing ones. Use your experiences, books, or information from other people to collect ideas. Write these ideas on your prewriting map.

6. **Arrange ideas and details.** Make sure your ideas and details are grouped into some kind of visual order on a **graphic organizer**. A form for a prewriting map has been provided on page 64 as a sample graphic organizer. Your teacher will tell you when to use this form.

7. **Keep your prewriting map.** Use it to write your rough draft. Then, place it in your Rough Draft folder.

Learn It: THE PREWRITING MAP

The information in the Prewriting Checklist will help you complete a prewriting map. This map will give you a visual aid of how you will organize your ideas. The example below shows you how ideas are organized into a prewriting map.

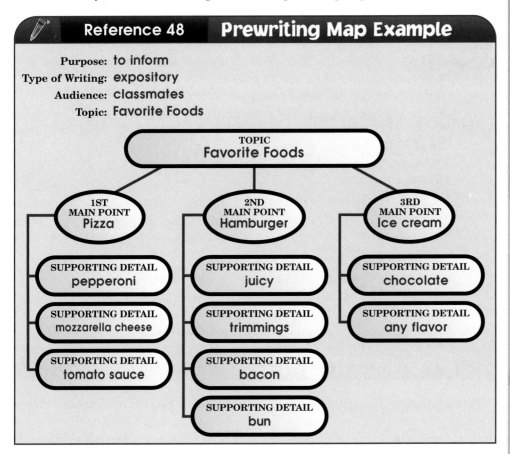

Reference 48 — Prewriting Map Example

Purpose: **to inform**
Type of Writing: **expository**
Audience: **classmates**
Topic: **Favorite Foods**

TOPIC
Favorite Foods

1ST MAIN POINT **Pizza** — 2ND MAIN POINT **Hamburger** — 3RD MAIN POINT **Ice cream**

SUPPORTING DETAIL **pepperoni** — SUPPORTING DETAIL **juicy** — SUPPORTING DETAIL **chocolate**

SUPPORTING DETAIL **mozzarella cheese** — SUPPORTING DETAIL **trimmings** — SUPPORTING DETAIL **any flavor**

SUPPORTING DETAIL **tomato sauce** — SUPPORTING DETAIL **bacon**

SUPPORTING DETAIL **bun**

Discuss It: FEATURES OF THE PREWRITING MAP EXAMPLE

First, look at the list in the top left corner of the map.

1. What is the purpose for writing?
2. What is the type of writing?
3. Who is the intended audience?
4. What is the topic?

As you can see, the topic is listed again as it is placed in the topic oval.

Plan It: MAKING A PREWRITING MAP

Next, brainstorm for ideas about the topic. If you don't know very much about your topic, you will have to look in the library or on the Internet to find information. In the example, the writer listed his favorite foods as main points in the ovals directly under the topic. His favorite foods, **pizza**, **hamburger**, and **ice cream** will be used as the main points in his three-point expository paragraph.

After the main points were listed, the writer had to think of some interesting details to tell about each of his favorite foods. For the food **pizza**, he listed the details *pepperoni, mozzarella cheese,* and *tomato sauce* on the prewriting map. For the food **hamburger**, he wrote the details *juicy, trimmings, bacon,* and *bun*. For the food **ice cream**, the writer listed the details *chocolate* and *any flavor*. Then, he checked to make sure each detail on his map supported its main point.

SHURLEY ENGLISH

In the example, all the ideas are organized into a simple map that shows the order in which the writer will write his three-point expository paragraph. Keep in mind, however, that this map is to help him get started. His ideas may change as he begins to write. He might add ideas to the map or even change them as he writes the actual paragraph.

Write It: WRITING ASSIGNMENT 1, PART 1

Look at Writing Assignment 1, Part 1. Follow the special instructions for this writing assignment. Use the prewriting map and the sentence outline on the next two pages to help you.

Writing Assignment [1] Part 1

Purpose: To inform

Type of Writing: Three-point Expository Paragraph

Audience: Classmates

Writing Topic: My Favorite Foods

Special Instructions:

1. Follow the Prewriting Checklist on page 62 and make a prewriting map, using your own brainstorming ideas. Write your ideas on a prewriting map.

2. Use your prewriting map as a guide and write the sentences for your expository paragraph on the form titled "Sentence Outline for an Expository Paragraph."

3. Use References 42–45 on pages 58–61 to help you write your paragraph.

4. Put your prewriting map and your sentence outline in your Rough Draft folder..

Prewriting Map

Name:_____ Date:_____

Purpose: _____

Type of Writing: _____

Audience: _____

Topic: _____

```
                              TOPIC

        1ST                   2ND                   3RD
     MAIN POINT            MAIN POINT            MAIN POINT

   SUPPORTING DETAIL     SUPPORTING DETAIL     SUPPORTING DETAIL

   SUPPORTING DETAIL     SUPPORTING DETAIL     SUPPORTING DETAIL

   SUPPORTING DETAIL     SUPPORTING DETAIL     SUPPORTING DETAIL
```

Sentence Outline for an Expository Paragraph

Name:_____ Date:_____

Purpose: _____

Type of Writing: _____

Audience: _____

Topic: _____

List 3 points about the topic:

1._____ 2._____ 3._____

Sentence 1 — Write a topic and number sentence.

_____

_____

Sentence 2 — Write a three-point sentence.

_____

_____

Sentence 3 — State your first point in a complete sentence.

_____

Sentence 4 — Write a supporting sentence for the first point.

_____

_____

Sentence 5 — State your second point in a complete sentence.

_____

Sentence 6 — Write a supporting sentence for the second point.

_____

_____

Sentence 7 — State your third point in a complete sentence.

_____

Sentence 8 — Write a supporting sentence for the third point.

_____

_____

Sentence 9 — Write a concluding general sentence.

_____

_____

START LESSON 10

Lesson 10

You will

- read and discuss rough draft (Step 2 in the writing process).
- write an expository paragraph for WA 1, Part 2.

Learn It: **WRITING A ROUGH DRAFT, THE SECOND STEP IN THE WRITING PROCESS**

 Reference 49 | **Rough Draft Checklist for Step 2 in the Writing Process**

The second step in the writing process is writing the rough draft.
Since you generally do not have a finished product the first time you write, your first writing attempt is called a **rough draft.** You do not have to worry about correcting mistakes as you write your rough draft because you will do that later. Use the rough draft guidelines below as you write a rough draft.

1. Your rough draft will be written in pencil on notebook paper.
2. On the left side of your paper, use the first seven lines to write the information below.
   Name:
   Date:
   WA: (Writing Assignment Number)
   Purpose: (to inform or explain, to persuade, to describe, or to entertain)
   Type of writing: (expository, persuasive, descriptive, narrative, creative, or comparison/contrast)
   Audience: (myself, classmates, friends, parents, relatives, teacher, principal, other)
   Topic: (name of assigned or chosen topic)
3. Skip the next line.
4. Begin writing your rough draft, using your prewriting map.
5. Use extra wide margins and skip every other line in your rough draft. This will give you room to revise and edit.
6. Skip two lines at the end of your rough draft and write the title on the left side of your paper.
   Title Information: You usually decide on a title after you write the rough draft. The title should not only tell what you are writing about but should also grab the reader's attention. You may use the topic as your title or choose another word or phrase that is interesting and that tells what your writing is about. Your title can be long or short. In your title, capitalize the first word, the last word, and all of the important words between them. Unless they are first or last words, prepositions, conjunctions, and articles are not normally capitalized.
7. Put the rough draft and prewriting map in your Rough Draft folder.

Discuss It: **STEPS IN WRITING A ROUGH DRAFT**

Look at the Rough Draft Example in Reference 50. This example demonstrates how to use the Rough Draft Checklist to write a rough draft.

Notice how the assignment information is placed on the left side of the paper on the first seven lines. Then, look at the extra wide margins that are used when writing a rough draft. Next, observe that every other line is skipped to give room for editing. Finally, a title is written at the end of the rough draft.

The mistakes in this rough draft have not been corrected. Learning how to correct a rough draft is presented in a later lesson.

Name: John Doe

Date: September ___, 20—

WA 1

Purpose: to inform

Type of writing: expository

Audience: classmates

Topic: My Favorite Foods

Of all the foods there is, my three favorites is the ones i eat the most. my

favorite foods are pizza hamburger and ice cream pizza is is

at the top of my list. I love the great italian taste of pizza with

crunchy peperoni mozarella cheese and lots of tomato sauce.

My brother also likes pizza. Another favorite foods of mine are a juicy

hamberger on an toasted bun. Too me the best hamburgers are loaded

with all the trimming, including onions. Ice cream is another favorite of mine.

I like choclate the best but ice cream in any flavor cant be beat i like foods

of all kinds but I enjoy my three favorite since I eat them all the time

Title: My Favorite Foods

Write It: WRITING ASSIGNMENT 1, PART 2

Look at Writing Assignment 1, Part 2.
Follow the special instructions for this writing assignment.

Writing Assignment 1 Part 2

Purpose: To inform

Type of Writing: Three-point Expository Paragraph

Audience: Classmates

Writing Topic: My Favorite Foods

Special Instructions:

1. Copy your sentences from your sentence outline onto notebook paper, putting them in paragraph form.

2. Follow the Rough Draft Checklist in Reference 49 on page 66 as you write your paragraph on paper.

3. Put your prewriting map and rough draft in your Rough Draft folder when you have finished.

Learn It: REVISING, THE THIRD STEP IN THE WRITING PROCESS

Lesson 11

You will
- read and discuss revising and editing (Steps 3–4 in the writing process).

Reference 51	Revising Checklist for Step 3 in the Writing Process

The third step in the writing process is called revising. Revising is finding ways to improve the content and meaning of your writing. Since you are dealing with content, you must read your rough draft several times. First, read your rough draft silently, and, then, read it aloud to yourself. Next, read it to others. When your rough draft is read aloud, you usually hear mistakes that you would not discover otherwise.

To revise your rough draft, draw a line through the words or phrases you want to change or delete. Write the revisions above the words or phrases you want to change. If you want to insert words, phrases, or sentences, use the insert symbol (∧) and write the added part above it.

The **checkpoints** below will help you improve the content and meaning of your writing as you revise your rough draft.

1. Have you written according to the purpose, type of writing, and audience assigned?

2. Have you stayed on the topic assigned? Does each paragraph have a topic sentence? Does each sentence within a paragraph support the topic sentence?

3. Check each sentence. Are your sentences in the right order? Do you need to combine, rearrange, or delete any of the sentences? Are your sentences interesting and descriptive with appropriate examples? Have you used a variety of simple, compound, and complex sentences?

4. Check the words. Have any words been left out? Are any words repeated or unnecessary? Do you need to replace any word or phrase with a clearer or more expressive one? Did you elaborate by using examples and descriptive words to support your ideas? Do the words make sense and express the thoughts you want to share?

5. Check the content for interest and creativity.

6. Check the voice of the writing. Does your writing sound original and genuinely express your own personal viewpoint?

>>>>>>>> Student Tip...

In the Revising Example, a line is drawn through words to be deleted, and the revised text is written above it. An insert symbol (∧) is used to indicate where to insert new text.

Discuss It:

This revising example demonstrates how to use the Revising Checklist to revise a rough draft. Compare the checkpoints in Reference 51 to the corrections made in the revising example in Reference 52.

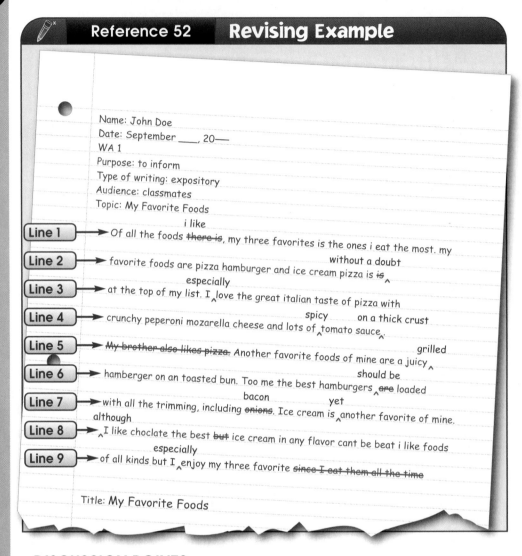

Reference 52 | **Revising Example**

Name: John Doe
Date: September ____, 20—
WA 1
Purpose: to inform
Type of writing: expository
Audience: classmates
Topic: My Favorite Foods

Line 1 → Of all the foods ~~there is~~, my three favorites is the ones i like eat the most. my

Line 2 → favorite foods are pizza hamburger and ice cream pizza is ~~is~~ without a doubt

Line 3 → at the top of my list. I love the great italian taste of pizza with especially

Line 4 → crunchy peperoni mozarella cheese and lots of tomato sauce. spicy on a thick crust

Line 5 → ~~My brother also likes pizza.~~ Another favorite foods of mine are a juicy grilled

Line 6 → hamberger on an toasted bun. Too me the best hamburgers ~~are~~ loaded should be

Line 7 → with all the trimming, including ~~onions~~. Ice cream is another favorite of mine. bacon yet

Line 8 → I like choclate the best ~~but~~ ice cream in any flavor cant be beat i like foods although

Line 9 → of all kinds but I enjoy my three favorite ~~since I eat them all the time~~ especially

Title: My Favorite Foods

DISCUSSION POINTS:

How did the writer use the Revising Checkpoints to revise his paragraph in Reference 52?

Checkpoint 1: Have you written according to the purpose, type of writing, and audience assigned?

Revising Example: The purpose, type of writing, and audience were identified because the writer used an expository paragraph to inform his classmates about his favorite foods.

Checkpoint 2: Have you stayed on the topic assigned? Does each paragraph have a topic sentence? Does each sentence within a paragraph support the topic sentence?

Revising Example: The writer checked over his sentences, looking for any sentence that did not support the topic. The sentence, **My brother also likes pizza**, does not support the topic, *My Favorite Foods*. The writer drew a line through the sentence, *My brother also likes pizza*, to indicate that it will be deleted when the final paper is written.

Checkpoint 3: Check each sentence. Are your sentences in the right order? Do you need to combine, rearrange, or delete any of the sentences? Are your sentences interesting and descriptive with appropriate examples? Have you used a variety of simple, compound, and complex sentences?

Revising Example: As the writer checked each sentence, he was satisfied with the sentence order. The writer then checked and was sure his sentences were interesting and descriptive with appropriate examples. Finally, he checked and verified that he had used different types of sentences.

Checkpoint 4: Check the words. Have any words been left out? Are any words repeated or unnecessary? Do you need to change any word or phrase for a clearer or more expressive one? Did you elaborate by using examples and descriptive words to support your ideas? Do the words make sense and express the thoughts you want to share?

Revising Example: The writer checked the words within each sentence. He found several things he wanted to change. On the first line, he drew a line through the words *there is* and changed them to the words *i like*. On the second line, he marked through the repeated word *is* because he wanted to delete it. He also decided to insert the words *without a doubt* at the end of the second line. Notice that he used the insert symbol (ᴧ) and wrote the words he wanted to insert above the symbol.

What are the other changes that the writer made as he continued using Checkpoint 4 to revise his paragraph?

Line 3: He inserted the word *especially* before the word *love*.

Line 4: He inserted the word *spicy* in front of *tomato;* he added the words *on a thick crust* after the word *sauce*.

Line 5: The sentence, *My brother also likes pizza,* was already discussed in Checkpoint 2. He added the word *grilled* after the word *juicy.*

Line 6: He drew a line through *are* and changed it to *should be*.

Line 7: He drew a line through *onions* and changed it to *bacon*; he inserted *yet* in front of the word *another*.

Line 8: He inserted *although* in front of *I like;* He marked through the word *but* in front of *ice cream* because he wanted to delete it.

Line 9: He inserted *especially* in front of *enjoy;* he marked through the unnecessary words *since I eat them all the time* because he wanted to delete them.

Checkpoint 5: Check the content for interest and creativity.

Revising Example: The writer read over his paragraph again with the revisions he had made up to this point. He was satisfied that it was interesting and creative.

Checkpoint 6: Check the voice of the writing. Does the writing sound original and genuinely express your own personal viewpoint?

Revising Example: The writer was satisfied that his paragraph sounded original and expressed his personal viewpoint.

Learn It: EDITING, THE FOURTH STEP IN THE WRITING PROCESS

Reference 53	**Editing Checklist for Step 4 in the Writing Process**

The fourth step in the writing process is called editing. When you check a sentence or a paragraph for mistakes in spelling, grammar, usage, capitalization, and punctuation, it is called **proofreading**. When you correct these mistakes, it is called **editing**.

After you have completed your revisions, you will use the **checkpoints** below to edit your rough draft. As you find capitalization, spelling, and usage mistakes, write the corrections above them. As you find punctuation mistakes, write the punctuation corrections within the sentence.

Continued on next page. >>>

Reference 53 continued from previous page.

1. Did you indent each paragraph?
2. Did you capitalize the first word and put an end mark at the end of every sentence? Did you follow all other capitalization and punctuation rules?
3. Did you check for misspelled words, for incorrect spellings of plural and possessive forms, and for incorrect homonym choices?
4. Did you check for correct construction and correct punctuation of a simple sentence, a simple sentence with compound parts, a compound sentence, and/or a complex sentence?
5. Did you check for usage mistakes? This includes subject-verb agreement, a/an choices, contractions, pronoun-antecedent agreement, pronoun cases, degrees of adjectives, double negatives, verb tenses, and singular/plural word choices.
6. You are now ready to put the revised and edited paper back in the Rough Draft folder.

Discuss It:

This editing example demonstrates how to use the Editing Checklist to edit a rough draft. Compare the checkpoints in Reference 50 to the corrections made in the editing example below.

Reference 54   **Editing Example**

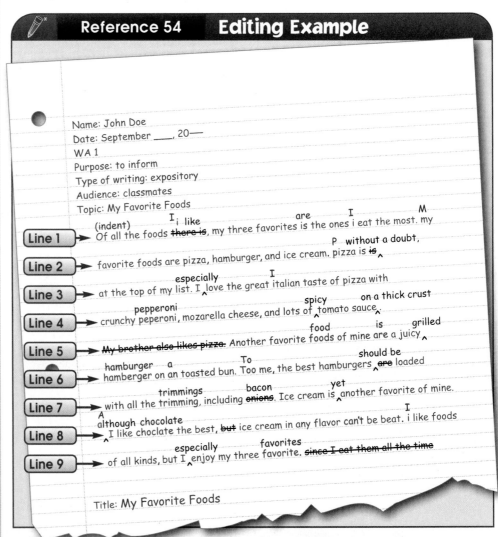

DISCUSSION POINTS:

How did the writer use the Editing Checkpoints to edit his paragraph in Reference 54?

Checkpoint 1: Did you indent each paragraph?

Editing Example: The writer wrote the word **indent** at the beginning of the paragraph to remind him to correct this mistake on the final paper.

Checkpoint 2: Did you capitalize the first word and put an end mark at the end of every sentence? Did you follow all other capitalization and punctuation rules?

Editing Example: First, the writer checked each sentence for first-word capitalization and end-mark punctuation. How many first-word capitalization mistakes did he find? He found four mistakes: **my** in Line 1; **pizza** in Line 2; **although** and **i** in Line 8.
How many end-mark punctuation mistakes did he find? He found three mistakes: **ice cream.** in Line 2; **beat.** in Line 8; and **favorite.** in Line 9.
He then checked the sentences for other capitalization and punctuation mistakes. He also corrected nine other capitalization and punctuation mistakes.

Checkpoint 3: Did you check for misspelled words, for incorrect spellings of plural and possessive forms, and for incorrect homonym choices?

Editing Example: The writer found and corrected three misspelled words. What are the misspelled words that were corrected?
(Line 4: **peperoni—pepperoni**, Line 6: **hamberger—hamburger**, Line 8: **choclate—chocolate**)
He also corrected one homonym spelling. Homonyms are words that sound alike but are spelled differently and have different meanings. Can you find the homonym mistake? (Line 6: **too—to**)

Checkpoint 4: Did you check for correct construction and correct punctuation of a simple sentence, a simple sentence with compound parts, a compound sentence, or a complex sentence?

Editing Example: The writer checked his sentences and found that he had already corrected a complex and a compound sentence punctuation mistake by adding commas during Checkpoint 2. (Line 8: Although I like chocolate the **best, ice cream** in any flavor can't be beat.
Lines 8-9: I like foods of all **kinds, but** I especially enjoy my three favorites.)

Checkpoint 5: Did you check for usage mistakes? This includes subject-verb agreement, a/an choices, contractions, pronoun-antecedent agreement, pronoun cases, degrees of adjectives, double negatives, verb tenses and singular/plural word choices.

Editing Example: The writer corrected two subject-verb agreement mistakes.
(Line 1: changed **favorites is** to **favorites are**, Line 5: changed mine **are** to mine **is**)
Then, he found one mistake for a/an choices. (Line 6: changed **an** toasted to **a** toasted)
Finally, he corrected three singular/plural word choice mistakes.
(Line 5: **foods** to **food**, Line 7: **trimming** to **trimmings**,
Line 9: **favorite** to **favorites**)

Checkpoint 6: You are now ready to put the revised and edited paper back in the Rough Draft folder.

You will use the Rough Draft Checklist, Revising Checklist, and the Editing Checklist in the next lesson as you write, revise, and edit your rough draft.

START LESSON 12

Lesson 12

You will

- read and discuss The Revising and Editing Schedule.
- revise and edit WA 1, Part 2.

Learn It: **THE REVISING AND EDITING SCHEDULE**

The schedule in Reference 55 has special instructions for revising and editing in the top portion and for writing a final paper in the bottom portion. You will revise and edit your rough draft today, and you will write your final paper in the next lesson. Since the revising and editing steps are so important, your rough draft will go through several stages of revising and editing before you write a final paper. Do not get in a hurry when you revise and edit. It is a slow, precise job because you are checking many areas.

Reference 55	Revising & Editing Schedule and Writing a Final Paper

SPECIAL INSTRUCTIONS FOR REVISING AND EDITING (Steps 3-4 in the writing process):

- Use the Revising and Editing Checklists in References 51 and 53 as you revise and edit your rough draft.
- Follow the revising and editing schedule below as directed by your teacher.

  1. **Individual.** First, read your rough draft to yourself. Use the Revising Checklist in Reference 51 on page 69. Go through your paper, checking each item on the list and making revisions to your rough draft. Then, use the Editing Checklist in Reference 53 on page 71. Go through your paper again, checking each item on the list and editing your rough draft.

  2. **Partner.** Next, get with your editing partner. Work together on each partner's rough draft, one paper at a time. Read each rough draft aloud and revise and edit it together, using the Revising and Editing Checklists. (The author of the paper should be the one to make the corrections on his own paper.)

  3. **Group.** Finally, read the rough draft to a revision group for feedback. Each student should read his paper while the others listen and offer possible revising and editing suggestions. (The author will determine whether to make corrections from the revision group's suggestions.)

SPECIAL INSTRUCTIONS FOR FINAL PAPER (Step 5 in the writing process):

- Write your final paper, using the Final Paper Checklist in Reference 56 on page 75.
- Staple your writing papers in this order: the final paper on top, the rough draft in the middle, and the prewriting map on the bottom. Place the stapled papers in the Final Paper folder.

>>>>>>>>>>>>**Student Tip...**

1. Be tactful and helpful in your comments during revising and editing time. The purpose of any suggestion should be to improve the writer's rough draft.

2. As you make your final corrections, you have the choice of accepting or rejecting any suggestions made by your partners or your revision group.

3. If you need to improve your handwriting, refer to the Resource Tools Section on page 521 for information on writing legibly.

Learn It: **FINAL PAPER,
THE FIFTH STEP IN THE WRITING PROCESS**

Lesson 13

You will

- discuss final paper (Step 5 in the writing process).
- discuss the Writing Evaluation Guide.
- review Steps in the Writing Process.
- write the final paper for WA 1, Part 2.
- discuss identifying one part of speech.

Reference 56	**Final Paper Checklist for Step 5 in the Writing Process**

The fifth step in the writing process is writing the final paper. A final paper is a neat, corrected copy of your rough draft. You should follow these guidelines as you write your final paper.

1. Read through your rough draft one last time and make final corrections before beginning your final paper.
2. Write your final paper neatly in pencil.
3. Center the title on the top line.
4. Center your name under the title with the word **By** in front of your name.
5. Skip a line after your name before you begin your writing assignment.
6. Single-space your final paper.
7. Use wide margins for your final paper.
8. Use the Writing Evaluation Guide to check your final paper one last time.
9. Staple your writing papers in this order: the final paper on top, the rough draft in the middle, and the prewriting map on the bottom. Place the stapled papers in the Final Paper folder.

Example of the Final Paper

My Favorite Foods
By John Doe

Of all the foods I like, my three favorites are the ones I eat the most. My favorite foods are pizza, hamburger, and ice cream. Pizza is, without a doubt, at the top of my list. I especially love the great Italian taste of pizza with crunchy pepperoni, mozzarella cheese, and lots of spicy tomato sauce on a thick crust. Another favorite food of mine is a juicy grilled hamburger on a toasted bun. To me, the best hamburgers should be loaded with all the trimmings, including bacon. Ice cream is yet another favorite of mine. Although I like chocolate the best, ice cream in any flavor can't be beat. I like foods of all kinds, but I especially enjoy my three favorites.

Learn It: **WRITING EVALUATION GUIDE**

You will have a Writing Evaluation Guide for each chapter. You will use it to check your final paper one last time. Your teacher will also use this guide to evaluate your writing and to discuss your final paper with you during writing conferences. Study the Writing Evaluation Guide on the next page.

Review It: **STEPS IN THE WRITING PROCESS**

Reference 57 | **The Steps in the Writing Process**

The steps below will take you through the writing process and will give you the location of each checklist.
1. **Prewriting.** Use the Prewriting Checklist to plan and organize your writing. (Reference 47, page 62)
2. **Rough Draft.** Use the Rough Draft Checklist to set up and write the rough draft. (Reference 49, page 66)
3. **Revising.** Use the Revising Checklist to revise the content of your writing. (Reference 51, page 69)
4. **Editing.** Use the Editing Checklist to edit your writing for spelling, grammar, usage, capitalization, and punctuation mistakes. (Reference 53, page 71)
5. **Final Paper.** Use the Final Paper Checklist to set up and write the final paper. (Reference 56, page 75)
6. **Publishing.** Use the publishing checklist to choose a publishing form for sharing with others. (Reference 67, page 102)

Write It: **WRITING A FINAL PAPER**
FOR WRITING ASSIGNMENT 1, PART 2

Get Writing Assignment 1, Part 2 from your Rough Draft folder, and write a final paper. Follow ALL the steps listed in the Final Paper Checklist. Make sure you use the Chapter 2 Writing Evaluation Guide on the next page to check your final paper one last time. After you have finished your paper, put it in your Final Paper folder.

Learn It: **IDENTIFYING ONE PART OF SPEECH**

You have been identifying the parts of a sentence by classifying every word. Now, you will use that knowledge to find only one part of speech on Part B of the Chapter Test. Use the steps below to learn the process for finding one part of speech.

1. Use the Question and Answer Flow to classify the sentence. Label each word mentally or with a pencil.
2. Start with the subject and verb. Continue classifying until you have classified the underlined word.
3. Look at the label of the underlined word.
4. Choose the answer that matches the classified word.

Example: Choose the part of speech for the underlined word.
The diamond necklace sparkled very <u>brightly</u>.
(a) noun (b) verb (c) adjective (d) adverb

Chapter 2 Writing Evaluation Guide

Name:_____ Date:_____

ROUGH DRAFT CHECK

_____ 1. Did you write your rough draft in pencil?

_____ 2. Did you write the correct headings on the first seven lines of your paper?

_____ 3. Did you use extra wide margins and skip every other line?

_____ 4. Did you write a title at the end of your rough draft?

_____ 5. Did you place your edited rough draft in your Rough Draft folder?

REVISING CHECK

_____ 6. Did you identify the purpose, type of writing, and audience?

_____ 7. Did you check for a topic, topic sentence, and sentences supporting the topic?

_____ 8. Did you check sentences for the right order, and did you combine, rearrange, or delete sentences when necessary?

_____ 9. Did you check for a variety of simple, compound, and complex sentences?

_____ 10. Did you check for any left out, repeated, or unnecessary words?

_____ 11. Did you check for the best choice of words by replacing or deleting unclear words?

_____ 12. Did you check the content for interest and creativity?

_____ 13. Did you check the voice to make sure the writing says what you want it to say?

EDITING CHECK

_____ 14. Did you indent each paragraph?

_____ 15. Did you put an end mark at the end of every sentence?

_____ 16. Did you capitalize the first word of every sentence?

_____ 17. Did you check for all other capitalization mistakes?

_____ 18. Did you check for all punctuation mistakes?
(commas, periods, apostrophes, quotation marks, underlining)

_____ 19. Did you check for misspelled words and for incorrect homonym choices?

_____ 20. Did you check for incorrect spellings of plural and possessive forms?

_____ 21. Did you check for correct construction and punctuation of your sentences?

_____ 22. Did you check for usage mistakes? (subject/verb agreement, a/an choices, contractions, verb tenses, pronoun/antecedent agreement, pronoun cases, degrees of adjectives, double negatives, etc.)

_____ 23. Did you put your revised and edited paper in the Rough Draft folder?

FINAL PAPER CHECK

_____ 24. Did you write the final paper in pencil?

_____ 25. Did you center the title on the top line and center your name under the title?

_____ 26. Did you skip a line before starting the writing assignment?

_____ 27. Did you single-space, use wide margins, and write the final paper neatly?

_____ 28. Did you staple your papers in this order: final paper on top, rough draft in the middle, and prewriting map on the bottom? Did you put them in the Final Paper folder?

START LESSON 14

Lesson 14

You will

- hand in WA 1, Part 2 for grading.
- respond to oral review questions.
- take Chapter 2 Test.

CHAPTER TEST

It is time to evaluate your knowledge of the skills you have learned in this chapter. Your teacher will give you the Chapter 2 Test to help you assess your progress.

Writing Time

Hand It In: **WRITING ASSIGNMENT 1, PART 2**

Get your stapled sheets for Writing Assignment 1, Part 2 from your Final Paper folder, and give them to your teacher.

LISTENING AND SPEAKING:
Oral Review Questions

Discuss It:

1. What are the three article adjectives?
2. What is the definition of a noun?
3. What is the definition of an adverb?
4. What is the definition of an adjective?
5. What are the three adverb questions?
6. What are the three adjective questions?
7. What are the four kinds of sentences?
8. What is the End Mark Flow for the declarative sentence?
9. What is the End Mark Flow for the imperative sentence?
10. What is the End Mark Flow for the exclamatory sentence?
11. What is the End Mark Flow for the interrogative sentence?
12. What are the five parts of a correct sentence?
13. What do you call a group of sentences that is written about one particular subject?
14. What do you call the sentence that tells what a paragraph is about?
15. What type of writing is used when your purpose is to inform, to give facts, to give directions, to explain, or to define something?

Learn It: **STANDARDIZED-TEST FORMAT**

There are two parts for the chapter test. The first part is called Chapter 2 Test, Part A. It looks like the Classroom Practices you have already been doing. The second part is called Chapter 2 Test, Part B. This part of the test is in a standardized-test format, so you will fill in the bubble beside the correct answer. Work each section of this page with your teacher to make sure you understand what to do.

>>>>>>>>>>>>>>>>>>>>>>>>>**Student Tip...**

For information about test-taking strategies, refer to the Resource Tools Section on page 520.

LISTENING AND SPEAKING:

Vocabulary & Analogy Time

Lesson 1

You will

- study new vocabulary; make Card 5; write own sentence using the vocabulary word.
- analyze new analogy; make Card 5; write own analogy.
- recite new jingles (Preposition, Object of the Preposition, and Prepositional Phrase).
- identify prepositions, objects of the preposition, and prepositional phrases.
- identify/compare adverbs and prepositions.
- classify Introductory Sentences.
- do a Skill Builder to identify nouns.
- recognize prepositions as a part of speech.
- write in your journal.

Learn It: Recite the new vocabulary and analogy words.

📖 Reference 58	Vocabulary & Analogy Words

Word: evade (ĭvād')

    Definition: to avoid something

    Synonym: elude   **Antonym:** confront

    Sentence: The suspect **evaded** the detective's questions.

Analogy: tuna : fish :: summer : season

    Type or kind relationship: Just as **tuna** is a type of **fish**, **summer** is a type of **season**.

Vocabulary Card 5: Record the vocabulary information above and write your own sentence, using the new word.

Analogy Card 5: Record the analogy information and write your own analogy, using the same relationship as the analogy above.

Jingle Time

Recite It: Recite the new jingles.

♪ Jingle 8	The Preposition Jingle

A prep, prep, preposition
Is an extra-special word
That connects a
Noun, noun, noun
Or a pro, pro, pronoun
To the rest of the sentence.

♪ Jingle 9	The Object of the Preposition Jingle

An object of the preposition   After the prep, prep, prep
Is a NOUN or PRONOUN.   After the prep, prep, prep
An object of the preposition   After the prep, prep, prep
Is a NOUN or PRONOUN   That answers **WHAT** or **WHOM**.

♪ Jingle 10	The Prepositional Phrase Jingle

I've been working with prepositions   When I put them all together,
'Til I can work no more.   The prep and its noun or pro,
They're connecting their objects   I get a prepositional phrase
To the rest of the sentence before.   That could cause my mind to blow!

Apply It: These Introductory Sentences are used to apply the new grammar concepts taught below. Classify these sentences orally with your teacher.

Introductory Sentences	Chapter 3: Lesson 1

1. _____ The old rooster crowed loudly at daybreak.

2. _____ The terrified little girl ran frantically inside the house!

3. _____ The crowd in the huge auditorium applauded warmly for the young magician.

Learn It: **PREPOSITIONS, OBJECTS OF THE PREPOSITIONS, AND PREPOSITIONAL PHRASES**

 Reference 59 | **Prepositions, Objects of the Prepositions, and Prepositional Phrases**

Prepositions

Prepositions join other words in a special way. They show how words in a sentence are related. Read Example 1.

Example 1: The black horse walked *beside* the gate.

Which word tells you where the horse is in relation to the gate? The word *beside* is placed before *gate* to show the relationship between *the horse* and *the gate*. The word *beside* is a preposition. If you use the preposition *near* or *behind*, this changes where the *horse* is in relation to the gate.

Example 2: The black horse walked **near** the gate.   **Example 3:** The black horse walked **behind** the gate.

The words *near* and *behind* give different ways of relating **horse** and **gate**. *Near* and *behind* are also prepositions. **A preposition relates the noun or pronoun that follows it to some other word in the sentence.** For example, the noun *gate* follows each of the prepositions. Therefore, each preposition relates *gate* to the word *horse* differently because they are different prepositions.

To find a preposition, say the preposition word and ask *WHAT* or *WHOM*. If the answer is a noun or pronoun, then the word is a preposition. A preposition is labeled with the abbreviation **P**.

Objects of the Prepositions

In Example 1 above, the noun *gate* follows the preposition *beside*. **The noun or pronoun following a preposition is called the object of the preposition.** *Gate* is the object of the preposition *beside*. *Gate* is also the object of the prepositions *near* and *behind* in Examples 2 and 3.

To find an object of the preposition, say the preposition and ask *WHAT* or *WHOM*. If the answer is the noun or pronoun after the preposition, the word is an object of the preposition. An *object of the preposition* is labeled with the abbreviation **OP**.

Continued on next page. >>>

Reference 59 continued from previous page.

Prepositional Phrases

A **prepositional phrase** starts with a preposition and ends with the object of the preposition. It also includes any words between the preposition and the object of the preposition. Prepositional phrases add meaning to sentences and can be located anywhere within a sentence.

Prepositional phrases are identified in the Question and Answer Flow after you say **Skill Check**. Mark prepositional phrases by putting parentheses around them. The examples below demonstrate how to identify prepositional phrases.

The black horse walked (beside the gate).   The bus drove (past my house).   We waved (at our friends).

Learn It: **IDENTIFYING ADVERBS AND PREPOSITIONS**

| Reference 60 | **Identifying Adverbs and Prepositions** |

Some words can be used as both **adverbs** and as **prepositions**. To tell the difference, find out how the word is used in a particular sentence. For example, the word *down* can be an adverb or a preposition. How do you decide if the word *down* is an adverb or a preposition?

If *down* is used alone, it is probably an adverb. Prepositions are never used alone. They are used in phrases and always have objects. If *down* has a noun or pronoun after it that answers the question *what* or *whom*, then *down* is a preposition, and the noun or pronoun after *down* is an object of the preposition.

In the first sentence below, the word *down* is an adverb because it is used alone. In the second sentence, the word *down* is a preposition because it is used in a phrase and has an object, *steps*.

Adv
1. Mark jumped **down**.

P   noun (OP)
2. Mark jumped **down the steps**.

How to classify adverbs and prepositions in the Question and Answer Flow

Mark jumped down.

Jumped where? **down - Adv (down—adverb)**

Mark jumped down the steps.

Down - P (down—preposition)

Down what? **steps - OP (steps—object of the preposition)**

>>>>>>>> Student Tip...

For a comprehensive list of the most commonly used abbreviations in Shurley English, refer to the Resource Tools Section on page 512.

Learn It: A SKILL BUILDER FOR A NOUN CHECK

You will use the sentences you have just classified to do a Skill Builder. A **Skill Builder** is an oral review of certain skills. The first skill introduced in the Skill Builder is a **Noun Check**. A Noun Check is a check to find the nouns in a sentence.

A noun can do many jobs in a sentence. The first noun job is the subject noun, and it is marked **SN**. The second noun job is the object of a preposition, and it is marked **OP**.

To find nouns, you will go to these jobs. An example of a Skill Builder for a Noun Check is given below.

FOR A noun CHECK

Circle the nouns in a Noun Check.

Sentence 1: Subject Noun rooster, yes, it is a noun;
Object of the Preposition daybreak, yes, it is a noun.

Sentence 2: Subject Noun girl, yes, it is a noun;
Object of the Preposition house, yes, it is a noun.

Sentence 3: Subject Noun crowd, yes, it is a noun;
Object of the Preposition auditorium, yes, it is a noun;
Object of the Preposition magician, yes, it is a noun.

Learn It: ADDING THE PREPOSITION TO THE PARTS OF SPEECH

A preposition is a part of speech. You have learned five of the eight parts of speech. What are these five parts of speech?

LISTENING AND SPEAKING:

Jingle Time

Lesson 2

You will
- practice Jingles 8–10.
- classify Practice Sentences.
- do a Skill Builder to identify singular/plural nouns, common/proper nouns, simple subject/ predicate, and complete subject/predicate.
- discuss and do a Noun Job Chart.
- do Classroom Practice 12.

Recite It: Practice Jingles 8–10 in the Jingle Section on page 500.

Grammar Time

Apply It: Classify the Practice Sentences orally with your teacher.

Practice Sentences	Chapter 3: Lesson 2

1. _____ The wild daffodils on the hill bloom profusely during the spring of the year.
2. _____ Carla dashed quickly toward the fountain for a drink of water before class.
3. _____ The muddy water of the Mississippi flowed freely from the river into the ocean.

Skill Time

Review It: A SKILL BUILDER FOR A NOUN CHECK

Skill Builder

FOR A NOUN CHECK

Circle the nouns in a Noun Check.

Sentence 1: Subject Noun **daffodils** *yes, it is a noun;*
Object of the Preposition **hill** *yes, it is a noun;*
Object of the Preposition **spring** *yes, it is a noun;*
Object of the Preposition **year** *yes, it is a noun.*

Sentence 2: Subject Noun **Carla** *yes, it is a noun;*
Object of the Preposition **fountain** *yes, it is a noun;*
Object of the Preposition **drink** *yes, it is a noun;*
Object of the Preposition **water** *yes, it is a noun;*
Object of the Preposition **class** *yes, it is a noun.*

Sentence 3: Subject Noun **water** *yes, it is a noun;*
Object of the Preposition **Mississippi** *yes, it is a noun;*
Object of the Preposition **river** *yes, it is a noun;*
Object of the Preposition **ocean** *yes, it is a noun.*

Learn It: SINGULAR AND PLURAL NOUNS

Study the definitions for singular and plural nouns in Reference 61.

Reference 61 — Definitions of Words Used in a Skill Builder

1. A **singular noun** means only one. Most singular nouns do not end in -s or -es. (**Examples:** *dog, child*) Some singular nouns, however, end in -s. (**Examples:** *grass, glass, gas*)
2. A **plural noun** means more than one. Most plural nouns add -s or -es to form the plural. (**Examples:** *dogs, glasses*) Some plural nouns, however, have different spellings for the plural. (**Examples:** *children, men*)

Read below and continue on next page. >>>

Apply It:

Add singular and plural nouns to the Skill Builder.

FOR A SINGULAR AND PLURAL CHECK

Mark the nouns with the letter **S** or **P**.

Sentence 1:

P
daffodils - plural *(write P)*;
S
hill - singular *(write S)*;
S
spring - singular *(write S)*;
S
year - singular *(write S)*.

Sentence 2:

S
Carla - singular *(write S)*;
S
fountain - singular *(write S)*;
S
drink - singular *(write S)*;
S
water - singular *(write S)*;
S
class - singular *(write S)*.

Sentence 3:

S
water - singular *(write S)*;
S
Mississippi - singular *(write S)*;
S
river - singular *(write S)*;
S
ocean - singular *(write S)*.

Learn It: COMMON AND PROPER NOUNS

Study the definitions for common and proper nouns in Reference 61.

Reference 61 continued from above.

3. A **common noun** names ANY person, place, or thing. A common noun is not capitalized because it does not name a specific person, place, or thing. (**Examples:** *boy, country*)
4. A **proper noun** is a noun that names a specific or particular person, place, or thing. Proper nouns are always capitalized no matter where they are located in the sentence. (**Examples:** *Carlos, Brazil*)

Continued on next page. >>>

Apply It:
Add common and proper nouns to the Skill Builder.

FOR A COMMON AND PROPER CHECK

Mark the nouns with the letter **C** or **P**.

Sentence 1:

C
daffodils – common *(write C)*;

C
hill – common *(write C)*;

C
spring – common *(write C)*;

C
year – common *(write C)*.

Sentence 2:

P
Carla – proper *(write P)*;

C
fountain – common *(write C)*;

C
drink – common *(write C)*;

C
water – common *(write C)*;

C
class – common *(write C)*.

Sentence 3:

C
water – common *(write C)*;

P
Mississippi – proper *(write P)*;

C
river – common *(write C)*;

C
ocean – common *(write C)*.

Learn It: COMPLETE SUBJECT AND COMPLETE PREDICATE
Study the definitions for complete subject and complete predicate in Reference 61.

Reference 61 continued from previous page.

5. The **complete subject** is the subject and all the words that modify it. The complete subject usually starts at the beginning of the sentence and includes every word up to the verb of the sentence.

6. The **complete predicate** is the verb and all the words that modify it. The complete predicate usually starts with the verb and includes every word after the verb.

Continued on next page. >>>

Apply It:
Add complete subject and complete predicate to the Skill Builder.

FOR A COMPLETE SUBJECT AND COMPLETE PREDICATE CHECK

Underline the complete subject once and the complete predicate twice.

Sentence 1: The wild daffodils on the hill bloom profusely during the spring of the year.

Sentence 2: Carla dashed quickly toward the fountain for a drink of water before class.

Sentence 3: The muddy water of the Mississippi flowed freely from the river into the ocean.

Learn It: SIMPLE SUBJECT AND SIMPLE PREDICATE

Study the definitions for simple subject and simple predicate in Reference 61.

Reference 61 continued from previous page.

7. A **simple subject** is another name for the subject noun or subject pronoun in a sentence. The simple subject is just the subject, without the words that modify it.

8. A **simple predicate** is another name for the verb in a sentence. The simple predicate is just the verb without the words that modify it.

Apply It:

Add simple subject and simple predicate to the Skill Builder.

FOR A SIMPLE SUBJECT AND SIMPLE PREDICATE CHECK

Circle the simple subject and the simple predicate.

Sentence 1: The wild daffodils on the hill bloom profusely during the spring of the year.

Sentence 2: Carla dashed quickly toward the fountain for a drink of water before class.

Sentence 3: The muddy water of the Mississippi flowed freely from the river into the ocean.

Learn It: THE NOUN JOB CHART

Reference 62   Noun Job Chart

Directions: Classify the sentence below. Underline the complete subject once and the complete predicate twice. Then, complete the table below.

SN V / Pl   A   Adj   SN   V   Adv   P   A   OP
         The experienced hikers / climbed steadily (toward the peak). D

List the Noun Used	List the Noun Job	Singular or Plural	Common or Proper	Simple Subject	Simple Predicate
hikers	SN	P	C	hikers	climbed
peak	OP	S	C		

Classroom Practice 12

It is time to practice the skills you are learning. You will use the classroom practice on the next page to apply these skills.

Classroom Practice 12

Name:_____ Date:_____

GRAMMAR

▶ **Exercise 1:** Classify each sentence. Underline the complete subject once and the complete predicate twice.

1. _____ The exhausted runners in the marathon ran slowly at the end of the race.

2. _____ The blanket of fog settled low in the wooded valley.

3. _____ Sara performed on the tightrope for the talent show.

▶ **Exercise 2:** Use sentence 3 above to complete the table below.

List the Noun Used	List the Noun Job	Singular or Plural	Common or Proper	Simple Subject	Simple Predicate

▶ **Exercise 3:** Name the five parts of speech that you have studied so far.
1. _____ 2. _____ 3. _____ 4. _____ 5. _____

▶ **Exercise 4:** Underline the complete subject once and the complete predicate twice.
1. The hardy cucumber vines grew well.
2. The rusty bicycle squeaked constantly.
3. Numerous football fans arrived early.
4. The enraged protesters shouted loudly.

▶ **Exercise 5:** Underline the simple subject once and the simple predicate twice.
1. A green caterpillar crawled up the twig.
2. A few glass marbles rolled away.
3. The five wheat rolls baked in the oven.
4. The crisp leaves fell from the tree.

SKILLS

▶ **Exercise 6:** Write **S** for singular or **P** for plural.

Noun	S or P
1. molecule	_____
2. pictures	_____
3. league	_____
4. voices	_____

▶ **Exercise 7:** Write **C** for common or **P** for proper.

Noun	C or P
1. plateau	_____
2. Australia	_____
3. Pasadena	_____
4. government	_____

EDITING

▶ **Exercise 8:** Put punctuation corrections within the sentence. Write all other corrections above the sentence.
Editing Guide: Capitals: 8 Commas: 4 Periods: 1 Misspelled Words: 1 End Marks: 1

ms baptise my french techer visited the eiffel tower in paris france in july

START LESSON 3

Lesson 3

You will

- study new vocabulary; make Card 6; write own sentence using the vocabulary word.
- analyze new analogy; make Card 6; write own analogy.
- recite the new jingle (Preposition Flow).
- classify Practice Sentences.
- do a Skill Builder.
- identify subject-verb agreement.
- do Classroom Practice 13.
- read and discuss Discovery Time.

LISTENING AND SPEAKING:
Vocabulary & Analogy Time

Learn It: Recite the new vocabulary and analogy words.

📖 * Reference 63	Vocabulary & Analogy Words

Word: shrewd (shrōōd)
   Definition: having keen insight or cunning
   Synonym: clever   **Antonym:** gullible
   Sentence: The **shrewd** fox covered his tracks.

Analogy: bucket : pail :: jacket : coat
   Synonym relationship: Just as **bucket** means nearly the same as **pail**, **jacket** means nearly the same as **coat**.

Vocabulary Card 6: Record the vocabulary information above and write your own sentence, using the new word.

Analogy Card 6: Record the analogy information and write your own analogy, using the same relationship as the analogy above.

Jingle Time

Recite It: Recite the new jingle.

♪ Jingle 11	The Preposition Flow Jingle

1. Preposition, Preposition,
   Starting with an **A**:
   **aboard, about, above,
   across, after, against,
   along, among, around, as, at!**

2. Preposition, Preposition,
   Starting with a **B**:
   **before, behind, below,
   beneath, beside, between,
   beyond, but,** and **by!**

3. Preposition, Preposition,
   Starting with a **D**:
   **despite, down, during
   despite, down, during!**

4. Oh, Preposition,
   Please, don't go away.
   Go to the middle of the alphabet,
   And see just what we say.
   E and **F** and **I** and **L**
   And **N** and **O** and **P**:
   **except, for, from,
   in, inside, into, like,
   near, of, off, on, out,
   outside, over, past!**

5. Preposition, Preposition,
   Almost through.
   Start with **S** and end with **W**:
   **since, through,
   throughout, to, toward,
   under, underneath,
   until, up, upon,
   with, within, without!**

6. Preposition, Preposition,
   Easy as can be.

   We just recited

   All **fifty-one**
   of these!

English Made Easy

Apply It: Classify the Practice Sentences orally with your teacher.

Practice Sentences	Chapter 3: Lesson 3

1. _____ The captain of the crew peered out the window into the blackness of space.

2. _____ The extremely hazardous trip ended after long hours on the river.

3. _____ An enthusiastic group of guitarists played loudly for the screaming crowd.

Using the three sentences just classified, follow the guidelines below for a Skill Builder.

1. **Identify the nouns in a Noun Check.**
   (Say the job and then say the noun. Circle each noun.)
2. **Identify the nouns as singular or plural.**
   (Write **S** or **P** above each noun.)
3. **Identify the nouns as common or proper.**
   (Follow established procedure for oral identification.)
4. **Identify the complete subject and the complete predicate.**
   (Underline the complete subject once and the complete predicate twice.)
5. **Identify the simple subject and the simple predicate.**
   (Circle the simple subject and the simple predicate.)

Learn It: **SUBJECT-VERB AGREEMENT**

Reference 64 — Subject-Verb Agreement Rules

The word **agreement** means *working together;* therefore, subject-verb agreement means the special way in which the subject and verb work together in a sentence. Whenever you work with subject-verb agreement, you must remember to look at only the subject and verb of a sentence.

RULE 1: A **singular** subject must use a singular verb that ends in **s** or **es**: *is, was, has, does, swims, pushes.*

In Rule 1, notice that all the singular verbs end in s or es. This should make them easier to identify as singular. If the subject is singular, use a singular verb that ends in s or es. Use Rule 1 to help you decide which verb to use with a singular subject.

Example 1. <u>kangaroo</u> <u>hops</u> (hop**s**—singular form)

Look at Example 1 above. The subject *kangaroo* is singular and needs a singular verb to be in agreement. According to Rule 1, adding an **s** to the verb *hop* makes it singular. The singular subject *kangaroo* agrees with the singular verb *hops*. Since the subject and verb are both singular, there is subject-verb agreement.

The following examples show subject-verb agreement for singular forms: *seal barks, bear climbs, pilot flies, child runs.* Each subject is singular; therefore, each verb must end in **s** or **es** for the singular form.

RULE 2: A **plural** subject, a compound subject, or the subject **YOU** must use a plural verb with **no s** or **es** ending: *are, were, have, do, swim, push.*

In Rule 2, notice that all plural verbs have a **plain form**. Plain form means that verbs do not end in **s** or **es**. This should make plural verbs easier to identify as plural. If the subject is plural, use a plural verb that does not end in **s** or **es**. Use Rule 2 to help you decide which verb to use with a plural subject.

Example 2. <u>kangaroos</u> <u>hop</u> (hop—plural form)

Look at Example 2 above. The subject *kangaroos* is plural and needs a plural verb to be in agreement. According to Rule 2, the plain form of the verb *hop* makes it plural. The plural subject *kangaroos* agrees with the plural verb *hop*. Since the subject and verb are both plural, there is subject-verb agreement.

The following examples show subject-verb agreement for plural forms: *seals bark, bears climb, pilots fly, children run.* Each subject is plural; therefore, each verb must not end in **s** or **es** for the plural form.

Example 3. <u>Mom and Dad</u> <u>cook</u> (cook—plural form)

Look at the compound subject in Example 3 above. A compound subject occurs when there are two or more subjects in the sentence. According to Rule 2, the plain form of the verb *cook* makes it plural. The compound subject *Mom and Dad* agrees with the plural verb *cook*. Since the subject and verb are both plural, there is subject-verb agreement.

The following examples show subject-verb agreement for compound subjects and the plural verb forms: *necklace and bracelet are, boys and girls play, Jennifer and Jonathan were.*

Example 4. <u>You</u> <u>cook</u> (cook—plural form)

Look at Example 4 above. The subject *you* always uses a plural verb to be in agreement. According to Rule 2, the plain form of the verb *cook* makes it plural. Since the subject *you* agrees with the plural verb *cook*, there is subject-verb agreement.

The following examples show subject-verb agreement for the subject *you* and the plural verb forms: *you walk, you run, you are, you were.*

Note: Subject-verb agreement is important only when verbs are in present tense. If a verb is past tense, it **does not** matter whether the subject is singular or plural because the verb remains in the same past-tense form. Even though the subject changes from singular to plural, the verb stays the same. (*dog barked; dogs barked; cat ran; cats ran*)

Continued on next page. >>>

Reference 64 continued from previous page.

RULE 1: A **singular** subject must use a singular verb that ends in **s** or **es**: *is, was, has, does, swims, pushes*.

RULE 2: A **plural** subject, a compound subject, or the subject **YOU** must use a plural verb with **no s** or **es** ending: *are, were, have, do, swim, push*.

Sample Exercise: For each sentence, do three things: (1) Write the subject. (2) Write **S** and **Rule 1** if the subject is singular, or write **P** and **Rule 2** if the subject is plural. (3) Underline the correct verb.

Subject	S or P	Rule #	
girl	S	1	1. The **girl** (enjoy, <u>enjoys</u>) her CD player.
girls	P	2	2. The **girls** (<u>enjoy</u>, enjoys) their CD players.
bat / glove	P	2	3. Your **bat** and **glove** (is, <u>are</u>) in the garage.
you	P	2	4. **You** (<u>help</u>, helps) rake leaves today.

Student Note:

1. The subject *I* is an exception. It presents a special case of subject-verb agreement. These examples demonstrate plural verb forms used with the pronoun *I*: *I* want; *I* walk; *I* talk; etc.

2. The singular subject *I* and the verb *be* also present a special case of subject-verb agreement. These examples demonstrate other verb forms used with the pronoun *I*: *I* am; *I* was.

Student Tip...

1. Recite the singular examples several times to hear the subject-verb agreement for singular forms: **seal barks, bear climbs, pilot flies, child runs.**

2. Recite the plural examples several times to hear the subject-verb agreement for plurals forms: **seals bark, bears climb, pilots fly, children run.**

Classroom Practice 13

It is time to practice the skills you are learning. You will use the classroom practice on the next page to apply these skills.

 Discovery Time

The Sun is a star that is made almost entirely of hydrogen and helium. The surface of the Sun is about 10,800°F, and its core can reach 15 million degrees. The Sun and the planets that orbit around it make up our solar system. The sun is more than 100 times bigger than the Earth.

Discovery Questions:
- The Sun is how many miles from the Earth?
- What do you think is the most interesting fact that you have learned about the Sun?

Are you interested in learning more about the Sun?

1. You may explore this topic further by using the resources listed below.
   Computer resources: Internet, encyclopedia software
   Library resources: encyclopedias, books, magazines, newspapers
   Home/community resources: books, interviews, newspapers, magazines

2. A Discovery Share Time is provided in Lesson 7 of Chapter 4 if you wish to share your investigation results. You may share orally, or you may prepare a written report. You will put your written report in a class booklet titled "Space Trivia." This booklet will be placed in the class library for everyone to enjoy.

 Student Tip...

For an introduction to computer terminology and using the Internet, refer to the Resource Tools Section on pages 532–535.

Classroom Practice 13

Name:_____ Date:_____

GRAMMAR

▶ **Exercise 1:** Classify each sentence. Underline the complete subject once and the complete predicate twice.

1. _____ The huge, colorful turkeys strutted proudly along the fence of the barnyard.

2. _____ A little boy glanced very shyly at the lifeguard on the sidewalk near the pool.

3. _____ The aroma of the homemade rolls drifted pleasantly into the office today.

▶ **Exercise 2:** Use sentence 3 above to complete the table below.

List the Noun Used	List the Noun Job	Singular or Plural	Common or Proper	Simple Subject	Simple Predicate

SKILLS

▶ **Exercise 3:** For each sentence, do three things: (1) Write the subject. (2) Write **S** and **Rule 1** if the subject is singular, or write **P** and **Rule 2** if the subject is plural. (3) Underline the correct verb.

> **Rule 1:** A singular subject must use a singular verb form that ends in **s** or **es**.
>
> **Rule 2:** A plural subject, a compound subject, or the subject **YOU** must use a plural verb form that has **no s** or **es** endings. (A plural verb form is also called the *plain form*.)

Subject	S or P	Rule
_____	_____	_____
_____	_____	_____
_____	_____	_____
_____	_____	_____
_____	_____	_____
_____	_____	_____
_____	_____	_____
_____	_____	_____
_____	_____	_____
_____	_____	_____

1. A barge (carry, carries) freight.
2. You (organize, organizes) your desk.
3. Kenneth and Kirk (plays, play) soccer.
4. The carnival (is, are) in town.
5. You and I (lives, live) on the same street.
6. A row of bushes (block, blocks) our view.
7. My mom's new car (have, has) an alarm.
8. The bluffs (is, are) very steep.
9. Daniel's toy soldier (march, marches) along.
10. They (looks, look) confused.

EDITING

▶ **Exercise 4:** Put punctuation corrections within the sentence. Write all other corrections above the sentence.
Editing Guide: Capitals: 10 Commas: 2 Apostrophe: 1 Subject-Verb Agreement: 1 Periods: 1 End Marks: 1

molly will you mails mr welchs package to mayor lee at 400 miller lane in albany new york

English Made Easy

LISTENING AND SPEAKING:
Vocabulary & Analogy Time

Learn It: Recite the new vocabulary and analogy words.

Reference 65	Vocabulary & Analogy Words

Word: colossal (kə lŏs'əl)
  Definition: extraordinarily great in size
  Synonym: gigantic   **Antonym:** tiny
  Sentence: My boss made a **colossal** advertising mistake.

Analogy: pilot : plane :: engineer : train
  Purpose or use relationship: Just as a **pilot** is in charge of a **plane**, an **engineer** is in charge of a **train**.

Vocabulary Card 7: Record the vocabulary information above and write your own sentence, using the new word.
Analogy Card 7: Record the analogy information and write your own analogy, using the same relationship as the analogy above.

Lesson 4

You will

- study new vocabulary; make card 7; write own sentence using the vocabulary word.
- analyze new analogy; make Card 7; write own analogy.
- practice Jingles 8–11.
- classify Practice Sentences.
- do a Skill Builder for a vocabulary check.
- edit a paragraph.
- do Classroom Practice 14.
- read and discuss Discovery Time.
- do a homework assignment.
- do a Home Connection activity.

Jingle Time

Recite It: Practice Jingles 8–11 in the Jingle Section on page 500.

Grammar Time

Apply It: Classify the Practice Sentences orally with your teacher.

Practice Sentences	Chapter 3: Lesson 4

1. _____ The aromatic yellow flowers bloom fairly often in the field.
2. _____ The girls broke into spontaneous laughter during the play.
3. _____ The sound of the melodious bells came from the two tall towers.

Learn It: **A SKILL BUILDER WITH A VOCABULARY CHECK**

A Vocabulary Check will be added to the Skill Builder. The purpose of this check is to improve your vocabulary. An example of a Skill Builder for a Vocabulary Check is given below.

FOR A VOCABULARY CHECK

For selected words, provide this information: a synonym, a new sentence, an antonym.

Sentence 1: The aromatic yellow flowers bloom fairly often in the field.

Sentence 2: The girls broke into spontaneous laughter during the play.

Sentence 3: The sound of the melodious bells came from the two tall towers.

SENTENCE 1

1. **aromatic:** **synonym:** fragrant, sweet-smelling
   new sentence: The aromatic scent filled the room.
   antonym: foul-smelling, rancid

2. A fun sentence, using antonyms or word changes for the words **aromatic, flowers,** and **often:** The **foul-smelling** yellow **onions seldom** bloomed in the field.

SENTENCE 2

1. **spontaneous:** **synonym:** unplanned, impromptu
   new sentence: We made a spontaneous trip to the lake.
   antonym: deliberate, planned

2. A fun sentence, using antonyms or word changes for the words **girls, spontaneous, laughter,** and **play:** The **fans** broke into a **planned moan** during the **game.**

SENTENCE 3

1. **melodious:** **synonym:** sweet-sounding, harmonious
   new sentence: The children's choir sang a melodious tune.
   antonym: out-of-tune, discordant

2. A fun sentence, using antonyms or word changes for the words **melodious, bells,** and **two towers:** The sound of the **discordant instruments** came from the elementary **band.**

Guidelines for a Vocabulary Check

1. Look over the sentences just classified.
2. Name a synonym or give a definition for any word selected.
3. Use the vocabulary word correctly in a new sentence.
4. Name an antonym for the word, if possible.
5. For fun, make a new sentence, using antonyms for several words in the original sentence. (*For an example, see the previous Skill Builder that introduces the Vocabulary Check.*)

Learn It: EDITING PARAGRAPHS

When you correct mistakes in your writing, it is called editing. You have been editing sentences for capitalization, punctuation, and spelling mistakes. Now, you will edit a paragraph instead of a single sentence.

When you edit a paragraph, you will still have an Editing Guide to help you, but it will be arranged a little differently. In Reference 66, notice that the **End Marks** title has been moved to the front of the Editing Guide so you will know how many sentences are in the paragraph.

To edit a paragraph, find each sentence and write the end mark for each one before editing the rest of the paragraph. This allows you to identify the sentences before the paragraph gets crowded with other corrections. It also helps you find the first word of each sentence to check for capitalization.

 Reference 66 **Editing a Paragraph**

Correct each mistake.

Editing Guide: End Marks: 2   Capitals: 19   Commas: 6   Subject-Verb Agreement: 2   Misspelled Words: 1

  W   I are   W   N   F   R   L   V   N   ESPN
walter and i is watching the wrangler national finals rodeo in las vegas, nevada, on espn tonight.

W hope C   J   S   A   T   tenth
we hopes charmayne james and her horse, scamper, from athens, texas, win their tinth world

barrel-racing title!

 Classroom Practice 14

It is time to practice the skills you are learning. You will use the classroom practice on the next page to apply these skills.

 **Discovery Time**

(Polish) 1473-1543 - Nicolaus Copernicus was the first scientist to theorize that the planets revolved around the Sun, not the Earth. The Copernican theory was not widely accepted until the late 17th century.

 Discovery Questions:
- **How do you think Copernicus felt when other scientists did not accept his theory?**
- **How do you think the Copernican theory was eventually proven true?**

Are you interested in learning more about Nicolaus Copernicus?

1. You may explore this topic further by using the resources listed below.
   Computer resources: Internet, encyclopedia software
   Library resources: encyclopedias, books, magazines, newspapers
   Home/community resources: books, interviews, newspapers, magazines

2. A Discovery Share Time is provided in Lesson 7 of Chapter 4 if you wish to share your investigation results. You may share orally, or you may prepare a written report. You will put your written report in a class booklet titled "Space Trivia." This booklet will be placed in the class library for everyone to enjoy.

Classroom Practice 14

Name:_____ Date:_____

GRAMMAR

▶ **Exercise 1:** Classify each sentence. Underline the complete subject once and the complete predicate twice.

1. _____ The ambulance raced to the scene of the accident!

2. _____ The newborn puppies snuggled together in a corner of the box.

3. _____ The wreckage of the boat floated to the shore with the tide.

▶ **Exercise 2:** Use sentence 2 above to complete the table below.

List the Noun Used	List the Noun Job	Singular or Plural	Common or Proper	Simple Subject	Simple Predicate

SKILLS

▶ **Exercise 3:** For each sentence, do three things: (1) Write the subject. (2) Write **S** and **Rule 1** if the subject is singular, or write **P** and **Rule 2** if the subject is plural. (3) Underline the correct verb.

Subject	S or P	Rule	
_____	_____	_____	1. A cello (make, makes) a soothing sound.
_____	_____	_____	2. Toads and frogs (is, are) similar in many ways.
_____	_____	_____	3. You (walk, walks) with me to the store.
_____	_____	_____	4. The firefighters (practices, practice) drills often.
_____	_____	_____	5. The tube of glue (are, is) in that drawer.
_____	_____	_____	6. You (wash, washes) your hands before dinner.
_____	_____	_____	7. The children (searches, search) through the toy box.
_____	_____	_____	8. The boxes in the corner (is, are) empty.
_____	_____	_____	9. Ron's guess (were, was) incorrect.

EDITING

▶ **Exercise 4:** Correct each mistake. **Editing Guide: End Marks: 4   Capitals: 15   Commas: 2   Apostrophes: 2   Subject-Verb Agreement: 5   Periods: 3   Misspelled Words: 1**

monica and mr boots is best friends mr boots eat the best brand of dog food watches tv in

monicas room and sleep by her bed at night they shop at dons grocery every saterday and talks

to all their friends monica loves mr boots and take good care of her seeing-eye dog

Homework 1

Complete this homework assignment on notebook paper.

1. Number your paper 1–7.
   For each sentence, do three things: (1) Write the subject. (2) Write **S** and **Rule 1** if the subject is singular, or write **P** and **Rule 2** if the subject is plural. (3) Write the correct verb.

> **Rule 1:** A singular subject must use a singular verb form that ends in **s** or **es**: *is, was, has, does, swims, pushes.*
>
> **Rule 2:** A plural subject, a compound subject, or the subject **YOU** must use a plural verb form that has **no s** or **es** endings: *are, were, have, do, swim, push.*

	Subject	S or P	Rule	
1.	_____	_____	_____	The vegetables (grow, grows) quite well in a sunny area.
2.	_____	_____	_____	Chris and Jamie (is, are) taking the kids to the zoo.
3.	_____	_____	_____	The tiger (was, were) performing in the ring.
4.	_____	_____	_____	You (was, were) in trouble at school yesterday.
5.	_____	_____	_____	(Doesn't, Don't) your mother work at the hospital?
6.	_____	_____	_____	(Do, Does) the college fans travel to games in other states?
7.	_____	_____	_____	The milk in the refrigerator (has, have) spoiled.

2. Rewrite the sentence below correctly. Use the editing guide to help you.
   Editing Guide: Capitals: 7   Commas: 1   Misspelled Words: 1   End Marks: 1

did abraham lincoln make his fameous "gettysburg address" in gettysburg pennsylvania

Home Connection

Family Activity for Prepositions

Some words can be either a preposition or an adverb. Have a timed contest between family members to see who can identify the underlined words as prepositions or adverbs. Write new sentences and do the activity again.

1. Just before the collision, I looked <u>out</u> the window. _____
2. He went <u>out</u> after the evening meal. _____
3. Because of the storm, we stayed <u>inside</u>. _____
4. We went <u>down</u> the water slide at the park. _____
5. He climbed <u>aboard</u> the bus. _____
6. He fell <u>down</u> and hurt his leg. _____
7. The candles <u>on</u> the mantel came from Italy. _____
8. She came <u>over</u> today. _____
9. They stood <u>near</u> the door. _____
10. We keep an extra loaf of bread <u>in</u> the freezer. _____

Family Activity for Common and Proper Nouns

1. Have students list a common noun for each of these proper nouns.

   • Brazil
   • Edgar Allan Poe
   • Oregon
   • Babe Ruth
   • Abraham Lincoln

2. Have students list a proper noun for the following common nouns: song, book, governor, city, school, product, famous person, pet, country, holiday, and river.

Chapter 3

START LESSON 5

Lesson 5

You will

- recite new jingle (Transition Words).
- classify Practice Sentences.
- Do a Skill Builder.
- do Chapter Checkup 15.
- write in your journal.

LISTENING AND SPEAKING:

Recite It: Recite the new jingle.

♪	Jingle 12	The Transition Words Jingle

Aw, listen, comrades, and you shall hear
About transition words
That make your writing smooth and clear.

Transition words are connecting words.
You add them to the beginning
Of sentences and paragraphs
To keep your ideas spinning and give your writing flow.

These words can clarify, summarize, or emphasize,
Compare or contrast, inform or show time.
Learn them now, and your writing will shine!

Transition, Transition,
For words that **SHOW TIME:**
first, second, third, before, during, after,
next, then, and *finally.*

Transition, Transition,
For words that **INFORM:**
for example, for instance, in addition, as well,
also, next, another, along with, and *besides.*

Transition, Transition,
For words that **CONTRAST:**
although, even though, but, yet, still,
otherwise, however, and *on the other hand.*

Transition, Transition,
For words that **COMPARE:**
as, also, like, and *likewise.*

Transition, Transition,
For words that **CLARIFY:**
for example, for instance, and *in other words.*

Transition, Transition,
For words that **EMPHASIZE:**
truly, again, for this reason, and *in fact.*

Transition, Transition,
For words that **SUMMARIZE:**
therefore, in conclusion, in summary, and *finally,*
to sum it up, all in all, as a result, and *last.*

TRANSITION WORD

Apply It: Classify the Practice Sentences orally with your teacher.

Practice Sentences | Chapter 3: Lesson 5

1. _____ The engine of the model helicopter worked very well during the trial performance.
2. _____ The windshield of the rusty antique car bulged rather noticeably in the heat.
3. _____ Ginny arrived too late for dinner at the Italian restaurant yesterday.

Skill Builder

Using the three sentences just classified, follow the guidelines below for a Skill Builder.

1. **Identify the nouns in a Noun Check.**
   (Say the job and then say the noun. Circle each noun.)
2. **Identify the nouns as singular or plural.**
   (Write **S** or **P** above each noun.)
3. **Identify the nouns as common or proper.**
   (Follow established procedure for oral identification.)
4. **Identify the complete subject and the complete predicate.**
   (Underline the complete subject once and the complete predicate twice.)
5. **Identify the simple subject and the simple predicate.**
   (Circle the simple subject and the simple predicate.)
6. **Do a Vocabulary Check.**
   (Follow established procedure.)

Chapter Checkup 15

It is time for a checkup of the skills you have learned in this chapter. You will use the chapter checkup on the next page to evaluate your progress.

JOURNAL WRITING **7**

Write an entry in your journal. Use Reference 9 on page 12 for ideas.

Chapter 3 Checkup 15

Name:_____ Date:_____

GRAMMAR

▶ **Exercise 1:** Classify each sentence. Underline the complete subject once and the complete predicate twice.

1. _____ The experiments in space occurred outside the cabin of the spacecraft.

2. _____ Deer hunters arrived early in the woods on the first day of hunting season.

3. _____ Lisa screamed with fear at the sight of the snake!

▶ **Exercise 2:** Use sentence 3 above to complete the table below.

List the Noun Used	List the Noun Job	Singular or Plural	Common or Proper	Simple Subject	Simple Predicate

▶ **Exercise 3:** Underline the simple subject once and the simple predicate twice.

1. An artifact from Egypt arrived at the museum.   2. At night, bears rummaged in the trash.

SKILLS

▶ **Exercise 4:** For each sentence, do three things: (1) Write the subject. (2) Write **S** and **Rule 1** if the subject is singular, or write **P** and **Rule 2** if the subject is plural. (3) Underline the correct verb.

Subject	S or P	Rule	
_____	_____	_____	1. You (sit, sits) on the sofa.
_____	_____	_____	2. That child (sleeps, sleep) soundly.
_____	_____	_____	3. Martin and I (eats, eat) in the cafeteria.
_____	_____	_____	4. The construction crews (begins, begin) early.

EDITING

▶ **Exercise 5:** Correct each mistake. **Editing Guide: End Marks: 5   Capitals: 9   Commas: 5   Apostrophes: 3
Subject-Verb Agreement: 4   Misspelled Words: 2**

on the weekends i sit on grandmas back pourch and feed the ducks they is so funny they

quacks and squawks to let me know its time to eat then they gobble up the food real fast later

they waddles down the path to the pond with bingo grandmas dog waddleing right behind them

Writing Time

Write It: WRITING ASSIGNMENT 2

Lesson 6

You will
- conference with teacher about WA 1, Part 2.
- write a creative writing piece for WA 2.

Writing Assignment [2]: Creative Expressions

Purpose: To entertain

Type of Writing: Creative

Audience: Classmates, family, or friends

Choose one of the writing topics below.

1. If you could have three wishes, what would you wish for and why? How would these wishes change your life? How would you be different?
2. What are three qualities an ideal family would possess? Tell about a family you know with these qualities.
3. Write a poem about wishes, family, or a topic of your choice.

Special Instructions:

1. A prewriting map is not required for this creative-writing assignment.
2. Follow the Rough Draft Checklist in Reference 49 on page 66.
3. Put your creative-writing paper in your Rough Draft folder when you have finished.

Note: Reference 57 on page 76 gives the steps in the writing process and the location for all the writing checklists.

>>>>>>>>>>>>>>>>>>>> Student Tip...

> For more information about writing poetry, look at Chapter 18, pages 456–474.

Conference Time

Discuss It: TEACHER-STUDENT CONFERENCES
FOR WRITING ASSIGNMENT 1

Meet with your teacher to discuss Writing Assignment 1, Part 2.
After the conference, place this group of papers in your Publishing folder.

START LESSON 7

Lesson 7

You will

- read and discuss publishing (Step 6 in the writing process).
- read and discuss Share Time Guidelines.
- publish WA 1.

Learn It: PUBLISHING, THE SIXTH STEP
IN THE WRITING PROCESS

Discuss the Publishing Checklist in Reference 67 with your teacher. Then, choose a publishing form and publish Writing Assignment 1. After rewriting your paper for publication, give the stapled papers (evaluation guide, graded final paper, rough draft, and prewriting map) to your teacher to be placed in your Writing Portfolio.

 Reference 67   **Publishing Checklist for Step 6 in the Writing Process**

The sixth step in the writing process is called publishing. Publishing is sharing your writing with others. With so many forms of publishing available, finding a match for every project and personality is easy. At times, a written work is best read aloud. Other times, the biggest impact is made when a written work is read silently. You can also use media sources to enhance any publication.

SPECIAL INSTRUCTIONS FOR PUBLISHING:

- Rewrite the graded paper in ink or type it on a computer, correcting any marked errors. *(Do not display or publish papers that have marked errors or grades on them.)*
- Give your teacher the set of stapled papers to place in your Writing Portfolio. *(Stapled papers: evaluation guide, graded final paper, rough draft, and prewriting map.)*
- Select a publishing form from the list below and publish your rewritten paper.

  1. Have classmates, family members, neighbors, or others read your writing at school or home.
  2. Share your writing with others during a Share Time. *(Refer to Reference 68 for sharing guidelines.)*
  3. Display your writing on a bulletin board or wall.
  4. Put your writing in the classroom library or in the school library for checkout.
  5. Send your writing as a letter or an e-mail to a friend or relative.
  6. Frame your writing by gluing it on colored construction paper and decorating it.
  7. Make a book of your writing for your classroom, your family, or others.
  8. Illustrate your writing and give it to others to read.
  9. Dramatize your writing in the form of a play, puppet show, or radio broadcast.
  10. Send your writing to be placed in a waiting room (doctor, veterinarian, dentist, etc.), senior-citizen center, or a nursing home.
  11. Send your writing to a school newspaper, local newspaper, or a magazine for publication.
  12. Make a videotape, cassette tape, or slide presentation of your writing.
  13. Choose another publishing form that is not listed.

Learn It: SHARE TIME GUIDELINES

Sharing is one of the publishing forms listed in Reference 68. Study the Share Time Guidelines to help you know what to do as a speaker or as a member of the audience.

 Reference 68 **Share Time Guidelines**

Speaker Presentation

1. Have your paper ready to read when called upon.
2. Tell the title of your writing selection.
3. Tell the purpose and type of writing used.

PRESENTATION TIPS:

4. Stand with your feet flat on the floor and your shoulders straight. Do not shift your weight as you stand.
5. Hold your paper about chin high to help you project your voice to your audience.
6. Make sure you do not read too fast.
7. Read in a clear voice that can be heard so that your audience does not have to strain to hear you.
8. Change your voice tone for different characters or for different parts of the writing selection.

Audience Response

1. Look at the speaker.
2. Turn your body toward the speaker.
3. Listen attentively. Do not let your thoughts wander.
4. Do not make distracting noises as you listen.
5. Do not make distracting motions as you listen.
6. Show interest in what the speaker is saying.
7. Silently summarize what the speaker is saying. Take notes if necessary.
8. Ask questions about anything that is not clear.
9. Show appreciation by clapping after the speaker has finished.

START LESSON 8

Lesson 8

You will
- practice Jingles 2 and 12.
- do Classroom Practice 16.
- write an independent expository paragraph (WA 3).

LISTENING AND SPEAKING:

Recite It: Practice Jingles 2 and 12 in the Jingle Section on pages 498, 501.

GRAMMAR & WRITING CONNECTION:
Practice and Revised Sentences

Apply It: BUILDING AND EXPANDING SENTENCES

Reference 69	A Guide for Using Prepositions and Objects of the Prepositions to Build and Expand Sentences

1. **P (preposition)** Use the Preposition Flow Jingle to help you think of a preposition for a prepositional phrase that describes and expands the subject and verb in your sentence. The preposition you choose must make sense with the noun you choose for the object of the preposition in your next step. Write the preposition you have chosen for your sentence. Repeat this step for each preposition you add to the sentence.

2. **OP (object of the preposition)** An object of the preposition is a noun or pronoun after a preposition. Think of an object of the preposition by asking **what** or **whom** after the preposition. The noun or pronoun you choose for an object of the preposition must make sense with the preposition and with the rest of the sentence. Write the word you have chosen for the object of the preposition in your sentence. Repeat this step for each object of the preposition you add to the sentence.

>>>>>>>>>>>>> **Student Tip...**

Use your vocabulary words in your Practice and Revised Sentences. Use a thesaurus, synonym-antonym book, or a dictionary to help you develop your writing vocabulary.

English Made Easy

Classroom Practice 16

It is time to practice the skills you are learning. You will use the classroom practice on the next page to apply these skills.

Writing Time

Write It: WRITING ASSIGNMENT 3

As you write a rough draft for your independent writing assignment, you will do two of the six steps in the writing process: prewriting and rough draft.

Writing Assignment ③

Purpose: To inform

Type of Writing: Three-point expository paragraph

Audience: Classmates

Writing Topics: Favorite school subject
Favorite colors
Favorite season
(Brainstorm for other ideas, individually or in groups.)

Special Instructions:

1. Follow the Prewriting and Rough Draft Checklists in References 47 and 49 on pages 62, 66.

2. Use References 42–46 on pages 58–61 to help you write your expository paragraph.

3. Put your prewriting map and rough draft in your Rough Draft folder when you have finished.

Note: Reference 57 on page 76 gives the steps in the writing process and the location of all the writing checklists.

Student Note: Some of your writing pieces will be selected for revision and editing later in the school year.

Classroom Practice 16

Name: _____   Date: _____

INDEPENDENT PRACTICE & REVISED SENTENCES

1. Write a Practice Sentence according to the labels you choose.
Use the **SN V** labels once. You may use the other labels in any order and as many times as you wish in order to make a Practice Sentence.
Chapter 3 labels for a Practice Sentence: SN, V, Adj, Adv, A, P, OP

2. Write a Revised Sentence. Use the following revision strategies: *synonym (syn), antonym (ant), word change (wc), added word (add), deleted word (delete),* or *no change (nc).* Under each word, write the abbreviation of the revision strategy you use.

Labels: _____

Practice: _____

Revised: _____

Strategies: _____

Labels: _____

Practice: _____

Revised: _____

Strategies: _____

Labels: _____

Practice: _____

Revised: _____

Strategies: _____

English Made Easy

LISTENING AND SPEAKING:

Jingle Time

Recite It: Practice Jingle 12 in the Jingle Section on page 501.

>>>>>> **Student Tip...**

> Reviewing the transition words will help you apply them in your writing.

Writing Time

Learn It: **DIFFERENT WRITING FORMS**

The information in Reference 70 will explain different ways to introduce the main points in a paragraph.

Lesson 9

You will
- practice Jingle 12.
- read and discuss writing forms and point of view.
- plan and write rough drafts for expository paragraphs (WA 4 and 5).

Reference 70 — Different Writing Forms

The way you introduce the points in your paragraph determines the form of the paragraph. Whichever form you choose must be used throughout the paragraph. You cannot mix forms within the same paragraph.

1. Standard Form – Uses possessive pronouns or article adjectives and *first, second, third.*

In the standard form, the main points begin with possessive pronouns or article adjectives followed by the time-order words, *first, second,* and *third.* The standard form is the easiest because it is the most consistent. For this reason, it is used often and is a good, reliable three-point writing form.

Standard words: My first, My second, My third. The first, The second, The third.

I enjoy participating in several outdoor games. Three of these games are volleyball, croquet, and lawn darts. **My first** favorite game is volleyball. I love playing a hard-hitting game of volleyball with my friends at the park. **My second** favorite game is croquet. Croquet has been around for years, but it is still lots of fun to play. **My third** favorite game is lawn darts. Lawn darts help me improve my aim and concentration. My three favorite outdoor games provide fun, fellowship, and good exercise for me.

2. Time-Order Form – Uses time-order words.

In the time-order form, the main points begin with transition words that suggest a definite time order, or number order, at the beginning of the sentence. Using time-order words is a superior way to accomplish sequence when it is important. The words, *first, second, third* or *first, next, last* or *finally,* are the most common time-order words. Whenever you use this form, you must put a comma after the time-order words at the beginning of the sentences because they are transitional words.

Time-order words: First, Second, Third. First, Next, Then, After that, Last, Lastly, Finally.

I enjoy participating in several outdoor games. Three of these games are volleyball, croquet, and lawn darts. **First,** I enjoy a good game of volleyball. I love playing a hard-hitting game of volleyball with my friends at the park. **Next,** I enjoy a peaceful game of croquet. Croquet has been around for years, but it is still lots of fun to play. **Finally,** I enjoy the challenge of lawn darts. Lawn darts help me improve my aim and concentration. My three favorite outdoor games provide fun, fellowship, and good exercise for me.

Continued on next page. >>>

Reference 70 continued from previous page.

3. Transition Form – Uses different types of transition words.

In the transition form, the main points are stated by using transition words that denote addition instead of time-order. These transition words may be added to the beginning of the sentences or added within the sentences. The transition form provides a chance for variety because the main points are all presented with different transition words. This makes your writing unlike others and is highly favored if you choose not to use time-order words.

Transition words: one, also, other, another, besides, besides that, in addition to, furthermore, too.

    I enjoy participating in several outdoor games. Three of these games are volleyball, croquet, and lawn darts. Volleyball is an exciting and competitive game for me. I love playing a hard-hitting game of volleyball with my friends at the park. Croquet is **another** favorite game of mine. Croquet has been around for years, but it is still lots of fun to play. I **also** enjoy the challenge of lawn darts. Lawn darts help me improve my aim and concentration. My three favorite outdoor games provide fun, fellowship, and good exercise for me.

Learn It: **POINT OF VIEW**
                AND WRITING IN FIRST AND THIRD PERSON

 Reference 71   **Point of View**

Point of view refers to the writer's use of personal pronouns to show who is telling a story. In order to use a point of view correctly, one must know the pronouns associated with the points of view listed below.

First-Person Point of View uses the first-person pronouns **I, me, my, mine, we, us, our,** and **ours** to name the speaker. If **any** of the first-person pronouns are used in a piece of writing, the writing is automatically considered a first-person writing, even though second- and third-person pronouns may also be used. **First person shows that you (the writer) are speaking, and that you (the writer) are personally involved in what is happening.**

(**Examples:** **I** am going for a ride in **my** new car. My cousin likes **my** new car.)

Third-Person Point of View uses the third-person pronouns *he, his, him, she, her, hers, it, its, they, their, theirs,* and *them* to name the person or thing spoken about. You may **not** use the first-person pronouns *I, me, my, mine, we, us, our,* and *ours* because using any first-person pronouns automatically puts the writing in a first-person point of view. **Third person means that you (the writer) must write as if you are observing the events that take place.** Third person shows that you are writing about another person, thing, or event, and you are not involved.

(**Examples:** **He** is going for a ride in **his** new car. **His** cousin likes **his** new car.)

Second-Person Point of View uses the second-person pronouns *you, your,* or *yours* to name the person or thing to whom you are speaking. Second-person point of view is not used very often in writing. Mostly, second-person point of view is used in giving directions, and it uses the pronoun **you** almost exclusively.

(**Examples:** (**You**) Turn left at the stoplight. **You** go three blocks, and the park is on the right.)

Continued on next page. >>>

Review It:

The examples on the next page illustrate the different points of view.
All the pronouns are in bold type so you will notice the change in the point
of view of each paragraph.

Reference 71 continued from previous page.

First-Person Point of View

Yesterday, **my** friends and **I** went on a short hiking trip to Devil's Den National Park. **We** put food, water, and hiking equipment into **our** backpacks and drove to the hiking trail entrance at daylight. **I** took along **my** new GPS navigation device so **I** would know exactly where **we** were at any time. **My** friends and **I** were interested in learning how this new piece of hiking equipment worked. **We** were able to explore new areas of the park with the confidence of returning safely, thanks to the GPS device!

Third-Person Point of View

Yesterday, William and **his** friends went on a short hiking trip to Devil's Den National Park. **They** put food, water, and hiking equipment into **their** backpacks and drove to the hiking trail entrance at daylight. William took along **his** new GPS navigation device so **he** would know exactly where **they** were at any time. William and **his** friends were interested in learning how this new piece of hiking equipment worked. William and **his** friends were able to explore new areas of the park with the confidence of returning safely, thanks to the GPS device!

Second-Person Point of View

You should go on a hiking trip to Devil's Den National Park. **You** will need to pack food, water, and hiking equipment in **your** backpack before heading to the hiking trail. **You** should take along a GPS navigation device so **you** will know exactly where **you** are at any time. **You** will be able to explore new areas of the park with the confidence of returning safely, thanks to the GPS device.

Look at the paragraph for third-person point of view again. Notice that all the first-person pronouns were changed to third-person pronouns or to a person's name. Remember that when you write in third person, you cannot use any of the first-person pronouns (*I, me, my, mine, we, us, our,* and *ours*) because this would automatically put your writing in a first-person point of view. As you look at the paragraph for second-person point of view, you can see why very few stories or paragraphs are written in second person.

Write It: WRITING ASSIGNMENTS 4 AND 5

As you write rough drafts for your two guided writing assignments, you will do two of the six steps in the writing process: prewriting and rough draft.

Writing Assignments 4 and 5

Purpose: To inform

Type of Writing: Three-point expository paragraphs

Audience: Classmates or family

Writing Topics: Favorite games/hobbies/countries
(Brainstorm for other ideas, individually or in groups.)

Special Instructions:

1. Write Rough Draft 4 in third-person point of view. Use Reference 71 on page 108 and third-person pronouns: *he, his, him, she, her, hers, it, its, they, their, theirs,* and *them.*
2. Write Rough Draft 5 in first-person point of view. Use Reference 71 and first-person pronouns: *I, me, my, mine, we, us, our, and ours..*
3. Follow the Prewriting and Rough Draft Checklists in References 47 and 49 on pages 62, 66.
4. Make only one prewriting map to use with both rough drafts.
5. Use References 42–46 on pages 58–61 to help you write your expository paragraphs.
6. Use standard, time-order, or transition writing form. See Reference 70 on page 107.

Note: Reference 57 on page 76 gives the steps in the writing process and the location of all the writing checklists.

START LESSON 10

Lesson 10

You will

• revise, edit, and write a final paper for WA 5.

Apply It: **REVISE, EDIT, AND WRITE A FINAL PAPER**

Following the schedule below, you will revise and edit Writing Assignment 5. Then, you will write a final paper. Use the Chapter 3 Writing Evaluation Guide on the next page to check your final paper one last time.

 | **Reference 55** | **Revising & Editing Schedule and Writing a Final Paper**

SPECIAL INSTRUCTIONS FOR REVISING AND EDITING (Steps 3-4 in the writing process):

• Use the Revising and Editing Checklists in References 51 and 53 as you revise and edit your rough draft.

• Follow the revising and editing schedule below as directed by your teacher.

1. **Individual.** First, read your rough draft to yourself. Use the Revising Checklist in Reference 51 on page 69. Go through your paper, checking each item on the list and making revisions to your rough draft. Then, use the Editing Checklist in Reference 53 on page 71. Go through your paper again, checking each item on the list and editing your rough draft.

2. **Partner.** Next, get with your editing partner. Work together on each partner's rough draft, one paper at a time. Read each rough draft aloud and revise and edit it together, using the Revising and Editing Checklists. (The author of the paper should be the one to make the corrections on his own paper.)

3. **Group.** Finally, read the rough draft to a revision group for feedback. Each student should read his paper while the others listen and offer possible revising and editing suggestions. (The author will determine whether to make corrections from the revision group's suggestions.)

SPECIAL INSTRUCTIONS FOR FINAL PAPER (Step 5 in the writing process):

• Write your final paper, using the Final Paper Checklist in Reference 56 on page 75.

• Staple your writing papers in this order: the final paper on top, the rough draft in the middle, and the prewriting map on the bottom. Place the stapled papers in the Final Paper folder.

>>>>>>>>>>>>> Student Tip...

1. Be tactful and helpful in your comments during revising and editing time. The purpose of any suggestion should be to improve the writer's rough draft.

2. As you make your final corrections, you have the choice of accepting or rejecting any suggestions made by your partners or your revision group.

3. Study Vocabulary Words and Analogies 5-7 for the chapter test in the next lesson.

4. If you need to improve your handwriting, refer to the Resource Tools Section on page 521 for information on writing legibly.

Chapter 3 Writing Evaluation Guide

Name:_____ Date:_____

ROUGH DRAFT CHECK

_____ 1. Did you write your rough draft in pencil?

_____ 2. Did you write the correct headings on the first seven lines of your paper?

_____ 3. Did you use extra wide margins and skip every other line?

_____ 4. Did you write a title at the end of your rough draft?

_____ 5. Did you place your edited rough draft in your Rough Draft folder?

REVISING CHECK

_____ 6. Did you identify the purpose, type of writing, and audience?

_____ 7. Did you check for a topic, topic sentence, and sentences supporting the topic?

_____ 8. Did you check sentences for the right order, and did you combine, rearrange, or delete sentences when necessary?

_____ 9. Did you check for a variety of simple, compound, and complex sentences?

_____ 10. Did you check for any left out, repeated, or unnecessary words?

_____ 11. Did you check for the best choice of words by replacing or deleting unclear words?

_____ 12. Did you check the content for interest and creativity?

_____ 13. Did you check the voice to make sure the writing says what you want it to say?

EDITING CHECK

_____ 14. Did you indent each paragraph?

_____ 15. Did you put an end mark at the end of every sentence?

_____ 16. Did you capitalize the first word of every sentence?

_____ 17. Did you check for all other capitalization mistakes?

_____ 18. Did you check for all punctuation mistakes?
(commas, periods, apostrophes, quotation marks, underlining)

_____ 19. Did you check for misspelled words and for incorrect homonym choices?

_____ 20. Did you check for incorrect spellings of plural and possessive forms?

_____ 21. Did you check for correct construction and punctuation of your sentences?

_____ 22. Did you check for usage mistakes? *(subject/verb agreement, a/an choices, contractions, verb tenses, pronoun/antecedent agreement, pronoun cases, degrees of adjectives, double negatives, etc.)*

_____ 23. Did you put your revised and edited paper in the Rough Draft folder?

FINAL PAPER CHECK

_____ 24. Did you write the final paper in pencil?

_____ 25. Did you center the title on the top line and center your name under the title?

_____ 26. Did you skip a line before starting the writing assignment?

_____ 27. Did you single-space, use wide margins, and write the final paper neatly?

_____ 28. Did you staple your papers in this order: final paper on top, rough draft in the middle, and prewriting map on the bottom? Did you put them in the Final Paper folder?

START LESSON 11

Lesson 11

You will

- hand in WA 5 for grading.
- respond to oral review questions.
- take Chapter 3 Test.

CHAPTER TEST

It is time to evaluate your knowledge of the skills you have learned in this chapter. Your teacher will give you the Chapter 3 Test to help you assess your progress.

Hand It In: **WRITING ASSIGNMENT 5**

Get your stapled papers for Writing Assignment 5 from your Final Paper folder. Check to make sure they are in the correct order: the final paper on top, the rough draft in the middle, and the prewriting map on the bottom. Hand them in to your teacher.

LISTENING AND SPEAKING:
Oral Review Questions

1. What is the word that connects its object to some other word in the sentence?
2. What is a noun or pronoun after a preposition called?
3. What begins with a preposition and ends with an object of a preposition?
4. What kind of noun means only one?
5. What kind of noun means more than one?
6. What kind of noun is not specific and is not capitalized?
7. What kind of noun is specific and is always capitalized?
8. What is another name for the subject and all the words that modify it?
9. What is another name for the verb and all the words that modify it?
10. What is another name for the subject noun or pronoun?
11. What is another name for the verb?
12. Are the verbs is, was, has, and does singular or plural verb forms?
13. Are the verbs sings, drives, and walks singular or plural verb forms?
14. Are the verbs are, were, have, and do singular or plural verb forms?
15. What are some time-order words used in writing?
16. Which point of view uses the pronouns I, me, my, mine, we, us, and our?
17. Which point of view uses the pronouns he, she, it, they, their, and them?
18. What type of writing is used to inform, to give facts, to give directions, to explain, or to define something?

>>>>>>>>>>>>> Student Tip...

For information about test-taking strategies, refer to the Resource Tools Section on page 520.

LISTENING AND SPEAKING:
Vocabulary & Analogy Time

Learn It: Recite the new vocabulary and analogy words.

 Reference 72 **Vocabulary & Analogy Words**

Word: petition (pə tĭsh'ən)
  Definition: a sincere request
  Synonym: appeal   **Antonym:** demand
  Sentence: The voters submitted a **petition** for lower taxes.

Analogy: letters : word :: sentences : paragraph
  Part-to-whole relationship: Just as **letters** are part of a **word**,
                sentences are part of a **paragraph.**

Vocabulary Card 8: Record the vocabulary information above and write your own
      sentence, using the new word.
Analogy Card 8: Record the analogy information and write your own analogy,
      using the same relationship as the analogy above.

 **Jingle Time**

Recite It: Recite the new jingles.

♪ **Jingle 13** **The Pronoun Jingle**

These little pronouns,   With a smile and a nod
Hangin' around,   And a twinkle of the eye,
Can take the place   Give those pronouns
Of any of the nouns.   A big high five! Yeah!

♪ **Jingle 14** **The Subject Pronoun Jingle**

There are seven subject pronouns
That are easy as can be.
SUBJECT PRONOUNS!
I and **We**,
He and **She**,
It and **They** and **You**.
Those are the subject pronouns!

♪ **Jingle 15** **The Possessive Pronoun Jingle**

There are seven possessive pronouns
That are easy as can be.
POSSESSIVE PRONOUNS!
My and **Our**,
His and **Her**,
Its and **Their** and **Your**.
Those are possessive pronouns!

Lesson 1
You will
- study new vocabulary; make Card 8; write own sentence using the vocabulary word.
- analyze new analogy; make Card 8; write own analogy.
- recite new jingles (Pronoun, Subject Pronoun, Possessive Pronoun).
- identify pronouns, subject pronouns, understood subject pronouns, and possessive pronoun adjectives.
- classify Introductory Sentences.
- do a Skill Builder to identify pronouns.
- recognize pronouns as a part of speech.
- write in your journal.

Apply It: These Introductory Sentences are used to apply the new grammar concepts taught below. Classify these sentences orally with your teacher.

Introductory Sentences	Chapter 4: Lesson 1

1. _____ She looked at the unusual flower through the powerful camera lens.
2. _____ Meet with the directors of the company at noon today.
3. _____ We floated lazily on our raft in the river behind our house.

Learn It: **PRONOUNS AND SUBJECT PRONOUNS**

📖 Reference 73	**Pronouns & Subject Pronouns**

1. A **pronoun** may take the place of any noun in a sentence. A pronoun may stand for a person, place, thing, or idea.
2. A **subject pronoun** takes the place of a noun that is used as the subject of a sentence.
3. The subject pronouns are *I, we, he, she, it, they,* and *you.* Use the Subject Pronoun Jingle to remember these subject pronouns.
4. To find a subject pronoun, ask the subject question *who* or *what.*
5. A *subject pronoun* is labeled with the abbreviation **SP**.

Learn It: **UNDERSTOOD SUBJECT PRONOUNS**

📖 Reference 74	**Understood Subject Pronouns**

1. A sentence has an **understood subject** when someone gives a command or makes a request and leaves the subject unwritten or unspoken. The unspoken subject will always be the pronoun *you*.
2. When a sentence has an understood subject and gives a command or makes a request, it is called an imperative sentence. It ends with a period and always has the word *you* understood, not expressed, as the subject. (**Example:** Do your homework.)
3. When you classify sentences, the understood subject pronoun *you* is always written in **parentheses** at the beginning of the sentence with the label **SP** beside it: **(You) SP**.
4. Whenever you read **(You) SP**, you will say, "*You – understood subject pronoun.*"
5. In the example, *Do your homework* who is being commanded to do your homework? Someone is being commanded to do your homework even though the name of that person is not mentioned. The person receiving the command is the understood subject pronoun, **YOU**.

Learn It: **POSSESSIVE PRONOUN ADJECTIVES**

📖 **Reference 75** | **Possessive Pronouns**

1. A **possessive pronoun** takes the place of a possessive noun, but a possessive pronoun does not use an apostrophe to make it possessive.
2. The possessive pronouns are *my, our, his, her, its, their,* and *your.*
   Use the Possessive Pronoun Jingle to remember these pronouns.
3. A possessive pronoun has two jobs: to show ownership or possession and to modify like an adjective.
4. A possessive pronoun's part of speech is an adjective.
5. When a possessive pronoun is classified, it is labeled as a possessive pronoun adjective in order to recognize both jobs. A **possessive pronoun adjective** is labeled with the abbreviation **PPA.**
   For the abbreviation **PPA,** say, "*Possessive pronoun adjective.*"
6. Include possessive pronoun adjectives when you are asked to identify pronouns, possessives, or adjectives.
7. To find a possessive pronoun adjective, ask "*whose*" before the noun. (**Example:** Whose coat? **his - PPA**)

Apply It: **A SKILL BUILDER FOR A NOUN CHECK WITH PRONOUNS**

Using the sentences just classified, do a Skill Builder orally with your teacher. The example below shows you what to do with pronouns in a Noun Check.

LISTENING AND SPEAKING:

FOR A NOUN CHECK WITH PRONOUNS

Circle the nouns in a Noun Check.

Sentence 1: Subject Pronoun **she**, *no, it is a pronoun;*
Object of the Preposition (flower), *yes, it is a noun;*
Object of the Preposition (lens), *yes, it is a noun.*

Sentence 2: Subject Pronoun **you**, *no, it is a pronoun;*
Object of the Preposition (directors), *yes, it is a noun;*
Object of the Preposition (company), *yes, it is a noun;*
Object of the Preposition (noon), *yes, it is a noun.*

Sentence 3: Subject Pronoun **we**, *no, it is a pronoun;*
Object of the Preposition (raft), *yes, it is a noun;*
Object of the Preposition (river), *yes, it is a noun;*
Object of the Preposition (house), *yes, it is a noun.*

JOURNAL WRITING 8

Write an entry in your journal. Use Reference 9 on page 12 for ideas.

Learn It: **ADDING PRONOUNS TO THE PARTS OF SPEECH**

A pronoun is a part of speech. You have learned six of the eight parts of speech. What are these six parts of speech?

START LESSON 2

Lesson 2

You will

- practice Jingles 13-15; recite new jingle (Conjunction).
- identify conjunctions and compound parts.
- classify Introductory Sentences.
- do a Skill Builder.
- recognize conjunctions as a part of speech.
- identify simple sentences, fragments, run-on sentences, and compound parts.
- do Classroom Practice 17.

LISTENING AND SPEAKING:

Recite It: 1. Practice Jingles 13–15 in the Jingle Section on pages 501–502.
2. Recite the new jingle.

| ♪ | Jingle 16 | **The Conjunction Sound-Off Jingle** |

Conjunctions are a part of speech.
Conjunctions are a part of speech.
They join words or sentences; it's quite a feat!
They join words or sentences; it's quite a feat!
Sound off! Conjunctions!   Sound off! AND, OR, BUT!
There are many conjunctions, but three stand out.
There are many conjunctions, but three stand out.
Put your hands together and give a shout!
Put your hands together and give a shout!
Sound off! Conjunctions!   Sound off! AND, OR, BUT!
Sound off! Conjunctions!   Sound off! AND, OR, BUT!

Apply It: These Introductory Sentences are used to apply the new grammar concepts taught below. Classify these sentences orally with your teacher.

| Introductory Sentences | Chapter 4: Lesson 2 |

1. _____ Two frisky chipmunks danced merrily and scampered around before dark.

2. _____ My brothers and I traveled to Canada during our summer vacation.

3. _____ Move forward to the center aisle for a green salad and two vegetables.

English Made Easy

Learn It: COORDINATE CONJUNCTIONS AND COMPOUND PARTS

 Reference 76 | **Coordinate Conjunctions and Compound Parts**

1. A **conjunction** is a word that joins words or groups of words together.

2. Conjunctions that join things of the same kind or of equal importance (like two subjects, two verbs, or two simple sentences) are called **coordinate conjunctions**.

3. The three most common coordinate conjunctions are **and**, **or**, and **but**. There are no questions used to find coordinate conjunctions; therefore, these conjunctions should be memorized.

4. A *coordinate conjunction* is labeled with the abbreviation **C**.

5. When words or groups of words in a sentence are joined by a coordinate conjunction, the parts that are joined are called **compound parts**. There are many parts of a sentence that can be **compound**. However, compound subjects and compound verbs are the most common.

6. The label **C** is also used to identify compound parts when it is used in front of regular labels. Examples of compound labels are **CSN, CSP, CV, CAdj, CAdv, COP**, etc. To classify a compound part, always say the word *compound* first. For example, read the label **CSN** as "*Compound Subject Noun.*"

>>>>>>>> **Student Tip...**

Swing your right hand to your chest and say <u>and</u>. Keeping your right hand at your chest, swing your left hand to your chest and say <u>or</u>. Then, swing both hands horizontally and say <u>but</u>. Repeat the chant and motions several times.

Discuss It:

What abbreviation is used for a compound subject noun?

What abbreviation is used for a compound subject pronoun?

What abbreviation is used for a compound verb?

What abbreviation is used for a compound adjective?

What abbreviation is used for a compound adverb?

What abbreviation is used for a compound object of the preposition?

FOR A NOUN CHECK WITH PRONOUNS

Using the sentences just classified, do a Skill Builder orally with your teacher.

1. **Identify the nouns in a Noun Check.**

2. **Identify the nouns.**

3. **Identify the pronouns.**

Learn It: ADDING THE CONJUNCTION TO THE PARTS OF SPEECH

A conjunction is a part of speech. You have learned seven of the eight parts of speech. What are these seven parts of speech?

Learn It: SIMPLE SENTENCES, SENTENCE FRAGMENTS,
RUN-ONS, AND COMPOUND PARTS

Reference 77 — Simple Sentences, Fragments, Run-ons, and Compound Parts

1. A **simple sentence** must have three core parts to be complete: a subject, a verb, and a complete thought. A simple sentence is independent and can stand alone. The label for a *simple sentence* is the letter **S**.
   Example: *My aunt cooks for her large family every day.*

2. A sentence **fragment** is an incomplete sentence. A fragment is missing one or more of the core sentence parts (subject, verb, or complete thought). The label for a *fragment* is the letter **F**.
   Example: *Cooks for her large family every day.*

3. A **run-on sentence** is two sentences written together as one sentence without correct punctuation.
   Example: *My aunt cooks for her large family every day she is an amazing woman.*

4. A simple sentence may also have **compound parts**. Compound parts are usually joined by the conjunction **and**. When it is used in front of regular labels, the label **C** is used to identify compound parts. Here are the meanings and labels of several compound parts: **CS**—*compound subject;*
   CV—*compound verb;* **SCS**—*simple sentence with a compound subject;*
   SCV—*simple sentence with a compound verb.*

Part 1: The examples below show how each sentence is identified by the label in parentheses.

1. A yellow bird flew into the window. (**S**)
2. The two dogs in the yard. (**F**)
3. My sister and brother played in the pool. (**SCS**)
4. Curtis waved and ran into the house. (**SCV**)

Part 2: Correct each sentence fragment by adding the part in parentheses that is underlined.

1. In the park after school. (subject part, predicate part, <u>both the subject and predicate</u>, sense)
   Example: The neighborhood children played in the park after school.
2. The dark, foreboding clouds. (subject part, <u>predicate part</u>, both the subject and predicate, sense)
   Example: The dark, foreboding clouds warned of the coming thunderstorm.
3. Was running away from the forest fire.
   (<u>subject part</u>, predicate part, both the subject and predicate, sense)
   Example: A family of wolves was running away from the forest fire.
4. As I ran happily along the beach. (subject part, predicate part, both the subject and predicate, <u>sense</u>)
   Example: Delete **As**. I ran happily along the beach.

Part 3: Use a slash to separate each run-on sentence below.
Then, correct each run-on sentence by rewriting it as indicated by the labels in parentheses at the end of the sentence.

1. The toddler fell down / he started crying. (**S, S**)
   The toddler fell down. He started crying.
2. The teacher eats in the cafeteria every day / the student eats in the cafeteria every day. (**SCS**)
   The teacher and student eat in the cafeteria every day.
3. The rocket rose slowly / it disappeared from sight. (**SCV**)
   The rocket rose slowly and disappeared from sight.

Part 4: Identify each type of sentence by writing the correct label in the blank. (**Labels: S, F, SCS, SCV**)

__S__ 1. The squirrel climbed higher in the tree.
__F__ 2. As I looked into the telescope.
__SCV__ 3. They laughed and shouted with their friends.
__SCS__ 4. Mother and I shop on Saturdays.

 Classroom Practice 17

It is time to practice the skills you are learning. You will use the classroom practice on the next page to apply these skills.

Classroom Practice 17

Name:_____ Date:_____

GRAMMAR

▶ **Exercise 1:** Classify each sentence. Underline the complete subject once and the complete predicate twice.

1. _____ Julie and Cecile walked with the grace and charm of professional models.

2. _____ Two huge boulders near the steep cliff balanced uneasily on their flat surfaces!

3. _____ Debbie and I darted around the track for our morning exercise.

SKILLS

▶ **Exercise 2:** Identify each type of sentence by writing the correct label in the blank. (**Labels: S, F, SCS, SCV**)

_____ 1. Meredith and Jonathan play the trumpet.
_____ 2. Before the intersection on Main Street.
_____ 3. The plaster on the east side of the building cracked and peeled in several places.
_____ 4. The trees and shrubs around my house provide shade on hot summer days.
_____ 5. Knows how to weld metal.
_____ 6. Sheila stood in line and waited for the ticket counter to open.
_____ 7. Nicole made a list of chores and completed each one.
_____ 8. The sun peaked over the horizon.
_____ 9. The high winds and heavy rain ended our picnic.

▶ **Exercise 3:** Use a slash to separate the two complete thoughts in each run-on sentence.
Correct the run-on sentences as indicated by the labels in parentheses at the end of each sentence.

1. The movers packed the boxes the movers loaded the truck. (**SCV**)
_____

2. My dad mowed the lawn my brother helped him. (**SCS**)
_____

3. The children went to the zoo their parents went to the zoo. (**SCS**)
_____

4. Grandfather fell asleep he began to snore. (**SCV**)
_____

EDITING

▶ **Exercise 4:** Correct each mistake.
Editing Guide: End Marks: 2   Capitals: 9   Commas: 7   Subject-Verb Agreement: 1   Misspelled Words: 2

the hurricane victims desperately need food clothing and shelter the red cross the

salvation army the united way churches american citizens and others is helping in many ways

START LESSON 3

Lesson 3

You will

- study new vocabulary; make Card 9; write own sentence using the vocabulary word.
- analyze new analogy; make Card 9; write own analogy.
- practice Jingles 13-16.
- classify Practice Sentences.
- do a Skill Builder.
- identify homonyms.
- do Classroom Practice 18.
- read and discuss Discovery Time.

LISTENING AND SPEAKING:

Vocabulary & Analogy Time

Learn It: Recite the new vocabulary and analogy words.

	Reference 78	**Vocabulary & Analogy Words**

Word: intricate (ĭn'trĭ kĭt)
   Definition: having many detailed parts
   Synonym: complex   **Antonym:** simple
   Sentence: The main character developed an **intricate** plan of escape.

Analogy: late : early :: arrival : departure
   Antonym relationship: Just as **late** is the opposite of **early**, **arrival** is the opposite of **departure**.

Vocabulary Card 9: Record the vocabulary information above and write your own sentence, using the new word.

Analogy Card 9: Record the analogy information and write your own analogy, using the same relationship as the analogy above.

Jingle Time

Recite It: Practice Jingles 13–16 in the Jingle Section on pages 501–502.

Grammar Time

Apply It: Classify the Practice Sentences orally with your teacher.

Practice Sentences	Chapter 4: Lesson 3

1. _____ Marksmen in the amateur competition aimed and fired accurately at their targets.
2. _____ Look at that breathtaking view and beautiful sunrise in Jasper Valley!
3. _____ The new baseball went astray and disappeared into a nearby sewer drain.

LISTENING AND SPEAKING:

Using the sentences just classified, do a Skill Builder orally with your teacher.

1. **Identify the nouns in a Noun Check.**
2. **Identify the nouns as singular or plural.**
3. **Identify the nouns as common or proper.**
4. **Identify the complete subject and the complete predicate.**
5. **Identify the simple subject and the simple predicate.**
6. **Do a Vocabulary Check.**

Learn It: HOMONYMS

The Homonym Chart contains a partial listing of the most common homonyms. Use a dictionary to look up other homonyms that you do not know.

📖 **Reference 79**	**Homonym Chart**

Homonyms are words which sound alike but have different meanings and different spellings.

1. **blew** – did blow	21. **its** - ownership pronoun	41. **sea** – large body of water; ocean
2. **blue** – a color	22. **it's** - contraction for *it is*	42. **see** – to look at
3. **buy** – to purchase	23. **knew** – did know	43. **son** – male child
4. **by** – near to	24. **new** – recently made or bought	44. **sun** – the star in our solar system
5. **capital** – main; wealth	25. **knot** – to tie or clump together	45. **stationary** - motionless
6. **capitol** - statehouse	26. **not** – refuse; deny; prevent	46. **stationery** - paper
7. **council** – assembly	27. **know** – to understand	47. **their** - belonging to them
8. **counsel** – to advise	28. **no** - not so; negative	48. **there** - in that place
9. **fore** - before	29. **lead** - metal	49. **they're** - contraction for *they are*
10. **four** – the number 4	30. **led** - did guide; did show the way	
11. **forth** - forward	31. **meat** – a type of food	50. **threw** - did throw
12. **fourth** - number in order	32. **meet** – to join or be introduced to	51. **through** - from end to end
13. **heal** – to make healthy	33. **peace** – not fighting or not at war	52. **to** - toward; a preposition
14. **heel** – part of the foot	34. **piece** – a part of something	53. **too** - denoting excess
15. **hear** – to listen	35. **pore** – a tiny opening in the skin	54. **two** - the number 2; a couple
16. **here** – in this place	36. **pour** – to send liquid flowing	55. **your** - owned by you; a pronoun
17. **hour** – sixty minutes	37. **principle** - a truth; rule; law	56. **you're** - contraction for you are
18. **our** – belonging to us	38. **principal** - primary; head person	57. **wait** – to delay action
19. **in** – included within	39. **right** – correct; direction	58. **weight** - amount of heaviness
20. **inn** – a small hotel	40. **write** – to form letters	59. **weak** - not strong
		60. **week** - period of seven days

Exercise: Underline the correct homonym.

1. He used the (<u>capital</u>, capitol) from his business to make another investment.

2. The tourists visited the state (capital, <u>capitol</u>) and talked with the governor.

Learn It: EDITING PARAGRAPHS WITH HOMONYMS

You have just learned about homonyms. You have been editing paragraphs already for different kinds of mistakes. Look at Reference 80. This reference shows how to find and correct homonym mistakes in a paragraph

Reference 80	**Editing a Paragraph with Homonyms**

Correct each mistake.

Editing Guide: End Marks: 2   Capitals: 9   Commas: 3   Homonyms: 7   Periods: 1   Misspelled Words: 3

   m   m L   two   principals   to their fourth   E H School

my friend, ms. lee, and too other principles went two there forth annual meeting at east high scool in

A   m   E   whole   to   improve   achievement

augusta, maine. educators from the hole state met too discuss ways to emprove student achevement.

✏️	**Classroom Practice 18**

It is time to practice the skills you are learning. You will use the classroom practice on the next page to apply these skills.

ENRICHMENT:

Mercury is the closest planet to the sun in our solar system. Since Mercury's atmosphere is too thin to provide any insulation, its temperature rises to 800°F during the day and drops to -300°F at night. Mercury is a very small planet; it would take twenty planets the size of Mercury to equal the size of Earth.

Discovery Questions:
- Do you think there would be a way humans could inhabit Mercury? Explain.
- Would you like to live on another planet?

Are you interested in learning more about Mercury?

1. You may explore this topic further by using the resources listed below.
   Computer resources: Internet, encyclopedia software
   Library resources: encyclopedias, books, magazines, newspapers
   Home/community resources: books, interviews, newspapers, magazines

2. A Discovery Share Time is provided in Lesson 7 if you wish to share your investigation results. You may share orally, or you may prepare a written report. You will put your written report in a class booklet titled "Space Trivia." This booklet will be placed in the class library for everyone to enjoy.

Classroom Practice 18

Name:_____ Date:_____

GRAMMAR

▶ **Exercise 1:** Classify each sentence. Underline the complete subject once and the complete predicate twice.

1. _____ We yelled frantically at the raging bull!

2. _____ An old cat lay cozily on the warm rug in front of the large fireplace for a nap.

3. _____ Hold tightly to the banister with your left hand.

SKILLS

▶ **Exercise 2:** Underline the correct homonym in each sentence.

1. The baker kneaded the (dough, doe).
2. The morning (due, dew) soaked my shoes.
3. The lion carefully stalked his (prey, pray).
4. Dad (threw, through) a sack in the trunk.
5. Our final paper is (do, due) on Friday.
6. A guide (led, lead) us through the cave.
7. Cory (mode, mowed) the lawn yesterday.
8. There are (know, no) pets allowed in here.

▶ **Exercise 3:** Identify each type of sentence by writing the correct label in the blank. (**Labels: S, F, SCS, SCV**)

_____ 1. Aluminum cans and glass bottles can be recycled.
_____ 2. I grabbed my coat and went outside for a walk.
_____ 3. Before we could start on the project.
_____ 4. Samantha washed the dishes for her mother.
_____ 5. We gathered wood and made a campfire.

▶ **Exercise 4:** Use a slash to separate the two complete thoughts in each run-on sentence. Correct the run-on sentences as indicated by the labels in parentheses at the end of each sentence.

1. The children were crying they were afraid. (**S, S**)

_____

2. The cow walks to the pond her calf walks to the pond. (**SCS**)

_____

3. The students studied hard they passed their test. (**SCV**)

_____

EDITING

▶ **Exercise 5:** Correct each mistake. **Editing Guide: End Marks: 4   Capitals: 11   Commas: 1   Apostrophes: 2   Homonyms: 3   Misspelled Words: 2**

on monday stans car had a blowout on the brooklyn bridge in the midle of morning traffick

he had know spare he called bobs wrecker service to fix his tire what a way too start the weak

START LESSON 4

Lesson 4

You will

- study new vocabulary; make Card 10; write own sentence using the vocabulary word.
- analyze new analogy; make Card 10; write own analogy.
- practice Jingles 5-11.
- classify Practice Sentences.
- do a Skill Builder.
- do Classroom Practice 19.
- read and discuss Discovery Time.
- write in your journal.
- do a homework assignment.
- do a Home Connection activity.

LISTENING AND SPEAKING:

Vocabulary & Analogy Time

Learn It: Recite the new vocabulary and analogy words.

Reference 81	Vocabulary & Analogy Words

Word: absurd (əb sûrd', –zûrd')
   Definition: making no sense
   Synonym: ridiculous   **Antonym:** sensible
   Sentence: His statement was one of the most **absurd** I had ever heard.

Analogy: beeper : sweeper :: swing : string
   Rhyming relationship: Just as **beeper** rhymes with **sweeper**, **swing** rhymes with **string**.

Vocabulary Card 10: Record the vocabulary information above and write your own sentence, using the new word.

Analogy Card 10: Record the analogy information and write your own analogy, using the same relationship as the analogy above.

Jingle Time

Recite It: Practice Jingles 5–11 in the Jingle Section on pages 499–500.

Grammar Time

Apply It: Classify the Practice Sentences orally with your teacher.

Practice Sentences	Chapter 4: Lesson 4

1. _____ A brilliant new satellite blinked continuously in the unusually dark sky.
2. _____ Dan and I flew to the summit for our interviews with world leaders.
3. _____ Move carefully through the winding trails of green foliage in our woods.

 Skill Builder

Using the sentences just classified, do a Skill Builder orally with your teacher.

1. **Identify the nouns in a Noun Check.**
2. **Identify the nouns as singular or plural.**
3. **Identify the nouns as common or proper.**
4. **Identify the complete subject and the complete predicate.**
5. **Identify the simple subject and the simple predicate.**
6. **Do a Vocabulary Check.**

Classroom Practice 19

It is time to practice the skills you are learning. You will use the classroom practice on the next page to apply these skills.

ENRICHMENT:

 **Discovery Time**

(Italian) 1564-1642— Galileo Galilei was an Italian physicist and astronomer. He invented a telescope based on hearing that such a device existed in Holland. He bought lenses from eyeglass shops to create his own three-powered and eight-powered telescopes.

 Discovery Questions:
- **What were some of Galileo's most remembered discoveries?**
- **How do you think Galileo would react to the modern equipment that astronomers use today?**
- **Have you ever been to a observatory? What impressed you most during your visit?**
- **Would you like to be an astronomer? Explain.**

Are you interested in learning more about Galileo Galilei?

1. You may explore this topic further by using the resources listed below.
   Computer resources: Internet, encyclopedia software
   Library resources: encyclopedias, books, magazines, newspapers
   Home/community resources: books, interviews, newspapers, magazines

2. A Discovery Share Time is provided in Lesson 7 if you wish to share your investigation results. You may share orally, or you may prepare a written report. You will put your written report in a class booklet titled "Space Trivia." This booklet will be placed in the class library for everyone to enjoy.

 JOURNAL WRITING 9

Write an entry in your journal. Use Reference 9 on page 12 for ideas.

Classroom Practice 19

Name:_____ Date:_____

GRAMMAR

▶ **Exercise 1:** Classify each sentence. Underline the complete subject once and the complete predicate twice.

1. _____ The pack of wild wolves howled at the large moon.

2. _____ Practice for your Spanish test with Pedro after lunch tomorrow.

3. _____ Tyler and I played in the orchestra and performed at the fall festival.

SKILLS

▶ **Exercise 2:** Underline the correct homonym in each sentence.

1. That shirt looks good on (you, ewe).

2. We need to win (for, four, fore) more games.

3. Will you help me (peal, peel) the potatoes?

4. Did you get a new (pair, pear, pare) of shoes?

5. I did (not, knot) understand your question.

6. Heavy (rain, reign, rein) flooded the streets.

7. Have you (scene, seen) my gloves?

8. This bowl of soup is (two, to, too) hot!

▶ **Exercise 3:** Identify each type of sentence by writing the correct label in the blank. (**Labels: S, F, SCS, SCV**)

_____ 1. Nikki looked frantically for her keys.

_____ 2. My dad's old truck coughed and sputtered down the street.

_____ 3. The boys and girls toasted marshmallows over the campfire.

_____ 4. Angie's old, gray cat.

_____ 5. The hens in the coop scratched the ground and searched for corn.

▶ **Exercise 4:** Use a slash to separate the two complete thoughts in each run-on sentence.
  Correct the run-on sentences as indicated by the labels in parentheses at the end of each sentence.

1. The teacher wore safety goggles during the experiment her students wore goggles, too. (**SCS**)

_____

2. Our team scored the most points our team won the game. (**SCV**)

_____

3. The workers were mining they found gold. (**S, S**)

_____

EDITING

▶ **Exercise 5:** Correct each mistake. **Editing Guide: End Marks: 3   Capitals: 19   Commas: 4   Apostrophes: 2**
  Homonyms: 1   Subject-Verb Agreement: 2   Underlining: 4   Misspelled Words: 2

the most famos early african-american newspaper the north star were started buy frederick

douglass in 1847 other poplar newspapers included freemans advocate freedoms journal and

the mirror of liberty these anti-slavery newspapers was influential during the civil war

Homework 2

Complete this homework assignment on notebook paper.

1. Number your paper 1–6. Write the correct homonym for each sentence. Write answers only.

1. I want a big (peace, piece) of cake.

2. The bride walked slowly down the (isle, aisle).

3. That (coarse, course) cloth irritates my skin.

4. We wanted ice cream, (to, two, too).

5. The tree put (fourth, forth) large, green leaves.

6. The traffic was (stationary, stationery) for an hour.

2. Write the names of the seven parts of speech you have studied so far.

1. _____ 2. _____ 3. _____ 4. _____

5. _____ 6. _____ 7. _____

3. Number your paper 1–4. Identify each type of sentence by writing the correct label (**S**, **F**, **SCS**, or **SCV**) beside each number.

_____ 1. I went to the fair with Jessie and Shane.   _____ 3. My puppy and kitten eat together.

_____ 2. We walked and ran in the marathon.   _____ 4. In the bus station.

4. Rewrite and correct each sentence fragment by adding the part in parentheses that is underlined.

1. Under the porch in the backyard.   (subject part, predicate part, <u>both the subject and predicate</u>, sense)

2. The raging forest fire.   (subject part, <u>predicate part</u>, both the subject and predicate, sense)

3. Soared high above the treetops.   (<u>subject part</u>, predicate part, both the subject and predicate, sense)

Home Connection

Family Activity for Pronouns

1. Have a contest with family members or friends to see who can go the longest without using any pronouns. Down the left side of a sheet of paper, make a list of the pronouns that are used in the pronoun jingles on Student Book p. 113. For an hour, do not use any pronouns in your conversations. Keep the list with you at all times. Every time you forget and say a pronoun, place a tally mark beside that pronoun. At the end of an hour, add up the number of times that you used pronouns. Which pronouns did you use most? Discuss the importance of pronouns in communication.

2. Expand the game to several hours on a weekend or all weekend. You could include relatives, guests, or friends in this activity.

Family Activity for Fragments

Divide into teams. See which team can make the longest sentence from each fragment below in the shortest time. Read and discuss the sentences. Write more fragments and do this activity again.

a. On a huge rock in the middle of the river

b. My brother and I

c. Everybody in the class

d. Beside the dusty road

e. Slithered out of its hole in broad daylight

START LESSON 5

Lesson 5

You will
- classify Practice Sentences.
- do Chapter Checkup 20.
- write in your journal.

JOURNAL WRITING 10

Write an entry in your journal. Use Reference 9 on page 12 for ideas.

LISTENING AND SPEAKING:

Grammar Time

Apply It: Classify the Practice Sentences orally with your teacher.

Practice Sentences	Chapter 4: Lesson 5

1. _____ We ski yearly in the Rockies during the months of December and January.
2. _____ Jennifer, Taylor, and Brittany flew to Europe for their vacation.
3. _____ Eat in the solarium with your grandfather and grandmother.

✎ Chapter Checkup 20

It is time for a checkup of the skills you have learned in this chapter. You will use the chapter checkup on the next page to evaluate your progress.

Chapter 4 Checkup 20

Name:_____ Date:_____

GRAMMAR

▶ **Exercise 1:** Classify each sentence. Underline the complete subject once and the complete predicate twice.

1. _____ Turn off the stove in the kitchen.

2. _____ They applauded loudly for the winners and losers in the spelling competition.

3. _____ The rival teams from nearby schools gathered for the final race of the season.

SKILLS

▶ **Exercise 2:** Underline the correct homonym in each sentence.

1. The pod of (whales, wails) swam away.

2. We have one (weak, week) to write a report.

3. Raise your (write, right) hand.

4. Edgar called a (tow, toe) truck.

5. The icing on the cake was too (sweet, suite).

6. I asked the teller for a (role, roll) of quarters.

▶ **Exercise 3:** Identify each type of sentence by writing the correct label in the blank. (**Labels: S, F, SCS, SCV**)

_____ 1. The photo lab technician processed and printed my pictures.

_____ 2. The lions, tigers, and bears performed perfectly in the circus act.

_____ 3. From the same community in their homeland.

_____ 4. The pilot narrowly escaped the crash.

_____ 5. The strong currents rushed over the rocks and carried the canoeist downstream.

▶ **Exercise 4:** Use a slash to separate the two complete thoughts in each run-on sentence.
Correct the run-on sentences as indicated by the labels in parentheses at the end of each sentence.

1. Johann Galle was a German astronomer he discovered Neptune. (**S, S**)

_____

2. My brother wanted pepperoni pizza My sister wanted pepperoni pizza, too. (**SCS**)

_____

3. We went to the zoo we saw many rare animals. (**SCV**)

_____

EDITING

▶ **Exercise 5:** Correct each mistake. **Editing Guide: End Marks: 4   Capitals: 17   Commas: 3   Apostrophes: 1   Homonyms: 5   Subject-Verb Agreement: 2   Misspelled Words: 2**

the presidents schedule fore the last two weaks in november is to hectic he have meetings

inn california michigan new york and florida he has a tv appearance just before thankgiving

he and his family plans to spend thanksgiving at the white house with there close freinds

START LESSON 6

Lesson 6

You will

- conference with teacher about WA 5.
- write a creative writing piece for WA6.

Writing Time

Write It: **WRITING ASSIGNMENT 6**

Writing Assignment 6 : Creative Expressions

Purpose: To entertain

Type of Writing: Creative

Audience: Classmates, family, or friends

Choose one of the writing topics below.

1. What does it take to be a good friend? Whom do you consider a good friend? Why?
2. If you could choose your future, what would it be? How would you prepare for it? How would it change you?
3. Write a poem about friends, the future, or a topic of your choice.

Special Instructions:

1. A prewriting map is not required for this creative-writing assignment.
2. Follow the Rough Draft Checklist in Reference 49 on page 66.
3. Put your creative-writing paper in your Rough Draft folder when you have finished.

   Note: Reference 57 on page 76 gives the steps in the writing process and the location of all the writing checklists.

>>>>>>>>>>>>>>>>>>>>>>>>> Student Tip...

For more information about writing poetry, look at Chapter 18, pages 456–474.

Conference Time

Discuss It: **TEACHER-STUDENT CONFERENCES FOR WRITING ASSIGNMENT 5**

Meet with your teacher to discuss Writing Assignment 5.
After the conference, place this group of papers in your Publishing folder.

Publishing Time

Publish It: **WRITING ASSIGNMENT 5**

Choose a publishing form and publish Writing Assignment 5. After rewriting your paper for publication, give the stapled papers (evaluation guide, graded final paper, rough draft, and prewriting map) to your teacher to be placed in your Writing Portfolio.

START LESSON 7

Lesson 7

You will
- publish WA 5.
- participate in Discovery Share Time.

Reference 67	Publishing Checklist for Step 6 in the Writing Process

The sixth step in the writing process is called publishing. Publishing is sharing your writing with others. With so many forms of publishing available, finding a match for every project and personality is easy. At times, a written work is best read aloud. Other times, the biggest impact is made when a written work is read silently. You can also use media sources to enhance any publication.

SPECIAL INSTRUCTIONS FOR PUBLISHING:

- Rewrite the graded paper in ink or type it on a computer, correcting any marked errors. *(Do not display or publish papers that have marked errors or grades on them.)*
- Give your teacher the set of stapled papers to place in your Writing Portfolio. *(Stapled papers: evaluation guide, graded final paper, rough draft, and prewriting map.)*
- Select a publishing form from the list below and publish your rewritten paper.

  1. Have classmates, family members, neighbors, or others read your writing at school or home.
  2. Share your writing with others during a Share Time. *(Refer to Reference 68 on page 103 for sharing guidelines.)*
  3. Display your writing on a bulletin board or wall.
  4. Put your writing in the classroom library or in the school library for checkout.
  5. Send your writing as a letter or an e-mail to a friend or relative.
  6. Frame your writing by gluing it on colored construction paper and decorating it.
  7. Make a book of your writing for your classroom, your family, or others.
  8. Illustrate your writing and give it to others to read.
  9. Dramatize your writing in the form of a play, puppet show, or radio broadcast.
  10. Send your writing to be placed in a waiting room (doctor, veterinarian, dentist, etc.), senior-citizen center, or a nursing home.
  11. Send your writing to a school newspaper, local newspaper, or a magazine for publication.
  12. Make a videotape, cassette tape, or slide presentation of your writing.
  13. Choose another publishing form that is not listed.

LISTENING AND SPEAKING:

Discovery Share Time

If you have chosen to investigate a topic introduced in Chapter 3 or in Chapter 4, you now have the opportunity to share your results in one of the following ways:

1. You may relate your information orally.
2. You may read a written report.
3. You may place your report in the booklet without reading it aloud.

After share time, all written reports should be turned in to be placed in the class booklet titled "Space Trivia." You are encouraged to check out this class booklet so you can enjoy the reports again.

START LESSON 8

Lesson 8

You will

- practice Jingle 2.
- do Classroom Practice 21.
- write an independent expository paragraph (WA 7).

LISTENING AND SPEAKING:

Recite It: Practice Jingle 2 in the Jingle Section on page 498.

GRAMMAR & WRITING CONNECTION:
Practice and Revised Sentences

Apply It: BUILDING AND EXPANDING SENTENCES

Reference 82	A Guide for Using Pronouns and Conjunctions to Build & Expand Sentences

1. **SP (subject pronoun)** Sing or recite the Subject Pronoun Jingle to help you think of a pronoun that you want to use as the subject. Write the subject pronoun you have chosen for your sentence. Repeat this step for each subject pronoun you add to the sentence.

2. **PPA (possessive pronoun adjective)** Sing or recite the Possessive Pronoun Jingle to help you think of a possessive pronoun that you want to use. Choose the possessive pronoun that makes the best sense in your sentence. Write the possessive pronoun you have chosen for your sentence. Repeat this step for each possessive pronoun adjective you add to the sentence.

3. **C (conjunction)** Sing or recite the Conjunction Jingle. Choose one of the three coordinate conjunctions (*and, but, or*) that makes sense in your sentence. Make sure the conjunction connects the compound parts in your sentence. Write the conjunction you have chosen for your sentence. Repeat this step for each conjunction you add to the sentence.

Classroom Practice 21

It is time to practice the skills you are learning. You will use the classroom practice on page 134 to apply these skills.

>>>>>>>>>>>> Student Tip...

Use your vocabulary words in your Practice and Revised Sentences. Use a thesaurus, synonym-antonym book, or a dictionary to help you develop your writing vocabulary.

Student Note: The conjunction allows any part of speech to be compound, including the core parts, Sn/SP V.

Writing Time

Write It: **WRITING ASSIGNMENT 7**

As you write a rough draft for your independent writing assignment, you will do two of the six steps in the writing process: prewriting and rough draft.

Writing Assignment [7]

Purpose: To inform

Type of Writing: Three-point expository paragraph

Audience: Classmates

Writing Topics: Favorite pets

Favorite sports

Favorite eating places

(Brainstorm for other ideas, individually or in groups.)

Special Instructions:

1. Follow the Prewriting and Rough Draft Checklists in References 47 and 49 on pages 62, 66.

2. Use References 42–46 on pages 58–61 to help you write your expository paragraph.

3. Use standard, time-order, or transition writing form. See Reference 70 on page 107.

4. Write in first or third person. See Reference 71 on page 108.
   (First-person pronouns: *I, me, my, mine, we, us, our,* and *ours.*)
   (Third-person pronouns: *he, his, him, she, her, hers, it, its, they, their, theirs,* and *them.*)

Note: Reference 57 on page 76 gives the steps in the writing process and the location of all the writing checklists.

Student Note: Some of your writing pieces will be selected for revision and editing later in the school year.

Classroom Practice 21

Name: _____ Date: _____

INDEPENDENT PRACTICE & REVISED SENTENCES

1. Write a Practice Sentence according to the labels you choose.
   Use **SN/SP V** as your main labels. You may use the other labels in any order and as many times as you wish in order to make a Practice Sentence.
   Chapter 4 labels for a Practice Sentence: **SN/SP**, V, Adj, Adv, A, P, OP, PPA, C

2. Write a Revised Sentence. Use the following revision strategies: *synonym (syn)*, *antonym (ant)*, *word change (wc)*, *added word (add)*, *deleted word (delete)*, or *no change (nc)*. Under each word, write the abbreviation of the revision strategy you use.

Labels:

Practice:

Revised:

Strategies:

Labels:

Practice:

Revised:

Strategies:

Labels:

Practice:

Revised:

Strategies:

LISTENING AND SPEAKING:

Recite It: Practice Jingle 12 in the Jingle Section on page 501.

 Student Tip...

> Reviewing the transition words will help you apply them in your writing.

Writing Time

Lesson 9

You will

- practice Jingle 12.
- read and discuss changing plural categories to singular points in your writing.
- read and discuss the parts of a three-paragraph expository essay.
- plan and write rough draft for expository essay (WA 8).

Learn It: CHANGING PLURAL CATEGORIES TO SINGULAR POINTS

Reference 83 — Changing Plural Categories to Singular Points

When you have a topic such as *My favorite animals*, you will usually name your favorite animals by categories, or groups, like spider monkeys, hedgehogs, and parrots. These categories, **spider monkeys, hedgehogs,** and **parrots,** are plural. When this happens, you need to change the plural categories to singular points as you write each point sentence.

CHANGING FROM PLURAL CATEGORIES TO SINGULAR POINTS
(First Person)

Topic: My favorite animals

Categories: 1. spider monkeys   2. hedgehogs   3. parrots

    I have **several** unusual **animals** that are my favorites. Even though I like all kinds of animals, my **favorites** are **spider monkeys, hedgehogs,** and **parrots.** My first favorite **animal is** the **spider monkey. Spider monkeys** live most of their lives in the treetops of the tropical rainforest and are agile, curious, and intelligent animals. My second favorite **animal is** the **hedgehog.** These little **animals** have raccoon-like faces, soft quills that make them look like a porcupine, and an affectionate nature. My third favorite **animal is** the **parrot. Parrots** are the world's most colorful and spectacular birds. For me, learning about my favorite animals is a challenging and exciting experience. Even though I enjoy other animals, I think spider monkeys, hedgehogs, and parrots are the most interesting of all.

CHANGING FROM PLURAL CATEGORIES TO SINGULAR POINTS
(Third Person)

Topic: Favorite animals

Categories: 1. spider monkeys   2. hedgehogs   3. parrots

    Jeffery has **several** unusual **animals** that are his favorites. Even though he likes all kinds of animals, his **favorites** are **spider monkeys, hedgehogs,** and **parrots.** Jeffery's first favorite **animal is** the **spider monkey. Spider monkeys** live most of their lives in the treetops of the tropical rainforest and are agile, curious, and intelligent animals. His second favorite **animal is** the **hedgehog.** These little **animals** have raccoon-like faces, soft quills that make them look like a porcupine, and an affectionate nature. His third favorite **animal is** the **parrot. Parrots** are the world's most colorful and spectacular birds. For Jeffery, learning about his favorite animals is a challenging and exciting experience. Even though he enjoys other animals, Jeffery thinks spider monkeys, hedgehogs, and parrots are the most interesting of all.

Learn It: WRITING AN ESSAY

When you write several paragraphs about a certain topic, it is called an essay. The **essay** is a written discussion of one idea and is made up of several paragraphs. An interesting fact is that the word *essay* comes from the French word *essai,* meaning "a trial" or "a try."

Learn It: **WRITING A THREE-PARAGRAPH EXPOSITORY ESSAY**

Expository essays give facts, directions, explain ideas, or define words, just like expository paragraphs. Any time you do an expository writing, whether it is an essay or a paragraph, you will have three parts: the **Introduction**, the **Body**, and the **Conclusion**.

The three parts will always be written in that order. Although a title will be the first item appearing at the top of your essay, you will not write the title until you have finished writing the essay. In effect, the title will become the fourth part of a three-paragraph essay. In a three-paragraph essay, there will be three paragraphs. The introduction forms the first paragraph, the body forms the second paragraph, and the conclusion forms the third paragraph of the essay.

Compare It:

As you study the two outlines below, notice that there are more sentences in the introduction and conclusion of the essay. In addition, the second paragraph of the essay, which is the body, contains all the points and supporting sentences.

 Reference 84

Outlines for the Three-Point Paragraph and the Three-Paragraph Essay

Outline of a Three-Point Paragraph

Paragraph
- A. Topic and number sentence
- B. Three-point sentence
- C. **First-point** sentence
- D. **Supporting** sentence for the first point
- E. **Second-point** sentence
- F. **Supporting** sentence for the second point
- G. **Third-point** sentence
- H. **Supporting** sentence for the third point
- I. Concluding general sentence

Title

Outline of a Three-Paragraph Essay

1. **Paragraph 1**—Introduction
   - A. Topic and number sentence
   - B. Extra-information sentence
   - C. Three-point sentence
2. **Paragraph 2**—Body
   - A. First-point sentence
   - B. One or two supporting sentences for the first point
   - C. Second-point sentence
   - D. One or two supporting sentences for the second point
   - E. Third-point sentence
   - F. One or two supporting sentences for the third point
3. **Paragraph 3**—Conclusion
   - A. Concluding general sentence
   - B. Concluding three-point sentence
4. **Title**

English Made Easy

Learn It: **WRITING THE INTRODUCTION**
FOR A THREE-PARAGRAPH EXPOSITORY ESSAY

The introduction forms the first paragraph. Two or three sentences make up the introduction. The first sentence in the introduction is called the **topic and number sentence**. The second sentence is the **extra-information sentence**, and the third sentence is called the **three-point sentence**.

Reference 85	**Writing the Introduction for a Three-Paragraph Expository Essay**

LIST THE THREE POINTS ABOUT THE TOPIC
Select three points to list about the topic. 1. **spider monkeys**   2. **hedgehogs**   3. **parrots**

THE INTRODUCTION
Paragraph 1

Writing Topic: Favorite animals

Sentence 1 – Topic and Number Sentence:
To write the topic sentence, use some or all of the words in your topic and add a general or specific number word that tells the number of points that will be discussed.

> **General number words:** *several, many, some,* etc.
> **Specific number words:** *two, three, four,* etc.

In the sample sentence, words from the topic (*favorite animals*) are used, and the general number word (*several*) is used instead of a specific number word.

> **I have several unusual animals that are my favorites.**

Sentence 2 – Extra-Information Sentence(s):
Sometimes, you need one or two extra sentences that will add information about the topic or embellish it. This sentence(s) is usually optional and can clarify, explain, define, or just be an extra interesting comment.

> **Because my favorite animals are so interesting, I try to learn as much as I can about them.**

Sentence 3 – Three-Point Sentence:
This sentence names the three points to be discussed in the order that you will present them in the body of your paper. You can list the points with or without the specific number in front. In the sample sentence, the points, *spider monkeys, hedgehogs,* and *parrots,* are named without using the specific number *three*.

> **Even though I enjoy all kinds of animals, my favorites are spider monkeys, hedgehogs, and parrots.**

Learn It: **WRITING THE BODY**
FOR A THREE-PARAGRAPH EXPOSITORY ESSAY

The body contains one paragraph. Notice that the three points and the supporting sentences for the three points form this paragraph.

Reference 86	**Writing the Body for a Three-Paragraph Expository Essay**

THE BODY
Paragraph 2

Sentence 4 – First Point:
Write a sentence stating your first point.

> **My first favorite animal is the spider monkey.**

Continued on next page. >>>

Reference 86 continued from previous page.

Sentences 5–6 – Supporting Sentence(s):
Write one or more sentences that give more information about your first point.

> Spider monkeys live most of their lives in the treetops of the tropical rainforest and are agile, curious, and intelligent animals. They do not have thumbs, and their long, flexible tails are used as a fifth limb.

Sentence 7 – Second Point:
Write a sentence stating your second point.

> My second favorite animal is the hedgehog.

Sentences 8–9 – Supporting Sentence(s):
Write one or more sentences that give more information about your second point.

> These little animals have raccoon-like faces, soft quills that make them look like a porcupine, and an affectionate nature. When they are frightened, hedgehogs roll up into a tight ball, raise their quills, and make a high-pitched hissing sound.

Sentence 10 – Third Point:
Write a sentence stating your third point.

> My third favorite animal is the parrot.

Sentences 11–12 – Supporting Sentence(s):
Write one or more sentences that give more information about your third point.

> Parrots are the world's most colorful and spectacular birds. They have two toes pointing forward and two toes pointing backward to help them hold onto branches and food.

Learn It: **WRITING THE CONCLUSION**
FOR A THREE-PARAGRAPH EXPOSITORY ESSAY

The conclusion forms the third paragraph. The conclusion should tie all the important points together with a restatement of the main idea and your final comments on it.

Two sentences make up the conclusion. The first sentence in the conclusion is called the **concluding general sentence**, and the second sentence is the **concluding three-point sentence**.

Reference 87

Writing the Conclusion for a Three-Paragraph Expository Essay

THE CONCLUSION
Paragraph 3

Sentence 13 – Concluding General Sentence:
Read the topic sentence again and then rewrite it, using some of the same words. The concluding general sentence is meant to be general in nature and restates the topic sentence. In the sample sentence, the word *animals* is used instead of the particular points, *spider monkeys*, *hedgehogs*, and *parrots*.

> For me, learning about my favorite animals is a challenging and exciting experience.

Sentence 14 – Concluding Three-Point Sentence:
Read the introductory three-point sentence again and then rewrite it, using some of the same words. The concluding three-point sentence restates the three-point sentence, listing the particular points and bringing the writing to a close. In the sample sentence, the particular points, *spider monkeys*, *hedgehogs*, and *parrots*, are named, along with another closing thought.

> Even though I enjoy other animals, I think spider monkeys, hedgehogs, and parrots are the most interesting of all.

Continued on next page. >>>

Reference 87 continued from previous page.

WRITING THE TITLE
Since there are many possibilities for titles, look at the topic and the three points listed about the topic. Use some of the words in the topic and write a phrase to tell what your essay is about. Your title can be short or long. Capitalize the first, last, and important words in your title.

Title: My Favorite Unusual Animals

Sample Three-Paragraph Essay

My Favorite Unusual Animals

    I have several unusual animals that are my favorites. Because my favorite animals are so interesting, I try to learn as much as I can about them. Even though I like all kinds of animals, my favorites are spider monkeys, hedgehogs, and parrots.

    My first favorite animal is the spider monkey. Spider monkeys live most of their lives in the treetops of the tropical rainforest and are agile, curious, and intelligent animals. They do not have thumbs, and their long, flexible tails are used as a fifth limb. My second favorite animal is the hedgehog. These little animals have raccoon-like faces, soft quills that make them look like a porcupine, and an affectionate nature. When they are frightened, hedgehogs roll up into a tight ball, raise their quills, and make a high-pitched hissing sound. My third favorite animal is the parrot. Parrots are the world's most colorful and spectacular birds. They have two toes pointing forward and two toes pointing backward to help them hold onto branches and food.

    For me, learning about my favorite animals is a challenging and exciting experience. Even though I enjoy other animals, I think spider monkeys, hedgehogs, and parrots are the most interesting of all.

Write It: WRITING ASSIGNMENT 8
As you write a rough draft for your guided writing assignment, you will do two of the six steps in the writing process: prewriting and rough draft.

Writing Assignment [8]

Purpose: To inform
Type of Writing: Three-paragraph expository essay
Audience: Classmates or family
Writing Topic: Favorite Animals

Special Instructions:
1. Follow the Prewriting and Rough Draft Checklists in References 47 and 49 on pages 62, 66.
2. Use Reference 83 on page 135 to help you change plural categories to singular points.
3. Use References 84–87 on pages 136–138 to help you write a three-paragraph expository essay.
4. Use standard, time-order, or transition writing form. See Reference 70 on page 107.
5. Write in first or third person. See Reference 71 on page 108.
(First-person pronouns: *I, me, my, mine, we, us, our,* and *ours.*)
(Third-person pronouns: *he, his, him, she, her, hers, it, its, they, their, theirs,* and *them.*)

Note: Reference 57 on page 76 gives the steps in the writing process and the location of all the writing checklists.

START LESSON 10

Lesson 10

You will

- revise, edit, and write a final paper for WA 8.

 Writing Time

Apply It: **REVISE, EDIT, AND WRITE A FINAL PAPER**

Following the schedule below, you will revise and edit Writing Assignment 8. Then, you will write a final paper. Use the Chapter 4 Writing Evaluation Guide on the next page to check your final paper one last time.

✎* **Reference 55**	**Revising & Editing Schedule and Writing a Final Paper**

SPECIAL INSTRUCTIONS FOR REVISING AND EDITING (Steps 3-4 in the writing process):

- Use the Revising and Editing Checklists in References 51 and 53 as you revise and edit your rough draft.
- Follow the revising and editing schedule below as directed by your teacher.

  1. **Individual.** First, read your rough draft to yourself. Use the Revising Checklist in Reference 51 on page 69. Go through your paper, checking each item on the list and making revisions to your rough draft. Then, use the Editing Checklist in Reference 53 on page 71. Go through your paper again, checking each item on the list and editing your rough draft.

  2. **Partner.** Next, get with your editing partner. Work together on each partner's rough draft, one paper at a time. Read each rough draft aloud and revise and edit it together, using the Revising and Editing Checklists. (The author of the paper should be the one to make the corrections on his own paper.)

  3. **Group.** Finally, read the rough draft to a revision group for feedback. Each student should read his paper while the others listen and offer possible revising and editing suggestions. (The author will determine whether to make corrections from the revision group's suggestions.)

SPECIAL INSTRUCTIONS FOR FINAL PAPER (Step 5 in the writing process):

- Write your final paper, using the Final Paper Checklist in Reference 56 on page 75.
- Staple your writing papers in this order: the final paper on top, the rough draft in the middle, and the prewriting map on the bottom. Place the stapled papers in the Final Paper folder.

>>>>>>>>>>>>> **Student Tip...**

1. Be tactful and helpful in your comments during revising and editing time. The purpose of any suggestion should be to improve the writer's rough draft.

2. As you make your final corrections, you have the choice of accepting or rejecting any suggestions made by your partners or your revision group.

3. Study Vocabulary Words and Analogies 8-10 for the chapter test in the next lesson.

4. If you need to improve your handwriting, refer to the Resource Tools Section on page 521 for information on writing legibly.

Chapter 4 Writing Evaluation Guide

Name:_____ Date:_____

ROUGH DRAFT CHECK

_____ 1. Did you write your rough draft in pencil?

_____ 2. Did you write the correct headings on the first seven lines of your paper?

_____ 3. Did you use extra wide margins and skip every other line?

_____ 4. Did you write a title at the end of your rough draft?

_____ 5. Did you place your edited rough draft in your Rough Draft folder?

REVISING CHECK

_____ 6. Did you identify the purpose, type of writing, and audience?

_____ 7. Did you check for a topic, topic sentence, and sentences supporting the topic?

_____ 8. Did you check sentences for the right order, and did you combine, rearrange, or delete sentences when necessary?

_____ 9. Did you check for a variety of simple, compound, and complex sentences?

_____ 10. Did you check for any left out, repeated, or unnecessary words?

_____ 11. Did you check for the best choice of words by replacing or deleting unclear words?

_____ 12. Did you check the content for interest and creativity?

_____ 13. Did you check the voice to make sure the writing says what you want it to say?

EDITING CHECK

_____ 14. Did you indent each paragraph?

_____ 15. Did you put an end mark at the end of every sentence?

_____ 16. Did you capitalize the first word of every sentence?

_____ 17. Did you check for all other capitalization mistakes?

_____ 18. Did you check for all punctuation mistakes?
(commas, periods, apostrophes, quotation marks, underlining)

_____ 19. Did you check for misspelled words and for incorrect homonym choices?

_____ 20. Did you check for incorrect spellings of plural and possessive forms?

_____ 21. Did you check for correct construction and punctuation of your sentences?

_____ 22. Did you check for usage mistakes? (subject/verb agreement, a/an choices, contractions, verb tenses, pronoun/antecedent agreement, pronoun cases, degrees of adjectives, double negatives, etc.)

_____ 23. Did you put your revised and edited paper in the Rough Draft folder?

FINAL PAPER CHECK

_____ 24. Did you write the final paper in pencil?

_____ 25. Did you center the title on the top line and center your name under the title?

_____ 26. Did you skip a line before starting the writing assignment?

_____ 27. Did you single-space, use wide margins, and write the final paper neatly?

_____ 28. Did you staple your papers in this order: final paper on top, rough draft in the middle, and prewriting map on the bottom? Did you put them in the Final Paper folder?

START LESSON 11

Lesson 11

You will

- hand in WA 8 for grading.
- respond to oral review questions.
- Take Chapter 4 Test.
- write Goal Evaluation paragraphs.

CHAPTER TEST

It is time to evaluate your knowledge of the skills you have learned in this chapter. Your teacher will give you the Chapter 4 Test to help you assess your progress.

Writing Time

Hand It In: WRITING ASSIGNMENT 8

Get your stapled papers for Writing Assignment 8 from your Final Paper folder. Check to make sure they are in the correct order: the final paper on top, the rough draft in the middle, and the prewriting map on the bottom. Hand them in to your teacher.

LISTENING AND SPEAKING:
Oral Review Questions

Discuss It:

1. What is the definition for a pronoun?
2. What are the seven subject pronouns?
3. What are the seven possessive pronouns?
4. What is the understood subject pronoun?
5. What is the End Mark Flow for the imperative sentence?
6. What are the seven parts of speech you have learned so far?
7. What are the three most common coordinate conjunctions?
8. What is an incomplete sentence called?
9. What are the three core parts of a simple sentence?
10. What abbreviation is used for a compound subject noun?
11. What abbreviation is used for a compound subject pronoun?
12. What abbreviation is used for a compound verb?
13. What are words called that sound alike but have different meanings and spellings?
14. What is a written discussion of one topic that is made up of several paragraphs?
15. What are the three parts of a paragraph or essay?
16. What type of writing is used when your purpose is to inform, to give facts, to give directions, to explain, or to define something?

Student Tip...

> For information about test-taking strategies, refer to the Resource Tools Section on page 520.

Review It: GOALS

Review the goals you wrote in your Goal Booklet at the beginning of the school year. Discuss your progress with your teacher or a student partner. Then, write a paragraph in your Goal Booklet that tells how well you are meeting your short-term goals. Give examples that support your evaluation of your progress. Next, write another paragraph to evaluate your long-term goals. Tell whether you want to change them or keep them the same. Give reasons to support either choice. Finally, return your Goal Booklet to your teacher when you have finished.

English Made Easy

LISTENING AND SPEAKING:
Vocabulary & Analogy Time

Learn It: Recite the new vocabulary and analogy words.

📖 Reference 88	Vocabulary & Analogy Words

Word: valor (văl'ər)
  Definition: personal bravery
  Synonym: courage   **Antonym:** cowardice
  Sentence: My dad received a medal for his **valor**.

Analogy: wait : weight :: clothes : close
  Homonym relationship: Just as **wait** is a homonym of **weight**,
              clothes is a homonym of **close**.

Vocabulary Card 11: Record the vocabulary information above and write your own
              sentence, using the new word.

Analogy Card 11: Record the analogy information and write your own analogy,
              using the same relationship as the analogy above.

 Jingle Time

Recite It: Recite the new jingle.

♪ Jingle 17	The 23 Helping Verbs of the Mean, Lean, Verb Machine Jingle

These twenty-three helping verbs
will be on my test.
I've gotta remember them so I can do my best.
I'll start out with eight and finish with fifteen.
Just call me the mean, lean, verb machine.

There are the eight **be** verbs
that are easy as can be.
    am, is, are - was and **were**
    am, is, are - was and **were**
    am, is, are - was and **were**
    be, being, and **been**

All together now, the eight **be** verbs:
am, is, are - was and **were - be, being,** and **been**
am, is, are - was and **were - be, being,** and **been**
am, is, are - was and **were - be, being,** and **been**

There are twenty-three helping verbs,
and I've recited eight.
That leaves fifteen more that I must relate.
Knowing all these verbs will save my grade.
The mean, lean, verb machine is here to stay.
    has, have, and **had - do, does,** and **did**
    has, have, and **had - do, does,** and **did**
    might, must, and **may -**
    might, must, and **may**
    can and **could - would** and **should**
    can and **could - would** and **should**
    shall and **will - shall** and **will**
    has, have, and **had - do, does,** and **did**
    might, must, and **may**
    can and **could, would** and **should**
    shall and **will**
In record time, I did this drill.
I'm the mean, lean, verb machine—STILL!

Lesson 1

You will
- study new vocabulary; make card 11; write own sentence using the vocabulary word.
- analyze new analogy; make Card 11; write own analogy.
- recite new jingle (23 Helping Verbs).
- identify helping verbs, the NOT adverb, and natural and inverted order.
- classify Introductory Sentences.
- do a Skill Builder.
- write in your journal.

Grammar Time

Apply It: These Introductory Sentences are used to apply the new grammar concepts taught below. Classify these sentences orally with your teacher.

Introductory Sentences	Chapter 5: Lesson 1

1. _____ My aunt and her husband have been looking for a new truck.
2. _____ Connie did not move into her apartment until this weekend.
3. _____ Are you going to our family reunion in July?

Learn It: HELPING VERBS

📖 **Reference 89**   **Helping Verbs**

1. When two or more verbs make up the simple predicate of a sentence, the verbs in front of the main verb are known as the **helping verbs**. Helping verbs are also called **auxiliary verbs**. Together, the main verb and the helping verbs are called the **verb phrase**.

2. When directions are given to underline the verb, or simple predicate, the helping verb and the main verb are underlined because they are both part of the verb phrase. In the following sentence, the phrase *is walking* makes up the verb phrase, and both verbs should be underlined:

   My son is walking to the store.

3. A *helping verb* is labeled with the abbreviation **HV**. If you are labeling the verb phrase, *is walking*, you would label the *helping verb* is with the abbreviation **HV** and the *main verb* walking with the abbreviation **V**.

                HV   V

   Example: **My son is walking to the store.**

4. When a sentence *begins with a helping verb and asks a question*, it is called an **interrogative** sentence and is labeled with the abbreviation **Int**.

         HV PPA SN   V   P A   OP

   Example: **Is my son walking (to the store)?** *Int*

Learn It: NOT ADVERB

📖 **Reference 90**   **The ПOT Adverb**

Sometimes, the helping verb can be split from the main verb by the adverb *NOT*. Even though the word *NOT* is an adverb, it is often confused as part of a verb phrase. The word *NOT* is an adverb telling *how*. Most negative words are adverbs telling *how* or *to what extent*.

Example: They <u>did</u> not <u>ride</u> in Dad's car.
(They did ride how? **not - adverb**)

Learn It: NATURAL AND INVERTED WORD ORDER

📖 Reference 91 — Natural and Inverted Word Order

A **Natural-Order** sentence has all subject parts before the verb and all predicate parts starting with the verb.

The word **inverted** means to reverse the position of something. Therefore, **Inverted Word Order** in a sentence means that some of the predicate words are located at the beginning of the complete subject, and the rest of the predicate words are located after the verb.

There are three ways a sentence can have inverted word order. An inverted-order sentence can have an **adverb**, a **helping verb**, or a **prepositional phrase** at the beginning of the sentence. Even though these words are located at the beginning of the complete subject, they modify the verb and are considered part of the predicate. These predicate words in the subject are inverted parts and cause the sentence to have an inverted word order. Using this inverted order in your writing is a way to give your sentences more variety.

1. **An adverb at the beginning of a sentence modifies the verb.**
   Inverted Order: Yesterday, we / talked on the phone.
   Natural Order: We / talked on the phone yesterday.

2. **A helping verb at the beginning of a sentence is part of the verb. It usually forms a question.**
   Inverted Order: Are you / listening to the radio?
   Natural Order: You / are listening to the radio.

3. **A prepositional phrase at the beginning of a sentence modifies the verb.**
   Inverted Order: Before the final performance, the musicians / practiced on the stage.
   Natural Order: The musicians / practiced on the stage before the final performance.

To add an inverted-order check to the Question and Answer Flow, ask,

"Is this sentence in a natural or inverted order?"

1. If there are no predicate words at the beginning of the complete subject, answer, **"Natural - No change."**
   Natural Order: Our family / went to the city park on Saturday.

2. If there are predicate words at the beginning of the complete subject, answer, **"Inverted - underline the subject parts once and the predicate parts twice."**
   Inverted Order: On Saturday, our family / went to the city park.

LISTENING AND SPEAKING:

Using the sentences just classified, do a Skill Builder orally with your teacher.

1. **Identify the nouns in a Noun Check.**
2. **Identify the nouns as singular or plural.**
3. **Identify the nouns as common or proper.**
4. **Identify the complete subject and the complete predicate.**
5. **Identify the simple subject and the simple predicate.**
6. **Do a Vocabulary Check.**

JOURNAL WRITING 11

Write an entry in your journal. Use Reference 9 on page 12 for ideas.

START LESSON 2

Lesson 2

You will
- practice Jingle 17.
- classify Practice Sentences.
- do a Skill Builder.
- identify compound sentences, comma splices, run-on sentences, coordinating conjunctions, and connective adverbs.
- do Classroom Practice 22.

LISTENING AND SPEAKING:

Recite It: Practice Jingle 17 in the Jingle Section on page 502.

Apply It: Classify the Practice Sentences orally with your teacher.

Practice Sentences	Chapter 5: Lesson 2

1. _____ Today, the horse was carefully groomed for his master.
2. _____ Casey and I will listen to our recorded speeches from our drama class.
3. _____ During the football game, the quarterback did not pass well.

Using the sentences just classified, do a Skill Builder orally with your teacher.
1. **Identify the nouns in a Noun Check.**
2. **Identify the nouns as singular or plural.**
3. **Identify the nouns as common or proper.**
4. **Identify the complete subject and the complete predicate.**
5. **Identify the simple subject and the simple predicate.**
6. **Do a Vocabulary Check.**

Learn It: COORDINATE CONJUNCTIONS AND CONNECTIVE ADVERBS

 Reference 92 **Coordinate Conjunctions and Connective Adverbs**

COORDINATE CONJUNCTIONS

Conjunctions join words or groups of words together. Conjunctions that join things of equal importance are called **coordinate**, or **coordinating conjunctions**. There are seven coordinate conjunctions: **and, or, but, nor, yet, for,** and **so**. The seven coordinate conjunctions and how they are used are listed below.

Add information	Show contrast or choice	Show logic or result
, and	, but	, for
, nor	, or	, so (as a result of)
	, yet	so (that)—no comma

Continued on next page. >>>

Reference 92 continued from previous page.

CONNECTIVE ADVERBS

When an adverb is used to connect sentences, it is called a **connective adverb**. Connective adverbs are often used as transition words between ideas. A connective adverb always uses two punctuation marks: a semicolon before it and a comma after it. A connective adverb is also called a **conjunctive adverb**. Some of the connective adverbs and how they are used are listed below.

Add information	Show contrast or choice	Show logic or result
; also,	; however,	; accordingly,
; besides,	; nevertheless,	; consequently,
; furthermore,	; otherwise,	; hence,
; likewise,		; so,
; moreover,		; therefore,
		; thus,

Learn It: COMPOUND SENTENCE

 Reference 93 **The Compound Sentence**

The word **compound** means two. A **compound sentence** is the result of two simple sentences being joined together. The abbreviation for a *compound sentence* is **CD**. To make a *compound sentence*, join two simple sentences in one of the ways listed below. The information in parentheses at the end of each sentence shows how the *compound sentence* was made.

1. **Compound sentence:** Use a comma and a coordinate conjunction.
    Example: I found the letter, but I did not open it. (CD, but)

2. **Compound sentence:** Use a semicolon, a connective adverb, and a comma.
    Example: I found the letter; however, I did not open it. (CD; however,)

3. **Compound sentence:** Use a semicolon only.
    Example: I found the letter; I did not open it. (CD;)

Compound sentences should be closely related in thought and importance.

Correct: I found the letter, but I did not open it.

Incorrect: I found the letter, but I am going to the library.

>>>>>>>>>> **Student Tip...**

> Use the following information as a visual aid to help you construct compound sentences.
>
> ### Simple Sentence + Simple Sentence = Compound Sentence
>
> Joining two simple sentences in one of the following ways forms a compound sentence.
>
> 1. Two simple sentences joined by a comma and a conjunction.
> _____, and _____.
> 2. Two simple sentences joined by a semicolon, a connective adverb, and a comma.
> _____; therefore, _____.
> 3. Two simple sentences joined by a semicolon.
> _____; _____.

Learn It: COMMA SPLICES AND RUN-ON SENTENCES

Reference 94 — Comma Splices and Run-on Sentences

Two common mistakes are often made when joining simple sentences together to make a compound sentence. The first mistake is called a **comma splice**. The second mistake is called a **run-on sentence**.

1. A *comma splice occurs* when simple sentences are connected with a comma but without a conjunction.

>   **Incorrect: I found the letter, I did not open it.**

>   *To correct a comma splice*, put a coordinate conjunction after the comma.

>   **Correct: I found the letter, but I did not open it.**

2. A *run-on sentence occurs* in one of two ways.
   a. When the simple sentences are written together with a conjunction but without a comma.

>   **Incorrect: I found the <u>letter but I</u> did not open it.**

   b. When the simple sentences are written together as one sentence without a comma or a conjunction.

>   **Incorrect: I found the <u>letter I did</u> not open it.**

Use one of three strategies *to correct a run-on sentence*.

1. Put a comma and a coordinate conjunction between the two simple sentences.

>   **Correct: I found the letter, but I did not open it.**

2. Put a semicolon, a connective adverb, and a comma between the two simple sentences.

>   **Correct: I found the letter; however, I did not open it.**

3. Put a semicolon between the two simple sentences.

>   **Correct: I found the letter; I did not open it.**

>>>>>>>>>>>>> Student Tip...

> There are two times when you should put a comma in front of the conjunction <u>and</u>:
>
> 1. When you have three or more items in a series.
>
> 2. When you are connecting two simple sentences using and as a coordinate conjunction to make a compound sentence.

Learn It: CORRECTING RUN-ON SENTENCES

Reference 95 — Using Compound Sentences to Correct Run-On Sentences

Use a slash to separate each run-on sentence below. Then, correct each run-on sentence by rewriting it as indicated by the labels in parentheses at the end of the sentence. **Example: (CD, but)** means to write a **compound sentence**, using a **comma** and the conjunction **but**.

PRACTICE EXAMPLES

1. Rita enjoyed the book / she didn't like the movie. **(CD, but)**
   Rita enjoyed the book, but she didn't like the movie.

2. The young girl attended school across town / she rode the bus every day. **(CD; therefore,)**
   The young girl attended school across town; therefore, she rode the bus every day.

3. I listen to my CD player every day / music makes me feel great! **(CD;)**
   I listen to my CD player every day; music makes me feel great!

Learn It: **IDENTIFYING TYPES OF SENTENCES**

Reference 96 — Identifying S, F, SCS, SCV, and CD

Directions: Identify each type of sentence by writing the correct label in the blank. (**Labels: S, F, SCS, SCV, CD**).

CD	1. Roberto wanted a pony; however, his family had no place to keep it.
SCS	2. Christopher and Megan eat lunch together every day.
F	3. Calling all their friends with the good news.
CD	4. I heard the doorbell, but I did not answer it.
SCV	5. My parents packed our suitcases and put them by the door.
S	6. After the hike in the woods, I drank two bottles of water.

Classroom Practice 22

It is time to practice the skills you are learning. You will use the classroom practice on the next page to apply these skills.

Classroom Practice 22

Name:_____ Date:_____

GRAMMAR

▶ **Exercise 1:** Classify each sentence.

1. _____ Were the frightened animals hiding during the storm yesterday?

2. _____ The manuscript deadline is approaching rapidly.

3. _____ Eddie and his family did not arrive at the ballpark in time for the game.

SKILLS

▶ **Exercise 2:** Identify each type of sentence by writing the correct label in the blank. (**Labels: S, F, SCS, SCV, CD**)

_____ 1. Makes an eerie noise.
_____ 2. Larry read the instructions, yet he could not put the bicycle together.
_____ 3. Anna and I played miniature golf at the park.
_____ 4. The frightened passengers on the stranded ship yelled and screamed for help.
_____ 5. Sally knocked on her neighbor's door, but no one answered.
_____ 6. Marilyn buys and sells real-estate.
_____ 7. I will not clean your room, nor will I do your laundry.
_____ 8. Set your alarm tonight, or you will be late.
_____ 9. Mom, Dad, and Blake arrived too late for their flight to Cancun.

▶ **Exercise 3:** Use a slash to separate each run-on sentence below. Then, correct the run-on sentences by rewriting them as indicated by the labels in parentheses at the end of each sentence.

1. Ms. Jackson offered us a snack we were very grateful. (**CD, and**)

_____

2. The homework was hard I finished it. (**CD; however,**)

_____

3. Robin shopped at the mall Paige and Regina shopped with her. (**SCS**)

_____

4. Benny is my brother we do not look alike. (**CD, yet**)

_____

5. The monkeys at the zoo jumped in their cage they screamed for bananas. (**SCV**)

_____

EDITING

▶ **Exercise 4:** Correct each mistake. **Editing Guide: End Marks: 3   Capitals: 14   Apostrophes: 2   Homonyms: 3   Misspelled Words: 1   Commas: 4   Underlining: 1   Periods: 4**

mr j d padgett a reporter for the austin times interviewed rob our team captain on

thursday before hour big game against the tuckerville tigers mr padgett said that wed bee

seeing his artical in the newspaper on saturday i cant weight

LISTENING AND SPEAKING:
Vocabulary & Analogy Time

Learn It: Recite the new vocabulary and analogy words.

📖 **Reference 97**	**Vocabulary & Analogy Words**

Word: **agile** (ăj'əl, –īl)
   Definition: able to move quickly and easily
   Synonym: nimble   **Antonym:** awkward
   Sentence: The **agile** quarterback broke several tackles for a touchdown!

Analogy: **oak : tree :: parrot : bird**
   Type or kind relationship: Just as an **oak** is a kind of **tree**,
                     a **parrot** is a kind of **bird**.

Vocabulary Card 12: Record the vocabulary information above and write your own
                     sentence, using the new word.

Analogy Card 12: Record the analogy information and write your own analogy,
                     using the same relationship as the analogy above.

Jingle Time

Recite It: Practice Jingles 13–17 in the Jingle Section on pages 501–502.

Grammar Time

Apply It: Classify the Practice Sentences orally with your teacher.

Practice Sentences	**Chapter 5: Lesson 3**

1. _____ Today, ancient Egyptian artifacts were placed on display
          at the museum.
2. _____ We slipped very quietly through the trees and came out at
          Crystal Lake.
3. _____ We could not see down the dark, narrow aisles of the
          large auditorium.

START LESSON 3

Lesson 3
You will

- study new vocabulary; make Card 12; write own sentence using the vocabulary word.
- analyze new analogy; make Card 12; write own analogy.
- practice jingles 13-17.
- classify Practice Sentences.
- do a Skill Builder.
- identify contractions.
- do Classroom Practice 23.
- write in your journal.
- read and discuss Discovery Time.

Using the sentences just classified, do a Skill Builder orally with your teacher.

1. **Identify the nouns in a Noun Check.**
2. **Identify the nouns as singular or plural.**
3. **Identify the nouns as common or proper.**
4. **Identify the complete subject and the complete predicate.**
5. **Identify the simple subject and the simple predicate.**
6. **Do a Vocabulary Check.**

Learn It: CONTRACTIONS

 Reference 98 | **Contraction Chart**

A **contraction** is two words combined into one. The new word always has an apostrophe that takes the place of the letter(s) that has (have) been left out. Sometimes, contractions may be confused with pronouns because they sound alike. Study the spellings of all contractions.

AM
I'm . . . . I am

IS
isn't . . . . is not
he's . . . . he is
she's . . . . she is
it's . . . . it is
who's . . . . who is
that's . . . . that is
what's . . . . what is
there's . . . . there is

ARE
aren't . . . . are not
you're . . . . you are
we're . . . . we are
they're . . . . they are

WAS, WERE
wasn't . . . . was not
weren't . . . . were not

HAS
hasn't . . . . has not
he's . . . . he has
she's . . . . she has

HAVE
haven't . . . . have not
I've . . . . I have
you've . . . . you have
we've . . . . we have
they've . . . . they have

HAD
hadn't . . . . had not
I'd . . . . I had
you'd . . . . you had
we'd . . . . we had
they'd . . . . they had

DO, DOES, DID
don't . . . . do not
doesn't . . . . does not
didn't . . . . did not

CAN
can't . . . . cannot

COULD
couldn't . . . . . could not

WOULD
wouldn't . . . . . would not
I'd . . . . I would
he'd . . . . he would
she'd . . . . she would
you'd . . . . you would
we'd . . . . we would
they'd . . . . . . they would

SHOULD
shouldn't . . . . . should not

WILL, SHALL
won't . . . . will not
I'll . . . . I will, I shall
he'll . . . . he will, he shall
she'll . . . . she will, she shall
you'll . . . . you will, you shall
we'll . . . . we will, we shall
they'll . . . . they will, they shall

LET
let's . . . . let us

Contractions That May Be Confused With Pronouns

Contractions:
it's . . . . (it is) . . . . *It's red.*
you're . . . . . (you are) . . . . *You're late.*
they're . . . . (they are) . . . *They're lost.*
who's . . . . . . (who is) . . . . . *Who's sick?*

Pronouns:
its . . . . (owns) . . . . . . *its nose*
your . . . . (owns) . . . . . . *your boat*
their . . . . (owns) . . . . . . *their friends*
whose . . . . . (owns) . . . . . . *whose pie*

English Made Easy

>>>>>>>>> **Student Tip...**

Make two sets of cards. On the first set, write the contractions. On the second set, write the words from which each contraction was made. Practice matching the contraction cards to the word cards. Find a partner and practice matching the word cards to the contraction cards.

✏️ Classroom Practice 23

It is time to practice the skills you are learning. You will use the classroom practice on the next page to apply these skills.

JOURNAL WRITING 12

Write an entry in your journal. Use Reference 9 on page 12 for ideas.

🧭 Discovery Time

Venus is the second planet from the sun in our solar system. Venus is known as the hottest planet because its atmosphere is so thick that it traps the heat from the sun. Its temperatures reach 875°F.

Discovery Questions:
- Why is Venus sometimes called the evening star?
- Why do you think no one lives on Venus?
- What do you think about the name, Venus?

Are you interested in learning more about Venus?

1. You may explore this topic further by using the resources listed below.
   Computer resources: Internet, encyclopedia software
   Library resources: encyclopedias, books, magazines, newspapers
   Home/community resources: books, interviews, newspapers, magazines

2. A Discovery Share Time is provided in Lesson 7 if you wish to share your investigation results. You may share orally, or you may prepare a written report. You will put your written report in a class booklet titled "Space Trivia." This booklet will be placed in the class library for everyone to enjoy.

Classroom Practice 23

Name:_____ Date:_____

GRAMMAR

▶ **Exercise 1:** Classify each sentence.

1. _____ He and I walked hurriedly to the crowded food court with our friends.

2. _____ Look at the angry bee around the President's head and arms.

3. _____ On the return flight, the spacecraft orbited around the Earth.

SKILLS

▶ **Exercise 2:** Write either the contraction or the contraction words in the blanks.

1. you will _____   2. we've _____   3. can not _____   4. won't _____

▶ **Exercise 3:** Identify each type of sentence by writing the correct label in the blank. (**Labels: S, F, SCS, SCV, CD**)

_____ 1. Michael ran around the bases and scored a run for his team.
_____ 2. The recliner fell from the moving van, yet it was not damaged.
_____ 3. The boxer and his opponent danced around the ring.
_____ 4. Emmett's short-term goals for the fifth grade.
_____ 5. Mom's new sewing machine would not work, so she took it back to the store.

▶ **Exercise 4:** Use a slash to separate each run-on sentence below. Then, correct the run-on sentences by rewriting them as indicated by the labels in parentheses at the end of each sentence.

1. Martina wanted to have lunch the café was closed. (**CD, but**)

_____

2. You go to bed I'll stay up. (**CD;**)

_____

3. Carmen built the props for the play Dean built the props for the play. (**SCS**)

_____

4. I returned several library books a week late I was not charged a late fee. (**CD; however,**)

_____

5. The tiger ate his dinner he cleaned his paws. (**SCV**)

_____

EDITING

▶ **Exercise 5:** Correct each mistake. **Editing Guide: End Marks: 2   Capitals: 12   Commas: 4   Apostrophes: 1
Homonyms: 3   Underlining: 1   Misspelled Words: 2**

a young virginian named thomas jefferson wrote won of our countrys most important

documents the declaration of independence it was aproved on july 4 1776 buy the continental

congress and the colonys declared there independence from great britain

English Made Easy

LISTENING AND SPEAKING:
Vocabulary & Analogy Time

Learn It: Recite the new vocabulary and analogy words.

Reference 99	Vocabulary & Analogy Words

Word: wary (wâr'ē)
  Definition: always on the alert
  Synonym: guarded   **Antonym:** trusting
  Sentence: We were a bit **wary** of the uninvited stranger.

Analogy: fake : false :: conceal : hide
  Synonym relationship: Just as **fake** means nearly the same as **false**, **conceal** means nearly the same as **hide**.

Vocabulary Card 13: Record the vocabulary information above and write your own sentence, using the new word.

Analogy Card 13: Record the analogy information and write your own analogy, using the same relationship as the analogy above.

Jingle Time

Recite It: Practice Jingles 3–11 in the Jingle Section on pages 499–500.

Grammar Time

Apply It: Classify the Practice Sentences orally with your teacher.

Practice Sentences	Chapter 5: Lesson 4

1. _____ For exercise, Donna has been walking and running around the track.

2. _____ They cheered loudly for the players and coach after the final buzzer.

3. _____ Today, Anthony did not study at the library after school.

Lesson 4
You will
- study new vocabulary; make Card 13; write own sentence using the vocabulary word.
- analyze new analogy; make Card 13; write own analogy.
- practice jingles 3-11.
- classify Practice Sentences.
- do a Skill Builder.
- identify a/an choices.
- do Classroom Practice 24.
- read and discuss Discovery Time.
- do a homework assignment.
- do a Home Connection activity.

Skill Builder

Using the sentences just classified, do a Skill Builder orally with your teacher.
1. **Identify the nouns in a Noun Check.**
2. **Identify the nouns as singular or plural.**
3. **Identify the nouns as common or proper.**
4. **Identify the complete subject and the complete predicate.**
5. **Identify the simple subject and the simple predicate.**
6. **Do a Vocabulary Check.**

Skill Time

Learn It: A/AN CHOICES

Reference 100	**Choosing A or An**

RULE 1: Use the word **a** when the next word begins with a consonant sound. (**Example: a r**ed apple.)

RULE 2: Use the word **an** when the next word begins with a vowel sound. (**Example: an a**pple.)

Directions: Write **a** or **an** in the blanks.
1. Would you like ___an___ orange?
2. Would you like ___a___ fresh orange?
3. We saw ___a___ covered wagon.
4. We saw ___an___ old covered wagon.

Classroom Practice 24

It is time to practice the skills you are learning. You will use the classroom practice on the next page to apply these skills.

ENRICHMENT:

Discovery Time

(English) 1656-1742 - Edmund Halley is given credit for discovering Halley's Comet, which comes within viewing distance of the Earth every seventy-six years.

Discovery Questions:
- **What do you think Halley thought the first time he saw the comet?**
- **What kind of equipment do you think Halley used to spot the comet?**
- **How would you like to have a comet named after you?**

Are you interested in learning more about Edmund Halley or Halley's Comet?
1. You may explore this topic further by using the resources listed below.
   Computer resources: Internet, encyclopedia software
   Library resources: encyclopedias, books, magazines, newspapers
   Home/community resources: books, interviews, newspapers, magazines
2. A Discovery Share Time is provided in Lesson 7 if you wish to share your investigation results. You may share orally, or you may prepare a written report. You will put your written report in a class booklet titled "Space Trivia." This booklet will be placed in the class library for everyone to enjoy.

Classroom Practice 24

Name:_____ Date:_____

GRAMMAR

▶ **Exercise 1:** Classify each sentence.

1. _____ The stoplight at the intersection is not flashing properly.

2. _____ Did Judy and Karen shop for souvenirs during their holiday break?

3. _____ Sit in the front seats for a better view of the concert.

SKILLS

▶ **Exercise 2:** Write **a** or **an** in the blanks.

1. _____ parasol is like _____ umbrella.   2. Read _____ epic poem.   3. _____ ostrich   4. _____ spout

▶ **Exercise 3:** Write either the contraction or the contraction words in the blanks.

1. they had _____   2. shouldn't _____   3. I am _____   4. let's _____

▶ **Exercise 4:** Identify each type of sentence by writing the correct label in the blank. (**Labels: S, F, SCS, SCV, CD**)

_____ 1. Levi and Ramon arrived early.
_____ 2. Remembered my dentist appointment.
_____ 3. I would like to learn how to sky dive, yet I have a fear of airplanes.
_____ 4. The farmer set traps and waited for the pesky raccoon.
_____ 5. Stacy tripped on her shoelaces; nevertheless, we won the race.

▶ **Exercise 5:** Use a slash to separate each run-on sentence below. Then, correct the run-on sentences by rewriting them as indicated by the labels in parentheses at the end of each sentence.

1. Write your appointment on the calendar you will forget it. (**CD; otherwise**)
_____

2. The boys misbehaved they were sent to the principal's office. (**CD;**)
_____

3. Lauren looked for a book by her favorite author she found it in the library. (**SCV**)
_____

4. Mr. Lane is a chaperon Mrs. Hayes is a chaperon, too. (**SCS**)
_____

5. You may do your homework you may read a book. (**CD, or**)
_____

EDITING

▶ **Exercise 6:** Correct each mistake. **Editing Guide: End Marks: 4   Capitals: 4   Commas: 6   Homonyms: 5   A/An: 1   Subject-Verb Agreement: 4**

leo my dog likes too roam threw the woods he crawls under the gait and hit the trails leo stir

up an rabbit or too and the chase is on then he jump in the creak cools off and head for home

 **Homework 3**

Complete this homework assignment on notebook paper.

1. Number your paper 1–10. Write the correct contraction for each set of words. Write answers only.

1. she is	_____	5. did not	_____	9. we had	_____
2. we are	_____	6. have not	_____	10. we will	_____
3. it is	_____	7. I have	_____		
4. they are	_____	8. he would	_____		

2. Number your paper 1–4. Write **a** or **an** for each sentence.

1. He shut _____ open door.   2. He shut _____ metal door.   3. _____ airplane   4. _____ computer

3. Copy the sentence below. Classify the sentence, using the Question and Answer Flow, as you label each part.

_____ They cheered loudly for the players and coach after the final buzzer.

4. Use the four ways listed below to correct the run-on sentence.
   Cody mowed the lawn Stacey helped him.

   1. CD, and   _____

   2. CD; furthermore,   _____

   3. CD;   _____

   4. SCS   _____

5. Write three compound sentences. For the first sentence, connect the two sentences with a comma and a conjunction (*and, but, or*). For the second sentence, connect the two sentences with a semicolon, connective adverb, and comma. For the third sentence, connect the two sentences with a semicolon only. Double-check each sentence for correct punctuation.

Home Connection

Family Activity for Helping Verbs

For this activity, use coloring books that contain children's stories. Divide family members into different teams. Give each team a different coloring book. Set the timer for three to five minutes. Have the teams circle as many helping verbs as they can find. When time is up, check each team's book for identified helping verbs. Teams can lose points by not circling helping verbs or by circling the wrong words. The team with the fewest mistakes wins the game. Each team member may color his favorite picture and autograph it. These coloring books may be used again for other parts of speech.

Family Activity for Vocabulary and Analogies

Divide into family teams. The first team will use vocabulary and analogy cards 1–6 to ask questions about the information on their cards. The second team will use vocabulary and analogy cards 7–13 to ask questions about the information on their cards.

For vocabulary words:
- What is the definition of the word?
- Name a synonym and antonym for the word.
- Create a new sentence using the word.
- Find the word in another source (dictionary, newspaper, magazine, advertisement).

For analogies:
- What is the answer to the analogy?
- What is the relationship of the analogy?
- Make another analogy with the same relationship.
- Make another analogy with a different relationship.

English Made Easy

LISTENING AND SPEAKING:

Grammar Time

Apply It: Classify the Practice Sentences orally with your teacher.

Practice Sentences	Chapter 5: Lesson 5

1. _____ The stately old mansion has completely collapsed from age and neglect.
2. _____ Today, Darren did not work on the engine with enthusiasm or confidence.
3. _____ During our vacation, Dad and I fished for salmon in a stream in Alaska.

Chapter Checkup 25

It is time for a checkup of the skills you have learned in this chapter. You will use the chapter checkup on the next page to evaluate your progress.

START LESSON 5

Lesson 5

You will
- classify Practice Sentences.
- do Chapter Checkup 25.
- write in your journal.

JOURNAL WRITING 13

Write an entry in your journal. Use Reference 9 on page 12 for ideas.

Chapter 5 Checkup 25

Name:_____ Date:_____

GRAMMAR

▶ **Exercise 1:** Classify each sentence.

1. _____ Lizards and scorpions slithered over the rocks and dashed to their hideaways.

2. _____ After the concert, wait backstage for your grandmother and grandfather.

3. _____ For several weeks, he did not travel well on his crutches.

SKILLS

▶ **Exercise 2:** Write either the contraction or the contraction words in the blanks.

1. we have _____   2. they had _____   3. wouldn't _____   4. didn't _____

▶ **Exercise 3:** Write **a** or **an** in the blanks.

1. _____ orange is _____ fruit.   2. _____ cello is _____ musical instrument.   3. _____ emu   4. _____ arch

▶ **Exercise 4:** Identify each type of sentence by writing the correct label in the blank. (**Labels: S, F, SCS, SCV, CD**)

_____ 1. The dancers bowed and curtsied after their performance.

_____ 2. My pantry is empty; therefore, I must go to the grocery store before dinner.

_____ 3. Leslie's kaleidoscope and pinwheel were gifts from her mother.

_____ 4. Our mail was not delivered today; thus, your package did not arrive.

_____ 5. Frank's job at the dry cleaners.

▶ **Exercise 5:** Use a slash to separate each run-on sentence below. Then, correct the run-on sentences by rewriting them as indicated by the labels in parentheses at the end of each sentence.

1. Norman lifts weights in the gym Patrick lifts weights in the gym. (**SCS**)

_____

2. Marcia washed the vegetables for our salad Marcia cut the vegetables for our salad. (**SCV**)

_____

3. Keith made us salsa it was too spicy. (**CD, but**)

_____

EDITING

▶ **Exercise 6:** Correct each mistake. **Editing Guide: End Marks: 4   Capitals: 8   Commas: 4   Homonyms: 2   Subject/Verb Agreement: 2   Misspelled Words: 3**

the game of marbles date back two ancient egypt rome and early north america marbles

were originaly made from pebbles nuts or fruit pits modern-day rules and names for marbel

games is varried children inn countries all over the world still love to play the game

Writing Time

Write It: **WRITING ASSIGNMENT 9**

Lesson 6

You will

- conference with teacher about WA 8.
- write a creative writing piece for WA 9.

Writing Assignment [9]: Creative Expressions

Purpose: To entertain

Type of Writing: Creative

Audience: Classmates, friends, or family members

Choose one of the writing topics below.

1. If you could choose another time period in which to live, when and where would it be? How would your life be different? What would you enjoy most about this time period? What would you be doing? What hardships and dangers would you face?

2. You are going on a long trip. Where will you go and how long will you be gone? What will you pack if you are allowed only one medium-sized suitcase?

3. Write a poem about a trip, another time period, or a topic of your choice.

Special Instructions:

1. A prewriting map is not required for this creative-writing assignment.

2. Follow the Rough Draft Checklist in Reference 49 on page 66.

3. Put your creative-writing paper in your Rough Draft folder when you have finished.

Note: Reference 57 on page 76 gives the steps in the writing process and the location of all the writing checklists.

>>>>>>>>>>>>>>>>>>>>>> Student Tip...

> For more information about writing poetry, look at Chapter 18 on pages 456–474.

Conference Time

Discuss It: **TEACHER-STUDENT CONFERENCES FOR WRITING ASSIGNMENT 8**

Meet with your teacher to discuss Writing Assignment 8.
After the conference, place this group of papers in your Publishing folder.

Lesson 7

You will

- publish WA 8.
- participate in Discovery Share Time.
- do Across the Curriculum activity.

Publishing Time

Publish It: WRITING ASSIGNMENT 8

Choose a publishing form and publish Writing Assignment 8. After rewriting your paper for publication, give the stapled papers (evaluation guide, graded final paper, rough draft, and prewriting map) to your teacher to be placed in your Writing Portfolio.

✐*	**Reference 67**	**Publishing Checklist for Step 6 in the Writing Process**

The sixth step in the writing process is called publishing. Publishing is sharing your writing with others. With so many forms of publishing available, finding a match for every project and personality is easy.

At times, a written work is best read aloud. Other times, the biggest impact is made when a written work is read silently. You can also use media sources to enhance any publication.

SPECIAL INSTRUCTIONS FOR PUBLISHING:

- Rewrite the graded paper in ink or type it on a computer, correcting any marked errors. *(Do not display or publish papers that have marked errors or grades on them.)*
- Give your teacher the set of stapled papers to place in your Writing Portfolio. *(Stapled papers: evaluation guide, graded final paper, rough draft, and prewriting map.)*
- Select a publishing form from the list below and publish your rewritten paper.
    1. Have classmates, family members, neighbors, or others read your writing at school or home.
    2. Share your writing with others during a Share Time. *(Refer to Reference 68 on page 103 for sharing guidelines.)*
    3. Display your writing on a bulletin board or wall.
    4. Put your writing in the classroom library or in the school library for checkout.
    5. Send your writing as a letter or an e-mail to a friend or relative.
    6. Frame your writing by gluing it on colored construction paper and decorating it.
    7. Make a book of your writing for your classroom, your family, or others.
    8. Illustrate your writing and give it to others to read.
    9. Dramatize your writing in the form of a play, puppet show, or radio broadcast.
    10. Send your writing to be placed in a waiting room (doctor, veterinarian, dentist, etc.), senior-citizen center, or a nursing home.
    11. Send your writing to a school newspaper, local newspaper, or a magazine for publication.
    12. Make a videotape, cassette tape, or slide presentation of your writing.
    13. Choose another publishing form that is not listed.

English Made Easy

LISTENING AND SPEAKING:

Discovery Share Time

If you have chosen to investigate a topic introduced in this chapter, you now have the opportunity to share your results in one of the following ways:

1. You may relate your information orally.

2. You may read a written report.

3. You may place your report in the booklet without reading it aloud.

After share time, all written reports should be turned in to be placed in the class booklet titled "Space Trivia." You are encouraged to check out this class booklet so you can enjoy the reports again.

Across the Curriculum

Science/Art Connection: Select a page in your science book. Make a list of all the verbs used on that page. Then, make a scribble-art page, drawing as many large loops or ovals as you have verbs listed. Write or print a verb inside each loop. Outline the loops in different colors to make them easier to identify. Write a title for your art page. Read your science verbs to a partner.

Social Studies/Art Connection: Select a page in your social studies book. Make a list of all the verbs used on that page. Then, make a scribble-art page, drawing as many large loops or ovals as you have verbs listed. Write or print a verb inside each loop. Outline the loops in different colors to make them easier to identify. Write a title for your art page. Read your social studies verbs to a partner.

Compare the types of verbs used in science and in social studies. How are they different? How are they alike?

Optional: Do the same activity, using nouns.

START LESSON 8

Lesson 8

You will
- practice Jingle 2.
- do Classroom Practice 26.
- write an independent expository essay (WA 10).

LISTENING AND SPEAKING:

Jingle Time

Recite It: Practice Jingle 2 in the Jingle Section on page 498.

GRAMMAR & WRITING CONNECTION:
Practice and Revised Sentences

Apply It: BUILDING AND EXPANDING SENTENCES

 Reference 101 | **A Guide for Using Helping Verbs and the Not Adverb to Build & Expand Sentences**

1. **HV** (*helping verb*) Recite the Helping Verb Jingle to help you choose a helping verb for your sentence. You may use more than one helping verb with your main verb. Before you write your helping verb, make sure it makes sense in your sentence. Repeat this step for each helping verb you add to the sentence. If you write an interrogative sentence, put a question mark at the end.
2. Sometimes, the helping verb can be split from the main verb by the *NOT* adverb . Even though the word *not* is an adverb, it is often confused as part of a verb phrase. The word *NOT* is an adverb telling *how*. Most negative words are adverbs telling *how* or *to what extent*. If you choose to use the NOT adverb, write it in your sentence.

Student Tip...

Use your vocabulary words in your Practice and Revised Sentences. Use a thesaurus, synonym-antonym book, or a dictionary to help you develop your writing vocabulary.

Classroom Practice 26

It is time to practice the skills you are learning. You will use the classroom practice on the next page to apply these skills.

Writing Time

Write It: WRITING ASSIGNMENT 10

As you write a rough draft for your independent writing assignment, you will do two of the six steps in the writing process: prewriting and rough draft.

Writing Assignment 10

Purpose: To inform
Type of Writing: Three-paragraph expository essay
Audience: Classmates
Writing Topics: Reasons for having a fire drill/for cleaning my room
Least favorite insects/foods/types of music
Favorite books/movies/activities
(Brainstorm for other ideas, individually or in groups.)

Special Instructions:
1. Follow the Prewriting and Rough Draft Checklists in References 47 and 49 on pages 62, 66.
2. Use References 84–87 on pages 136–138 to help you write a three-paragraph expository essay.
3. Use standard, time-order, or transition writing form. See Reference 70 on page 107.
4. Write in first or third person. See Reference 71 on page 108.
(First-person pronouns: *I, me, my, mine, we, us, our,* and *ours.*)
(Third-person pronouns: *he, his, him, she, her, hers, it, its, they, their, theirs,* and *them.*)
Note: Reference 57 on page 76 gives the steps in the writing process and the location of all the writing checklists.

Student Note: Some of your writing pieces will be selected for revision and editing later in the school year.

Classroom Practice 26

Name: _____   Date: _____

INDEPENDENT PRACTICE & REVISED SENTENCES

1. Write a Practice Sentence according to the labels you choose.
Use **SN/SP V** as your main labels. You may use the other labels in any order and as many times as you wish in order to make a Practice Sentence.
Chapter 5 labels for a Practice Sentence: **SN/SP**, **V**, Adj, Adv, A, P, OP, PPA, C, HV

2. Write a Revised Sentence. Use the following revision strategies: *synonym (syn)*, *antonym (ant)*, *word change (wc)*, *added word (add)*, *deleted word (delete)*, or *no change (nc)*. Under each word, write the abbreviation of the revision strategy you use.

Labels:

Practice:

Revised:

Strategies:

Labels:

Practice:

Revised:

Strategies:

Labels:

Practice:

Revised:

Strategies:

START LESSON 9

Lesson 9

You will

- practice Jingle 12.
- read and discuss a five-paragraph essay.
- plan and write rough draft for expository essay (WA 11).

LISTENING AND SPEAKING:

Recite It: Practice Jingle 12 in the Jingle Section on page 501.

>>>> **Student Tip...**

> Reviewing the transition words will help you apply them in your writing.

Compare It:

As you compare the paragraph and the essay below, notice the similarities and the differences.

Reference 102 — Comparing a Three-Point Paragraph and a Three-Paragraph Essay

THREE-POINT EXPOSITORY PARAGRAPH

Topic: My Favorite animals

Three points: 1. **spider monkeys** 2. **hedgehogs** 3. **parrots**

    I have several unusual animals that are my favorites. Even though I like all kinds of animals, my favorites are spider monkeys, hedgehogs, and parrots. My first favorite animal is the spider monkey. Spider monkeys live most of their lives in the treetops of the tropical rain forest and are agile, curious, and intelligent animals. My second favorite animal is the hedgehog. These little animals have raccoon-like faces, soft quills that make them look like a porcupine, and an affectionate nature. My third favorite animal is the parrot. Parrots are the world's most colorful and spectacular birds. For me, learning about my favorite animals is a challenging and exciting experience. Even though I enjoy other animals, I think spider monkeys, hedgehogs, and parrots are the most interesting of all.

THREE-PARAGRAPH EXPOSITORY ESSAY

Topic: Favorite animals

Three points: 1. **spider monkeys** 2. **hedgehogs** 3. **parrots**

My Favorite Unusual Animals

    I have several unusual animals that are my favorites. Because my favorite animals are so interesting, I try to learn as much as I can about them. Even though I like all kinds of animals, my favorites are spider monkeys, hedgehogs, and parrots.

    My first favorite animal is the spider monkey. Spider monkeys live most of their lives in the treetops of the tropical rain forest and are agile, curious, and intelligent animals. They do not have thumbs, and their long, flexible tails are used as a fifth limb. My second favorite animal is the hedgehog. These little animals have raccoon-like faces, soft quills that make them look like a porcupine, and an affectionate nature. When they are frightened, hedgehogs roll up into a tight ball, raise their quills, and make a high-pitched hissing sound. My third favorite animal is the parrot. Parrots are the world's most colorful and spectacular birds. They have two toes pointing forward and two toes pointing backward to help them hold onto branches and food.

    For me, learning about my favorite animals is a challenging and exciting experience. Even though I enjoy other animals, I think spider monkeys, hedgehogs, and parrots are the most interesting of all.

Compare It:

As you study the two outlines below, notice that the introduction and conclusion are the same for both essays. In the body of the three-paragraph essay, all the points and their supporting sentences are in one paragraph. However, the body of the five-paragraph essay has three paragraphs. In the body of the five-paragraph essay, each point and its supporting sentences are a separate paragraph.

Reference 103 — **Outlines for the Three-Paragraph Essay and the Five-Paragraph Essay**

Outline of a Three-Paragraph Essay

1. **Paragraph 1 – Introduction**
   A. Topic and number sentence
   B. Extra-information sentence(s)
   C. Three-point sentence

2. **Paragraph 2 – Body**
   A. **First-point** sentence
   B. One or more **supporting** sentences for the first point
   C. **Second-point** sentence
   D. One or more **supporting** sentences for the second point
   E. **Third-point** sentence
   F. One or more **supporting** sentences for the third point

3. **Paragraph 3 – Conclusion**
   A. Concluding general sentence
   B. Concluding three-point sentence

4. **Title**

Outline of a Five-Paragraph Essay

1. **Paragraph 1 – Introduction**
   A. Topic and number sentence
   B. Extra-information sentence(s)
   C. Three-point sentence

2. **Paragraph 2 – First Point (Body)**
   A. **First-point** sentence
   B. Two or more **supporting** sentences for the first point

3. **Paragraph 3 – Second Point (Body)**
   A. **Second-point** sentence
   B. Two or more **supporting** sentences for the second point

4. **Paragraph 4 – Third Point (Body)**
   A. **Third-point** sentence
   B. Two or more **supporting** sentences for the third point

5. **Paragraph 5 – Conclusion**
   A. Concluding general sentence
   B. Concluding three-point sentence

6. **Title**

Review It: PARTS OF A FIVE-PARAGRAPH ESSAY

You have learned that an essay has three main parts: **introduction**, **body**, and **conclusion**. The five-paragraph essay has these same main parts. The **introduction** is the first paragraph, the **body** includes the second, third, and fourth paragraphs, and the **conclusion** is the fifth paragraph of the essay. The title will be the fourth part of a five-paragraph essay. In a five-paragraph essay, there will be five paragraphs.

Learn It: WRITING THE INTRODUCTION FOR A FIVE-PARAGRAPH EXPOSITORY ESSAY

Three or more sentences make up the introduction. The first sentence in the introduction is called the **topic and number sentence**. The second sentence is the **extra-information sentence**, and the third sentence is called the **three-point sentence**.

Continued on next page. >>>

Reference 104

Writing the Introduction for a Five-Paragraph Expository Essay

LIST THREE POINTS ABOUT THE TOPIC.
Select three points to list about the topic. 1. **spider monkeys**   2. **hedgehogs**   3. **parrots**

THE INTRODUCTION
Paragraph 1

Writing Topic: Favorite animals

Sentence 1 – Topic and Number Sentence
To write the topic sentence, use some or all of the words in your topic and add a general or specific number word that tells the number of points that will be discussed.

> **General number words:** *several, many, some*, etc.
> **Specific number words:** *two, three, four*, etc.

In the sample sentence below, words from the topic (*favorite animals*) are used, and the general number word (*several*) is used instead of a specific number word.

> **I have several unusual animals that are my favorites.**

Sentence 2 – Extra-Information Sentence
Sometimes, you need one or more extra sentences that will add information about the topic or embellish it. This sentence is usually optional and can clarify, explain, define, or just be an extra interesting comment.

> **Because my favorite animals are so interesting, I try to learn as much as I can about them.**

Sentence 3 – Three-Point Sentence
This sentence names the three points to be discussed in the order that you will present them in the body of your paper. You can list the points with or without the specific number in front. In the sample sentence, the points, *spider monkeys, hedgehogs,* and *parrots*, are named without using the specific number *three*.

> **Even though I like all kinds of animals, my favorites are spider monkeys, hedgehogs, and parrots.**

Learn It: **WRITING THE BODY**
FOR A FIVE-PARAGRAPH EXPOSITORY ESSAY

The body contains three paragraphs. Each of the three points forms a new paragraph. After the sentence for each point is written, notice that there are at least two or more supporting sentences that are added.

Reference 105

Writing the Body for a Five-Paragraph Expository Essay

THE BODY
Paragraph 2

Sentence 4 – First Point
Write a sentence stating your first point.

> **My first favorite animal is the spider monkey.**

Sentences 5–7 – Supporting Sentences
Write two or more sentences that give additional information about your first point.

> **Spider monkeys live most of their lives in the treetops of the tropical rain forest and are agile, curious, and intelligent animals. They do not have thumbs, and their long, flexible tails are used as a fifth limb. Spider monkeys do not make good pets because they can damage an owner's home, and they can carry dangerous diseases**

Continued on next page. >>>

Reference 105 continued from previous page.

Paragraph 3

Sentence 8 – Second Point
Write a sentence stating your second point.

> **My second favorite animal is the hedgehog.**

Sentences 9–12 – Supporting Sentences
Write two or more sentences that give additional information about your second point.

> **These little animals have raccoon-like faces, soft quills that make them look like a porcupine, and an affectionate nature. When they are frightened, hedgehogs roll up into a tight ball, raise their quills, and make a high-pitched hissing sound. When they are happy, they purr quietly. Hedgehogs make very good pets because they have very little odor, are easily litter-trained, are disease-resistant, do not require a special diet, and bond with an owner for life.**

Paragraph 4

Sentence 13 – Third Point
Write a sentence stating your third point.

> **My third favorite animal is the parrot.**

Sentences 14–17 – Supporting Sentences
Write two or more sentences that give additional information about your third point.

> **Parrots are the world's most colorful and spectacular birds. They have two toes pointing forward and two toes pointing backward to help them hold onto branches and food. They have hooked beaks for eating fruits, seeds, and nuts, and they have a remarkable sense of hearing. As pets, larger parrots can live up to seventy-five years and can be taught to mimic people and noisy objects..**

Learn It: **WRITING THE CONCLUSION**
FOR A FIVE-PARAGRAPH EXPOSITORY ESSAY

The conclusion forms the fifth paragraph. The closing paragraph, or conclusion, should tie all the important points together with a restatement of the main idea and your final comments on it. Two sentences make up the conclusion. The first sentence in the conclusion is called the **concluding general sentence**, and the second sentence is the **concluding three-point sentence**.

Reference 106

Writing the Conclusion for a Five-Paragraph Expository Essay

THE CONCLUSION
Paragraph 5

Sentence 18 – Concluding General Sentence
Read the topic sentence again and then rewrite it, using some of the same words. The Concluding General Sentence is meant to be general in nature and restates the topic sentence. In the sample sentence, the word, *animals,* is used instead of the particular points, *spider monkeys, hedgehogs,* and *parrots.*

> **For me, learning about my favorite animals is a challenging and exciting experience.**

Sentence 19 – Concluding Three-Point Sentence
Read the introductory three-point sentence again and then rewrite it, using some of the same words. The Concluding Three-Point Sentence restates the three-point sentence, listing the particular points and bringing the writing to a close. In the sample sentence, the particular points, *spider monkeys, hedgehogs,* and *parrots,* are named, along with another closing thought.

> **Even though I enjoy other animals, I think spider monkeys, hedgehogs, and parrots are the most interesting of all.**

Continued on next page. >>>

Reference 106 continued from previous page.

WRITING THE TITLE
Since there are many possibilities for titles, look at the topic and the three points listed about the topic. Use some of the words in the topic and write a phrase to tell what your paragraph is about. Your title can be short or long. Capitalize the first, last, and important words in your title.

Title: My Favorite Unusual Animals

Sample Five-Paragraph Essay
My Favorite Unusual Animals

I have several unusual animals that are my favorites. Because my favorite animals are so interesting, I try to learn as much as I can about them. Even though I like all kinds of animals, my favorites are spider monkeys, hedgehogs, and parrots.

My first favorite animal is the spider monkey. Spider monkeys live most of their lives in the treetops of the tropical rain forest and are agile, curious, and intelligent animals. They do not have thumbs, and their long, flexible tails are used as a fifth limb. Spider monkeys do not make good pets because they can damage an owner's home, and they can carry dangerous diseases.

My second favorite animal is the hedgehog. These little animals have raccoon-like faces, soft quills that make them look like a porcupine, and an affectionate nature. When they are frightened, hedgehogs roll up into a tight ball, raise their quills, and make a high-pitched hissing sound. When they are happy, they purr quietly. Hedgehogs make very good pets because they have very little odor, are easily litter-trained, are disease-resistant, do not require a special diet, and bond with an owner for life.

My third favorite animal is the parrot. Parrots are the world's most colorful and spectacular birds. They have two toes pointing forward and two toes pointing backward to help them hold onto branches and food. They have hooked beaks for eating fruits, seeds, and nuts, and they have a remarkable sense of hearing. As pets, larger parrots can live up to seventy-five years and can be taught to mimic people and noisy objects.

For me, learning about my favorite animals is a challenging and exciting experience. Even though I enjoy other animals, I think spider monkeys, hedgehogs, and parrots are the most interesting of all.

Write It: WRITING ASSIGNMENT 11
As you write a rough draft for your guided writing assignment, you will do two of the six steps in the writing process: prewriting and rough draft.

Writing Assignment 11

Purpose: To inform
Type of Writing: Five-paragraph expository essay
Audience: Classmates
Writing Topics: New things I would like to learn
Ways to be happy/to bird watch/to catch fish
Reasons I could/could not be a baby-sitter
(Brainstorm for other ideas, individually or in groups.)

Special Instructions:
1. Follow the Prewriting and Rough Draft Checklists in References 47 and 49 on pages 62, 66.
2. Use References 102–106 on pages 166–169 to help you write your five-paragraph expository essay.
3. Use standard, time-order, or transition writing form. See Reference 70 on page 107.
4. Write in first or third person. See Reference 71 on page 108.
(First-person pronouns: *I, me, my, mine, we, us, our,* and *ours*.)
(Third-person pronouns: *he, his, him, she, her, hers, it, its, they, their, theirs,* and *them*.)
Note: Reference 57 on page 76 gives the steps in the writing process and the location of all the writing checklists.

Writing Time

START LESSON 10

Apply It: REVISE, EDIT, AND WRITE A FINAL PAPER

Following the schedule below, you will revise and edit Writing Assignment 11. Then, you will write a final paper. Use the Chapter 5 Writing Evaluation Guide on the next page to check your final paper one last time.

Lesson 10

You will
- revise, edit, and write a final paper for WA 11.

✏* **Reference 55** | **Revising & Editing Schedule and Writing a Final Paper**

SPECIAL INSTRUCTIONS FOR REVISING AND EDITING (Steps 3-4 in the writing process):
- Use the Revising and Editing Checklists in References 51 and 53 as you revise and edit your rough draft.
- Follow the revising and editing schedule below as directed by your teacher.
  1. **Individual.** First, read your rough draft to yourself. Use the Revising Checklist in Reference 51 on page 69. Go through your paper, checking each item on the list and making revisions to your rough draft. Then, use the Editing Checklist in Reference 53 on page 71. Go through your paper again, checking each item on the list and editing your rough draft.
  2. **Partner.** Next, get with your editing partner. Work together on each partner's rough draft, one paper at a time. Read each rough draft aloud and revise and edit it together, using the Revising and Editing Checklists. (The author of the paper should be the one to make the corrections on his own paper.)
  3. **Group.** Finally, read the rough draft to a revision group for feedback. Each student should read his paper while the others listen and offer possible revising and editing suggestions. (The author will determine whether to make corrections from the revision group's suggestions.)

SPECIAL INSTRUCTIONS FOR FINAL PAPER (Step 5 in the writing process):
- Write your final paper, using the Final Paper Checklist in Reference 56 on page 75.
- Staple your writing papers in this order: the final paper on top, the rough draft in the middle, and the prewriting map on the bottom. Place the stapled papers in the Final Paper folder.

>>>>>>>> **Student Tip...**

1. Be tactful and helpful in your comments during revising and editing time. The purpose of any suggestion should be to improve the writer's rough draft.

2. As you make your final corrections, you have the choice of accepting or rejecting any suggestions made by your partners or your revision group.

3. Study Vocabulary Words and Analogies 11-13 for the chapter test in the next lesson.

4. If you need to improve your handwriting, refer to the Resource Tools Section on page 521 for information on writing legibly.

Chapter 5 Writing Evaluation Guide

Name:_____ Date:_____

ROUGH DRAFT CHECK

_____ 1. Did you write your rough draft in pencil?

_____ 2. Did you write the correct headings on the first seven lines of your paper?

_____ 3. Did you use extra wide margins and skip every other line?

_____ 4. Did you write a title at the end of your rough draft?

_____ 5. Did you place your edited rough draft in your Rough Draft folder?

REVISING CHECK

_____ 6. Did you identify the purpose, type of writing, and audience?

_____ 7. Did you check for a topic, topic sentence, and sentences supporting the topic?

_____ 8. Did you check sentences for the right order, and did you combine, rearrange, or delete sentences when necessary?

_____ 9. Did you check for a variety of simple, compound, and complex sentences?

_____ 10. Did you check for any left out, repeated, or unnecessary words?

_____ 11. Did you check for the best choice of words by replacing or deleting unclear words?

_____ 12. Did you check the content for interest and creativity?

_____ 13. Did you check the voice to make sure the writing says what you want it to say?

EDITING CHECK

_____ 14. Did you indent each paragraph?

_____ 15. Did you put an end mark at the end of every sentence?

_____ 16. Did you capitalize the first word of every sentence?

_____ 17. Did you check for all other capitalization mistakes?

_____ 18. Did you check for all punctuation mistakes?
(commas, periods, apostrophes, quotation marks, underlining)

_____ 19. Did you check for misspelled words and for incorrect homonym choices?

_____ 20. Did you check for incorrect spellings of plural and possessive forms?

_____ 21. Did you check for correct construction and punctuation of your sentences?

_____ 22. Did you check for usage mistakes? (subject/verb agreement, a/an choices, contractions, verb tenses, pronoun/antecedent agreement, pronoun cases, degrees of adjectives, double negatives, etc.)

_____ 23. Did you put your revised and edited paper in the Rough Draft folder?

FINAL PAPER CHECK

_____ 24. Did you write the final paper in pencil?

_____ 25. Did you center the title on the top line and center your name under the title?

_____ 26. Did you skip a line before starting the writing assignment?

_____ 27. Did you single-space, use wide margins, and write the final paper neatly?

_____ 28. Did you staple your papers in this order: final paper on top, rough draft in the middle, and prewriting map on the bottom? Did you put them in the Final Paper folder?

English Made Easy

Writing Time

Hand It In: **WRITING ASSIGNMENT 11**

Get your stapled papers for Writing Assignment 11 from your Final Paper folder. Check to make sure they are in the correct order: the final paper on top, the rough draft in the middle, and the prewriting map on the bottom. Hand them in to your teacher.

LISTENING AND SPEAKING:

Discuss It:

1. What are the eight be verbs?

2. What are verbs called that are used with a main verb?

3. What is it called when a helping verb and a main verb are used together?

4. What type of sentence has all subject parts first and all predicate parts after the verb?

5. What type of sentence has predicate words at the beginning of the sentence?

6. What are the three ways to form an inverted-order sentence?

7. When you use the article a, should the next word begin with a consonant or vowel sound?

8. When you use the article an, should the next word begin with a consonant or vowel sound?

9. What does a contraction have that takes the place of the letter(s) that has(have) been left out?

10. What punctuation is used in a contraction to show that letters have been left out?

11. What are the three ways to write a compound sentence?

12. What are two run-on sentence mistakes?

13. What do you call a group of sentences that is written about one particular subject?

14. What do you call the sentence that tells what a paragraph is about?

15. What is a written discussion of one idea that is made up of several paragraphs?

16. What type of writing is used when your purpose is to inform, to give facts, to give directions, to explain, or to define something?

Lesson 11

You will
- hand in WA 11 for grading.
- respond to oral review questions.
- take Chapter 5 Test.

CHAPTER TEST

It is time to evaluate your knowledge of the skills you have learned in this chapter. Your teacher will give you the Chapter 5 Test to help you assess your progress.

>>>>>>>>>>>>> **Student Tip...**

For information about test-taking strategies, refer to the Resource Tools Section on page 520.

START LESSON 1

Lesson 1

You will

- study new vocabulary; make Card 14; write own sentence using the vocabulary word.
- analyze new analogy; make Card 14; write own analogy.
- recite new jingles (Interjection, Possessive Noun).
- identify interjections and possessive nouns.
- classify Introductory Sentences.
- do a Skill Builder to identify possessive nouns.
- recognize interjections as a part of speech.
- identify all eight parts of speech.
- write in your journal.

LISTENING AND SPEAKING:

Learn It: Recite the new vocabulary and analogy words.

Reference 107	**Vocabulary & Analogy Words**

Word: vigilant (vĭj'ə lənt)
  Definition: watchful, alert to danger
  Synonym: wary   **Antonym:** negligent
  Sentence: The islanders were **vigilant** in their search for poisonous snakes.

Analogy: plane : plain :: seen : scene
  Homonym relationship: Just as **plane** is a homonym of **plain**,
                seen is a homonym of **scene**.

Vocabulary Card 14: Record the vocabulary information above and write your own
                sentence, using the new word.

  Analogy Card 14: Record the analogy information and write your own analogy,
                using the same relationship as the analogy above.

Jingle Time

Recite It: Recite the new jingles.

♪ Jingle 18	**The Interjection Jingle**

Oh, Interjection, Interjection, Interjection, who are you?
  I'm a part of speech through and through.
Well, Interjection, Interjection, Interjection, what do you do?
  I show strong or mild emotion; need a review?
Oh, Interjection, Interjection, I still don't have a clue.
  I show strong emotion, like Wow! Great! or Yahoo!
  I show mild emotion, like Oh, Yes, Fine, or Toodle-oo.
Well, Interjection, Interjection, you really know how to groove!
  That's because I'm a part of speech through and through!

♪ Jingle 19	**The Possessive Noun Jingle**

A possessive noun just can't be beat.
It shows ownership, and that is neat.
Add an apostrophe to show possession.
This is a great ownership lesson.
Adjective is its part of speech.
Ask **WHOSE** to find it as you speak.
Whose house? Tommy's house.
Possessive Noun Adjective!

Grammar Time

Apply It: These Introductory Sentences are used to apply the new grammar concepts taught below. Classify these sentences orally with your teacher.

Introductory Sentences · Chapter 6: Lesson 1

1. _____ Mercy! Those stallions pawed and reared wildly during the thunderstorm!
2. _____ Leo's pickup sputtered and clanged noisily on the way to the mechanic's shop.
3. _____ Did the circus clowns sail through the air and land in foam barrels?

Learn It: INTERJECTIONS

Reference 108 · Interjections

1. An **interjection** is one or more words used to express mild or strong emotion.
2. An interjection is usually located at the beginning of a sentence and is separated from the rest of the sentence with a punctuation mark.
3. A mild interjection is followed by a comma or a period; a strong interjection is followed by an exclamation point.
4. There are no questions to ask to find interjections. Interjections are not connected grammatically to the rest of the sentence. For this reason, interjections are not underlined as subject parts or predicate parts. Likewise, interjections should not be considered when deciding whether a sentence is declarative, interrogative, exclamatory, or imperative.
5. An *interjection* is labeled with the abbreviation **I**.

Learn It: POSSESSIVE NOUNS

Reference 109 · Possessive Nouns

1. A **possessive noun** is the name of a person, place, or thing that owns something.
2. A possessive noun will always have an apostrophe after it. It will have either an *apostrophe* before the *s* ('s) or an *apostrophe* after the *s* (s'). The apostrophe makes a noun show ownership. (*Maria's lunch*)
3. A possessive noun has two jobs: to show ownership or possession and to modify like an adjective.
4. A possessive noun's part of speech is an adjective.
5. When a possessive noun is classified, it is labeled as a possessive noun adjective to recognize both jobs. A *possessive noun adjective* is labeled with the abbreviation **PNA**. For the abbreviation **PNA**, say, "*possessive noun adjective.*"
6. Include possessive nouns when you are asked to identify possessive nouns or adjectives.
7. To find a possessive noun, begin with the question *whose*. (Whose lunch? **Maria's - PNA**)

Since you use the *whose* question to find a possessive noun and a possessive pronoun, you must remember one important fact about each one in order to tell them apart. All possessive nouns have an apostrophe at the end. You can remember the possessive pronouns by reciting the Possessive Pronoun Jingle.

Learn It: **A SKILL BUILDER FOR A NOUN CHECK WITH POSSESSIVE NOUNS**

The example below shows you what to do with possessive nouns when you are identifying nouns for a Noun Check.

FOR A NOUN CHECK WITH POSSESSIVE NOUNS

Sentence 1: Subject Noun *stallions,* yes, it is a noun;
Object of the Preposition *thunderstorm,* yes, it is a noun.

Sentence 2: Subject Noun *pickup,* yes, it is a noun;
Object of the Preposition *way,* yes, it is a noun;
Object of the Preposition *shop,* yes, it is a noun.

Sentence 3: Subject Noun *clowns,* yes, it is a noun;
Object of the Preposition *air,* yes, it is a noun;
Object of the Preposition *barrels,* yes, it is a noun.

Are there any possessive nouns in the sentences? **(Yes)**
Name them. **(Leo's and mechanic's)**

What part of speech is a possessive noun? **(adjective)**.

JOURNAL WRITING 14

Write an entry in your journal. Use Reference 9 on page 12 for ideas.

Learn It: **ADDING THE INTERJECTION TO THE PARTS OF SPEECH**

An interjection is a part of speech. You have now learned the eight parts of speech. What are the eight parts of speech?

English Made Easy

LISTENING AND SPEAKING:

Lesson 2

You will
- practice Jingles 18–19; recite new jingle (Eight Parts of Speech).
- classify Practice Sentences.
- do a Skill Builder.
- review eight parts of speech.
- identify clauses, subordinate conjunctions, and complex sentences.
- review types of sentences.
- do Classroom Practice 27.

Recite It: 1. Practice Jingles 18–19 in the Jingle Section on page 503.
2. Recite the new jingle.

♪ Jingle 20	**The Eight Parts of Speech Jingle**

Want to know how to write?
Use the eight parts of speech.
They're dynamite!

Nouns, **V**erbs, and **P**ronouns.
They rule!
They're called the **NVP's**, and they're really cool!
The **Double A's** are on the move.
Adjectives and **A**dverbs help you to groove.
Next come the **PIC's**, and then we're done.
They're **P**reposition, **I**nterjection, and **C**onjunction!

All together now.
The eight parts of speech, abbreviations, please.
NVP—**AA**—and—**PIC**!

Apply It: Classify the Practice Sentences orally with your teacher.

Practice Sentences	Chapter 6: Lesson 2

1. _____ The new ambassador sat quietly outside the President's office.
2. _____ Horrors! Jay tripped and tumbled down the steep ravine during his hike!
3. _____ Mother's pet parakeet chattered loudly and talked to my sister and her friend.

Using the sentences just classified, do a Skill Builder orally with your teacher.

1. **Identify the nouns in a Noun Check.**
2. **Identify the nouns as singular or plural.**
3. **Identify the nouns as common or proper.**
4. **Identify the complete subject and the complete predicate.**
5. **Identify the simple subject and the simple predicate.**
6. **Do a Vocabulary Check.**

Review It: THE EIGHT PARTS OF SPEECH

You have learned a jingle to help you remember the eight parts of speech.
What are the eight parts of speech? Recite the jingle for the eight parts of speech.

Learn It: CLAUSES AND SUBORDINATE CONJUNCTIONS

Reference 110   Clauses and Subordinate Conjunctions

CLAUSES

A **clause** is a group of words that has a subject and a verb. There are two kinds of clauses: independent and subordinate. An **independent clause** has a subject and a verb and expresses a complete thought. An independent clause is also called a simple sentence.

> Independent clause: **The bell rang for a fire drill.**

A **subordinate** (or **dependent**) **clause** has a subject and a verb but does not express a complete thought because it begins with a subordinate conjunction. Since it does not express a complete thought, it is a fragment and cannot stand alone.

> Subordinate clause: <u>**When**</u> **the bell rang for a fire drill.**

SUBORDINATE CONJUNCTIONS

The word **subordinate** means "to place below another in rank or importance." When a subordinate conjunction is added to the beginning of a simple sentence, that sentence becomes a fragment because it no longer expresses a complete thought. This fragment is called a subordinate (or dependent) clause and is unequal to an independent clause. To use a subordinate clause correctly, the subordinate clause must be connected to an independent clause. A **subordinate conjunction** is the word that makes a clause subordinate and, at the same time, connects it to an independent clause.

Some of the most common subordinate conjunctions are listed below.

after	because	except	so that	though	when
although	before	if	than	unless	where
as, or as soon as	even though	since	that	until	while

Learn It: COMPLEX SENTENCES

Reference 111   The Complex Sentence

A **complex sentence** is the result of two clauses, a <u>subordinate</u> (or dependent) clause and an <u>independent</u> clause being joined together. The abbreviation for a *complex sentence* is **CX**. Remember that a subordinate clause must be joined to an independent clause in order to complete its meaning. To make a complex sentence, combine a subordinate clause and an independent clause in one of the two ways listed below.

1. If the subordinate clause comes first, a comma is required between the clauses.
    Complex sentence: <u>**When the bell rang for a fire drill**</u>, the students left the building.

2. If the subordinate clause comes last, a comma is normally not required between the clauses.
    Complex sentence: The students left the building <u>**when the bell rang for a fire drill**</u>.

A REVIEW

1. To make a complex sentence, join an independent clause and a subordinate clause together.

2. An independent clause can be made subordinate (dependent) by simply adding a subordinate conjunction to the beginning of that clause. (**The bell rang: As** the bell rang, **Before** the bell rang, **After** the bell rang.)

3. A subordinate (or dependent) clause can be made independent by removing the subordinate conjunction at the beginning of the clause. (~~**As**~~ the bell rang, ~~**Before**~~ the bell rang, ~~**After**~~ the bell rang: **The bell rang.**)

PRACTICE EXERCISE

Below is a set of run-on sentences. First, use a slash between the two simple sentences. Next, follow the set of directions given in parentheses to make complex sentences. The abbreviation (**CX**) tells you to make a complex sentence. The words **when** and **after** tell you which subordinate conjunction to use. The numbers (**1**) or (**2**) tell you whether to put the <u>subordinate conjunction</u> at the beginning of the first clause (**1**) or the second clause (**2**).

> **Example 1:** the bell rang for a fire drill / the students left the building. (**CX, when**) (**1**)
>   **When** the bell rang for a fire drill, the students left the building.

> **Example 2:** the students left the building / the bell rang for a fire drill. (**CX, after**) (**2**)
>   The students left the building **after** the bell rang for a fire drill.

⟩⟩⟩⟩⟩⟩⟩ Student Tip...

Use the following information as a visual aid to help you construct complex sentences.

Subordinate clause + Independent clause = Complex sentence
Independent clause + Subordinate clause = Complex sentence

A complex sentence is formed when a subordinate clause is joined to an independent clause.
A complex sentence can be punctuated in one of two ways.

1. A comma is needed when the subordinate clause comes first.
   (Subordinate Conjunction) _____ , _____ .

2. A comma is usually not needed when the independent clause comes first.
   _____ (subordinate conjunction) _____ .

SHURLEY ENGLISH

Review It: TYPES OF SENTENCES

The sentence chart will help you to identify each type of sentence quickly.

Reference 112	A Review of the Types of Sentences
F............ A fragment	does not contain a subject. *(Swimming in the pool.)* does not contain a verb. *(The cars and trucks.)* has a subject and a verb but does not make sense. *(Before the movie began.)*
S............ A simple sentence (or independent sentence)	has a subject, a verb, and makes sense. *(Fans cheered.)*
SCS........ A simple sentence with a compound subject	has multiple subjects connected by a conjunction but only one verb. *(The young **players** and anxious **coaches** ran onto the field.)*
SCV........ A simple sentence with a compound verb	has multiple verbs connected by a conjunction but only one subject. *(The antelope **leaped** and **dashed** across the valley.)*
CD........... A compound sentence	is two independent sentences joined 1. by a comma and a conjunction. *(Carl ate pizza, **and** Curtis ate tacos.)* 2. by a semicolon, connective adverb, comma. *(Carl ate pizza; **however**, Curtis ate tacos.)* 3. by a semicolon only. *(Carl ate pizza; Curtis ate tacos.)*
CX........... A complex sentence	is an independent clause joined with a subordinate clause. 1. *(I bought a new coat before the store closed.)* 2. *(Before the store closed, I bought a new coat.)*

IDENTIFYING THE TYPES OF SENTENCES

Identify each type of sentence by writing the correct label in the blank. **(Labels: S, F, SCS, SCV, CD, CX)**

     _S_   1. My baby brother chewed on my sister's new eraser.

     _F_   2. After we climbed down the steep mountain.

   SCS   3. After their nap, the mother cat and her kittens played on the porch.

   SCV   4. We stopped at the store and asked for directions.

    _CD_   5. My sister talked on the phone, and my brother played on the computer.

    _CX_   6. After you finish your meal, you may go outside.

    _CX_   7. We paid a late fee because the movies were overdue.

Classroom Practice 27

It is time to practice the skills you are learning. You will use the classroom practice on the next page to apply these skills.

Classroom Practice 27

Name:_____ Date:_____

GRAMMAR

▶ **Exercise 1:** Classify each sentence.

1. _____ Goodness! We have not gone to my grandfather's house in a long time.

2. _____ Wow! Johnny's giant hawk swooped down on the enormous rodent in the field.

SKILLS

▶ **Exercise 2:** Use a slash to separate each run-on sentence below. Then, correct the run-on sentences by rewriting them as indicated by the labels in parentheses at the end of each sentence.

1. Timothy and Marty left the meeting the speaker made his presentation. (**CX, before**) (**2**)
   _____

2. He left the party Corey thanked the hostess. (**CX, before**) (**1**)
   _____

3. I did not understand the directions I had trouble with the test. (**CX, since**) (**1**)
   _____

4. I watered my plants they died. (**CX, even though**) (**1**)
   _____

5. We went to the movies we ate dinner. (**CX, after**) (**2**)
   _____

▶ **Exercise 3:** Identify each type of sentence by writing the correct label in the blank. (**Labels: S, F, SCS, SCV, CD, CX**)

_____ 1. We must paint the deck; otherwise, it may rot.
_____ 2. You must fertilize and water the plants in your garden.
_____ 3. Walking across the street to the neighbor's house.
_____ 4. Tamara called me when I got home.
_____ 5. My brother entered the sweepstakes and won.
_____ 6. The farmer harvested honey from the beehive.
_____ 7. Owls and opossums are nocturnal creatures.
_____ 8. Since our plane was delayed, we missed our connecting flight.
_____ 9. The ducks flew away after the dog barked.

EDITING

▶ **Exercise 4:** Correct each mistake. **Editing Guide: End Marks: 5   Capitals: 13   Commas: 4   Apostrophes: 2   Homonyms: 8   A/An: 1   Subject-Verb Agreement: 4   Misspelled Words: 1**

i has to pay to much for a pear of socks at socks galore store when they gets wholes in them

a month latter i feel bad tomorrow i think ill by a cheap pare at an discount store inn downtown

reno nevada where my mother live wouldnt that make more cents i no my mother agree

START LESSON 3

Lesson 3

You will

- study new vocabulary; make Card 15; write own sentence using the vocabulary word.
- analyze new analogy; make Card 15; write own analogy.
- practice Jingles 13–20.
- classify Practice Sentences.
- do a Skill Builder.
- do Classroom Practice 28.
- write in your journal.
- read and discuss Discovery Time.

LISTENING AND SPEAKING:
Vocabulary & Analogy Time

Learn It: Recite the new vocabulary and analogy words.

📖 *	Reference 113	**Vocabulary & Analogy Words**

Word: endorse (ĕn·dôrs')
  Definition: to approve
  Synonym: support   **Antonym:** disapprove
  Sentence: Our senator **endorsed** the new trade policy.

Analogy: toothpaste : teeth :: shampoo : hair
  Purpose or use relationship: Just as **toothpaste** cleans **teeth**, **shampoo** cleans **hair**.

Vocabulary Card 15: Record the vocabulary information above and write your own sentence, using the new word.

Analogy Card 15: Record the analogy information and write your own analogy, using the same relationship as the analogy above.

Jingle Time

Recite It: Practice Jingles 13–20 in the Jingle Section on pages 501–503.

Grammar Time

Apply It: Classify the Practice Sentences orally with your teacher.

Practice Sentences	**Chapter 6: Lesson 3**

1. _____ Good grief! Our neighbor's bull snorted and pushed against our rickety fence!

2. _____ Residents and guests at the apartments met and talked together during the picnic.

3. _____ The colorful peacocks from India strutted proudly through the zoo grounds.

Skill Builder

Using the sentences just classified, do a Skill Builder orally with your teacher.

1. **Identify the nouns in a Noun Check.**
2. **Identify the nouns as singular or plural.**
3. **Identify the nouns as common or proper.**
4. **Identify the complete subject and the complete predicate.**
5. **Identify the simple subject and the simple predicate.**
6. **Do a Vocabulary Check.**

Classroom Practice 28

It is time to practice the skills you are learning. You will use the classroom practice on the next page to apply these skills.

ENRICHMENT:

Discovery Time

Earth is the third planet from the sun in our solar system. From a distance, Earth looks like a blue planet because three fourths of its surface is covered with water. It has more water than any other planet.

 Discovery Questions:
• **What do you like the most about Earth?**
• **What do you think it would be like to see Earth from space?**
• **What would it be like to be an astronaut?**

Are you interested in learning more about Earth?

1. You may explore this topic further by using the resources listed below.
   Computer resources: Internet, encyclopedia software
   Library resources: encyclopedias, books, magazines, newspapers
   Home/community resources: books, interviews, newspapers, magazines
2. A Discovery Share Time is provided in Lesson 7 if you wish to share your investigation results. You may share orally, or you may prepare a written report. You will put your written report in a class booklet titled "Space Trivia." This booklet will be placed in the class library for everyone to enjoy.

JOURNAL WRITING **15**

Write an entry in your journal. Use Reference 9 on page 12 for ideas.

Classroom Practice 28

Name:_____ Date:_____

GRAMMAR

▶ **Exercise 1:** Classify each sentence.

1. _____ Do not read in poor lighting.

2. _____ Whew! My eraser flew across the room and landed in Mr. Dillard's coffee!

SKILLS

▶ **Exercise 2:** Identify each type of sentence by writing the correct label in the blank. (**Labels: S, F, SCS, SCV, CD, CX**)

_____ 1. The skydiver did not hesitate before he jumped from the airplane.

_____ 2. Colorful aspens and fragrant firs dotted the mountainside.

_____ 3. Into the Northern and Southern Hemispheres.

_____ 4. Al was late for his interview; consequently, he was not offered the job.

_____ 5. My pants were too long, so Mother hemmed the length to shorten them.

_____ 6. Yesterday, Takesha and Marcus went to the dentist.

_____ 7. Before you begin the test, you must give me your homework.

_____ 8. Hummingbirds and bumblebees darted around the flowers.

_____ 9. The seed of oats, rice, corn, and other cereal plants.

_____ 10. My bicycle rusted because I left it in the rain.

▶ **Exercise 3:** Use a slash to separate each run-on sentence below. Then, correct the run-on sentences by rewriting them as indicated by the labels in parentheses at the end of each sentence.

1. I studied hard I did not score well on my science test. (**CX, although**) **(1)**

_____

2. The jury will return with a verdict they come to an agreement. (**CX, when**) **(2)**

_____

3. I gave him detailed directions Dale could not find my house. (**CX, even though**) **(1)**

_____

4. You cannot ride your new scooter you wear a helmet. (**CX, unless**) **(2)**

_____

5. The filter is changed regularly the air conditioner will run more efficiently. (**CX, if**) **(1)**

_____

EDITING

▶ **Exercise 4:** Correct each mistake. **Editing Guide: End Marks: 3 Capitals: 20 Commas: 4 Homonyms: 3 A/An: 1**
Subject-Verb Agreement: 2 Misspelled Words: 2

atheletes from the united states and canada gathered in july 1968 at soldier field stadium inn

chicago illinois four the first special olympics games they was an success the special olympics

organization were founded six months latter with chapters inn the united states canada and france

LISTENING AND SPEAKING:
Vocabulary & Analogy Time

Learn It: Recite the new vocabulary and analogy words.

Reference 114	Vocabulary & Analogy Words

Word: illiterate (ĭlĭt'ərĭt)
  Definition: unable to read or write
  Synonym: uneducated   **Antonym:** scholarly
  Sentence: Even today, thousands of people in this country are **illiterate**.

Analogy: cold : winter :: hot : summer
  Descriptive or characteristic relationship: Just as **cold** describes **winter**, **hot** describes **summer**.

Vocabulary Card 16: Record the vocabulary information above and write your own sentence, using the new word.

Analogy Card 16: Record the analogy information and write your own analogy, using the same relationship as the analogy above.

Jingle Time

Recite It: Practice Jingles 3–11 in the Jingle Section on pages 499–500.

Grammar Time

Apply It: Classify the Practice Sentences orally with your teacher.

Practice Sentences	Chapter 6: Lesson 4

1. _____ The families of the space crew waited near the launch site for liftoff.
2. _____ Gee! Andy's old truck slid into Mr. Cole's new car on the side of the street!
3. _____ On liftoff, a huge cloud of smoke mushroomed over the Atlantic.

START LESSON 4

Lesson 4

You will

- study new vocabulary; make Card 16; write own sentence using the vocabulary word.
- analyze new analogy; make Card 16; write own analogy.
- practice Jingles 3-11.
- classify Practice Sentences.
- do a Skill Builder.
- do Classroom Practice 29.
- read and discuss Discovery Time.
- do a homework assignment.
- do a Home Connection activity.

Skill Builder

Using the sentences just classified, do a Skill Builder orally with your teacher.

1. **Identify the nouns in a Noun Check.**
2. **Identify the nouns as singular or plural.**
3. **Identify the nouns as common or proper.**
4. **Identify the complete subject and the complete predicate.**
5. **Identify the simple subject and the simple predicate.**
6. **Do a Vocabulary Check.**

Classroom Practice 29

It is time to practice the skills you are learning. You will use the classroom practice on the next page to apply these skills.

ENRICHMENT:

Discovery Time

(American) 1930-present— Neil Armstrong was the first man on the moon.

Discovery Questions:
- **What were Neil Armstrong's first words as he walked on the moon?**
- **What do you think it would be like to walk on the moon?**
- **If you could interview Neil Armstrong, what would you ask him?**

Are you interested in learning more about Neil Armstrong?

1. You may explore this topic further by using the resources listed below.
   Computer resources: Internet, encyclopedia software
   Library resources: encyclopedias, books, magazines, newspapers
   Home/community resources: books, interviews, newspapers, magazines

2. A Discovery Share Time is provided in Lesson 7 if you wish to share your investigation results. You may share orally, or you may prepare a written report. You will put your written report in a class booklet titled "Space Trivia." This booklet will be placed in the class library for everyone to enjoy.

Classroom Practice 24

Name:_____ Date:_____

GRAMMAR

▶ **Exercise 1:** Classify each sentence.

1. _____ Yesterday, the pictures of the moon's craters were transmitted back to Earth.

2. _____ Wow! Look at Rosa's prize-winning painting!

SKILLS

▶ **Exercise 2:** Use a slash to separate each run-on sentence below. Then, correct the run-on sentences by rewriting them as indicated by the labels in parentheses at the end of each sentence.

1. I will go to the museum on Tuesday I have homework. (**CX, unless**) (**2**)

_____

2. Her daughters were still sleeping Tina read the morning newspaper. (**CX, while**) (**1**)

_____

3. The kitchen looked spotless I cleaned it. (**CX, after**) (**2**)

_____

4. The toddler played in the mud his clothes were dirty. (**CX, because**) (**1**)

_____

5. Arteries become blocked blood cannot flow through them easily. (**CX, if**) (**1**)

_____

▶ **Exercise 3:** Identify each type of sentence by writing the correct label in the blank. (**Labels: S, F, SCS, SCV, CD, CX**)

_____ 1. Smoking is very unhealthy; nevertheless, many people continue this habit.
_____ 2. My dryer broke; hence, I hung the wet clothes on a line in the backyard.
_____ 3. Sudden chest pains and shortness of breath are common signs of a heart attack.
_____ 4. Walked right up to me and shook my hand.
_____ 5. As I drive to work, I listen to the radio.
_____ 6. Oral hygiene is important to me, so I go to the dentist twice a year.
_____ 7. The little dog wagged its tail and begged for food.
_____ 8. Since it was raining, we did not go on our picnic.
_____ 9. Terrance caught the pass and ran for a touchdown.
_____ 10. I saw the black snake before it slithered away.

EDITING

▶ **Exercise 4:** Correct each mistake. **Editing Guide: End Marks: 2   Capitals: 7   Commas: 2   Homonyms: 1   Subject-Verb Agreement: 2   Misspelled Words: 1**

habitat for humanity international a nonprofit organization help people build there own homes

the organization have attracted the help of president jimmy carter and many other famus people

Homework 4

Complete this homework assignment on notebook paper.

1. Copy the sentence below. Classify the sentence, using the Question and Answer Flow, as you label each part.

_____ Oh, no! The puppies are digging in Grandmother's flower and vegetable garden during their playtime.

2. Correct the run-on sentences on notebook paper by rewriting them as indicated by the labels in parentheses at the end of each sentence.

1. Arliss fell asleep he missed the movie. (**CX, when**) (**1**)

_____

2. I went to the dentist I had a toothache. (**CX, because**) (**2**)

_____

3. Our vegetable garden will dry up it does not rain. (**CX, if**) (**2**)

_____

4. The plane took off we fastened our seat belts. (**CX, before**) (**1**)

_____

3. Write two complex sentences on notebook paper. For the first complex sentence, write the subordinate clause first and write the independent clause last. For the second complex sentence, write the independent clause first and write the subordinate clause last. Punctuate each complex sentence correctly.

Home Connection

Family Activity for Possessive Nouns

Divide into two teams. One team will write a set of directions, using prepositional phrases instead of possessive nouns. See the example below.

Directions to the office of **Mr. Grant:**
Turn left after you leave the **school of Sara**. Go straight for six blocks until you reach the stoplight. Turn right on Main Street. Go one mile. When you reach the **office of the mayor**, turn left on Miller Street. The **diner of Debbie** is on the left, and the **office of Mr. Grant** is in the red brick building beside it. You will see the **car of Mr. Grant** in the **parking lot of Joe**. Tell the **secretary of Mr. Grant** that you are here to see him. Sit patiently in the **office of Mr. Grant** until he can see you.

The second team will rewrite the directions, using possessive nouns as shown in the example below.

Directions to Mr. Grant's office:
Turn left after you leave **Sara's school**. Go straight for six blocks until you reach the stoplight. Turn right on Main Street. Go one mile. When you reach the **mayor's office**, turn left on Miller Street. **Debbie's Diner** is on the left, and **Mr. Grant's office** is in the red brick building beside it. You will see **Mr. Grant's car** in **Joe's Parking Lot**. Tell **Mr. Grant's secretary** that you are here to see him. Sit patiently in **Mr. Grant's office** until he can see you.

After both teams have finished, each team will read its paragraph aloud. Discuss the importance of possessive nouns in everyday conversation.

Family Activity for Vocabulary and Analogies

Divide into family teams. The first team will use vocabulary and analogy cards 1–8 to ask questions about the information on their cards. The second team will use vocabulary and analogy cards 9–16 to ask questions about the information on their cards.

English Made Easy

LISTENING AND SPEAKING:

Grammar Time

Apply It: Classify the Practice Sentences orally with your teacher.

Practice Sentences	Chapter 6: Lesson 5

1. _____ Great! All the newborn calves in the barn bawled loudly throughout the night!

2. _____ Yesterday, the new students arrived early for their first year of college.

3. _____ Mercy! That large stack of papers fell and scattered over the wooden floor!

✏ Chapter Checkup 30

It is time for a checkup of the skills you have learned in this chapter. You will use the chapter checkup on the next page to evaluate your progress.

Lesson 5

You will
- classify Practice Sentences.
- do Chapter Checkup 30.
- write in your journal.

JOURNAL WRITING 16

Write an entry in your journal. Use Reference 9 on page 12 for ideas.

SHURLEY ENGLISH

Chapter 6 Checkup 30

Name:_____ Date:_____

GRAMMAR

▶ **Exercise 1:** Classify each sentence.

1. _____ Wow! Our halfback zigzagged through Delta's defense and scored!

2. _____ He and I laughed uncontrollably with our friends during the afternoon tea.

3. _____ The brave army men advanced cautiously through the minefield.

SKILLS

▶ **Exercise 2:** Identify each type of sentence by writing the correct label in the blank. (**Labels: S, F, SCS, SCV, CD, CX**)

_____ 1. Allen will not be in class today because he is sick.
_____ 2. Donovan went to the library; I stayed home.
_____ 3. Although there was three feet of snow on the ground, we still had school.
_____ 4. We split the wood and stacked it into neat piles.
_____ 5. Received the message I left for you on your phone.
_____ 6. I have a pen pal in Germany.
_____ 7. Marie and I saw the Statue of Liberty from our ship.
_____ 8. Emma wanted to swim, but the water was too cold.

▶ **Exercise 3:** Use a slash to separate each run-on sentence below. Then, correct the run-on sentences by rewriting them as indicated by the labels in parentheses at the end of each sentence.

1. The door was open we walked in. (**CX, because**) (**1**)

_____

2. He was playing video games his dinner burned. (**CX, while**) (**1**)

_____

3. All my friends laughed you told that joke. (**CX, when**) (**2**)

_____

4. I won't make a decision about the wallpaper I hear from you. (**CX, until**) (**2**)

_____

EDITING

▶ **Exercise 4:** Correct each mistake. **Editing Guide: End Marks: 3 Capitals: 18 Commas: 4 Apostrophes: 2 Homonyms: 3 A/An: 2 Subject-Verb Agreement: 1 Underlining: 2 Misspelled Words: 2**

on august 16 1896 george carmack spotted an small nuggett of gold while fishing inn the

klondike river jack london were among the fortune seakers that flocked to canadas yukon

territory fore gold although he didnt find gold london later found fame as a author with his

memorable alaskan tails call of the wild and white fang

Writing Time

Write It: **WRITING ASSIGNMENT 12**

Lesson 6

You will

- conference with teacher about WA 11.
- write a creative writing piece for WA 12.

Writing Assignment 12: Creative Expressions

Purpose: To entertain

Type of Writing: Creative

Audience: Classmates or family members

Use the writing prompt below.

Write to your best friend about your new home on another planet. The following is a list of the things you must describe for your friend.

1. Name and describe your planet.
2. Tell how you get air, food, and water.
3. Describe the types of transportation used.
4. Describe the houses.
5. Describe the clothing.
6. Add other details that you choose.
   (School, friends, teachers, subjects, entertainment, etc.)

Special Instructions:

1. A prewriting map is not required for this creative-writing assignment.

2. Follow the Rough Draft Checklist in Reference 49, page 66.

3. Put your creative-writing paper in your Rough Draft folder when you have finished.

Note: Reference 57 on page 76 gives the steps in the writing process and the location of all the writing checklists.

Conference Time

Discuss It: **TEACHER-STUDENT CONFERENCES FOR WRITING ASSIGNMENT 11**

Meet with your teacher to discuss Writing Assignment 11.
After the conference, place this group of papers in your Publishing folder.

START LESSON 7

Lesson 7

You will

- publish WA 11.
- participate in Discovery Share Time.
- do Across the Curriculum activity.

Publishing Time

Publish It: **WRITING ASSIGNMENT 11**

Choose a publishing form and publish Writing Assignment 11. After rewriting your paper for publication, give the stapled papers (evaluation guide, graded final paper, rough draft, and prewriting map) to your teacher to be placed in your Writing Portfolio.

Reference 67	Publishing Checklist for Step 6 in the Writing Process

The sixth step in the writing process is called publishing. Publishing is sharing your writing with others. With so many forms of publishing available, finding a match for every project and personality is easy.

At times, a written work is best read aloud. Other times, the biggest impact is made when a written work is read silently. You can also use media sources to enhance any publication.

SPECIAL INSTRUCTIONS FOR PUBLISHING:

- Rewrite the graded paper in ink or type it on a computer, correcting any marked errors. (*Do not display or publish papers that have marked errors or grades on them.*)
- Give your teacher the set of stapled papers to place in your Writing Portfolio. (*Stapled papers: evaluation guide, graded final paper, rough draft, and prewriting map.*)
- Select a publishing form from the list below and publish your rewritten paper.
  1. Have classmates, family members, neighbors, or others read your writing at school or home.
  2. Share your writing with others during a Share Time. (*Refer to Reference 68 on page 103 for sharing guidelines.*)
  3. Display your writing on a bulletin board or wall.
  4. Put your writing in the classroom library or in the school library for checkout.
  5. Send your writing as a letter or an e-mail to a friend or relative.
  6. Frame your writing by gluing it on colored construction paper and decorating it.
  7. Make a book of your writing for your classroom, your family, or others.
  8. Illustrate your writing and give it to others to read.
  9. Dramatize your writing in the form of a play, puppet show, or radio broadcast.
  10. Send your writing to be placed in a waiting room (doctor, veterinarian, dentist, etc.), senior-citizen center, or a nursing home.
  11. Send your writing to a school newspaper, local newspaper, or a magazine for publication.
  12. Make a videotape, cassette tape, or slide presentation of your writing.
  13. Choose another publishing form that is not listed.

LISTENING AND SPEAKING:

Discovery Share Time

If you have chosen to investigate a topic introduced in this chapter, you now have the opportunity to share your results in one of the following ways:

1. You may relate your information orally.

2. You may read a written report.

3. You may place your report in the booklet without reading it aloud.

After share time, all written reports should be turned in to be placed in the class booklet titled "Space Trivia." You are encouraged to check out this class booklet so you can enjoy the reports again.

Across the Curriculum

Vocabulary/Social Studies Connection:

1. Make a vocabulary booklet, using a folder with brads. Divide your booklet into subject sections with these titles: **Science**, **Social Studies**, **English**, **Math**, and **Reading**. Keep a list of vocabulary words in each subject. Continue adding to the lists throughout the year. Compare your lists with other students' lists. Discuss how the words listed are important to the understanding of the subjects.

2. Read a story about another culture. Make a vocabulary booklet, listing the vocabulary from that culture. Explain the words and tell the customs associated with the words.

Lesson 8

You will

- practice Jingle 2.
- do Classroom Practice 31.
- write an independent expository essay (WA 13).

LISTENING AND SPEAKING:

Jingle Time

Recite It: Practice Jingle 2 in the Jingle Section on page 498.

GRAMMAR & WRITING CONNECTION:
Practice and Revised Sentences

Apply It: **BUILDING AND EXPANDING SENTENCES**

 Reference 115 | **A Guide for Using Possessive Nouns and Interjections to Build & Expand Sentences**

1. **PNA (possessive noun adjective)** Think of a possessive noun that answers the question "whose." The possessive noun should make sense in your sentence. Write the apostrophe correctly as you write the possessive noun adjective you have chosen for your sentence. Repeat this step for each possessive noun adjective you add to the sentence.

2. **I (interjection)** Choose an interjection that makes the best sense in your sentence. Make sure you punctuate the interjection with an exclamation point, a period, or a comma. Write the interjection you have chosen for your sentence.

Student Tip...

Use your vocabulary words in your Practice and Revised Sentences. Use a thesaurus, synonym-antonym book, or a dictionary to help you develop your writing vocabulary.

Classroom Practice 31

It is time to practice the skills you are learning. You will use the classroom practice on the next page to apply these skills.

Writing Time

Write It: **WRITING ASSIGNMENT 13**

As you write a rough draft for your independent writing assignment, you will do two of the six steps in the writing process: prewriting and rough draft.

Writing Assignment [13]

Purpose: To inform
Type of Writing: Five-paragraph expository essay
Audience: Classmates, family, or friends
Writing Topics: Things I like to do with my family
Dangers of drugs/fire/disobeying your parents
Favorite vacations/clothes/holidays
(Brainstorm for other ideas, individually or in groups.)

Special Instructions:

1. Follow the Prewriting and Rough Draft Checklists in References 47 and 49 on pages 62, 66.

2. Use References 102–106 on pages 166–169 to help you write your expository essay.

3. Use standard, time-order, or transition writing form. See Reference 70 on page 107.

4. Write in first or third person. See Reference 71 on page 108.
(First-person pronouns: *I, me, my, mine, we, us, our,* and *ours*.)
(Third-person pronouns: *he, his, him, she, her, hers, it, its, they, their, theirs,* and *them*.)

Note: Reference 57 on page 76 gives the steps in the writing process and the location of all the writing checklists.

Student Note: Some of your writing pieces will be selected for revision and editing later in the school year.

Classroom Practice 31

Name: _____

Date: _____

INDEPENDENT PRACTICE & REVISED SENTENCES

1. Write a Practice Sentence according to the labels you choose.
   Use **SN/SP V** as your main labels. You may use the other labels in any order and as many times as you wish in order to make a Practice Sentence.
   Chapter 6 labels for a Practice Sentence: SN/SP, V, Adj, Adv, A, P, OP, PPA, C, HV, I, PNA

2. Write a Revised Sentence. Use the following revision strategies: *synonym (syn), antonym (ant), word change (wc), added word (add), deleted word (delete), or no change (nc)*. Under each word, write the abbreviation of the revision strategy you use.

Labels:

Practice:

Revised:

Strategies:

Labels:

Practice:

Revised:

Strategies:

Labels:

Practice:

Revised:

Strategies:

Lesson 9

You will

- practice Jingle 12.
- read and discuss a persuasive paragraph and a three-paragraph persuasive essay.
- plan and write rough draft for persuasive essay (WA 14).

LISTENING AND SPEAKING:

Recite It: Practice Jingle 12 in the Jingle Section on page 501.

>>>> Student Tip...

> Reviewing the transition words will help you apply them in your writing.

Learn It: **PERSUASIVE WRITING**

You have been studying expository writing. Now, you will learn about persuasive writing. As you study persuasive writing, try to answer the following questions.

1. What does persuasion mean?
2. How is persuasive writing organized?
3. How is persuasive writing different from expository writing?

| Reference 116 | **Persuasive Writing** |

Persuasion is getting other people to see things your way. When you write a persuasive paragraph or essay, you are encouraging, or **persuading**, your audience to take a certain action or to feel the same way you do. Persuasive writing expresses an opinion and tries to convince the reader that this opinion is correct. An **opinion** is a belief or feeling that cannot be proven. It is a personal judgment. A **fact** is a statement that can be proved as true. Persuasive writing uses facts to support opinions of the writer.

As the writer, you must make the issue clear and present facts and reasons that strongly support your opinion. It is VERY important to consider who your audience is and to use arguments that will appeal to that audience. You would not use the same kind of argument to persuade your five-year-old sister to tell you where she hid your skates that you would use to persuade your parents to allow you to have friends over.

The three-point writing format is one of the best ways to present your persuasive argument because it gives you an organized way of stating your opinion and supporting it. The persuasive-writing format is the same as the expository-writing format. They both use the three-point organization. The differences between persuasive and expository writing are your purpose for writing and the wording of your sentences.

In persuasive writing, the topic sentence is an opinion statement. In addition, all the points and supporting sentences are persuasive in nature and are intended to back up the opinion statement. Persuasive writing states your opinion and backs it up with supporting facts that try to convince your reader to agree with you.

There are certain words that signal when a writer is expressing an opinion. Opinion Words: think, believe, feel, hope, seem, best, better, worse, worst, probably, excellent, terrible, should, love, hate, etc.

Learn It: WRITING A PERSUASIVE PARAGRAPH

Any time you do persuasive writing, whether it is a paragraph or an essay, you will have three parts: the **Introduction**, the **Body**, and the **Conclusion**.

The three parts will always be written in that order. Although a title will be the first item appearing at the top of a paragraph or essay, you will not finalize the title until you have finished writing the persuasive piece. The title becomes the fourth part of a paragraph or essay.

As you study the persuasive paragraph, you should notice that most of the sentences used in a persuasive paragraph are opinion statements. Factual statements are used to support opinion statements.

Reference 117 — Writing a Persuasive Paragraph

Writing Topic: A new swimming pool for Madison County

Sentence 1 – Topic Sentence:
State your opinion in the topic sentence.
> **Madison County needs to build a new public swimming pool.**

Sentence 2 – General Number Sentence:
You will use a general number word and restate the main idea in the topic sentence.
> **An up-to-date pool is needed for many reasons.**

Sentence 3 – First Point:
You will give your first reason to support your opinion.
> **The first reason we need a new pool is because our old pool is not as safe as it needs to be and may have to be closed before long.**

Sentence 4 – Supporting Sentence(s):
You will give an example that supports and explains your first point. Write one or two sentences.
> **We all have noticed that the paint and even the concrete are beginning to chip and fall from the sides of the pool.**

Sentence 5 – Second Point:
You will give your second reason to support your opinion.
> **The second reason for the new pool is to provide summer swimming in a location that is convenient for all residents of the county.**

Sentence 6 – Supporting Sentence(s):
You will give an example that supports and explains your second point. Write one or two sentences.
> **The old pool is located on the north side of the county, and most of the growth in the last ten years has been on the east side.**

Sentence 7 – Third Point:
You will give your third reason to support your opinion.
> **The third reason we need a new pool is because the old Madison pool does not have all the facilities of a first-rate, modern pool.**

Sentence 8 – Supporting Sentence(s):
You will give an example that supports and explains your third point. Write one or two sentences.
> **It needs many extra features to make the pool area more inviting for county residents.**

Sentence 9 – First Concluding Sentence:
The first concluding sentence is a restatement sentence that forcefully restates your original opinion in the topic sentence and usually starts with the words, *In conclusion*.
> **In conclusion, there are several reasons why our county officials should seriously consider building a new swimming pool.**

Sentence 10 – Final Concluding Sentence:
This sentence summarizes one or more of the reasons stated.
> **A new pool would be safer, more convenient for everybody, and would be more fun for us all.**

WRITING THE TITLE

The Title. Since there are many possibilities for titles, look at the topic and the three points listed about the topic. Use some of the words in the topic and write a phrase to tell what your paragraph is about. Your title can be short or long. Capitalize the first, last, and important words in your title.
Title: A Pool for the Twenty-First Century

Continued on next page. >>>

Reference 117 continued from previous page.

A Pool for the Twenty-First Century

Madison County needs to build a new public swimming pool. An up-to-date pool is needed for many reasons. The first reason we need a new pool is because our old pool is not as safe as it needs to be and may have to be closed before long. We all have noticed that the paint and even the concrete are beginning to chip and fall from the sides of the pool. The second reason for the new pool is to provide summer swimming in a location that is convenient for all residents of the county. The old pool is located on the north side of the county, and most of the growth in the last ten years has been on the east side. The third reason we need a new pool is because the old Madison pool does not have all the facilities of a first-rate, modern pool. It needs many extra features to make the pool area more inviting for county residents. In conclusion, there are several reasons why our county officials should seriously consider building a new swimming pool. A new pool would be safer, more convenient for everybody, and would be more fun for us all.

Compare It:

As you study the two outlines below, notice that there are more sentences in the introduction and conclusion for the essay. Also, note that in the essay, the second paragraph contains all the points and supporting sentences.

Reference 118 | **Outlines for the Persuasive Paragraph and the Three-Paragraph Persuasive Essay**

Guidelines for a Persuasive Paragraph

Paragraph

- A. **Topic** sentence (opinion statement)
- B. **General number** sentence
- C. **First-point** persuasive sentence
- D. One or two **supporting** sentences for the first point
- E. **Second-point** persuasive sentence
- F. One or two **supporting** sentences for the second point
- G. **Third-point** persuasive sentence
- H. One or two **supporting** sentences for the third point
- I. **First concluding** sentence (Restate topic idea)
- J. **Final concluding** sentence (Summarize reasons)

Title

Guidelines for a Three-Paragraph Persuasive Essay

1. **Paragraph 1—** Introduction
   - A. **Topic** sentence (opinion statement)
   - B. **Reason** sentence
   - C. **General number** sentence

2. **Paragraph 2—** Body
   - A. **First-point** persuasive sentence
   - B. One or two **supporting** sentences for the first point
   - C. **Second-point** persuasive sentence
   - D. One or two **supporting** sentences for the second point
   - E. **Third-point** persuasive sentence
   - F. One or two **supporting** sentences for the third point

3. **Paragraph 3—** Conclusion
   - A. **First concluding** sentence (Restate topic idea)
   - B. **Final concluding** sentence (Summarize reasons)

4. **Title**

Learn It: WRITING THE INTRODUCTION FOR A THREE-PARAGRAPH PERSUASIVE ESSAY

The organization of a three-paragraph persuasive essay has three parts: the introduction forms the first paragraph, the body forms the second paragraph, and the conclusion forms the third paragraph.

Three sentences make up the introduction. The first sentence is the **topic sentence**. The second sentence is the added sentence that gives a **reason** why the topic sentence is true. The third sentence in the introduction is called a **general number sentence**. This is the sentence you will add when writing any persuasive essay. It gives a general or specific number of points (reasons or proofs) that will be mentioned to reinforce the topic sentence. You will NOT list your three points as you usually do in the expository three-point writing you have studied.

| Reference 119 | Writing the Introduction for a Three-Paragraph Persuasive Essay |

THE INTRODUCTION
Paragraph 1

Writing Topic: **A new swimming pool for Madison County**

Sentence 1 – **Topic Sentence:**
State your opinion in the topic sentence.
> **Madison County needs to build a new public swimming pool.**

Sentence 2 – **Reason Sentence:**
You will give a general reason why you think the topic sentence is true.
> **Although the old pool has served our county for many years, the time has come to plan for a modern facility.**

Sentence 3 – **General Number Sentence:**
You will use a general number word and restate the main idea in the topic sentence.
> **An up-to-date pool is needed for many reasons.**

Learn It: WRITING THE BODY
FOR A THREE-PARAGRAPH PERSUASIVE ESSAY

After the introduction, you are ready to write the body. The body of a three-paragraph essay contains one paragraph. This paragraph lists each of the three persuasive points. Also, notice that each of the three main points has one or two supporting sentences.

| Reference 120 | Writing the Body for a Three-Paragraph Persuasive Essay |

THE BODY
Paragraph 2

Sentence 4 – **First Point:**
You will give your first reason to support your opinion.
> **The first reason we need a new pool is because our old pool is not as safe as it needs to be and may have to be closed before long.**

Sentence 5 – **Supporting Sentence:**
You will give an example that supports and explains your first point. Write one or more supporting sentences.
> **We all have noticed that the paint and even the concrete are beginning to chip and fall from the sides of the pool.**

Continued on next page. >>>

Reference 120 continued from previous page.

Sentence 6 – Second Point:
You will give your second reason to support your opinion.

The second reason for the new pool is to provide summer swimming in a location that is convenient for all residents of the county.

Sentences 7–8 – Supporting Sentences:
You will give an example that supports and explains your second point. Write one or more supporting sentences.

The old pool is located on the north side of the county, and most of the growth in the last ten years has been on the east side. A new, larger pool could be built in the center of the county so everyone could get to it easily.

Sentence 9 – Third Point:
You will give your third reason to support your opinion.

The third reason we need a new pool is because the old Madison pool does not have all the facilities of a first-rate, modern pool.

Sentence 10 – Supporting Sentence:
You will give an example that supports and explains your third point. Write one or more supporting sentences.

It needs many extra features to make the pool area more inviting for county residents.

Learn It: WRITING THE CONCLUSION
FOR A THREE-PARAGRAPH PERSUASIVE ESSAY

The conclusion forms the third paragraph. The closing paragraph, or conclusion, should tie all the important points together with a restatement of the main idea and your final comments.

Two or more sentences make up the conclusion. The first sentence in the conclusion is called the **first concluding sentence**. To write this sentence, you should refer to the third sentence in the introduction. Using the general or specific number and topic as stated in that introductory sentence, you can write a similar concluding sentence. The **final concluding sentences** summarize one or more of the reasons stated.

 Reference 121 **Writing the Conclusion for a Three-Paragraph Persuasive Essay**

THE CONCLUSION
Paragraph 3

Sentence 11 – First Concluding Sentence:
The first concluding sentence is a restatement sentence that forcefully restates your original opinion in the topic sentence and usually starts with the words, *In conclusion*. Write one sentence.

In conclusion, there are several reasons why our county officials should seriously consider building a new swimming pool.

Sentences 12–13 – Final Concluding Sentences:
These final sentences summarize one or more of the reasons stated. Write one or two sentences.

A new pool would be safer, more convenient for everybody, and would be more fun for us all. Madison County residents would be proud to have a modern pool for the twenty-first century.

WRITING THE TITLE
Since there are many possibilities for titles, look at the topic and the three points listed about the topic. Use some of the words in the topic and write a phrase to tell what your paragraph is about. Your title can be short or long. Capitalize the first, last, and important words in your title.

Title: A Pool for the Twenty-First Century

Continued on next page. >>>

Reference 121 continued from previous page.

A Sample Three-Paragraph Persuasive Essay

A Pool for the Twenty-First Century

Madison County needs to build a new public swimming pool. Although the old pool has served our county for many years, the time has come to plan for a modern facility. An up-to-date pool is needed for many reasons.

The first reason we need a new pool is because our old pool is not as safe as it needs to be and may have to be closed before long. We all have noticed that the paint and even the concrete are beginning to chip and fall from the sides of the pool. The second reason for the new pool is to provide summer swimming in a location that is convenient for all residents of the county. The old pool is located on the north side of the county, and most of the growth in the last ten years has been on the east side. A new, larger pool could be built in the center of the county so everyone could get to it easily. The third reason we need a new pool is because the old Madison pool does not have all the facilities of a first-rate, modern pool. It needs many extra features to make the pool area more inviting for county residents.

In conclusion, there are several reasons why our county officials should seriously consider building a new swimming pool. A new pool would be safer, more convenient for everybody, and would be more fun for us all. Madison County residents would be proud to have a modern pool for the twenty-first century.

Writing Time

Write It: **WRITING ASSIGNMENT 14**

As you write a rough draft for your guided writing assignment, you will do two of the six steps in the writing process: prewriting and rough draft.

Writing Assignment

Purpose: To persuade

Type of Writing: Three-paragraph persuasive essay

Audience: Classmates

Writing Topics: Reasons why reading is important
Why a healthy diet/sleep is important
Why I should have less homework/should have musical training/should have my own room
(Brainstorm for other ideas, individually or in groups.)

Special Instructions:

1. Follow the Prewriting and Rough Draft Checklists in References 47 and 49 on pages 62, 66.

2. Use References 116–121 on pages 196–200 to help you write your persuasive essay.

3. Use standard, time-order, or transition writing form. See Reference 70 on page 107.

4. Write in first or third person. See Reference 71 on page 108.
(First-person pronouns: *I, me, my, mine, we, us, our,* and *ours.*)
(Third-person pronouns: *he, his, him, she, her, hers, it, its, they, their, theirs,* and *them.*)

Note: Reference 57 on page 76 gives the steps in the writing process and the location of all the writing checklists.

START LESSON 10

Lesson 10

You will

- revise, edit, and write a final paper for WA 14.

Apply It: **REVISE, EDIT, AND WRITE A FINAL PAPER**
Following the schedule below, you will revise and edit Writing Assignment 14. Then, you will write a final paper. Use the Chapter 6 Writing Evaluation Guide on the next page to check your final paper one last time.

Reference 55 | **Revising & Editing Schedule and Writing a Final Paper**

SPECIAL INSTRUCTIONS FOR REVISING AND EDITING (Steps 3-4 in the writing process):

- Use the Revising and Editing Checklists in References 51 and 53 as you revise and edit your rough draft.
- Follow the revising and editing schedule below as directed by your teacher.
  1. **Individual.** First, read your rough draft to yourself. Use the Revising Checklist in Reference 51 on page 69. Go through your paper, checking each item on the list and making revisions to your rough draft. Then, use the Editing Checklist in Reference 53 on page 71. Go through your paper again, checking each item on the list and editing your rough draft.
  2. **Partner.** Next, get with your editing partner. Work together on each partner's rough draft, one paper at a time. Read each rough draft aloud and revise and edit it together, using the Revising and Editing Checklists. (The author of the paper should be the one to make the corrections on his own paper.)
  3. **Group.** Finally, read the rough draft to a revision group for feedback. Each student should read his paper while the others listen and offer possible revising and editing suggestions. (The author will determine whether to make corrections from the revision group's suggestions.)

SPECIAL INSTRUCTIONS FOR FINAL PAPER (Step 5 in the writing process):

- Write your final paper, using the Final Paper Checklist in Reference 56 on page 75.
- Staple your writing papers in this order: the final paper on top, the rough draft in the middle, and the prewriting map on the bottom. Place the stapled papers in the Final Paper folder.

>>>>>>>>>>>>> **Student Tip...**

1. Be tactful and helpful in your comments during revising and editing time. The purpose of any suggestion should be to improve the writer's rough draft.

2. As you make your final corrections, you have the choice of accepting or rejecting any suggestions made by your partners or your revision group.

3. Study Vocabulary Words and Analogies 14-16 for the chapter test in the next lesson.

4. If you need to improve your handwriting, refer to the Resource Tools Section on page 521 for information on writing legibly.

Chapter 6 Writing Evaluation Guide

Name:_____ Date:_____

ROUGH DRAFT CHECK

_____ 1. Did you write your rough draft in pencil?

_____ 2. Did you write the correct headings on the first seven lines of your paper?

_____ 3. Did you use extra wide margins and skip every other line?

_____ 4. Did you write a title at the end of your rough draft?

_____ 5. Did you place your edited rough draft in your Rough Draft folder?

REVISING CHECK

_____ 6. Did you identify the purpose, type of writing, and audience?

_____ 7. Did you check for a topic, topic sentence, and sentences supporting the topic?

_____ 8. Did you check sentences for the right order, and did you combine, rearrange, or delete sentences when necessary?

_____ 9. Did you check for a variety of simple, compound, and complex sentences?

_____ 10. Did you check for any left out, repeated, or unnecessary words?

_____ 11. Did you check for the best choice of words by replacing or deleting unclear words?

_____ 12. Did you check the content for interest and creativity?

_____ 13. Did you check the voice to make sure the writing says what you want it to say?

EDITING CHECK

_____ 14. Did you indent each paragraph?

_____ 15. Did you put an end mark at the end of every sentence?

_____ 16. Did you capitalize the first word of every sentence?

_____ 17. Did you check for all other capitalization mistakes?

_____ 18. Did you check for all punctuation mistakes?
(commas, periods, apostrophes, quotation marks, underlining)

_____ 19. Did you check for misspelled words and for incorrect homonym choices?

_____ 20. Did you check for incorrect spellings of plural and possessive forms?

_____ 21. Did you check for correct construction and punctuation of your sentences?

_____ 22. Did you check for usage mistakes? *(subject/verb agreement, a/an choices, contractions, verb tenses, pronoun/antecedent agreement, pronoun cases, degrees of adjectives, double negatives, etc.)*

_____ 23. Did you put your revised and edited paper in the Rough Draft folder?

FINAL PAPER CHECK

_____ 24. Did you write the final paper in pencil?

_____ 25. Did you center the title on the top line and center your name under the title?

_____ 26. Did you skip a line before starting the writing assignment?

_____ 27. Did you single-space, use wide margins, and write the final paper neatly?

_____ 28. Did you staple your papers in this order: final paper on top, rough draft in the middle, and prewriting map on the bottom? Did you put them in the Final Paper folder?

START LESSON 11

Lesson 11

You will

- hand in WA 14 for grading.
- respond to oral review questions.
- take Chapter 6 Test.

CHAPTER TEST

It is time to evaluate your knowledge of the skills you have learned in this chapter. Your teacher will give you the Chapter 6 Test to help you assess your progress.

Writing Time

Hand It In: **WRITING ASSIGNMENT 14**

Get your stapled papers for Writing Assignment 14 from your Final Paper folder. Check to make sure they are in the correct order: the final paper on top, the rough draft in the middle, and the prewriting map on the bottom. Hand them in to your teacher.

LISTENING AND SPEAKING:
Oral Review Questions

Discuss It:

1. What are the eight parts of speech?

2. What part of speech is used to show emotion?

3. What is the name of a noun that shows ownership and modifies like an adjective?

4. What are the two jobs of a possessive noun?

5. What punctuation mark is used to show that a noun is possessive?

6. What type of clause has a subject and verb but does not express a complete thought?

7. What two types of clauses make up a complex sentence?

8. What type of conjunction is used in a complex sentence?

9. What type of writing is used when your purpose is to express an opinion and to convince the reader that this opinion is correct?

>>>>>>>>>>>>> **Student Tip...**

For information about test-taking strategies, refer to the Resource Tools Section on page 520

English Made Easy

LISTENING AND SPEAKING:
Vocabulary & Analogy Time

Learn It: Recite the new vocabulary and analogy words.

📖 **Reference 122** **Vocabulary & Analogy Words**

Word: commotion (kə mō'shən)
> **Definition:** a disturbance or uproar
> **Synonym:** hubbub   **Antonym:** calm
> **Sentence:** We were alarmed by the **commotion** in the airport.

Analogy: least : most :: raise : lower
> **Antonym relationship:** Just as **least** is the opposite of **most**,
> **raise** is the opposite of **lower**.

Vocabulary Card 17: Record the vocabulary information above and write your own
sentence, using the new word.

Analogy Card 17: Record the analogy information and write your own analogy,
using the same relationship as the analogy above.

Jingle Time

Recite It: Recite the new jingle.

♪ **Jingle 21** **The Direct Object Jingle**

A **direct object** is a NOUN or a PRO,
> Is a noun or a pro, is a noun or a pro.

A **direct object** completes the meaning,
> Completes the meaning of the sentence.

A **direct object** follows the verb,
> Follows the **verb-transitive**.

To find a direct object,
> Ask *WHAT* or *WHOM*
> Ask *WHAT* or *WHOM* after the verb.

Lesson 1

You will

- study new vocabulary; make Card 17; write own sentence using the vocabulary word.
- analyze new analogy; make Card 17; write own analogy.
- recite new jingle (Direct Object).
- identify direct object, transitive verb, and Pattern 2.
- classify Introductory Sentences.
- do a Skill Builder to identify a direct object.
- write in your journal.

Apply It: These Introductory Sentences are used to apply the new grammar concepts taught below. Classify these sentences orally with your teacher.

Introductory Sentences	Chapter 7: Lesson 1

1. _____ George bought a new car.
2. _____ Yesterday, George bought a beautiful red convertible for his wife.
3. _____ Wow! I beat my older brother in an exciting game of pool!

Learn It: **DIRECT OBJECTS AND TRANSITIVE VERBS**

A Pattern 1 sentence has only one noun and an action verb as its main parts. The new sentence pattern, Pattern 2, has two nouns and an action verb as the sentence core.

Reference 123 — Direct Object, Verb-transitive, and Pattern 2

1. A **direct object** is a noun or a pronoun.

2. A direct object completes the meaning of a sentence and is located in the predicate.

3. To find the direct object, ask *WHAT* or *WHOM* after the verb. Ask *WHAT* when the direct object is a place, thing, or idea. Ask *WHOM* when the direct object is a person.

4. A direct object must be someone or something different from the subject noun. The direct object receives the action of the verb.

5. A direct object is labeled with the abbreviation **DO**.

6. In a sentence containing a direct object, the verb is transitive. A **transitive-verb** is an action verb that tells what the subject does, and it is followed by a direct object. The transitive verb transfers the action from the subject to the direct object. The *transitive verb* is labeled **V-t** and can be called **verb-transitive**.

7. A Pattern 2 sentence has a subject noun, transitive verb, and direct object as its core. A Pattern 2 sentence is labeled **SN V-t DO P2**. A Pattern 2 sentence has two noun jobs in its core: the subject noun and the direct-object noun. *If the subject is a pronoun, it is labeled as a subject pronoun in the sentence, but the pattern is still identified as SN V-t DO P2.*

8. **A review:**
   Pattern 1 is **SN V**. It has a noun-verb (**N V**) core.
   Pattern 2 is **SN V-t DO**. It has a noun-verb-noun (**N V N**) core.

The location of each noun determines its job in a sentence. Only certain noun jobs form the pattern parts of a sentence. For each pattern, the order of the core nouns does not change. A noun that is an object of the preposition is not part of a sentence pattern.

Continued on next page. >>>

Reference 123 continued from previous page.

Question and Answer Flow for the Practice Sentence, Adding Direct Objects

Practice Sentence: Nana made a cake.

1. Who made a cake? **Nana - SN**
2. What is being said about Nana? **Nana made - V**
3. Nana made what? **cake - verify the noun**
4. Does cake mean the same thing as Nana? **No.**
5. **Cake - DO**   (Say: *Cake* - direct object.)
6. **Made - V-t**   (Say: *Made* - verb-transitive.)
7. **A - A**
8. **SN V-t DO P2**   (Say: Subject noun, verb-transitive, direct object, Pattern 2.)
9. Skill Check
10. Verb-transitive - check again (This check is to make sure the "t" is added to the verb.)
11. **No prepositional phrases**
12. **Period, statement, declarative sentence**
13. Go back to the verb. Divide the complete subject from the complete predicate.
14. Is this sentence in a natural or inverted order? **Natural - no change.**

```
        SN    V-t A DO
SN V-t     Nana / made a cake. D
DO P2
```

Discuss It:

1. What is the pattern in a Pattern 2 sentence?
2. What are the core parts of a Pattern 2 sentence?
3. What parts of speech are used in a Pattern 2 sentence?

Learn It: A SKILL BUILDER FOR A NOUN CHECK WITH DIRECT OBJECTS

The example below shows you what to do with direct objects when you are identifying nouns for a Noun Check.

JOURNAL WRITING 17

Write an entry in your journal. Use Reference 9 on page 12 for ideas.

Skill Builder

FOR A NOUN CHECK WITH DIRECT OBJECTS

Circle the nouns in a Noun Check.

Sentence 1: Subject Noun (George) *yes, it is a noun;*
Direct Object (car) *yes, it is a noun.*

Sentence 2: Subject Noun (George) *yes, it is a noun;*
Direct Object (convertible) *yes, it is a noun;*
Object of the Preposition (wife) *yes, it is a noun.*

Sentence 3: Subject Pronoun I, *no, it is a pronoun;*
Direct Object (brother) *yes, it is a noun;*
Object of the Preposition (game), *yes, it is a noun.*
Object of the Preposition (pool) *yes, it is a noun.*

START LESSON 2

Lesson 2

You will

- practice Jingle 21.
- classify Practice Sentences.
- identify verb tenses and regular/irregular verbs.
- do a Skill Builder verb chant.
- do Classroom Practice 32.

LISTENING AND SPEAKING:

Recite It: Practice Jingle 21 in the Jingle Section on page 504.

Apply It: Classify the Practice Sentences orally with your teacher.

Practice Sentences	Chapter 7: Lesson 2
1. _____ Alas! An unwelcome mole invaded my yard and destroyed my garden.	
2. _____ Mail a reunion invitation to Aunt Rebecca in New York City.	
3. _____ Abruptly, the boxer in the ring threw a knockout punch at his opponent!	

Learn It: SIMPLE VERB TENSES

📖* Reference 124   Simple Verb Tenses

Verbs are time-telling words. They not only tell of an action, but they also tell the time of the action. The time of the action is called the tense of the verb. The word *tense* means *time*.

There are three basic verb tenses that show when an action takes place: **present tense**, **past tense**, and **future tense**. These tenses are known as the **simple verb tenses**. When you are writing paragraphs, you should use verbs that are in the same tense.

1. The **present tense** shows that something is happening now, in the present. Present tense verbs can be singular or plural. Singular present tense verbs end in **-s**. Plural present tense verbs have **no -s** added.

Present Tense with a Singular Subject	**Present Tense with a Plural Subject**
The girl <u>dances</u>. The girl <u>sings</u>.	The girls <u>dance</u>. The girls <u>sing</u>.

2. The **simple past** tense shows that something has happened at some time in the past. Most past tense verbs end in **-ed** or have a middle vowel change. Past tense verbs are the same for singular or plural subjects.

Past Tense with a Singular Subject	**Past Tense with a Plural Subject**
The girl <u>danced</u>. The girl <u>sang</u>.	The girls <u>danced</u>. The girls <u>sang</u>.

3. The **future tense** shows that something will happen at some time in the future. Future tense verbs use the helping verb **_will_** or **_shall_** before the main verb. Future tense verbs are the same for singular or plural subjects.

Future Tense with a Singular Subject	**Future Tense with a Plural Subject**
The girl <u>will dance</u>. The girl <u>will sing</u>.	The girls <u>will dance</u>. The girls <u>will sing</u>.

Continued on next page. >>>

Reference 124 continued from previous page.

Present Tense	Past Tense	Future Tense
Ends with **-s** or has **no** -s ending.	Ends with **-ed** or has a middle vowel change.	Has the helping verb **will** or **shall** before the main verb.
1. He <u>walks</u> to the office.	3. He <u>walked</u> to the office.	5. He <u>will walk</u> to the office.
2. He <u>drives</u> to the office.	4. He <u>drove</u> to the office.	6. He <u>will drive</u> to the office.

Learn It: REGULAR AND IRREGULAR VERBS

Reference 125 ### Regular and Irregular Verbs

Verbs are divided into two groups: regular and irregular.

Regular Verbs:

Most verbs are **regular** if you make the main verb past tense by **adding -ed** to the end. Most verbs are regular verbs because you add letters to the end of the verbs to make them past tense.

> (**Examples:** want and want**ed**, jump and jump**ed**, laugh and laugh**ed**)

Irregular Verbs:

Most verbs are **irregular** if you make the main verb past tense by **changing a vowel in the middle of the word**. Irregular verbs do not form their past tense by adding letters to the end of a verb. They form their past tense by making a new verb with the vowel change.

> (**Examples:** bec**o**me and bec**a**me, fr**ee**ze and fr**o**ze, t**e**ll and t**o**ld)

To decide if a verb is regular or irregular, remember these three things:

1. Look only at the main verb.
2. If the main verb is made past tense by **adding** an **-ed** ending, it is a regular verb.
3. If the main verb is made past tense by a **middle vowel change**, it is an irregular verb.

Some of the most common irregular verbs are listed on the irregular verb chart located in Reference 126 on page 210 Refer to this chart whenever necessary.

Exercise: Write the past-tense form for the verbs 1-4. Then, Write **R** for regular or **I** for irregular.

1. open........ *R* **Past tense:** *opened*   3. sell............. *I* **Past tense:** *sold*
2. swim........ *I* **Past tense:** *swam*   4. cry............. *R* **Past tense:** *cried*

Learn It: A SKILL BUILDER FOR A VERB CHANT

A verb chant will now be added to the Skill Builder. The verb chart you will use is located in Reference 126. As you can see, two of the irregular verb forms use helping verbs with the main verbs. Only the helping verbs listed in a column can be used with the main verbs in that column. The verb chart shows only a partial listing of regular and irregular verbs, but you can add others. You will learn more about these verbs later.

 Student Tip...

Recite a set of five verbs in Reference 126 in a lively manner. Follow the example below.

Say: (become)	(became)	(<u>has</u> become)	(<u>is</u> becoming)
Say: (begin)	(began)	(<u>has</u> begun)	(<u>is</u> beginning)
Say: (blow)	(blew)	(<u>has</u> blown)	(<u>is</u> blowing)
Say: (break)	(broke)	(<u>has</u> broken)	(<u>is</u> breaking)
Say: (bring)	(brought)	(<u>has</u> brought)	(<u>is</u> bringing)

Reference 126 | **Verb Chart for Principal Parts**

Irregular Verbs

PRESENT	PAST	PAST PARTICIPLE		PRESENT PARTICIPLE	
become	became	(**has**, have, had)	become	(am, **is**, are, was, were)	becoming
begin	began	(**has**, have, had)	begun	(am, **is**, are, was, were)	beginning
blow	blew	(**has**, have, had)	blown	(am, **is**, are, was, were)	blowing
break	broke	(**has**, have, had)	broken	(am, **is**, are, was, were)	breaking
bring	brought	(**has**, have, had)	brought	(am, **is**, are, was, were)	bringing
buy	bought	(**has**, have, had)	bought	(am, **is**, are, was, were)	buying
choose	chose	(**has**, have, had)	chosen	(am, **is**, are, was, were)	choosing
come	came	(**has**, have, had)	come	(am, **is**, are, was, were)	coming
cut	cut	(**has**, have, had)	cut	(am, **is**, are, was, were)	cutting
do	did	(**has**, have, had)	done	(am, **is**, are, was, were)	doing
drink	drank	(**has**, have, had)	drunk	(am, **is**, are, was, were)	drinking
drive	drove	(**has**, have, had)	driven	(am, **is**, are, was, were)	driving
eat	ate	(**has**, have, had)	eaten	(am, **is**, are, was, were)	eating
fall	fell	(**has**, have, had)	fallen	(am, **is**, are, was, were)	falling
fly	flew	(**has**, have, had)	flown	(am, **is**, are, was, were)	flying
freeze	froze	(**has**, have, had)	frozen	(am, **is**, are, was, were)	freezing
get	got	(**has**, have, had)	gotten	(am, **is**, are, was, were)	getting
give	gave	(**has**, have, had)	given	(am, **is**, are, was, were)	giving
go	went	(**has**, have, had)	gone	(am, **is**, are, was, were)	going
grow	grew	(**has**, have, had)	grown	(am, **is**, are, was, were)	growing
know	knew	(**has**, have, had)	known	(am, **is**, are, was, were)	knowing
lay	laid	(**has**, have, had)	laid	(am, **is**, are, was, were)	laying
lie	lay	(**has**, have, had)	lain	(am, **is**, are, was, were)	lying
lose	lost	(**has**, have, had)	lost	(am, **is**, are, was, were)	losing
make	made	(**has**, have, had)	made	(am, **is**, are, was, were)	making
ride	rode	(**has**, have, had)	ridden	(am, **is**, are, was, were)	riding
ring	rang	(**has**, have, had)	rung	(am, **is**, are, was, were)	ringing
rise	rose	(**has**, have, had)	risen	(am, **is**, are, was, were)	rising
run	ran	(**has**, have, had)	run	(am, **is**, are, was, were)	running
say	said	(**has**, have, had)	said	(am, **is**, are, was, were)	saying
see	saw	(**has**, have, had)	seen	(am, **is**, are, was, were)	seeing
sell	sold	(**has**, have, had)	sold	(am, **is**, are, was, were)	selling
sing	sang	(**has**, have, had)	sung	(am, **is**, are, was, were)	singing
sink	sank	(**has**, have, had)	sunk	(am, **is**, are, was, were)	sinking
set	set	(**has**, have, had)	set	(am, **is**, are, was, were)	setting
shoot	shot	(**has**, have, had)	shot	(am, **is**, are, was, were)	shooting
sit	sat	(**has**, have, had)	sat	(am, **is**, are, was, were)	sitting
speak	spoke	(**has**, have, had)	spoken	(am, **is**, are, was, were)	speaking
swim	swam	(**has**, have, had)	swum	(am, **is**, are, was, were)	swimming
take	took	(**has**, have, had)	taken	(am, **is**, are, was, were)	taking
teach	taught	(**has**, have, had)	taught	(am, **is**, are, was, were)	teaching
tell	told	(**has**, have, had)	told	(am, **is**, are, was, were)	telling
throw	threw	(**has**, have, had)	thrown	(am, **is**, are, was, were)	throwing
wear	wore	(**has**, have, had)	worn	(am, **is**, are, was, were)	wearing
write	wrote	(**has**, have, had)	written	(am, **is**, are, was, were)	writing

Regular Verbs

PRESENT	PAST	PAST PARTICIPLE		PRESENT PARTICIPLE	
call	called	(**has**, have, had)	called	(am, **is**, are, was, were)	calling
cry	cried	(**has**, have, had)	cried	(am, **is**, are, was, were)	crying
hop	hopped	(**has**, have, had)	hopped	(am, **is**, are, was, were)	hopping
play	played	(**has**, have, had)	played	(am, **is**, are, was, were)	playing

English Made Easy

 Student Tip...

Consult a dictionary if you are in doubt about the spelling of regular or irregular verb forms.

Classroom Practice 32

It is time to practice the skills you are learning. You will use the classroom practice on the next page to apply these skills.

Classroom Practice 32

Name:_____ Date:_____

GRAMMAR

▶ **Exercise 1:** Classify each sentence.

1. _____ Clouds of mosquitoes from Lake Erie covered my uncle's farm in May.

2. _____ For lunch, my sister and brother raided the refrigerator for sandwiches.

▶ **Exercise 2:** Use sentence 1 and complete the table below.

List the Noun Used	List the Noun Job	Singular or Plural	Common or Proper	Simple Subject	Simple Predicate

SKILLS

▶ **Exercise 3:** (1) Underline the verb or verb phrase. (2) Identify the verb tense by writing **1** for present tense, **2** for past tense, or **3** for future tense. (3) Write the past-tense form. (4) Write **R** for Regular or **I** for Irregular.

	Verb Tense	Main Verb Past Tense Form	R or I
1. Michael watches television for one hour after school.			
2. Daniel will give you directions to his house.			
3. I saw the long black snake near the porch.			
4. I worked in the office on Saturday.			
5. The quarterback broke his foot during practice.			
6. My brother sells motorcycles.			
7. We played basketball in the park.			
8. We will eat pancakes for breakfast.			
9. My uncle hunts in the woods behind my house.			⟨
10. Jake writes in his journal every day.			

EDITING

▶ **Exercise 4:** Correct each mistake. **Editing Guide: End Marks: 3 Capitals: 18 Commas: 6 Apostrophes: 1 Homonyms: 2 A/An: 2 Subject-Verb Agreement: 2 Periods: 1 Misspelled Words: 1**

in 1792 james hoban a irish-born architect one an contest to desine the presidents home

during the war of 1812 the british set fire too the white house the white house were rebuilt and

it still stand at 1600 pennsylvania avenue in washington dc

LISTENING AND SPEAKING:
Vocabulary & Analogy Time

Learn It: Recite the new vocabulary and analogy words.

Reference 127	Vocabulary & Analogy Words

Word: inquisitive (ĭn kwĭz ə tĭv)
   Definition: particularly curious
   Synonym: inquiring **Antonym:** indifferent
   Sentence: She is one of the most **inquisitive** children I know.

Analogy: reaching : teaching :: crash : clash
   Rhyming relationship: Just as **reaching** rhymes with **teaching**,
   crash rhymes with **clash**.

Vocabulary Card 18: Record the vocabulary information above and write your own
   sentence, using the new word.

Analogy Card 18: Record the analogy information and write your own analogy,
   using the same relationship as the analogy above.

Jingle Time

Recite It: Practice Jingles 13–21 in the Jingle Section on pages 501–504.

Grammar Time

Apply It: Classify the Practice Sentences orally with your teacher.

Practice Sentences	Chapter 7: Lesson 3

1. _____ Ray and I recorded the prices and discounts for the new
   electronic games.

2. _____ Bob keeps his rabbits and chickens in a coop at the back
   of his house.

3. _____ Did Sam and Jeff buy two copies of the new book on football?

START LESSON 3

Lesson 3

You will

- study new vocabulary;
  make Card 18;
  write own sentence using
  the vocabulary word.
- analyze new analogy; make
  Card 18; write own analogy.
- practice Jingles 13-21.
- classify Practice Sentences.
- do a Skill Builder.
- identify tenses
  of helping verbs.
- do Classroom Practice 33.
- read and discuss
  Discovery Time.

Using the sentences just classified, do a Skill Builder orally with your teacher.

1. **Identify the nouns in a Noun Check.**
2. **Identify the nouns as singular or plural.**
3. **Identify the nouns as common or proper.**
4. **Identify the complete subject and the complete predicate.**
5. **Identify the simple subject and the simple predicate.**
6. **Do a Vocabulary Check.**
7. **Do a Verb Chant.**

Learn It: TENSES OF HELPING VERBS

📖	**Reference 128**	**Tenses of Helping Verbs**

To determine the tense of a verb, you must first know if the sentence has a main verb only, or if it has a main verb and a helping verb. Then, you will use one of the two ways below to determine the verb tense.

1. If there is only a main verb in a sentence, the tense is determined by the main verb and will be either present tense or past tense.
2. If there is a helping verb with a main verb, the tense of both verbs is determined by the helping verb, not the main verb. If there is more than one helping verb, the tense is determined by the first helping verb.

Since the helping verb determines the tense, it is important to learn the tenses of the 14 helping verbs you will be using. You should memorize the list below so you will never have trouble with tenses.

> **Present-tense helping verbs:** am, is, are, has, have, do, does
> **Past-tense helping verbs:** was, were, had, did, been
> **Future-tense helping verbs:** will, shall

Some present-tense helping verbs keep verb phrases in present tense even though the main verbs have a past-tense form. *Has* and *have* are the two present-tense helping verbs used most often with past-tense main verbs. When *has* and *have* are used with a past-tense main verb, it describes an actin that began in the past and continues into the present or that occurred in the recent past. (*I have washed the car today.* .)

Example 1: (1) Underline the verb or verb phrase.

(2) Identify the verb tense by writing **1** for present tense, **2** for past tense, or **3** for future tense.

(3) Write the past-tense form.

(4) Write **R** for Regular or **I** for Irregular.

	Verb Tense	Main Verb Past Tense Form	R or I
1. The boy <u>is wearing</u> a warm jacket.	1	wore	I
2. My sister <u>was trying</u> a new recipe.	2	tried	R
3. The man <u>will ride</u> on the noon train.	3	rode	I

Example 2: List the present-tense and past-tense helping verbs in the blanks below.						
Present Tense	1. am	2. is	3. are	4. has	5. have	6. do	7. does
Past Tense	1. was	2. were	3. had	4. did	5. been		

Classroom Practice 33

It is time to practice the skills you are learning. You will use the classroom practice on the next page to apply these skills.

>>>>>>>>> **Student Tip...**

Verb-Tense Game:

Write each of the present-, past-, and future-tense helping verbs on the front of index cards. On the back of the cards, write either present, past, or future tense for each helping verb. (Make several sets of cards.)

Present-tense helping verbs: **am, is, are, has, have, do, does**

Past-tense helping verbs: **was, were, had, did, been**

Future-tense helping verbs: **will, shall**

Divide into several groups with three or four students in each group. Give each group a set of cards. Have the "dealer" in each group place a card on the desk, "verb side" up. The first person in the group to name the tense gets to keep the card. Continue until all the cards have been played. Rotate until each student has had a turn to be the dealer.

 **Discovery Time**

Mars is the fourth planet from the sun in our solar system. It is named for the Roman god of war. Mars has a thin atmosphere and less gravity than Earth. We have several missions to Mars currently in progress.

Discovery Questions:
- Why is Mars called the Red Planet?
- What do you think it is like to be a scientist receiving information for the first time from space probes on Mars?

Discovery Activity:

- Have you heard any funny jokes or seen any TV shows or movies about life on Mars?
  If so, tell about one of your favorites.

Are you interested in learning more about Mars?

1. You may explore this topic further by using the resources listed below.
   Computer resources: Internet, encyclopedia software
   Library resources: encyclopedias, books, magazines, newspapers
   Home/community resources: books, interviews, newspapers, magazines

2. A Discovery Share Time is provided in Lesson 7 if you wish to share your investigation results. You may share orally, or you may prepare a written report. You will put your written report in a class booklet titled "Space Trivia." This booklet will be placed in the class library for everyone to enjoy.

SHURLEY ENGLISH

Classroom Practice 33

Name:_____ Date:_____

GRAMMAR

▶ **Exercise 1:** Classify each sentence.

1. _____ Yesterday, Sandy and I drove a red convertible around town.

2. _____ Give a reason and an apology to Joe and Amy for your tardiness to dinner.

▶ **Exercise 2:** Use sentence 2 above and complete the table below.

List the Noun Used	List the Noun Job	Singular or Plural	Common or Proper	Simple Subject	Simple Predicate

SKILLS

▶ **Exercise 3:** (1) Underline the verb or verb phrase. (2) Identify the verb tense by writing **1** for present tense, **2** for past tense, or **3** for future tense. (3) Write the past-tense form. (4) Write **R** for Regular or **I** for Irregular.

	Verb Tense	Main Verb Past Tense Form	R or I
1. Curtis will take my books to the library.			
2. Katie and Kelly skated across the frozen pond.			
3. The teacher had told that story several times.			
4. My cousin is eating pizza at the party.			
5. The play begins at four o'clock.			
6. I will wash those dirty dishes.			
7. My brothers have been playing baseball.			
8. Chris needs a ride to school.			

▶ **Exercise 4:** List the present-tense and past-tense helping verbs below. (These verbs are listed in Reference 128.)

Present Tense	1.	2.	3.	4.	5.	6.	7.
Past Tense	1.	2.	3.	4.	5.		

EDITING

▶ **Exercise 5:** Correct each mistake. **Editing Guide: End Marks: 5   Capitals: 15   Commas: 5   Apostrophes: 3   Homonyms: 3   Subject-Verb Agreement: 2   Underlining: 1   Periods: 2   Misspelled Words: 2**

i think ill weight for the train even through it is late some passengers believes it will be hear

shortly it is delayed in detroit because of the blizard im just glad it's on its way to hour

station until the train arrive ill read my book the lion the witch and the wardrobe by c s lewis

English Made Easy

LISTENING AND SPEAKING:
Vocabulary & Analogy Time

Learn It: Recite the new vocabulary and analogy words.

Lesson 4

You will
- study new vocabulary; make Card 19; write own sentence using the vocabulary word.
- analyze new analogy; make Card 19; write own analogy.
- practice Jingles 3–11.
- classify Practice Sentences.
- do a Skill Builder.
- do Classroom Practice 34.
- write in your journal.
- read and discuss Discovery Time.
- do a homework assignment.
- do Home Connection activity.

📖 Reference 129	Vocabulary & Analogy Words

Word: lenient (lē nē ənt, lēn yənt)
  Definition: not strict
  Synonym: permissive   **Antonym:** stern
  Sentence: The new parents were very **lenient** with their first child.

Analogy: carpenter : hammer :: doctor : stethoscope
  Purpose or use relationship: Just as a **carpenter** uses a **hammer**, a **doctor** uses a **stethoscope**.

Vocabulary Card 19: Record the vocabulary information above and write your own sentence, using the new word.

Analogy Card 19: Record the analogy information and write your own analogy, using the same relationship as the analogy above.

Jingle Time

Recite It: Practice Jingles 3–11 in the Jingle Section on pages 499–500.

Grammar Time

Apply It: Classify the Practice Sentences orally with your teacher.

Practice Sentences	Chapter 7: Lesson 4

1. _____ Our coach has built a good team by hard work and daily practice.
2. _____ After three hours, I found the solution to the complex problem.
3. _____ Dozens of pigeons lined the rooftop of the old abandoned warehouse.

Skill Builder

Using the Practice Sentences just classified, do a Skill Builder orally with your teacher.

1. **Identify the nouns in a Noun Check.**
2. **Identify the nouns as singular or plural.**
3. **Identify the nouns as common or proper.**
4. **Identify the complete subject and the complete predicate.**
5. **Identify the simple subject and the simple predicate.**
6. **Do a Vocabulary Check.**
7. **Do a Verb Chant.**

JOURNAL WRITING 18

Write an entry in your journal. Use Reference 9 on page 12 for ideas.

Classroom Practice 34

It is time to practice the skills you are learning. You will use the classroom practice on the next page to apply these skills.

>>> **Student Tip...**

Play the verb-tense game from Lesson 3 again. The directions are reprinted below for your convenience.

Write each of the present-, past-, and future-tense helping verbs on the front of index cards. On the back of the cards, write either present, past, or future tense for each helping verb. (Make several sets of cards.)

Present-tense helping verbs: **am, is, are, has, have, do, does**

Past-tense helping verbs: **was, were, had, did, been**

Future-tense helping verbs: **will, shall**

Divide into several groups with three or four students in each group. Give each group a set of cards. Have the "dealer" in each group place a card on the desk, "verb side" up. The first person in the group to name the tense gets to keep the card. Continue until all the cards have been played. Rotate until each student has had a turn to be the dealer.

ENRICHMENT:

Discovery Time

(American) 1889-1953 — Edwin Powell Hubble was an American astronomer who showed that there were other galaxies beyond our own. He is considered the founder of extragalactic astronomy. The Hubble Space Telescope is named in his honor. The Hubble Space Telescope weighs 12 tons and is 43 feet long.

Discovery Questions:
- **What do you imagine other galaxies are like?**
- **Do you think there could be life in other galaxies? Explain.**
- **Are you interested in extragalactic astronomy?**

Are you interested in learning more about Edward Hubble or the Hubble Space Telescope?

1. You may explore this topic further by using the resources listed below.
   Computer resources: Internet, encyclopedia software
   Library resources: encyclopedias, books, magazines, newspapers
   Home/community resources: books, interviews, newspapers, magazines

2. A Discovery Share Time is provided in Lesson 7 if you wish to share your investigation results. You may share orally, or you may prepare a written report. You will put your written report in a class booklet titled "Space Trivia." This booklet will be placed in the class library for everyone to enjoy.

Classroom Practice 34

Name:_____ Date:_____

GRAMMAR

▶ **Exercise 1:** Classify each sentence.

1. _____ For an hour, the children drew pictures quietly with their new crayons.

2. _____ Oh, no! Diane broke her father's expensive new telescope!

3. _____ The rice farmers do not plant rice during the winter months.

SKILLS

▶ **Exercise 2:** (1) Underline the verb or verb phrase. (2) Identify the verb tense by writing **1** for present tense, **2** for past tense, or **3** for future tense. (3) Write the past-tense form. (4) Write **R** for Regular or **I** for Irregular.

	Verb Tense	Main Verb Past Tense Form	R or I
1. We are delivering a piano to that apartment.			
2. An orange rolled across the table.			
3. My brother will not sleep in a tent by the lake.			
4. Tonya had not finished her book report.			
5. That brown colt has been sleeping in the barn.			
6. Our equipment will be sold at the auction.			
7. The artist paints beautiful landscapes.			
8. Will your dog growl at the mailman?			
9. Have you studied for the semester exam?			
10. That boy was drinking a glass of lemonade.			

▶ **Exercise 3:** List the present-tense and past-tense helping verbs below.

Present Tense	1.	2.	3.	4.	5.	6.	7.
Past Tense	1.	2.	3.	4.	5.		

EDITING

▶ **Exercise 4:** Correct each mistake. **Editing Guide: End Marks: 4   Capitals: 9   Commas: 6   Homonyms: 2   A/An: 1   Subject-Verb Agreement: 3   Misspelled Words: 2**

beth is finally arriving in key west florida for her belated summer vaction the first morning

she go to the beach for fore hours in the afternoon she go deep-sea fishing with a groop of

college students from akron ohio for the rest of the weak she nurse a ugly case of sunburn

 **Homework 5**

Complete this homework assignment on notebook paper.

1. Write the **helping verbs** for each verb tense listed.

   Present Tense:

   Past Tense:

   Future Tense:

2. Number your paper 1–8. For each sentence, do four things. (1) Write the verb or verb phrase. (2) Identify the verb tense by writing **1** for present tense, **2** for past tense, or **3** for future tense. (3) Write the past-tense form. (4) Write **R** for Regular or **I** for Irregular.

	Verb Tense	Main Verb Past Tense Form	R or I
1. The baby is crying in his crib.			
2. The doctor handed the patient a prescription.			
3. The thirsty horses will drink water at the pond.			
4. Rabbits have been eating the cabbage.			
5. My dog barks at strangers.			
6. What will we see at the movies?			
7. The chocolate pie was eaten before dinner.			
8. The vegetable soup is simmering on the stove.			

Home Connection

Family Activity for Direct Objects

Have each family member (or team) choose a different historical figure from the Discovery Time list in the Resource Tools section of the Student Text Book. Look up information about the historical figure in books, encyclopedias, or on the Internet. On one side of an index card, write at least five sentences with direct objects that give clues to the identity of the person chosen. Put the most revealing clues last. Write the mystery person's name on the opposite side of the index card. Read the clues, one at a time, to a member of the family. In order for a family member to guess the mystery person's name, he must first identify the direct-object word in the clue sentence that is read. See how many clues have to be read before the mystery person can be identified. The person or team that is the first to guess the correct historical figure is the winner.

Example: Clues with direct objects for Benjamin Franklin:
- He began the first **library** in America.
- He established the first **hospital** in America.
- He published a **newspaper** and an **almanac**.
- He invented a **stove** for heating homes.
- He wrote a **book** on electricity.
- He performed **experiments** in electricity.
- He and other famous Americans wrote the **Declaration of Independence**.

Family Activity for Vocabulary and Analogies

Divide into family teams. The first team will use vocabulary and analogy cards 1–8 to ask questions about the information on their cards. The second team will use vocabulary and analogy cards 9–18 to ask questions about the information on their cards.

For vocabulary words:
- What is the definition of the word?
- Name a synonym and antonym for the word.
- Create a new sentence using the word.
- Find the word in another source (dictionary, newspaper, magazine, advertisement).

For analogies:
- What is the answer to the analogy?
- What is the relationship of the analogy?
- Make another analogy with the same relationship.
- Make another analogy with a different relationship.

LISTENING AND SPEAKING:

Grammar Time

Apply It: Classify the Practice Sentences orally with your teacher.

Practice Sentences	Chapter 7: Lesson 5

1. _____ Did archaeologists discover dinosaur bones in the desert of Arizona?
2. _____ The football did not reach the receiver at the far end of the field.
3. _____ Gather some earthworms for the fishing tournament on Saturday.

Chapter Checkup 35

It is time for a checkup of the skills you have learned in this chapter. You will use the chapter checkup on the next page to evaluate your progress.

Lesson 5

You will
- classify Practice Sentences.
- do Chapter Checkup 35.
- write in their journal.

JOURNAL WRITING [19]

Write an entry in your journal. Use Reference 9 on page 12 for ideas.

Chapter 7 Checkup 35

Name:_____ Date:_____

GRAMMAR

▶ **Exercise 1:** Classify each sentence.

1. _____ The club's president devised a new plan for the election campaign.

2. _____ Does your sister take violin lessons at the music academy?

3. _____ The unusually crowded runway delayed the departure of planes on our trip.

SKILLS

▶ **Exercise 2:** (1) Underline the verb or verb phrase. (2) Identify the verb tense by writing **1** for present tense, **2** for past tense, or **3** for future tense. (3) Write the past-tense form. (4) Write **R** for Regular or **I** for Irregular.

	Verb Tense	Main Verb Past Tense Form	R or I
1. My boss leaves for Texas in the morning.			
2. The horse was galloping slowly across the field.			
3. My sister likes bananas in her cereal.			
4. The children are sitting on the grass by the creek.			
5. Jared will come to the parade with his friends.			
6. I have heard that song on the radio.			
7. I know the answer to that question.			
8. My dad was talking to my teacher about my grades.			
9. My friend tells very funny jokes.			
10. My brother had been kicking the ball over the fence.			

▶ **Exercise 3:** List the present-tense and past-tense helping verbs below.

Present Tense	1.	2.	3.	4.	5.	6.	7.
Past Tense	1.	2.	3.	4.	5.		

EDITING

▶ **Exercise 4:** Correct each mistake. **Editing Guide: End Marks: 5 Capitals: 8 Commas: 2 Apostrophes: 2 Homonyms: 5 A/An: 2 Subject-Verb Agreement: 4 Misspelled Words: 2**

joe eight so much for thanksgiving that he cant bend over too tie his shoelaces he feel like an

water bufalo and he dont no what to do he wish that he could make his miserie disappear he

may has two go on an diet after all he must lose wait before his christmas feast in december

Writing Time

Write It: **WRITING ASSIGNMENT 15**

Writing Assignment 15 : Creative Expressions

Purpose: To persuade

Type of Writing: Creative/persuasive

Audience: Parents

Writing Prompt: The governor of your state wants to cancel summer vacation. Using what you have learned about persuasive essays, write a letter to the governor or to the editor of a newspaper, expressing your views about the situation. Make sure you edit your letter carefully, or your mistakes may convince the governor that he is right.

Special Instructions:

1. Write a response to the writing prompt above.

2. A prewriting map is not required for this creative-writing assignment.

3. Follow the Rough Draft Checklist in Reference 49 on page 66.

4. Put your creative-writing paper in your Rough Draft folder when you have finished.

Note: Reference 57 on page 76 lists the steps in the writing process and the location of all the writing checklists.

Lesson 6

You will

- conference with teacher about WA 14.
- write a creative writing piece for WA 15.

Conference Time

Discuss It: **TEACHER-STUDENT CONFERENCES FOR WRITING ASSIGNMENT 14**

Meet with your teacher to discuss Writing Assignment 14.
After the conference, place this group of papers in your Publishing folder.

START LESSON 7

Lesson 7

You will

- publish WA 14.
- participate in Discovery Share Time.
- do Across the Curriculum activity.

Publishing Time

Publish It: **WRITING ASSIGNMENT 14**

Choose a publishing form and publish Writing Assignment 14. After rewriting your paper for publication, give the stapled papers (evaluation guide, graded final paper, rough draft, and prewriting map) to your teacher to be placed in your Writing Portfolio.

✐* **Reference 67**	**Publishing Checklist for Step 6 in the Writing Process**

The sixth step in the writing process is called publishing. Publishing is sharing your writing with others. With so many forms of publishing available, finding a match for every project and personality is easy.

At times, a written work is best read aloud. Other times, the biggest impact is made when a written work is read silently. You can also use media sources to enhance any publication.

SPECIAL INSTRUCTIONS FOR PUBLISHING:

- Rewrite the graded paper in ink or type it on a computer, correcting any marked errors. *(Do not display or publish papers that have marked errors or grades on them.)*
- Give your teacher the set of stapled papers to place in your Writing Portfolio. *(Stapled papers: evaluation guide, graded final paper, rough draft, and prewriting map.)*
- Select a publishing form from the list below and publish your rewritten paper.
    1. Have classmates, family members, neighbors, or others read your writing at school or home.
    2. Share your writing with others during a Share Time.
       (Refer to Reference 68 on page 103 for sharing guidelines.)
    3. Display your writing on a bulletin board or wall.
    4. Put your writing in the classroom library or in the school library for checkout.
    5. Send your writing as a letter or an e-mail to a friend or relative.
    6. Frame your writing by gluing it on colored construction paper and decorating it.
    7. Make a book of your writing for your classroom, your family, or others.
    8. Illustrate your writing and give it to others to read.
    9. Dramatize your writing in the form of a play, puppet show, or radio broadcast.
    10. Send your writing to be placed in a waiting room (doctor, veterinarian, dentist, etc.), senior-citizen center, or a nursing home.
    11. Send your writing to a school newspaper, local newspaper, or a magazine for publication.
    12. Make a videotape, cassette tape, or slide presentation of your writing.
    13. Choose another publishing form that is not listed.

LISTENING AND SPEAKING:

If you have chosen to investigate a topic introduced in this chapter, you now have the opportunity to share your results in one of the following ways:

1. You may relate your information orally.

2. You may read a written report.

3. You may place your report in the booklet without reading it aloud.

After share time, all written reports should be turned in to be placed in the class booklet titled "Space Trivia." You are encouraged to check out this class booklet so you can enjoy the reports again.

Spelling/Language Arts Connection:

1. Team up with a partner. Write as many homonyms as you can. Study the different spellings and compare the meanings. Then, compare your list with the lists of other students. Add new homonyms to your list.

2. Write a story, using as many homonyms from your list as possible. Use complex sentence structure with conjunctions, such as while, when, if, because, after, and since. Exchange stories with others in your class. Discuss whether the homonyms were used correctly. Illustrate your story.

3. Compare the types of verbs you used in your story. Did you use more regular or irregular verbs? Did you use any helping verbs? Make a chart listing the types of verbs you used.

START LESSON 8

Lesson 8

You will
- practice Jingle 21.
- do Classroom Practice 36.
- write an independent persuasive essay (WA 16).

LISTENING AND SPEAKING:

Recite It: Practice Jingle 21 in the Jingle Section on page 504.

GRAMMAR & WRITING CONNECTION:
Practice and Revised Sentences

Apply It: BUILDING AND EXPANDING SENTENCES

	Reference 130	A Guide for Using a Pattern 2 Core (Sn V-t DO) to Build and Expand Sentences

1. **SN** or **SP** (**subject**) Think of a noun or pronoun that you want to use as the subject. Write the noun or pronoun you have chosen as the subject of your sentence.

2. **V-t** (**verb-transitive**) The transitive verb tells what the subject does, and it is followed by a direct object. First, choose a verb for your sentence. Then, after you have chosen a direct object, verify that the verb is transitive and keep it as the verb of your Pattern 2 core.

3. **DO** (**direct object**) The direct object is a noun or pronoun after the verb that answers the question *whom* or *what*. The direct object receives the action of a transitive verb and does not mean the same thing as the subject. To help you think of a **direct object**, ask the question *WHAT* or *WHOM* after the verb. Write the direct object you have chosen in the predicate part of your sentence.

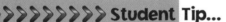 Student Tip...

Use your vocabulary words in your Practice and Revised Sentences. Use a thesaurus, synonym-antonym book, or a dictionary to help you develop your writing vocabulary.

Classroom Practice 36

It is time to practice the skills you are learning. You will use the classroom practice on the next page to apply these skills.

Writing Time

Write It: **WRITING ASSIGNMENT 16**

As you write a rough draft for your independent writing assignment, you will do two of the six steps in the writing process: prewriting and rough draft.

Writing Assignment 16

Purpose: To persuade

Type of Writing: Three-paragraph persuasive essay

Audience: Classmates

Writing Topics: The importance of knowing our family history/of wearing a seat belt
What makes camping/swimming fun
Benefits of playing sports/learning to dance/reading books
(Brainstorm for other ideas, individually or in groups.)

Special Instructions:

1. Follow the Prewriting and Rough Draft Checklists in References 47 and 49 on pages 62, 66.

2. Use References 116–121 on pages 196–200 to help you write your persuasive essay.

3. Use standard, time-order, or transition writing form. See Reference 70 on page 107.

4. Write in first or third person. See Reference 71 on page 108.
(First-person pronouns: *I, me, my, mine, we, us, our,* and *ours.*)
(Third-person pronouns: *he, his, him, she, her, hers, it, its, they, their, theirs,* and *them.*)

Note: Reference 57 on page 76 lists the steps in the writing process and the location of all the writing checklists.

Student Note: Some of your writing pieces will be selected for revision and editing later in the school year.

Classroom Practice 36

Name: _____

Date: _____

INDEPENDENT PRACTICE & REVISED SENTENCES

1. Write a Practice Sentence according to the labels you choose.
   Use **SN/SP V-t DO** as your main labels. You may use the other labels in any order and as many times as you wish in order to make a Practice Sentence. Chapter 7 labels for a Practice Sentence: **SN/SP, V-t, DO,** Adj, Adv, A, P, OP, PPA, C, HV, I, PNA

2. Write a Revised Sentence. Use the following revision strategies: *synonym (syn), antonym (ant), word change (wc), added word (add), deleted word (delete), or no change (nc).* Under each word, write the abbreviation of the revision strategy you use.

Labels:

Practice:

Revised:

Strategies:

Labels:

Practice:

Revised:

Strategies:

Labels:

Practice:

Revised:

Strategies:

LISTENING AND SPEAKING:

Lesson 9

You will
- practice Jingle 12.
- read and discuss a persuasive five-paragraph essay.
- plan and write rough draft for persuasive essay (WA 17).

Recite It: Practice Jingle 12 in the Jingle Section on page 501.

>>>>> Student Tip...

> Reviewing the transition words will help you apply them in your writing.

Learn It: **WRITING A FIVE-PARAGRAPH PERSUASIVE ESSAY**

As you learned earlier, a **persuasive essay** expresses an opinion and tries to convince the reader that this opinion is correct. Any time you do persuasive writing, whether it is a three- or five-paragraph essay, you will have three parts: the **Introduction**, the **Body**, and the **Conclusion**. The three parts will always be written in that order.

In a five-paragraph essay, there will be five paragraphs. The introduction forms the first paragraph; the body forms the second, third, and fourth paragraphs; and the conclusion forms the fifth paragraph of the essay. Although a title will be the first item appearing at the top of your essay, you will not finalize the title until you have finished writing the essay.

Learn It: **WRITING THE INTRODUCTION**
FOR A FIVE-PARAGRAPH PERSUASIVE ESSAY

The introduction forms the first paragraph. Notice that the word *Although* has been added to the beginning of the second sentence in the introduction. The transitional word *Although* is needed to help the sentences "flow together." Three sentences make up the introduction.

Reference 131 | **Writing the Introduction for a Five-Paragraph Persuasive Essay**

THE INTRODUCTION
Paragraph 1

Writing Topic: A new swimming pool for Madison County

Sentence 1 – Topic Sentence:
State your opinion in the topic sentence.
Madison County needs to build a new public swimming pool.

Sentence 2 – Reason Sentence:
Give a general reason why you think the topic sentence is true.
Although the old pool has served our county for many years, the time has come to plan for a modern facility.

Sentence 3 – General Number Sentence:
Use a general number word and restate the main idea in the topic sentence.
An up-to-date pool is needed for many reasons.

Learn It: **WRITING THE BODY**
FOR A FIVE-PARAGRAPH PERSUASIVE ESSAY

After the introduction, you are ready to write the body. The body of a five-paragraph essay contains three paragraphs. Each of the three persuasive points forms a new paragraph. Also, notice that each of the three paragraphs has two or more supporting sentences.

Reference 132

Writing the Body
for a Five-Paragraph Persuasive Essay

THE BODY
Paragraph 2

Sentence 4 – First Point:
Give your first reason to support your opinion.

> **The first reason we need a new pool is because our old pool is not as safe as it needs to be and may have to be closed before long.**

Sentences 5–7 – Supporting Sentences:
Give an example that supports and explains your first point. Write two or more supporting sentences.

> **We all have noticed that the paint and even the concrete are beginning to chip and fall from the sides of the pool. The last inspection by the state pointed out that a lot of repair on this pool is needed. These repairs could be very costly to the county.**

Paragraph 3

Sentence 8 – Second Point:
Give your second reason to support your opinion.

> **The second reason for the new pool is to provide summer swimming in a location that is convenient for all residents of the county.**

Sentences 9–11 – Supporting Sentences:
Give an example that supports and explains your second point. Write two or more supporting sentences.

> **The old pool is located on the north side of the county, and most of the growth in the last ten years has been on the east side. A new, larger pool could be built in the center of the county so everyone could get to it easily. All county residents would see an immediate benefit from this investment.**

Paragraph 4

Sentence 12 – Third Point:
Give your third reason to support your opinion.

> **The third reason we need a new pool is because the old Madison pool does not have all the facilities of a first-rate, modern pool.**

Sentences 13–15 – Supporting Sentences:
Give an example that supports and explains your third point. Write two or more supporting sentences.

> **It needs many extra features to make the pool area more inviting for county residents. For instance, the new pool in Stafford County has a double water slide and two fiberglass diving boards. Fayette County's new pool was built with large picnic and playground areas.**

Learn It: **WRITING THE CONCLUSION**
FOR A FIVE-PARAGRAPH PERSUASIVE ESSAY

The conclusion forms the fifth paragraph of a five-paragraph essay. The closing paragraph, or conclusion, should tie all the important points together with a restatement of the main idea and your final comments on it.

Two or more sentences make up the conclusion. The first sentence in the conclusion is called the **first concluding sentence**. To write this sentence, you should refer to the third sentence in the introduction. Using the general or specific number and topic as stated in that introductory sentence, you can write a similar concluding sentence. The **final concluding sentences** summarize one or more of the reasons stated.

Reference 133

Writing the Conclusion
for a Five-Paragraph Persuasive Essay

THE CONCLUSION
Paragraph 5

Sentence 16 – First Concluding Sentence:
The first concluding sentence is a restatement sentence that forcefully restates your original opinion in the topic sentence and usually starts with the words, *in conclusion*. Write one sentence.

> **In conclusion, there are several reasons why our county officials should seriously consider building a new swimming pool.**

Sentences 17–18 – Final Concluding Sentences:
These final sentences summarize one or more of the reasons stated. Write one or more sentences.

> **A new pool would be safer, more convenient for everybody, and would be more fun for us all. Madison County residents would be proud to have a modern pool for the twenty-first century.**

WRITING THE TITLE
Since there are many possibilities for titles, look at the topic and the three points listed about the topic. Use some of the words in the topic and write a phrase to tell what your paragraph is about. Your title can be short or long. Capitalize the first, last, and important words in your title.

Title: A Pool for the Twenty-First Century

Sample Five-Paragraph Persuasive Essay

A Pool for the Twenty-First Century

Madison County needs to build a new public swimming pool. Although the old pool has served our county for many years, the time has come to plan for a modern facility. An up-to-date pool is needed for many reasons.

The first reason we need a new pool is because our old pool is not as safe as it needs to be and may have to be closed before long. We all have noticed that the paint and even the concrete are beginning to chip and fall from the sides of the pool. The last inspection by the state pointed out that a lot of repair on this pool is needed. These repairs could be very costly to the county.

The second reason for the new pool is to provide summer swimming in a location that is convenient for all residents of the county. The old pool is located on the north side of the county, and most of the growth in the last ten years has been on the east side. A new, larger pool could be built in the center of the county so everyone could get to it easily. All county residents would see an immediate benefit from this investment.

The third reason we need a new pool is because the old Madison pool does not have all the facilities of a first-rate, modern pool. It needs many extra features to make the pool area more inviting for county residents. For instance, the new pool in Stafford County has a double water slide and two fiberglass diving boards. Fayette County's new pool was built with large picnic and playground areas.

In conclusion, there are several reasons why our county officials should seriously consider building a new swimming pool. A new pool would be safer, more convenient for everybody, and would be more fun for us all. Madison County residents would be proud to have a modern pool for the twenty-first century.

Write It: WRITING ASSIGNMENT 17

As you write a rough draft for your guided writing assignment, you will do two of the six steps in the writing process: prewriting and rough draft.

Writing Assignment 17

Purpose: To persuade

Type of Writing: Five-paragraph persuasive essay

Audience: Classmates

Writing Topics: Why public speaking/using good manners/learning to cook is important
Why everyone needs to pick up litter/needs to ride a bicycle
Why everyone should vote/keep their promises
(Brainstorm for other ideas, individually or in groups.)

Special Instructions:

1. Expand your three-paragraph persuasive essay from Writing Assignment 14 to a five-paragraph persuasive essay or choose a new topic from the ones listed above.

2. Follow the Prewriting and Rough Draft Checklists in References 47 and 49 on pages 62, 66.

3. Use References 131–133 on pages 229–231 to help you write your persuasive paragraph.

4. Use standard, time-order, or transition writing form.
See Reference 70 on page 107.

5. Write in first or third person. See Reference 71 on page 108.
(First-person pronouns: *I, me, my, mine, we, us, our, and ours.*)
(Third-person pronouns: *he, his, him, she, her, hers, it, its, they, their, theirs,* and *them.*)

Note: Reference 57 on page 76 gives the steps in the writing process and the location of all the writing checklists.

Writing Time

Apply It: **REVISE, EDIT, AND WRITE A FINAL PAPER**

Following the schedule below, you will revise and edit Writing Assignment 17. Then, you will write a final paper. Use the Chapter 7 Writing Evaluation Guide on the next page to check your final paper one last time.

Lesson 10

You will
- revise, edit, and write a final paper for WA 17.

Reference 55 | **Revising & Editing Schedule and Writing a Final Paper**

SPECIAL INSTRUCTIONS FOR REVISING AND EDITING (Steps 3-4 in the writing process):

- Use the Revising and Editing Checklists in References 51 and 53 as you revise and edit your rough draft.
- Follow the revising and editing schedule below as directed by your teacher.

  1. **Individual.** First, read your rough draft to yourself. Use the Revising Checklist in Reference 51 on page 69. Go through your paper, checking each item on the list and making revisions to your rough draft. Then, use the Editing Checklist in Reference 53 on page 71. Go through your paper again, checking each item on the list and editing your rough draft.

  2. **Partner.** Next, get with your editing partner. Work together on each partner's rough draft, one paper at a time. Read each rough draft aloud and revise and edit it together, using the Revising and Editing Checklists. (The author of the paper should be the one to make the corrections on his own paper.)

  3. **Group.** Finally, read the rough draft to a revision group for feedback. Each student should read his paper while the others listen and offer possible revising and editing suggestions. (The author will determine whether to make corrections from the revision group's suggestions.)

SPECIAL INSTRUCTIONS FOR FINAL PAPER (Step 5 in the writing process):

- Write your final paper, using the Final Paper Checklist in Reference 56 on page 75.
- Staple your writing papers in this order: the final paper on top, the rough draft in the middle, and the prewriting map on the bottom. Place the stapled papers in the Final Paper folder.

>>>>>>>>>> **Student Tip...**

1. Be tactful and helpful in your comments during revising and editing time. The purpose of any suggestion should be to improve the writer's rough draft.

2. As you make your final corrections, you have the choice of accepting or rejecting any suggestions made by your partners or your revision group.

3. Study Vocabulary Words and Analogies 17-19 for the chapter test in the next lesson.

4. If you need to improve your handwriting, refer to the Resource Tools Section on page 521 for information on writing legibly.

Chapter 7 Writing Evaluation Guide

Name:_____ Date:_____

ROUGH DRAFT CHECK

_____ 1. Did you write your rough draft in pencil?

_____ 2. Did you write the correct headings on the first seven lines of your paper?

_____ 3. Did you use extra wide margins and skip every other line?

_____ 4. Did you write a title at the end of your rough draft?

_____ 5. Did you place your edited rough draft in your Rough Draft folder?

REVISING CHECK

_____ 6. Did you identify the purpose, type of writing, and audience?

_____ 7. Did you check for a topic, topic sentence, and sentences supporting the topic?

_____ 8. Did you check sentences for the right order, and did you combine, rearrange, or delete sentences when necessary?

_____ 9. Did you check for a variety of simple, compound, and complex sentences?

_____ 10. Did you check for any left out, repeated, or unnecessary words?

_____ 11. Did you check for the best choice of words by replacing or deleting unclear words?

_____ 12. Did you check the content for interest and creativity?

_____ 13. Did you check the voice to make sure the writing says what you want it to say?

EDITING CHECK

_____ 14. Did you indent each paragraph?

_____ 15. Did you put an end mark at the end of every sentence?

_____ 16. Did you capitalize the first word of every sentence?

_____ 17. Did you check for all other capitalization mistakes?

_____ 18. Did you check for all punctuation mistakes?
(*commas, periods, apostrophes, quotation marks, underlining*)

_____ 19. Did you check for misspelled words and for incorrect homonym choices?

_____ 20. Did you check for incorrect spellings of plural and possessive forms?

_____ 21. Did you check for correct construction and punctuation of your sentences?

_____ 22. Did you check for usage mistakes? (*subject/verb agreement, a/an choices, contractions, verb tenses, pronoun/antecedent agreement, pronoun cases, degrees of adjectives, double negatives, etc.*)

_____ 23. Did you put your revised and edited paper in the Rough Draft folder?

FINAL PAPER CHECK

_____ 24. Did you write the final paper in pencil?

_____ 25. Did you center the title on the top line and center your name under the title?

_____ 26. Did you skip a line before starting the writing assignment?

_____ 27. Did you single-space, use wide margins, and write the final paper neatly?

_____ 28. Did you staple your papers in this order: final paper on top, rough draft in the middle, and prewriting map on the bottom? Did you put them in the Final Paper folder?

Writing Time

Hand It In: **WRITING ASSIGNMENT 17**

Get your stapled papers for Writing Assignment 17 from your Final Paper folder. Check to make sure they are in the correct order: the final paper on top, the rough draft in the middle, and the prewriting map on the bottom. Hand them in to your teacher.

LISTENING AND SPEAKING:

Oral Review Questions

Discuss It:

1. What word receives the action of the verb and answers the question what or whom?

2. What type of verb is used with a direct object?

3. What are the core parts of a Pattern 2 sentence?

4. What kind of verb makes the past tense by adding -ed, -d, or -t to the main verb?

5. What kind of verb makes the past tense by a vowel-spelling change?

6. What are the three simple verb tenses?

7. If there is a helping verb and main verb, which verb determines the tense?

8. What are the seven present-tense helping verbs?

9. What are the five past-tense helping verbs?

10. What are the two future-tense helping verbs?

11. What type of writing is used when your purpose is to express an opinion and to convince the reader that this opinion is correct?

12. What type of writing is used when your purpose is to inform, to give facts, to give directions, to explain, or to define something?

>>>>>>>>>>>>> **Student Tip...**

> **For information about test-taking strategies, refer to the Resource Tools Section on page 520.**

START LESSON 11

Lesson 11

You will

- hand in WA 17 for grading.
- respond to oral review questions.
- take Chapter 7 Test.

CHAPTER TEST

It is time to evaluate your knowledge of the skills you have learned in this chapter. Your teacher will give you the Chapter 7 Test to help you assess your progress.

START LESSON 1

Lesson 1

You will

- study new vocabulary;
  make Card 20;
  write own sentence using
  the vocabulary word.
- analyze new analogy;
  make Card 20;
  write own analogy.
- recite new jingle
  (Object Pronoun).
- identify object pronouns
  and Mixed Patterns 1-2.
- classify Introductory
  Sentences.
- do a Skill Builder to
  identify object pronouns.
- change verb tenses
  in paragraphs.
- do Classroom Practice 37.
- write in your journal.

LISTENING AND SPEAKING:

Vocabulary & Analogy Time

Learn It: Recite the new vocabulary and analogy words.

📖 * Reference 134	Vocabulary & Analogy Words

Word: sinister (sĭn'ĭstər)
  Definition: suggesting evil
  Synonym: threatening   **Antonym:** harmless
  Sentence: The unknown actor played a **sinister** role in the movie.

Analogy: break : brake :: sweet : suite
  Homonym relationship: Just as **break** is a homonym of **brake**,
              sweet is a homonym of **suite**.

Vocabulary Card 20: Record the vocabulary information above and write your own
                sentence, using the new word.

Analogy Card 20: Record the analogy information and write your own analogy,
              using the same relationship as the analogy above.

Jingle Time

Recite It: Recite the new jingle.

♪ Jingle 22	The Object Pronoun Jingle

There are seven object pronouns
That are easy as can be.
OBJECT PRONOUNS!
Me and **us**,
Him and **her**,
It and **them** and **you**.
Those are the object pronouns.

Grammar Time

Apply It: These Introductory Sentences are used to apply the new grammar
concepts taught below. Classify these sentences orally with your teacher.

Introductory Sentences	Chapter 8: Lesson 1

1. _____ My friend helps me in the afternoon with my homework.
2. _____ Will you ride on the chartered bus with Loren and me
         in December?
3. _____ My aunt and uncle are taking Chris and me to the
         Smoky Mountains.

Learn It: OBJECT PRONOUNS

What are the names of the two types of pronouns you have studied? The new type of pronoun you will learn is called the object pronoun. Recite the jingles to help you remember the different types of pronouns.

Reference 135 **Object Pronouns**

1. **Object pronouns** are used as *objects* of prepositions, direct *objects*, and indirect *objects*. Did you notice that all of these jobs have the word *object* in them?

2. The object pronouns are listed in your Object Pronoun Jingle: **me, us, him, her, it, them,** and **you.**

3. An object pronoun does not have an object pronoun label. An *object pronoun* keeps the **OP, DO,** or **IO** label that names its job.

OP	DO	IO

Example 1: Tom gave the keys to *him*.   **Example 2:** The speaker encouraged *us*.   **Example 3:** Dad gave *me* advice.

Other object pronouns can be substituted for the object pronouns in the examples in Reference 135.

Tom gave the keys **to me, to us, to her, to them,** or **to you.**

The speaker encouraged **me, him, her, them,** or **you.**

Dad gave **us, him, her, them,** or **you** advice.

Learn It: MIXED GRAMMAR PATTERNS 1–2

The sentences classified in this chapter will be Patterns 1 and 2. They are called **Mixed Patterns** because there are two different patterns from which to choose. Be alert to the parts of speech and where they are located in each sentence. Use the sentence cores to determine the patterns of the sentences.

Learn It: A SKILL BUILDER FOR A NOUN CHECK
WITH OBJECT PRONOUNS

The example below shows you what to do with object pronouns when you are identifying nouns for a Noun Check.

FOR A NOUN CHECK WITH OBJECT PRONOUNS

Circle the nouns in a Noun Check.

Sentence 1: Subject Noun (friend) *yes, it is a noun;*
Direct Object **me,** *no, it is a pronoun;*
Object of the Preposition (afternoon) *yes, it is a noun;*
Object of the Preposition (homework) *yes, it is a noun.*

Sentence 2: Subject Pronoun **you,** *no, it is a pronoun;*
Object of the Preposition (bus) *yes, it is a noun;*
Compound Object of the Preposition (Lauren) *yes, it is a noun;*
Compound Object of the Preposition **me,** *no, it is a pronoun;*
Object of the Preposition (December) *yes, it is a noun.*

Continued on next page. >>>

JOURNAL WRITING 20

Write an entry in your journal. Use Reference 9 on page 12 for ideas.

Continued from previous page.

Sentence 3: Compound Subject Noun *aunt*, *yes, it is a noun;*
Compound Subject Noun *uncle*, *yes, it is a noun;*
Compound Direct Object *Chris*, *yes, it is a noun;*
Compound Direct Object **me**, *no, it is a pronoun;*
Object of the Preposition *Smoky Mountains*, *yes, it is a noun.*

Skill Time

Learn It: **CHANGING VERBS TO DIFFERENT TENSES IN PARAGRAPHS**

 Reference 136 **Changing Present Tense to Past Tense in Paragraphs**

It is very important to study verb tenses because they tell the reader the time period in which an event takes place. If your tense is not consistent, it makes it difficult for your reader to know the time of an event. It takes knowledge and practice to work well with verb tenses. To check the tense of your writing, you must check each verb to make sure it is written in the tense you have chosen. It helps to read a paragraph aloud so you can train your ear to hear the tense of the verbs.

Paragraph 1: Present Tense

Troy's dad **keeps** a steady pace as he **throws** sacks of feed in the back of the farm truck. Sweat **pours** down Troy's face as he **struggles** to keep up with his dad. Troy **strains** as he **lifts** the fifty-pound sacks, one after another. He **is gaining** new respect for his dad as they **work** without a break.

To Check the Verb Tense

To make sure each verb in Paragraph 1 is written in the present tense, identify each verb and check for present tense. You must make sure there are no past-tense forms mixed with your present-tense verbs. It is best to separate the verbs from the paragraph so that you can check each verb individually. (*keeps, throws, pours, struggles, strains, lifts, is gaining, work*)

To Change the Verb Tense

If you want to change a present-tense paragraph to a past-tense paragraph, you must change each verb to past tense, one at a time. Again, it is best to separate the verbs from the paragraph so that you can check each verb individually. (*keeps-kept, throws-threw, pours-poured, struggles-struggled, strains-strained, lifts-lifted, is gaining-was gaining, work-worked*)

Paragraph 2: Past Tense

Troy's dad **kept** a steady pace as he **threw** sacks of feed in the back of the farm truck. Sweat **poured** down Troy's face as he **struggled** to keep up with his dad. Troy **strained** as he **lifted** the fifty-pound sacks, one after another. He **was gaining** new respect for his dad as they **worked** without a break.

 ## Classroom Practice 37

It is time to practice the skills you are learning. You will use the classroom practice on the next page to apply these skills.

Classroom Practice 37

Name:_____ Date:_____

GRAMMAR

▶ **Exercise 1:** Classify each sentence.

1. _____ Call me at my office for an appointment with the personnel manager.

2. _____ Good grief! That bottle fell on the floor and shattered into a million pieces!

3. _____ Would you come to the outdoor concert with Joy, Judy, and me?

SKILLS

▶ **Exercise 2:** Change the underlined present-tense verbs in Paragraph 1 to past-tense verbs in Paragraph 2.

Paragraph 1: Present Tense

Today my family and I **move** to another state because my dad **changes** jobs. My parents **plan** our move very carefully. They **pack** the household things while my sister and I **run** errands and **tell** our friends good-bye. My sister **cries** over her boyfriend, but I **cry** over the thought of leaving behind those big, delicious banana splits from E-zee Freezee. Our mom and dad **talk** with us about our mixed-up feelings, and they **assure** us that boys and banana splits **are** plentiful in our new town.

Paragraph 2: Past Tense

Yesterday my family and I _____ to another state because my dad _____ jobs. My parents _____ our move very carefully. They _____ the household things while my sister and I _____ errands and _____ our friends good-bye. My sister _____ over her boyfriend, but I _____ over the thought of leaving behind those big, delicious banana splits from E-zee Freezee. Our mom and dad _____ with us about our mixed-up feelings, and they _____ us that boys and banana splits _____ plentiful in our new town.

EDITING

▶ **Exercise 3:** Correct each mistake. **Editing Guide: End Marks: 5   Capitals: 5   Commas: 4   Apostrophes: 1 Homonyms: 6   A/An: 3   Subject-Verb Agreement: 2**

jackie loves entomology the study of insects jackies latest interest is the mantis because

of there familiar hunting pose mantises is often called praying mantises when an mantis raise

it's head and holds its front legs together it is actually waiting four food as soon as a insect comes

along the mantis snatches its pray and brings it too its mouth inn less than an second

START LESSON 2

Lesson 2

You will

- practice Jingle 22.
- classify Practice Sentences.
- do a Skill Builder.
- change mixed tenses to one tense in paragraphs.
- do Classroom Practice 38.

LISTENING AND SPEAKING:

Recite It: Practice Jingle 22 in the Jingle Section on page 504.

Apply It: Classify the Practice Sentences orally with your teacher.

Practice Sentences	Chapter 8: Lesson 2

1. _____ The shipwrecked crew showed courage in the face of adversity.
2. _____ Mr. Green was not impressed with Hal's feeble excuse for the lost textbook.
3. _____ The strong prescription relieved the patient's excruciating pain.

Using the sentences just classified, do a Skill Builder orally with your teacher.

1. **Identify the nouns in a Noun Check.**
2. **Identify the nouns as singular or plural.**
3. **Identify the nouns as common or proper.**
4. **Identify the complete subject and the complete predicate.**
5. **Identify the simple subject and the simple predicate.**
6. **Do a Vocabulary Check.**
7. **Do a Verb Chant.**

Skill Time

Learn It: **CHANGING MIXED TENSES TO PAST OR PRESENT TENSE IN A PARAGRAPH**

Reference 137	Changing Mixed Tenses to Past or Present Tense in a Paragraph

In writing, one of the most common mistakes made is mixing present-tense and past-tense verbs. Mixing verb tenses can make your writing awkward and confusing to your reader.

Mixed Tenses: The door **opened** and my mom **comes** into the kitchen and **grinned**.

In this sentence, *opened* and *grinned* are past tense, and *comes* is present tense. The shift from past to present and back to past leaves your reader wondering about the time these actions take place. To make your writing clear and effective, choose a verb tense for your writing and stick to it.

Past Tense: The door **opened** and my mom **came** into the kitchen and **grinned**.

Present Tense: The door **opens** and my mom **comes** into the kitchen and **grins**.

Directions: Change the underlined mixed-tense verbs in Paragraph 1 to <u>past-tense</u> verbs in Paragraph 2 and to <u>present-tense</u> verbs in Paragraph 3.

Paragraph 1: Mixed Tenses

Molly, our calico cat, **wakes** me early every morning. She **meows** hungrily and **rubbed** her purring body against my legs. I **stumble** to the pantry for her food; then I sleepily **filled** her bowl. I **yawned** as she **eats** slowly. Then, she carefully **washed** her face and paws. Finally, she **settles** down for a nap in the sun. I **yawn** again, and I **trudged** back upstairs to get dressed. Someone **has** to work in this family, and it sure **isn't** Molly!

Paragraph 2: Past Tense

Molly, our calico cat, <u>woke</u> me early every morning. She <u>meowed</u> hungrily and <u>rubbed</u> her purring body against my legs. I <u>stumbled</u> to the pantry for her food; then I sleepily <u>filled</u> her bowl. I <u>yawned</u> as she <u>ate</u> slowly. Then, she carefully <u>washed</u> her face and paws. Finally, she <u>settled</u> down for a nap in the sun. I <u>yawned</u> again, and I <u>trudged</u> back upstairs to get dressed. Someone <u>had</u> to work in this family, and it sure <u>wasn't</u> Molly!

Paragraph 3: Present Tense

Molly, our calico cat, <u>wakes</u> me early every morning. She <u>meows</u> hungrily and <u>rubs</u> her purring body against my legs. I <u>stumble</u> to the pantry for her food; then I sleepily <u>fill</u> her bowl. I <u>yawn</u> as she <u>eats</u> slowly. Then, she carefully <u>washes</u> her face and paws. Finally, she <u>settles</u> down for a nap in the sun. I <u>yawn</u> again, and I <u>trudge</u> back upstairs to get dressed. Someone <u>has</u> to work in this family, and it sure <u>isn't</u> Molly!

Classroom Practice 38

It is time to practice the skills you are learning. You will use the classroom practice on the next page to apply these skills.

SHURLEY ENGLISH

Classroom Practice 38

Name:_____ Date:_____

GRAMMAR

▶ **Exercise 1:** Classify each sentence.

1. _____ On Saturday, Dad and I will paint the walls and woodwork in my bedroom.

2. _____ Will you make a copy of these important papers before lunch?

3. _____ The old yellow taxi has completely stopped in the middle of the freeway.

SKILLS

▶ **Exercise 2:** Change the underlined mixed-tense verbs in Paragraph 1 to present-tense verbs in Paragraph 2.

Paragraph 1: Mixed Tense

　　　I **hear** the shatter of glass. Then I **heard** the groaning of wood as something heavy **moved** across the porch. I **huddle** on the couch, and terror **grips** me as my eyes **were glued** to the front door. The door **bursts** open, and a horrible swamp creature **stomped** into the house. He **drips** slime and swamp water all over the furniture and carpet. He **knocked** over lamps and chairs as he **reached** for the couch. Frantically, I **push** the remote control button. As the television **switched** off, I **vowed** never to watch another horror movie again!

Paragraph 2: Present Tense

　　　I _____ the shatter of glass. Then I _____ the groaning of wood as something heavy _____ across the porch. I _____ on the couch, and terror _____ me as my eyes _____ _____ to the front door. The door _____ open, and a horrible swamp creature _____ into the house. He _____ slime and swamp water all over the furniture and carpet. He _____ over lamps and chairs as he _____ for the couch. Frantically, I _____ the remote control button. As the television _____ off, I _____ never to watch another horror movie again!

EDITING

▶ **Exercise 3:** Correct each mistake. **Editing Guide: End Marks: 3　Capitals: 18　Commas: 4　Apostrophes: 2　Homonyms: 4　A/An: 1　Subject/Verb Agreement: 1　Underlining: 1　Misspelled Words: 2**

maurice sendak a american artist and auther is best known fore his illustrated childrens

books in 1962 he won the caldecot medal four his book where the wild things are he were

the sun of polish immigrants and recieved his formal art training at the art students league inn

new york city

LISTENING AND SPEAKING:
Vocabulary & Analogy Time

Learn It: Recite the new vocabulary and analogy words.

Reference 138	Vocabulary & Analogy Words

Word: allegiance (ə lēˈjəns)
  Definition: loyalty to a person or cause
  Synonym: devotion   **Antonym:** betrayal
  Sentence: He pledged his **allegiance** to his country.

Analogy: bulb : lamp :: drawer : dresser
  Part-to-whole relationship: Just as a **bulb** is a part of a **lamp**,
            a **drawer** is a part of a **dresser**.

Vocabulary Card 21: Record the vocabulary information above and write your own
            sentence, using the new word.

Analogy Card 21: Record the analogy information and write your own analogy,
            using the same relationship as the analogy above.

Jingle Time

Recite It: Practice Jingles 13–22 in the Jingle Section on pages 501–504.

Grammar Time

Apply It: Classify the Practice Sentences orally with your teacher.

Practice Sentences	Chapter 8: Lesson 3

1. _____ Jennifer had an acute pain in her side for an hour after lunch.
2. _____ Aunt Nadine worked diligently in her flower garden during
   the weekends.
3. _____ The smoke from the smokestack polluted the air with
   destructive chemicals.

START LESSON 3

Lesson 3

You will
- study new vocabulary; make Card 21; write own sentence using the vocabulary word.
- analyze new analogy; make Card 21; write own analogy.
- practice Jingles 13–22.
- classify Practice Sentences.
- do a Skill Builder.
- identify principal parts of verbs.
- do Classroom Practice 39.
- read and discuss Discovery Time.

Skill Builder

Using the sentences just classified, do a Skill Builder orally with your teacher.

1. **Identify the nouns in a Noun Check.**
2. **Identify the nouns as singular or plural.**
3. **Identify the nouns as common or proper.**
4. **Identify the complete subject and the complete predicate.**
5. **Identify the simple subject and the simple predicate.**
6. **Do a Vocabulary Check.**
7. **Do a Verb Chant.**

Skill Time

Learn It: **PRINCIPAL PARTS OF VERBS**

| Reference 139 | **Principal Parts of Verbs** |

Every main verb has four principal parts, or forms. The four principal parts of main verbs are called **present**, **past**, **past participle**, and **present participle**. All forms of a main verb are made by using one of the four principal parts. The names of the four principal parts are the same for regular and irregular verbs.

1. The **PRESENT** (principal part) has a present-tense main verb and no helping verb.
   (**Regular:** I <u>walk</u>. He <u>walks</u>. We <u>walk</u>.) (**Irregular:** I <u>eat</u>. He <u>eats</u>. We <u>eat</u>.)

2. The **PAST** (principal part) has a past-tense main verb and no helping verb.
   (**Regular:** I <u>walked</u>. He <u>walked</u>. We <u>walked</u>.) (**Irregular:** I <u>ate</u>. He <u>ate</u>. We <u>ate</u>.)

3. The **PAST PARTICIPLE** (principal part) has a main verb (past-participle form) and one of these helping verbs: *has, have,* or *had.*
   (**Regular:** I have <u>walked</u>. He has <u>walked</u>. We have <u>walked</u>. She had <u>walked</u>.)
   (**Irregular:** I have <u>eaten</u>. He has <u>eaten</u>. We have <u>eaten</u>. She had <u>eaten</u>.)

4. The **PRESENT PARTICIPLE** (principal part) has a main verb ending in -ing (present-participle form) and one of these helping verbs: *am, is, are, was,* or *were.*
   (**Regular:** I am <u>walking</u>. He is <u>walking</u>. We are <u>walking</u>. She was <u>walking</u>. They were <u>walking</u>.)
   (**Irregular:** I am <u>eating</u>. He is <u>eating</u>. We are <u>eating</u>. She was <u>eating</u>. They were <u>eating</u>.)

The **four principal parts** of the regular verb *walk:* **walk(s), walked, (has) walked, (is) walking**

The **four principal parts** of the irregular verb *eat:* **eat(s), ate, (has) eaten, (is) eating**

The present and past principal parts have no helping verbs. The principal parts for present participles and past participles <u>always</u> have helping verbs. Study the examples below and use the Verb Chart in Reference 126 on page 210 to help you learn the four principal parts of some regular and irregular main verbs.

	PRESENT	PAST	PAST PARTICIPLE		PRESENT PARTICIPLE	
IRREGULAR:	begin	began	(has, have, had)	begun	(am, is, are, was, were)	beginning
IRREGULAR:	break	broke	(has, have, had)	broken	(am, is, are, was, were)	breaking
REGULAR:	call	called	(has, have, had)	called	(am, is, are, was, were)	calling
REGULAR:	dance	danced	(has, have, had)	danced	(am, is, are, was, were)	dancing

Classroom Practice 39

It is time to practice the skills you are learning. You will use the classroom practice on the next page to apply these skills.

ENRICHMENT:

Jupiter is the fifth planet from the sun in our solar system. Jupiter is the largest planet and spins faster than any other planet. It is made mostly of hydrogen and helium. Galileo discovered four of Jupiter's sixteen moons in 1610.

Discovery Questions:
- What do you think Galileo was thinking when he spotted Jupiter's moons for the first time?
- What do you think he would say about all we have learned about the planets since his discoveries?
- What else do you think is in space? Explain.

Are you interested in learning more about Jupiter?

1. You may explore this topic further by using the resources listed below.
   Computer resources: Internet, encyclopedia software
   Library resources: encyclopedias, books, magazines, newspapers
   Home/community resources: books, interviews, newspapers, magazines

2. A Discovery Share Time is provided in Lesson 7 if you wish to share your investigation results. You may share orally, or you may prepare a written report. You will put your written report in a class booklet titled "Space Trivia." This booklet will be placed in the class library for everyone to enjoy.

Classroom Practice 39

Name:_____ Date:_____

GRAMMAR

▶ **Exercise 1:** Classify each sentence.

1. _____ Shhh! The baby is finally napping after a long day of sneezing and coughing!

2. _____ The doctors performed extensive research on the effects of the procedure.

SKILLS

▶ **Exercise 2:** Write the four principal parts of the following verbs: **give** and **clap**.

PRESENT	PAST	PAST PARTICIPLE	PRESENT PARTICIPLE
1._____	3._____	5. (**has**) _____	7. (**is**) _____
2._____	4._____	6. (**has**) _____	8. (**is**) _____

▶ **Exercise 3:** Change the underlined mixed-tense verbs in Paragraph 1 to present-tense verbs in Paragraph 2.

Paragraph 1: Mixed Tenses

My mom and dad **invited** their best friends to our house for the weekend. They **hadn't seen** their friends for years. They **recruited** me for major cleaning chores. I **kept telling** my mom that I **did** not **understand** all this fuss just because some people **were coming** to visit. I **cleaned** and **grumbled** all week. As their friends **were getting** out of their car, I **caught** my breath. They **had** a good-looking son, and he **looks** just my age! I **raced** into the house and **changed** clothes. Then, I quickly **checked** my hair again. Mom **said** that she **did** not **understand** all this fuss just because a boy **came** to visit.

Paragraph 2: Present Tense

My mom and dad _____ their best friends to our house for the weekend. They _____ _____ their friends for years. They _____ me for major cleaning chores. I _____ _____ my mom that I _____ not _____ all this fuss just because some people _____ _____ to visit. I _____ and _____ all week. As their friends _____ _____ out of their car, I _____ my breath. They _____ a good-looking son, and he _____ just my age! I _____ into the house and _____ clothes. Then, I quickly _____ my hair again. Mom _____ that she _____ not _____ all the fuss just because a boy_____ to visit.

EDITING

▶ **Exercise 4:** Correct each mistake.
   Editing Guide: End Marks: 3   Capitals: 21   Commas: 2   Homonyms: 2   A/An: 1   Misspelled Words: 2

after the british parliament passed the tea act an group of american colonists dresed like

native americans and borded ships in the boston harbor on december 16 1773 they through

chests of tee from the british east india company into the water to protest unfair taxes this act of

rebellion against england became known as the boston tea party

English Made Easy

LISTENING AND SPEAKING:
Vocabulary & Analogy Time

Learn It: Recite the new vocabulary and analogy words.

📖 Reference 140	Vocabulary & Analogy Words

Word: meager (mē'gər)
   Definition: not enough
   Synonym: sparse   **Antonym:** plentiful
   Sentence: He was still hungry after the **meager** meal.

Analogy: soccer : sport :: grizzly : bear
   Type or kind relationship: Just as **soccer** is a kind of **sport**,
                    grizzly is a kind of **bear**.

Vocabulary Card 22: Record the vocabulary information above and write your own
                 sentence, using the new word.

Analogy Card 22: Record the analogy information and write your own analogy,
             using the same relationship as the analogy above.

Recite It: Practice Jingles 3–11 in the Jingle Section on pages 499–500.

Apply It: Classify the Practice Sentences orally with your teacher.

Practice Sentences	Chapter 8: Lesson 4

1. _____ The approaching meteor caused global panic.
2. _____ A huge boulder rolled down the mountain and landed in the middle of the road.
3. _____ Julie's little sister cooked and seasoned the mashed potatoes very carefully.

START LESSON 4

Lesson 4

You will

- study new vocabulary; make Card 22; write own sentence using the vocabulary word.
- analyze new analogy; make Card 22; write own analogy.
- practice Jingles 3–11.
- classify Practice Sentences.
- do Classroom Practice 40.
- write in your journal.
- read and discuss Discovery Time.
- do a homework assignment.
- do Home Connection activity.

JOURNAL WRITING 21

Write an entry in your journal. Use Reference 9 on page 12 for ideas.

✏ Classroom Practice 40

It is time to practice the skills you are learning. You will use the classroom practice on the next page to apply these skills.

ENRICHMENT:

 ## Discovery Time

(Soviet) 1957 — Sputnik 1 was the first satellite launched by man, beginning the space age. The Soviet Union launched Sputnik 1 on October 4, 1957. It circled the Earth every 96 minutes and remained in orbit until 1958.

 **Discovery Questions:**

- What do you think the other nations of the world thought when they heard about the Soviet Union's launching of Sputnik 1?

- What do you think would be an exciting "first" in space exploration? Explain.

Are you interested in learning more about Sputnik I or the Soviet space program?

1. You may explore this topic further by using the resources listed below.
   Computer resources: Internet, encyclopedia software
   Library resources: encyclopedias, books, magazines, newspapers
   Home/community resources: books, interviews, newspapers, magazines

2. A Discovery Share Time is provided in Lesson 7 if you wish to share your investigation results. You may share orally, or you may prepare a written report. You will put your written report in a class booklet titled "Space Trivia." This booklet will be placed in the class library for everyone to enjoy.

Classroom Practice 40

Name:_____ Date:_____

GRAMMAR

▶ **Exercise 1:** Classify each sentence.

1. _____ Annie's room had a yellow bed, a yellow chair, and a yellow table.

2. _____ We rode from one side of the mountain to the other side through the tunnel.

3. _____ We congratulated him on his victory.

SKILLS

▶ **Exercise 2:** Write the four principal parts of the following verbs: **ride** and **explore**.

PRESENT	PAST	PAST PARTICIPLE	PRESENT PARTICIPLE
1._____	3._____	5. (**has**) _____	7. (**is**) _____
2._____	4._____	6. (**has**) _____	8. (**is**) _____

▶ **Exercise 3:** Change the underlined mixed-tense verbs in Paragraph 1 to past-tense verbs in Paragraph 2.

Paragraph 1: Mixed Tenses

Dad **sank** tiredly into his easy chair and **mopped** sweat from his forehead. His push mower **rests** beside the steps. Mom **watches** out the window anxiously until she **saw** the mailman. She **grinned** as the mailman **hands** the package to Dad. Then, Dad **cut** the tape and slowly **unwrapped** the box. Inside **is** a note and a key. Dad **rose** and **walks** outside. Mom and I **follow** him to the backyard. Dad **smiled** broadly as he **sees** a new riding lawn mower in the shed.

Paragraph 2: Past Tense

Dad _____ tiredly into his easy chair and _____ sweat from his forehead. His push mower _____ beside the steps. Mom _____ out the window anxiously until she _____ the mailman. She _____ as the mailman _____ the package to Dad. Then, Dad _____ the tape and slowly _____ the box. Inside _____ a note and a key. Dad _____ and _____ outside. Mom and I _____ him to the backyard. Dad _____ broadly as he _____ a new riding lawn mower in the shed.

EDITING

▶ **Exercise 4:** Correct each mistake in the present-tense paragraph. **Editing Guide: End Marks: 7   Capitals: 10   Commas: 2   Apostrophes: 1   Homonyms: 6   Subject-Verb Agreement: 3   Misspelled Words: 2**

there are too chores i doesn't enjoy taking out the garbage on trash day is one of them

taking out the garbage isnt very much fun usually the garbege can is to heavy fore me

washing the dishes is the second chore i dew not like when i wash dishes my hands get

wrinkled and looks like their a hunderd years old these chores makes me old before my time

SHURLEY ENGLISH

Homework 6

Complete this homework assignment on notebook paper.

1. Number your paper 1–3. Write Present Tense beside Number 1 and list the present-tense helping verbs. Write Past Tense beside Number 2 and list the past-tense helping verbs. Write Future Tense beside Number 3 and list the future-tense helping verbs.

   Present Tense:

   Past Tense:

   Future tense:

2. Number your paper 1–7. For each sentence, do four things. (1) Write the verb or verb phrase. (2) Identify the verb tense by writing **1** for present tense, **2** for past tense, or **3** for future tense. (3) Write the past-tense form. (4) Write **R** for Regular or **I** for Irregular.

	Verb Tense	Main Verb Past Tense Form	R or I
1. My sister works hard on her schoolwork.			
2. The children are talking loudly at recess.			
3. I have known Keisha for a long time.			
4. We will freeze vegetables from our garden.			
5. His compass fell out of his pocket.			
6. She drinks hot tea with her meals.			
7. Did you leave early for school?			

3. Write a Practice Sentence, using the labels below. You may expand the sentence by adding more labels.
   SN V-t A DO P A OP

Home Connection

Family Activity for Irregular Verbs

1. Complete the rhymes below with the correct form of the irregular verb in parentheses.

   For dinner, my brother (bring) the huge catfish he had (catch).

   The little girl (cry) when her little fishy (die).

   We were happy when we were (tell) that our old car had (sell).

   A can of paint was (spill) on the deck that Dad just (build).

   When the bride got (marry), a bouquet of roses she (carry).

   The bed was (make), and the bills were (pay).

2. Divide into two teams. Each team should make up rhymes that are similar to the ones above. Then, each team should read its rhymes, and the other team should tell the correct verb forms.

3. Divide into teams and divide the irregular-verb chart (Reference 126 on page 210) into as many sections as teams. Each team, using its designated verb section, will recite a present-tense verb, and the other team(s) must respond by reciting the verb forms for the past tense, present participle, and past participle.

Answers for number 1: brought-caught, cried-died, told-sold, spilt-built, married-carried, made-paid

LISTENING AND SPEAKING:

Grammar Time

Lesson 5

You will
- classify Practice Sentences.
- do Chapter Checkup 41.
- write in your journal.

Apply It: Classify the Practice Sentences orally with your teacher.

Practice Sentences	Chapter 8: Lesson 5

1. _____ Jody's tall glass of tea tipped over and spilled onto the floor.
2. _____ Carlos set a new record in the distance relay over the weekend.
3. _____ The new cashier would not take a check on my account.

JOURNAL WRITING 22

Write an entry in your journal. Use Reference 9 on page 12 for ideas.

✏ Chapter Checkup 41

It is time for a checkup of the skills you have learned in this chapter. You will use the chapter checkup on the next page to evaluate your progress.

Chapter 8 Checkup 41

Name:_____ Date:_____

GRAMMAR

▶ **Exercise 1:** Classify each sentence.

1. _____ The workers cleaned and painted the exterior of the tall building.

2. _____ He went with Rosa and me to the airport early yesterday.

3. _____ Would you like butter and syrup on your pancakes?

SKILLS

▶ **Exercise 2:** Write the four principal parts of the following verbs: **sleep** and **watch**.

PRESENT	PAST	PAST PARTICIPLE	PRESENT PARTICIPLE
1. _____	3. _____	5. (has) _____	7. (is) _____
2. _____	4. _____	6. (has) _____	8. (is) _____

▶ **Exercise 3:** Change the underlined mixed-tense verbs in Paragraph 1 to past-tense verbs in Paragraph 2.

Paragraph 1: Mixed Tenses

    I **don't like** baby-sitting Jeffrey Logan. He **is** forty pounds of human tornado. Jeffrey **does** unbelievable things. He **bounces** from his bed and **lands** on top of the bookcase. He **fishes** in the family aquarium for Mr. Logan's prized tiger fish. He even **smears** peanut butter and jelly sandwiches all over Mrs. Logan's living room. He also **does** fifty other things that I **try** to forget. I **am** glad Jeffrey **doesn't live** at my house.

Paragraph 2: Past Tense

    I _____ _____ baby-sitting Jeffrey Logan. He _____ forty pounds of human tornado. Jeffrey _____ unbelievable things. He _____ from his bed and _____ on top of the bookcase. He _____ in the family aquarium for Mr. Logan's prized tiger fish. He even _____ peanut butter and jelly sandwiches all over Mrs. Logan's living room. He also _____ fifty other things that I _____ to forget. I _____ glad Jeffrey _____ _____ at my house.

EDITING

▶ **Exercise 4:** Correct each mistake.
    Editing Guide: End Marks: 4 Capitals: 14 Commas: 5 Apostrophes: 1 Homonyms: 2 A/An: 1 Periods: 2

    ms baptise the schools french teacher and her students visited the eiffel tower and other

sights in paris france in july they had an blast while ms baptise checked everyone into the hotel

sum students tried too order lunch in french they ended up with snail soup and fish eggs

Writing Time

Write It: WRITING ASSIGNMENT 18

Lesson 6

You will

- conference with teacher about WA 17.
- write a creative writing piece for WA 18.

Writing Assignment 18 : Creative Expressions

Purpose: To entertain

Type of Writing: Creative

Audience: Classmates, relatives, or friends

Choose one of the writing topics below.

1. Describe what it would be like to live in a city underwater/in space?
2. You have won a fabulous trip anywhere in the world with all expenses paid for you and a guest. Where would you go, who would you take, and what would you do?
3. Write a poem about new places or about new friends or about a topic of your choice.

Special Instructions:

1. A prewriting map is not required for this creative-writing assignment.
2. Follow the Rough Draft Checklist in Reference 49 on page 66.
3. Put your creative-writing paper in your Rough Draft folder when you have finished.

Note: Reference 57 on page 76 gives the steps in the writing process and the location of all the writing checklists..

 **Student Tip...**

> **For more information about writing poetry, look at Chapter 18 on pages 456–474.**

Conference Time

Discuss It: TEACHER-STUDENT CONFERENCES FOR WRITING ASSIGNMENT 17

Meet with your teacher to discuss Writing Assignment 17.
After the conference, place this group of papers in your Publishing folder.

START LESSON 7

Lesson 7

You will

- publish WA 17.
- participate in Discovery Share Time.
- write an independent persuasive essay (WA 19).

Publish It: **WRITING ASSIGNMENT 17**

Choose a publishing form and publish Writing Assignment 17. After rewriting your paper for publication, give the stapled papers (evaluation guide, graded final paper, rough draft, and prewriting map) to your teacher to be placed in your Writing Portfolio.

 Reference 67 | **Publishing Checklist for Step 6 in the Writing Process**

The sixth step in the writing process is called publishing. Publishing is sharing your writing with others. With so many forms of publishing available, finding a match for every project and personality is easy.

At times, a written work is best read aloud. Other times, the biggest impact is made when a written work is read silently. You can also use media sources to enhance any publication.

SPECIAL INSTRUCTIONS FOR PUBLISHING:

- Rewrite the graded paper in ink or type it on a computer, correcting any marked errors. *(Do not display or publish papers that have marked errors or grades on them.)*
- Give your teacher the set of stapled papers to place in your Writing Portfolio. *(Stapled papers: evaluation guide, graded final paper, rough draft, and prewriting map.)*
- Select a publishing form from the list below and publish your rewritten paper.
    1. Have classmates, family members, neighbors, or others read your writing at school or home.
    2. Share your writing with others during a Share Time. *(Refer to Reference 68 on page 103 for sharing guidelines.)*
    3. Display your writing on a bulletin board or wall.
    4. Put your writing in the classroom library or in the school library for checkout.
    5. Send your writing as a letter or an e-mail to a friend or relative.
    6. Frame your writing by gluing it on colored construction paper and decorating it.
    7. Make a book of your writing for your classroom, your family, or others.
    8. Illustrate your writing and give it to others to read.
    9. Dramatize your writing in the form of a play, puppet show, or radio broadcast.
    10. Send your writing to be placed in a waiting room (doctor, veterinarian, dentist, etc.), senior-citizen center, or a nursing home.
    11. Send your writing to a school newspaper, local newspaper, or a magazine for publication.
    12. Make a videotape, cassette tape, or slide presentation of your writing.
    13. Choose another publishing form that is not listed.

LISTENING AND SPEAKING:

If you have chosen to investigate a topic introduced in this chapter, you now have the opportunity to share your results in one of the following ways:

1. You may relate your information orally.

2. You may read a written report.

3. You may place your report in the booklet without reading it aloud.

After share time, all written reports should be turned in to be placed in the class booklet titled "Space Trivia." You are encouraged to check out this class booklet so you can enjoy the reports again.

Writing Time

Write It: **WRITING ASSIGNMENT 19**

As you write a rough draft for your independent writing assignment, you will do two of the six steps in the writing process: prewriting and rough draft.

Writing Assignment ⟨19⟩

Purpose: To persuade

Type of Writing: Five-paragraph persuasive essay

Audience: Classmates

Writing Topics: Why homes should have a smoke detector/air conditioning/a basement
The importance of encouraging others/spending time with my family
Why everyone should go on a cruise/ spend time outdoors
(Brainstorm for other ideas, individually or in groups.)

Special Instructions:

1. Follow the Prewriting and Rough Draft Checklists in References 47 and 49 on pages 62, 66.

2. Use References 131–133 on pages 229–231 to help you write your persuasive essay.

3. Use standard, time-order, or transition writing form. See Reference 70, page 107.

4. Write in first or third person. See Reference 71, page 108.
(First-person pronouns: *I, me, my, mine, we, us, our,* and *ours.*)
(Third-person pronouns: *he, his, him, she, her, hers, it, its, they, their, theirs,* and *them.*)

Note: Reference 57 on page 76 gives the steps in the writing process and the location of all the writing checklists.

Student Note: Some of your writing pieces will be selected for revision and editing later in the school year.

START LESSON 8

Lesson 8

You will

- practice Jingle 12.
- read and discuss descriptive paragraphs.
- plan and write rough draft for descriptive paragraph (WA 20).

>> **Student Tip...**

Reviewing the transition words will help you apply them in your writing.

LISTENING AND SPEAKING:

Recite It: Practice Jingle 12 in the Jingle Section on page 501.

Learn It: **DESCRIPTIVE WRITING**

An artist paints a picture on canvas with paint. A descriptive writer paints a picture on paper with words. Both the artist and writer must select what they will include in their picture.

Reference 141	**Descriptive Writing**

Descriptive writing shows the reader what is being described. It does not just tell him about it. Descriptive writing paints a picture on paper with words. Even though you can use description in expository, narrative, and persuasive writing, sometimes you are asked to write only a descriptive piece of writing. Then, you must understand that a descriptive paragraph gives a detailed picture of a person, place, thing, or idea.

A descriptive paragraph will usually start with an overall impression of what you are describing. That will be your topic sentence. Then, you will add supporting sentences that give details about the topic. To make a description clear and vivid, these detail sentences should include as much information as possible about how the topic looks, sounds, feels, tastes, or smells. The sensory details that you include will depend on what you are describing. Since all the senses are not significant in all situations, the following guidelines about descriptive writing will give you the types of details that you should consider when you are describing certain topics.

Descriptive Guidelines

WHEN DESCRIBING PEOPLE

Use these types of details:

1. Appearance, walk, voice, mannerisms, gestures, personality traits
2. Any special situations related to the person being described
3. Striking details that make that person stand out

WHEN DESCRIBING PLACES

Use these types of details:

1. Sensory details that create a clear picture of the place's physical features (colors, textures, sights, shapes, age, sounds, smells, and feelings)
2. Unusual or unique features
3. Special circumstances related to the place
4. Why the place is special

WHEN DESCRIBING ANIMALS, PLANTS, OR OBJECTS

Use these types of details:

1. Sensory details that create a clear picture of the animal, plant, or object's physical features (colors, textures, sights, shapes, age, sounds, smells, and feelings)
2. Unusual or unique features
3. Special situations related to the animal, plant, or object
4. Why the animal, plant, or object is special

WHEN DESCRIBING NATURE

Use these types of details:

1. Special features of the season or scene
2. Sensory details that create a clear picture of the scene (colors, textures, sights, sounds, smells, and feelings)
3. Any plants, insects, birds, or other animals in the scene
4. Any special conditions related to the scene

Continued on next page. >>>

Reference 141 continued from previous page.

WHEN DESCRIBING AN INCIDENT OR EVENT	WHEN DESCRIBING A FEELING
Use these types of details: 1. The order in which things happen 2. Facts that help the action move along smoothly from a beginning to an ending 3. Any of the who, what, when, where, why, and how questions 4. Sensory details that create a clear picture of the incident or event (sights, sounds, smells, and feelings)	**Use these types of details:** 1. The cause of this feeling or emotion 2. Physical signs that occur as a result of this feeling (smile, frown, tears, hugs, sobs, laughter, red face) 3. Figurative language for comparison (similes, metaphors, personification)

Learn It: **WRITING A DESCRIPTIVE PARAGRAPH**

Reference 142 — Writing a Descriptive Paragraph

Writing Topic: A day in the summer heat

Sentence 1 – Topic Sentence:
Introduces what is being described.

It was in the hottest part of the summer, and our air conditioner was broken.

Following Sentences – Body of Paragraph:
Uses some of the descriptive details in Reference 141.

Our whole household was in a sour, irritable mood. The ceiling fans groaned noisily and tried desperately to circulate the hot, humid air. The doors and windows were open, and big black flies buzzed in and out at will. Even my little puppy sprawled in the doorway, trying to catch a faint breeze. Dad and my brother were outside, working on the air conditioner. As they finally walked wearily through the open door, my brother tripped over the sleeping puppy and knocked over Mom's lamp. As the lamp crashed to the floor, my poor puppy yelped and howled loudly, scrambling frantically under the couch. All the noise woke the baby from her nap, and she started screaming. As everyone dashed in all directions, it was a hot, sweltering, noisy madhouse! After everyone had calmed down, my dad looked sympathetically at his heat-drenched family. He pulled himself up to his full height, squared his shoulders, and walked to the telephone. He called the air-conditioner repairman. Then, Dad loaded us all in the car for a trip to the ice-cream shop.

Last Sentence – Concluding Sentence:
Restates or relates back to the topic sentence.

For the rest of the afternoon, we left the heat and worries far behind as we enjoyed our "cool" family time.

A Sample Descriptive Paragraph

A Heated Problem

It was in the hottest part of the summer, and our air conditioner was broken. Our whole household was in a sour, irritable mood. The ceiling fans groaned noisily and tried desperately to circulate the hot, humid air. The doors and windows were open, and big black flies buzzed in and out at will. Even my little puppy sprawled in the doorway, trying to catch a faint breeze. Dad and my brother were outside, working on the air conditioner. As they finally walked wearily through the open door, my brother tripped over the sleeping puppy and knocked over Mom's lamp. As the lamp crashed to the floor, my poor puppy yelped and howled loudly, scrambling frantically under the couch. All the noise woke the baby from her nap, and she started screaming. As everyone dashed in all directions, it was a hot, sweltering, noisy madhouse! After everyone had calmed down, my dad looked sympathetically at his heat-drenched family. He pulled himself up to his full height, squared his shoulders, and walked to the telephone. He called the air-conditioner repairman. Then, Dad loaded us all in the car for a trip to the ice-cream shop. For the rest of the afternoon, we left the heat and worries far behind as we enjoyed our "cool" family time.

Discuss It:

The example shows how the writer followed the Descriptive Writing Guidelines to write a descriptive paragraph.

What is the writing topic?

What title did the author decide to use?

What is being described in the topic sentence?

In the body of the descriptive paragraph, the writer uses sights, sounds, and feelings to describe a day in the hottest part of the summer when the air conditioner at her house was broken. What are some of the examples of what she sees, hears, and feels?

Which sentence do you think is the most descriptive?

Compare the topic sentence to the concluding sentence. How do they relate to each other?

Write It: **WRITING ASSIGNMENT 20**

As you write a rough draft for your guided writing assignment, you will do two of the six steps in the writing process: prewriting (descriptive guidelines) and rough draft.

Writing Assignment 20

Purpose: To describe

Type of Writing: Descriptive paragraph

Audience: Classmates

Writing Topics: An amazing person/sunrise/night sky
An unforgettable dream/person/outing
My room/a game/city scene
(Brainstorm for other ideas, individually or in groups.)

Special Instructions:

1. Follow the Prewriting and Rough Draft Checklists in References 47 and 49 on pages 62, 66.

2. Make a prewriting map using the descriptive guidelines in References 141–142 on pages 256–257 to help you write your descriptive paragraph.

3. Write in first or third person. See Reference 71, page 108.
   (First-person pronouns: *I, me, my, mine, we, us, our,* and *ours.*)
   (Third-person pronouns: *he, his, him, she, her, hers, it, its, they, their, theirs,* and *them.*)

Note: Reference 57 on page 76 gives the steps in the writing process and the location of all the writing checklists.

Writing Time

Apply It: **REVISE, EDIT, AND WRITE A FINAL PAPER**

Following the schedule below, you will revise and edit Writing Assignment 20. Then, you will write a final paper. Use the Chapter 8 Writing Evaluation Guide on the next page to check your final paper one last time.

Lesson 9

You will
- revise, edit, and write a final paper for WA 20.

Reference 55 | **Revising & Editing Schedule and Writing a Final Paper**

SPECIAL INSTRUCTIONS FOR REVISING AND EDITING (Steps 3-4 in the writing process):
- Use the Revising and Editing Checklists in References 51 and 53 as you revise and edit your rough draft.
- Follow the revising and editing schedule below as directed by your teacher.
  1. **Individual.** First, read your rough draft to yourself. Use the Revising Checklist in Reference 51 on page 69. Go through your paper, checking each item on the list and making revisions to your rough draft. Then, use the Editing Checklist in Reference 53 on page 71. Go through your paper again, checking each item on the list and editing your rough draft.
  2. **Partner.** Next, get with your editing partner. Work together on each partner's rough draft, one paper at a time. Read each rough draft aloud and revise and edit it together, using the Revising and Editing Checklists. (The author of the paper should be the one to make the corrections on his own paper.)
  3. **Group.** Finally, read the rough draft to a revision group for feedback. Each student should read his paper while the others listen and offer possible revising and editing suggestions. (The author will determine whether to make corrections from the revision group's suggestions.)

SPECIAL INSTRUCTIONS FOR FINAL PAPER (Step 5 in the writing process):
- Write your final paper, using the Final Paper Checklist in Reference 56 on page 75.
- Staple your writing papers in this order: the final paper on top, the rough draft in the middle, and the prewriting map on the bottom. Place the stapled papers in the Final Paper folder.

>>>>>>>>> **Student Tip...**

1. Be tactful and helpful in your comments during revising and editing time. The purpose of any suggestion should be to improve the writer's rough draft.

2. As you make your final corrections, you have the choice of accepting or rejecting any suggestions made by your partners or your revision group.

3. Study Vocabulary Words and Analogies 20-22 for the chapter test in the next lesson.

4. If you need to improve your handwriting, refer to the Resource Tools Section on page 521 for information on writing legibly.

Chapter 8 Writing Evaluation Guide

Name:_____ Date:_____

ROUGH DRAFT CHECK

_____ 1. Did you write your rough draft in pencil?

_____ 2. Did you write the correct headings on the first seven lines of your paper?

_____ 3. Did you use extra wide margins and skip every other line?

_____ 4. Did you write a title at the end of your rough draft?

_____ 5. Did you place your edited rough draft in your Rough Draft folder?

REVISING CHECK

_____ 6. Did you identify the purpose, type of writing, and audience?

_____ 7. Did you check for a topic, topic sentence, and sentences supporting the topic?

_____ 8. Did you check sentences for the right order, and did you combine, rearrange, or delete sentences when necessary?

_____ 9. Did you check for a variety of simple, compound, and complex sentences?

_____ 10. Did you check for any left out, repeated, or unnecessary words?

_____ 11. Did you check for the best choice of words by replacing or deleting unclear words?

_____ 12. Did you check the content for interest and creativity?

_____ 13. Did you check the voice to make sure the writing says what you want it to say?

EDITING CHECK

_____ 14. Did you indent each paragraph?

_____ 15. Did you put an end mark at the end of every sentence?

_____ 16. Did you capitalize the first word of every sentence?

_____ 17. Did you check for all other capitalization mistakes?

_____ 18. Did you check for all punctuation mistakes?
(commas, periods, apostrophes, quotation marks, underlining)

_____ 19. Did you check for misspelled words and for incorrect homonym choices?

_____ 20. Did you check for incorrect spellings of plural and possessive forms?

_____ 21. Did you check for correct construction and punctuation of your sentences?

_____ 22. Did you check for usage mistakes? (subject/verb agreement, a/an choices, contractions, verb tenses, pronoun/antecedent agreement, pronoun cases, degrees of adjectives, double negatives, etc.)

_____ 23. Did you put your revised and edited paper in the Rough Draft folder?

FINAL PAPER CHECK

_____ 24. Did you write the final paper in pencil?

_____ 25. Did you center the title on the top line and center your name under the title?

_____ 26. Did you skip a line before starting the writing assignment?

_____ 27. Did you single-space, use wide margins, and write the final paper neatly?

_____ 28. Did you staple your papers in this order: final paper on top, rough draft in the middle, and prewriting map on the bottom? Did you put them in the Final Paper folder?

Hand It In: WRITING ASSIGNMENT 20

Get your stapled papers for Writing Assignment 20 from your Final Paper folder. Check to make sure they are in the correct order: the final paper on top, the rough draft in the middle, and the prewriting map (descriptive guidelines) on the bottom. Hand them in to your teacher.

LISTENING AND SPEAKING:
Oral Review Questions

Discuss It:

1. What are the seven object pronouns?

2. What are the core parts of a Pattern 2 sentence?

3. What kind of verb makes the past tense by adding -ed to the main verb?

4. What kind of verb makes the past tense by a vowel-spelling change?

5. What are the three simple verb tenses?

6. If there is a helping verb and main verb, which verb determines the tense?

7. What are the seven present-tense helping verbs?

8. What are the five past-tense helping verbs?

9. What are the two future-tense helping verbs?

10. Name the four principal parts of a verb?

11. Which two principal parts have helping verbs?

12. Which two principal parts do not have helping verbs?

13. What type of writing is used when your purpose is to paint a picture with words?

14. What type of writing is used when your purpose is to express an opinion and to convince the reader that this opinion is correct?

15. What type of writing is used when your purpose is to inform, to give facts, to give directions, to explain, or to define something?

>>>>>>>>>>>>>> Student Tip...

> For information about test-taking strategies, refer to the **Resource Tools Section on page 520.**

Review It: GOALS

Review the goals you wrote in your Goal Booklet at the beginning of the school year. Discuss your progress with your teacher or a student partner. Then, write a paragraph in your Goal Booklet that tells how well you are meeting your short-term goals. Give examples that support your evaluation of your progress. Next, write another paragraph to evaluate your long-term goals. Tell whether you want to change them or keep them the same. Give reasons to support either choice. Finally, return your Goal Booklet to your teacher when you have finished.

START LESSON 10

Lesson 10

You will

- hand in WA 20 for grading.
- respond to oral review questions.
- take Chapter 8 Test.
- discuss and evaluate goals.
- write a paragraph in your goal booklet.

CHAPTER TEST

It is time to evaluate your knowledge of the skills you have learned in this chapter. Your teacher will give you the Chapter 8 Test to help you assess your progress.

Lesson 1

You will

- study new vocabulary; make Card 23; write own sentence using the vocabulary word.
- analyze new analogy; make Card 23; write own analogy.
- recite new jingle (Indirect Object).
- identify indirect objects and Pattern 3.
- classify Introductory Sentences.
- do a Skill Builder to identify indirect objects.
- write in your journal.

LISTENING AND SPEAKING:

Vocabulary & Analogy Time

Learn It: Recite the new vocabulary and analogy words.

 | **Reference 143** | **Vocabulary & Analogy Words**

Word: immaculate (ĭ mǎk' yə lĭt)
   Definition: perfectly clean
   Synonym: spotless   **Antonym:** filthy
   Sentence: Our grandmother was an **immaculate** housekeeper.

Analogy: error : mistake :: independence : freedom
   Synonym relationship: Just as **error** means nearly the same thing as **mistake, independence** means nearly the same thing as **freedom.**

Vocabulary Card 23: Record the vocabulary information above and write your own sentence, using the new word.

Analogy Card 23: Record the analogy information and write your own analogy, using the same relationship as the analogy above.

Jingle Time

Recite It: Recite the new jingle.

♪ | **Jingle 23** | **The Indirect Object Jingle**

Indirect, oh, indirect, oh, indirect object.
Give me that indirect, oh, indirect, oh, indirect object.

An indirect object is a NOUN or a PRONOUN
That receives what the direct, the direct object names.
An indirect object is found between the **verb, verb-transitive,**
And the **direct object.**
    To find the indirect object,   *(sha-bop)*
    Ask **TO WHOM** or **FOR WHOM**   *(sha-bop)*
    After the direct object.   *(sha-bop)*

An indirect, indirect, indirect, indirect, yeah!
An **INDIRECT OBJECT!**
    Just give me that indirect, oh, indirect, oh, indirect object.
    Give me that indirect, oh, indirect, oh, indirect object.
    Give me that object, oh, indirect, oh, indirect object.
An **INDIRECT OBJECT!**

Apply It: These Introductory Sentences are used to apply the new grammar concepts taught below. Classify these sentences orally with your teacher.

Introductory Sentences — Chapter 9: Lesson 1

1. _____ Grandfather built me a birdhouse.
2. _____ During the summer, my grandfather built me an elaborate birdhouse.
3. _____ I handed the students five study questions for their history quiz on Friday.

Learn It: **INDIRECT OBJECTS**

A Pattern 1 sentence has only one noun and an action verb as the sentence core. A Pattern 2 sentence has two nouns and an action verb as the sentence core. The new sentence pattern, Pattern 3, has three nouns and an action verb as the sentence core.

Reference 144 — Indirect Object and Pattern 3

1. An **indirect object** is a noun or pronoun.

2. An indirect object receives what the direct object names. The indirect object tells *to whom* or *for whom or to what or for what* the action is done. It does not receive the action of the verb.

3. An indirect object is located between the verb-transitive and the direct object.

4. To find an indirect object, ask TO WHOM or FOR WHOM, TO WHAT or FOR WHAT after the direct object. Use WHOM when the indirect object is a person. Use WHAT when the indirect object is a place, thing, or idea.

5. An *indirect object* is labeled with the abbreviation **IO**.

6. A Pattern 3 sentence has a subject noun, transitive verb, indirect object, and a direct object as its core. A Pattern 3 sentence is labeled **SN V-t IO DO P3**. A Pattern 3 sentence has three noun jobs in its pattern: the subject noun, the indirect-object noun, and the direct-object noun. *(If the subject is a subject pronoun, it is labeled as a pronoun in the sentence, but the pattern is still identified as SN V-t IO DO P3.)*

7. A review:
   Pattern 1 is **SN V**. It has a noun-verb (**N V**) core.
   Pattern 2 is **SN V-t DO**. It has a noun-verb-noun (**N V N**) core.
   Pattern 3 is **SN V-t IO DO**. It has a noun-verb-noun-noun (**N V N N**) core.

   The location of each noun determines its job in a sentence. Only certain noun jobs form the pattern parts of a sentence. For each pattern, the order of the core nouns does not change. A noun that is an object of the preposition is not part of a sentence pattern.

Continued on next page. >>>

Reference 144 continued from previous page.

Question and Answer Flow for the Practice Sentence, adding Indirect Objects

Practice Sentence: Aaron gave me a CD.

1. Who gave me a CD? **Aaron - SN**
2. What is being said about Aaron?
   Aaron gave - V
3. Aaron gave what? **CD - verify the noun**
4. Does CD mean the same thing as Aaron? **No.**
5. **CD - DO**
6. **Gave - V-t**
7. Aaron gave CD to whom?
   me - IO (Say: *me - indirect object.*)
8. **A - A**

9. **SN V-t IO DO P3** (Say: *Subject Noun, Verb-transitive, Indirect Object, Direct Object, Pattern 3.*)
10. Skill Check
11. Verb-transitive - check again
12. **No prepositional phrases**
13. **Period, statement, declarative sentence**
14. Go back to the verb. Divide the complete subject from the complete predicate.
15. Is this sentence in a natural or inverted order? **Natural - no change.**

SN V-t
IO DO P3   SN   V-t IO A DO
Aaron / gave me a CD. D

Discuss It:

1. What is the pattern in a Pattern 3 sentence?
2. What are the core parts of a Pattern 3 sentence?
3. What parts of speech are used in a Pattern 3 sentence?

Learn It: **A SKILL BUILDER FOR A NOUN CHECK WITH INDIRECT OBJECTS**

The example below shows you what to do with indirect objects when you are identifying nouns for a Noun Check

Skill Builder

FOR A NOUN CHECK WITH INDIRECT OBJECTS

Circle the nouns in a Noun Check.

Sentence 1: Subject Noun (grandfather) *yes, it is a noun;*
Indirect Object me, *no, it is a pronoun;*
Direct Object (birdhouse) *yes, it is a noun.*

Sentence 2: Object of the Preposition (summer) *yes, it is a noun;*
Subject Noun (grandfather) *yes, it is a noun;*
Indirect Object me, *no, it is a pronoun;*
Direct Object (birdhouse) *yes, it is a noun.*

Sentence 3: Subject Pronoun I, *no, it is a pronoun;*
Indirect Object (students) *yes, it is a noun;*
Direct Object (questions) *yes, it is a noun;*
Object of the Preposition (quiz) *yes, it is a noun.*
Object of the Preposition (Friday) *yes, it is a noun.*

JOURNAL WRITING 23

Write an entry in your journal. Use Reference 9 on page 12 for ideas.

English Made Easy

LISTENING AND SPEAKING:

Jingle Time

Recite It: Practice Jingle 23 in the Jingle Section on page 504.

Grammar Time

Apply It: Classify the Practice Sentences orally with your teacher.

Practice Sentences	Chapter 9: Lesson 2

1. _____ Today, Dad and Mom started me a college fund at our bank.
2. _____ Mr. Miller asked Joe a question about the math problem on the board.
3. _____ Before their tour of the island, the guide gave them an itinerary of events.

Skill Builder

Using the sentences just classified, do a Skill Builder orally with your teacher.

1. **Identify the nouns in a Noun Check.**
2. **Identify the nouns as singular or plural.**
3. **Identify the nouns as common or proper.**
4. **Identify the complete subject and the complete predicate.**
5. **Identify the simple subject and the simple predicate.**
6. **Do a Vocabulary Check.**
7. **Do a Verb Chant.**

START LESSON 2

Lesson 2

You will

- practice Jingle 23.
- classify Practice Sentences.
- do a Skill Builder.
- identify and punctuate quotations (beginning, ending, and split).
- do Classroom Practice 42.

LISTENING AND SPEAKING:

 *Skill Time*

Compare It:

The following stories have the same topic, but they are written differently. Tell which story you enjoyed more, Story 1 or Story 2.

STORY 1

Sandra called her friend, Jennifer, who had just returned from summer camp. Sandra wanted Jennifer to tell her everything that had happened.

Jennifer told her about swimming every day, riding horses, and playing lots of games. Then, she wanted to know if Sandra would be able to go to camp with her next summer.

Sandra was so excited and said that her parents had already given her permission to go with Jennifer next summer. Then, Sandra wanted to get together and make a list of everything that she would need. She got excited just thinking about it.

Jennifer agreed that it would be lots of fun to share ideas and begin making plans.

STORY 2

Sandra called her friend, Jennifer, who had just returned from summer camp. As soon as Jennifer answered the phone, Sandra squealed excitedly, "Jenny, tell me everything about summer camp!"

Jennifer laughed as she drew a deep breath and said, "We went swimming everyday. I got sunburned just a little bit, but I survived. We rode horses through forest trails and had picnic lunches. In the evenings, we played lots of games! We got up early and went to bed late. I sure hated for camp to end, but it is good to be home. Everyone was so nice and helpful that I can't wait to go back. Do you think you can go with me next summer?"

"Well, I sure want to go," said Sandra. "It sounds awesome! Mom and Dad have already given me permission, so I'm saving my money. There is so much that I need to know, so let's get together and make a list of everything I'll need. I get so excited just thinking about it!"

Jennifer laughed again as she said, "You are the organized one. It will be lots of fun to share ideas and make big plans. We will be busy the rest of the year!"

Learn It: BEGINNING QUOTES

Quotations help build pictures for readers as a story unfolds. Writers use three types of quotations: the beginning quote, the end quote, and the split quote.

Reference 145 **Rules for Punctuating Beginning Quotes**

Quotations are words spoken by someone, and quotation marks are used to set off the spoken words. The words set off by quotation marks are called a **direct quotation**. **Explanatory words** are the words that explain who is talking, but they are not part of the actual quote.

When writers use quotations in a story, it is called **dialogue**, or **conversation**. Dialogue helps move the plot along and helps the reader to understand the characters.

There are special rules for punctuating quotations. You will use five rules to punctuate a beginning quote. Each rule tells you how to punctuate a specific part of the sample sentence below. Before you begin, read the sample sentence aloud.

Sample Sentence: the girls and i are going fishing on friday with c j smith my mom said

RULE 1: Underline **end explanatory words** and place a period at the end of the explanatory words. If the quote is at the beginning of the sentence, the explanatory words are at the end. (*Explanatory words are the words that explain who is talking but which are not part of the actual quote.*)

Following Rule 1, the explanatory words are underlined, and a period is placed at the end of the explanatory words in the sample sentence below.

1. the girls and i are going fishing on friday with c j smith <u>**my mom said.**</u>

RULE 2: Place quotation marks at the beginning and end of what is said. For a beginning quote, put a comma, question mark, or exclamation point (no period) after the last word of the quote but in front of the quotation mark. Use a comma if the quote is a statement; use a question mark if the quote is a question; use an exclamation point if the quote is an exclamation and shows strong feeling.

Following Rule 2, quotation marks are placed at the beginning and end of what is said in the sample sentence below. A comma is placed at the end of the quote but in front of the quotation mark.

2. "the girls and i are going fishing on friday with c j smith**,"** <u>my mom said.</u>

RULE 3: **Capitalize** the beginning of a quote and any proper nouns or the pronoun *I*.

Following Rule 3, the beginning of the quote is capitalized, the proper nouns are capitalized, and the pronoun I is capitalized in the sample sentence below. The noun, mom, is not capitalized because it has a possessive pronoun in front of it.

3. "**T**he girls and **I** are going fishing on **F**riday with **C J S**mith," <u>my mom said.</u>

RULE 4: **Punctuate** the rest of the sentence by checking for any apostrophes, periods, or commas that may be needed within the sentence.

Following Rule 4, the rest of the sentence is checked for any words needing apostrophes, periods, or commas.

4. "The girls and I are going fishing on Friday with C**.** J**.** Smith," <u>my mom said.</u>

RULE 5: Use the **beginning quotation pattern** to check the punctuation of a beginning quote.

Beginning Quotation Pattern: "C (quote) **(,!?)"** (explanatory words) **(.)**

Translation of the Beginning Quotation Pattern: beginning quotation marks, capital letter to begin the quote, the quote itself, choices for an end mark (**,!?**), ending quotation marks, explanatory words, and a period.

Corrected Sentence: "The girls and I are going fishing on Friday with C. J. Smith," <u>my mom said.</u>

Learn It: ENDING QUOTES

| Reference 146 | **Rules for Punctuating Ending Quotes** |

You will use five rules to punctuate an ending quote. Each rule tells you how to punctuate a specific part of the sample sentence below. Before you begin, read the sample sentence aloud.

Sample Sentence: my mom said the girls and i are going fishing on friday with c j smith

RULE 1: Underline **beginning explanatory words** and place a comma at the end of the explanatory words. If the quote is at the end of the sentence, the explanatory words are at the beginning. (*Explanatory words are the words that explain who is talking but which are not part of the actual quote.*)

Following Rule 1, the explanatory words are underlined, and a comma is placed at the end of the explanatory words in the sample sentence below.

1. **my mom said,** the girls and i are going fishing on friday with c j smith

RULE 2: Place quotation marks at the beginning and end of what is said. For an end quote, put an end-mark punctuation (no comma) after the quote but in front of the quotation mark. Use a period if the quote is a statement; use a question mark if the quote is a question; use an exclamation point if the quote is an exclamation and shows excitement or strong feeling.

Following Rule 2, quotation marks are placed at the beginning and end of what is said in the sample sentence below. A period is placed at the end of the quote but in front of the quotation mark.

2. my mom said, **"**the girls and i are going fishing on friday with c j smith.**"**

RULE 3: **Capitalize** the first word of the explanatory words, the first word of the quote, and any proper nouns or the pronoun I.

Following Rule 3, the first word of the explanatory words is capitalized, the beginning of the quote is capitalized, the proper nouns are capitalized, and the pronoun I is capitalized in the sample sentence below. The noun, *mom*, is not capitalized because it has a possessive pronoun in front of it.

3. **M**y mom said, "**T**he girls and **I** are going fishing on **F**riday with **C J S**mith."

RULE 4: **Punctuate** the rest of the sentence by checking for any apostrophes, periods, or commas that may be needed.

Following Rule 4, the rest of the sentence is checked for any words needing apostrophes, periods, or commas.

4. My mom said, "The girls and I are going fishing on Friday with C**.** J**.** Smith."

RULE 5: Use the **ending quotation pattern** to check the punctuation of an end quote.

Ending Quotation Pattern: C (explanatory words) **(,) "C** (quote) **(.!?)"**

Translation of the Ending Quotation Pattern: capital letter to begin the explanatory words, the explanatory words, comma, beginning quotation marks, capital letter to begin the quote, the quote itself, choices for an end mark (.!?), ending quotation marks.

Corrected Sentence: My mom said, "The girls and I are going fishing on Friday with C. J. Smith."

Learn It: SPLIT QUOTES

Reference 147 | Rules for Punctuating Split Quotes

When one sentence has a quote that is split by explanatory words, it is called a **split quotation**. You will use the five rules below to punctuate a split quote. Each rule tells you how to punctuate a specific part of the sample sentence below. Before you begin, read the sample sentence aloud.

Sample Sentence: the girls and i my mom said are going fishing on friday with c j smith

RULE 1: Underline the **middle explanatory words** and place a comma at the end of the explanatory words. If the quote is split, the explanatory words are in the middle of the sentence. (*Explanatory words are the words that explain who is talking but which are not part of the actual quote.*)

Following Rule 1, the explanatory words are underlined, and a comma is placed at the end of the explanatory words in the sample sentence below.

   1. the girls and i **my mom said,** are going fishing on friday with c j smith

RULE 2: **For the first part of a split quote**, place quotation marks at the beginning and end of the first part of what is said. Put a comma after the last word of the first part of the quote but in front of the quotation mark.

For the second part of a split quote, place quotation marks at the beginning and end of the second part of what is said. Put an end-mark punctuation (no comma) after the quote but in front of the quotation mark. Use a period if the quote is a statement; use a question mark if the quote is a question; use an exclamation point if the quote is an exclamation and shows excitement or strong feeling.

Following Rule 2, quotation marks are placed at the beginning and end of what is said in the sample sentence below. A comma is placed at the end of the first part of the quote but in front of the quotation mark. For this example, the end mark is a period and is placed at the end of the second part of the quote but in front of the quotation mark.

   2. "the girls and i**,**" my mom said, "are going fishing on friday with c j smith**.**"

RULE 3: **Capitalize** the beginning of the quote and any proper nouns or the pronoun **I**.

Following Rule 3, the beginning of the quote is capitalized, the proper nouns are capitalized, and the pronoun **I** is capitalized in the sample sentence below. The noun, *mom*, is not capitalized because it has a possessive pronoun in front of it.

   3. "The girls and **I**," my mom said, "are going fishing on **F**riday with **C J S**mith."

RULE 4: **Punctuate** the rest of the sentence by checking for any apostrophes, periods, or commas that may be needed.

Following Rule 4, the rest of the sentence is checked for any words needing apostrophes, periods, or commas.

   4. "The girls and I," my mom said, "are going fishing on Friday with C**.** J**.** Smith."

RULE 5: Use the **split quotation pattern** to check the punctuation of a split quote.

Split Quotation Pattern:
"C (first part of the quote) **(,)"** **c** (explanatory words) **(,)** **"c** (second part of the quote) **(.!?)"**

Translation of the Split Quotation Pattern: beginning quotation marks, capital letter to begin the quote, first part of the split quote, comma, ending quotation marks, lowercase letter unless there is a proper noun, explanatory words, comma, beginning quotation marks for the second part of the split quote, lowercase letter unless there is a proper noun, second part of the split quote, choices for an end mark (.!?), ending quotation marks.

Corrected Sentence: **"The girls and I,"** my mom said, "are going fishing on Friday with C. J. Smith."

Note: When consecutive sentences are part of a quotation, you do not have a split quotation.

   Example: "The girls and I are going fishing on Friday," my mom said. "I think they need the experience."

SHURLEY ENGLISH

Classroom Practice 42

It is time to practice the skills you are learning. You will use the classroom practice on the next page to apply these skills.

Student Note: Anytime the word "exclaimed" is used in explanatory words, the end mark for the quote should be an exclamation point, not a period.

Classroom Practice 42

Name:_____ Date:_____

GRAMMAR

▶ **Exercise 1:** Classify each sentence.

1. _____ Ed and Brad painted their dad a huge poster with deer and turkeys on it.

2. _____ Their teacher has assigned them several science experiments.

3. _____ Goodness! Troy has not sent me an e-mail in a long time!

SKILLS & EDITING

▶ **Exercise 2:** Punctuate the sentences and underline the explanatory words. Use the Editing Guide below.
    (1.) 13 mistakes   (2.) 13 mistakes   (3.) 15 mistakes   (4.) 24 mistakes

1. misty could you walk ms millers dog on tuesday mom asked

2. mom asked misty could you walk ms millers dog on tuesday

3. misty mom asked could you walk ms millers dog on tuesday

4. misty could you walk ms millers dog on tuesday mom asked she will be in

   destin florida until wednesday she has offered to pay you ten dollars

SKILLS & EDITING

▶ **Exercise 3:** Punctuate the sentences and underline the explanatory words. Use the Editing Guide below.
    (1.) 13 mistakes   (2.) 13 mistakes   (3.) 16 mistakes   (4.) 19 mistakes

1. julie exclaimed kelly and i are going to the mall of america in bloomington minnesota

2. kelly and i are going to the mall of america in bloomington minnesota exclaimed julie

3. kelly and i julie exclaimed are going to the mall of america in bloomington minnesota

4. julie exclaimed kelly and i are going to the mall of america in bloomington minnesota

   it is one of the largest indoor shopping malls in the united states would you like to go with us

START LESSON 3

Lesson 3

You will

- study new vocabulary; make Card 24; write own sentence using the vocabulary word.
- analyze new analogy; make Card 24; write own analogy.
- practice Jingles 13-23.
- classify Practice Sentences.
- do a Skill Builder.
- identify other quotation rules.
- do Classroom Practice 43.
- read and discuss Discovery Time.

LISTENING AND SPEAKING:

Vocabulary & Analogy Time

Learn It: Recite the new vocabulary and analogy words.

📖 * Reference 148	Vocabulary & Analogy Words

Word: sabotage (săb'ə täzh')
  Definition: to secretly interfere
  Synonym: undermine   **Antonym:** support
  Sentence: The agent **sabotaged** the computer's database.

Analogy: sponge : absorb :: fan : circulate
  Purpose or use relationship: Just as a **sponge** is used to **absorb** liquid, a **fan** is used to **circulate** air.

Vocabulary Card 24: Record the vocabulary information above and write your own sentence, using the new word.

Analogy Card 24: Record the analogy information and write your own analogy, using the same relationship as the analogy above.

Jingle Time

Recite It: Practice Jingles 13–23 in the Jingle Section on pages 501–504.

Grammar Time

Apply It: Classify the Practice Sentences orally with your teacher.

Practice Sentences	Chapter 9: Lesson 3

1. _____ Would your dad loan you his new convertible for the prom?
2. _____ Hank showed David and Adam the new aquarium in his office.
3. _____ The beautician gave my mom and me a shampoo and haircut.

Skill Builder

Using the sentences just classified, do a Skill Builder orally with your teacher.

1. **Identify the nouns in a Noun Check.**
2. **Identify the nouns as singular or plural.**
3. **Identify the nouns as common or proper.**
4. **Identify the complete subject and the complete predicate.**
5. **Identify the simple subject and the simple predicate.**
6. **Do a Vocabulary Check.**
7. **Do a Verb Chant.**

Skill Time

Learn It: OTHER QUOTATION RULES

Reference 149   Other Quotation Rules

1. Longer Quotes

A. The examples below show how to punctuate quotations with more than one sentence.

> Dad said, "Saturday is our day for chores. Two of you will help me rake the leaves and mow the grass. The other two will help Mom clean the house."

> "Saturday is our day for chores. Two of you will help me rake the leaves and mow the grass. The other two will help Mom clean the house," said Dad.

> "Saturday is our day for chores," said Dad. "Two of you will help me rake the leaves and mow the grass. The other two will help Mom clean the house."

B. When a speaker has a lengthy quote that is longer than one paragraph, quotation marks are used at the beginning of each paragraph but only at the end of the last paragraph of that speaker's quote. Then, when the speaker changes, a new paragraph is started with another set of quotation marks.

> Cindy told her friends, "I am going shopping with my sister on Saturday. Do you want to meet us at the mall for lunch? We will have a great time.   } speaker begins

> "In fact, my sister said we could stop by all the cool places. I have my birthday money to spend."   } same speaker continues and ends

> "That sounds like lots of fun," said Cindy's friends. "We'll ask our parents."   } new speaker begins and ends

2. A Quote Within a Quote

Single quotation marks are used to punctuate a quotation within a quotation.

> My brother asked, "Did you hear Dad say, 'Get ready for bed'?"

3. Quotation Marks to Punctuate Titles

Quotation marks are used to punctuate titles of songs, short stories, poems, articles, essays, radio and television programs, short plays, and book chapters. (*Capitalize the first word, last word, and every word in between except for articles, short prepositions, and short conjunctions.*)

> I can recite several stanzas of "Casey at the Bat."

4. Direct Quotations, Indirect Quotations, and Statements

A. A direct quotation occurs when you show exactly what someone says by using quotation marks.

> **Direct quotation:** Anthony said, "I want a large order of fries."

B. An indirect quotation occurs when you describe what someone says without using his exact words.

> **Indirect quotation:** Anthony said he wanted a large order of fries.

C. A statement occurs when no speaker is mentioned and no quotation is used.

> **Statement:** Anthony wants a large order of fries.

✏️ Classroom Practice 43

It is time to practice the skills you are learning. You will use the classroom practice on the next page to apply these skills.

ENRICHMENT:

 Discovery Time

Saturn is the sixth planet from the sun in our solar system. Saturn is the second biggest planet and has more moons than any other planet. It is so light that it could float in water.

 Discovery Questions:
- What do you find most interesting about Saturn?
- Imagine living on Saturn. What would it be like?

Discovery Activity:
- Draw and color Saturn, its rings, and its moons. Make up a title to fit your illustration.

Are you interested in learning more about Saturn?

1. You may explore this topic further by using the resources listed below.
   Computer resources: Internet, encyclopedia software
   Library resources: encyclopedias, books, magazines, newspapers
   Home/community resources: books, interviews, newspapers, magazines

2. A Discovery Share Time is provided in Lesson 7 if you wish to share your investigation results. You may share orally, or you may prepare a written report. You will put your written report in a class booklet titled "Space Trivia." This booklet will be placed in the class library for everyone to enjoy.

Classroom Practice 43

Name:_____ Date:_____

GRAMMAR

▶ **Exercise 1:** Classify each sentence.

1. _____ Has Emma sent you any unusual postcards for your collection?

2. _____ The song director gave the pianist a new sheet of music for the concert.

3. _____ Give Kenny and Bonnie their spelling test today.

SKILLS & EDITING

▶ **Exercise 2:** Punctuate the sentences and underline the explanatory words. Use the Editing Guide below.
   (1.) 13 mistakes   (2.) 12 mistakes   (3.) 11 mistakes   (4.) 10 mistakes

1. martina i had to miss mr wilsons science class yesterday ricky said

2. martina replied yes i noticed that you werent there where were you

3. do you remember the kites we made in ms lincolns art class asked ricky

4. oh yes mine was red and yellow replied martina

▶ **Exercise 3:** Punctuate the sentences and underline the explanatory words. Use the Editing Guide below.
   (5.) 16 mistakes   (6.) 9 mistakes   (7.) 10 mistakes   (8.) 15 mistakes

5. well ms lincoln wanted me to move everyones kites to the storage building as i was

   moving them a huge gust of wind lifted the kites and me up into the air ricky declared loudly

6. amazing were you able to hang on to them martina wanted to know

7. ricky answered mischievously sure i floated with the kites until i dropped into my backyard

8. martina glared at ricky and muttered that is the lamest excuse ive ever heard you will

   have to come up with a better story than that for mr wilson

START LESSON 4

Lesson 4

You will

- study new vocabulary; make Card 25; write own sentence using the vocabulary word.
- analyze new analogy; make Card 25; write own analogy.
- practice Jingles 3–11.
- classify Practice Sentences.
- do a Skill Builder.
- do Classroom Practice 44.
- write in your journal.
- read and discuss Discovery Time.
- do a homework assignment.
- do Home Connection activity.

LISTENING AND SPEAKING:

Vocabulary & Analogy Time

Learn It: Recite the new vocabulary and analogy words.

📖 Reference 150	Vocabulary & Analogy Words

Word: incessant (ĭn sĕs'ənt)
    Definition: continuing without interruption
    Synonym: constant   **Antonym:** periodic
    Sentence: The **incessant** dripping of water from the faucet kept me awake all night.
Analogy: moo : cow :: meow : cat
    Descriptive or characteristic relationship: Just as **moo** is a characteristic of a **cow**, **meow** is a characteristic of a **cat**.

Vocabulary Card 25: Record the vocabulary information above and write your own sentence, using the new word.

Analogy Card 25: Record the analogy information and write your own analogy, using the same relationship as the analogy above.

Jingle Time

Recite It: Practice Jingles 3–11 in the Jingle Section on pages 499–500.

Grammar Time

Apply It: Classify the Practice Sentences orally with your teacher.

Practice Sentences	Chapter 9: Lesson 4

1. _____ The building inspector showed us the damage from the hailstorm.
2. _____ Has the realtor given you a tour of the beach homes near the ocean?
3. _____ Did you give Alex and Lewis an alternate date for band rehearsal?

 # Skill Builder

Using the sentences just classified, do a Skill Builder orally with your teacher.

1. **Identify the nouns in a Noun Check.**
2. **Identify the nouns as singular or plural.**
3. **Identify the nouns as common or proper.**
4. **Identify the complete subject and the complete predicate.**
5. **Identify the simple subject and the simple predicate.**
6. **Do a Vocabulary Check.**
7. **Do a Verb Chant.**

Classroom Practice 44

It is time to practice the skills you are learning. You will use the classroom practice on the next page to apply these skills.

ENRICHMENT:

 ## Discovery Time

(Soviet) 1934-1968 — Yury Gagarin was the first man to travel into space. He completed a single orbit around the Earth in 1961.

(American) 1923-1998 — Alan B. Shepard, Jr. was the first American astronaut in space.

 **Discovery Questions:**

- If you were the first person to travel into space, what would your feelings be before your space flight? What would your feelings be after your flight?
- What do you think the first space suit looked like?
- What do you think Gagarin's space ship looked like?
- Do you think Shepard's space ship looked similar to Gagarin's ship?
- Compare the first space ships to the present-day space ships.

Are you interested in learning more about Yury Gagarin or Alan Shepard, Jr.?

1. You may explore these topics further by using the resources listed below.
   Computer resources: Internet, encyclopedia software
   Library resources: encyclopedias, books, magazines, newspapers
   Home/community resources: books, interviews, newspapers, magazines
2. A Discovery Share Time is provided in Lesson 7 if you wish to share your investigation results. You may share orally, or you may prepare a written report. You will put your written report in a class booklet titled "Space Trivia." This booklet will be placed in the class library for everyone to enjoy.

JOURNAL WRITING 24

Write an entry in your journal. Use Reference 9 on page 12 for ideas.

Classroom Practice 44

Name:_____ Date:_____

GRAMMAR

▶ **Exercise 1:** Classify each sentence.

1. _____ My newspaper carrier did not leave me a receipt in my mailbox.

2. _____ Manuel's brother loaned me several comfortable chairs for the reception.

3. _____ For an afternoon snack, my aunt gave Jan and Lee cinnamon rolls and milk.

SKILLS & EDITING

▶ **Exercise 2:** Punctuate the sentences and underline the explanatory words. Use the Editing Guide below.
(1.) 9 mistakes (2.) 9 mistakes (3.) 11 mistakes (4.) 19 mistakes

1. dad said heath i want to show you how to change a flat tire

2. heath i want to show you how to change a flat tire dad said

3. heath dad said i want to show you how to change a flat tire

4. heath i want to show you how to change a flat tire said dad youll be old enough to drive

   soon and this is a skill youll need to know you dont want to be stranded on the side of the road

SKILLS & EDITING

▶ **Exercise 3:** Punctuate the sentences and underline the explanatory words. Use the Editing Guide below.
(1.) 17 mistakes (2.) 7 mistakes (3.) 22 mistakes

1. rosie my three sisters and i said katie had to change a flat tire in five minutes before we

   could date my dad timed us until we met his standard he said he didnt want us stranded

2. rosie asked did you ever have to change a flat tire

3. yes i did replied katie it was on my second date we had a flat and my date didnt know

   how to change it i changed it in five minutes for some reason he never asked me out again

Homework 7

Complete this homework assignment on notebook paper.

1. Copy the sentence below. Classify the sentence, using the Question and Answer Flow, as you label each part.

_____ Did you give Alex and Lewis an alternate date for band rehearsal?

2. Rewrite the sentences below, using the Quotation Rules to help you capitalize and punctuate each sentence correctly. Underline the explanatory words.

1. cedric asked during dinner dad may i watch a special on television tonight

2. dad may i watch a special on television tonight cedric asked during dinner

3. dad cedric asked during dinner may i watch a special on television tonight

4. dad may i watch a special on television tonight cedric asked during dinner it is on from

seven o clock until eight o clock and is about the exploration of mars it should be very interesting

Home Connection

Family Activity for Quotations

1. You want an allowance or a raise in your allowance. Write a convincing conversation between you and your parents about this topic or another topic of your choice.

2. A fable is a short story that teaches a moral lesson. It often uses animals as the characters. One of the most famous books about fables is Aesop's Fables. Use the internet or library to look up one of Aesop's fables. Then, write a fable of your own, using dialogue. Recruit family members to help you dramatize your fable.

3. You are giving someone in your family an important award. Create the certificate for the award. Then, write a presentation speech that you will read to the family member. Include quotes from other family members and friends.

Family Activity for Vocabulary and Analogies

Divide into family teams. The first team will use vocabulary and analogy cards 1–12 to ask questions about the information on their cards. The second team will use vocabulary and analogy cards 13–25 to ask questions about the information on their cards.

For vocabulary words:
- What is the definition of the word?
- Name a synonym and antonym for the word.
- Create a new sentence using the word.
- Find the word in another source (dictionary, newspaper, magazine, advertisement).

For analogies:
- What is the answer to the analogy?
- What is the relationship of the analogy?
- Make another analogy with the same relationship.
- Make another analogy with a different relationship.

START LESSON 5

Lesson 5

You will

- classify Practice Sentences.
- do Classroom Practice 45.
- write in your journal.

LISTENING AND SPEAKING:

Apply It: Classify the Practice Sentences orally with your teacher.

Practice Sentences	Chapter 9: Lesson 5

1. _____ Mitchell gave his insurance agent an estimate of the damage to his car.

2. _____ Did the detective ask the employees many questions after the robbery?

3. _____ Cindy and Karen bought their mom some antique plates at the estate sale.

JOURNAL WRITING 25

Write an entry in your journal. Use Reference 9 on page 12 for ideas.

Chapter Checkup 45

It is time for a checkup of the skills you have learned in this chapter. You will use the chapter checkup on the next page to evaluate your progress.

Chapter 9 Checkup 45

Name:_____ Date:_____

GRAMMAR

▶ **Exercise 1:** Classify each sentence.

1. _____ Will your mother order you the black leather coat from the winter catalog?

2. _____ Hand me the keys to the computer room at the east end of the building.

3. _____ My faithful dog gave me a slight nudge with his nose.

SKILLS & EDITING

▶ **Exercise 2:** Punctuate the sentences and underline the explanatory words. Use the Editing Guide below.
            (1.) 18 mistakes   (2.) 23 mistakes

1. sir said thomas politely i think youre standing on my toes would you please move a little

   to the left or right my toes are complaining and i must rescue them

2. oops i am so sorry the old gentleman apologized as he quickly stepped to the right my

   feet are so cold that i didnt notice i couldnt find a taxi and had to walk several blocks through

   this blizzard since im here on vacation from florida my feet are not used to this cold weather

SKILLS & EDITING

▶ **Exercise 3:** Punctuate the sentences and underline the explanatory words. Use the Editing Guide below.
            (1.) 11 mistakes   (2.) 19 mistakes

1. i understand what you mean thomas replied with a big grin as he looked outside at the few

   snowflakes falling on the dry sidewalk the weather here can be pretty harsh during early winter

2. the stranger nodded in agreement yes the weather is definitely harsh today however i

   am visiting some Northern friends this week and they think floridas summers are harsh too i

   just dont understand how some people get excited over nothing

START LESSON 6

Lesson 6

You will

- conference with teacher about WA 20.
- write a creative writing piece for WA 21.

Writing Time

Write It: **WRITING ASSIGNMENT 21**

Writing Assignment 21 : Creative Expressions

Purpose: To entertain

Type of Writing: Creative

Audience: Classmates, family, or friends

Choose one of the writing prompts below.

1. You are going on a ski trip with your friend and his/her family. You have never skied before, and you have just discovered that your friend's seven-year-old brother is an advanced skier. Write a story about what happens on your ski trip.

2. What do you wish you had done at an earlier age that would help you now?

3. Write a poem about skiing, about your early life, or about a topic of your choice.

Special Instructions:

1. A prewriting map is not required for this creative-writing assignment.

2. Follow the Rough Draft Checklist in Reference 49 on page 66.

3. Put your creative-writing paper in your Rough Draft folder when you have finished.

Note: Reference 57 on page 76 gives the steps in the writing process and the location of all the writing checklists.

>>>>>>>>>>>>>>>>>>>>>>>>>>> **Student Tip...**

> For more information about writing poetry, look at Chapter 18, pages 456–474.

Conference Time

Discuss It: **TEACHER-STUDENT CONFERENCES FOR WRITING ASSIGNMENT 20**

Meet with your teacher to discuss Writing Assignment 20.
After the conference, place this group of papers in your Publishing folder.

English Made Easy

Publishing Time

Publish It: WRITING ASSIGNMENT 20

Choose a publishing form and publish Writing Assignment 20. After rewriting your paper for publication, give the stapled papers (evaluation guide, graded final paper, rough draft, and prewriting) to your teacher to be placed in your Writing Portfolio.

Lesson 7

You will

• publish WA 20.

• participate in Discovery Share Time.

• do Across the Curriculum activity.

✏* Reference 67	Publishing Checklist for Step 6 in the Writing Process

The sixth step in the writing process is called publishing. Publishing is sharing your writing with others. With so many forms of publishing available, finding a match for every project and personality is easy.

At times, a written work is best read aloud. Other times, the biggest impact is made when a written work is read silently. You can also use media sources to enhance any publication.

SPECIAL INSTRUCTIONS FOR PUBLISHING:

• Rewrite the graded paper in ink or type it on a computer, correcting any marked errors. *(Do not display or publish papers that have marked errors or grades on them.)*

• Give your teacher the set of stapled papers to place in your Writing Portfolio. *(Stapled papers: evaluation guide, graded final paper, rough draft, and prewriting map.)*

• Select a publishing form from the list below and publish your rewritten paper.

1. Have classmates, family members, neighbors, or others read your writing at school or home.

2. Share your writing with others during a Share Time. *(Refer to Reference 68 on page 103 for sharing guidelines.)*

3. Display your writing on a bulletin board or wall.

4. Put your writing in the classroom library or in the school library for checkout.

5. Send your writing as a letter or an e-mail to a friend or relative.

6. Frame your writing by gluing it on colored construction paper and decorating it.

7. Make a book of your writing for your classroom, your family, or others.

8. Illustrate your writing and give it to others to read.

9. Dramatize your writing in the form of a play, puppet show, or radio broadcast.

10. Send your writing to be placed in a waiting room (doctor, veterinarian, dentist, etc.), senior-citizen center, or a nursing home.

11. Send your writing to a school newspaper, local newspaper, or a magazine for publication.

12. Make a videotape, cassette tape, or slide presentation of your writing.

13. Choose another publishing form that is not listed.

LISTENING AND SPEAKING:

Discovery Share Time

If you have chosen to investigate a topic introduced in this chapter, you now have the opportunity to share your results in one of the following ways:

    1. You may relate your information orally.

    2. You may read a written report.

    3. You may place your report in the booklet without reading it aloud.

After share time, all written reports should be turned in to be placed in the class booklet titled "Space Trivia." You are encouraged to check out this class booklet so you can enjoy the reports again.

Across the Curriculum

Social Studies/Writing Connection: Leo is a character who travels all over the world. Write a story about Leo's travels. Use past-tense verbs and underline each verb. Then, rewrite the story, changing the past-tense verbs to present-tense verbs. Read the two stories in small groups. Discuss whether the story sounds better in past tense or in present tense.

LISTENING AND SPEAKING:

Jingle Time

Recite It: Practice Jingle 23 in the Jingle Section on page 504.

GRAMMAR & WRITING CONNECTION:
Practice and Revised Sentences

Apply It: **BUILDING AND EXPANDING SENTENCES**

Lesson 8

You will
- practice Jingle 23.
- do Classroom Practice 46.
- write an independent descriptive paragraph (WA 22).

Reference 151	A Guide for Using a Pattern 3 Core (SN V-t IO DO) to Build & Expand Sentences

1. **SN or SP (subject)** Think of a noun or pronoun that you want to use as the *subject*. Write the noun or pronoun you have chosen as the *subject* of your sentence.

2. **V-t (verb transitive)** The *transitive-verb* does two things. It tells what the subject does, and it is followed by a direct object. First, choose a verb for your sentence. Then, after you have chosen a direct object, verify that the verb is transitive and keep it as the verb of your Pattern 3 core.

3. **DO (direct object)** The *direct object* is a noun or pronoun after the verb that answers the question *what* or *whom*. The *direct object* receives the action of a transitive verb and does not mean the same thing as the subject. To help you think of a *direct object,* ask the question WHAT or WHOM after the verb. Write the direct object you have chosen.

4. **IO (indirect object)** An *indirect object* receives what the direct object names. The indirect object tells *to whom* or *for whom* the action is done. It does not receive the action of the verb. To help you think of an *indirect object,* ask the question TO WHOM or FOR WHOM, TO WHAT or FOR WHAT after the direct object. Write the indirect object you have chosen. The indirect object will always be located between the verb and direct object.

>>>>>>>> Student Tip...

Use your vocabulary words in your Practice and Revised Sentences. Use a thesaurus, synonym-antonym book, or a dictionary to help you develop your writing vocabulary.

Classroom Practice 46

It is time to practice the skills you are learning. You will use the classroom practice on the next page to apply these skills.

Write It: **WRITING ASSIGNMENT 22**

As you write a rough draft for your independent writing assignment, you will do two of the six steps in the writing process: prewriting and rough draft.

Writing Assignment 22

Purpose: To describe

Type of Writing: Descriptive paragraph

Audience: Classmates

Writing Topics: Interesting person/animal/scenery
Unusual bird/snake/fish/food
Crazy clothing/habit(s)/custom/game
(Brainstorm for other ideas, individually or in groups.)

Special Instructions:

1. Follow the Prewriting and Rough Draft Checklists in References 47 and 49 on pages 62, 66.

2. Make a prewriting map using the descriptive guidelines to help you write your descriptive paragraph. Use References 141–142 on pages 256–257.

3. Write in first or third person. See Reference 71 on page 108.
   (First-person pronouns: *I, me, my, mine, we, us, our,* and *ours.*)
   (Third-person pronouns: *he, his, him, she, her, hers, it, its, they, their, theirs,* and *them.*)

Note: Reference 57 on page 76 gives the steps in the writing process and the location of all the writing checklists.

Student Note: Some of your writing pieces will be selected for revision and editing later in the school year.

Classroom Practice 46

Name: _____   Date: _____

INDEPENDENT PRACTICE & REVISED SENTENCES

1. Write a Practice Sentence according to the labels you choose.
   Use **SN/SP V-t IO DO** as your main labels. You may use the other labels in any order and as many times as you wish in order to make a Practice Sentence.
   Chapter 9 labels for a Practice Sentence: **SN/SP, V-t, IO, DO**, Adj, Adv, A, P, OP, PPA, C, HV, I, PNA

2. Write a Revised Sentence. Use the following revision strategies: *synonym (syn), antonym (ant), word change (wc), added word (add), deleted word (delete), or no change (nc)*. Under each word, write the abbreviation of the revision strategy you use.

Labels:

Practice:

Revised:

Strategies:

Labels:

Practice:

Revised:

Strategies:

Labels:

Practice:

Revised:

Strategies:

START LESSON 9

Lesson 9

You will

- practice Jingle 12.
- read and discuss narrative writing and story elements outline.
- plan and write rough draft for narrative with dialogue (WA 23).

LISTENING AND SPEAKING:

Recite It: Practice Jingle 12 in the Jingle Section on page 501.

>>>> Student Tip...

> Reviewing the transition words will help you apply them in your writing.

Learn It: STORY ELEMENTS FOR A NARRATIVE WITH DIALOGUE

Reference 152	Story Elements for a Narrative With Dialogue

Narrative writing is simply the telling of a story. When you compose stories, you are actually writing what professional writers call narratives, or short stories. Short stories have certain characteristics that make them different from other types of writing. These characteristics are known as story elements.

Writers use five story elements. The story elements are **main idea, setting, characters, plot,** and **ending**. Narrative writing skills are developed through the use of these elements. A Story Elements Outline will help you keep your writing focused, and it will help you choose details and events that support the main idea of your story. Narrative writing has a beginning, middle, and end, and it can be written with or without dialogue (quotations).

STORY ELEMENTS OUTLINE

1. **Main Idea:**
   Tell the problem or situation that needs a solution.
   The writer is trying to think of a name for his new horse.

2. **Setting:**
   Tell when and where the story takes place, either clearly stated or implied.
   When — The story takes place in the summertime.
   Where — The story takes place at the writer's home and Mr. Hunter's ranch.

3. **Characters:**
   Tell whom or what the story is about.
   The main characters are the writer, his father, Mr. Hunter, and the new horse.

4. **Plot:**
   Tell what the characters in the story do and what happens to them.
   The story is about a boy who goes with his father to pick up his new horse at Mr. Hunter's ranch.
   The boy cannot think of a name for his horse, so he is waiting until he meets him to select a name.

5. **Ending:**
   Use a strong ending that will bring the story to a close.
   The story ends with the writer thinking of a name for his horse as he meets him.

Continued on next page. >>>

Reference 152 continued from previous page.

Example of Narrative Writing With Dialogue

A Horse Named…?

My excitement grew as the afternoon approached. I knew my dad would take me to Mr. Hunter's ranch to pick up my new horse as soon as the afternoon chores were finished. I had tried to think of a name all week, but I knew it would come to me as soon as I saw him. I tagged along behind Dad until he finally leaned on the barn door, wiped his forehead with his red bandanna, and said, "Well, do you reckon it's time to pick up your horse?"

Mr. Hunter met us as we got out of the truck. He shook hands with my dad, and then he shook hands with me. I remembered my manners and waited respectfully for Mr. Hunter to finish his weather and crop talk with my dad. Finally, Mr. Hunter turned to me and asked, "Well, boy, are you ready to meet your new horse?"

Mr. Hunter grinned and winked at Dad as I about fell over myself in my eagerness to find out where my horse was. Mr. Hunter was watching my excitement with amusement as he said teasingly, "Well, now. Let's see if I can remember where I put that puny little horse. Oh, yes! I do recall that I put him in the corral behind the barn. He's there waiting for you."

Instantly, I raced toward the corral. As I neared the barn, I could hear the steady rhythm of hooves beating the hard-packed earth. As I burst around the corner to the corral, I stopped in awe. My eyes followed a giant horse, a glistening chestnut. His mane and tail flowed gracefully behind him as he thundered around the corral. I could scarcely believe that this beauty was mine. I listened to his thundering hooves pounding the ground. Then, I smiled and whispered, "I shall call you Thunder!"

There is another special element that makes narrative writing especially interesting, and that is conversation. Another word for conversation is **dialogue**. Writers use dialogue, or conversation, in their short stories because it helps move the plot along, and it helps the reader understand the characters better.

Writers like to use dialogue because it "shows" instead of "tells" in narratives. Dialogue "shows" what a character is like. A character's personal quotations show the readers a great deal about the character.

Review It: MAIN PUNCTUATION RULES TO OBSERVE WITH DIALOGUE

1. Dialogue is always placed INSIDE quotation marks. This placement will separate dialogue from any explanatory words or other words that develop the plot of the story.

2. Periods, commas, question marks, and exclamation points that punctuate dialogue always go INSIDE the quotation marks. You should follow the rules that you have already learned for punctuating quotations.

3. If more than one character is speaking, you must indent and create a new paragraph each time the speaker changes.

Write It: **WRITING ASSIGNMENT 23**

As you write a rough draft for your guided writing assignment, you will do two of the six steps in the writing process: prewriting and rough draft.

Writing Assignment 23

Purpose: To tell a story

Type of Writing: Narrative

Audience: Classmates

Writing Topics: The day I was in charge
A big mistake/A big storm
The best gift/compliment I ever gave or received
(Brainstorm for other ideas, individually or in groups.)

Special Instructions:

1. Follow the Prewriting and Rough Draft Checklists in References 47 and 49 on pages 62, 66.

2. Use Reference 152 on page 288 to help you write your narrative. Make a Story Elements Outline instead of a prewriting map.

3. Write your narrative with dialogue. Use the review below and References 145–147 and 149 on pages 267– 269 and 273 to help you punctuate quotations.

   • Dialogue is always placed INSIDE quotation marks. This placement will separate dialogue from any explanatory words or other words that develop the plot of the story.

   • Periods, commas, question marks, and exclamation points that punctuate dialogue always go INSIDE the quotation marks.

   • If more than one character is speaking, you must indent and create a new paragraph each time the speaker changes.

4. Write in first or third person. See Reference 71 on page 108.
   (First-person pronouns: *I, me, my, mine, we, us, our,* and *ours.*)
   (Third-person pronouns: *he, his, him, she, her, hers, it, its, they, their, theirs,* and *them.*)

Note: Reference 57 on page 76 gives the steps in the writing process and the location of all the writing checklists.

Apply It: **REVISE, EDIT, AND WRITE A FINAL PAPER**

Following the schedule below, you will revise and edit Writing Assignment 23. Then, you will write a final paper. Use the Chapter 9 Writing Evaluation Guide on the next page to check your final paper one last time.

Lesson 10

You will

- revise, edit, and write a final paper for WA 23.

Reference 55   **Revising & Editing Schedule and Writing a Final Paper**

SPECIAL INSTRUCTIONS FOR REVISING AND EDITING (Steps 3-4 in the writing process):

- Use the Revising and Editing Checklists in References 51 and 53 as you revise and edit your rough draft.
- Follow the revising and editing schedule below as directed by your teacher.
  1. **Individual.** First, read your rough draft to yourself. Use the Revising Checklist in Reference 51 on page 69. Go through your paper, checking each item on the list and making revisions to your rough draft. Then, use the Editing Checklist in Reference 53 on page 71. Go through your paper again, checking each item on the list and editing your rough draft.
  2. **Partner.** Next, get with your editing partner. Work together on each partner's rough draft, one paper at a time. Read each rough draft aloud and revise and edit it together, using the Revising and Editing Checklists. (The author of the paper should be the one to make the corrections on his own paper.)
  3. **Group.** Finally, read the rough draft to a revision group for feedback. Each student should read his paper while the others listen and offer possible revising and editing suggestions. (The author will determine whether to make corrections from the revision group's suggestions.)

SPECIAL INSTRUCTIONS FOR FINAL PAPER (Step 5 in the writing process):

- Write your final paper, using the Final Paper Checklist in Reference 56 on page 75.
- Staple your writing papers in this order: the final paper on top, the rough draft in the middle, and the prewriting map on the bottom. Place the stapled papers in the Final Paper folder.

>>>>>>>> Student Tip...

1. Be tactful and helpful in your comments during revising and editing time. The purpose of any suggestion should be to improve the writer's rough draft.

2. As you make your final corrections, you have the choice of accepting or rejecting any suggestions made by your partners or your revision group.

3. Study Vocabulary Words and Analogies 23–25 for the chapter test in the next lesson.

4. If you need to improve your handwriting, refer to the Resource Tools Section on page 521 for information on writing legibly.

Chapter 9 Writing Evaluation Guide

Name:_____ Date:_____

ROUGH DRAFT CHECK

_____ 1. Did you write your rough draft in pencil?

_____ 2. Did you write the correct headings on the first seven lines of your paper?

_____ 3. Did you use extra wide margins and skip every other line?

_____ 4. Did you write a title at the end of your rough draft?

_____ 5. Did you place your edited rough draft in your Rough Draft folder?

REVISING CHECK

_____ 6. Did you identify the purpose, type of writing, and audience?

_____ 7. Did you check for a topic, topic sentence, and sentences supporting the topic?

_____ 8. Did you check sentences for the right order, and did you combine, rearrange, or delete sentences when necessary?

_____ 9. Did you check for a variety of simple, compound, and complex sentences?

_____ 10. Did you check for any left out, repeated, or unnecessary words?

_____ 11. Did you check for the best choice of words by replacing or deleting unclear words?

_____ 12. Did you check the content for interest and creativity?

_____ 13. Did you check the voice to make sure the writing says what you want it to say?

EDITING CHECK

_____ 14. Did you indent each paragraph?

_____ 15. Did you put an end mark at the end of every sentence?

_____ 16. Did you capitalize the first word of every sentence?

_____ 17. Did you check for all other capitalization mistakes?

_____ 18. Did you check for all punctuation mistakes?
(*commas, periods, apostrophes, quotation marks, underlining*)

_____ 19. Did you check for misspelled words and for incorrect homonym choices?

_____ 20. Did you check for incorrect spellings of plural and possessive forms?

_____ 21. Did you check for correct construction and punctuation of your sentences?

_____ 22. Did you check for usage mistakes? (*subject/verb agreement, a/an choices, contractions, verb tenses, pronoun/antecedent agreement, pronoun cases, degrees of adjectives, double negatives, etc.*)

_____ 23. Did you put your revised and edited paper in the Rough Draft folder?

FINAL PAPER CHECK

_____ 24. Did you write the final paper in pencil?

_____ 25. Did you center the title on the top line and center your name under the title?

_____ 26. Did you skip a line before starting the writing assignment?

_____ 27. Did you single-space, use wide margins, and write the final paper neatly?

_____ 28. Did you staple your papers in this order: final paper on top, rough draft in the middle, and prewriting map on the bottom? Did you put them in the Final Paper folder?

Writing Time

Hand It In: **WRITING ASSIGNMENT 23**

Get your stapled papers for Writing Assignment 23 from your Final Paper folder. Check to make sure they are in the correct order: the final paper on top, the rough draft in the middle, and the prewriting map on the bottom. Hand them in to your teacher.

LISTENING AND SPEAKING:

Oral Review Questions

Discuss It:

1. What word receives what the direct object names?

2. What type of verb is used with an indirect object?

3. What are the core parts of a Pattern 3 sentence?

4. What are the core parts of a Pattern 2 sentence?

5. What are the core parts of a Pattern 1 sentence?

6. What punctuation is used to set off the exact words that are spoken by someone?

7. In writing, what is dialogue?

8. What is another name for dialogue?

9. What are the three types of quotes?

10. What are the End Mark choices for a beginning quote?

11. What are the End Mark choices for an end quote?

12. What type of writing is used when your purpose is to tell a story?

13. What type of writing is used when your purpose is to paint a picture with words?

14. What type of writing is used when your purpose is to express an opinion and to convince the reader that this opinion is correct?

15. What type of writing is used when your purpose is to inform, to give facts, to give directions, to explain, or to define something?

>>>>>>>>>>>>>> **Student Tip...**

For information about test-taking strategies, refer to the Resource Tools Section on page 520.

START LESSON 11

Lesson 11

You will

- hand in WA 23 for grading.
- respond to oral review questions.
- take Chapter 9 Test.

CHAPTER TEST

It is time to evaluate your knowledge of the skills you have learned in this chapter. Your teacher will give you the Chapter 9 Test to help you assess your progress.

Lesson 1

You will

- study new vocabulary; make Card 26; write own sentence using the vocabulary word.
- analyze new analogy; make Card 26; write own analogy.
- practice Jingles 18–23.
- identify Mixed Patterns 1–3.
- classify Introductory Sentences.
- do a Skill Builder.
- write in your journal.

LISTENING AND SPEAKING:

Vocabulary & Analogy Time

Learn It: Recite the new vocabulary and analogy words.

Reference 153	Vocabulary & Analogy Words

Word: coax (kōks)
    Definition: to persuade by gentle urging
    Synonym: cajole   **Antonym:** command
    Sentence: She **coaxed** the kitten down from the tree.

Analogy: never : always :: absent : present
    Antonym relationship: Just as **never** is the opposite of **always**, **absent** is the opposite of **present**.

Vocabulary Card 26: Record the vocabulary information above and write your own sentence, using the new word.

Analogy Card 26: Record the analogy information and write your own analogy, using the same relationship as the analogy above.

Jingle Time

Recite It: Practice Jingles 18–23 in the Jingle Section on pages 503–504.

Grammar Time

Apply It: These Introductory Sentences are used to apply the new grammar concepts taught below. Classify these sentences orally with your teacher.

Introductory Sentences	Chapter 10: Lesson 1

1. _____ The receptionist gave the customer my extension number.
2. _____ A bear's body stores large amounts of fat for the winter.
3. _____ The gnats flew in my face and hovered over my picnic basket.

Learn It: **MIXED GRAMMAR PATTERNS 1–3**

The sentences classified in this chapter will be Patterns 1–3. They are called **Mixed Patterns** because there are three different patterns from which to choose. Be alert to the parts of speech and where they are located in each sentence. Use the sentence cores to help determine the patterns of the sentences.

Skill Builder

Using the sentences just classified, do a Skill Builder orally with your teacher.

1. **Identify the nouns in a Noun Check.**
2. **Identify the nouns as singular or plural.**
3. **Identify the nouns as common or proper.**
4. **Identify the complete subject and the complete predicate.**
5. **Identify the simple subject and the simple predicate.**
6. **Do a Vocabulary Check.**
7. **Do a Verb Chant.**

JOURNAL WRITING 26

Write an entry in your journal. Use Reference 9 on page 12 for ideas.

START LESSON 2

Lesson 2

You will

- practice Jingles 13-17.
- classify Practice Sentences.
- do a Skill Builder.
- identify ten spelling rules for the plurals of nouns.
- make a spelling rule book.
- do Classroom Practice 47.

LISTENING AND SPEAKING:

 **Jingle Time**

Recite It: Practice Jingles 13–17 in the Jingle Section on pages 501-502.

 **Grammar Time**

Apply It: Classify the Practice Sentences orally with your teacher.

Practice Sentences	Chapter 10: Lesson 2
1. _____ Mary and Ellen left in a hurry and ran toward the bus station.	
2. _____ Gary's older brother gave him a guitar amplifier for his birthday.	
3. _____ Will our school broadcast the football games on the radio?	

 **Skill Builder**

Using the sentences just classified, do a Skill Builder orally with your teacher.

1. **Identify the nouns in a Noun Check.**
2. **Identify the nouns as singular or plural.**
3. **Identify the nouns as common or proper.**
4. **Identify the complete subject and the complete predicate.**
5. **Identify the simple subject and the simple predicate.**
6. **Do a Vocabulary Check.**
7. **Do a Verb Chant.**

 **Skill Time**

Learn It: **RULES FOR MAKING NOUNS PLURAL**

This list of rules will help you form the plurals of nouns correctly.

Reference 154 — Rules for Making Nouns Plural

Nouns are regular or irregular according to how they are made plural. **A regular noun is made plural by adding -s or -es to the end of the word.** Use Rules 1–8 below for making regular nouns plural.

Irregular nouns are made plural in ways other than adding -s or -es. The following lists of irregular nouns should be memorized. Use Rules 9–10 below for making irregular nouns plural.

- Some irregular nouns are made plural by a complete spelling change. **(Rule 9)**

Singular:	child	foot	goose	man	mouse	ox	tooth	woman
Plural:	children	feet	geese	men	mice	oxen	teeth	women

- Other irregular nouns are spelled the same for both singular and plural. **(Rule 10)**

Singular/Plural: aircraft, deer, fish, fowl, headquarters, moose, salmon, series, sheep, scissors, species, and trout.

RULES FOR MAKING REGULAR NOUNS PLURAL

Add -s to nouns without special endings.

1. most singular nouns.

Add -es to nouns with these special endings:

2. **ch, sh, z, s, ss, x.**
3. a consonant plus **o**.
4. a consonant plus **y**, change **y** to **i** before adding **es**.
5. **f** or **fe**, change **f** or **fe** to **v** before adding **es**.

Add -s to nouns with these special endings:

6. **f** or **ff**.
7. a vowel plus **o**.
8. a vowel plus **y**.

RULES FOR MAKING IRREGULAR NOUNS PLURAL

9. Change the spelling completely for the plural form.
10. Spell the same for both the singular and plural form.

Directions: For each noun, write the rule number and the plural form that follows the rule. Some nouns have two acceptable plural forms, but you should use the plural spellings that can be verified by these rules.

	Rule	Plural Form		Rule	Plural Form
1. clock	1	clocks	6. roof	6	roofs
2. compass	2	compasses	7. patio	7	patios
3. potato	3	potatoes	8. key	8	keys
4. penny	4	pennies	9. woman	9	women
5. half	5	halves	10. moose	10	moose

Discuss It:

Look at the word **clock**. What is the rule number that tells you what to do when you want to make most singular nouns plural? What does Rule 1 tell you to do to make **clock** plural? How do you spell the plural of **clock**?

Look at the word **compass**. What are the two letters at the end of **compass**? What is the number of the rule that tells you what to do when you have **ss** at the end of a word? What does Rule 2 tell you to do to make **compass** plural? How do you spell the plural of **compass**?

Look at the words **potato** and **penny**. Is the letter before the **o** in **potato** a consonant or a vowel? What rule number is used for a consonant plus **o**? What does Rule 3 tell you to do to make **potato** plural? How do you spell the plural of **potato**?

Is the letter before the **y** in **penny** a consonant or vowel? What rule number is used for a consonant plus **y**? What does Rule 4 tell you to do to make **penny** plural? How do you spell the plural of **penny**?

Continued on next page. >>>

Look at the words **half** and **roof**. What is the letter at the end of each of these words? What two rules deal with the letter **f**? By just reading these two rules, can you tell how to make **roof** and **half** plural? Words that end only in **f**, like **half** and **roof**, must be looked up in the dictionary or memorized if you do not already know how to form their plurals.

Look at the words **patio** and **key**. Is the letter before the **o** in **patio** a consonant or a vowel? What rule number is used for a vowel plus **o**? What does Rule 7 tell you to do to make **patio** plural? How do you spell the plural of **patio**?

Is the letter before the **y** in **key** a consonant or vowel? What rule number is used for a vowel plus **y**? What does Rule 8 tell you to do to make **key** plural? How do you spell the plural of **key**?

Look at the words **woman** and **moose**. What rule number is used in making **woman** plural? What does Rule 9 tell you to do to make **woman** plural? How do you spell the plural of **woman**? Since these words are irregular nouns, they must be memorized or looked up in the dictionary if you do not already know how to form their plurals. A list of the most common words that fit this rule is provided in the reference. You should memorize this list.

What rule number is used in making **moose** plural? What does Rule 10 tell you to do to make **moose** plural? How do you spell the plural of **moose**? A list of the most common words that fit this rule is provided in the reference. You should memorize this list.

Classroom Practice 47

It is time to practice the skills you are learning. You will use the classroom practice on the next page to apply these skills.

Student Activity

How to make a spelling rule book.

1. Write the title of each spelling rule at the top of lined notebook paper (one sheet per rule).

2. On each page, make two columns. Write **singular** at the top of the first column and **plural** at the top of the second column.

3. Use a folder or two sheets of construction paper as the cover of your book. Write the book title **My Spelling Rule Book** and your name on the front cover.

4. Put the pages in order according to the rule numbers. Staple the pages on the left-hand side if you do not use a folder with brads.

5. Illustrate the cover page. (*Suggestions: rulers, books, pencils, pictures of singular and plural nouns, etc.*)

6. During your study of singular and plural nouns, write the singular and plural forms for the nouns you have learned on the appropriate rule page.

7. At various times, get into small groups to compare and expand lists. You can also quiz fellow group members on plural spellings and the spelling rules.

Classroom Practice 47

Name:_____   Date:_____

GRAMMAR

▶ **Exercise 1:** Classify each sentence.

1. _____ Ashley's supervisor gave her the password for the company's computer files.

2. _____ Dangerous germs spread extremely fast in unsanitary environments.

3. _____ The magician astonished the audience with his amazing tricks.

SKILLS

▶ **Exercise 2:** For each noun, write the rule number and the plural form that follows the rule. Some nouns have two acceptable plural forms, but you should use the plural spellings that can be verified by these rules.

> **RULES FOR MAKING REGULAR NOUNS PLURAL**
> **Add -s to nouns without special endings.**
> 1. most singular nouns.
> **Add -es to nouns with these special endings:**
> 2. *ch, sh, z, s, ss, x*.
> 3. a consonant plus *o*.
> 4. a consonant plus *y*,
>   change *y* to *i* before adding *es*.
> 5. *f* or *fe*, change *f* or *fe* to *v* before adding *es*.
>
> **Add -s to nouns with these special endings:**
> 6. *f* or *ff*.
> 7. a vowel plus *o*.
> 8. a vowel plus *y*.
> **RULES FOR MAKING IRREGULAR NOUNS PLURAL**
> 9. Change the spelling completely
>   for the plural form.
> 10. Spell the same for both the singular
>   and plural form.

	Rule	Plural Form		Rule	Plural Form
1. airman			11. life		
2. patio			12. victory		
3. knife			13. mouse		
4. bluff			14. radio		
5. sample			15. Sunday		
6. veto			16. drapery		
7. volley			17. business		
8. bunch			18. mansion		
9. shovel			19. potato		
10. reef			20. fowl		

EDITING

▶ **Exercise 3:** Punctuate the story, "Here Comes George." (Part 1 of 5) **Editing Guide: End Marks: 3   Capitals: 5   Commas: 2   Quotation Marks: 4   Apostrophes: 2   Homonyms: 4   A/An: 1   Misspelled Words: 1**

i dont think were going to make it in time julie said as she gasped fore heir

i no we can make it if we hurry shouted george he motioned for everyone too

follow him as he swurved to take an shortcut

START LESSON 3

Lesson 3

You will

- study new vocabulary; make Card 27; write own sentence using the vocabulary word.
- analyze new analogy; make Card 27; write own analogy.
- practice Jingles 8–11.
- classify Practice Sentences.
- do a Skill Builder.
- do Classroom Practice 48.
- write in your journal.
- read and discuss Discovery Time.

LISTENING AND SPEAKING:
Vocabulary & Analogy Time

Learn It: Recite the new vocabulary and analogy words.

📖 *	Reference 155	Vocabulary & Analogy Words

Word: solitary (sŏl'ĭtĕr'ē)
Definition: standing alone
Synonym: sole   **Antonym:** accompanied
Sentence: He was the **solitary** dissenter in a recent show of hands.

Analogy: countries : continent :: stars : constellation
Part-to-whole relationship: Just as **countries** are part of a **continent**, **stars** are part of a **constellation**

Vocabulary Card 27: Record the vocabulary information above and write your own sentence, using the new word.

Analogy Card 27: Record the analogy information and write your own analogy, using the same relationship as the analogy above.

Jingle Time

Recite It: Practice Jingles 8–11 in the Jingle Section on page 500.

Grammar Time

Apply It: Classify the Practice Sentences orally with your teacher.

Practice Sentences	Chapter 10: Lesson 3

1. _____ Joseph has memorized the lyrics to his favorite songs on the radio.

2. _____ Horrors! That plane veered from its course and crashed into a grove of trees!

3. _____ Rebecca's doctor prescribed her the medicine for her illness.

Skill Builder

Using the sentences just classified, do a Skill Builder orally with your teacher.

1. **Identify the nouns in a Noun Check.**
2. **Identify the nouns as singular or plural.**
3. **Identify the nouns as common or proper.**
4. **Identify the complete subject and the complete predicate.**
5. **Identify the simple subject and the simple predicate.**
6. **Do a Vocabulary Check.**
7. **Do a Verb Chant.**

Classroom Practice 48

It is time to practice the skills you are learning. You will use the classroom practice on the next page to apply these skills.

ENRICHMENT:

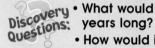

Uranus is the seventh planet from the sun in our solar system. Uranus is a giant gas planet that looks blue-green because it has oceans of liquid methane that give the planet its color. Uranus takes about 84 years to make one orbit around the Sun. This makes winters and summers last approximately 20 Earth years.

Discovery Questions:
- **What would it be like to have a summer that was twenty years long?**
- **How would it affect your education and recreation activities?**
- **If you could create a planet, what would it be like?**

Are you interested in learning more about Uranus?

1. You may explore this topic further by using the resources listed below.
   Computer resources: Internet, encyclopedia software
   Library resources: encyclopedias, books, magazines, newspapers
   Home/community resources: books, interviews, newspapers, magazines
2. A Discovery Share Time is provided in Lesson 8 if you wish to share your investigation results. You may share orally, or you may prepare a written report. You will put your written report in a class booklet titled "Space Trivia." This booklet will be placed in the class library for everyone to enjoy.

JOURNAL WRITING **27**

Write an entry in your journal. Use Reference 9 on page 12 for ideas.

Classroom Practice 48

Name:_____ Date:_____

GRAMMAR

▶ **Exercise 1:** Classify each sentence.

1. _____ Yes! Curtis scored a basket from the middle of the court!

2. _____ Angela's best friend bought her a locket for her graduation.

3. _____ Will you work with me after school on our science and math projects?

SKILLS

▶ **Exercise 2:** For each noun, write the rule number and the plural form that follows the rule. Some nouns have two acceptable plural forms, but you should use the plural spellings that can be verified by these rules.

RULES FOR MAKING REGULAR NOUNS PLURAL

Add -s to nouns without special endings.
  1. most singular nouns.
Add -es to nouns with these special endings:
  2. *ch, sh, z, s, ss, x*.
  3. a consonant plus *o*.
  4. a consonant plus *y*,
     change **y** to **i** before adding **es**.
  5. *f* or *fe*, change **f** or **fe** to **v** before adding **es**.

Add -s to nouns with these special endings:
  6. *f* or *ff*.
  7. a vowel plus *o*.
  8. a vowel plus *y*.
RULES FOR MAKING IRREGULAR NOUNS PLURAL
  9. Change the spelling completely for the plural form.
  10. Spell the same for both the singular and plural form.

	Rule	Plural Form		Rule	Plural Form
1. hoax			11. wolf		
2. tooth			12. gulf		
3. series			13. byway		
4. lawn			14. yacht		
5. potato			15. domino		
6. shelf			16. match		
7. foot			17. chef		
8. puff			18. salary		
9. forty			19. studio		
10. wax			20. journey		

EDITING

▶ **Exercise 3:** Punctuate the story, "Here Comes George." (Part 2 of 5) **Editing Guide: End Marks: 5   Capitals: 6   Commas: 1   Quotation Marks: 6   Apostrophes: 3   Homonyms: 2   A/An: 1   Subject-verb Agreement: 1   Misspelled Words: 1**

what will we dew if were not in time panted randy as he followed the others at an hard run

we wont worry about that now george replied grimly we only has a few more blocks two

go lets put on more speede

LISTENING AND SPEAKING:
Vocabulary & Analogy Time

Learn It: Recite the new vocabulary and analogy words.

📖 Reference 156	Vocabulary & Analogy Words

Word: tranquil (trăng'kwəl)
  Definition: free from turmoil
  Synonym: serene   **Antonym:** turbulent
  Sentence: The painting depicted a **tranquil** scene beside the lake.

Analogy: brainless : painless :: giggle : jiggle
  Rhyming relationship: Just as **brainless** rhymes with **painless**,
  giggle rhymes with **jiggle**.

Vocabulary Card 28: Record the vocabulary information above and write your own sentence, using the new word.

Analogy Card 28: Record the analogy information and write your own analogy, using the same relationship as the analogy above.

Jingle Time

Recite It: Practice Jingles 3–7 in the Jingle Section page 499.

Grammar Time

Apply It: Classify the Practice Sentences orally with your teacher.

Practice Sentences	Chapter 10: Lesson 4

1. _____ Did Marsha's dog bring her the newspaper from the neighbor's driveway?

2. _____ The petite fairy danced gracefully across the stage during the school play.

3. _____ Her fictitious story did not fool the crime investigators.

START LESSON 4

Lesson 4
You will

- study new vocabulary; make Card 28; write own sentence using the vocabulary word.
- analyze new analogy; make Card 28; write own analogy.
- practice Jingles 3–7.
- classify Practice Sentences.
- do Classroom Practice 49.
- read and discuss Discovery Time.
- do a homework assignment.
- do Home Connection activity.

Classroom Practice 49

It is time to practice the skills you are learning. You will use the classroom practice on the next page to apply these skills.

ENRICHMENT:

(German/English) 1738-1822 — Sir William Herschel was a German-born British astronomer who discovered the planet Uranus. The name Uranus was given to this planet, according to the tradition of naming planets for the gods of Greek and Roman mythology.

Discovery Questions:
- What interesting information can you find about the names of the planets?
- If you could name a planet, what name would you choose?
- What do you think it would be like to discover a new planet?
- Would you like to be an astronomer? Why or why not?

Are you interested in learning more about Sir William Herschel?

1. You may explore this topic further by using the resources listed below.
   Computer resources: Internet, encyclopedia software
   Library resources: encyclopedias, books, magazines, newspapers
   Home/community resources: books, interviews, newspapers, magazines

2. A Discovery Share Time is provided in Lesson 8 if you wish to share your investigation results. You may share orally, or you may prepare a written report. You will put your written report in a class booklet titled "Space Trivia." This booklet will be placed in the class library for everyone to enjoy.

Classroom Practice 49

Name:_____ Date:_____

GRAMMAR

▶ **Exercise 1:** Classify each sentence.

1. _____ Change the arrival times for the incoming flights from Memphis and Jackson.

2. _____ Today, a large number of hickory nuts fell among the leaves in my yard.

3. _____ Shawn's lieutenant gave him special recognition for his outstanding leadership.

SKILLS

▶ **Exercise 2:** For each noun, write the rule number and the plural form that follows the rule. Some nouns have two acceptable plural forms, but you should use the plural spellings that can be verified by these rules.

RULES FOR MAKING REGULAR NOUNS PLURAL
Add -s to nouns without special endings. 　1. most singular nouns. **Add -es to nouns with these special endings:** 　2. *ch, sh, z, s, ss, x*. 　3. a consonant plus *o*. 　4. a consonant plus *y*, 　　change *y* to *i* before adding **es**. 　5. *f* or *fe*, change *f* or *fe* to *v* before adding **es**.

Add -s to nouns with these special endings:
　6. *f* or *ff*.
　7. a vowel plus *o*.
　8. a vowel plus *y*.

RULES FOR MAKING IRREGULAR NOUNS PLURAL
　9. Change the spelling completely for the plural form.
　10. Spell the same for both the singular and plural form.

	Rule	Plural Form		Rule	Plural Form
1. mango			10. deer		
2. finch			11. Friday		
3. cyclist			12. tariff		
4. joy			13. punch		
5. trout			14. lady		
6. zoo			15. hotel		
7. toy			16. berry		
8. scarf			17. thief		
9. goof			18. groomsman		

EDITING

▶ **Exercise 3:** Punctuate the story, "Here Comes George." (Part 3 of 5) **Editing Guide: End Marks: 4　Capitals: 7　Commas: 2　Quotation Marks: 4　Apostrophes: 2　Homonyms: 3　Misspelled Words: 2**

nick grined as he turned to george and whooped i sea your house were going to make

it i cant weight

george glansed anxiously at his watch and gulped i sure hope sew

Homework 8

On notebook paper, number 1–12. For each noun, write the rule number and the plural form that follows the rule. If a noun has two acceptable plural forms, use the plural spelling that can be verified by these rules.

RULES FOR MAKING REGULAR NOUNS PLURAL

Add -s to nouns without special endings.
1. most singular nouns.

Add -es to nouns with these special endings:
2. ch, sh, z, s, ss, x.
3. a consonant plus o.
4. a consonant plus y, change y to i before adding es.
5. f or fe, change f or fe to v before adding es.

Add -s to nouns with these special endings:
6. f or ff.
7. a vowel plus o.
8. a vowel plus y.

RULES FOR MAKING IRREGULAR NOUNS PLURAL
9. Change the spelling completely for the plural form.
10. Spell the same for both the singular and plural form.

	Rule	Plural Form		Rule	Plural Form
1. treaty			7. torpedo		
2. patio			8. shelf		
3. trolley			9. mouse		
4. belief			10. ax		
5. tomato			11. wolf		
6. journey			12. child		

Home Connection

Family Activity for Vocabulary and Analogies

Divide into family teams. The first team will use vocabulary and analogy cards 1–14 to ask questions about the information on their cards. The second team will use vocabulary and analogy cards 15–28 to ask questions about the information on their cards.

Family Activity for Plurals of Nouns

Write the plurals of the nouns in the blanks. Then, circle them in the word search below. Words may appear across or down.

elf _____

fly _____

hoof _____

latch _____

man _____

patio _____

pulley _____

scissors _____

sheep _____

tooth _____

```
Q E R H Y G H C P M S W A U V
W X F J A S D C P T E E T H S
O J S W I N S I T U M P E E F
Z K C O Q D F U A T D W E P O
F U I G P U L L E Y S Q A O T
P O S E L R E C O V Z C A O Q
L A S R U Y E E L V E S L F S
H O O V E S G E A C G Z S E Z
L O R F E S O Z T A P S H S R
D B S T T E N U C T A H E I L
S R E O T A B R H T T S E M A
Z G S Q I F L I E S I O P E P
E S H E R I F F S O O S D N N
A R S E T T O R N G S T S O R
```

Puzzle Answers: elf/elves fly/flies hoof/hooves latch/latches man/men patio/patios pulley/pulleys scissors/scissors sheep/sheep tooth/teeth

English Made Easy

LISTENING AND SPEAKING:

Grammar Time

Apply It: Classify the Practice Sentences orally with your teacher.

Practice Sentences	Chapter 10: Lesson 5

1. _____ Laboratory mice made the trip to the satellite during the last flight.
2. _____ She is drawing her friends a map to her new home in the city.
3. _____ Were the tropical plants in the foyer watered yesterday?

Chapter Checkup 50

It is time for a checkup of the skills you have learned in this chapter. You will use the chapter checkup on the next page to evaluate your progress.

START LESSON 5

Lesson 5

You will
- classify Practice Sentences.
- do Chapter Checkup 50.
- write in your journal.

JOURNAL WRITING 28

Write an entry in your journal. Use Reference 9 on page 12 for ideas.

Chapter 10 Checkup 50

Name:_____ Date:_____

GRAMMAR

▶ **Exercise 1:** Classify each sentence.

1. _____ She is mailing her cousin in Australia a wedding announcement.

2. _____ Remind me of my dentist appointment on Friday.

3. _____ Yikes! The aircraft is landing in the middle of an electrical storm!

SKILLS

▶ **Exercise 2:** For each noun, write the rule number and the plural form that follows the rule. Some nouns have two acceptable plural forms, but you should use the plural spellings that can be verified by these rules.

RULES FOR MAKING REGULAR NOUNS PLURAL
Add -s to nouns without special endings.
  1. most singular nouns.
Add -es to nouns with these special endings:
  2. *ch, sh, z, s, ss, x.*
  3. a consonant plus *o.*
  4. a consonant plus *y,*
     change **y** to **i** before adding **es.**
  5. **f** or **fe,** change **f** or **fe** to **v** before adding **es.**

Add -s to nouns with these special endings:
  6. **f** or **ff.**
  7. a vowel plus *o.*
  8. a vowel plus *y.*
RULES FOR MAKING IRREGULAR NOUNS PLURAL
  9. Change the spelling completely
     for the plural form.
  10. Spell the same for both the singular
      and plural form.

	Rule	Plural Form		Rule	Plural Form
1. galaxy			9. rodeo		
2. cliff			10. sheep		
3. moose			11. lily		
4. pistachio			12. waltz		
5. banjo			13. detour		
6. half			14. delay		
7. canopy			15. citizen		
8. woman			16. indigo		

EDITING

▶ **Exercise 3:** Punctuate the story, "Here Comes George." (Part 4 of 5) **Editing Guide: End Marks: 3   Capitals: 5   Commas: 4   Quotation Marks: 4   Apostrophes: 2   Homonyms: 2   Subject-verb Agreement: 1   Misspelled words: 2**

georges mom looked up as the gang burst into her kitchen you and your freinds almost didnt

make it george she said as she pointed two the clock

mom your fryed apple pies and ice cream is worth running fore george said happily as he

settled down with the others and dug into the scrumptious desert his mother had on the counter

Literature Time

Learn It: **FICTION AND NONFICTION BOOKS**

START LESSON 6

Lesson 6

You will
- read and discuss fiction, nonfiction, autobiography, and biography.
- read and discuss card catalog and how to find fiction books in the library.
- read and discuss how to write a fiction book review.
- write a fiction book review for WA 24.

Reference 157 — Two Kinds of Books

When you go to the library to check out a book, you need to know which books are available and how to find them. There are two large categories of books, fiction and nonfiction.

1. FICTION

Fiction books contain stories about people, places, or things that are not true even though the author may use ideas based on real people or events. Fiction writers use their imagination and make up stories for the reader's enjoyment. There are several types of fictional writings. Some of these include fables, myths, novels, plays, science fiction, short stories, horror stories, and mysteries. Fiction books are grouped together in a special section of the library and are arranged alphabetically by the author's last name.

2. NONFICTION

Nonfiction books contain factual information and stories that are true. You can find a nonfiction book on just about any subject. Nonfiction books have been written about plants, animals, oceans, planets, space, countries, history, and all kinds of other topics. In most libraries, these nonfiction books are grouped together in numerical order, according to a call number. A call number is the number that is seen on the spine of all nonfiction books.

Autobiographies and biographies are special types of nonfiction writings. An autobiography tells about the writer's own life. In a biography, on the other hand, a writer writes about another person's life. Details and facts are true and cannot be changed or embellished. Even though autobiographies and biographies are nonfiction, they are not arranged by call numbers like other nonfiction books. Instead, they are grouped together by the last name of the person about whom they are written.

Learn It: **THE CARD CATALOG**

Reference 158 — Card Catalogs

The **card catalog** is an index to the books in a library. A book is listed in the card catalog in three ways—by author, by title, and by subject. An electronic or traditional card catalog can help you find any book in the library.

A computerized card catalog is an electronic file where you can search by author, title, or subject to find the same information that you would get by searching for a card in the traditional card catalog. Many community libraries have websites that offer access to the card catalog from home. After the book's title, the author's name, or the subject of the book has been entered in an electronic card catalog, the computer will search its library database for your request. The information you requested will be displayed on a computer screen if it is available in that particular library. You can print or copy the information received to help you find the book.

A traditional card catalog is a file of cards, arranged alphabetically, that is usually placed in the drawers of a card catalog cabinet. Labels on the drawers tell which cards are in each drawer. The catalog cards contain information about every book and nearly all the other materials located in the library.

Continued on next page. >>>

Reference 158 continued from previous page.

CARD CATALOG CARDS

The card catalog has three kinds of cards for every book: an **author card**, a **title card**, and a **subject card**. All three kinds of cards are arranged alphabetically by the word(s) on the top line. All three kinds of cards give the name of the book, the name of the author, and the call number of the book. They also give the place and date of publication, the publisher, the number of pages in the book, and other important information. The main difference in the cards is how the information is arranged.

Author cards have the name of the author of the book on the top line, and they are filed alphabetically by the author's last name. **Title cards** have the title of the book on the top line, and they are filed alphabetically by the first word of the title (except for *A*, *An*, or *The*). **Subject cards** have the subject of the book on the top line, and they are filed alphabetically by the first word of the subject (except for *A*, *An*, or *The*).

Author Card	Title Card	Subject Card

DiC
Author: DiCamillo, Kate
  Title: The Tale of Despereaux
    Illustrated by Timothy Ering
    Candlewick Press, Cambridge
    (c2003) 269p.
	DiC
	  Title: The Tale of Despereaux
	Author: DiCamillo, Kate
	    Illustrated by Timothy Ering
	    Candlewick Press, Cambridge
	    (c2003) 269p.
		DiC
		  Subject: Fantasy
		  Author: DiCamillo, Kate
		    Title: The Tale of Despereaux
		    Illustrated by Timothy Ering
		    Candlewick Press, Cambridge
		    (c2003) 269p.

Learn It: FINDING FICTION BOOKS IN THE LIBRARY

Reference 159 — How to Find Fiction Books in the Library

To find out if a library has a certain fiction book, look in the card catalog for the title card of that book. If you don't know the title but know the author, look for the author card. If you don't know the title or the author, look under the subject of the book. Also, look under the subject if you are interested in finding several books about your topic. Sometimes, fiction books are not classified by subject like other books. You must then look for the title or author of the book.

After you find the card for the book you want in the card catalog, you must know how to find the book. Fiction books are arranged on the shelves in **alphabetical order** according to the **authors' last name**; therefore, a fiction book can be located only if you know the author's last name.

If you look on the spine of a fiction book, you will see only a letter(s). This is the first letter in the author's last name, and all three catalog cards will have the first letter of the author's last name in the top left corner of each card. Be sure to write the author's last name and the book title down on paper before you look for the book.

When you go to the library shelf, look at the letter printed on the spines of the books until you find the same letter(s) on the book that you copied from the catalog card. If two authors have the same last name, their books are arranged in alphabetical order according to the authors' first names. If there are two or more books by the same author, they are arranged in alphabetical order by titles.

Learn It: WRITING A BOOK REVIEW FOR A FICTION BOOK

Reference 160 — Writing a Book Review for a Fiction Book

Writing a book review gives you an opportunity to tell what a book is about and what you think about the book. The things you share in your review could influence others as they decide whether or not to read the book. Therefore, it is important that you consider carefully the information and opinion you share. Use the following guidelines to help you decide what to include in a book review for a **fiction book**.

Continued on next page. >>>

Reference 160 continued from previous page.

1. List the title and author.

2. Tell the type of book: Fiction.

3. Write an introductory paragraph to describe the main character(s) and the problem he/she/they faced. In the second paragraph, write a short version (summary) of the main events in the story. In the third paragraph, tell how the problem was resolved and/or how the story ended.

4. In the last paragraph, give your opinion of the book. In this paragraph, tell why you liked or disliked the book.

The example below shows one way to write a book review for a fiction book.

<u>My Life as a Fifth-Grade Comedian</u>

by Elizabeth Levy

Fiction Book

   In this book, the main character is a boy named Bobby. Bobby is the fifth-grade class clown at his school. He can always be counted on to make other students laugh during class, and he is famous for his practical jokes. Bobby also tries to use humor to deal with the tension and problems he faces at home.

   Things finally sour for Bobby at school when he refuses to do his homework because of a bet with his friend, Tyrone. The bet is that Bobby can't get into the Book of Records for not doing his homework. The bet between Bobby and Tyrone ends up with serious consequences for Bobby. His constant bad behavior has the principal threatening to send him to the School for Intervention. Bobby is given one last chance to prove to his teachers, his principal, and his parents that he can be taken seriously. Bobby must organize a schoolwide laugh-off and get teachers and students to compete. Bobby knows he has to make the contest a success. The only problem is that he has no clue where to begin.

   Bobby's perseverance does pay off in the end, and Bobby discovers he can't use humor to hide from his troubles. Bobby learns that he must face his real problems at home and at school. He learns to deal with his problems in a more constructive way.

   I liked this book a lot because it made me laugh, and it taught me other ways that problems can be handled. I also learned a lot about friendship and family. Some of my favorite parts were the jokes and riddles.

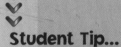

Student Tip...

For additional information and activities about fiction and nonfiction books, the library, and the card catalog, refer to Study Skills in the Resource Tools Section on pages 524–525.

Write It: **WRITING ASSIGNMENT 24**

Even though this writing assignment for a book review of a fiction book is given today, your book review is not due until Lesson 6 of Chapter 11.

Writing Assignment 24 : Fiction Book Review

Purpose: To provide information about events or persons in a book and to express an opinion

Type of Writing: Book review of a fiction book

Audience: Classmates, family, or friends

Writing Topics: Choose a fiction book.

Special Instructions:

1. Choose a fiction book about which to write a book review.

2. Use References 157–160 on pages 309-310 to guide you in writing a book review of a fiction book of your choice.

3. Write a rough draft, then revise and edit it, and write a final paper of your book review during a study time or outside of class..

4. Finish Book Review 24 by Lesson 6 of Chapter 11 and give it to your teacher.

5. Keep your book review in the Final Paper folder if you finish early.

START LESSON 7

Lesson 7

You will

- conference with teacher about WA 23.
- read a fiction book.

Reading Time

Read It: **FICTION BOOK**

Use this reading time to read the fiction book you have selected for a book review. When you finish your book, you may begin working on your book review assignment, Writing Assignment 24.

Conference Time

Discuss It: **TEACHER-STUDENT CONFERENCES FOR WRITING ASSIGNMENT 23**

Meet with your teacher to discuss Writing Assignment 23.
After the conference, place this group of papers in your Publishing folder.

>>>>>>>>>>>>>>>>>>>>>>> **Student Tip...**

> To review the information about fiction book reviews, look at Reference 160 on page 310.

English Made Easy

Publishing Time

Publish It: **WRITING ASSIGNMENT 23**

Choose a publishing form and publish Writing Assignment 23. After rewriting your paper for publication, give the stapled papers (evaluation guide, graded final paper, rough draft, and Story Elements Outline) to your teacher to be placed in your Writing Portfolio.

Lesson 8

You will

- publish WA 23.
- participate in Discovery Share Time.
- write an independent narrative with dialogue (WA 25).

Reference 67	Publishing Checklist for Step 6 in the Writing Process

The sixth step in the writing process is called publishing. Publishing is sharing your writing with others. With so many forms of publishing available, finding a match for every project and personality is easy.

At times, a written work is best read aloud. Other times, the biggest impact is made when a written work is read silently. You can also use media sources to enhance any publication.

SPECIAL INSTRUCTIONS FOR PUBLISHING:

- Rewrite the graded paper in ink or type it on a computer, correcting any marked errors. *(Do not display or publish papers that have marked errors or grades on them.)*
- Give your teacher the set of stapled papers to place in your Writing Portfolio. *(Stapled papers: evaluation guide, graded final paper, rough draft, and prewriting map.)*
- Select a publishing form from the list below and publish your rewritten paper.

    1. Have classmates, family members, neighbors, or others read your writing at school or home.
    2. Share your writing with others during a Share Time.
       (Refer to Reference 68 on page 103 for sharing guidelines.)
    3. Display your writing on a bulletin board or wall.
    4. Put your writing in the classroom library or in the school library for checkout.
    5. Send your writing as a letter or an e-mail to a friend or relative.
    6. Frame your writing by gluing it on colored construction paper and decorating it.
    7. Make a book of your writing for your classroom, your family, or others.
    8. Illustrate your writing and give it to others to read.
    9. Dramatize your writing in the form of a play, puppet show, or radio broadcast.
    10. Send your writing to be placed in a waiting room (doctor, veterinarian, dentist, etc.), senior-citizen center, or a nursing home.
    11. Send your writing to a school newspaper, local newspaper, or a magazine for publication.
    12. Make a videotape, cassette tape, or slide presentation of your writing.
    13. Choose another publishing form that is not listed.

LISTENING AND SPEAKING:

Discovery Share Time

If you have chosen to investigate a topic introduced in this chapter, you now have the opportunity to share your results in one of the following ways:

1. You may relate your information orally.

2. You may read a written report.

3. You may place your report in the booklet without reading it aloud.

After share time, all written reports should be turned in to be placed in the class booklet titled "Space Trivia." You are encouraged to check out this class booklet so you can enjoy the reports again.

Writing Time

Write It: **WRITING ASSIGNMENT 25**

As you write a rough draft for your independent writing assignment, you will do two of the six steps in the writing process: prewriting and rough draft.

Writing Assignment 25

Purpose: To tell a story

Type of Writing: Narrative

Audience: Classmates, relatives, or friends

Writing Topics: The band contest/The art show/The dog show
An argument with my best friend
The night I couldn't sleep/The night I dreamed about....
(Brainstorm for other ideas, individually or in groups.)

Special Instructions:

1. Follow the Prewriting and Rough Draft Checklists in References 47 and 49 on pages 62, 66.

2. Use Reference 152 on page 288 to help you write your narrative. Make a Story Elements Outline instead of a prewriting map

3. Write your narrative with dialogue.

4. Write in first or third person. See Reference 71 on page 108.
(First-person pronouns: *I, me, my, mine, we, us, our,* and *ours.*)
(Third-person pronouns: *he, his, him, she, her, hers, it, its, they, their, theirs,* and *them.*)

Note: Reference 57 on page 76 gives the steps in the writing process and the location of all the writing checklists.

Student Note:

Some of your writing pieces will be selected for revision and editing later in the school year.

English Made Easy

LISTENING AND SPEAKING:

Jingle Time

Recite It: Practice Jingle 12 in the Jingle Section on page 501.

>>>>>>>>>>>>>>>>>>>>>>>>>> **Student Tip...**

> Reviewing the transition words will help you apply them in your writing.

Writing Time

Learn It: **NARRATIVE WRITING WITHOUT DIALOGUE**

Some narratives are written without dialogue. The Story Elements Outline is still used because it keeps your writing focused and helps you choose details and events that support the main idea of your story.

Lesson 9
You will
- practice Jingle 12.
- read and discuss a narrative essay without dialogue.
- plan and write rough draft for narrative without dialogue (WA 26).

 Reference 161 | **Story Elements for a Narrative Without Dialogue**

STORY ELEMENTS OUTLINE

1. Main Idea:
Tell the problem or situation that needs a solution.

> **Grandmother wants to learn to ski for her sixty-fifth birthday.**

2. Setting:
Tell when and where the story takes place, either clearly stated or implied.

> **When:** **The story takes place during the winter.**
> **Where:** **The story takes place at a ski resort in Colorado.**

3. Characters:
Tell whom or what the story is about.

> **The main characters are Grandmother and her grandchildren.**

4. Plot:
Tell what the characters in the story do and what happens to them.

> **The story is about how Grandmother handles the challenges of learning to ski down the bunny slope for the first time.**

5. Ending:
Use a strong ending that will bring the story to a close.

> **Snow skiing was the first project Grandmother wanted her grandchildren to help her do for her sixty-fifth birthday.**

Continued on next page. >>>

Reference 161 continued from previous page.

Example of Narrative Writing Without Dialogue

Grandmother's Birthday

My grandmother had never skied before; so, for her sixty-fifth birthday, we took her to Colorado to snow ski. It was the best trip of our lives. We waited while Grandmother went into a local store to be outfitted. When she came out, she had a bright yellow jacket, black ski pants with yellow stripes, a yellow and black hat, and a pair of bright yellow skis. As we stared, she held up her orange gloves and said she decided to add a little color to her outfit. Except for the gloves, she looked like a well-bundled bumblebee.

The next step was getting Grandmother on the beginner's lift. They had to stop the chair lift for five minutes while Grandmother tried to figure out the best way to get on. Next, came getting off the lift. Another five minutes! Finally, we all made it to the bunny slope. Then, we waited another 30 minutes for Grandmother to reassure herself that she could go down the slope like all those little kids.

As she started down, we heard her yelling at everyone to get out of the way. And everyone did. At the bottom, Grandmother did a victory dance, along with a lot of shouting and high-fives for everyone. She soon had a crowd clapping and cheering for her. Some of the them even took her picture! Then, she looked triumphantly at all of us and said that she was taking us to a victory lunch.

As we watched Grandmother waddle confidently to the cafeteria in her bulky ski boots, we all experienced a feeling of success, too. Grandmother had been such an important part of our lives for so many years that we were more than eager to help her with her birthday projects. Snow skiing was the first one.

Write It: **WRITING ASSIGNMENT 26**

As you write a rough draft for your guided writing assignment, you will do two of the six steps in the writing process: prewriting and rough draft.

Writing Assignment 26

Purpose: To tell a story

Type of Writing: Narrative

Audience: Classmates, relatives, or friends

Writing Topics: A summer/winter job
A natural disaster in my room/locker/town
A crazy idea/funny story/day to forget
(Brainstorm for other ideas, individually or in groups.)

Special Instructions:

1. Follow the Prewriting and Rough Draft Checklists in References 47 and 49 on pages 62, 66.

2. Use Reference 161 on page 315 to help you write your narrative. Make a Story Elements Outline instead of a prewriting map.

3. Write your narrative without dialogue.

4. Write in first or third person. See Reference 71 on page 108
(First-person pronouns: *I, me, my, mine, we, us, our,* and *ours.*)
(Third-person pronouns: *he, his, him, she, her, hers, it, its, they, their, theirs,* and *the*

Note: Reference 57 on page 76 gives the steps in the writing process and the locat of all the writing checklists.

Writing Time

Apply It: **REVISE, EDIT, AND WRITE A FINAL PAPER**

Following the schedule below, you will revise and edit Writing Assignment 26. Then, you will write a final paper. Use the Chapter 10 Writing Evaluation Guide on the next page to check your final paper one last time.

Reference 55   Revising & Editing Schedule and Writing a Final Paper

SPECIAL INSTRUCTIONS FOR REVISING AND EDITING (Steps 3-4 in the writing process):

- Use the Revising and Editing Checklists in References 51 and 53 as you revise and edit your rough draft.
- Follow the revising and editing schedule below as directed by your teacher.
    1. **Individual.** First, read your rough draft to yourself. Use the Revising Checklist in Reference 51 on page 69. Go through your paper, checking each item on the list and making revisions to your rough draft. Then, use the Editing Checklist in Reference 53 on page 71. Go through your paper again, checking each item on the list and editing your rough draft.
    2. **Partner.** Next, get with your editing partner. Work together on each partner's rough draft, one paper at a time. Read each rough draft aloud and revise and edit it together, using the Revising and Editing Checklists. (The author of the paper should be the one to make the corrections on his own paper.)
    3. **Group.** Finally, read the rough draft to a revision group for feedback. Each student should read his paper while the others listen and offer possible revising and editing suggestions. (The author will determine whether to make corrections from the revision group's suggestions.)

SPECIAL INSTRUCTIONS FOR FINAL PAPER (Step 5 in the writing process):

- Write your final paper, using the Final Paper Checklist in Reference 56 on page 75.
- Staple your writing papers in this order: the final paper on top, the rough draft in the middle, and the prewriting map on the bottom. Place the stapled papers in the Final Paper folder.

>>>>>>>> **Student Tip...**

1. Be tactful and helpful in your comments during revising and editing time. The purpose of any suggestion should be to improve the writer's rough draft.

2. As you make your final corrections, you have the choice of accepting or rejecting any suggestions made by your partners or your revision group.

3. Study Vocabulary Words and Analogies 26-28 for the chapter test in the next lesson.

4. If you need to improve your handwriting, refer to the Resource Tools Section on page 521 for information on writing legibly.

Chapter 10 Writing Evaluation Guide

Name:_____ Date:_____

ROUGH DRAFT CHECK

_____ 1. Did you write your rough draft in pencil?

_____ 2. Did you write the correct headings on the first seven lines of your paper?

_____ 3. Did you use extra wide margins and skip every other line?

_____ 4. Did you write a title at the end of your rough draft?

_____ 5. Did you place your edited rough draft in your Rough Draft folder?

REVISING CHECK

_____ 6. Did you identify the purpose, type of writing, and audience?

_____ 7. Did you check for a topic, topic sentence, and sentences supporting the topic?

_____ 8. Did you check sentences for the right order, and did you combine, rearrange, or delete sentences when necessary?

_____ 9. Did you check for a variety of simple, compound, and complex sentences?

_____ 10. Did you check for any left out, repeated, or unnecessary words?

_____ 11. Did you check for the best choice of words by replacing or deleting unclear words?

_____ 12. Did you check the content for interest and creativity?

_____ 13. Did you check the voice to make sure the writing says what you want it to say?

EDITING CHECK

_____ 14. Did you indent each paragraph?

_____ 15. Did you put an end mark at the end of every sentence?

_____ 16. Did you capitalize the first word of every sentence?

_____ 17. Did you check for all other capitalization mistakes?

_____ 18. Did you check for all punctuation mistakes?
(*commas, periods, apostrophes, quotation marks, underlining*)

_____ 19. Did you check for misspelled words and for incorrect homonym choices?

_____ 20. Did you check for incorrect spellings of plural and possessive forms?

_____ 21. Did you check for correct construction and punctuation of your sentences?

_____ 22. Did you check for usage mistakes? (*subject/verb agreement, a/an choices, contractions, verb tenses, pronoun/antecedent agreement, pronoun cases, degrees of adjectives, double negatives, etc.*)

_____ 23. Did you put your revised and edited paper in the Rough Draft folder?

FINAL PAPER CHECK

_____ 24. Did you write the final paper in pencil?

_____ 25. Did you center the title on the top line and center your name under the title?

_____ 26. Did you skip a line before starting the writing assignment?

_____ 27. Did you single-space, use wide margins, and write the final paper neatly?

_____ 28. Did you staple your papers in this order: final paper on top, rough draft in the middle, and prewriting map on the bottom? Did you put them in the Final Paper folder?

Writing Time

Hand It In: **WRITING ASSIGNMENT 26**

Get your stapled papers for Writing Assignment 26 from your Final Paper folder. Check to make sure they are in the correct order: the final paper on top, the rough draft in the middle, and the Story Elements Outline on the bottom. Hand them in to your teacher.

LISTENING AND SPEAKING:

Oral Review Questions

Discuss It:

1. What are the core parts of a Pattern 3 sentence?

2. What are the core parts of a Pattern 2 sentence?

3. What are the core parts of a Pattern 1 sentence?

4. True or False. Most regular nouns are made plural by adding an **-s**.

5. What is the rule number for making nouns plural that end in **ch, sh, z, s, ss,** or **x**?

6. Do you add an **-s** or an **-es** to the word **sandwich** to make it plural?

7. What is the rule number for making nouns plural that end in a consonant plus **y**?

8. Do you add an **-s** or an **-es** to the word **berry** to make it plural?

9. What else do you do to the word **berry** to make it plural?

10. What is the rule number for making nouns plural that end in a vowel plus **y**?

11. Do you add an **-s** or an **-es** to the word **birthday** to make it plural?

12. What kinds of books contain stories that are not true?

13. What kinds of books contain stories and information that are true?

14. Name two different types of nonfiction writing?

15. What is an autobiography?

16. What is a biography?

17. How are fiction books arranged in the library?

18. How are nonfiction books arranged in the library?

19. What type of writing is used when your purpose is to tell a story?

20. What type of writing is used when your purpose is to paint a picture with words?

21. What type of writing is used when your purpose is to express an opinion and to convince the reader that this opinion is correct?

22. What type of writing is used when your purpose is to inform, to give facts, to give directions, to explain, or to define something?

 **Student Tip...**

> For information about test-taking strategies, refer to the Resource Tools Section on page 520.

START LESSON 11

Lesson 11
You will
- hand in WA 26 for grading.
- respond to oral review questions.
- take Chapter 10 Test.

CHAPTER TEST

It is time to evaluate your knowledge of the skills you have learned in this chapter. Your teacher will give you the Chapter 10 Test to help you assess your progress.

Lesson 1

You will

- study new vocabulary; make Card 29; write own sentence using the vocabulary word.
- analyze new analogy; make Card 29; write own analogy.
- recite new jingle (Predicate Noun).
- identify predicate noun, linking verb, and Pattern 4.
- classify Introductory Sentences.
- do a Skill Builder to identify predicate nouns.
- write in your journal.

LISTENING AND SPEAKING:
Vocabulary & Analogy Time

Learn It: Recite the new vocabulary and analogy words.

Reference 162	Vocabulary & Analogy Words

Word: contemplate (kŏn'təm plāt')
Definition: to consider carefully
Synonym: ponder **Antonym:** disregard
Sentence: The principal **contemplated** putting a hiking trail on the school grounds.

Analogy: possessions : belongings :: delicious : tasty
  Synonym relationship: Just as **possessions** means nearly the same as **belongings**, **delicious** means nearly the same as **tasty**.

Vocabulary Card 29: Record the vocabulary information above and write your own sentence, using the new word.
Analogy Card 29: Record the analogy information and write your own analogy, using the same relationship as the analogy above.

Jingle Time

Recite It: Recite the new jingle.

♪ Jingle 24	The Predicate Noun Jingle

A predicate, predicate noun
Is a special, special noun
In the predicate, predicate, predicate
That means the **same as the subject**,
The simple, simple subject.
A predicate, predicate noun
Follows after a linking verb.

To locate a predicate noun,
Ask **WHAT** or **WHO** after the verb
And verify the answer.
Verify that the noun in the predicate
Means the **same thing as the subject**,
The simple, simple subject.

Grammar Time

Apply It: These Introductory Sentences are used to apply the new grammar concepts taught below. Classify these sentences orally with your teacher.

Introductory Sentences	Chapter 11: Lesson 1

1. _____ A bear is an animal.
2. _____ A bear is a large, shaggy animal with a short tail.
3. _____ China is a country on the other side of the world.

Learn It: PREDICATE NOUNS AND LINKING VERBS

Earlier, you learned that nouns can have different jobs, or functions, in a sentence. You have already studied four of these jobs. A noun can be a subject, an object of a preposition, an indirect object, or a direct object. You have also learned that not all nouns are part of a sentence pattern.

You have been studying Patterns 1–3. A Pattern 1 sentence has only one noun and an action verb as the sentence core. A Pattern 2 sentence has two nouns and an action verb as the sentence core. A Pattern 3 sentence has three nouns and an action verb as the sentence core. Now, we will learn a new sentence pattern. The new sentence pattern, Pattern 4, has two nouns and a linking verb as the sentence core.

📖 **Reference 163**	**Predicate Noun or Pronoun, Linking Verb, and Pattern 4**

1. A **predicate noun** is located in the predicate and means the same thing as the simple subject.

2. A predicate noun is located after a linking verb.

3. A *predicate noun* is labeled with the abbreviation **PrN**.

4. A predicate pronoun can take the place of a predicate noun. Label a *predicate pronoun* as **PrP**.

5. A predicate noun or pronoun is also known as a **predicate nominative**.

6. To find a predicate noun or pronoun, ask WHAT or WHO after the verb.

7. A **linking verb** is a verb that expresses a state of **being** instead of **action**. A linking verb states that someone or something exists. It shows no action. A linking verb links, or connects, the subject to a predicate noun or pronoun that means the same thing. A *linking verb* is labeled with the abbreviation **LV**. (**Common linking verbs:** *am, is, are, was, were, being, been, appear, become, feel, grow, look, remain, seem, smell, sound,* and *taste.*)

8. A Pattern 4 sentence has a subject noun, linking verb, and predicate noun as its core. A Pattern 4 sentence is labeled **SN LV PrN P4**. A Pattern 4 sentence has two noun jobs in its core: the subject noun and the predicate noun. (*If the subject is a pronoun, it is labeled as a subject pronoun in the sentence, but the pattern is still identified as SN LV PrN P4.*)

9. **A review:**
   Pattern 1 is **SN V**. It has a noun-verb (**N V**) core.
   Pattern 2 is **SN V-t DO**. It has a noun-verb-noun (**N V N**) core.
   Pattern 3 is **SN V-t IO DO**. It has a noun-verb-noun-noun (**N V N N**) core.
   Pattern 4 is **SN LV PrN**. It has a noun-linking verb-noun (**N LV N**) core.

The location of each noun determines its job in a sentence. Only certain noun jobs form the pattern parts of a sentence. For each pattern, the order of the core nouns does not change. A noun that is an object of the preposition is not part of a sentence pattern.

Question and Answer Flow for the Practice Sentence, adding Predicate Nouns

Practice Sentence: Mom is a talented singer.

1. Who is a talented singer? **Mom - SN**

2. What is being said about Mom? **Mom is - V**

3. Mom is what? **singer - verify the noun**

4. Does singer mean the same thing as Mom? **Yes.**

5. Singer - **PrN** (Say: *Singer - predicate noun.*)

6. Is - **LV** (Say: *Is - linking verb.*)

7. What kind of singer? **talented - Adj**

8. **A - A**

9. **SN LV PrN P4** (Say: *Subject Noun, Linking Verb, Predicate Noun, Pattern 4.*)

10. Skill Check

11. Linking verb - check again

12. **No prepositional phrases**

13. **Period, statement, declarative sentence**

14. Go back to the verb. Divide the complete subject from the complete predicate.

15. Is this sentence in a natural or inverted order? **Natural - no change.**

```
            SN   LV A  Adj   PrN
 SN  LV     Mom / is a talented singer.  D
 PrN  P4
```

JOURNAL WRITING 29

Write an entry in your journal. Use Reference 9 on page 12 for ideas.

Discuss It: **PREDICATE NOUNS AND LINKING VERBS**

1. What is the pattern in a Pattern 4 sentence?
2. What are the core parts of a Pattern 4 sentence?
3. What parts of speech are used in a Pattern 4 sentence?

Learn It: **A SKILL BUILDER FOR A NOUN CHECK WITH PREDICATE NOUNS**

The example below shows you what to do with predicate nouns when you are identifying nouns for a Noun Check.

Skill Builder
FOR A noun CHECK WITH PREDICATE nouns

Sentence 1: Subject Noun **bear**, *yes, it is a noun;*
Predicate Noun **animal**, *yes, it is a noun.*

Sentence 2: Subject Noun **bear**, *yes, it is a noun;*
Predicate Noun **animal**, *yes, it is a noun;*
Object of the Preposition **tail**, *yes, it is a noun.*

Sentence 3: Subject Noun **China**, *yes, it is a noun;*
Predicate Noun **country**, *yes, it is a noun;*
Object of the Preposition **side**, *yes, it is a noun,*
Object of the Preposition **world**, *yes, it is a noun.*

English Made Easy

LISTENING AND SPEAKING:

Recite It: Practice Jingle 24 in the Jingle Section on page 504.

Apply It: Classify the Practice Sentences orally with your teacher.

Practice Sentences	Chapter 11: Lesson 2

1. _____ Vixen is the name for a female fox.
2. _____ The dictionary is a valuable source of information for students.
3. _____ The papyrus plant is a giant reed along the Nile River.

Using the sentences just classified, do a Skill Builder orally with your teacher.

1. **Identify the nouns in a Noun Check.**
2. **Identify the nouns as singular or plural.**
3. **Identify the nouns as common or proper.**
4. **Identify the complete subject and the complete predicate.**
5. **Identify the simple subject and the simple predicate.**
6. **Do a Vocabulary Check.**
7. **Do a Verb Chant.**

Lesson 2

You will
- practice Jingle 24.
- classify Practice Sentences.
- do a Skill Builder.
- identify how to make nouns possessive.
- do Classroom Practice 51.

Learn It: **RULES FOR MAKING NOUNS POSSESSIVE**

In order to form nouns that show ownership (possessive nouns), you must first decide if the noun is singular or plural before you add the apostrophe. After you know whether a noun is singular or plural, you can then use three rules to help you decide how to make the noun possessive.

Reference 164	**Rules for Making Nouns Possessive**

A **possessive noun** is the name of a person, place, or thing that owns something. A possessive noun will always have an **apostrophe** after it. It will have either an *apostrophe* before the *s* ('s) or an *apostrophe* after the *s* (s'). The apostrophe makes a noun show ownership (*Darren's truck*). Follow the rules below to make nouns possessive.

RULE 1: boy's	**RULE 2: boys'**	**RULE 3: men's**
For a singular noun — add ('s)	For a plural noun that ends in s — add (')	For a plural noun that does not end in s — add ('s)

Directions: For Part A, underline each noun to be made possessive. Write **S** for singular or **P** for plural, the rule number, and the possessive form. **For Part B**, write the singular possessive and plural possessive of each noun.

Part A	S-P	Rule	Possessive Form	Part B	Singular Poss	Plural Poss
1. <u>baby</u> crib	S	1	baby's	5. James	James's	Jameses'
2. <u>birds</u> wings	P	2	birds'	6. men	man's	men's
3. <u>mice</u> cheese	P	3	mice's	7. wolf	wolf's	wolves'
4. <u>carpenter</u> ladder	S	1	carpenter's	8. Wilson	Wilson's	Wilsons'

Discuss It: **RULES FOR MAKING NOUNS POSSESSIVE**

Look at Number 1 under Part A.
1. Which noun should be made possessive, baby or crib?
2. Is the word baby singular or plural?
3. Which rule is used to make the word baby possessive?
4. What is Rule 1?
5. How do you spell the possessive form of baby?
(Continue Numbers 2–4 under Part A

Look at Number 5 under Part B.
1. Is the word James singular or plural?
2. Which rule is used to make the word James possessive?
3. What is Rule 1?
4. How do you spell the possessive form of the word James?
5. What is the plural spelling of James?
6. Which rule is used to make the word Jameses possessive?
7. What is Rule 2?
8. How do you spell the possessive form of the word Jameses?
(Continue Numbers 6–8 under Part B

Classroom Practice 51

It is time to practice the skills you are learning. You will use the classroom practice on the next page to apply these skills.

Classroom Practice 51

Name:_____ Date:_____

GRAMMAR

▶ **Exercise 1:** Classify each sentence.

1. _____ The young man in the brick house on the corner is a carpenter.

2. _____ Elephants and whales are very large animals.

3. _____ Will Cindy be a volunteer at the hospital on weekends?

SKILLS

▶ **Exercise 2: For Part A**, underline each noun to be made possessive. Write **S** for singular or **P** for plural, the rule number, and the possessive form. **For Part B**, write the singular possessive and plural possessive of each noun.

RULE 1: boy's	RULE 2: boys'	RULE 3: men's
For a singular noun — add ('s)	For a plural noun that ends in s — add (')	For a plural noun that does not end in s — add ('s)

Part A	S-P	Rule	Possessive Form	Part B	Singular Poss	Plural Poss
1. cat toy				10. Charles		
2. children books				11. mouse		
3. Wests cars				12. parrot		
4. turkeys feathers				13. woman		
5. Thomas desk				14. child		
6. speaker speech				15. baby		
7. Chris backpack				16. wife		
8. kittens whiskers				17. boy		
9. animal tracks				18. goose		

EDITING

▶ **Exercise 3:** Punctuate the story, "George and His Mom." (Part 1 of 5) **Editing Guide: End Marks: 6   Capitals: 13   Commas: 5   Quotation Marks: 6   Apostrophes: 3   Homonyms: 5   A/An: 1   Misspelled Words: 2**

mom may i have to friends over two spend the knight shouted george as he rushed into the

room with randy and nick write behind him

well i suppose it will be all right his mother ansered slowly she didnt like george asking for

permission in front of his freinds

george wasnt threw asking his mom for favors he said mom may we go to randys house

for an dip in his pool

START LESSON 3

Lesson 3

You will

- study new vocabulary; make Card 30; write own sentence using the vocabulary word.
- analyze new analogy; make Card 30; write own analogy.
- practice Jingles 20–24.
- classify Practice Sentences.
- do a Skill Builder.
- identify pronoun cases.
- do Classroom Practice 52.
- write in your journal.
- read and discuss Discovery Time.

LISTENING AND SPEAKING:

Learn It: Recite the new vocabulary and analogy words.

 Reference 165   **Vocabulary & Analogy Words**

Word: controversy (kŏn'trə vûr'sē)
  Definition: argument of opposing views
  Synonym: disagreement   **Antonym:** harmony
  Sentence: The **controversy** between members of the city council is over!

Analogy: chicken : meat :: lemonade : drink
  Type or kind relationship: Just as **chicken** is a kind of **meat**, **lemonade** is a kind of **drink**.

Vocabulary Card 30: Record the vocabulary information above and write your own sentence, using the new word.

Analogy Card 30: Record the analogy information and write your own analogy, using the same relationship as the analogy above.

Recite It: Practice Jingles 20–24 in the Jingle Section on pages 503–504.

Apply It: Classify the Practice Sentences orally with your teacher.

Practice Sentences	Chapter 11: Lesson 3
1. _____ Milton and I are the most accurate spellers in our class.	
2. _____ Tarantulas are large, hairy spiders in the southwestern United States.	
3. _____ My sister's kitten is a very lovable animal.	

English Made Easy

Skill Builder

Using the sentences just classified, do a Skill Builder orally with your teacher.

1. **Identify the nouns in a Noun Check.**
2. **Identify the nouns as singular or plural.**
3. **Identify the nouns as common or proper.**
4. **Identify the complete subject and the complete predicate.**
5. **Identify the simple subject and the simple predicate.**
6. **Do a Vocabulary Check.**
7. **Do a Verb Chant.**

Skill Time

Learn It: PRONOUN CASES

📖 Reference 166 — Subjective, Objective, and Possessive Pronoun Cases

Personal pronouns can function in any of the ways in which nouns function: as subjects, predicate nouns, and as objects. Nouns do not change forms in the different jobs. However, most pronouns change forms according to how they are used in a sentence. A pronoun's form and how it is used are known as its **case**. Understanding pronoun cases will help you choose pronouns correctly.

> **Incorrect:** Mom and **her** made a cake for **he** and **I**.
> **Correct:** Mom and **she** made a cake for **him** and **me**.

PRONOUN CASES

1. **Subjective Case:** Pronouns that are used as <u>subjects</u> or <u>predicate pronouns</u> are in the subjective (sometimes called nominative) case. (**He** *went home. This is* **he**.)

   Subjective Case Pronouns: I, we, he, she, it, they, and **you.**

2. **Objective Case:** Pronouns that are used as <u>objects</u> are in the objective case: <u>objects</u> of prepositions, direct <u>objects</u>, or indirect <u>objects</u>. (*Dan gave* **me** *a card from* **him** *and* **her.** *Ray found* **us** *in the hall.*)

   Objective Case Pronouns: me, us, him, her, it, them, and **you.**

3. **Possessive Case:** Pronouns that are used <u>to show ownership</u> are in the possessive case. Unlike nouns, pronouns are not made possessive by using an apostrophe.

   Possessive Case Pronouns: my, our, his, her, its, their, and **your.**

Use these steps to help you choose the correct pronoun and pronoun case.

- Identify the job for the pronoun choices in parentheses by deciding if the pronoun is used as a subject, object of the preposition, a direct object, indirect object, or predicate pronoun.

- If the pronoun is used as a subject or as a predicate pronoun, it is in the subjective (nominative) case. Write **S** in the blank for subjective case. Recite the Subject Pronoun Jingle. Look at the two pronouns in parentheses. Underline the one that was recited in the jingle.

- If the pronoun is used as an object of the preposition, a direct object, or an indirect object, it is in the objective case. Write **O** in the blank for objective case. Recite the Object Pronoun Jingle. Look at the two pronouns in parentheses. Underline the one that was recited in the jingle.

Continued on next page. >>>

Reference 166 continued from previous page.

Directions: Write **S** for subjective, **O** for objective, or **P** for possessive in the blank.
Underline the correct pronoun in parentheses.

S	1. (<u>She</u>, Her) and (<u>I</u>, me) are looking for Sue.	O	4. Teresa gave (he and I, <u>him and me</u>) a photo.
P	2. (Me, <u>My</u>) puppy ate (he, <u>his</u>) food.	P	5. We took (us, <u>our</u>) grandmother to the store.
O	3. Joseph will ride with Roger and (I, <u>me</u>).	S	6. The leaders are Keith and (her, <u>she</u>).

Classroom Practice 52

It is time to practice the skills you are learning. You will use the classroom practice on the next page to apply these skills.

JOURNAL WRITING 30

Write an entry in your journal. Use Reference 9 on page 12 for ideas.

ENRICHMENT:

Discovery Time

Neptune is the eighth planet from the sun in our solar system. Neptune is another giant gas planet that has a cobalt blue color because of the oceans of liquid methane on the planet. Neptune has a moon named Triton that is so cold that ice erupts from its volcanoes.

Discovery Questions:
- **What do you think a volcano from which ice erupted would look like?**
- **What is the most amazing fact that you discovered about Neptune in your research?**

Discovery Activity:
- **For fun, use your imagination to make up creatures that might live on Neptune. Name your creatures and describe them. Draw a picture or write a description or short story about Neptune's moon, Triton.**

Are you interested in learning more about Neptune?

1. You may explore this topic further by using the resources listed below.
   Computer resources: Internet, encyclopedia software
   Library resources: encyclopedias, books, magazines, newspapers
   Home/community resources: books, interviews, newspapers, magazines

2. A Discovery Share Time is provided in Lesson 8 if you wish to share your investigation results. You may share orally, or you may prepare a written report. You will put your written report in a class booklet titled "Space Trivia." This booklet will be placed in the class library for everyone to enjoy.

Classroom Practice 52

Name:_____ Date:_____

GRAMMAR

▶ **Exercise 1:** Classify each sentence.

1. _____ My grandmother from Memphis is the best cook in the world.

2. _____ On the weekends, my mom is a clerk at the supermarket in town.

SKILLS

▶ **Exercise 2: For Part A**, underline each noun to be made possessive. Write **S** for singular or **P** for plural, the rule number, and the possessive form. **For Part B**, write the singular possessive and plural possessive of each noun.

RULE 1: boy's	RULE 2: boys'	RULE 3: men's
For a singular noun — add ('s)	For a plural noun that ends in s — add (')	For a plural noun that does not end in s — add ('s)

Part A	S-P	Rule	Possessive Form	Part B	Singular Poss	Plural Poss
1. senator wife				9. wife		
2. boss phone				10. snake		
3. students desks				11. jockey		
4. Williamses boys				12. mouse		
5. keyboard keys				13. patio		
6. men meeting				14. foot		
7. teachers jobs				15. calf		
8. children toys				16. bench		

▶ **Exercise 3:** Identify the pronoun case by writing **S** for subjective or **O** for objective in the blank. Underline the correct pronoun in parentheses.

1. Read a book to Dad and (I, me).	5. Will you ride with James and (I, me)?
2. The skaters were Lorenzo and (I, me).	6. (They, Them) are my sisters.
3. Momma made Tina and (I, me) sweaters.	7. (We, Us) kids couldn't sleep last night.
4. Jermaine and (he, him) mowed Jen's yard.	8. Draw a picture for (we, us) teachers.

EDITING

▶ **Exercise 4:** Punctuate the story, "George and His Mom." (Part 2 of 5)
**Editing Guide: End Marks: 6   Capitals: 15   Commas: 8   Quotation Marks: 6   Apostrophes: 6   Homonyms: 1
A/An: 1   Subject-Verb Agreement: 1   Misspelled Words: 1**

george his mother answered with an glint in her eye i dont mind your going swimming but

i dont think you will have time the yard still has not been mowed and the yard are your responsibility

george replied dont worry mom ill be back in plenty of time theres a tv special on tonite

that andy steve and i have been dying to sea ill mow the yard this afternoon and still have plenty of

time to get cleaned up before the movie

START LESSON 4

Lesson 4

You will

- study new vocabulary; make Card 31; write own sentence using the vocabulary word.
- analyze new analogy; make Card 31; write own analogy.
- recite new jingle (The Noun Job).
- classify Practice Sentences.
- identify noun jobs.
- do a Skill Builder to identify noun jobs.
- do Classroom Practice 53.
- read and discuss Discovery Time.
- do a homework assignment.
- do Home Connection activity.

LISTENING AND SPEAKING:
Vocabulary & Analogy Time

Learn It: Recite the new vocabulary and analogy words.

Reference 167	**Vocabulary & Analogy Words**

Word: mandatory (măn'də tôr'ē)
 Definition: commanded by an authority
 Synonym: required   **Antonym:** unnecessary
 Sentence: Four years of math are **mandatory** for all students.

Analogy: stationary : stationery :: principal : principle
 Homonym relationship: Just as **stationary** is a homonym of **stationery**, **principal** is a homonym of **principle**.

Vocabulary Card 31: Record the vocabulary information above and write your own sentence, using the new word.

Analogy Card 31: Record the analogy information and write your own analogy, using the same relationship as the analogy above.

Jingle Time

Recite It: Recite the new jingle.

♪ Jingle 25	**The Noun Job Jingle**

Nouns will give you a run for your money.
They do so many jobs
That it's not even funny.
A noun—person, place, thing, or idea—
is very appealing!
But it's the noun job *(noun job)*
That is so revealing!

To find the nouns in a sentence,
Go to their jobs *(go to their jobs)*
Nouns can do objective jobs *(objective jobs)*
They're the **IO** *(IO)*, **DO** *(DO)*, and **OP** jobs *(OP jobs)*.
And nouns can do subjective jobs *(subjective jobs)*.
They're the **SN** *(SN)* and **PrN** jobs *(PrN jobs)*.
Jobs. Jobs. Noun Jobs! Yeah!

Grammar Time

Apply It: These Practice Sentences are used to apply grammar concepts taught. Classify these sentences orally with your teacher.

Practice Sentences	**Chapter 11: Lesson 4**

1. _____ Braille is an alphabet for the blind.
2. _____ Guppies are the most popular fish for aquariums.
3. _____ The faded tapestry on the wall is a priceless family heirloom.

Learn It: NOUN JOBS

Reference 168   noun Jobs

Every word in a sentence has a job. A word's position and function in a sentence determine its job. Nouns are the only part of speech that can be used in different jobs and still be identified as a noun. If you can recognize noun jobs in a sentence, you will identify nouns more accurately.

In the sentences below, the word *refrigerator* is used in several noun-job positions and in one adjective position. You must always look at the position of a word instead of its meaning to determine if it is a noun. For example, *kitchen* is an adjective in Sentence 3, and *refrigerator* is an adjective in Sentence 6.

1. Nouns have many jobs in a sentence. These jobs include the following: **subject, object of the preposition, direct object, indirect object,** and **predicate noun.**

2. These jobs give nouns specific identification to show their function in a sentence. It is easier to find nouns in a sentence if you look at the noun-job positions.

3. The noun jobs can be divided into **subjective jobs** (subject noun and predicate noun) and **objective jobs** (object of the preposition, direct object, and indirect object). The possessive form of a noun functions as an adjective and is not considered a noun job.

The examples below demonstrate the importance of looking at noun jobs to help identify nouns.

1. **The <u>refrigerator</u> was very old.** Look at the noun jobs: **<u>SN</u>, OP, DO, IO, PrN.**
   Refrigerator is a noun that is used as a subject.

2. **Mom put the milk in the <u>refrigerator</u>.** Look at the noun jobs: **SN, <u>OP</u>, DO, IO, PrN.**
   Mom is a noun in the SN job position. Milk is a noun in the DO position.
   Refrigerator is a noun in the OP position.

3. **Joe saw the <u>refrigerator</u> through the kitchen window.** Look at the noun jobs: **SN, OP, <u>DO</u>, IO, PrN.**
   Joe is a noun in the SN job position. Refrigerator is a noun in the DO position.
   Window is a noun in the OP position. Kitchen is an adjective. An adjective is not a noun job.

4. **The repairman gave the <u>refrigerator</u> a final inspection.** Look at the noun jobs: **SN, OP, DO, <u>IO</u>, PrN.**
   Repairman is a noun in the SN job position. Refrigerator is a noun in the IO position.
   Inspection is a noun in the DO position. There is no OP position in this sentence.

5. **Mom's favorite gift was a new <u>refrigerator</u> from Dad.** Look at the noun jobs: **SN, OP, DO, IO, <u>PrN</u>.**
   Gift is a noun in the SN job position. Refrigerator is a noun in the PrN position.
   Dad is a noun in the OP position.

6. **Tim and Jim looked in the <u>refrigerator</u> door for ketchup.** Look at the noun jobs: **SN, OP, DO, IO, PrN.**
   Tim and Jim are nouns in the SN job position. Door is a noun in the OP position.
   Ketchup is a noun in the OP position. Refrigerator is an adjective. An adjective is not a noun job.

Learn It: **A SKILL BUILDER FOR A NOUN JOB CHECK**

The example below shows you how to identify nouns and their jobs in a Noun Job Check.

LISTENING AND SPEAKING:

FOR A NOUN JOB CHECK

Identify the nouns and their jobs in a Noun Job Check.

Sentence 1:	Sentence 2:	Sentence 3:
Braille - Subject noun	**guppies** - Subject noun	**tapestry** - Subject noun
alphabet – Predicate noun	**fish** – Predicate noun	**wall** - Object of the preposition
blind - Object of the preposition	**aquariums** - Object of the preposition	**heirloom** – Predicate noun

⟫⟫⟫⟫⟫⟫⟫ **Student Tip...**

1. Finding a noun is easier if you know the noun job. The nouns below are just nouns until you label each noun with a special name that identifies its job.

noun	noun	noun	noun	noun
boys	boys	boys	boys	boys
SN	OP	DO	IO	PrN

SN
The **boys** were swimming.   Dad swam with the **boys**.   *OP*   The lifeguard watched the **boys**.   *DO*

IO   *DO*
Mom gave the boys a big beachball.   The **swimmers** were the **boys**.   *SN*   *PrN*

2. As you review each pattern, notice how the Shurley patterns relate to the traditional patterns.

	Pattern 1	OP	Pattern 2	Pattern 3	Pattern 4
Traditional	N V	N	N V N	N V N N	N LV N
Shurley	SN V	OP	SN V-t DO	SN V-t IO DO	SN LV PrN

Classroom Practice 53

It is time to practice the skills you are learning. You will use the classroom practice on the next page to apply these skills.

ENRICHMENT:

(American) 1958 — NASA stands for National Aeronautics and Space Administration. NASA began in 1958 with approximately 8,000 employees and a budget of 100 million dollars. In 1962, NASA launched the first communications satellite that transmitted the first live television images between the United States and Europe.

Discovery Questions:
- **What was the name of the first communications satellite, and what company owned it?**
- **What do you think it would be like to work at NASA?**
- **What subjects in school do you think would prepare you for a career at NASA?**

Are you interested in learning more about NASA?

1. You may explore this topic further by using the resources listed below.
   Computer resources: Internet, encyclopedia software
   Library resources: encyclopedias, books, magazines, newspapers
   Home/community resources: books, interviews, newspapers, magazines

2. A Discovery Share Time is provided in Lesson 8 if you wish to share your investigation results. You may share orally, or you may prepare a written report. You will put your written report in a class booklet titled "Space Trivia." This booklet will be placed in the class library for everyone to enjoy.

Classroom Practice 53

Name:_____ Date:_____

GRAMMAR

▶ **Exercise 1:** Classify each sentence.

1. _____ The breeze beneath the willow tree is a cool and restful relief.

2. _____ For camping trips, a tent, an emergency kit, and cooking utensils are necessary items.

SKILLS

▶ **Exercise 2: For Part A**, underline each noun to be made possessive. Write **S** for singular or **P** for plural, the rule number, and the possessive form. **For Part B**, write the singular possessive and plural possessive of each noun.

RULE 1: boy's	RULE 2: boys'	RULE 3: men's
For a singular noun — add ('s)	For a plural noun that ends in s — add (')	For a plural noun that does not end in s — add ('s)

Part A	S-P	Rule	Possessive Form	Part B	Singular Poss	Plural Poss
1. banana peel				8. comet		
2. robins beaks				9. ox		
3. doctor bag				10. loaf		
4. problem answer				11. wife		
5. barbers scissors				12. monkey		
6. women shoes				13. box		
7. Jess grandma				14. glass		

▶ **Exercise 3:** Identify the pronoun case by writing **S** for subjective or **O** for objective in the blank. Underline the correct pronoun in parentheses.

1. (We, Us) students worked on our projects.	5. For (we, us), Daddy took a day off.
2. Please buy (he and I, him and me) a kite.	6. (We, Us) clapped for the magician.
3. Janelle took (we, us) girls to a movie.	7. Samuel visited (I, me) in the hospital.
4. Will you give (I, me) more time?	8. My daughter's teacher is (she, her).

EDITING

▶ **Exercise 4:** Punctuate the story, "George and His Mom." (Part 3 of 5) **Editing Guide: End Marks: 6   Capitals: 14   Commas: 7   Quotation Marks: 8   Apostrophes: 4   A/An: 1   Misspelled Words: 2**

well i really dont think you should wait until the last minute to mow the yard mom said quitely

mom dont worry i wont forget ill mow the yard before this day is over george promised

if i know george he will forget to mow the yard before dark mom thought to herself

as she watched her son leave with his friends mom then chuckled to herself and said this time

george will learn an valuble lesson

Homework 9

Complete this homework assignment on notebook paper.

1. Number your paper 1–12. **For Part A**, write each noun to be made possessive. Write **S** for singular or **P** for plural, the rule number, and the possessive form. **For Part B**, write the singular possessive and plural possessive of each noun.

RULE 1: boy's	RULE 2: boys'	RULE 3: men's
For a singular noun — add ('s)	For a plural noun that ends in s — add (')	For a plural noun that does not end in s — add ('s)

Part A	S-P	Rule	Possessive Form	Part B	Singular Poss	Plural Poss
1. father haircut				7. wolf		
2. James brother				8. potato		
3. planes wings				9. child		
4. men hats				10. goose		
5. flowers petals				11. moose		
6. Darrell bike				12. fox		

2. Number your paper 1–4. Identify the pronoun case by writing **S** for subjective case or **O** for objective case beside the number. Then, write the correct pronoun within the parentheses.

1. A mosquito bit (I, me) on the arm.	3. Can you find (he and I, him and me) at the game?
2. The winner was obviously (he, him).	4. My uncle took (they, them) home yesterday.

Home Connection

Family Activity for Vocabulary and Analogies

Divide into family teams. The first team will use vocabulary and analogy cards 1–15 to ask questions about the information on their cards. The second team will use vocabulary and analogy cards 16–31 to ask questions about the information on their cards.

Family Activity for Linking Verbs

Get three sheets of colored paper. You will need two sheets of one color and one sheet of a second color. Cut each page lengthwise into five long strips. Write the subject nouns and predicate nouns from the list below on the strips that are the same color. Write the linking verbs from the list on the other-colored strips.

Choose a subject noun, a linking verb, and a predicate noun that make sense together. Fasten the ends of the subject-noun strip together to form a paper link. Do the same with the predicate-noun strip. Now, loop the linking-verb strip to connect the subject-noun and predicate-noun strips. Fasten the ends of the linking-verb strip together. Your sentence chain should follow this order: subject noun, linking verb, and predicate noun.

Subject Nouns	Predicate Nouns	Linking Verbs
They	sisters	are
Ramona and Juanita	co-workers	were
Bach and Beethoven	composers	were
Laurence and I	friends	are
Mars and Venus	planets	are

START LESSON 5

Lesson 5

You will

- classify Practice Sentences.
- do Chapter Checkup 54.
- write in your journal.

JOURNAL WRITING 31

Write an entry in your journal. Use Reference 9 on page 12 for ideas.

LISTENING AND SPEAKING:

 **Grammar Time**

Apply It: Classify the Practice Sentences orally with your teacher.

Practice Sentences	Chapter 11: Lesson 5

1. _____ Her speech was an impassioned plea about the dangers of toxic waste.
2. _____ Dominoes is a game of dots on small rectangular tiles.
3. _____ The organizer of the holiday parade is a patient and energetic man.

Chapter Checkup 54

It is time for a checkup of the skills you have learned in this chapter. You will use the chapter checkup on the next page to evaluate your progress.

Chapter 11 Checkup 54

Name:_____ Date:_____

GRAMMAR

▶ **Exercise 1:** Classify each sentence.

1. _____ Wow! That bookcase is a passageway to a hidden cellar!

2. _____ The moon is our nearest neighbor in the sky.

SKILLS

▶ **Exercise 2: For Part A**, underline each noun to be made possessive. Write **S** for singular or **P** for plural, the rule number, and the possessive form. **For Part B**, write the singular possessive and plural possessive of each noun.

RULE 1: boy's	RULE 2: boys'	RULE 3: men's
For a singular noun — add ('s)	For a plural noun that ends in s — add (')	For a plural noun that does not end in s — add ('s)

Part A	S-P	Rule	Possessive Form	Part B	Singular Poss	Plural Poss
1. butterfly wings				8. elf		
2. players uniforms				9. fox		
3. train engine				10. house		
4. twins room				11. wolf		
5. monkeys tails				12. mouse		
6. men boats				13. child		
7. officers tents				14. tomato		

▶ **Exercise 3:** Identify the pronoun case by writing **S** for subjective or **O** for objective in the blank. Underline the correct pronoun in parentheses.

1. Cassie sat with (we, us) at the game.	5. (He, Him) traveled to Chicago yesterday.
2. Jared invited (he, him) to our meeting.	6. Mother made dinner for (they, them).
3. Yes, this is (she, her).	7. (We, Us) will visit Aunt Tina on Monday.
4. Look in the library for (she, her).	8. Carlos gave (I, me) a ride to school.

EDITING

▶ **Exercise 4:** Punctuate the story, "George and His Mom." (Part 4 of 5) **Editing Guide: End Marks: 7   Capitals: 11   Commas: 5   Quotation Marks: 6   Apostrophes: 3   Homonyms: 1   Misspelled Words: 2**

mom heard george and his friends laughing and talking as they returned home just before dark

as she studied her sons happy-go-lucky face mom thought to herself now is the time for his lesson

i hope hes big enough to take it

just a minit young man mom said firmly i believe you said the yard wood be mowed

before the day was over well youd better hurry if you expect to finish before this day is over

you have until midnite

START LESSON 6

Lesson 6

You will

- hand in WA 24.
- read and discuss the parts of a nonfiction book and how to find a nonfiction book in the library.
- read and discuss how to write a nonfiction book review.
- write a nonfiction book review for WA 27.

Literature Time

Hand It In: **WRITING ASSIGNMENT 24**

Get the book review for your fiction book ready to hand in when your teacher asks for it. Your review will be given back to you for sharing in Chapter 12.

Learn It: **PARTS OF A NONFICTION BOOK**

Reference 169 — Parts of a Nonfiction Book

A **nonfiction book** can be divided into three parts: the front, the body, and the back. Any time you use a nonfiction book to help you with an assignment, you must understand how to use that book efficiently. Knowing the parts of a book will help you make full use of the special features that are frequently found in nonfiction books.

THE FRONT OF A BOOK

1. **Title Page**
   This page has the full title of the book, the author's name, the illustrator's name, the name of the publishing company, and the city where the book was published.

2. **Copyright Page**
   This page is right after the title page and tells the year in which the book was published and who owns the copyright. If the book has an ISBN (International Standard Book Number), it is listed here.

3. **Preface** (also called **introduction**)
   If a book has this page, it will come before the table of contents and will usually tell you briefly why the book was written and what it is about.

4. **Table of Contents**
   This section lists the major divisions of the book by units or chapters and tells their beginning page numbers.

THE BODY OF A BOOK

5. **Body**
   This is the main section, or text, of the book.

THE BACK OF A BOOK

6. **Appendix**
   This section includes extra informative material such as maps, charts, tables, diagrams, and letters. It is always wise to find out what is in the appendix, since it may contain supplementary material that you could otherwise find only by going to the library.

7. **Glossary**
   This section is like a dictionary and gives the meanings of some of the important words in the book.

8. **Bibliography**
   This section includes a list of sources used by the author. It could serve as a guide for further reading on a topic.

9. **Index**
   This will probably be your most useful section. The purpose of the index is to help you quickly locate information about the topics in the book. It contains an alphabetical list of specific topics and tells the page on which that information can be found. It is similar to the table of contents, but it is much more detailed.

Learn It: HOW TO FIND NONFICTION BOOKS IN THE LIBRARY

📖 Reference 170 | How to Find Nonfiction Books in the Library

To find out if a library has a certain nonfiction book, look in the card catalog for the title card of that book. If you don't know the title but do know the author, look for the author card. If you don't know the title or the author, look under the subject of the book. Also, look under the subject if you are interested in finding several books about your topic.

After you find the card in the card catalog, you must find the book on the library shelves. Nonfiction books are arranged on the shelves in **numerical order** according to a **call number**. A *call number* is the number on the spine of all nonfiction books.

The **Dewey Decimal System** is the means of identifying nonfiction books by number. All nonfiction books are given a *call number*, which will identify where they are located on the shelf. All three catalog cards for a book will have the same call number in the top left corner.

Be sure to write the call number down on paper before you look for the book. When you go to the library shelf, look at the call numbers printed on the spines of the books until you find the same number you copied from the catalog card.

Note: Individual biographies and autobiographies are arranged alphabetically on a separate shelf by the last name of the person about whom they are written.

Learn It: WRITING A BOOK REVIEW FOR A NONFICTION BOOK

✏️ Reference 171 | Writing a Book Review for a Nonfiction Book

A book review gives you an opportunity to tell what a book is about and what you think about the book. The following guidelines will help you know what to include in a book review for a nonfiction book.

BOOK REVIEW FOR A NONFICTION BOOK

1. List the title and author.
2. Tell the type of book: **Nonfiction**.
3. Write an introductory paragraph to tell what the book is about (the topic), and list one, two, or three major facts that you will discuss. In the body of the review, write about each fact you have listed in the introductory paragraph and provide supporting details.
4. In the last paragraph, give your opinion of the book. In this paragraph, tell why you liked or disliked the book. The example below shows you one way to write a nonfiction book review.

<u>Gorillas</u>
by Seymour Simon
Nonfiction Book

    This book gives fun and interesting facts and statistics about gorillas and about their family structure. The author presents insights and information in a way that is highly enjoyable as he reveals that gorillas are usually peaceful and quite shy.

    Gorillas are sometimes called anthropoid (manlike) apes because their bodies are like a human's body. A gorilla has five fingers on each hand, five toes on each foot, and thirty-two teeth. Gorillas do have much bigger stomachs than humans which helps them handle all the plants they eat. Gorillas can shriek, chuckle, hiccup, and even belch.

    Family units are headed by a male silverback and usually have five or more members. They have a daily routine of eating, grooming, and burping together. Babies usually weigh about five pounds when they are born, but adults can weigh more than 400 pounds. Baby gorillas do summersaults, climb trees, and slide down hills on their stomachs. They play by chasing, tackling, and wrestling.

Continued on next page. >>>

Reference 171 continued from previous page.

This is a wonderful book for animal lovers, but it will also intrigue non-animal lovers. It provides the factual information needed to help people understand and respect these remarkable creatures.

BOOK REVIEW FOR AN AUTOBIOGRAPHY OR BIOGRAPHY

1. List the title and author.
2. Tell the type of book: **Autobiography**.
3. Write an introductory paragraph to tell who the book is about, and list one, two, or three major facts or events that you will present. In the body of the review, write about each fact or event you have listed in the introductory paragraph and provide supporting details.
4. In the last paragraph, give your opinion of the book. In this paragraph, tell why you liked or disliked the book. The example below shows you one way to write an autobiographical book review.

<u>Laura: The Life of Laura Ingalls Wilder</u>
by Donald Zochert
Biography

Donald Zochert wrote a biography of Laura Ingalls Wilder. He did a lot of research because he wanted readers to know the woman behind the stories that have become American classics. He writes about Laura's story from before she was born until her death in 1957.

Laura's biography begins with her grandparents. They were pioneers who moved a lot in search of land for themselves and their children. Laura's parents, Charles Ingalls and Caroline Quiner, met and married in Wisconsin. Laura was born on February 7, 1867. She was the second child and had three sisters and one brother. Laura did not attend school regularly because the family kept moving from place to place. She was thirteen when her family settled down so she could go to school on a regular basis.

Laura married her husband, Almanzo Wilder, on August 25, 1885. Their daughter, Rose, was born on December 5, 1886. Laura told her daughter many stories about her parents and her life as a child. Rose wanted her mother to write down the stories, so at the age of 65, Laura wrote and published her first book entitled, <u>Little House in the Big Woods</u>. This led to an entire series of Little House books about the frontier and the people who settled there. Laura Ingalls Wilder died on February 10, 1957.

I enjoyed reading this biography because it gave a lot of detail about the life of Laura Ingalls Wilder and her family. She was an important person because her books brought to life the memories of pioneers and of the frontier. I think other people would enjoy reading this book, too.

Write It: WRITING ASSIGNMENT 27

Even though this writing assignment for a book review of a nonfiction book is given today, it is not due until Lesson 4 of Chapter 12.

Writing Assignment 27 : Nonfiction Book Review

Purpose: To provide information about events or persons in a book and to express an opinion

Type of Writing: Biography/autobiography/nonfiction book review

Audience: Classmates, family, or friends

Writing Topics: Choose a biography/autobiography/nonfiction book.

Special Instructions:

1. Choose a biography/autobiography/nonfiction book about which to write a book review.

2. Use References 169–171 on pages 338–339 to guide you in writing a book review of a biography/autobiography/nonfiction book of your choice.

3. Write a rough draft. Next, revise and edit it. Then, write a final paper for your book review during a study time or outside of class.

4. Finish Book Review 27 by Lesson 4 of Chapter 12 and give it to your teacher.

5. Keep your book review in the Final Paper folder if you finish early.

>>>>>>>>>>>>>>>>>>>>>>>>>>>>> **Student Tip...**

For additional information and activities about nonfiction books, the table of contents, and the index, refer to Study Skills in the Resource Tools Section on pages 524–528.

START LESSON 7

Lesson 7

You will

- conference with teacher about WA 26.
- read nonfiction book during conferences.

Read It: **NONFICTION BOOK**

Use this reading time to read the nonfiction book you have selected for a book review. When you finish your book, you may begin working on your book review assignment, Writing Assignment 27.

Discuss It: **TEACHER-STUDENT CONFERENCES FOR WRITING ASSIGNMENT 26**

Meet with your teacher to discuss Writing Assignment 26.
After the conference, place this group of papers in your Publishing folder.

English Made Easy

Publishing Time

Publish It: **WRITING ASSIGNMENT 26**

Choose a publishing form and publish Writing Assignment 26. After rewriting your paper for publication, give the stapled papers (evaluation guide, graded final paper, rough draft, and prewriting) to your teacher to be placed in your Writing Portfolio.

Lesson 8

You will
- publish WA 26.
- participate in Discovery Share Time.
- do Across the Curriculum activity.

Reference 67	Publishing Checklist for Step 6 in the Writing Process

The sixth step in the writing process is called publishing. Publishing is sharing your writing with others. With so many forms of publishing available, finding a match for every project and personality is easy.

At times, a written work is best read aloud. Other times, the biggest impact is made when a written work is read silently. You can also use media sources to enhance any publication.

SPECIAL INSTRUCTIONS FOR PUBLISHING:

- Rewrite the graded paper in ink or type it on a computer, correcting any marked errors. *(Do not display or publish papers that have marked errors or grades on them.)*
- Give your teacher the set of stapled papers to place in your Writing Portfolio. *(Stapled papers: evaluation guide, graded final paper, rough draft, and prewriting map.)*
- Select a publishing form from the list below and publish your rewritten paper.
  1. Have classmates, family members, neighbors, or others read your writing at school or home.
  2. Share your writing with others during a Share Time. *(Refer to Reference 68 on page 103 for sharing guidelines.)*
  3. Display your writing on a bulletin board or wall.
  4. Put your writing in the classroom library or in the school library for checkout.
  5. Send your writing as a letter or an e-mail to a friend or relative.
  6. Frame your writing by gluing it on colored construction paper and decorating it.
  7. Make a book of your writing for your classroom, your family, or others.
  8. Illustrate your writing and give it to others to read.
  9. Dramatize your writing in the form of a play, puppet show, or radio broadcast.
  10. Send your writing to be placed in a waiting room (doctor, veterinarian, dentist, etc.), senior-citizen center, or a nursing home.
  11. Send your writing to a school newspaper, local newspaper, or a magazine for publication.
  12. Make a videotape, cassette tape, or slide presentation of your writing.
  13. Choose another publishing form that is not listed.

LISTENING AND SPEAKING:

If you have chosen to investigate a topic introduced in this chapter, you now have the opportunity to share your results in one of the following ways:

1. You may relate your information orally.

2. You may read a written report.

3. You may place your report in the booklet without reading it aloud.

After share time, all written reports should be turned in to be placed in the class booklet titled "Space Trivia." You are encouraged to check out this class booklet so you can enjoy the reports again.

Literature/Language Development Connection:

1. Look in the library for a book that you have never read that has an interesting title or an interesting illustration on the cover. Using only the title or cover illustration, write a narrative that tells what you think the book is about. Later, read the book to see if the title or illustration accurately depicts the original story. Then, compare your story to the original. How are they different? How are they the same?

2. Get in small groups. Retell the order of events from your book, but do not tell the ending. Have others in the group predict the ending of your book. Then, compare the predictions of the ending of the story to the original. Tell how they are different. Tell how they are the same.

LISTENING AND SPEAKING:

Jingle Time

Lesson 9

You will
- practice Jingles 24–25.
- do Classroom Practice 55.
- write an independent narrative without dialogue (WA 28).

Recite It: Practice Jingles 24–25 in the Jingle Section on pages 504–505.

GRAMMAR & WRITING CONNECTION:
Practice and Revised Sentences

Apply It: **BUILDING AND EXPANDING SENTENCES**

| Reference 172 | A Guide for Using a Pattern 4 Core (Sn LV Prn) to Build & Expand Sentences |

1. **SN or SP (subject)** Think of a noun or pronoun that you want to use as the *subject*. Write the noun or pronoun you have chosen as the *subject* of your sentence.

2. **LV (linking verb)** A *linking verb* links the subject with a word in the predicate. You may choose a linking verb from this list: *am, is, are, was, were, be, being, been, appear, become, feel, grow, look, remain, seem, smell, sound, stay,* and *taste*. First, choose a verb for your sentence. Then, wait until you have chosen a predicate noun to verify that it is a linking verb. If the verb is verified as linking, keep it as the verb of your Pattern 4 core.

3. **PrN (predicate noun)** The *predicate noun* is a noun or pronoun after the verb that renames and means the same thing as the subject. To help you think of a *predicate noun,* ask the question WHAT or WHO after the verb. Check to make sure it renames the subject of the sentence. Write the predicate noun you have chosen in the predicate part of your sentence.

Classroom Practice 55

It is time to practice the skills you are learning. You will use the classroom practice on the next page to apply these skills.

Student Tip...

Use your vocabulary words in your Practice and Revised Sentences. Use a thesaurus, synonym-antonym book, or a dictionary to help you develop your writing vocabulary.

Write It: **WRITING ASSIGNMENT 28**

As you write a rough draft for your independent writing assignment, you will do two of the six steps in the writing process: prewriting and rough draft.

Writing Assignment 28

Purpose: To tell a story
Type of Writing: Narrative
Audience: Classmates, family, or friends
Writing Topics: A holiday adventure/tradition/disaster
The problem with winter/summer clothes or activities
The big party/celebration/meeting
(Brainstorm for other ideas, individually or in groups.)

Special Instructions:

1. Follow the Prewriting and Rough Draft Checklists in References 47 and 49 on pages 62, 66.

2. Use Reference 161 on page 315 to help you write your narrative. Make a Story Elements Outline instead of a prewriting map.

3. Write your narrative without dialogue.

4. Write in first or third person. See Reference 71 on page 108.
(First-person pronouns: *I, me, my, mine, we, us, our,* and *ours.*)
(Third-person pronouns: *he, his, him, she, her, hers, it, its, they, their, theirs,* and *them.*)

Note: Reference 57 on page 76 gives the steps in the writing process and the location of all the writing checklists.

Student Note:

Some of your writing pieces will be selected for revision and editing later in the school year.

Classroom Practice 55

Name: _____   Date: _____

INDEPENDENT PRACTICE & REVISED SENTENCES

1. Write a Practice Sentence according to the labels you choose.
Use **SN/SP LV PrN** as your main labels. You may use the other labels in any order and as many times as you wish in order to make a Practice Sentence.
Chapter 11 labels for a Practice Sentence: **SN/SP, LV, PrN,** Adj, Adv, A, P, OP, PPA, C, HV, I, PNA

2. Write a Revised Sentence. Use the following revision strategies: *synonym (syn), antonym (ant), word change (wc), added word (add), deleted word (delete),* or *no change (nc)*. Under each word, write the abbreviation of the revision strategy you use.

Labels: _____

Practice: _____

Revised: _____

Strategies: _____

Labels: _____

Practice: _____

Revised: _____

Strategies: _____

Labels: _____

Practice: _____

Revised: _____

Strategies: _____

LISTENING AND SPEAKING:
Jingle Time

Recite It: Practice Jingle 12 in the Jingle Section on page 501.

>>>>> **Student Tip...**

> Reviewing the transition words will help you apply them in your writing.

Writing Time

Learn It: **WRITING A COMPARISON-CONTRAST ESSAY**

START LESSON 10

Lesson 10

You will
- practice Jingle 12.
- read and discuss a comparison/contrast essay.
- plan and write rough draft for comparison/contrast essay (WA 29).

Reference 173   **Writing a Comparison-Contrast Essay**

When you **compare** subjects, you tell how they are alike.

When you **contrast** subjects, you tell how they are different.

First, you must choose two subjects that can be easily compared and contrasted. Next, you should make a pre-writing map. For this type of writing, make a Venn diagram by drawing two large overlapping circles. Show how the subjects are alike and how they are different by writing the differences in the outer circles and the similarities in the inner circle. Make sure the differences are balanced. This means that for every fact you list about the first subject, you must list a contrasting fact for the second subject. *(See the Venn diagram.)* Brainstorm for details to compare and contrast. Ideas could include the following: size, shape, color, texture, behavior, purpose, location, degree of importance, unusual facts, accomplishments, etc.

The transitional words and phrases that are used to **compare** subjects include the following:
also, and, another, as, besides, furthermore, in addition, like, likewise, same, similarly, too, which, etc.

The transitional words and phrases that are used to **contrast** subjects include the following:
although, but, different, even though, however, in contrast, in other ways, on the other hand, otherwise, still, while, yet, etc.

A comparison-contrast essay has four parts.

1. Write an **introduction**. The introduction should name the subjects you will compare and contrast. Keep the interest high by asking a question, by stating an interesting or unusual fact, or by citing an incident.

2. Write a **paragraph of comparison** that tells how the two subjects are similar. Use the similarities listed in the inner section of the Venn diagram to help you write the sentences for this paragraph.

3. Write a **paragraph of contrast** that tells how the two subjects are different. Use the differences listed in the outer sections of the Venn diagram to help you write the sentences for this paragraph.

4. Write a **conclusion**. The conclusion should include a summary of your ideas. It can also include what you think about the likeness and differences and/or a final comment that ties your ideas together and draws the writing to a close. Use the following words to help you write a conclusion: *all in all, as a result, finally, in conclusion, in summary, last, therefore, to sum it up.*

Continued on next page. >>>

Reference 173 continued from previous page.

Example of a Venn Diagram

Reading a Book

Is published before the movie

Read a book in many hours or days

Use imagination

Feel involved in the story

Enjoy words

Similarities of Both

Entertaining

Tell a story

Contain the story elements: main idea, setting, characters, plot, and ending

Watching a Movie

Is produced after the book

Watch a movie in hours

Don't use imagination

Watch the story develop

Enjoy pictures

My sister and I both love stories. I love to read books, but my sister prefers to watch movies. After I read a book, I tell my sister all about how great the story is. My descriptions of the characters and events are usually vivid enough to cause great anticipation as my sister waits for the movie to come out. As we watch the movie together on opening day, I subconsciously compare the book to the movie. In the end, I still think reading the book is better, but my sister still thinks watching the movie is better.

My sister and I admit that books and movies have their similar points. Both are entertaining because they tell a great story. Each has a setting that tells or shows where the story takes place. Also, they have characters that are faced with a problem. Likewise, books and movies both have a plot that tells what happens and an ending that brings the story to a close.

Even though they have similar points, books and movies are also very different. I like the fact that the book comes out first. This gives me a chance to read and enjoy it before it is released as a movie. My sister likes the idea of watching a movie in one to three hours; it takes me several days to read a book. I am encouraged to use my imagination when I read a book. Reading a book gets you involved in the story. In contrast, watching a movie takes the imagination out of it. You are on the outside looking in.

All in all, my sister and I have decided that our love for stories is more important than whether we read the book or watch the movie. Since I love words, I will continue to read books and enjoy them. In the same way, my sister loves pictures, and she will continue watching and enjoying movies.

Write It: **WRITING ASSIGNMENT 29**

As you write a rough draft for your independent writing assignment, you will do two of the six steps in the writing process: prewriting (Venn diagram) and rough draft.

Writing Assignment 〔 29 〕

Purpose: To show how subjects are alike and how they are different

Type of Writing: Comparison-contrast

Audience: Family or friends

Writing Topics: Old friends/new friends
Dogs/cats
Small dogs/big dogs
Two songs or books on the same subject
(Brainstorm for other ideas, individually or in groups.)

Special Instructions:

1. Follow the Prewriting and Rough Draft Checklists in References 47 and 49 on pages 62, 66.

2. Use Reference 173 on page 347 to help you write your comparison-contrast essay. Make a Venn diagram instead of a prewriting map.

3. Use standard, time-order, or transition writing form. See Reference 70 on page 107.

4. Write in first or third person. See Reference 71 on page 108.
(First-person pronouns: *I, me, my, mine, we, us, our,* and *ours.*)
(Third-person pronouns: *he, his, him, she, her, hers, it, its, they, their, theirs,* and *them.*)

Note: Reference 57 on page 76 gives the steps in the writing process and the location of all the writing checklists.

START LESSON 11

Lesson 11

You will

- revise, edit, and write a final paper for WA 29.

Apply It: **REVISE, EDIT, AND WRITE A FINAL PAPER**

Following the schedule below, you will revise and edit Writing Assignment 29. Then, you will write a final paper. Use the Chapter 11 Writing Evaluation Guide on the next page to check your final paper one last time.

Reference 55 — Revising & Editing Schedule and Writing a Final Paper

SPECIAL INSTRUCTIONS FOR REVISING AND EDITING (Steps 3-4 in the writing process):

- Use the Revising and Editing Checklists in References 51 and 53 as you revise and edit your rough draft.
- Follow the revising and editing schedule below as directed by your teacher.

    1. **Individual.** First, read your rough draft to yourself. Use the Revising Checklist in Reference 51 on page 69. Go through your paper, checking each item on the list and making revisions to your rough draft. Then, use the Editing Checklist in Reference 53 on page 71. Go through your paper again, checking each item on the list and editing your rough draft.

    2. **Partner.** Next, get with your editing partner. Work together on each partner's rough draft, one paper at a time. Read each rough draft aloud and revise and edit it together, using the Revising and Editing Checklists. (The author of the paper should be the one to make the corrections on his own paper.)

    3. **Group.** Finally, read the rough draft to a revision group for feedback. Each student should read his paper while the others listen and offer possible revising and editing suggestions. (The author will determine whether to make corrections from the revision group's suggestions.)

SPECIAL INSTRUCTIONS FOR FINAL PAPER (Step 5 in the writing process):

- Write your final paper, using the Final Paper Checklist in Reference 56 on page 75.
- Staple your writing papers in this order: the final paper on top, the rough draft in the middle, and the prewriting map on the bottom. Place the stapled papers in the Final Paper folder.

>>>>>>>>>>> Student Tip...

1. Be tactful and helpful in your comments during revising and editing time. The purpose of any suggestion should be to improve the writer's rough draft.

2. As you make your final corrections, you have the choice of accepting or rejecting any suggestions made by your partners or your revision group.

3. Study Vocabulary Words and Analogies 29–31 for the chapter test in the next lesson.

4. If you need to improve your handwriting, refer to the Resource Tools Section on page 521 for information on writing legibly.

Chapter 11 Writing Evaluation Guide

Name:_____ Date:_____

ROUGH DRAFT CHECK

_____ 1. Did you write your rough draft in pencil?

_____ 2. Did you write the correct headings on the first seven lines of your paper?

_____ 3. Did you use extra wide margins and skip every other line?

_____ 4. Did you write a title at the end of your rough draft?

_____ 5. Did you place your edited rough draft in your Rough Draft folder?

REVISING CHECK

_____ 6. Did you identify the purpose, type of writing, and audience?

_____ 7. Did you check for a topic, topic sentence, and sentences supporting the topic?

_____ 8. Did you check sentences for the right order, and did you combine, rearrange, or delete sentences when necessary?

_____ 9. Did you check for a variety of simple, compound, and complex sentences?

_____ 10. Did you check for any left out, repeated, or unnecessary words?

_____ 11. Did you check for the best choice of words by replacing or deleting unclear words?

_____ 12. Did you check the content for interest and creativity?

_____ 13. Did you check the voice to make sure the writing says what you want it to say?

EDITING CHECK

_____ 14. Did you indent each paragraph?

_____ 15. Did you put an end mark at the end of every sentence?

_____ 16. Did you capitalize the first word of every sentence?

_____ 17. Did you check for all other capitalization mistakes?

_____ 18. Did you check for all punctuation mistakes?
(*commas, periods, apostrophes, quotation marks, underlining*)

_____ 19. Did you check for misspelled words and for incorrect homonym choices?

_____ 20. Did you check for incorrect spellings of plural and possessive forms?

_____ 21. Did you check for correct construction and punctuation of your sentences?

_____ 22. Did you check for usage mistakes? (*subject/verb agreement, a/an choices, contractions, verb tenses, pronoun/antecedent agreement, pronoun cases, degrees of adjectives, double negatives, etc.*)

_____ 23. Did you put your revised and edited paper in the Rough Draft folder?

FINAL PAPER CHECK

_____ 24. Did you write the final paper in pencil?

_____ 25. Did you center the title on the top line and center your name under the title?

_____ 26. Did you skip a line before starting the writing assignment?

_____ 27. Did you single-space, use wide margins, and write the final paper neatly?

_____ 28. Did you staple your papers in this order: final paper on top, rough draft in the middle, and prewriting map on the bottom? Did you put them in the Final Paper folder?

START LESSON 12

Lesson 12

You will

- hand in WA 29 for grading.
- respond to oral review questions.
- take Chapter 11 Test.

CHAPTER TEST

It is time to evaluate your knowledge of the skills you have learned in this chapter. Your teacher will give you the Chapter 11 Test to help you assess your progress.

Hand It In: **WRITING ASSIGNMENT 29**

Get your stapled papers for Writing Assignment 29 from your Final Paper folder. Check to make sure they are in the correct order: the final paper on top, the rough draft in the middle, and the prewriting map on the bottom. Hand them in to your teacher.

LISTENING AND SPEAKING:

Discuss It:

1. What word in the predicate means the same thing as the subject?
2. What is another name for a predicate noun?
3. What type of verb is used with a predicate noun?
4. What are the core parts of a Pattern 4 sentence?
5. What are the core parts of a Pattern 3 sentence?
6. What are the core parts of a Pattern 2 sentence?
7. What are the core parts of a Pattern 1 sentence?
8. What punctuation mark is used to make a noun show ownership?
9. How do you make a singular noun possessive?
10. How do you make a plural noun that ends in 's' possessive?
11. What are the subjective-case pronouns?
12. How are subjective pronouns used?
13. What are the objective-case pronouns?
14. How are objective pronouns used?
15. What are the possessive-case pronouns?
16. How are possessive pronouns used?
17. What are the five noun jobs?
18. What type of writing is used when your purpose is to show similarities and differences?
19. What type of writing is used when your purpose is to tell a story?
20. What type of writing is used when your purpose is to paint a picture with words?
21. What type of writing is used when your purpose is to express an opinion and to convince the reader that this opinion is correct?
22. What type of writing is used when your purpose is to inform, to give facts, to give directions, to explain, or to define something?

>>>>>>>>>>>>>>>>>>>>>>>>>> **Student Tip...**

> **For information about test-taking strategies, refer to the Resource Tools Section on page 520.**

English Made Easy

LISTENING AND SPEAKING:

Jingle Time

Recite It: Practice Jingles 20–25 in the Jingle Section on pages 503-505.

Grammar Time

Apply It: These Introductory Sentences are used to apply the new grammar concepts taught below. Classify these sentences orally with your teacher.

Introductory Sentences	Chapter 12: Lesson 1

1. _____ The Earth's driest geographical areas are deserts.
2. _____ Were these wagons used for floats and rides during the festival?
3. _____ Show me the way to your summer cabin.
4. _____ The reporter bombarded me with questions about the mayor's health.

Learn It: **MIXED GRAMMAR PATTERNS 1–4**

The sentences classified in this chapter will be Patterns 1–4. They are called **Mixed Patterns** because there are four different patterns from which to choose. Be alert to the parts of speech and where they are located in each sentence. Use the sentence cores to help determine the pattern of the sentences.

Skill Builder

Using the sentences just classified, do a Skill Builder orally with your teacher.
1. **Identify the nouns in a Noun Check.**
2. **Identify the nouns as singular or plural.**
3. **Identify the nouns as common or proper.**
4. **Identify the complete subject and the complete predicate.**
5. **Identify the simple subject and the simple predicate.**
6. **Do a Vocabulary Check.**
7. **Do a Verb Chant.**

Lesson 1

You will
- practice Jingles 20-25.
- identify Mixed Patterns 1-4.
- classify Introductory Sentences.
- do a Skill Builder.
- identify pronoun and antecedent agreement.
- do Classroom Practice 56.
- write in your journal.

Skill Time

Learn It: PERSONAL PRONOUNS AND THEIR ANTECEDENTS

 Reference 174 **Personal Pronouns and Their Antecedents**

The most common pronouns are known as personal pronouns. A personal pronoun refers to the one speaking (first person), the one spoken to (second person), or the one spoken about (third person).

Any time a personal pronoun is used in a sentence, it refers to a noun. The noun to which a pronoun refers is called the **antecedent** of that pronoun. The antecedent can come before a pronoun or even in a preceding sentence.

    antecedent pronoun   antecedent pronoun pronoun
1. The *girl* loved *her* new bedroom.   2. The *girl* smiled. *She* loved *her* new bedroom.

Since antecedents determine the pronouns used, it is important for the pronoun to agree with the antecedent in number (singular/plural) and gender (male/female). See the two rules below for number and gender.

1. **Number: Decide if the antecedent is singular or plural; choose the pronoun that agrees in number.**

   If the antecedent is singular, the pronoun must be singular. (For the antecedent *man*, use *he*, *him*, *his*.)

   If the antecedent is plural, the pronoun must be plural. (For the antecedent *men*, use *they*, *them*, *their*.)

2. **Gender: Decide if the antecedent is male or female; choose the pronoun that agrees in gender.**

   If the antecedent is masculine, the pronoun must be of masculine gender. (antecedent *boy*—pronoun *he*)

   If the antecedent is feminine, the pronoun must be of feminine gender. (antecedent *girl*—pronoun *she*)

   If the gender of the antecedent is not specified, the general rule is to use the masculine form of the pronoun. (For the antecedent *musician*, *pilot*, *doctor*, *nurse*, etc., use the pronouns *he*, *him*, *his*, etc.)

   If the antecedent is not a person and is neither masculine nor feminine, the pronoun must be of neuter gender. (antecedent *book*—pronoun *it*) The plural pronouns *they* and *them* also show neuter gender. (The *logs* were very dry. *They* quickly burned in the fireplace.)

Examples of Pronoun-Antecedent Agreement

                   antecedent pronoun   antecedent pronoun pronoun
Incorrect: 1a. The *girl* loved *their* new bedroom. 2a. The *girl* smiled. *He* loved *his* new bedroom.

                   antecedent pronoun   antecedent pronoun pronoun
Correct: 1b. The *girl* loved *her* new bedroom. 2b. The *girl* smiled. *She* loved *her* new bedroom.

PRACTICE FOR PRONOUN-ANTECEDENT AGREEMENT

Complete the table. Then, underline the correct pronoun in the parentheses that agrees with its antecedent.

Pronoun-Antecedent Agreement	Antecedent	S or P	Pronoun S or P
1. The birds chirped in (its, <u>their</u>) nest.	birds	P	P
2. The musician was in (<u>his</u>, their) practice room.	musician	S	S
3. Every person needs (<u>his</u>, their) computer today.	person	S	S

JOURNAL WRITING  **32**

Write an entry in your journal. Use Reference 9 on page 12 for ideas.

Classroom Practice 56

It is time to practice the skills you are learning. You will use the classroom practice on the next page to apply these skills.

Classroom Practice 56

Name:_____ Date:_____

GRAMMAR

▶ **Exercise 1:** Classify each sentence.

1. _____ He made a soft impression in the snow with his foot.

2. _____ My uncle is the new director of an art gallery in Springdale.

3. _____ Oops! Jody's tall glass of tea tipped over and spilled onto the white carpet!

4. _____ Did your family send Grandmother this beautiful arrangement of cut flowers?

SKILLS

▶ **Exercise 2:** Complete the table. Then, underline the pronoun in parentheses that agrees with its antecedent.

Pronoun-Antecedent Agreement	Antecedent	S or P	Pronoun S or P
1. The president of the company is (he, them).			
2. The boys played with (his, their) games.			
3. The artist signed (his, their) drawing for me.			
4. The snake escaped from (its, their) cage.			
5. The salesman misplaced (his, their) cell phone.			
6. The teachers were in (his, their) meeting.			
7. Rose made belts and sold (it, them).			

▶ **Exercise 3:** Identify the pronoun case by writing **S** for subjective or **O** for objective in the blank. Underline the correct pronoun in parentheses.

1. Antonio saw (we, us) at the theater.	5. The trucks passed (I, me) on the freeway.
2. This is (he, him).	6. Do (we, us) have any bread for sandwiches?
3. Terrance gave (she, her) some water.	7. Please wrap this gift for Tracy and (he, him).
4. (We, Us) are lucky to sit in the front.	8. (They, Them) leave for Dallas on Sunday.

EDITING

▶ **Exercise 4:** Punctuate the story, "George and His Mom." (Part 1 of 5) **Editing Guide: End Marks: 3   Capitals: 7   Commas: 5   Quotation Marks: 8   Homonyms: 3   Subject-Verb Agreement: 1   Misspelled Words: 1**

if i have to tell you to cleen up your room won more time mother said impatiently their will bee big-time consequences

but mother george complained what do you want me to clean up i knows exactly where everything is

START LESSON 2

Lesson 2

You will

- practice Jingles 13-19.
- classify Practice Sentences.
- do a Skill Builder.
- identify indefinite pronouns.
- do Classroom Practice 57.

LISTENING AND SPEAKING:

Recite It: Practice Jingles 13-19 in the Jingle Section on pages 501–503.

Apply It: Classify the Practice Sentences orally with your teacher.

Practice Sentences	Chapter 12: Lesson 2
1. _____	Marcus is the most qualified employee for the job in marketing.
2. _____	The calf in the fenced pasture bawled continuously for its mother.
3. _____	The smoke from the campfire did not permit insects into our campsite.

Using the sentences just classified, do a Skill Builder orally with your teacher.

1. **Identify the nouns in a Noun Check.**
2. **Identify the nouns as singular or plural.**
3. **Identify the nouns as common or proper.**
4. **Identify the complete subject and the complete predicate.**
5. **Identify the simple subject and the simple predicate.**
6. **Do a Vocabulary Check.**
7. **Do a Verb Chant.**

Learn It: INDEFINITE PRONOUNS

 Reference 175   **Indefinite Pronouns**

Indefinite means not definite or not specific. A pronoun that does not refer to a definite person, place, or thing is called an **indefinite pronoun**. In order to prevent problems in subject-verb agreement and in pronoun-antecedent agreement, it is important to know which indefinite pronouns are always singular, which indefinite pronouns are always plural, and which indefinite pronouns can be either singular or plural.

Continued on next page. >>>

Reference 175 continued from previous page.

1. INDEFINITE PRONOUNS THAT ARE ALWAYS SINGULAR:

end in -**one**	*(anyone, everyone, someone, no one)*
end in -**body**	*(anybody, everybody, somebody, nobody)*
end in -**thing**	*(anything, everything, something)*
imply **one** or **nothing**	*(one, each, either, neither, nothing, another)*

Subject-verb agreement. Singular indefinite subject pronouns use singular verbs.

> **Example: Someone** in the class **gets** a prize.

Pronoun-antecedent agreement. When singular indefinite pronouns are antecedents, use singular personal pronouns for agreement. Since gender is not specified, the general rule is to use the masculine form or rewrite the sentence.

> **Examples: Everyone** gave **his** report. **No one** did the homework assigned.

2. INDEFINITE PRONOUNS THAT ARE ALWAYS PLURAL:

both, few, many, others, several

Subject-verb agreement. Plural indefinite subject pronouns use plural verbs.

> **Example: Several** on the plane **eat** peanuts.

Pronoun-antecedent agreement. When plural indefinite pronouns are antecedents, use plural personal pronouns for agreement.

> **Example: Many** should receive **their** diplomas.

3. INDEFINITE PRONOUNS THAT CAN BE EITHER SINGULAR OR PLURAL:

all, most, none, some, any, half

If a prepositional phrase follows any of the indefinite pronouns in this third group, the object of the preposition determines whether the indefinite pronoun is singular or plural.

> **Example of *singular* object of the preposition: Some** (of the **candy**) **is** chocolate.

> **Example of *plural* object of the preposition: Some** (of the **books**) **are** mysteries.

If these indefinite pronouns are used alone, they are usually considered plural. Only the "either singular or plural" pronouns depend on prepositional phrases to determine whether they are singular or plural.

> **Example of *no* prepositional phrase: Some are** listening to the jazz recordings.

4. WAYS INDEFINITE PRONOUNS CAN BE USED

Indefinite pronouns can be used as subjects or objects, but if an indefinite word is used as an adjective, then it is not an indefinite pronoun.

> **Example of an indefinite <u>pronoun</u> used as a *subject*: Many** hope to see the concert.

> **Example of an indefinite <u>pronoun</u> used as an *object*:** The teacher helps **many** of her students.

> **Example of an indefinite <u>word</u> used as an *adjective*: Many** pilots are completing their training.

Directions: Complete the table. Then, underline the correct verb. **N/Pro** means to identify the subject as a noun or pronoun. Use **S** for singular and **P** for plural.

Subject-Verb Agreement	Subject	N/Pro	S or P	Verb S or P
1. Nobody in the class (<u>likes</u>, like) liver and onions.	Nobody	Pro	S	S
2. Your shoes (was, <u>were</u>) in the closet.	shoes	N	P	P
3. All of your shoes (is, <u>are</u>) in the closet.	All	Pro	P	P

Classroom Practice 57

It is time to practice the skills you are learning. You will use the classroom practice on the next page to apply these skills.

Classroom Practice 57

Name:_____ Date:_____

GRAMMAR

▶ **Exercise 1:** Classify each sentence.

1. _____ He gave his secretary a copy of the legal documents.

2. _____ Computer games and music videos are excellent birthday presents.

3. _____ The top of the large cedar tree touched the ceiling of our den.

SKILLS

▶ **Exercise 2:** Complete the table. Then, underline the pronoun in parentheses that agrees with its antecedent.

Pronoun-Antecedent Agreement	Antecedent	S or P	Pronoun S or P
1. The bears slept in (her, their) cave.			
2. Roberto stayed in (his, their) bedroom.			
3. No one could hear (his, their) name called.			
4. Anyone can see (his, their) own grades.			
5. Others gave (his, their) help, also.			

▶ **Exercise 3:** Complete the table and underline the correct verb. **N/Pro** means to identify the subject as a noun or pronoun. Use **S** for singular and **P** for plural.

Subject-Verb Agreement	Subject	N/Pro	S or P	Verb S or P
1. Neither of the winners (is, are) present.				
2. Three boxes of books (was, were) stacked in the back.				
3. A box of books (was, were) stacked in the back.				
4. Everyone in our class (don't, doesn't) ride on the bus.				
5. All of the club members (know, knows) your name.				

▶ **Exercise 4:** Identify these indefinite pronouns as singular (**S**), plural (**P**), or either (**E**) singular or plural.
1. ___ nobody   2. ___ most   3. ___ nothing   4. ___ several   5. ___ everybody

EDITING

▶ **Exercise 5:** Punctuate the story, "George and His Mom." (Part 2 of 5) **Editing Guide: End Marks: 6   Capitals: 11   Commas: 4   Quotation Marks: 8   Apostrophes: 2   Homonyms: 1   Misspelled Words: 1**

mom studied george and said what if i let this house get into the same mess that your room is in

one of these days you will understand why its important to have a cleen and orderly home george

but why george asked im perfectly happy with my room he looked at his mom and

grinned as he added mom you could just close your eyes every time you walk bye

LISTENING AND SPEAKING:
Vocabulary & Analogy Time

Learn It: Recite the new vocabulary and analogy words.

Reference 176	Vocabulary & Analogy Words

Word: catastrophe (kə tăs'trə fē)
  Definition: sudden, widespread disaster
  Synonym: calamity   **Antonym:** triumph
  Sentence: The tsunami was a **catastrophe**, to say the least.

Analogy: day : month :: second : minute
  Part-to-whole relationship: Just as a **day** is a part of a **month**,
                                            a **second** is a part of a **minute.**

Vocabulary Card 32: Record the vocabulary information above and write your own
                              sentence, using the new word.

Analogy Card 32: Record the analogy information and write your own analogy,
                           using the same relationship as the analogy above.

Jingle Time

Recite It: Practice Jingles 3-7 in the Jingle Section on page 499.

Grammar Time

Apply It: Classify the Practice Sentences orally with your teacher.

Practice Sentences	Chapter 12: Lesson 3

1. _____ The captain gave his teammates high-fives at the end
            of the game.
2. _____ Paul is a safety inspector for the shipping industry on the coast.
3. _____ Lightning crackled and sizzled in the night sky during the
            summer storm.

Lesson 3
You will
- study new vocabulary;
  make Card 32;
  write own sentence using
  the vocabulary word.
- analyze new analogy;
  make Card 32;
  write own analogy.
- practice Jingles 3-7.
- classify Practice Sentences.
- do a Skill Builder.
- do Classroom Practice 58.
- read and discuss
  Discovery Time.

Skill Builder

Using the sentences just classified, do a Skill Builder orally with your teacher.

1. Identify the nouns in a Noun Check.
2. Identify the nouns as singular or plural.
3. Identify the nouns as common or proper.
4. Identify the complete subject and the complete predicate.
5. Identify the simple subject and the simple predicate.
6. Do a Vocabulary Check.
7. Do a Verb Chant.

Classroom Practice 58

It is time to practice the skills you are learning. You will use the classroom practice on the next page to apply these skills.

ENRICHMENT:

Discovery Time

Aurora or northern and southern lights are often visible from the surface of the Earth. Aurora is the result of space weather which is generated by the sun.

Discovery Questions:
- **What is the name of the northern aurora?** *(Aurora Borealis)*
- **What is the name of the southern aurora?** *(Aurora Australis)*
- **Where are the best places to see auroras?** *(Near the magnetic poles.)*

Are you interested in learning more about auroras?

1. You may explore this topic further by using the resources listed below.
   Computer resources: Internet, encyclopedia software
   Library resources: encyclopedias, books, magazines, newspapers
   Home/community resources: books, interviews, newspapers, magazines

2. A Discovery Share Time is provided in Lesson 7 if you wish to share your investigation results. You may share orally, or you may prepare a written report. You will put your written report in a class booklet titled "Space Trivia." This booklet will be placed in the class library for everyone to enjoy

Classroom Practice 58

Name:_____ Date:_____

GRAMMAR

▶ **Exercise 1:** Classify each sentence.

1. _____ Look in the dictionary for the correct spelling and definition of that word.

2. _____ Did Shelly offer you another serving of apple dumplings for dessert?

3. _____ The Earth's largest bodies of water are oceans.

SKILLS

▶ **Exercise 2:** Complete the table. Then, underline the pronoun in parentheses that agrees with its antecedent.

Pronoun-Antecedent Agreement	Antecedent	S or P	Pronoun S or P
1. Everyone paid for (his, their) own ticket.			
2. The tourists stayed in (his, their) rooms.			
3. Few brought money for (his, their) lunch.			
4. Someone in the line gave away (his, their) seat.			
5. Everybody heard (his, their) name announced.			

▶ **Exercise 3:** Complete the table and underline the correct verb. **N/Pro** means to identify the subject as a noun or pronoun. Use **S** for singular and **P** for plural.

Subject-Verb Agreement	Subject	N/Pro	S or P	Verb S or P
1. Some of the mail (was, were) lost.				
2. Anyone in our office (has, have) a chance to win.				
3. A vase of flowers (sit, sits) on the piano.				
4. None of the children (is, are) hungry.				
5. He and I (visit, visits) Grandpa every day.				

▶ **Exercise 4:** Identify these indefinite pronouns as singular (**S**), plural (**P**), or either (**E**) singular or plural.
1. ____ nobody   2. ____ everything   3. ____ either   4. ____ someone   5. ____ both

EDITING

▶ **Exercise 5:** Punctuate the story, "George and His Mom." (Part 3 of 5)
**Editing Guide: End Marks: 4   Capitals: 5   Commas: 1   Quotation Marks: 6   Apostrophes: 1   Homonyms: 1   A/An: 2
Subject-Verb Agreement: 1   Misspelled Words: 1**

thats what you think now mother said as she looked at him with an misterious twinkle in her

eyes you just thinks you are perfectly happy with an messy room

i wonder what she mint by that george thought to himself as he left for school

Chapter 12

START LESSON 4

Lesson 4

You will

- study new vocabulary; make Card 33; write own sentence using the vocabulary word.
- analyze new analogy; make Card 33; write own analogy.
- hand in your nonfiction book review (WA 27).
- classify Practice Sentences.
- do Chapter Checkup 59.
- read and discuss Discovery Time.

Hand It In: **WRITING ASSIGNMENT 27**
Get the book review for your nonfiction book ready to hand in when your teacher asks for it. Your review will be given back to you for sharing in the next lesson.

LISTENING AND SPEAKING:

Learn It: Recite the new vocabulary and analogy words.

Reference 177	Vocabulary & Analogy Words

Word: inconspicuous (ĭn'kən spĭk'yoo əs)
    Definition: hardly noticeable
    Synonym: indistinct   **Antonym:** prominent
    Sentence: In the crowd of shoppers, she was totally **inconspicuous**.

Analogy: hop : frog :: slither : snake
Descriptive or characteristic relationship: Just as **hop** is a characteristic of a **frog**, **slither** is a characteristic of a **snake**.

Vocabulary Card 33: Record the vocabulary information above and write your own sentence, using the new word.

Analogy Card 33: Record the analogy information and write your own analogy, using the same relationship as the analogy above.

Apply It: Classify the Practice Sentences orally with your teacher.

Practice Sentences	Chapter 12: Lesson 4

1. _____ The captain of the hockey team is the player with the star on his helmet.
2. _____ Kate kept her car keys on a hook beside the kitchen door.
3. _____ My parents traveled throughout Europe for their summer vacation.

 Chapter Checkup 59

It is time for a checkup of the skills you have learned in this chapter. You will use the chapter checkup on the next page to evaluate your progress.

ENRICHMENT:

(American) 1973 — Skylab was the first space station the United States launched into orbit. Astronauts on Skylab have been able to prove that humans can live in space for extended periods of time.

 Discovery Questions:
- What do you think it would be like to live on Skylab?
- What do you think the future will be like when whole families can live on space stations far from Earth?
- Describe what a day might be like living on a space station.

Are you interested in learning more about Skylab?

1. You may explore this topic further by using the resources listed below.
   Computer resources: Internet, encyclopedia software
   Library resources: encyclopedias, books, magazines, newspapers
   Home/community resources: books, interviews, newspapers, magazines

2. A Discovery Share Time is provided in Lesson 7 if you wish to share your investigation results. You may share orally, or you may prepare a written report. You will put your written report in a class booklet titled "Space Trivia." This booklet will be placed in the class library for everyone to enjoy.

Chapter 12 Checkup 59

Name:_____ Date:_____

GRAMMAR

▶ **Exercise 1:** Classify each sentence.

1. _____ Her poem was the first selection in the poetry collection.

2. _____ Despite the forecast, the winter storm did not bring a lot of snow to our state.

3. _____ Take the dead leaves in the front yard to the garden.

SKILLS

▶ **Exercise 2:** Complete the table. Then, underline the pronoun in parentheses that agrees with its antecedent.

Pronoun-Antecedent Agreement	Antecedent	S or P	Pronoun S or P
1. All of the toddlers took (his, their) naps.			
2. Does everyone have (his, their) report ready?			
3. Many of the flowers lost (his, their) petals.			
4. None of the students saw (his, their) scores.			

▶ **Exercise 3:** Complete the table and underline the correct verb. **N/Pro** means to identify the subject as a noun or pronoun. Use **S** for singular and **P** for plural.

Subject-Verb Agreement	Subject	N/Pro	S or P	Verb S or P
1. Some of the pizza (was, were) still left.				
2. Each of the girls (has, have) a new puppy.				
3. Tina and Gina (isn't, aren't) twins.				
4. Most of the animals (was, were) in good health.				
5. Others (was, were) present for the meeting.				

▶ **Exercise 4:** Identify these indefinite pronouns as singular (**S**), plural (**P**), or either (**E**) singular or plural.
1. ____ many   2. ____ most   3. ____ neither   4. ____ everyone   5. ____ someone

EDITING

▶ **Exercise 5:** Punctuate the story, "George and His Mom." (Part 4 of 5) **Editing Guide: End Marks: 8   Capitals: 11   Commas: 3   Quotation Marks: 8   Apostrophes: 3   Homonyms: 2   Subject-Verb Agreement: 1**

that afternoon george rushed all the weigh home from school his girlfriend were coming over to

study with him and he sure wanted to impress her ill just close the door to my room he said to

himself cindy and i will study in the den where its clean and orderly

george entered the house whistling the whistle froze on his lips as his horrified eyes viewed

total disaster throughout the house mom george wailed in despair you cant dew this to me

Publishing Time

Share It: BOOK REVIEWS, WRITING ASSIGNMENTS 24 AND 27

Look over Writing Assignments 24 and 27 after your teacher returns them. Prepare to share your reviews in cooperative-learning groups.

You will be assigned to two different groups. Share the fiction book review from Writing Assignment 24 in your first cooperative-learning group. After this group has finished sharing, each of you will pass your book review around so everyone in your group can record the title and author of each book in his journal. Under each book title, add a brief comment to help you remember whether you would like to read that particular book.

In your second group, you will share the nonfiction book review from Writing Assignment 27, following the same procedure of sharing and recording. Your teacher will tell you when to change groups.

Choose It: A FICTION OR NONFICTION BOOK

Choose a fiction or nonfiction book to read for enjoyment and have it ready to read during Conference Time in the next lesson.

START LESSON 5

Lesson 5

You will

- share book reviews.
- choose a book to be read in the next lesson.
- write in your journal.

JOURNAL WRITING 33

Write an entry in your journal. Use Reference 9 on page 12 for ideas.

Chapter 12

START LESSON 6

Lesson 6

You will

- conference with teacher about WA 29.
- read a book.
- do student reading activity.
- write in your journal.

Reading Time

Read It: **FICTION OR NONFICTION BOOK**

Use your reading time to read the fiction or nonfiction book you selected in the previous lesson. This book is for enjoyment, and there is no book review required.

Conference Time

Discuss It: **TEACHER-STUDENT CONFERENCES FOR WRITING ASSIGNMENT 29**

Meet with your teacher to discuss Writing Assignment 29.
After the conference, place this group of papers in your Publishing folder.

Student Tip...

Form an after-school book club. A book club is a small group of students who are reading the same book and who meet together to talk about the book. Meet at different times to read and discuss the book with each other. Talk about the different characters and the plot. Keep a notebook about the books you read, your opinions, and quotes from other students about the books.

Student Reading Activity

1. Write a poem to describe a character in the book you are reading. To find information on poems, study the different types of poems in Chapter 18 on pages 456-474. Share your poem with friends and family.

2. Write a different ending for the book you are reading. Think about how your ending compares with the book ending. Write the comparison in your journal.

JOURNAL WRITING 34

Write an entry in your journal. Use Reference 9 on page 12 for ideas.

Publishing Time

Publish It: **WRITING ASSIGNMENT 29**

Choose a publishing form and publish Writing Assignment 29. After rewriting your paper for publication, give the stapled papers (evaluation guide, graded final paper, rough draft, and Venn diagram) to your teacher to be placed in your Writing Portfolio.

Lesson 7

You will
- publish WA 29.
- participate in Discovery Share Time.
- write an independent comparison-contrast essay (WA 30).

Reference 67	Publishing Checklist for Step 6 in the Writing Process

The sixth step in the writing process is called publishing. Publishing is sharing your writing with others. With so many forms of publishing available, finding a match for every project and personality is easy.

At times, a written work is best read aloud. Other times, the biggest impact is made when a written work is read silently. You can also use media sources to enhance any publication.

SPECIAL INSTRUCTIONS FOR PUBLISHING:

- Rewrite the graded paper in ink or type it on a computer, correcting any marked errors. *(Do not display or publish papers that have marked errors or grades on them.)*

- Give your teacher the set of stapled papers to place in your Writing Portfolio. *(Stapled papers: evaluation guide, graded final paper, rough draft, and prewriting map.)*

- Select a publishing form from the list below and publish your rewritten paper.

  1. Have classmates, family members, neighbors, or others read your writing at school or home.

  2. Share your writing with others during a Share Time. *(Refer to Reference 68 on page 103 for sharing guidelines.)*

  3. Display your writing on a bulletin board or wall.

  4. Put your writing in the classroom library or in the school library for checkout.

  5. Send your writing as a letter or an e-mail to a friend or relative.

  6. Frame your writing by gluing it on colored construction paper and decorating it.

  7. Make a book of your writing for your classroom, your family, or others.

  8. Illustrate your writing and give it to others to read.

  9. Dramatize your writing in the form of a play, puppet show, or radio broadcast.

  10. Send your writing to be placed in a waiting room (doctor, veterinarian, dentist, etc.), senior-citizen center, or a nursing home.

  11. Send your writing to a school newspaper, local newspaper, or a magazine for publication.

  12. Make a videotape, cassette tape, or slide presentation of your writing.

  13. Choose another publishing form that is not listed.

LISTENING AND SPEAKING:

Discovery Share Time

If you have chosen to investigate a topic introduced in this chapter, you now have the opportunity to share your results in one of the following ways:

  1. You may relate your information orally.

  2. You may read a written report.

  3. You may place your report in the booklet without reading it aloud.

After share time, all written reports should be turned in to be placed in the class booklet titled "Space Trivia." You are encouraged to check out this class booklet so you can enjoy the reports again.

Write It: WRITING ASSIGNMENT 30

As you write a rough draft for your comparison-contrast essay assignment, you will do two of the six steps in the writing process: prewriting and rough draft.

Writing Assignment [30]

Purpose: To show how subjects are alike and how they are different
Type of Writing: Comparison-contrast
Audience: Classmates, parents, or friends
Writing Topics: Learning to play a band instrument and a sport
　　　　　　　Chocolate shakes and strawberry shakes
　　　　　　　Pop music and country-western music
　　　　　　　(Brainstorm for other ideas, individually or in groups.)

Special Instructions:

1. Follow the Prewriting and Rough Draft Checklists in References 47 and 49 on pages 62, 66.

2. Use Reference 173 on page 347 to help you write your comparison-contrast essay. Make a Venn diagram instead of a prewriting map.

3. Use standard, time-order, or transition writing form. See Reference 70 on page 107.

4. Write in first or third person. See Reference 71 on page 108.
   (First-person pronouns: *I, me, my, mine, we, us, our,* and *ours.*)
   (Third-person pronouns: *he, his, him, she, her, hers, it, its, they, their, theirs,* and *them.*)

Note: Reference 57 on page 76 gives the steps in the writing process and the location of all the writing checklists.

Student Note:

Some of your writing pieces will be selected for revision and editing later in the school year.

LISTENING AND SPEAKING:

Recite It: Practice Jingle 12 in the Jingle Section on page 501.

⟩⟩⟩⟩ Student Tip...

> Reviewing the transition words will help you apply them in your writing.

Writing Time

Learn It: **WRITING TALL TALES**

A **tall tale** is a humorous story that uses fabrication (a big lie), surprise, something funny, something clever, something unexpected, or something that leaves the reader guessing to make it an unbelievable tale.

Lesson 8

You will
- practice Jingle 12.
- read and discuss Tall Tales.
- plan and write rough draft for Tall Tale (WA 31).

✎ Reference 178   Writing a Tall Tale

A **tall tale** is a humorous story that makes use of exaggeration, but it also includes believable events and situations. A tall tale is a story that "stretches" people, places, or events into unbelievable proportions. Pecos Bill's roping a tornado is an example of a tall tale. The story of Paul Bunyan, the giant lumberjack, and his blue ox, Babe, is also a tall tale.

A tall tale may take on different forms, but every tall tale is a "far-fetched" story that is hard to believe. It usually takes something believable, such as a man fishing, and "stretches" the story into an unbelievable tale. Although you know the story is "stretched," you still find it fun to read or hear. The speech in a tall tale is almost always colloquial, or informal, and characters speak in dialect. The way characters speak is very much a part of the charm of the story. The guidelines below will help you write a tall tale.

1. Make a Story Elements Outline for your tall tale.
2. Choose a believable story and "stretch" the story to make it unbelievable in some way.
3. Tell the story in the order that you want the events to happen.
4. Use the following list of words for the purpose of exaggeration: *extraordinary, never before, unbelievable, outlandish, worst, biggest, horrendous, million, faster than, impossible, tremendous, meanest, longest, heaviest, terrible, cleverest, most unexpected, strangest, etc.*
5. Use colloquial, or informal, speech for your characters.
6. Think of a title that will tell what your story is about. The title is usually written after the story is finished.

Example of a Tall Tale

The Truth and Nothing but the Truth

Just before the dismissal bell on Friday afternoon, Ms. Lenardo assigned us homework. My eyes automatically rolled up and back down again. "I do NOT need homework today! It will interfere with my skateboard tournament," I whispered impatiently to my best friend, Todd, as we left the room.

Bursting into the house, I yelled at no one in particular, "I do NOT need homework this weekend! Why can't everyone understand that I cannot spend a SINGLE minute doing homework!"

"Oh, well," I grumbled. "I might as well get it over with!" And I sat down right then and wrote my story. "Wow! What a fantastic story!" I gloated to myself. "Now, I'll make a snack before I head to the park."

As I poured a glass of milk, I knocked the glass over, and the milk drowned my newly-finished homework. I tried desperately to wipe it off, but it just smeared and disintegrated into mush. I stared

Continued on next page. >>>

Reference 178 continued from previous page.

unbelievingly at what had just happened. "Oh, well," I muttered through clenched teeth. "I didn't like that story anyway. I'll just write another one!"

After I finished my second story, I felt better. This time, I carefully carried my homework upstairs and laid it on my backpack. Then, I dashed downstairs with my skateboard. As I opened the front door, I heard a horrendous crash from my room. I raced back upstairs. There, happily chewing my homework paper under my overturned desk, was my overgrown puppy, Jumbo. I could not speak.

My heart was pounding as I walked slowly toward Ms. Lenardo on Monday morning. I wondered how I was going to explain the unfortunate circumstances surrounding my homework. I took a deep breath and blurted, "Ms. Lenardo, I need to talk to you about my homework! I know you are not going to believe this, but my homework was totally destroyed six times this weekend!"

I took another breath and continued, "First, I spilled milk on it. Then, my puppy ate it. Next, my little brother scribbled all over it. After that, my mom accidentally shredded it. Then, my dad used it to help start a fire in the grill. I wrote a new story after every catastrophe. Each story was more wonderful than the one before it. The most fantastic story of all was the last one. Then, on the way to school this morning, my friend threw my best story out the window of the bus! This is the truth and nothing but the truth! I promise!"

Ms. Lenardo's eyes automatically rolled up and back down again as she whispered impatiently to me, "I do NOT need homework excuses today! It will interfere with my compassionate spirit!"

Write It: WRITING ASSIGNMENT 31

As you write a rough draft for your independent writing assignment, you will do two of the six steps in the writing process: prewriting (the Story Elements Outline) and rough draft.

Writing Assignment 31

Purpose: To tell a story
Type of Writing: Tall tale (narrative)
Audience: Classmates, parents, or friends
Writing Topics: The impossible homework assignment
The fastest mouth/feet in the country
The smartest/strangest computer game in the world
(Brainstorm for other ideas, individually or in groups.)

Special Instructions:

1. Use Reference 178 to help you write your tall-tale narrative.
2. Make a Story Elements Outline instead of a prewriting checklist. See References 152 and 161 on pages 288, 315.
3. Write your tall tale with or without dialogue.
4. You will rewrite your tall tale in Lesson 8 of Chapter 13. You will share it in Lessons 9 and 10. If you wish, you may dress the part of a character in your tall tale, make and show illustrations, or just do a dramatic reading. Keep this in mind as you write your tall tale.
5. Write in first or third person. See Reference 71 on page 108.
(First-person pronouns: *I, me, my, mine, we, us, our,* and *ours*.)
(Third-person pronouns: *he, his, him, she, her, hers, it, its, they, their, theirs,* and *them*.)

Note: Reference 57 on page 76 gives the steps in the writing process and the location of all the writing checklists.

>>>>>>>>>>>>> Student Tip...

Check out a collection of tall tales from the school and/or city library to read and enjoy. Pick a few to read aloud to your friends or family.

Writing Time

Apply It: REVISE, EDIT, AND WRITE A FINAL PAPER

Following the schedule below, you will revise and edit Writing Assignment 31. Then, you will write a final paper. Use the Chapter 12 Writing Evaluation Guide on the next page to check your final paper one last time.

Lesson 9

You will
- revise, edit, and write a final paper for WA 31.

 Reference 55   **Revising & Editing Schedule and Writing a Final Paper**

SPECIAL INSTRUCTIONS FOR REVISING AND EDITING (Steps 3-4 in the writing process):

- Use the Revising and Editing Checklists in References 51 and 53 as you revise and edit your rough draft.
- Follow the revising and editing schedule below as directed by your teacher.

1. **Individual.** First, read your rough draft to yourself. Use the Revising Checklist in Reference 51 on page 69. Go through your paper, checking each item on the list and making revisions to your rough draft. Then, use the Editing Checklist in Reference 53 on page 71. Go through your paper again, checking each item on the list and editing your rough draft.

2. **Partner.** Next, get with your editing partner. Work together on each partner's rough draft, one paper at a time. Read each rough draft aloud and revise and edit it together, using the Revising and Editing Checklists. (The author of the paper should be the one to make the corrections on his own paper.)

3. **Group.** Finally, read the rough draft to a revision group for feedback. Each student should read his paper while the others listen and offer possible revising and editing suggestions. (The author will determine whether to make corrections from the revision group's suggestions.)

SPECIAL INSTRUCTIONS FOR FINAL PAPER (Step 5 in the writing process):

- Write your final paper, using the Final Paper Checklist in Reference 56 on page 75.
- Staple your writing papers in this order: the final paper on top, the rough draft in the middle, and the prewriting map on the bottom. Place the stapled papers in the Final Paper folder.

>>>>>>>> Student Tip...

1. Be tactful and helpful in your comments during revising and editing time. The purpose of any suggestion should be to improve the writer's rough draft.

2. As you make your final corrections, you have the choice of accepting or rejecting any suggestions made by your partners or your revision group.

3. Study Vocabulary Words and Analogies 32–33 for the chapter test in the next lesson.

4. If you need to improve your handwriting, refer to the Resource Tools Section on page 521 for information on writing legibly.

Chapter 12 Writing Evaluation Guide

Name:_____ Date:_____

ROUGH DRAFT CHECK

_____ 1. Did you write your rough draft in pencil?

_____ 2. Did you write the correct headings on the first seven lines of your paper?

_____ 3. Did you use extra wide margins and skip every other line?

_____ 4. Did you write a title at the end of your rough draft?

_____ 5. Did you place your edited rough draft in your Rough Draft folder?

REVISING CHECK

_____ 6. Did you identify the purpose, type of writing, and audience?

_____ 7. Did you check for a topic, topic sentence, and sentences supporting the topic?

_____ 8. Did you check sentences for the right order, and did you combine, rearrange, or delete sentences when necessary?

_____ 9. Did you check for a variety of simple, compound, and complex sentences?

_____ 10. Did you check for any left out, repeated, or unnecessary words?

_____ 11. Did you check for the best choice of words by replacing or deleting unclear words?

_____ 12. Did you check the content for interest and creativity?

_____ 13. Did you check the voice to make sure the writing says what you want it to say?

EDITING CHECK

_____ 14. Did you indent each paragraph?

_____ 15. Did you put an end mark at the end of every sentence?

_____ 16. Did you capitalize the first word of every sentence?

_____ 17. Did you check for all other capitalization mistakes?

_____ 18. Did you check for all punctuation mistakes?
(commas, periods, apostrophes, quotation marks, underlining)

_____ 19. Did you check for misspelled words and for incorrect homonym choices?

_____ 20. Did you check for incorrect spellings of plural and possessive forms?

_____ 21. Did you check for correct construction and punctuation of your sentences?

_____ 22. Did you check for usage mistakes? (subject/verb agreement, a/an choices, contractions, verb tenses, pronoun/antecedent agreement, pronoun cases, degrees of adjectives, double negatives, etc.)

_____ 23. Did you put your revised and edited paper in the Rough Draft folder?

FINAL PAPER CHECK

_____ 24. Did you write the final paper in pencil?

_____ 25. Did you center the title on the top line and center your name under the title?

_____ 26. Did you skip a line before starting the writing assignment?

_____ 27. Did you single-space, use wide margins, and write the final paper neatly?

_____ 28. Did you staple your papers in this order: final paper on top, rough draft in the middle, and prewriting map on the bottom? Did you put them in the Final Paper folder?

Writing Time

Hand It In: **WRITING ASSIGNMENT 31**

Get your stapled papers for Writing Assignment 31 from your Final Paper folder. Check to make sure they are in the correct order: the final paper on top, the rough draft in the middle, and the Story Elements Outline on the bottom. Hand them in to your teacher.

LISTENING AND SPEAKING:
Oral Review Questions

Discuss It:

1. What is an antecedent?

2. True or False. A pronoun should agree with the antecedent in number and gender.

3. True or False. A pronoun that does not refer to a definite person, place, or thing is called an indefinite pronoun.

4. Name the five plural indefinite pronouns.

5. Name the six indefinite pronouns that can be either singular or plural.

6. Name the seventeen singular indefinite pronouns.

7. What are the core parts of a Pattern 4 sentence?

8. What are the seven subjective-case pronouns?

9. How are subjective pronouns used?

10. What are the seven objective-case pronouns?

11. How are objective pronouns used?

12. What are the seven most common possessive-case pronouns?

13. How are possessive pronouns used?

14. What type of writing is a humorous story that makes use of exaggeration?

15. What type of writing is used when your purpose is to show similarities and differences?

>>>>>>>>>>>>>>>>>>> **Student Tip...**

For information about test-taking strategies, refer to the Resource Tools Section on page 520.

Review It: **GOALS**

Review the goals you wrote in your Goal Booklet at the beginning of the school year. Discuss your progress with your teacher or a student partner. Then, write a paragraph in your Goal Booklet that tells how well you are meeting your short-term goals. Give examples that support your evaluation of your progress. Next, write another paragraph to evaluate your long-term goals. Tell whether you want to change them or keep them the same. Give reasons to support either choice. Finally, return your Goal Booklet to your teacher when you have finished.

START LESSON 10

Lesson 10

You will

- hand in WA 31 for grading.
- respond to oral review questions.
- take Chapter 12 Test.
- discuss and evaluate goals.
- write a paragraph in your goal booklet.

CHAPTER TEST

It is time to evaluate your knowledge of the skills you have learned in this chapter. Your teacher will give you the Chapter 12 Test to help you assess your progress.

START LESSON 1

Lesson 1

You will

- recite new jingle (Predicate Adjective).
- identify predicate adjectives and Pattern 5.
- classify Introductory Sentences.
- do a Skill Builder to identify predicate adjectives.
- write in your journal.

Student Note:

Beginning with this chapter, you will no longer have Vocabulary and Analogy Time. You will work word analogies independently during practice and test times. This will develop your ability to analyze word relationships on your own.

LISTENING AND SPEAKING:

Recite It: Recite the new jingle.

♪	Jingle 26	**The Predicate Adjective Jingle**

A predicate, predicate, predicate adjective
Is a special, special adjective
In the predicate, predicate, predicate
That modifies, modifies, **modifies**
The simple, simple **subject**.

A predicate, predicate, predicate adjective
Follows after a linking verb.
To find a predicate adjective,
Ask **WHAT KIND** of subject and verify the answer.
Verify that the adjective in the predicate
Modifies, modifies, **modifies**
The simple, simple **subject**.

Apply It: These Introductory Sentences are used to apply the new grammar concepts taught below. Classify these sentences orally with your teacher.

Introductory Sentences	Chapter 13: Lesson 1

1. _____ A wild rose is very beautiful.
2. _____ The wild roses behind our house are spectacular!
3. _____ My winter coat is so cozy and very warm.

Learn It: **PREDICATE ADJECTIVES**

You have studied five jobs of nouns: subject, object of a preposition, indirect object, direct object, and predicate noun. You have learned that certain nouns form parts of different sentence patterns, and you have learned that these patterns have either action verbs or linking verbs. The new sentence pattern, Pattern 5, has an adjective as one of its pattern parts.

📖	Reference 179	**Predicate Adjective and Pattern 5**

1. A **predicate adjective** is an adjective that is located in the predicate and modifies the simple subject.
2. A predicate adjective is located after a linking verb. A linking verb links, or connects, the subject and the predicate adjective.
3. A predicate adjective tells **what kind** of subject.

Continued on next page. >>>

Reference 179 continued from previous page.

4. To find the predicate adjective, ask WHAT KIND OF SUBJECT after the verb.
5. A *predicate adjective* is labeled with the abbreviation **PA**.
6. A Pattern 5 sentence has a subject noun, linking verb, and predicate adjective as its core. A Pattern 5 is labeled **SN LV PA P5**. A Pattern 5 sentence has one noun job and one adjective job in its core: the subject noun and the predicate adjective. *(If the subject is a pronoun, it is labeled as a subject pronoun in the sentence, but the pattern is still identified as SN LV PA P5.)*
7. **A review:**
   <u>Pattern 1</u> is SN V. It has a noun-verb (**N V**) core.
   <u>Pattern 2</u> is SN V-t DO. It has a noun-verb-noun (**N V N**) core.
   <u>Pattern 3</u> is SN V-t IO DO. It has a noun-verb-noun-noun (**N V N N**) core.
   <u>Pattern 4</u> is SN LV PrN. It has a noun-linking verb-noun (**N LV N**) core.
   <u>Pattern 5</u> is SN LV PA. It has a noun-linking verb-adjective (**N LV Adj**) core.

   In Patterns 1–4, adjectives are not part of the pattern core. However, in Pattern 5, an adjective is part of the pattern core because it is located in the predicate and modifies the subject.

Question and Answer Flow for the Practice Sentence, adding Predicate Adjectives

Practice Sentence: Her new baby is absolutely adorable!

1. Who is absolutely adorable? **baby - SN**
2. What is being said about baby? **baby is - V**
3. Baby is what? **adorable - verify the adjective**
4. What kind of baby? **adorable - PA**
   (**Say:** *adorable - predicate adjective.*)
5. **Is - LV** (**Say:** *is - linking verb.*)
6. How adorable? **absolutely - Adv**
7. What kind of baby? **new - Adj**
8. Whose baby? **her - PPA**

9. **SN LV PA P5** (**Say:** *subject noun, linking verb, predicate adjective, Pattern 5.*)
10. Skill Check
11. Linking verb - check again
12. **No prepositional phrases**
13. **Exclamation point, strong feeling, exclamatory sentence**
14. Go back to the verb. Divide the complete subject from the complete predicate.
15. Is this sentence in a natural or inverted order? **Natural - no change.**

<u>SN LV</u> PPA Adj SN LV Adv PA
<u>PA P5</u> Her new baby / is absolutely adorable! *E*

Discuss It:

1. What is the pattern in a Pattern 5 sentence?
2. What are the core parts of a Pattern 5 sentence?
3. What parts of speech are used in a Pattern 5 sentence?

Learn It: A SKILL BUILDER FOR A NOUN CHECK WITH PREDICATE ADJECTIVES

The example below shows you what to do with predicate adjectives when you are identifying nouns for a Noun Check.

JOURNAL WRITING 35

Write an entry in your journal. Use Reference 9 on page 12 for ideas.

Skill Builder

FOR A NOUN CHECK WITH PREDICATE ADJECTIVES

Sentence 1: Subject Noun (rose) *yes, it is a noun.*

Sentence 2: Subject Noun (roses) *yes, it is a noun;*
   Object of the Preposition (house) *yes, it is a noun.*

Sentence 3: Subject Noun (coat) *yes, it is a noun.*

START LESSON 2

Lesson 2

You will

- practice Jingle 26.
- classify Practice Sentences.
- do a Skill Builder.
- identify degrees of comparison of adjectives.
- do Classroom Practice 60.

LISTENING AND SPEAKING:

Recite It: Practice Jingle 26 in the Jingle Section on page 505.

Apply It: Classify the Practice Sentences orally with your teacher.

Practice Sentences	Chapter 13: Lesson 2
1. _____ The weathered barn was dilapidated and barely visible.	
2. _____ The red carnations in the glass vase on the mantle are plastic.	
3. _____ After a week in the hospital, he was weak and wobbly.	

Using the sentences just classified, do a Skill Builder orally with your teacher.

1. **Identify the nouns in a Noun Check.**
2. **Identify the nouns as singular or plural.**
3. **Identify the nouns as common or proper.**
4. **Identify the complete subject and the complete predicate.**
5. **Identify the simple subject and the simple predicate.**
6. **Do a Vocabulary Check.**
7. **Do a Verb Chant.**

Learn It: DEGREES OF COMPARISON OF ADJECTIVES

Reference 180	Degrees of Comparison of Adjectives

When adjectives are describing one noun, they are usually in a simple form, as indicated in Rule 1 below. However, when adjectives are used to compare two or more nouns, they change to comparative or superlative forms, as in Rule 2 and Rule 3 below. **Simple, comparative, and superlative forms of adjectives are called degrees of comparison.** Study the rules to help you understand the degrees of comparison.

Continued on next page. >>>

Reference 180 continued from previous page.

RULE 1: **Simple Form.** This is also known as the positive form. This form is the one used most often because it describes **ONE** person, place, or thing. Use the **Simple Form** when no comparison is being made.

Simple Form: **slow** (one syllable), **anxious** (two syllables), **good** (irregular)

RULE 2: **Comparative Form.** Use the comparative form to compare **TWO** people, places, or things. **To make the comparative form, add *-er* or MORE to the simple form.** Use *-er* with one-syllable adjectives and some two-syllable adjectives. Use **more** with some two-syllable adjectives and all adjectives of three or more syllables.

Comparative Form: **slower** (one syllable), **more anxious** (two syllables), **better** (irregular)

RULE 3: **Superlative Form.** The superlative form is used to compare **THREE** or more people, places, or things. **To make the superlative form, add *-est* or MOST to the simple form.** Use *-est* with one-syllable adjectives and some two-syllable adjectives. Use **most** with some two-syllable adjectives and all adjectives of three or more syllables.

Superlative Form: **slowest** (one syllable), **most anxious** (two syllables), **best** (irregular)

Most adjectives use regular forms in the comparative and superlative degrees, but some adjectives have irregular forms in the comparative and superlative degrees. You must memorize the irregular forms.

IRREGULAR ADJECTIVES MUST BE MEMORIZED

Simple	Comparative	Superlative
good	better	best
bad, ill	worse	worst
little (amount)	less or lesser	least
much, many	more	most

Avoid double comparisons. **Do not** use both *-er* and **more** or *-est* and **most** to form the comparative or superlative degrees. (**Your house is <u>more newer</u> than mine.**)

Classroom Practice 60

It is time to practice the skills you are learning. You will use the classroom practice on the next page to apply these skills.

Student Note: Look at the editing section at the bottom of the Classroom Practice 60. Starting with this practice, the editing guide will give only a total number of mistakes. The editing guide will no longer give a detailed list of each kind of mistake.

Classroom Practice 60

Name:_____ Date:_____

GRAMMAR

▶ **Exercise 1:** Classify each sentence.

1. _____ Mother's strawberry cake is rich, moist, and delicious.

2. _____ The hunting dogs were exhausted after the long chase.

3. _____ The steps to the top of the monument are too steep and narrow for us.

SKILLS

▶ **Exercise 2:** Write the different forms for the adjectives below.

RULE 1: Simple form	RULE 2: Comparative form (er, more)	RULE 3: Superlative form (est, most)

Simple Form	Comparative Form	Superlative Form
1.	worse	
2. intelligent		
3.		happiest
4.	better	
5. respectful		
6.	more beautiful	

▶ **Exercise 3:** In each blank, write the correct form of the adjective in parentheses to complete the sentences.

1. Cedric sat in the _____ recliner in the store. **(comfortable)**

2. This dress is _____ than the one you bought yesterday. **(pretty)**

3. William handled a very _____· problem with skill. **(difficult)**

4. The fudge brownies tasted _____ than the orange cake. **(good)**

5. Of all the composers, I like Beethoven the _____. **(good)**

▶ **Exercise 4:** Write the letter of the word that best completes each analogy.

1. **books : reading :: ____ : driving**   a. beds   b. chairs   c. cars   d. library

2. **blow : blew :: sleep : ____**   a. walked   b. eat   c. sleeping   d. slept

EDITING

▶ **Exercise 5:** Correct the sentences below. **Editing Guide: 20 mistakes**

the membership in hour book club are increasing every week i said to my friend you should

join us we discuss diferent books eat snacks and play games we always have an great time

LISTENING AND SPEAKING:

START LESSON 3

Lesson 3

You will
- practice Jingles 20–26.
- classify Practice Sentences.
- do a Skill Builder.
- identify double negatives.
- do Classroom Practice 61.
- read and discuss Discovery Time.

Recite It: Practice Jingles 20–26 in the Jingle Section on pages 503-505.

Apply It: Classify the Practice Sentences orally with your teacher.

Practice Sentences	Chapter 13: Lesson 3

1. _____ The rings around Saturn are usually visible with a telescope.
2. _____ During the extended drought, the wheat crop looked pathetic.
3. _____ The water over the road was deep and treacherous after the downpour.

Using the sentences just classified, do a Skill Builder orally with your teacher.

1. **Identify the nouns in a Noun Check.**
2. **Identify the nouns as singular or plural.**
3. **Identify the nouns as common or proper.**
4. **Identify the complete subject and the complete predicate.**
5. **Identify the simple subject and the simple predicate.**
6. **Do a Vocabulary Check.**
7. **Do a Verb Chant.**

Learn It: DOUBLE NEGATIVES

📖	Reference 181	Double Negatives

Double means TWO. Negative means NOT. You have a **double-negative** mistake when you use two negative words in the same sentence. Most negative words begin with the letter n. Other negative words do not begin with the letter n but are negative in meaning. There are also some prefixes that give words a negative meaning.

Negative Words that Begin with *N*			Other Negative Words	Negative Prefixes
• neither	• no	• no one	• barely	• dis
• not (n't)	• nowhere	• never	• hardly	• non
• nobody	• none	• nothing	• scarcely	• un

Continued on next page. >>>

Reference 181 continued from previous page.

THREE WAYS TO CORRECT A DOUBLE NEGATIVE

RULE 1: Change the second negative to a positive:
    Incorrect: Janice <u>couldn't</u> hear <u>nothing</u>.   **Correct:** Janice **couldn't** hear **anything**.

RULE 2: Take out the negative part of a contraction:
    Incorrect: Janice <u>couldn't</u> hear <u>nothing</u>.   **Correct:** Janice **could** hear **nothing**.

RULE 3: Remove the first negative word (possibility of a verb change):
    Incorrect: Janice <u>didn't</u> hear <u>nothing</u>.   **Correct:** Janice **heard nothing**.

CHANGING NEGATIVE WORDS TO POSITIVE WORDS

1. Change *no* or *none* to *any*.
2. Change *nobody* to *anybody*.
3. Change *no one* to *anyone*.
4. Change *nothing* to *anything*.
5. Change *nowhere* to *anywhere*.
6. Change *never* to *ever*.
7. Change *neither* to *either*.
8. Remove the *n't* from a contraction.

Directions: Underline the negative words in each sentence. Rewrite each sentence and correct the double-negative mistake as indicated by the rule number at the end of the sentence.

She <u>doesn't</u> have <u>no</u> books in her locker.   **(Rule 3)** *She has no books in her locker.*

He <u>can't hardly</u> wait for the movie tonight.   **(Rule 2)** *He can hardly wait for the movie tonight.*

He <u>hasn't</u> done <u>nothing</u> on his vacation.   **(Rule 1)** *He hasn't done anything on his vacation.*

>>>> Student Tip...

For more information about writing poetry, look at Chapter 18 on pages 456–474.

Classroom Practice 61

It is time to practice the skills you are learning. You will use the classroom practice on the next page to apply these skills.

ENRICHMENT:

Discovery Time

The Moon is a cold ball of rock that circles around the Earth continuously. It has no light of its own, but shines at night because it reflects the Sun's light. The word "month" comes from moon and the time it takes the Moon to go around the Earth once.

Discovery Questions:
- **Is there water on the Moon?**
- **Would you want to explore the moon? Explain.**
- **What would living on the moon be like?**

Discovery Activity:
- **Many poems, songs, and stories have been written about the moon. Name as many as you can. Which are your favorites? Write your own poem, song, or story about the moon.**

Are you interested in learning more about the moon?

1. You may explore this topic further by using the resources listed below.
   Computer resources: Internet, encyclopedia software
   Library resources: encyclopedias, books, magazines, newspapers
   Home/community resources: books, interviews, newspapers, magazines

2. A Discovery Share Time is provided in Lesson 8 if you wish to share your investigation results. You may share orally, or you may prepare a written report. You will put your written report in a class booklet titled "Space Trivia." This booklet will be placed in the class library for everyone to enjoy.

Classroom Practice 61

Name:_____ Date:_____

GRAMMAR

▶ **Exercise 1:** Classify each sentence.

1. _____ The skies will be clear and blue tomorrow.

2. _____ The fog in the valley during the mornings is dense.

3. _____ On the train trip, we were cold and hungry.

SKILLS

▶ **Exercise 2:** Write the different forms for the adjectives below.

RULE 1: Simple form	RULE 2: Comparative form (er, more)	RULE 3: Superlative form (est, most)

Simple Form	Comparative Form	Superlative Form
1. wonderful		
2.	more peaceful	
3.		least

▶ **Exercise 3:** In each blank, write the correct form of the adjective in parentheses to complete the sentences.

1. Tamika's story is the _____ of the two. **(interesting)**

2. Josh's team is _____ than Donald's team. **(good)**

3. Janette is the _____ baby I've ever seen! **(pretty)**

▶ **Exercise 4:** Underline the negative words in each sentence. Rewrite each sentence and correct the double-negative mistake as indicated by the rule number in parentheses at the end of the sentence.

RULE 1:	RULE 2:	RULE 3:
Change the second negative to a positive.	Take out the negative part of a contraction.	Remove the first negative word (verb change).

1. Sara couldn't find no food at home. **(Rule 2)** _____

2. She doesn't have no athletic shoes. **(Rule 3)** _____

3. We didn't hear nothing but the wind. **(Rule 1)** _____

4. Tim hadn't never played soccer. **(Rule 2)** _____

5. There wasn't no pizza left. **(Rule 1)** _____

▶ **Exercise 5:** Write the letter of the word that best completes each analogy.

1. **do : due :: sight** ____   a. sound   b. sense   c. dew   d. site

2. **flood : drought :: problem :** ____   a. math   b. solution   c. dry   d. trouble

EDITING

▶ **Exercise 6:** Correct the sentence below. **Editing Guide: 12 mistakes**

mariana father said tell samantha that youll call her back when youve finished your chores

START LESSON 4

Lesson 4

You will

- practice Jingles 13-19.
- classify Practice Sentences.
- do Classroom Practice 62.
- read and discuss Discovery Time.
- do a homework assignment.
- do Home Connection activity.

LISTENING AND SPEAKING:

Jingle Time

Recite It: Practice Jingles 13–19 in the Jingle Section on pages 501–503.

Grammar Time

Apply It: Classify the Practice Sentences orally with your teacher.

Practice Sentences	Chapter 13: Lesson 4
1. _____ The children were noisy and restless after the parade.	
2. _____ Grandma's cast-iron pot was black from years of use.	
3. _____ The salsa dip at the Mexican restaurant on Lewis Road is extremely hot.	

✏ Classroom Practice 62

It is time to practice the skills you are learning. You will use the classroom practice on the next page to apply these skills.

ENRICHMENT:

Discovery Time

(Soviet) 1966—Luna 9 was the first spacecraft to land on the moon successfully. Previous spacecraft tried to land on the moon but had crashed.

Discovery Questions:
- What do you think it would it be like to explore the moon?
- What other information can you discover about early spacecraft?
- Do you think space travel is safer today? Explain.
- What would it be like to design, make, and fly a spaceship?

Discovery Activity:
- Get into groups and create plans for your own private spaceship. Make a list of necessary features and draw a picture of your spaceship.

Are you interested in learning more about Luna 9 or space travel?

1. You may explore this topic further by using the resources listed below.
   Computer resources: Internet, encyclopedia software
   Library resources: encyclopedias, books, magazines, newspapers
   Home/community resources: books, interviews, newspapers, magazines

2. A Discovery Share Time is provided in Lesson 8 if you wish to share your investigation results. You may share orally, or you may prepare a written report. You will put your written report in a class booklet titled "Space Trivia." This booklet will be placed in the class library for everyone to enjoy.

Classroom Practice 62

Name:_____ Date:_____

GRAMMAR

▶ **Exercise 1:** Classify each sentence.

1. _____ The paint on the bench in the park is wet.

2. _____ The life of a spy is very dangerous.

3. _____ Winters in some countries are terribly cold and harsh.

SKILLS

▶ **Exercise 2:** Write the different forms for the adjectives below.

RULE 1: Simple form	RULE 2: Comparative form (er, more)	RULE 3: Superlative form (est, most)

Simple Form	Comparative Form	Superlative Form
1.	funnier	
2. helpful		
3. bad		

▶ **Exercise 3:** In each blank, write the correct form of the adjective in parentheses to complete the sentences.

1. Our gymnastics coach was _____ than usual. **(anxious)**

2. Malcolm scored the _____ points of all the players on the team. **(many)**

3. Mr. Schultz is a very _____ band director. **(good)**

4. Kenny's family had the _____ camper in the park. **(cool)**

▶ **Exercise 4:** Underline the negative words in each sentence. Rewrite each sentence and correct the double-negative mistake as indicated by the rule number in parentheses at the end of the sentence.

RULE 1: Change the second negative to a positive.	RULE 2: Take out the negative part of a contraction.	RULE 3: Remove the first negative word (verb change).

1. Jan didn't find nothing at the store. **(Rule 3)** _____

2. Ray hasn't never driven a motorcycle. **(Rule 2)** _____

3. I wouldn't take nothing without paying. **(Rule 1)** _____

4. I couldn't find no correct answer. **(Rule 3)** _____

5. She hasn't had no dessert. **(Rule 1)** _____

▶ **Exercise 5:** Write the letter of the word that best completes the analogy.

1. **curious : toddler :: ____ : grandmother**   a. grandpa   b. grandma   c. aunt   d. loving

EDITING

▶ **Exercise 6:** Correct the sentence below. **Editing Guide: 13 mistakes**

we wont be able to sea the speaker very well mrs blackburn said from our balcony seats

Homework 10

Complete this homework assignment on notebook paper.

1. Number your paper 1–6. Write the correct form of the adjective listed in parentheses at the end of the sentence.

1. My mom is _____ than I am. **(busy)**

2. Kendrell Smith is _____ than his brother, Kendrick. **(tall)**

3. My dad is the _____ of anyone in our family. **(active)**

4. Snowboarding is _____ than snow skiing. **(difficult)**

5. My little brother has the _____ nightmares. **(bad)**

6. My best friend is _____ than I in math. **(smart)**

2. Number your paper 1–4. Write the negative words in each sentence. Then, rewrite each sentence and correct the double-negative mistake as indicated by the rule number in parentheses at the end of the sentence.

RULE 1:	RULE 2:	RULE 3:
Change the second negative to a positive.	Take out the negative part of a contraction.	Remove the first negative word (verb change).

1. The sick baby didn't want nothing to eat.   **(Rule 3)** _____

2. The thief didn't leave no clues for the police. **(Rule 1)** _____

3. My mom hadn't never seen a shooting star.   **(Rule 2)** _____

4. Our teacher doesn't give no homework.   **(Rule 1)** _____

Home Connection

Family Activity for Double Negatives

1. Pretend that you and your classmates have entered a poster contest for a anti-litter campaign at your school. Below are some of the slogans with double negatives your classmates have written. Rewrite the slogans, correcting the errors. See how many ways each slogan can be corrected.

Don't never litter.

I won't never litter.

Litter doesn't never look good.

Litter isn't no good.

Litter ain't no joke.

2. Write your own slogans about a subject of your choice.

3. Divide into family teams. Each team should write slogans with double-negative errors for another team to correct. After each team has corrected the other team's slogans, the teams could choose a way to illustrate or dramatize the corrected slogans.

LISTENING AND SPEAKING:

Grammar Time

Apply It: Classify the Practice Sentences orally with your teacher.

Practice Sentences	Chapter 13: Lesson 5

1. _____ The yellow letters looked great on the navy background.
2. _____ Frontier life was extremely difficult for the pioneers.
3. _____ Terrance was impressed with the new computer program.

Chapter Checkup 63

It is time for a checkup of the skills you have learned in this chapter. You will use the Chapter Checkup on the next page to evaluate your progress.

START LESSON 5

Lesson 5

You will
- classify Practice Sentences.
- do Chapter Checkup 63.
- write in your journal.

JOURNAL WRITING 36

Write an entry in your journal. Use Reference 9 on page 12 for ideas.

Chapter 13 Checkup 63

Name:_____ Date:_____

GRAMMAR

▶ **Exercise 1:** Classify each sentence.

1. _____ The day before the storm was dark and dreary.

2. _____ The memory for my digital camera is very expensive.

3. _____ The children were hungry after their long hiking trip.

SKILLS

▶ **Exercise 2:** Write the different forms for the adjectives below.

RULE 1: Simple form	RULE 2: Comparative form (er, more)	RULE 3: Superlative form (est, most)

Simple Form	Comparative Form	Superlative Form
1.	sadder	
2. delighted		
3. bad		

▶ **Exercise 3:** In each blank, write the correct form of the adjective in parentheses to complete the sentences.

1. Will the radio or television give _____ advertising results? **(good)**

2. These cartoons are much _____ than the ones I watched last week. **(funny)**

3. Carl had the _____ case of homesickness he had ever had. **(bad)**

4. Lindsay read her book _____ than anyone in the book club. **(quick)**

▶ **Exercise 4:** Underline the negative words in each sentence. Rewrite each sentence and correct the double-negative mistake as indicated by the rule number in parentheses at the end of the sentence.

RULE 1:	RULE 2:	RULE 3:
Change the second negative to a positive.	Take out the negative part of a contraction.	Remove the first negative word (verb change).

1. My friend hasn't never called me. **(Rule 2)** _____

2. Kendra isn't making nothing for lunch. **(Rule 1)** _____

3. Terrell doesn't want nothing to eat. **(Rule 3)** _____

4. She didn't wear no coat outside. **(Rule 1)** _____

▶ **Exercise 5:** Write the letter of the word that best completes the analogy.

1. **oar : ____ :: read : reed**   a. canoe   b. ore   c. chore   d. book

EDITING

▶ **Exercise 6:** Correct the sentence below. **Editing Guide: 14 mistakes**

corey ill take you and a freind to the mid-america museum on sunday after lunch mother said

LISTENING AND SPEAKING:

 Jingle Time

Recite It: Practice Jingle 26 in the Jingle Section on page 505.

GRAMMAR & WRITING CONNECTION:
Practice and Revised Sentences

Apply It: BUILDING AND EXPANDING SENTENCES

START LESSON 6

Lesson 6

You will

- practice Jingle 26.
- do Classroom Practice 64.
- choose a book to read for enjoyment in the next lesson.
- do Across the Curriculum activity.
- write in your journal.

> **Reference 182** — **A Guide for Using a Pattern 5 Core (Sn LV PA) to Build & Expand Sentences**
>
> 1. **SN** or **SP** (**subject**) Think of a noun or pronoun that you want to use as the *subject*. Write the noun or pronoun you have chosen as the *subject* of your sentence.
> 2. **LV** (**linking verb**) A *linking verb* links the subject with a word in the predicate. You may choose a linking verb from this list: *am, is, are, was, were, be, being, been, appear, become, feel, grow, look, remain, seem, smell, sound, stay,* and *taste.* First, choose a verb for your sentence. Then, wait until you have chosen a predicate adjective to verify that it is a linking verb. If the verb is verified as linking, keep it as the verb of your Pattern 5 core.
> 3. **PA** (**predicate adjective**) A *predicate adjective* is an adjective in the predicate that tells **what kind** of subject is in the sentence. To find a predicate adjective, ask the question WHAT KIND of subject after the verb. Check to make sure the predicate adjective describes the subject. Write the predicate adjective you have chosen in the predicate part of your sentence.

 Classroom Practice 64

It is time to practice the skills you are learning. You will use the classroom practice on the next page to apply these skills.

Choose It: A FICTION OR NONFICTION BOOK

Choose a fiction or nonfiction book to read for enjoyment and have it ready to read during Reading Time in the next lesson.

 **Across the Curriculum**

Drama/Social Studies Connection: Divide into small groups. Select an invention from history. Write a short play, using the inventor as the main character. Use your imagination and the information you have researched to write the dialogue for your play. When you write a play, you do not use quotation marks. On the left side of your paper, write the character's name, followed by a colon. Then, write the words that are spoken after the character's name. Start a new line each time the dialogue changes from one character to another.

Additional instructions, or cues, for the actors are always written in parentheses and italicized. These instructions tell the actor where to stand, when to leave the stage, and what type of voice inflections to use: soft, loud, irritable, proud, etc..

 Student Tip...

Use your vocabulary words in your Practice and Revised Sentences. Use a thesaurus, synonym-antonym book, or a dictionary to help you develop your writing vocabulary.

  JOURNAL WRITING 37

Write an entry in your journal. Use Reference 9 on page 12 for ideas.

Classroom Practice 64

Name: _____ Date: _____

INDEPENDENT PRACTICE & REVISED SENTENCES

1. Write a Practice Sentence according to the labels you choose. Use **SN/SP LV PA** as your main labels. You may use the other labels in any order and as many times as you wish in order to make a Practice Sentence. Chapter 13 labels for a Practice Sentence: **SN/SP, LV, PA,** Adj, Adv, A, P, OP, PPA, C, HV, I, PNA

2. Write a Revised Sentence. Use the following revision strategies: *synonym (syn), antonym (ant), word change (wc), added word (add), deleted word (delete),* or *no change (nc).* Under each word, write the abbreviation of the revision strategy you use.

Labels:

Practice:

Revised:

Strategies:

Labels:

Practice:

Revised:

Strategies:

Labels:

Practice:

Revised:

Strategies:

Read It: A FICTION OR NONFICTION BOOK

Use your reading time to read the fiction or nonfiction book you selected in the previous lesson. This book is for enjoyment, and there is no book review required.

Conference Time

Discuss It: TEACHER-STUDENT CONFERENCES
FOR WRITING ASSIGNMENT 31

Meet with your teacher to discuss Writing Assignment 31.
After the conference, place this group of papers in your Publishing folder.

START LESSON 7

Lesson 7

You will
- conference with teacher about WA 31.
- read book for enjoyment during conferences.

START LESSON 8

Lesson 8

You will

- participate in Discovery Share Time.
- read and discuss guidelines for dramatic presentations.
- begin publishing WA 31 by rewriting your tall tale.

LISTENING AND SPEAKING:

If you have chosen to investigate a topic introduced in this chapter, you now have the opportunity to share your results in one of the following ways:

1. You may relate your information orally.
2. You may read a written report.
3. You may place your report in the booklet without reading it aloud.

After share time, all written reports should be turned in to be placed in the class booklet titled "Space Trivia." You are encouraged to check out this class booklet so you can enjoy the reports again.

Learn It: **DRAMATIC PRESENTATIONS OF TALL TALES**

You will publish your tall tale by presenting it to the class in a dramatic presentation. Your teacher will give you a presentation schedule to follow. If you are in Group 1, you will share in Lesson 9. If you are in Group 2, you will share in Lesson 10. Use the guidelines below as you prepare for your presentation.

Reference 183	**Guidelines for Dramatic Presentations**

1. Your teacher will post a presentation schedule.
2. Stay seated until the current presenter has finished.
3. When it is your turn, go to the designated area. Make all preparations necessary for your presentation before you begin.
4. Introduce yourself and your presentation. Be sure to say your first and last name. Here are two examples.

    Say: "Hello, my name is (*your first and last name*). The title of my story is (*the title of your story*)."

    Say: "(*the title of your story*) by (*your first and last name*)."

5. Read clearly, slowly, and loudly enough for everyone to hear. Read with expression. Do not be afraid to raise your voice and read with feeling. Look at your audience from time to time.
6. If you make a mistake, correct it or ignore it and keep going. Most people do not notice minor mistakes if the speaker recovers quickly and smoothly. It takes practice to become a calm and fluent speaker.
7. You are part of the audience when you are not presenting. You must be as quiet as possible and give the speaker your full attention. Show appreciation by clapping after the speaker has finished.
8. The information in the Share Time Guidelines applies to all presentations. If you need to review this information, look at Reference 68 on page 391.

Review It:

| Reference 68 | **Share Time Guidelines** |

Speaker Presentation

1. Have your paper ready to read when called upon.
2. Tell the title of your writing selection.
3. Tell the purpose and type of writing used.

PRESENTATION TIPS:

4. Stand with your feet flat on the floor and your shoulders straight. Do not shift your weight as you stand.
5. Hold your paper about chin high to help you project your voice to your audience.
6. Make sure you do not read too fast.
7. Read in a clear voice that can be heard so that your audience does not have to strain to hear you.
8. Change your voice tone for different characters or for different parts of the writing selection.

Audience Response

1. Look at the speaker.
2. Turn your body toward the speaker.
3. Listen attentively. Do not let your thoughts wander.
4. Do not make distracting noises as you listen.
5. Do not make distracting motions as you listen.
6. Show interest in what the speaker is saying.
7. Silently summarize what the speaker is saying. Take notes if necessary.
8. Ask questions about anything that is not clear.
9. Show appreciation by clapping after the speaker has finished.

Write It: **REWRITE WRITING ASSIGNMENT 31, TALL TALE**

Correct any errors in your tall tale before you rewrite it in ink or type it on a computer. After rewriting your paper for publication, give the stapled papers (evaluation guide, graded final paper, rough draft, and story elements outline) to your teacher to be placed in your Writing Portfolio.

>>>>>>>>> **Student Tip...**

1. **Dress the part of a character in your tall tale or make and use illustrations.**
2. **Take your rewritten tall tale home to practice before your presentation.**

START LESSON 9

Lesson 9

You will

- review guidelines for dramatic presentations.
- continue publishing WA 31 by sharing your tall tale in a dramatic presentation.

Publishing Time

Publish It: WRITING ASSIGNMENT 31

Review the Guidelines for Dramatic Presentations. If you are in Group 1, you will share your tall tale today. If you are in Group 2, you will share during the next lesson. Use the Share Time Guidelines as presentations are made. After each presentation, you should write the title of the tall tale and the student author in your journal.

Reference 183	Guidelines for Dramatic Presentations

1. Your teacher will post a presentation schedule.

2. Stay seated until the current presenter has finished.

3. When it is your turn, go to the designated area. Make all preparations necessary for your presentation before you begin.

4. Introduce yourself and your presentation. Be sure to say your first and last name. Here are two examples.

   Say: "**Hello, my name is (*your first and last name*). The title of my story is (*the title of your story*).**"

   Say: "**(*the title of your story*) by (*your first and last name*).**"

5. Read clearly, slowly, and loudly enough for everyone to hear. Read with expression. Do not be afraid to raise your voice and read with feeling. Look at your audience from time to time.

6. If you make a mistake, correct it or ignore it and keep going. Most people do not notice minor mistakes if the speaker recovers quickly and smoothly. It takes practice to become a calm and fluent speaker.

7. You are part of the audience when you are not presenting. You must be as quiet as possible and give the speaker your full attention. Show appreciation by clapping after the speaker has finished.

8. The information in the Share Time Guidelines applies to all presentations. If you need to review this information, look at Reference 68 on page 391.

Publishing Time

Publish It: **WRITING ASSIGNMENT 31**

Review the Guidelines for Dramatic Presentations. If you are in Group 2, you will share your tall tale today. Use the Share Time Guidelines on page 391 as presentations are made. After each presentation, you should write the title of the tall tale and the student author in your journal.

START LESSON 10

Lesson 10

You will

- review guidelines for dramatic presentations.
- finish publishing WA 31 by sharing your tall tale in a dramatic presentation.

START LESSON 11

Lesson 11

You will

- read and discuss evaluations of dramatic presentations.
- write an evaluation of your own dramatic presentation and a classmate's presentation for WA 32.

 Writing Time

Learn It: **EVALUATION OF DRAMATIC PRESENTATIONS**

Use the questions below to help you evaluate your dramatic presentation and the presentation of a classmate for Writing Assignment 32.

Reference 184 **Evaluation Prompts for Dramatic Presentations**

Choose the evaluation prompt below that describes your presentation. Write your answers and comments in complete sentences. Try to be as objective as possible. This evaluation will help you improve your next dramatic presentation.

Character Portrayal

1. Explain why you made the choice to do a character portrayal.

2. Which character did you choose to portray? Explain how you made your choice.

3. How did you look? (Describe your hair, face, and costume or outfit.)

4. Did you use any other props? If so, what were they? Did they add to your presentation? Did they distract from it?

5. Were you aware of nonverbal cues in your presentation? Did you hold your paper so that your face could be seen? Did you look at the audience from time to time? Did you use facial expressions and body gestures effectively? Did you move around or did you stand still?

Illustration

1. Explain why you made the choice to use illustrations for your presentation.

2. How did you illustrate your story? Did you use paint, markers, chalk, crayons, pencils, or other media? Were your illustrations easy for the audience to see? Did you use them effectively?

3. Did you use any other props? If so, what were they? Did they add to your presentation? Did they distract from it?

4. Were you aware of nonverbal cues in your presetion? Did you hold your paper so that your face could be seen? Did you look at the audience from time to time? Did you use facial expressions and body gestures effectively? Did you move around or did you stand still?

Reading Dramatization

1. Explain why you made the choice to do a dramatic reading of your story.

2. Were you aware of nonverbal cues in your presentation? Did you hold your paper so that your face could be seen? Did you look at the audience from time to time? Did you use facial expressions and body gestures effectively? Did you move around or did you stand still?

3. Did you speak clearly and loudly enough to be heard? Did you use inflections in your voice to make the characters come alive?

4. How could you enhance your presentation? What would you change and what would you not change?

Continued on next page. >>>

Reference 184 continued from previous page.

6. Did you speak clearly and loudly enough to be heard? Did you use inflections in your voice to make the characters come alive?	5. Did you speak clearly and loudly enough to be heard? Did you use inflections in your voice to make the characters come alive?	5. What is your honest opinion of your presentation? What were the strong points, and what areas needed improvement?
7. How could you enhance your presentation? What would you change and what would you not change?	6. How could you enhance your presentation? What would you change and what would you not change?	
8. What is your honest opinion of your presentation? What were the strong points, and what areas needed improvement?	7. What is your honest opinion of your presentation? What were the strong points, and what areas needed improvement?	

Write It: WRITING ASSIGNMENT 32

Write two evaluations in your journal. Evaluate your dramatic presentation and evaluate the presentation of one classmate.

Writing Assignment [32]

1. **Personal Evaluation:** The evaluation of the dramatic presentation of your own tall tale will be written in your journal. At the top of the page, write today's date and the title of your presentation. Next, choose the evaluation prompt according to the way you made your presentation. *(Refer to Reference 184 on page 394 for the evaluation prompts.)* For example, if you portrayed a character, use the evaluation section under **Character Portrayal**. Write your answers and comments in complete sentences. Try to be as objective as possible.

2. **Evaluation of a Classmate:** At the top of another journal page, write today's date, the title, and the author of your favorite tall-tale presentation by another classmate. Use your list of titles and the names of the student authors to help you. Tell your favorite part of your classmate's tall tale. Try to include as many details as you can remember. End your evaluation by telling why you liked the presentation.

START LESSON 12

Lesson 12

You will

- respond to oral review questions.
- take Chapter 13 Test.

CHAPTER TEST

It is time to evaluate your knowledge of the skills you have learned in this chapter. Your teacher will give you the Chapter 13 Test to help you assess your progress.

LISTENING AND SPEAKING:

Oral Review Questions

Discuss It:

1. What word in the predicate describes or tells what kind of subject?
2. What type of verb is used with a predicate adjective?
3. What are the core parts of a Pattern 5 sentence?
4. What are the core parts of a Pattern 4 sentence?
5. What are the core parts of a Pattern 3 sentence?
6. What are the core parts of a Pattern 2 sentence?
7. What are the core parts of a Pattern 1 sentence?
8. What are the three degrees of comparison for adjectives?
9. Which comparison form is used to compare three or more nouns?
10. What are the three degrees of the word happy?
11. What is it called when two negative words are used in a sentence?
12. Most negative words begin with which letter?
13. Name four negative words that begin with the letter **n**.
14. Name a negative word that does not begin with the letter **n**.
15. What type of writing is a humorous story that makes use of exaggeration?

>>>>>>>>>>>>>>>>>>>>>> **Student Tip...**

> For information about test-taking strategies, refer to the Resource Tools Section on page 520.

English Made Easy

LISTENING AND SPEAKING:
Grammar Time

Apply It: These Introductory Sentences are used to apply the new grammar concepts taught below. Classify these sentences orally with your teacher.

Introductory Sentences	Chapter 14: Lesson 1

1. _____ My cats are very fussy about their food in the mornings.
2. _____ The foreman sounded the whistle at the end of the day.
3. _____ My sister is a computer genius.

Lesson 1

You will
- identify Mixed Patterns 1-5.
- classify Introductory Sentences.
- read and discuss the parts of a friendly letter and a friendly letter envelope.
- read and discuss commonly used abbreviations.
- do Classroom Practice 65.
- write in your journal.

>>> Student Tip...

	Pattern 1	Pattern 2	Pattern 3	Pattern 4	Pattern 5
Traditional	N V	N V N	N V N N	N LV N	N LV Adj
Shurley English	SN V	SN V-t DO	SN V-t IO DO	SN LV PrN	SN LV PA

As you review each pattern, study how the Shurley patterns relate to the traditional patterns.

Learn It: MIXED PATTERNS 1–5

The sentences classified in this chapter will be Patterns 1–5. They are called **Mixed Patterns** because there are five different patterns from which to choose. Use the sentence cores to help determine the pattern of the sentences.

Skill Time

Learn It: TIPS FOR WRITING A FRIENDLY LETTER

Reference 185	Tips for Writing Friendly Letters

Writing letters is a great way to preserve memories of people you care about and who care about you. A letter written to or received from friends or relatives is called a **friendly letter**. Follow the tips below to write a friendly letter.

Tip 1: Write as if you were talking to the person face-to-face. Share information about yourself and mutual friends. Tell stories, conversations, or jokes. Share photographs, articles, drawings, poems, etc. Avoid saying something about someone else that you'll be sorry for later.

Tip 2: If you are writing a return letter, be sure to answer any questions that were asked. Repeat the question so that your reader will know what you are writing about. (You asked about...)

Tip 3: End your letter in a positive way so that your reader will want to write a return letter.

Learn It: **THE FIVE PARTS OF A FRIENDLY LETTER**

The language used in a friendly letter is conversational and informal.
Each part of a friendly letter has a specific place and purpose.

Reference 186 — The Five Parts of a Friendly Letter

1. Heading:
- Box or street address of writer
- City, state, zip code of writer
- Full date letter was written

2. Friendly Greeting or Salutation:
- Begins with *Dear*
- Names the person receiving the letter
- Has a comma after the person's name

3. Body:
- Tells the reason the letter is being written
- Can have one or more paragraphs
- Has indented paragraphs

4. Closing:
- Closes the letter with a personal phrase (*Your friend,*)
- Capitalizes only the first word
- Is followed by a comma

5. Signature:
- Tells who has written the letter
- Is usually signed in cursive
- Uses your first name only unless there is a question as to which friend or relative you are

EXAMPLE OF THE FRIENDLY LETTER

Friendly letter style:

The modified-block style is used in writing friendly letters. In the modified-block style, place the heading, closing, and signature in the middle of the page. Indent each paragraph and do not skip a line between paragraphs.

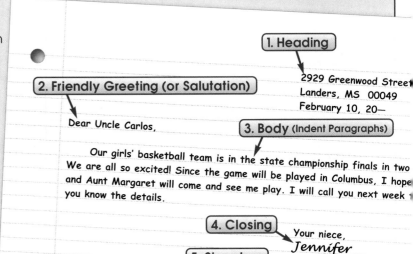

1. Heading

2929 Greenwood Street
Landers, MS 00049
February 10, 20—

2. Friendly Greeting (or Salutation)

Dear Uncle Carlos,

3. Body (Indent Paragraphs)

Our girls' basketball team is in the state championship finals in two
We are all so excited! Since the game will be played in Columbus, I hope
and Aunt Margaret will come and see me play. I will call you next week
you know the details.

4. Closing

Your niece,
Jennifer

5. Signature

Learn It: **THE PARTS OF AN ENVELOPE**

Each part of an envelope for a friendly letter has a specific place and purpose.

Reference 187 — Envelope Parts for a Friendly Letter

The Return Address:
- Name of the person writing the letter
- Box or street address of the writer
- City, state, and zip code of the writer

The Mailing Address:
- Name of the person receiving the letter
- Street address of the person receiving the letter
- City, state, and zip code of the person receiving the letter

Return Address

Jennifer Rodriguez
2929 Greenwood Street
Landers, MS 00049

Mailing Address

Carlos Juarez
124 Baker Road
Columbus, MS 00048

Learn It: COMMONLY USED ABBREVIATIONS

Reference 188 — Commonly Used Abbreviations

Addresses

Apartment	Apt.
Avenue	Ave.
Building	Bldg.
Boulevard	Blvd.
Circle	Cir.
County	Co.
Court	Ct.
Drive	Dr.
Fort	Ft.
Headquarters	Hq.
Highway	Hwy.
Lane	Ln.
Mount	Mt.
Mountain	Mt./Mtn.
Parkway	Pkwy.
Place	Pl.
Point	Pt.
Post Office	P.O./PO
Road	Rd.
Route	Rt.
School	Sch.
Street	St.
Terrace	Ter./Terr.
University	Univ.

Math Abbreviations

foot	ft.
hour	hr.
inch	in.
mile	mi.
minute	min.
month	mo.
ounce	oz.
pint	pt.
pound	lb.
quart	qt.
second	sec.
week	wk.
yard	yd.
year	yr.

Titles

Attorney	Atty.
Doctor	Dr.
Governor	Gov.
Honorable	Hon.
Junior	Jr.
Manager	Mgr.
Miss/Mistress	Ms.
Mistress	Mrs.
Mister	Mr.
President	Pres.
Professor	Prof.
Representative	Rep.
Reverend	Rev.
Senator	Sen.
Senior	Sr.
Superintendent	Supt.

Business Titles

Company	Co.
Corporation	Corp.
Department	Dept.
Incorporated	Inc.

Military Titles

Admiral	Adm.
Captain	Capt.
Colonel	Col.
Commander	Cmdr.
Corporal	Cpl.
Ensign	Ens.
General	Gen.
Lieutenant	Lt.
Major	Maj.
Private	Pvt.
Sergeant	Sgt.
Specialist	Spec.

States and Postal Abbreviations

Alabama	AL		Montana	MT
Alaska	AK		Nebraska	NE
Arizona	AZ		Nevada	NV
Arkansas	AR		New Hampshire	NH
California	CA		New Jersey	NJ
Colorado	CO		New Mexico	NM
Connecticut	CT		New York	NY
Delaware	DE		North Carolina	NC
Florida	FL		North Dakota	ND
Georgia	GA		Ohio	OH
Hawaii	HI		Oklahoma	OK
Idaho	ID		Oregon	OR
Illinois	IL		Pennsylvania	PA
Indiana	IN		Rhode Island	RI
Iowa	IA		South Carolina	SC
Kansas	KS		South Dakota	SD
Kentucky	KY		Tennessee	TN
Louisiana	LA		Texas	TX
Maine	ME		Utah	UT
Maryland	MD		Vermont	VT
Massachusetts	MA		Virginia	VA
Michigan	MI		Washington	WA
Minnesota	MN		West Virginia	WV
Mississippi	MS		Wisconsin	WI
Missouri	MO		Wyoming	WY

Days

Monday	Mon.
Tuesday	Tues.
Wednesday	Wed.
Thursday	Thurs.
Friday	Fri.
Saturday	Sat.
Sunday	Sun.

Directions

North	N
South	S
East	E
West	W
Northeast	NE
Northwest	NW
Southeast	SE
Southwest	SW

Months

January	Jan.
February	Feb.
March	Mar.
April	Apr.
May	——
June	——
July	——
August	Aug.
September	Sept.
October	Oct.
November	Nov.
December	Dec.

Others

District of Columbia	D.C./DC
afternoon	p.m.
before noon	a.m.

Classroom Practice 65

It is time to practice the skills you are learning. You will use the classroom practice on the next page to apply these skills.

JOURNAL WRITING 38

Write an entry in your journal. Use Reference 9 on page 12 for ideas.

Classroom Practice 65

Name:_____ Date:_____

GRAMMAR

▶ **Exercise 1:** Classify each sentence.

1. _____ Sara showed Anna and Janna her science project.

2. _____ Elections will be held on the fifth day of November.

3. _____ The leaves of the plant were brown from the lack of water.

4. _____ Pumpkins are popular fall decorations.

5. _____ Ah! Mom made bouquets of daisies for the bridesmaids!

SKILLS

▶ **Exercise 2:** Use the letter parts below to fill in the blanks of the friendly letter.

TITLE PARTS of a Friendly Letter: Closing   Signature   Heading   Greeting   Body

SAMPLE PARTS of a Friendly Letter: Judith   Dear Kate,   West Plains, OK 00267   Your cousin,
April 18, 20—   2925 Wilmington Blvd.   Grandmother's sixtieth birthday is the first Saturday in
June. I am making arrangements for a special surprise
party for her that weekend. Would you and Grant be
willing to help? Let me hear from you soon.

Friendly Letter

1. Title: _____

_____

_____

_____

2. Title: _____

_____

3. Title: _____

_____

_____

4. Title: _____

_____

5. Title: _____

_____

English Made Easy

LISTENING AND SPEAKING:

Recite It: Practice Jingles 20–26 in the Jingle Section on pages 503–505.

Apply It: Classify the Practice Sentences orally with your teacher.

Practice Sentences	Chapter 14: Lesson 2
1. _____ The design on the expensive rug was intricate and beautiful.	
2. _____ Look at the flower arrangement in the center of the table.	
3. _____ Good grief! Daniel made that stray dog a bed in my bathtub!	

Skill Time

Learn It: **EDITING A FRIENDLY LETTER, USING RULE NUMBERS**

The friendly letter in Classroom Practice 66 has already been punctuated. Write the capitalization and punctuation rule numbers for each correction that appears in **bold** type. There are thirty-nine rule numbers that you must write.

Lesson 2

You will

- practice Jingles 20–26.
- classify Practice Sentences.
- edit a friendly letter for rule numbers only.
- do Classroom Practice 66.
- read and discuss Discovery Time.
- do a homework assignment.
- do Home Connection activity.

Classroom Practice 66

It is time to practice the skills you are learning. You will use the classroom practice on the next page to apply these skills.

ENRICHMENT:

Constellations are patterns of stars in the night sky. Astronomers have identified 88 constellations. One of the best known constellations is the Big Dipper.

Discovery Questions:

- What are the names of the constellations that you are able to recognize in the night sky?
- In the past, how did people use constellations to give them directions at night?
- Today, why is it important to read directions on a compass? Explain.

Discovery Activity:

- Using a compass, track the directions from your classroom to various locations in the school building.

Are you interested in learning more about constellations?

1. You may explore this topic further by using the resources listed below.
   Computer resources: Internet, encyclopedia software
   Library resources: encyclopedias, books, magazines, newspapers
   Home/community resources: books, interviews, newspapers, magazines

2. A Discovery Share Time is provided in Lesson 4 if you wish to share your investigation results. You may share orally, or you may prepare a written report. You will put your written report in a class booklet titled "Space Trivia." This booklet will be placed in the class library for everyone to enjoy.

Student Tip...

Make sure you are aware of the homework note that tells you to bring an envelope from home for a letter-writing assignment in Lesson 6.

Classroom Practice 66

Name:_____ Date:_____

GRAMMAR

▶ **Exercise 1:** Classify each sentence.

1. _____ Bobby, Henry, and Thomas are good friends at school.

2. _____ Would you change the water filter before dark today?

3. _____ The crust of Mom's homemade pizza was too thin.

4. _____ The spry little boy jumped from the tree and darted across the yard.

5. _____ Will you loan me your bicycle for my paper route tomorrow?

SKILLS AND EDITING

▶ **Exercise 2:** Write the capitalization and punctuation rule numbers for each correction in **bold**. Use References 11, 13, and 14 on pages 13, 17–18 to look up rule numbers. (Total rule numbers required: 49.)

808 **B**roken **A**rrow **T**r

Cheyenne **WY** 00333

July 22 20—

Dear **D**ottie

Im enjoying summer camp at **S**ugar **L**oaf **M**ountain **M**r **H**enry our camp director

encourages us to write letters to our family every day **I**ve sent letters to **M**om **D**ad **B**uster

Grandma **G**randpa **A**unt **S**ue and **U**ncle **J**oe **I** guess you deserve a letter too

Your loving brother

Duke

Homework **11**

Complete the homework assignment on notebook paper. Choose one of the following writing prompts:

1. Write a friendly letter to the author of your favorite book.

2. Pretend you are writing a friendly letter to a pen pal in another country for the first time. You must tell your new pen pal some interesting things about yourself so that he/she can get to know you. Use a social studies book, the library, or the internet to help you pick the city and country where your imaginary friend lives.

Follow the friendly-letter form. Make up a reasonable name and address. You could research names from the country you choose. Even though this is a pretend pen pal, make sure you always use writing etiquette, or manners. This means you should not write anything that would embarrass your family, teacher, or school.

Note: For a letter-writing assignment in Lesson 6, you should bring an envelope from home. Also, bring the name and address of a friend or family member to whom you will write and mail your friendly letter.

Home Connection

The following activity can be performed at home to enrich language skills and to practice concepts taught.

Family Activity for the Friendly Letter

Glue the friendly letter below onto cardstock or construction paper. Cut the sections apart at the dotted lines and glue or write the number and the title for each friendly-letter part on the back of the corresponding strip.

Divide into teams. Time each team as members put the pieces of the friendly-letter puzzle together and identify each part. Check the correct answers with the number and title on the back of each piece. The team that completes the puzzle correctly in the shortest time is the winner.

Friendly Letter

Titles: | 1. Heading | 2. Greeting or Salutation | 3. Body | 4. Closing | 5. Signature |

231 Stoneridge Court
Overton, KS 00078
February 13, 20—

Dear Elaine,

    I can't wait to see you in March! Our families will have so much fun on Henderson Mountain. There are horseback riding trails and a fishing lake near our campsite. This will be the best Spring Break ever! See you soon!

Your friend,

Kayla

Kayla	**5. Signature**
Your friend,	**4. Closing**
I can't wait to see you in March! Our families will have so much fun on Henderson Mountain. There are horseback riding trails and a fishing lake near our campsite. This will be the best Spring Break ever! See you soon!	**3. Body**
Dear Elaine,	**2. Greeting or Salutation**
231 Stoneridge Court Overton, KS 00078 February 13, 20—	**1. Heading**

English Made Easy

LISTENING AND SPEAKING:

Jingle Time

Recite It: Practice Jingles 13–19 in the Jingle Section on pages 501-503.

Grammar Time

Apply It: Classify the Practice Sentences orally with your teacher.

Practice Sentences	Chapter 14: Lesson 3
1. _____ Today, the hurricane blew furiously from the ocean onto the shore.	
2. _____ The young man was completely disoriented after the accident.	
3. _____ The Mississippi is a very important river to our country.	

Skill Time

Learn It: **EDITING A FRIENDLY LETTER, USING CORRECTIONS ONLY**

The friendly letter in Classroom Practice 67 has not been punctuated. Write capitalization corrections above the capitalization mistakes, and write the punctuation corrections where they belong in the letter. Look at the editing guide to find the total number of errors you need to correct.

START LESSON 3

Lesson 3

You will
- practice Jingles 13–19.
- classify Practice Sentences.
- edit a friendly letter for corrections only.
- do Classroom Practice 67.
- write in your journal.
- read and discuss Discovery Time.

JOURNAL WRITING 39

Write an entry in your journal. Use Reference 9 on page 12 for ideas.

Classroom Practice 67

It is time to practice the skills you are learning. You will use the classroom practice on the next page to apply these skills.

ENRICHMENT:

Asteroids are large chunks in space that are made of rock, iron, or a mixture of rock and iron. Most asteroids in our solar system are located in the Asteroid Belt between Mars and Jupiter, but some asteroids orbit the Sun separately.

Comets are large balls in space that are made of ice and rock. Once a comet gets closer to the Sun, the ice starts to evaporate, leaving a tail made of ice and dust that has a bluish or brownish tint.

Meteors are mainly the debris that falls off of asteroids and comets. Usually they are the size of dust or peas, but some are larger. When the tiny particles from a meteor enter the Earth's atmosphere, they burn up in bright flashes of light. Depending on the size and amount of the particles, these meteors can be called shooting stars or, if there are a large number of them together, a meteor shower. Meteorites are the remaining part of meteors that land on the Earth because they have not burnt up as they entered the Earth's atmosphere.

Discovery Questions:
- How might asteroids, comets, and meteors affect Earth?
- Do you think an asteroid, comet, or meteor has ever hit Earth?
- What are the names of books or movies that are about space objects hitting Earth?

Discovery Activity:
- Write a story or play about an asteroid, comet, or meteor hitting Earth or other planets.

Are you interested in learning more about asteroids, comets, and meteors?

1. You may explore this topic further by using the resources listed below.
   Computer resources: Internet, encyclopedia software
   Library resources: encyclopedias, books, magazines, newspapers
   Home/community resources: books, interviews, newspapers, magazines

2. A Discovery Share Time is provided in Lesson 4 if you wish to share your investigation results. You may share orally, or you may prepare a written report. You will put your written report in a class booklet titled "Space Trivia." This booklet will be placed in the class library for everyone to enjoy.

Classroom Practice 67

Name:_____ Date:_____

GRAMMAR

▶ **Exercise 1:** Classify each sentence.

1. _____ The author gave us an autographed copy of his new book.

2. _____ Carol's daughter made a chocolate cake for our bake sale.

3. _____ The teenagers were standing in the crowded lobby of the theater.

4. _____ Lightning is a big spark of electricity during a storm.

5. _____ That joke is funny!

SKILLS AND EDITING

▶ **Exercise 2:** Write the capitalization and punctuation corrections only.
  Editing Guide: End marks: 4 Capitals: 20 Commas: 7 Underlining: 1

1945 state line road

nantucket ny 00004

may 4 20—

dear lawrence

    i am in charge of publishing a special patriotic edition of the nantucket news our local

newspaper would you like to contribute an article or a special poem i will need all submissions

by saturday june 7 this is a marvelous opportunity to display your talent and i hope you will

participate

your favorite uncle

phil

START LESSON 4

Lesson 4

You will
- practice Jingles 5–11.
- classify Practice Sentences.
- read and discuss thank-you notes.
- write an independent thank-you note for WA 33.
- participate in Discovery Share Time.

LISTENING AND SPEAKING:

Recite It: Practice Jingles 5–11 in the Jingle Section on pages 499–500.

Apply It: Classify the Practice Sentences orally with your teacher.

Practice Sentences	Chapter 14: Lesson 4

1. _____ The glass figurine was very fragile.
2. _____ Pollen causes allergic reactions in some people.
3. _____ David saved his friend a seat at the basketball game.
4. _____ Pecan pie and sugar cookies are delicious Christmas treats.
5. _____ Over the weekend, Stanley gave me a short ride on his new motorcycle.

Learn It: **WRITING THANK-YOU NOTES**

You usually write thank-you notes to thank someone for a gift or for doing something nice for you. In either case, a thank-you note should include at least three statements.

1. You should tell the person **what** you are thanking him for.

2. You should tell the person **how the gift was used** or **how it helped**.

3. You should tell the person **how much you appreciated the gift or action**.

A thank-you note should follow the same form as a friendly letter: heading, greeting, body, closing, and signature.

Reference 189	**Thank-You Notes**

For a Gift

  What: Thank you for... (describe the gift)

    Use: Tell how the gift is used.

Thanks: I appreciate your remembering me with this special gift.

For an Action

  What: Thank you for... (tell action)

Helped: Tell how the action helped.

Thanks: I appreciate your thinking of me at this time.

Continued on next page. >>>

Reference 189 continued from previous page.

Example of a Gift Thank-You Note

202 Hardy Circle
Oxford, NE 00016
June 30, 20—

Dear Aunt Sara,

Thank you for the new DVD that you gave me for my birthday. I have already watched it three times. It was a perfect gift, and I appreciate your thoughtfulness.

Love,
Elizabeth

Example of an Action Thank-You Note

700 Poplar Street
Clifton, UT 00045
August 16, 20—

Dear Jason,

Thank you for feeding my dog when I had to go to my grandfather's after his accident. It was a relief to know that Buddy was in good care. I appreciate your kindness.

Your friend,
Sam

Write It: WRITING ASSIGNMENT 33

Write a thank-you note to a real or imaginary person. After your teacher has checked it, take it home to share with family members.

Writing Assignment 33

Purpose: To thank someone
Type of Writing: Thank-you note
Audience: Person who gave a gift
Special Instructions:

1. Think of a person who has done something nice for you or who has given you a gift (including the gift of time).

2. Write that person a thank-you note, using the information in Reference 189 on page 408 as a guide.

3. Write in first person. See Reference 71 on page 108.
   (First-person pronouns: *I, me, my, mine, we, us, our,* and *ours.*)

Discovery Share Time

If you have chosen to investigate a topic introduced in this chapter, you now have the opportunity to share your results in one of the following ways:

1. You may relate your information orally.

2. You may read a written report.

3. You may place your report in the booklet without reading it aloud.

After share time, all written reports should be turned in to be placed in the class booklet titled "Space Trivia." You are encouraged to check out this class booklet so you can enjoy the reports again.

START LESSON 5

Lesson 5

You will

- practice Jingles 1-4.
- classify Practice Sentences.
- do Chapter Checkup 68.
- write in your journal.
- bring envelopes from home.

JOURNAL WRITING **40**

Write an entry in your journal. Use Reference 9 on page 12 for ideas.

LISTENING AND SPEAKING:

Recite It: Practice Jingles 1–4 in the Jingle Section on pages 498–499.

Apply It: Classify the Practice Sentences orally with your teacher.

Practice Sentences	Chapter 14: Lesson 5
1. _____ The fingernail polish was red with glittery sparkles.	
2. _____ The earthquake in California shook violently with a destructive force.	
3. _____ The eagle is the symbol of strength and courage.	

 Chapter Checkup 68

It is time for a checkup of the skills you have learned in this chapter. You will use the Chapter Checkup on the next page to evaluate your progress.

Student Note:

Bring an envelope from home if you have not done so. You will use the envelope in the next lesson. Also, bring the name and address of a friend or family member to whom you will write.

Chapter 14 Checkup 68

Name:_____ Date:_____

GRAMMAR

▶ **Exercise 1:** Classify each sentence.

1. _____ During baseball season, Mr. Green is the announcer at the games.

2. _____ That woman looks very familiar to me.

3. _____ Did the custodian leave us extra paper towels in the bathroom?

4. _____ Has Eddie's family subscribed to the daily newspaper?

5. _____ Today, the photographer snapped our picture for the paper.

SKILLS AND EDITING

▶ **Exercise 2:** Write the capitalization and punctuation corrections only.
   Editing Guide: End marks: 4   Capitals: 17   Commas: 6   Apostrophes: 4

8905 rosemary court

lexington ky 00287

october 25 20—

dear mark

i cant believe that halloween is only a few days away i hope youre planning on coming

to my monster mash on october 31 i will be making witchs brew stew pumpkin pie and

boo-berry cobbler dont forget to wear your scariest costume

with love

aunt nancy

START LESSON 6

Lesson 6

You will

- write an independent friendly letter for WA 34.
- revise and edit WA 34.
- address an envelope for a friendly letter.

Writing Time

Write It: **WRITING ASSIGNMENT 34**

Writing Assignment [34]

Purpose: To write a letter

Type of Writing: Friendly letter

Audience: Family member or friend

Special Instructions:

1. Use References 185-188 on pages 397-399 to help you write your friendly letter.

2. Write a friendly letter to a family member or a friend.

3. Address an envelope for the friendly letter.

4. Revise and edit the friendly letter and envelope by yourself. Then, write a final copy. Write it neatly or type it on a computer.

5. Take the final copy of your letter home in the unsealed envelope. Mail the friendly letter after your parent has looked over the letter one last time.

>>>>>>>>>>>> Student Tip...

If you need to improve your handwriting, refer to the Resource Tools Section on page 521 for information on writing legibly.

LISTENING AND SPEAKING:
Oral Review Questions

Discuss It:

1. What kind of letter is written to or received from friends or relatives?

2. What are the five parts of a friendly letter?

3. What two kinds of addresses are used for an envelope?

4. What information is contained in the heading?

5. What punctuation mark is used after the greeting in a friendly letter?

6. Whose name appears in the greeting?

7. Why do you write a thank-you note?

8. What type of writing is used when your purpose is to inform, to give facts, to give directions, to explain, or to define something?

9. What type of writing is used when your purpose is to express an opinion and to convince the reader that this opinion is correct?

10. What type of writing is used when your purpose is to tell a story?

11. What type of writing is used when your purpose is to paint a picture with words?

12. What type of writing is used when your purpose is to show similarities and differences?

 **Student Tip...**

> For information about test-taking strategies, refer to the Resource Tools Section on page 520.

START LESSON 7

Lesson 7

You will
- respond to oral review questions.
- take Chapter 14 Test.

CHAPTER TEST

It is time to evaluate your knowledge of the skills you have learned in this chapter. Your teacher will give you the Chapter 14 Test to help you assess your progress.

START LESSON 1

Lesson 1

You will
- classify Practice Sentences.
- take Posttest.
- write in your journal.

JOURNAL WRITING **41**

Write an entry in your journal. Use Reference 9 on page 12 for ideas.

LISTENING AND SPEAKING:

Grammar Time

Apply It: Classify the Practice Sentences orally with your teacher.

Practice Sentences	Chapter 15: Lesson 1

1. _____ A family of deer was eating silently in the garden by the light of the moon.
2. _____ Rats! Stacy's surprise party was a complete disaster!
3. _____ The rising floodwater was very dangerous to the people in our community.
4. _____ Does your math tutor give your mother updated progress reports?
5. _____ Mail the campaign stickers and signs to the office in Florida.

Posttest

Take the posttest. After it has been checked, compare the Pretest with the Posttest to evaluate how much you have learned during the year.

Learn It: THE FOUR TYPES OF BUSINESS LETTERS

Sometimes, you may need to write a letter to someone you do not know about something that is not personal in nature. This kind of letter is called a **business letter**. Even if you are not in business, there are several reasons why you may need to write a business letter.

Lesson 2

You will

- read and discuss four types of business letters.
- read and discuss the parts of a business letter.
- read and discuss a business-letter envelope.
- do Classroom Practice 69.

Reference 190 — **Four Types of Business Letters**

There are four common reasons to write business letters.

1. If you need to send for information, write a letter of inquiry.
2. If you want to order a product, write a letter of request or order.
3. If you want to express an opinion, write a letter to an editor or official.
4. If you want to complain about a product, write a letter of complaint.

Letter of Inquiry	Letter of Request or Order
1. Ask for information or answers to your questions.	1. Carefully and clearly describe the product.
2. Keep the letter short and to the point.	2. Keep the letter short and to the point.
3. Word the letter so that there can be no question as to what it is you need to know.	3. Include information on how and where the product should be shipped.
	4. Include information on how you will pay for the product.

Letter to an Editor or Official	Letter of Complaint About a Product
1. Clearly explain the problem or situation.	1. Carefully and clearly describe the product.
2. Offer your opinion of the cause and possible solutions.	2. Describe the problem and what may have caused it. (Don't spend too much time explaining how unhappy you are.)
3. Support your opinions with facts and examples.	3. Explain any action you have already taken to solve the problem.
4. Suggest ways to change or improve the situation.	4. End your letter with the action you would like the company to take to solve the problem.

Learn It: THE SIX PARTS OF A BUSINESS LETTER

Each part of a business letter has a specific place and purpose. The language used in a business letter is formal and to the point. Business people do not have time to read a "friendly" business letter.

Reference 191 **The Six Parts of a Business Letter**

1. Heading:
- Post office box or street address of writer
- City, state, zip code of writer
- Full date letter was written

2. Inside Address:
- Name of person or company receiving the letter (Place a person's title after his name. Separate the title from the name with a comma. If the title is long, place the title separately on the next line.)
- Post office box or street address of the company
- City, state, zip code of company

3. Salutation (Formal Greeting):
- Begins with *Dear*
- Names the person receiving the letter (For a specific person, use a greeting like Dear Mr. (*last name*) or Ms. (*last name*). For a letter addressed to a person by title, use Dear Sir, Dear Madam, or Dear (*Title*). For a company or organization, use Gentlemen or Dear Sirs.)
- Has a colon at the end of the greeting

4. Body:
- Tells the reason the letter is being written (The information should be clearly and briefly written.)
- Can have one or more paragraphs

5. Closing:
- Closes the letter with a formal phrase (*Very truly, Yours truly, Sincerely,* etc.)
- Capitalizes only the first word
- Is followed by a comma

6. Signature:
- Tells who wrote the letter
- Is usually signed in cursive and in ink
- Uses your first and last name (If you are typing your letter, skip four lines and type your full name. Then, sign your name in ink between the closing and typed name.)

Business letter styles: There are several letter styles that are used in business. Two popular styles are the full block and the modified block. In the full-block style, begin all lines at the left margin and skip a line between each paragraph. In the modified-block style, place the heading, closing, and signature in the middle of the page. Indent each paragraph and do not skip a line between paragraphs.

Review It: THE BUSINESS LETTER

1. A business letter has an inside address above the greeting that tells who is receiving the letter. The inside address saves companies or business people time because they do not have to read the entire letter in order to know which person in the company should receive the letter.

2. How you write the inside address will depend on what you know about the business or company that will receive the letter. If you know the name of a person in the company who can help you, you will use that person's name as part of the inside address. If you do not know the name of a person in the company who can help you, you will just use the name of the company.

3. Greetings in business letters are formal. This means that you use the title and last name of the person who is receiving the letter followed by a colon. If you do not know the name of the person receiving the letter, you should use **Sir** or **Madam**.

4. For the signature of a business letter, you should sign your first and last name in ink between the closing and typed name.

5. Two popular styles are usually used to write business letters. The full-block style is demonstrated in Reference 192, and the modified-block style is demonstrated in Reference 193.

Learn It: **THE FULL-BLOCK BUSINESS LETTER**
AND THE MODIFIED-BLOCK BUSINESS LETTER

Reference 192 **Example of the Full-Block Business Letter**

1. Heading

113 Shady Lane
Morgantown, PA 00033
January 11, 20—

2. Inside Address

Mr. Henry Worthington, Travel Agent
Beyond Horizons Travel Co.
505 Milky Way Ave.
Hershey, PA 00049

3. Salutation (Formal Greeting)

Dear Mr. Worthington:

4. Body (Space Between Paragraphs)

My wife and I want to book a summer cruise. You and your company have been highly recommended by our friends and associates.

Please send me information on cruises leaving from any Eastern port. I am particularly interested in those embarking in June. I would like brochures and pricing information. Thank you for your prompt response.

Sincerely yours, **5. Formal Closing**

Cecil Brown

Cecil Brown **6. Signature**

Example of the Modified-Block Business Letter

1. Heading

113 Shady Lane
Morgantown, PA 00033
January 11, 20—

2. Inside Address

Mr. Henry Worthington, Travel Agent
Beyond Horizons Travel Co.
505 Milky Way Ave.
Hershey, PA 00049

3. Salutation (Formal Greeting)

4. Body (Indent Paragraphs)

Dear Mr. Worthington:

My wife and I want to book a summer cruise. You and your company have been highly recommended by our friends and associates.
Please send me information on cruises leaving from any Eastern port. I am particularly interested in those embarking in June. I would like brochures and pricing information. Thank you for your prompt response.

5. Formal Closing → Sincerely yours,

Cecil Brown

6. Signature → Cecil Brown

Learn It: ADDRESSING THE ENVELOPE FOR A BUSINESS LETTER

 Reference 194 | **Parts Of A Business Envelope**

In order to address the envelope for your business letter correctly, you must know **how** and **where** to write the two addresses used for a business-letter envelope. The addresses of a business-letter envelope are similar to the addresses of a friendly-letter envelope. There are two differences, however, in the mailing address for the business envelope that you should remember.

1. You must put the name of the person within the company to whom you are writing and his title (if you know it) on the first line of the mailing address. If you do not know the name of the person who would handle your request or problem, write the name of the department (such as, SALES, SHIPPING, ACCOUNTING, etc.) on the first line of the mailing address. If you do not know the name of the person or the department, you may choose to leave the first line blank.

2. You must put the name of the company on the second line of the mailing address.

The Return Address:

- Name of the person writing the letter
- Box or street address of the writer
- City, state, and zip code of the writer

The Mailing Address:

- Name and title of the person receiving the letter
- Name of the company receiving the letter
- Street address of the company receiving the letter
- City, state, and zip code of the company receiving the letter

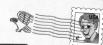

Cecil Brown
113 Shady Lane
Morgantown, PA 00033

Return Address

Mailing Address

Mr. Henry Worthington, Travel Agent
Beyond Horizons Travel Co.
505 Milky Way Ave.
Hershey, PA 00049

 **Student Tip...**

A two-letter abbreviation is used for states in most business letters. For a list of commonly used abbreviations, refer to Reference 188 on page 399.

Classroom Practice 69

It is time to practice the skills you are learning. You will use the classroom practice on the next page to apply these skills.

Classroom Practice 69

Name:_____ Date:_____

SKILLS

Use the letter parts below to fill in the blanks of the business letter.

TITLE PARTS of a Business Letter:

Closing   Signature   Heading

Salutation   Body   Inside Address

SAMPLE PARTS of a Business Letter:

Sincerely yours,   Donald A. Devlin   Senator Peter Samler
                                                    Texas Legislature

Dear Senator Samler: 266 Oak Drive   227 North Avenue
                          Dallas, TX 00032   Austin, TX 00091   October 11, 20—

I want to express my support for your work on funding the new highway project. This project is invaluable to the people of Texas. Thank you for all the progress you have made in this area.

Business Letter

1. Title:

2. Title:

3. Title:

4. Title:

5. Title:

6. Title:

Skill Time

Learn It: EDITING A BUSINESS LETTER, USING RULE NUMBERS

The business letter in Classroom Practice 70 has already been punctuated. Write the capitalization and punctuation rule numbers for each correction that appears in **bold** type. There are fifty-three rule numbers that you must write.

Classroom Practice 70

It is time to practice the skills you are learning. You will use the classroom practice on the next page to apply these skills.

>>>>>>>>>>>>>>>>>>>>>>>> **Student Note...**

Make sure you are aware of the homework note that tells you to bring an envelope from home for a letter-writing assignment in Lesson 6.

START LESSON 3

Lesson 3

You will

- edit a business letter using rule numbers.
- do Classroom Practice 70.
- do a homework assignment.
- do Home Connection activity.

Classroom Practice 70

Name:_____ Date:_____

SKILLS AND EDITING

Write the capitalization and punctuation rule numbers for each correction in **bold**. Use References 11, 13, and 14 to look up rule numbers. (Total rule numbers required: 53)

P.O. Box 9049

Big **F**alls, **MN** 00017

July 20, 20—

Representative **L**ucas **J. B**radwell

225 **C**apitol **A**venue

St. Paul**, MN** 00029

Dear **R**epresentative **B**radwell**:**

   Last year**,** we saw a disturbing decline in the local elk population**. It** is imperative that our state

officials take swift action before this beautiful animal is gone forever**. A**s chairman of the **B**ig **F**alls

Conservation **S**ociety**, I** strongly urge you to support **H**ouse **B**ill 292**. I** look forward to hearing your

response about this important matter**.**

Sincerely yours**,**

J. T. Lambert

Homework 12

Complete this homework assignment on notebook paper.

Write, revise, and edit a business letter to the Chamber of Commerce in a city you would like to visit. Ask for brochures and information about hotels, restaurants, unique attractions, and local history. Also, use the Internet, library, or telephone directories to find information that would help you. When you get a response, bring the information you receive to school and share it with your teacher and classmates. Use References 190–194 on pages 415–419.

Note: You should bring an envelope from home for a business-letter assignment in Lesson 6.

Home Connection

Family Activity for a Business Letter

First, glue the business letter below onto cardstock or construction paper. Next, cut the sections apart at the dotted lines. Then, glue or write the number and the title for each business-letter part on the back of the corresponding strip.

Divide into teams. Time each team as members put the pieces of the business-letter puzzle together and identify each part. Check the correct answers with the number and title on the back of each piece. The team that completes the puzzle correctly in the shortest time is the winner.

Business Letter

Titles: | 1. Heading | 2. Inside Address | 3. Salutation | 4. Body | 5. Closing | 6. Signature

931 Ocean Drive
Ward, Iowa 00029
May 16, 20—

Mr. Pete Lewis
Magic Shop, Inc.
99 Kite Lane
Earl, TX 00077

Dear Mr. Lewis:

    You have an excellent catalog with a large variety of materials. I would like to order a Mr. Magic Kit for my grandson. Enclosed is a check for $29.95. This will cover the item and the shipping. Thank you for a quick response.

Sincerely,

Justin P. Morgan
Justin P. Morgan

---

6. Signature

5. Closing

4. Body

3. Salutation

2. Inside Address

1. Heading

START LESSON 4

Lesson 4

You will

- edit a business letter for corrections only.
- do Classroom Practice 71.
- do Across the Curriculum activity.

Skill Time

Learn It: **EDITING A BUSINESS LETTER, USING CORRECTIONS ONLY**

The business letter in Classroom Practice 71 has not been punctuated. Write capitalization corrections above the capitalization mistakes, and put the punctuation corrections where they belong in the letter. Look at the editing guide to find the total number of errors you need to correct.

Classroom Practice 71

It is time to practice the skills you are learning. You will use the classroom practice on the next page to apply these skills.

Across the Curriculum

Social Studies Connection: Write the President of the United States a letter about an important matter that concerns your area or the country. Make sure your letter follows the correct business-letter form. Double check spelling, punctuation, and content

The President's address is shown below.

**The White House
1600 Pennsylvania Ave.
Washington, D.C. 20500**

Reference 196 continued from previous page.

COMMON PROPAGANDA TECHNIQUES

1. **Loaded Words.** This technique uses words that appeal to our emotions. Loaded words can give pleasant or unpleasant feelings, such as *new, best, exciting, tired, dull,* and *boring.* This technique is used to make us accept or reject something without examining the evidence.

   Example: You can buy everything for your pet at Pets Best, the most exciting pet place in the country!

   To Evaluate: Leaving the loaded words out, what are the key facts?
   (Everything for your pet can be bought at Pets Best.)

2. **Important/Famous People.** This technique uses an important or famous person to recommend that you do, buy, or believe something. When a person that we admire is used to recommend something, we are likely to accept what is said. On the other hand, when a person that we do not admire is used to recommend something, we are more likely to question the creditability of the product or idea.

   Example: Improve your catch! Use baseball's Al Hero glove!

   To Evaluate: Is the product or idea advertised partly responsible for a famous person's success?
   (Do baseball players use the Al Hero glove with great success?)

3. **Bandwagon.** This technique is used to make you feel that something is good because it is popular. It is also referred to as the everybody-does-it technique. The key approach is to make you feel left out if you don't join the crowd. Since no one wants to be left out, this technique can be quite successful.

   Example: We're having a home redecorating class! All of your friends and neighbors have been here and have gone home with some great ideas. Don't be left out!

   To Evaluate: If no one else was interested, would you still want this product or support this idea?
   (Do I really want or need what everyone else is buying or supporting?)

4. **Mudslinging.** This technique is used to indicate that something is wrong with the competition but gives no facts to support these claims. This technique uses a negative image in the hope that individuals will reject a person or an issue based on that negative image instead of looking at the facts. Mudslinging is a common technique used in political campaigns.

   Example: After the prison scandals, can you really trust Sheriff Davis with your safety? Vote for the man with values. Vote for Bob Young, the candidate you can trust.

   To Evaluate: Check out what was claimed about both candidates or about both sides of an issue.
   (How was Sheriff Davis involved with the prison scandals? What values do these candidates support?)

5. **Fact/Opinion.** A fact is often followed by a reasonable opinion that appears to be true. This technique is used in the hope that individuals will also accept the opinion as fact.

   Example: We've sold thousands of pizzas. People trust us because we are the best!

   To Evaluate: Can every statement be checked to see if it is true? Do any of the statements use opinion words? Have any of the important facts been left out?
   (The first statement can be proven, true or false. The second statement uses the opinion word "best" and cannot be proven. An important fact about how long it took to sell the pizzas has been left out.)

6. **Stereotyping.** This technique is used to give specific groups certain characteristics, images, or attitudes based on assumptions. Stereotyping implies that all members of a group are alike or believe the same way.

   Example: All business owners in town support the new bypass.

   To Evaluate: Is it correct to assume that everyone in a certain group believes the same way?
   (Do ALL the business owners in town support the new bypass?)

Classroom Practice 73

It is time to practice the skills you are learning. You will use the classroom practice on the next page to apply these skills.

Classroom Practice 73

Name:_____ Date:_____

SKILLS

▶ **Exercise 1:** For each statement, write **O** (opinion) or **F** (fact) in the blank.

_____ 1. A whale is a mammal living in the ocean.

_____ 2. Scuba diving is an exciting experience.

_____ 3. Everyone should exercise daily.

_____ 4. My dad gets paid every week.

_____ 5. That is a fair appraisal of the antique watch.

_____ 6. The capital of Texas is Austin.

▶ **Exercise 2:** Classify each of these sentences in terms of the propaganda technique it contains. **L** (loaded words), **I** (important/famous people), **B** (bandwagon), **M** (mudslinging), **S** (stereotyping), **F/O** (fact/opinion)

_____ 1. The first Olympic games were held in Greece. Everyone enjoys the Olympic games.

_____ 2. Famous marathon runners eat Flash Energy Bars for strong, healthy bodies. Eat Flash Bars!

_____ 3. Try our thick, savory, triple-decker bacon burger. It will make you come back for more!

_____ 4. Buy Moo-Milk. It is good for you. The other brand, Purr-Milk, is only fit for cats!

_____ 5. Dogs are loyal and make the best pets.

_____ 6. The whole community turns out for our football games. You should come, too!

▶ **Exercise 3:** Write **True** or **False** before each statement.

_____ 1. Opinions that are widely accepted are true.

_____ 2. Mudslinging is a form of propaganda.

_____ 3. A fact can be verified.

_____ 4. Propaganda is used to spread the truth.

_____ 5. Propaganda is an effort to change the opinions and actions of people.

_____ 6. Certain opinion words help identify opinion statements: hope, seem, best, think, etc.

▶ **Exercise 4:** Answer the questions below, using the information in the following article.

[1]Our city does not have an ambulance service. A city ambulance service could save many lives. [2]Most surrounding towns have an ambulance service, and we need one, too! [3]This would provide emergency care and transportation for sick or injured citizens. [4]The committee working against funding this ambulance service must not be concerned about saving lives. [5]Everyone who cares about our community will vote yes for the tax increase. You should vote yes, too. [6]Your "yes" vote will allow us to provide this absolutely essential service.

By Mayor Sidney Shaw

1. Who wrote this information? _____

2. What is the purpose? _____

_____

3. Write the propaganda technique for each numbered sentence above.

(1) _____   (4) _____

(2) _____   (5) _____

(3) _____   (6) _____

Classroom Practice 71

Name:_____ Date:_____

SKILLS AND EDITING

Write the capitalization and punctuation corrections only.
Editing Guide: End Marks: 5   Capitals: 35   Commas: 7   Periods: 4   Underlining: 1   Colons: 1

22 saddle creek pkwy

newark oh 00056

april 2 20—

intellitrax inc

ms cindy miller president

5041 apple valley road

milltown vt 00492

dear ms miller

   i am responding to your classified advertisement in the vermont democrat gazette for the

accounting position enclosed is my resume i am a quick learner and a hard worker and i believe

that my skills and experience would be an asset to intellitrax i am available at your convenience

to discuss a position within your company thank you for your time and consideration

                                                            sincerely

                                                            ramon valdez

START LESSON 5

Lesson 5

You will
- do Chapter Checkup 72.
- write in your journal.
- bring envelopes from home.

JOURNAL WRITING 42

Write an entry in your journal. Use Reference 9 on page 12 for ideas.

Chapter Checkup 72

It is time for a checkup of the skills you have learned in this chapter. You will use the chapter checkup on the next page to evaluate your progress.

Student Note: Bring an envelope from home if you have not done so. You will use the envelope in the next lesson.

Chapter 15 Checkup 72

Name:_____ Date:_____

SKILLS AND EDITING

Write the capitalization and punctuation corrections only.

Editing Guide: End Marks: 4 Capitals: 36 Commas: 8 Apostrophes: 1 Periods: 3 Colons: 1

2001 b street ste 101

rolling plains mi 00342

june 3 20—

picture perfect photography

mr chuck nolan owner

mountain ridge road

lansing mi 00048

dear mr nolan

    i heard your companys advertisement on a local fm station about free photography classes

since i am an amateur photographer i am very interested please send me more information

about these classes i appreciate your time and i look forward to receiving your information

sincerely

ginger conner

START LESSON 6

Lesson 6

You will

- write a independent business letter for WA 35.
- revise and edit WA 35.
- address an envelope for a business letter.

Writing Time

Write It: WRITING ASSIGNMENT 35

Writing Assignment 35

Purpose: To write a letter
Type of Writing: Business letter
Audience: Principal
Writing Topics: A Request to the Principal

Special Instructions:

1. Use References 190–194 on pages 416–419 to help you write your business letter.

2. Write a business letter to the principal of your school. The purpose of your business letter is to request something for the school or classroom, ask about something the students can do for the school or community, or choose a reason of your own. Before you begin your letter, make a list of the things you want to say.

3. Address an envelope for the business letter. Draw a stamp on the envelope in the correct position.

4. Revise and edit the business letter and envelope by yourself and then with an editing partner. Next, write a final copy. Write it neatly or type it on a computer.

5. Put your letter in the envelope but do not seal it until your teacher looks over it.

6. Mail the business letter to the principal via school mail.

>>>>>>>>>>>>> **Student Tip...**

If you need to improve your handwriting, refer to the Resource Tools Section on page 521 for information on writing legibly.

LISTENING AND SPEAKING:
Oral Review Questions

Lesson 7

You will
- respond to oral review questions.
- take Chapter 15 Test.

CHAPTER TEST

It is time to evaluate your knowledge of the skills you have learned in this chapter. Your teacher will give you the Chapter 15 Test to help you assess your progress.

Discuss It:

1. What kind of letter is written about something that is not personal in nature?

2. What are the four types of business letters?

3. What are the six parts of a business letter?

4. What information that is not contained in a friendly letter is added to the business letter?

5. What information is included in the inside address?

6. What two business letter styles were introduced?

7. Which style uses indented heading, closing, signature, and paragraphs?

8. What two kinds of addresses are used for a business envelope?

9. What extra information is added to the mailing addresses of the business envelope?

10. What punctuation mark is used after the greeting in a business letter?

11. If you do not know the name of the person receiving the business letter, what should be used in the greeting?

12. How should a business letter be signed?

 **Student Tip...**

> For information about test-taking strategies, refer to the Resource Tools Section on page 520.

Lesson 1

You will

- read and discuss fact and opinion and propaganda techniques.
- do Classroom Practice 73.

 Skill Time

Learn It: **FACT, OPINION, AND PROPAGANDA TECHNIQUES**

| 📖 **Reference 195** | **Recognizing Fact and Opinion** |

You are bombarded daily with information from television, radio, movies, printed materials, and advertisements. This information is designed to attract your attention and influence your way of thinking. Some information is based on facts and can be checked for accuracy. Other information is based on opinion or other factors that cannot be proved or disproved. You must be able to tell the difference between fact and opinion in order to make an informed judgement about the information you are receiving.

A **fact** is a specific statement that can be looked up, measured, counted, or otherwise proved or disproved.

Example: Susan is five feet tall.
(This is a statement that can be proved or disproved. Either Susan is five feet tall or she isn't. It can be proved or disproved by measuring Susan's height.)

An **opinion** is a belief, estimate, judgment, or feeling held by one or more people that cannot be proven. It is a personal judgment.

Example: Lilly is a respectful young woman.
(This is a statement that cannot be proved or disproved. Each person has his own definition of *respectful*. Some people may think Lilly respectful; others may not.)

Facts are statements that can be proved or disproved. Opinions are statements that cannot be proved or disproved. Opinions that are widely accepted often appear to be factual when they are not. Recognizing whether a statement is a fact or an opinion will help you make informed choices.

There are certain words that signal when a writer is expressing an opinion.
Opinion Words: *think, believe, feel, hope, seem, best, better, worse, worst, probably, excellent, terrible, should, love, hate,* etc.

Learn It: **PROPAGANDA**

| 📖 **Reference 196** | **Propaganda** |

Propaganda is a form of language used to spread ideas or information in an attempt to change the opinions and actions of a group of people. Propaganda usually contains some accurate facts along with exaggerations and untruths.

The information that you see and hear on television, radio, newspapers, and magazines often leaves out facts or uses techniques to persuade you in a specific direction. You need to evaluate these techniques by asking questions and by thinking about the information first. Then, you can make better decisions.

Some propaganda techniques are listed below. Learn to recognize and evaluate these techniques so they will not mislead you.

Continued on next page. >>>

Skill Time

START LESSON 2

Lesson 2

You will
- read and discuss different media sources.
- read and discuss propaganda techniques of the media.
- do Classroom Practice 74.
- do student activity on media advertisement.

Learn It: **DIFFERENT MEDIA SOURCES**

| Reference 197 | **Propaganda and Mass Media** |

Newspapers, radio, television, billboards, magazines, and the Internet are types of **mass media**. Mass media use verbal and visual communication to send information to large numbers of people. Their purpose is to inform, educate, entertain, or persuade.

Different media use their own ways of presenting a message. They will use fact, opinion, and some or all of the propaganda techniques. Sometimes, the propaganda techniques will be so subtle that you have to read or listen very carefully to detect them. Other times, the propaganda techniques will be obvious. Even so, individuals can interpret the same media message in different ways.

Learn It: **EVALUATING PROPAGANDA
IN THE DIFFERENT MEDIA SOURCES**

| Reference 198 | **Evaluating Propaganda Techniques in the Media** |

Look at and listen to the news, the stories, and the advertisements on television, radio, billboards, the Internet, and in newspapers and magazines. Use the questions below to help you evaluate the stories and the advertisements in the media.

1. Think about how the information is organized. Which stories appear first? Do you think they are the most important stories? How much time or space is devoted to each story? Does the newspaper or magazine include a large headline or photograph? Does the television program use visuals or video footage?

2. What is the purpose of the information? Does the information focus on a product, person, or idea? Decide whether it is intended to inform, persuade, advertise, or entertain. Ask yourself what the information wants you to think or do. How does it make you feel?

3. Can you tell if the information you read or hear is fair and truthful? Can you tell if the story is based on fact or opinion? Is there a way to verify the facts of the story?

4. Consider whether important information is missing. Does the story tell you all there is to know?

5. What kinds of commercials are shown during the program? What kinds of advertisements are in the newspapers and magazines or on the radio? Do you think any of the advertising companies influenced the story in any way?

6. Which propaganda techniques are used to attract your attention or to influence your way of thinking? Why do you think these techniques were chosen?

Classroom Practice 74

It is time to practice the skills you are learning. You will use the classroom practice on the next page to apply these skills.

Student Activity

1. Divide into five cooperative-learning groups. Each group should choose a product/person/idea to promote or a news story to publish. Select a media source for your advertisement/story (television, radio, newspaper, magazine, billboard, or Internet).

2. Make a presentation of your advertisement or story.

3. Discuss the purpose and success of each advertisement or story and the propaganda techniques used.

Classroom Practice 74

Name:_____ Date:_____

SKILLS

▶ **Exercise 1:** For each statement, write **O** (opinion) or **F** (fact) in the blank.

_____ 1. The highway department is building a new bridge across the lake.

_____ 2. I made three withdrawals from my checking account on Friday.

_____ 3. Owning chickens is a relaxing hobby.

_____ 4. We have a great community for young families.

_____ 5. The soccer players washed cars this weekend to raise money for their camp.

▶ **Exercise 2:** Classify each of these sentences in terms of the propaganda technique it contains. **L** (loaded words), **I** (important/famous people), **B** (bandwagon), **M** (mudslinging), **S** (stereotyping), **F/O** (fact/opinion)

_____ 1. Attend Harvard College, the alma mater of all successful people.

_____ 2. All famous chefs are men.

_____ 3. Tornadoes are very destructive storms. Everyone should have a storm shelter.

_____ 4. The city treasurer can't account for the surplus money! Should he receive your vote?

_____ 5. Retire in the beautiful Florida Keys. Live alongside Florida's most rich and famous!

_____ 6. Buy our luxurious vinyl siding and have a beautiful house like all of your neighbors.

▶ **Exercise 3:** Write **True** or **False** before each statement.

_____ 1. Mass media are designed to reach large numbers of people.

_____ 2. Television, radio, and newspapers are types of mass media.

_____ 3. All people will interpret the same media message in the same way.

_____ 4. Certain opinion words help identify opinion statements: believe, feel, should, etc.

_____ 5. Most propaganda techniques are subtle.

▶ **Exercise 4:** Answer the questions below, using the information in the following advertisement.

Buy your next computer at... truman's technology

[1] MOST PEOPLE DO.

Even the [2] Mayor of Skyview, Lucy Jones, drove from the next county to purchase computers for the city hall at Skyview. Truman's closest competitors have good prices, but [3] their merchandise is of inferior quality. Nobody wants to pay less for computers that will not hold up. [4] Even though Truman's competitors have lower prices, Truman's continues to outsell them. Simply put, people buy from Truman's because Truman's can be trusted. [5] Truman's has outstanding prices and excellent products.

[6] Smart shoppers know the difference between quality products and inferior ones.

TRUMAN'S TECHNOLOGY
9876 SKRETE STREET
TRUMAN, TX 78910
(555) 234-9876

1. What is the purpose?

_____

_____

_____

2. Write the propaganda technique for each numbered set of underlined words.

(1) _____

(2) _____

(3) _____

(4) _____

(5) _____

(6) _____

START LESSON 3

Lesson 3

You will

- read and discuss reasons for reading.
- read and discuss how to read subject-matter (skim, question, read, scan).
- do Classroom Practice 75.
- do Across the Curriculum activity.

Skill Time

Learn It: REASONS FOR READING AND READING SPEEDS

Have you ever run out of time when doing an assignment that requires you to read information and look up answers to questions? Do you enjoy reading books for fun but dislike subjects in school like social studies, reading, and science because you get frustrated looking for answers to study questions?

Whether or not this describes you, everyone can use some tips to help save time when reading for information.

 Reference 199 — **Reasons for Reading and Reading Speeds**

Do you know that not all reading material should be read slowly and carefully? How fast or slowly you read should depend on your reason for reading.

REASONS FOR READING:	READING SPEED:
1. **To enjoy** yourself	**Read slowly** enough to absorb details and enjoy the author's style.
2. **To understand** main ideas and details	**Read slowly** so you can stop and think about what is being said.
3. **To get an idea** about the topic	**Read quickly**, looking for titles, topic headings, underlining, and words in bold type.
4. **To locate answers** to specific questions. . .	**Read quickly**, looking for titles, topic headings, underlining, and words in bold type to find the key words in your question. Then, **read slowly** to find the answers to your specific questions.

Learn It: STEPS FOR READING SUBJECT MATTER

Remember that your purpose for reading will determine how quickly or slowly you read. When you have a reading assignment in a subject area like science or social studies, it is called **subject-matter** reading.

Reference 200 — **Steps for Reading Subject Matter: Skim, Question, Read, Scan**

When you read **subject matter**, such as topics in the areas of science and social studies, *you should use a combination of reading speeds.* Your reading should be done in four steps.

Step 1. **SKIM - read quickly to get a general idea of the article.**
Your purpose is to get an idea about the topic. This is called **skimming**. Look quickly over titles, topic headings, topic sentences of each paragraph, and underlined or bold type.

Step 2. **QUESTION - turn headings into questions to establish a purpose for reading.**
Some headings are written as questions. You have to turn other headings into **questions**. These heading questions will give you a reason for reading. You are more likely to pick out and remember the main facts when you are looking for answers to questions.

Step 3. **READ - read slowly to find and understand details about topic headings.**
The purpose of this step is to **read the whole article slowly** enough to find answers to the questions you asked in the question step. Read carefully to understand and remember the main ideas and details of the article.

Continued on next page. >>>

Reference 200 continued from previous page.

Step 4. **SCAN - read quickly to locate specific answers to study questions.**
The purpose is to locate specific answers to study questions from your book or worksheet. This is called **scanning**. First, find the key words in your study questions. Then, quickly look over titles, topic headings, topic sentences, and underlined or bold type to find the section that discusses your question. Finally, read that section carefully to find the answer.

THE TLINGIT INDIANS

SECTION 1 **Where the Tlingit Lived**

The Tlingit people lived along the Pacific Coast of what is now southern Alaska and British Columbia. There were many advantages to living here. Even though this area was in the north, the climate was mild and moist because of the warm Pacific Ocean breezes. Trees, plants, and animals were plentiful. The Tlingit Indians were able to find food and shelter easily, so they had plenty of time to make and decorate many things. The women made beautiful woven blankets, and the men became skilled woodcarvers.

SECTION 2 **How the Tlingit Got Their Food**

Tlingit Indians were hunters and gatherers. Much of the Tlingit food came from the ocean. Seals, porpoises, sea otters, fish, and clams were an important part of the Tlingit diet. **Oolakan**, oil from the candlefish, was used as a sauce. The Tlingit dipped almost everything they ate into this oil. Tlingit men hunted deer, elk, and mountain goats, and the women gathered berries, plant roots, and seaweed.

Mealtime was a very important time for the Tlingit. There were two meals a day - one in the middle of the morning and one in the late afternoon. During these meals, good manners were emphasized. They wiped their oily hands on napkins made of shredded cedar bark.

SECTION 3 **What the Tlingit Wore**

Tlingit clothing was usually made from deer skins. In warm weather, most Tlingit men and women worked in or near the sea. Because the weather was warm and they were in and out of the water frequently, most of the men wore only a small **breechcloth**, or loincloth, and the women wore only a short skirt made from deerskin. In cool weather, men and women covered their upper bodies with wool blankets and cedar bark. No matter how cold it was, Tlingit people did not wear shoes.

SECTION 4 **How the Tlingit Lived**

The Tlingit Indians lived in large wooden houses that were big enough to hold several families. Most Tlingit villages only had two or three of these houses. Boards were made by pounding wedges into the ends of cedar logs causing long flat pieces to split off. Each house had a central fireplace where the women cooked. There were no windows, and the doorways always faced the ocean. The chief and his family lived in a separate house. The entrance to a chief's house was usually a **totem pole** with a large hole at the bottom. The totem pole contained intricately carved and painted figures of animals. The Tlingit believed these animals held magical powers that protected the chief's family.

A Tlingit chief often held a **potlatch**, a great feast lasting several days, at which he told stories about his family and gave away blankets and fur robes to chiefs from surrounding villages. Of course, those receiving the gifts were expected to give potlatches of their own. Not to do so would be an insult and cause war.

Discuss It: THE SKIMMING STEP

1. What is the first step of reading subject matter?

2. What is the purpose of skimming?

3. What is the reading speed for skimming?

4. What parts of an article do you skim?

Use the article about Tlingit Indians to practice skimming for the title, topic headings, topic sentences, and underlined or bold type. Look at the article at the bottom of the reference.

1. What is the title of the article?

2. Find the topic headings. Where are they?

Continued on next page. >>>

3. Name them.

4. Where are the topic sentences for each paragraph?

5. Name the topic sentences for each paragraph.

6. What are the bold-type words in each section?

Skimming is used **before** you actually read an article. Skimming gives you a general idea of what you are about to read.

1. What is the article about?

2. Where did the Tlingit live?

3. Where did the Tlingit get their food?

4. What type of houses did they have?

Discuss It: THE QUESTIONING STEP

In this step, change your topic headings into questions.

1. How would you turn the first topic heading into a question?

2. How would you turn the second topic heading into a question?

3. How would you turn the third topic heading into a question?

4. How would you turn the fourth topic heading into a question?

5. What is the purpose of the questioning step?

Discuss It: THE READING STEP

1. What is the third step of reading subject matter?

2. What is the purpose of the reading step?

3. What is the reading speed for the reading step?

4. What parts of an article do you read?

Now, slowly read the article about the Tlingit Indians. Make a mental note of the details that will answer these questions as you read: *Where did the Tlingit live? How did the Tlingit get their food? What did the Tlingit wear? How did the Tlingit live?*

Discuss It: THE SCANNING PROCESS

1. What is the fourth step of reading subject matter?

2. What is the purpose of the scanning step?

3. What is the reading speed for the scanning step?

4. What procedures do you follow in the scanning step?

Apply It: THE SCANNING PROCESS

Sample Question: **"What is potlatch?"**

1. What is the key word in the sample question?

2. In what section do you find the answer?

3. What made it easy and fast for you to find the answer as you scanned?

4. What is the next step after you find the section?

5. What is the answer?

Continued on next page. >>>

Discuss It: **HOW TO READ SUBJECT MATTER MATERIAL**

    1. What is Step 1?

    2. What is Step 2?

    3. What is Step 3?

    4. What is Step 4?

Classroom Practice 75

It is time to practice the skills you are learning. You will use the classroom practice on the next page to apply these skills.

Across the Curriculum

Social Studies/Science Connection: Do this activity in small groups. Select a lesson in your science or social studies book. Study the lesson. Make up two questions with multiple choice answers. Make up two questions with fill-in-the-blank answers. Make up two questions that require answers to be written in paragraph or essay form. Make an answer key on another piece of paper. Exchange your questions with other students. Use the four steps in Reference 200 to help you find answers to the questions. Compare answers when you have finished. Discuss the advantages of using the steps to read and understand subject matter material. Keep your questions to use as a study guide for the chapter.

Classroom Practice 75

Name:_____ Date:_____

SKILLS

▶ **Exercise 1:** Underline the key word or words in each question. The word *Tlingit* cannot be used as a key word. Scan for the answers in the article in Reference 200. Write only the section number where you will find the answer.

Section:_____ 1. What is the oolakan?

Section:_____ 2. What kind of food did the Tlingit eat?

Section:_____ 3. What did the Tlingit make their clothing from?

Section:_____ 4. What is a breechcloth?

Section:_____ 5. What did the Tlingit believe about the animals on the totem poles?

▶ **Exercise 2:** Using Reference 200, write the answers in the blanks below and put the numbers of the sections where the answers were found in the box on the left.

Section:_____ 1. The _____ on the coast of southern Alaska is mild and moist.

Section:_____ 2. Tlingit women gathered _____, _____, and _____.

Section:_____ 3. During Tlingit mealtimes, good _____ were important.

Section:_____ 4. Tlingit men wore _____ and women wore skirts of _____.

Section:_____ 5. The Tlingit lived in large, cedar houses that had _____ in the center for cooking.

Section:_____ 6. Intricately carved _____ containing figures of animals stood at the entrance to the chiefs' houses.

▶ **Exercise 3:** Using the article in Reference 200, write the answers in the blanks below and put the number of the section where it is found in the box on the left.

Section:_____ 1. Give two advantages the Tlingit had in living on the Pacific Coast.

a. _____

b. _____

c. _____

Section:_____ 2. List two activities that took place at a potlatch.

a. _____

b. _____

c. _____

English Made Easy

Learn It: OUTLINES

START LESSON 4

Lesson 4

You will
- read and discuss outlining.
- do Classroom Practice 76.

Reference 201 | **Outlines**

Making an outline will give you a visual map of your report. There are two reasons to use an outline when you plan to write. First, outlining helps to put ideas and information in the correct order for writing. Second, outlining helps you remember information more easily and keeps you focused as you write.

There are two kinds of outlines: the **topic outline** and the **sentence outline**. In a *topic outline*, information is written in single words or phrases. In a *sentence outline*, information is written in complete sentences. Outlines have very rigid rules about how they are organized and formatted. Even though the topic outline and the sentence outline are formatted the same, you cannot mix the two styles by using phrases and complete sentences in the same outline. The topic outline is the easiest and most commonly used outline. Outlines have a vocabulary and set of rules that are unique to outlining and follow the same basic plan.

1. **Write a TITLE.**
   - At first, your outline title should be the same or similar to your narrowed topic. This will help you stay focused on the main idea of your report. If you decide to change the title for your final paper, you must remember to change your outline title.
   - Capitalization rules for titles are the same for outlines as for final papers: Capitalize the first word, the last word, and all important words in your title. Conjunctions, articles, and prepositions with fewer than five letters are not usually capitalized unless they are the first or last word. Titles for outlines are not underlined or placed in quotation marks unless the title is a quote.

2. **Use Roman numerals to indicate the MAIN TOPICS. (I., II., III., IV.)**
   - Outlines must always have two or more Roman numerals. Never use just one. Each Roman numeral has a paragraph in the <u>body</u> of the report. *(Three Roman numerals indicate three paragraphs in the body. The Introduction and the Conclusion will each have a paragraph, but they do not have Roman numerals.)*
   - Periods after the Roman numerals must be lined up, one under the other.
   - Information following a Roman numeral is called the main topic and gives the main idea or the main point of each paragraph. It will be used to form the topic sentence of the paragraph.
   - The first word in a main topic is always capitalized.

3. **Use capital letters to indicate SUBTOPICS. (A., B., C., D.)**
   - An outline must always have two or more capital letters. If you only have one subtopic, do not put it in the outline. Each capital letter is indented under the first word of the main topic.
   - Periods after the capital letters must be lined up, one under the other.
   - Information beside a capital letter is called the subtopic and gives details that support the main topic, or main point, of the paragraph that is stated in the Roman numeral above it.
   - The first word in a subtopic is always capitalized.

Continued on next page. >>>

Reference 201 continued from previous page.

4. Use Arabic numerals to indicate DETAILS. (1., 2., 3., 4.)

- Outlines must always have two or more Arabic numerals. If you only have one detail, do not put it in the outline. Each Arabic numeral is indented under the first word of the subtopic.
- Periods after the Arabic numerals must be lined up, one under the other.
- Information beside an Arabic numeral is called a detail and tells specific information about the subtopic of the paragraph that is stated in the capital letter above it.
- The first word in a detail is always capitalized.

5. Use these basic rules to punctuate an outline.

- You cannot have a **I.** without a **II.**, an **A.** without a **B.**, or a **1.** without a **2.** because outlining is a process of dividing. You cannot divide something into fewer than two parts.
- Put periods after Roman numerals, capital letters, Arabic numerals, and anything else that would require a period in a sentence.
- Capitalize the first word of each entry and any word that would be capitalized in a sentence.
- Follow the outline guide in Reference 202 to line up the parts of an outline correctly.

6. Use parallel form for outlines.

- All the main topics in an outline should be in parallel form. This means that all the main topics should begin in the same way: all nouns, all verbs, all noun phrases, all verb phrases, all prepositional phrases, etc. If necessary, change or rearrange the words of your outline so they are parallel. *(See Reference 203, number one, for examples of parallel form for main topics.)*
- All the subtopics under a specific Roman numeral must have the same parallel form, but these subtopics do not have to be in the same parallel form as the subtopics under another Roman numeral. For example, the subtopics under Roman numeral **I** must be parallel, and even though the subtopics under Roman numeral **II** must also be parallel, they do not have to be in the same form as the subtopics under Roman numeral **I**, etc. *(See Reference 203, number two, for examples of parallel form for subtopics.)*
- All the details under a specific letter must have the same parallel form, but these details do not have to be in the same form as the details under another letter. For example, the details under the letter **A** must be parallel, and even though the details under letter **B** must also be parallel, they do not have to be in the same parallel form as the details under letter **A**, etc. *(See Reference 203, number three, for examples of parallel form for details.)*

Learn It: **HOW THE OUTLINE RULES ARE APPLIED**

Reference 202 | **Outline Guide and Example**

Notice that the introduction and the conclusion do not have Roman numerals. They are automatically the first and last paragraphs of a report. The outline applies only to the body of the report. Since main topics are identified by Roman numerals, the body of a report contains as many paragraphs as there are Roman numerals in the outline.

Continued on next page. >>>

Reference 202 continued from previous page.

A report written from this outline example will have three paragraphs in the body because there are three Roman numerals. There will be a total of five paragraphs after the introduction and conclusion paragraphs are added.

OUTLINE GUIDE	EXAMPLE

Topic: Kinds of Animals
Title
Introduction
  I. Main Topic (First main point)
    A. Subtopic (Supports first main point)
      1. Details (Supports subtopic)
      2. Details (Supports subtopic)
      3. Details (Supports subtopic)
    B. Subtopic (Supports first main point)
      1. Details (Supports subtopic)
      2. Details (Supports subtopic)
    C. Subtopic (Supports first main point)
  II. Main Topic (Second main point)
    A. Subtopic (Supports second main point)
    B. Subtopic (Supports second main point)
  III. Main Topic (Third main point)
    A. Subtopic (Supports third main point)
    B. Subtopic (Supports third main point)
Conclusion
	Kinds of Animals
	Introduction
	  I. Birds
	    A. Hunting birds
	      1. Eagles
	      2. Hawks
	      3. Owls
	    B. Tropical Birds
	      1. Are usually colorful
	      2. Can live in the rain forest
	    C. Antarctic birds
	  II. Reptiles
	    A. On land
	    B. In water
	  III. Insects
	    A. Insects that crawl
	    B. Insects that fly
	Conclusion

Learn It: **HOW THE OUTLINE RULES ARE APPLIED**

Reference 203 — Rules and Examples for Parallel Form in an Outline

1. All the main topics in an outline should be in parallel form. This means that all the main topics should begin in the same way: all nouns, all verbs, all noun phrases, all verb phrases, all prepositional phrases, etc. If necessary, change or rearrange the words of your outline so they are parallel. It does not matter how a main topic begins; it is just important that all topics have the same form.

    I. Birds   **I. Animals that are birds**
    II. Reptiles   **II. Animals that are reptiles**
    III. Insects   **III. Animals that are insects**

2. All the subtopics under a specific Roman numeral must have the same parallel form, but these subtopics do not have to be in the same parallel form as the subtopics under another Roman numeral. For example, the subtopics under Roman numeral **I** must be parallel, and even though the subtopics under Roman numeral **II** must also be parallel, they do not have to be in the same form as the subtopics under Roman numeral **I**, etc.

Parallel form, using adjectives	**Parallel form, using prepositions**	**Parallel form, using nouns**
I. Birds	II. Reptiles	III. Insects
A. **Hunting** birds	A. **On** Land	A. **Insects** that crawl
B. **Tropical** birds	B. **In** Water	B. **Insects** that fly
C. **Antarctic** birds		

Continued on next page. >>>

Reference 203 continued from previous page.

3. All the details under a specific letter must have the same parallel form, but these details do not have to be in the same parallel form as the details under another letter. For example, the details under the letter **A** must be parallel, and even though the details under letter **B** must also be parallel, they do not have to be in the same form as the details under letter **A**, etc.

Parallel form, using nouns	**Parallel form, using verbs**
A. Hunting birds	B. Tropical birds
1. **Eagles**	1. **Are** usually colorful
2. **Hawks**	2. **Can** live in the rain forest
3. **Owls**	

Classroom Practice 76

It is time to practice the skills you are learning. You will use the classroom practice on the next page to apply these skills.

Classroom Practice 76

Name:_____ Date:_____

SKILLS

▶ **Exercise 1:** Copy the notes below into an outline. Use the correct outline form.
(The notes are in correct parallel form.)

NOTES:	OUTLINE:
exercises	
Introduction	
inside exercises	
exercises for weight loss	
stationary bike	
treadmill	
jump rope	
exercises for muscle building	
weights	
t-bar row	
outside exercises	
running	
walking	
inside and outside exercises	
swimming	
track	
Conclusion	

▶ **Exercise 2:** Place an **X** in front of the items that are parallel.

_____ 1. lying in the leaves   _____ 3. hiding places

_____ 2. hiding under rocks   _____ 4. buried in the sand

START LESSON 5

Lesson 5

You will

- do Chapter Checkups 77 and 78.
- write in your journal.

JOURNAL WRITING 43

Write an entry in your journal. Use Reference 9 on page 12 for ideas.

Chapter Checkups 77 and 78

It is time for a checkup of the skills you have learned in this chapter. You will use the chapter checkups on the next two pages to evaluate your progress.

Chapter 16 Checkup 77

Name:_____ Date:_____

SKILLS

▶ **Exercise 1:** For each statement, write **O** (opinion) or **F** (fact) in the blank.

_____ 1. The technical school in our town is a two-year college.

_____ 2. Math is an easy subject.

_____ 3. It is two miles from my home to my school.

_____ 4. Aunt Jo Jo is the best cook in town.

_____ 5. Everyone should have a college degree.

_____ 6. My neighbor drives a 1995 van.

_____ 7. I ate four slices of apple pie.

▶ **Exercise 2:** Classify each of these sentences in terms of the propaganda technique it contains. **L** (loaded words), **I** (important/famous people), **B** (bandwagon), **M** (mudslinging), **S** (stereotyping), **F/O** (fact/opinion)

_____ 1. Don't be the only student without an mp3 player. Get your mp3 player today!

_____ 2. The best cyclists go to Ben's Bike Shop. We have the largest selection in the state.

_____ 3. Mayor Alton Morris drinks Power Coffee. Buy your Power Coffee at Dan's Grocery today!

_____ 4. Camp at Jones Lake for unbelievable fun, incredible relaxation, and fantastic discounts!

_____ 5. Vote against inexperience in Congress. Vote for experience! Vote for Kelly Johnson.

_____ 6. Good cooks use Steel Bright Cookware. Moms should buy Steel Bright Cookware today.

▶ **Exercise 3:** Answer the questions below, using the information in the following article.

[1]Every fit person in our community owns a treadmill. [2]The fitness level in our area is very high, and the treadmill is the reason everyone is healthy. [3]A trusty treadmill is an outstanding purchase because it provides healthy aerobic exercise in any weather. [4]No other exercise equipment can do the job as well as the treadmill. [5]Most people in our neighborhood own a treadmill, and you need to get one, too.

1. What is the purpose? _____

2. Write the propaganda technique for each numbered sentence above.

(1) _____   (4) _____

(2) _____   (5) _____

(3) _____

Chapter 16 Checkup 78

Name:_____ Date:_____

SKILLS

▶ **Exercise 1:** Put the notes into a two-point outline form. Wording must be changed for correct parallel form.

NOTES:	OUTLINE:
two types of playgrounds	
carefully-planned playgrounds	
are large with lots of grassy areas	
safe equipment	
poorly-planned playgrounds	
small with lots of concrete or gravel areas	
have unsafe equipment	

▶ **Exercise 2:** Place an **X** in front of the items that are parallel.

_____ 1. in damp places _____ 3. has no roots

_____ 2. forms on rocks and logs _____ 4. draws moisture from the air

▶ **Exercise 3:** Write the correct word beside each definition. **Use these words:** skim, question, read, scan.

_____ 1. Process completed slowly to find and understand details about topic headings.

_____ 2. Process in which you change section headings to get a purpose for reading.

_____ 3. Process completed quickly to get a general idea of the article.

_____ 4. Process completed quickly to locate answers to specific questions.

▶ **Exercise 4:** Write **True** or **False** before each statement.

_____ 1. Skimming is the first step of subject matter reading.

_____ 2. Scanning is done slowly to get a general idea of the article.

_____ 3. You should read slowly to understand details.

_____ 4. You are more likely to pick out and remember the main facts when you are looking for answers to specific questions.

_____ 5. How fast or slowly you read should not depend on your reason for reading.

_____ 6. Titles, topic headings, topic sentences for each paragraph, and underlining or boldface type are parts of an article that you would skim.

_____ 7. Skimming is used after you actually read an article.

_____ 8. Turning topic headings into questions gives you a purpose for reading.

LISTENING AND SPEAKING:
Oral Review Questions

Lesson 6

You will
- respond to oral review questions.
- take Chapter 16 Test.
- discuss and evaluate goals.
- write a paragraph in your goal booklet.

Discuss It:

1. What is a fact?
2. What is an opinion?
3. What is propaganda?
4. What are six propaganda techniques?
5. What are six media sources?
6. True or False. You read slowly for enjoyment.
7. True or False. You read quickly for understanding main ideas and details.
8. True or False. You read slowly to get an idea about the topic.
9. What is subject-matter reading?
10. What are the four steps to subject-matter reading?
11. What are the two kinds of outlines?
12. What are the parts of an outline?
13. How are the main topics designated in an outline?
14. How are the subtopics designated in an outline?
15. How are the details designated in an outline?
16. What is parallel form in an outline?
17. What is the parallel form for these examples?

Example 1: A. <u>Walked</u> the dog   B. <u>Watered</u> the flowers   C. <u>Emptied</u> the trash

Example 2: A. <u>Air</u> travel   B. <u>Land</u> travel   C. <u>Water</u> travel

CHAPTER TEST

It is time to evaluate your knowledge of the skills you have learned in this chapter. Your teacher will give you the Chapter 16 Test to help you assess your progress.

>>>>>>>>>>>>>>>>>>>> **Student Tip...**

> For information about test-taking strategies, refer to the Resource Tools Section on page 520.

Review It: GOALS

Review the goals you wrote in your Goal Booklet at the beginning of the school year. Discuss your progress with your teacher or a student partner. Then, write a paragraph in your Goal Booklet that tells how well you are meeting your short-term goals. Give examples that support your evaluation of your progress. Next, write another paragraph to evaluate your long-term goals. Tell whether you want to change them or keep them the same. Give reasons to support either choice. Finally, return your Goal Booklet to your teacher when you have finished.

START LESSON 1

Lesson 1

You will

- revise and edit WA 19 independently.
- write a final paper for WA 19.
- write in your journal.

JOURNAL WRITING 44

Write an entry in your journal. Use Reference 9 on page 12 for ideas.

Writing Time

Apply It: REVISING, EDITING, AND WRITING A FINAL PAPER

Revise and edit Writing Assignment 19 from your Rough Draft folder. First, revise and edit your rough draft by yourself. Next, exchange papers with your editing partner. Then, make the final revisions and corrections to your rough draft as you write a **final paper**. After you have finished your final paper, put it in your Final Paper folder.

As you begin, refer to Reference 57. This reference will tell you where to find the Final Paper Checklist and will give you a visual check of all the steps you should have completed at this point. Always make it a habit to review these steps mentally to make sure you do not miss a step in the writing process.

Reference 57	The Steps in the Writing Process

The steps below will take you through the writing process and will give you the location of each checklist.

1. **Prewriting.** Use the Prewriting Checklist to plan and organize your writing. See Reference 47 on page 62.

2. **Rough Draft.** Use the Rough Draft Checklist to set up and write the rough draft. See Reference 49 on page 66.

3. **Revising.** Use the Revising Checklist to revise the content of your writing. See Reference 51 on page 69.

4. **Editing.** Use the Editing Checklist to edit your writing for spelling, grammar, usage, capitalization, and punctuation mistakes. See Reference 53 on page 71.

5. **Final Paper.** Use the Final Paper Checklist to set up and write the final paper. See Reference 56 on page 75.

6. **Publishing.** Use the Publishing Checklist to choose a publishing form for sharing your writing with others. (Reference 67, page 102)

>>>>>>>>>>>>> Student Tip...

If you need to improve your handwriting, refer to the Resource Tools Section on page 521 for information on writing legibly.

Writing Time

Apply It: **REVISING, EDITING, AND WRITING A FINAL PAPER**

Choose Writing Assignment 25 or 28 from your Rough Draft folder to revise and edit. First, revise and edit your rough draft by yourself. Next, exchange papers with your editing partner. Then, make the final revisions and corrections to your rough draft as you write a **final paper**. After you have finished your final paper, put it in your Final Paper folder.

As you begin, refer to Reference 57 on page 450. This reference will tell you where to find the Final Paper Checklist and will give you a visual check of all the steps you should have completed at this point.

START LESSON 2

Lesson 2

You will

- revise and edit WA 25 or WA 28 with a partner.
- write a final paper for WA 25 or WA 28.
- write in your journal.

JOURNAL WRITING **45**

Write an entry in your journal. Use Reference 9 on page 12 for ideas.

START LESSON 3

Lesson 3

You will

- revise and edit a selected creative writing assignment independently.
- write a final paper for the creative writing selection.
- write in your journal.

JOURNAL WRITING 46

Write an entry in your journal. Use Reference 9 on page 12 for ideas.

Writing Time

Apply It: **REVISING, EDITING, AND WRITING A FINAL PAPER**

Select a creative writing assignment of your choice from your Rough Draft folder to revise and edit. Revise and edit your rough draft by yourself. Then, write a **final paper**. After you have finished your final paper, put it in your Final Paper folder.

As you begin, refer to Reference 57. This reference will tell you where to find the Final Paper Checklist and will give you a visual check of all the steps you should have completed at this point.

| Reference 57 | The Steps in the Writing Process |

The steps below will take you through the writing process and will give you the location of each checklist.

1. **Prewriting.** Use the Prewriting Checklist to plan and organize your writing. Reference 47, page 62
2. **Rough Draft.** Use the Rough Draft Checklist to set up and write the rough draft. Reference 49, page 66
3. **Revising.** Use the Revising Checklist to revise the content of your writing. Reference 51, page 69
4. **Editing.** Use the Editing Checklist to edit your writing for spelling, grammar, usage, capitalization, and punctuation mistakes. Reference 53, page 71
5. **Final Paper.** Use the Final Paper Checklist to set up and write the final paper. Reference 56, page 75
6. **Publishing.** Use the Publishing Checklist to choose a publishing form for sharing with others. Reference 67, page 102

Writing Time

Apply It: REVISING, EDITING, AND WRITING A FINAL PAPER

Choose Writing Assignment 22 or 30 from your Rough Draft folder to revise and edit. First, revise and edit your rough draft by yourself. Next, exchange papers with your editing partner. Then, make the final revisions and corrections to your rough draft as you write a **final paper**. After you have finished your final paper, put it in your Final Paper folder.

As you begin, refer to Reference 57 on page 452. This reference will tell you where to find the Final Paper Checklist and will give you a visual check of all the steps you should have completed at this point.

Plan It:

Your teacher will give you a presentation schedule to follow as you share a writing selection with your class in the next two lessons. If you are in Group 1, you will share in Lesson 5. If you are in Group 2, you will share in Lesson 6.

START LESSON 4

Lesson 4

You will
- revise and edit WA 22 or WA 30 with a partner.
- write a final paper for WA 22 or WA 30.
- write in your journal.

JOURNAL WRITING **47**

Write an entry in your journal. Use Reference 9 on page 12 for ideas.

START LESSON 5

Lesson 5

You will

- select a final paper and share it with classmates.

Publishing Time

Publish It: SHARE A WRITING SELECTION

Select a favorite writing piece from your Final Paper folder to share with your classmates on your presentation day. If you are in Group 1, you will share today. If you are in Group 2, you will share during the next lesson. Use the Share Time Guidelines as presentations are made.

Reference 68 — Share Time Guidelines

Speaker Presentation

1. Have your paper ready to read when called upon.
2. Tell the title of your writing selection.
3. Tell the purpose and type of writing used.

PRESENTATION TIPS:

4. Stand with your feet flat on the floor and your shoulders straight. Do not shift your weight as you stand.
5. Hold your paper about chin high to help you project your voice to your audience.
6. Make sure you do not read too fast.
7. Read in a clear voice that can be heard so that your audience does not have to strain to hear you.
8. Change your voice tone for different characters or for different parts of the writing selection.

Audience Response

1. Look at the speaker.
2. Turn your body toward the speaker.
3. Listen attentively. Do not let your thoughts wander.
4. Do not make distracting noises as you listen.
5. Do not make distracting motions as you listen.
6. Show interest in what the speaker is saying.
7. Silently summarize what the speaker is saying. Take notes if necessary.
8. Ask questions about anything that is not clear.
9. Show appreciation by clapping after the speaker has finished.

End of
Lesson 5

START LESSON 6

Lesson 6

You will

- select a final paper and share it with classmates.

Publishing Time

Publish It: SHARE A WRITING SELECTION

If you are in Group 2, you will share your selected writing piece with your classmates today. Use the Share Time Guidelines as presentations are made.

Chapter 17 Writing Evaluation Guide

Name:_____ Date:_____

ROUGH DRAFT CHECK

_____ 1. Did you write your rough draft in pencil?

_____ 2. Did you write the correct headings on the first seven lines of your paper?

_____ 3. Did you use extra wide margins and skip every other line?

_____ 4. Did you write a title at the end of your rough draft?

_____ 5. Did you place your edited rough draft in your Rough Draft folder?

REVISING CHECK

_____ 6. Did you identify the purpose, type of writing, and audience?

_____ 7. Did you check for a topic, topic sentence, and sentences supporting the topic?

_____ 8. Did you check sentences for the right order, and did you combine, rearrange, or delete sentences when necessary?

_____ 9. Did you check for a variety of simple, compound, and complex sentences?

_____ 10. Did you check for any left out, repeated, or unnecessary words?

_____ 11. Did you check for the best choice of words by replacing or deleting unclear words?

_____ 12. Did you check the content for interest and creativity?

_____ 13. Did you check the voice to make sure the writing says what you want it to say?

EDITING CHECK

_____ 14. Did you indent each paragraph?

_____ 15. Did you put an end mark at the end of every sentence?

_____ 16. Did you capitalize the first word of every sentence?

_____ 17. Did you check for all other capitalization mistakes?

_____ 18. Did you check for all punctuation mistakes?
(commas, periods, apostrophes, quotation marks, underlining)

_____ 19. Did you check for misspelled words and for incorrect homonym choices?

_____ 20. Did you check for incorrect spellings of plural and possessive forms?

_____ 21. Did you check for correct construction and punctuation of your sentences?

_____ 22. Did you check for usage mistakes? *(subject/verb agreement, a/an choices, contractions, verb tenses, pronoun/antecedent agreement, pronoun cases, degrees of adjectives, double negatives, etc.)*

_____ 23. Did you put your revised and edited paper in the Rough Draft folder?

FINAL PAPER CHECK

_____ 24. Did you write the final paper in pencil?

_____ 25. Did you center the title on the top line and center your name under the title?

_____ 26. Did you skip a line before starting the writing assignment?

_____ 27. Did you single-space, use wide margins, and write the final paper neatly?

_____ 28. Did you staple your papers in this order: final paper on top, rough draft in the middle, and prewriting map on the bottom? Did you put them in the Final Paper folder?

Lesson 1

You will

- read and discuss the genre of poetry.
- read and analyze an Alfred Lord Tennyson poem.
- read and discuss a color poem.
- write a poem for WA 36.
- write a report on Alfred Lord Tennyson for Homework WA 37.

Literature Time

Learn It: POETRY

Reference 204   Poetry

Artistic writing includes many literary genres—essays, poems, short stories, plays, etc. A **genre** identifies what type of writing a piece of literature is. One of the oldest forms of literature is poetry. Throughout history, people have used poetry to pass along news, create songs and stories, and record historical events.

Poetry is a very compact and focused form of writing that spurs the imagination and calls up sensory images and emotional responses. Poetry says a lot in a few words. It allows you to share your thoughts and feelings in a unique way. With its multiple images, poetry relates to the heart as well as to the mind. A poem is a delicate juggling act of rhythm, figurative language, and sometimes rhyme.

The poem, whether it rhymes or not, is probably the most artistic of all genres. The poem, as an art form, is both visual and auditory. Poetry looks different. Without reading words, you can look at a poem and know it is a poem by its appearance on the page. Most poetry is pleasing to the ear. You can hear a poem read aloud and know it is a poem because it sounds like one. A poem should be read aloud in order to be fully appreciated and enjoyed. By reading a poem silently, you miss its music and, perhaps, even its meaning.

Poetry often says things in a special way by using figurative language. **Figurative language** uses words to draw pictures of things being compared. There are three figures of speech that create images that compare one thing to another. They are *simile, metaphor,* and *personification*.

1. **Simile** compares two or more things by using the words **like** or **as**.
   Example: He is **as** gentle **as** a lamb. She is **as** curious **as** a cat.
   My dad sings **like** a frog.

2. **Metaphor** compares things by stating that one thing is something else. It uses linking verbs such as **am, is, are, was,** and **were.**
   Example: His new **car was a rocket** on the open road.
   My **brother is a little monkey** after school.

3. **Personification** compares things by giving human qualities to something nonhuman.
   Example: The **trees sang a soothing song to the baby birds in their nest.**

Poems sometimes contain sound devices. The four principal **sound devices** are *alliteration, assonance, repetition,* and *rhyme*.

1. **Alliteration** is the repetition of initial consonant sounds (at the beginning of words).
   Example: <u>F</u>our <u>f</u>riendly <u>f</u>oxes (**f sounds**)

2. **Assonance** is the repetition of internal vowel sounds (within words).
   Example: H<u>i</u>gh fl<u>y</u>ing k<u>i</u>tes (**i sounds**)

3. **Repetition** refers to the repeating, or restating, of any words, phrases, or sentences. Words, phrases, or sentences can be repeated anywhere within the poem.

4. **Rhyme** is the sound-alike quality of words, regardless of their spellings (*say/sleigh, him/gym*). Rhyme may be of two types: end rhymes and internal rhymes. End rhymes are rhymes at the end of lines whereas internal rhymes are rhymes within lines.

A poem will most often be organized into sections called **stanzas.**

LISTENING AND SPEAKING:

Discuss It: POETRY

1. What genre of writing is one of the oldest forms of literature?

2. What is figurative language?

3. What are three figures of speech?

4. Which figure of speech uses the words **like** or **as** to make a comparison?

5. Which figure of speech makes a comparison by stating that one thing is something else?

6. Which figure of speech gives human qualities to something nonhuman?

7. What are four sound devices used in poetry?

8. Which sound device repeats beginning consonant sounds?

9. Which sound device repeats vowel sounds within words?

10. How are poems organized?

Read It:

 Reference 205   **Alfred Lord Tennyson**

The Eagle

He clasps the crag with crooked hands;
Close to the sun in lonely lands,
Ring'd with the azure world, he stands.

The wrinkled sea beneath him crawls;
He watches from his mountain walls,
And like a thunderbolt he falls.

— *Alfred Lord Tennyson*

Discuss It: ANALYZING "THE EAGLE"

1. In this poem, what does Alfred Lord Tennyson describe?

2. Look up the word crag in a dictionary. What does it mean?
   a. a steep rugged mountain rock
   b. a branch of a tree
   c. a small rabbit

3. Look up the word azure in a dictionary. What does it mean?
   a. sparkling
   b. sky blue
   c. a gem

4. In this poem, where is the eagle?
   a. soaring high in the blue sky
   b. in a nest in the zoo
   c. high on a mountain cliff overlooking the sea

5. Which sound devices are used?

6. What are some examples of rhyme?

Continued on next page. >>>

7. What are some examples of alliteration?

8. This poem uses figurative language to create images in order to compare one thing to another. Which types of figurative language are used?

9. What are some examples of personification?

10. What are some examples of simile?

11. The last line says the eagle falls like a thunderbolt. That means he fell quickly. Tennyson does not tell us why he fell. Can you think of some reasons why the eagle would fall like a thunderbolt?

Learn It: COLOR POEMS

Reference 206   **Color Poems**

Directions: Pick a color as your title. Tell about your color in complete sentences. Your sentences do not have to rhyme.

Green is...
Green is a freshly mowed lawn.

Green is a forest of summer trees.

It is grapes, limes, and kiwi slices.

It is clover and jade and pretty cat's eyes.

Green is an emerald jewel.

Green is the birth of spring.

Red and the Senses
Red looks like valentines.

Red smells like apples with cinnamon.

Red tastes as good as a cherry pie.

Red sounds like a fire engine clanging.

Red feels like Christmas morning.

Write It: WRITING ASSIGNMENT 36

Writing Assignment 36

Choose one of the options below about which to write your poem.

1. In the last line of Alfred Lord Tennyson's poem "The Eagle," he describes the eagle falling like a thunderbolt, but he ends the poem without telling us why the eagle fell. Write another verse to the poem, explaining why the eagle fell.

2. Write a poem about another animal that interests you, such as an otter, a rabbit, a snake, or a lizard. Think about where the animal lives and other special facts about the animal that you could include in your poem. Use descriptive words.

3. Write a color poem, using similes or metaphors.

4. Make up a poem of your own. Try to use similes or metaphors in your poem.

Activity:

Look up poems by poets Eve Merriam and Kate Greenaway. Pick out the poem you like the best. Why do you like this poem? What is your interpretation of the poem? Read and discuss it with a partner. What does your partner think about the poem?

Special Instructions:

1. Type this assignment on the computer or write it neatly on notebook paper.

2. Illustrate your poem with your own artwork, clip art, or magazine pictures.

3. Read your poem to a family member or a friend.

4. Give the finished poem to your teacher in the next lesson.

Write It: HOME WRITING ASSIGNMENT 37

Home Writing Assignment 37

Purpose: To inform

Type of Writing: Expository paragraph or essay

Audience: Classmates

Writing Topic: Alfred Lord Tennyson

Special Instructions:

1. You have been studying a poem by Alfred Lord Tennyson. Look up more information about him, using the Internet, a poetry reference, and/or an encyclopedia.

2. Write a paragraph or essay that includes the following information.
   Introduction: Tell who Alfred Lord Tennyson was and what he did.
   Body: Tell one or more important or unusual facts about Alfred Lord Tennyson's early life. Tell one or more important or unusual facts about Alfred Lord Tennyson's later life. Mention one or more important works written by Alfred Lord Tennyson.
   Conclusion: Give a summation, or wrap-up, of what the paragraph/essay is about.

3. Type your paragraph or essay on the computer or write it neatly on notebook paper. Everyone's report will be compiled into a classroom booklet.

4. Use standard, time-order, or transition writing form.
   See Reference 70 on page 107.

5. Write in third person. See Reference 71 on page 108.

>>>>>>>> Student Tip...

If you need to improve your handwriting, refer to the Resource Tools Section on page 521 for information on writing legibly.

START LESSON 2

Lesson 2

You will
- share reports and poems.

Literature Time

Discuss It: **WRITING ASSIGNMENT 37**

What did you learn about Alfred Lord Tennyson in your writing assignment?

Did you discover anything about Alfred Lord Tennyson's life that could have influenced him to write "The Eagle"?

Give your report about Alfred Lord Tennyson to your teacher to be placed in a class booklet. This booklet will be available to you for checkout so you may enjoy the research that was done.

Share It: **WRITING ASSIGNMENT 36**

A poem should be read aloud in order to be fully appreciated and enjoyed. When listening to a poem, you are enjoying one of the oldest forms of literature. Reading poems aloud gives us a chance to hear their rhythms and understand their images. However, since poems are also a personal expression of your thoughts, you have several ways of sharing your poem.

1. You may share your poem aloud.
2. You may have your poem put in the class poetry booklet for everyone to read.
3. You may give your poem to your teacher.

If you do not want to display your poem in the class booklet, you must write "return" in the lower right corner of your paper. It will be returned in a few days. The poems in the class booklet will be returned before the end of the school year. This will give everyone a chance to read and enjoy the poems.

Literature Time

Read It:

START LESSON 3

Lesson 3

You will

- read and analyze a Robert Louis Stevenson poem.
- read and discuss a parts-of-speech poem, a couplet, a triplet, and a quatrain.
- write a poem for WA 38.
- write a report on Robert Louis Stevenson for Homework WA 39.

> **Reference 207** **Robert Louis Stevenson**
>
> ### The Wind
>
> I saw you toss the kites on high
> And blow the birds about the sky;
> And all around I heard you pass,
> Like ladies' skirts across the grass—
>   O wind, a-blowing all day long,
>   O wind, that sings so loud a song!
> I saw the different things you did,
> But always you yourself you hid.
> I felt you push, I heard you call,
> I could not see yourself at all—
>   O wind, a-blowing all day long,
>   O wind, that sings so loud a song!
> O you that are so strong and cold,
> O blower, are you young or old?
> Are you a beast of field and tree,
> Or just a stronger child than me?
>   O wind, a-blowing all day long,
>   O wind, that sings so loud a song!
>
> —Robert Louis Stevenson

LISTENING AND SPEAKING:

Discuss It: ANALYZING "THE WIND"

1. The poet names a number of actions that the wind performed. What is the action that he does not name?
   a. toss b. blow c. hid d. push e. call f. sing g. dance

2. Why do you think the poet is puzzled by the wind?

3. In the last verse, the poet tries to guess what the wind is. What are some of his guesses?

4. Does the poem "The Wind" use sound devices?

5. Which sound devices are used?

6. What are some examples of alliteration?

7. What are some examples of assonance?

8. What are some examples of repetition?

9. What are some examples of rhyme?

Continued on next page. >>>

10. The poem uses figurative language to create images in order to compare one thing to another. Which figurative language is used?
How is personification used?
How is simile used?

11. Action imagery results from the use of action verbs.
Name the action verbs that help create an image.

12. What does this poem mean to you?

Learn It: **PARTS-OF-SPEECH, COUPLET, TRIPLET, AND QUATRAIN POEMS**

Reference 208 — Parts-of-Speech, Couplet, Triplet, and Quatrain Poems

Parts-of-Speech Poem: Follow the directions and use the parts of speech listed to write this poem.

Line 1. Write a noun. (*the topic of your poem*)

Line 2. Write two adjectives that describe the noun.

Line 3. Write one verb and one prepositional phrase.

Line 4. Write two adverbs describing the verb in Line 3.

Line 5. Write a sentence about the noun.

Snow

Soft and cold

Falls on the ground

Quietly and slowly

Snow is a silent mystery.

A **couplet** has two lines that rhyme. Some poems are written entirely in couplets. Other poems have only one couplet. Couplets are often silly and are usually about one subject.

My best friend's poems always rhyme,
I think her verses are sublime!

My best friend's poems always rhyme,
I think her verses are sublime!

She's always thinking of poems that are funny,
One day she could make lots of money.

A **triplet** has three lines that rhyme.

As John sped down the road in his Cooper

He was feeling really super-duper

Until he spied that hidden state trooper!

A **quatrain** is a four-line poem with at least two lines that rhyme. There are several rhyming schemes possible. For example, the first and second lines rhyme, and the third and fourth lines rhyme (aabb). Some other rhyming combinations include abab, abba, aaba, abcb, etc.

(aabb)

My dog, the Great Dane, likes to sleep with me,
He thinks it comes with the pedigree.
I've got news for that huge hound—
"Stay off my bed, or you're going to the pound!"

(abab)

I met a cowboy singer named Willy
From Texas he did come;
To sing songs that were foolish and silly
A big star he hoped to become.

Writing Time

Write It: WRITING ASSIGNMENT 38

Writing Assignment 38

Choose one of the options below about which to write your poem.

1. Robert Louis Stevenson observes the wind and describes what it does. Choose something in nature, such as a gentle rain, flocks of birds migrating in the fall, or trees and plants budding in the spring. Then, write a poem to describe it. It sometimes helps to go outside and pay careful attention to what you are describing. Try to use as many action verbs as you can in your poem.

2. Write a parts-of-speech poem about a friend or yourself.

3. Write a couplet, triplet, or quatrain.

4. Make up a poem of your own.

Activity:

Look up poems by poets Shel Silverstein and Sara Teasdale. Pick out the poem you like the best. Why do you like this poem? What is your interpretation of the poem? Read and discuss it with a partner. What does your partner think about the poem?

Special Instructions:

1. Type this assignment on the computer or write it neatly on notebook paper.

2. Illustrate your poem with your own artwork, clip art, or magazine pictures.

3. Read your poem to a family member or a friend.

4. Give the finished poem to your teacher in the next lesson.

Write It: HOME WRITING ASSIGNMENT 39

Home Writing Assignment 39

Purpose: To inform
Type of Writing: Expository paragraph or essay
Audience: Classmates
Writing Topic: Robert Louis Stevenson
Special Instructions:

1. You have been studying a poem by Robert Louis Stevenson. Look up more information about him, using the Internet, a poetry reference, and/or an encyclopedia.

2. Write a paragraph or essay that includes the following information.
Introduction: Tell who Robert Louis Stevenson was and what he did.
Body: Tell one or more important or unusual facts about Robert Louis Stevenson's early life. Tell one or more important or unusual facts about Robert Louis Stevenson's later life. Mention one or more important works written by Robert Louis Stevenson.
Conclusion: Give a summation, or wrap-up, of what the paragraph/essay is about.

3. Type your paragraph or essay on the computer or write it neatly on notebook paper. Everyone's report will be compiled into a classroom booklet.

4. Use standard, time-order, or transition writing form.
See Reference 70 on page 107.

5. Write in third person. See Reference 71 on page 108.

Chapter 18

START LESSON 4

Lesson 4

You will
- share reports and poems.

Literature Time

Discuss It: **WRITING ASSIGNMENT 39**

What did you learn about Robert Louis Stevenson in your writing assignment?

Did you discover anything about Robert Louis Stevenson's life that could have influenced him to write "The Wind"?

Give your report about Robert Louis Stevenson to your teacher to be placed in a class booklet. This booklet will be available to you for checkout so you may enjoy the research that was done.

Share It: **WRITING ASSIGNMENT 38**

You have several ways of sharing your poem.

1. You may share your poem aloud.
2. You may have your poem put in the class poetry booklet for everyone to read.
3. You may give your poem to your teacher.

If you do not want to display your poem in the class booklet, you must write "return" in the lower right corner of your paper. It will be returned in a few days. The poems in the class booklet will be returned before the end of the school year. This will give everyone a chance to read and enjoy the poems.

Literature Time

Read It:

START LESSON 5

Lesson 5

You will
- read and analyze a Christina Rossetti poem.
- read and discuss an acrostic and a haiku poem.
- write a poem for WA 40.
- write a report on Christina Rossetti for Homework WA 41.

> **Reference 209**   **Christina Rossetti**
>
> ### Hope is Like a Harebell
> Hope is like a harebell trembling from its birth,
> Love is like a rose the joy of all the earth;
> Faith is like a lily lifted high and white,
> Love is like a lovely rose the world's delight;
> Harebells and sweet lilies show a thornless growth,
> But the rose with all its thorns excels them both.
>
> — *Christina Rossetti*

LISTENING AND SPEAKING:

Discuss It: **ANALYZING "HOPE IS LIKE A HAREBELL"**

1. The poet names three qualities.
   What is the quality that she does not name?
       a. faith   b. hope   c. courage   d. love

2. What is hope compared to?
   Look in the dictionary to find the definition of a harebell. What is it?

3. What is love compared to?
   What is faith compared to?

4. In the last two lines, the author tells which quality she thinks is the best.
   Which is it? How do you know?

5. Does the poem "Hope is like a harebell" use sound devices?

6. Which sound devices are used?

7. What are some examples of alliteration?

8. What are some examples of repetition?

9. What are some examples of rhyme?

10. The poem uses figurative language to create images in order to compare one thing to another. What types of figurative language are used? How is personification used? How is simile used?

11. What does this poem mean to you?

Learn It: ACROSTIC POETRY

Reference 210 | Acrostic Poem

In an **acrostic** poem, the letters that begin each line often spell the subject of the poem. To write an acrostic, think of a person (or thing) to describe. Write the letters of the name vertically. Beside each letter, write an adjective or short phrase that starts with that letter and describes the person or thing.

ACROSTIC POEM 1
B – best friend
R – red hair and blue eyes
E – energy high
N – natural athlete
T – too cool

ACROSTIC POEM 2
P – perfect all-around food
I – irresistible to eat
Z – zesty sauce and cheese
Z – zippy delivery with a friendly smile
A – always a favorite

Learn It: HAIKU POETRY

Reference 211 | Haiku

Haiku is a form of Japanese poetry. Historically, haiku reflected some subject of nature, but modern haiku is more inclusive and the subject matter is not restricted to nature. Most traditional haiku have the following characteristics.

- Haiku has only three lines.
- Haiku does not rhyme.
- Haiku describes a specific moment in time, using present-tense verbs.
- The whole haiku has a total of seventeen syllables.
- The first line has five syllables.
- The second line has seven syllables.
- The third line has five syllables.
- The haiku uses descriptive words and poetic imagery to create one clear image, or word picture. It freezes a moment in time. It does not matter whether or not a haiku uses complete sentences. Only the first word of a haiku may be capitalized, or the first word of each line may be capitalized. Put a period at the end of a haiku.

HAIKU 1
Green berries turn red
Along September fence rows.
Dog days of summer.
—Nature

HAIKU 2
Traffic lights play games
of stop and go; motorists
inch their way to work.
—Non-nature

Continued on next page. >>>

Reference 211 continued from previous page.

STEPS FOR WRITING HAIKU

1. Select something that appeals to you. Narrow your subject down to a specific idea about your subject. (**Subject:** *crocus flowers*   **Specific idea:** *the crocus is braver than other flowers*)

2. Write the subject down in noun form, possibly with an adjective or two. (*brave crocus blossoms*)
   Note: *Your haiku does not always have to start with a noun phrase. It can begin with an adjective, an adverb, or whatever YOU choose. Use words that tell about the specific idea you are trying to portray.*

3. Count the syllables to see if you have enough to meet the five-syllable requirement for your first line. (*cro•cus blos•soms*) *Since your first line needs to be five syllables, you are one syllable short.*)

4. If necessary, add another adjective or a verb that has the number of syllables you need for the first line to be complete. (*Brave cro•cus blos•soms*) *Now you have the five syllables needed for your first line.*)

5. For the second line, think of something special about your subject. You might want to use a verb or two to tell the action or a few words to describe what is special about the subject. Try to use imagery or personification to create a vivid mental picture. Remember that you need seven syllables, and your end word should **not** rhyme with the end word in the first line. Add extra modifiers as needed to achieve the desired seven syllables. (*break through the heav•y snow•drifts*)

6. For the last line, try to give your haiku an effective conclusion by adding an unusual ending to the specific idea you have developed. Remember that you need five syllables and your words should **not** rhyme. (*Daf•fo•dils fol•low*)

7. Check your completed haiku to be sure it has all nine characteristics of a haiku.

   > **Brave crocus blossoms**
   > **break through the heavy snow drifts.**
   > **Daffodils follow.**

8. Decide how you want to capitalize the lines of your haiku. Put periods and commas where they are needed. Title your three-line poem "Haiku."

Write It: **WRITING ASSIGNMENT 40**

Writing Assignment

Choose one of the options below about which to write your poem.

1. Make up your own poem about one or more qualities, such as truth, kindness, or beauty.

2. Rhyming poems can be taken out of rhyme; unrhymed poems can be put into rhyme. Whether or not a poem rhymes has little to do with its being a good poem. Take the poem "Hope is Like a Harebell" out of rhyme. Here are the first two lines unrhymed. You continue with the rest of the poem.

   > *Hope is like a budding new harebell.*
   > *Love is like a rose that gives joy to everyone.*

3. Write an acrostic.

4. Write a haiku poem.

5. Make up a poem of your own.

Activity:

Look up poems by poets Ogden Nash and Alieen Fisher. Pick out the poem you like the best. Why do you like this poem? What is your interpretation of the poem? Read and discuss it with a partner. What does your partner think about the poem?

Special Instructions:

1. Type this assignment on the computer or write it neatly on notebook paper.

2. Illustrate your poem with your own artwork, clip art, or magazine pictures.

3. Read your poem to a family member or a friend.

4. Give the finished poem to your teacher in the next lesson.

Write It: HOME WRITING ASSIGNMENT 41

Home Writing Assignment 41

Purpose: To inform

Type of Writing: Expository paragraph or essay

Audience: Classmates

Writing Topic: Christina Rossetti

Special Instructions:

1. You have been studying a poem by Christina Rossetti. Look up more information about her, using the Internet, a poetry reference, and/or an encyclopedia.

2. Write a paragraph or essay that includes the following information.
   Introduction: Tell who Christina Rossetti was and what she did.
   Body: Tell one or more important or unusual facts about Christina Rossetti's early life. Tell one or more important or unusual facts about Christina Rossetti's later life. Mention one or more important works written by Christina Rossetti.
   Conclusion: Give a summation, or wrap-up, of what the paragraph/essay is about.

3. Type your paragraph or essay on the computer or write it neatly on notebook paper. Everyone's report will be compiled into a classroom booklet.

4. Use standard, time-order, or transition writing form.
   See Reference 70 on page 107.

5. Write in third person. See Reference 71 on page 108.

Literature Time

Discuss It: WRITING ASSIGNMENT 41

What did you learn about Christina Rossetti in your writing assignment?

Did you discover anything about Christina Rossetti's life that could have influenced her to write "Hope is Like a Harebell"?

Give your report about Christina Rossetti to your teacher to be placed in a class booklet. This booklet will be available to you for checkout so you may enjoy the research that was done.

Share It: WRITING ASSIGNMENT 40

You have several ways of sharing your poem.

1. You may share your poem aloud.
2. You may have your poem put in the class poetry booklet for everyone to read.
3. You may give your poem to your teacher.

If you do not want to display your poem in the class booklet, you must write "return" in the lower right corner of your paper. It will be returned in a few days. The poems in the class booklet will be returned before the end of the school year. This will give everyone a chance to read and enjoy the poems.

START LESSON 7

Literature Time

Lesson 7

You will

- read and analyze a Henry Wadsworth Longfellow poem.
- read and discuss a diamante and a limerick.
- write a poem for WA 42.
- write a report on Henry Wadsworth Longfellow for Homework WA 43.

Read It:

📖 **Reference 212**   **Henry Wadsworth Longfellow**

Paul Revere's Ride

1. Listen my children and you shall hear
        Of the midnight ride of Paul Revere,
    On the eighteenth of April, in Seventy-five;
        Hardly a man is now alive.
    Who remembers that famous day and year.

2. He said to his friend, "If the British march
        By land or sea from the town to-night,
    Hang a lantern aloft in the belfry arch
        Of the North Church tower as a signal light—
    One if by land, and two if by sea;
        And I on the opposite shore will be,
    Ready to ride and spread the alarm
        Through every Middlesex village and farm,
    For the country folk to be up and to arm."

3. Then he said "Good-night!" and with muffled oar
        Silently rowed to the Charleston shore,
    Just as the moon rose over the bay,
        Where swinging wide at her moorings lay
    The Somerset, British man-of war;
        A phantom ship, with each mast and spar
    Across the moon like a prison bar,
        And a huge black hulk, that was magnified
    By its own reflection in the tide.

4. Meanwhile, his friend through alley and street
        Wanders and watches, with eager ears,
    Till in the silence around him he hears
        The muster of men at the barrack door,
    The sound of arms, and the tramp of feet,
        And the measured tread of the grenadiers,
    Marching down to their boats on the shore.

5. Then he climbed the tower of the Old North Church,
        By the wooden stairs, with stealthy tread,
    To the belfry chamber overhead,
        And startled the pigeons from their perch
    On the sombre rafters, that round him made
        Masses and moving shapes of shade,—
    By the trembling ladder, steep and tall,
        To the highest window in the wall,
    Where he paused to listen and look down
        A moment on the roofs of the town
    And the moonlight flowing over all.

Continued on next page. >>>

Reference 212 continued from previous page.

6. Beneath, in the churchyard, lay the dead,
    In their night encampment on the hill,
Wrapped in silence so deep and still
    That he could hear, like a sentinel's tread,
The watchful night-wind, as it went
    Creeping along from tent to tent,
    And seemed to whisper, "All is well!"
    A moment only he feels the spell
Of the place and the hour, and the secret dead;
    For suddenly all his thoughts are bent
On a shadowy something far away,
    Where the river widens to meet the bay,—
A line of black that bends and floats
    On the rising tide like a bridge of boats.

7. Meanwhile, impatient to mount and ride,
    Booted and spurred, with a heavy stride
On the opposite shore walked Paul Revere.
    Now he patted his horse's side,
Now he gazed at the landscape far and near,
    Then, impetuous, stamped the earth,
And turned and tightened his saddle girth;
    But mostly he watched with eager search
The belfry tower of the Old North Church,
    As it rose above the graves on the hill,
Lonely and spectral and sombre and still.
    And lo! as he looks on, the belfry burns.

8. A hurry of hoofs in a village street,
    A shape in the moonlight, a bulk in the dark,
    And beneath, from the pebbles, in passing, a spark
    Struck out by a steed flying fearless and fleet;
That was all! And yet, through the gloom and the light,
    The fate of a nation was riding that night;
And the spark struck out by that steed, in his flight,
    Kindled the land into flame with its heat.
He has left the village and mounted the steep,
    And beneath him, tranquil and broad and deep,
Is the Mystic, meeting the ocean tides;
    And under the alders that skirt its edge,
Now soft on the sand, now loud on the ledge,
    Is heard the tramp of his steed as he rides.

9. It was twelve by the village clock
    When he crossed the bridge into Medford town.
He heard the crowing of the cock,
    And the barking of the farmer's dog,
And felt the damp of the river fog,
    That rises after the sun goes down.

10. It was one by the village clock,
    When he galloped into Lexington.
    He saw the gilded weathercock
Swim in the moonlight as he passed,
    And the meeting-house windows, black and bare,
Gaze at him with a spectral glare,
    As if they already stood aghast
At the bloody work they would look upon.

11. It was two by the village clock,
    When he came to the bridge in Concord town.
He heard the bleating of the flock,
    And the twitter of birds among the trees,
And felt the breath of the morning breeze
    Blowing over the meadow brown.
And one was safe and asleep in his bed
    Who at the bridge would be first to fall,
Who that day would be lying dead,
    Pierced by a British musket ball.

12. You know the rest. In books you have read
    How the British Regulars fired and fled,—
How the farmers gave them ball for ball,
    From behind each fence and farmyard wall,
Chasing the Redcoats down the lane,
    Then crossing the fields to emerge again
Under the trees at the turn of the road,
    And only pausing to fire and load.

13. So through the night Paul Revere;
    And so through the night went his cry of alarm
To every Middlesex village and farm,—
    A cry of defiance, and not of fear,
A voice in the darkness, a knock at the door,
    And a word that shall echo for evermore!
For, borne on the night-wind of the Past,
    Through all our history, to the last,
In the hour of darkness and peril and need,
    The people will waken and listen to hear
The hurrying hoof-beats of that steed,
    And the midnight message of Paul Revere.

—*Henry Wadsworth Longfellow*

LISTENING AND SPEAKING:
Discussion Questions for Analyzing "Paul Revere's Ride"

1. What historical event is this poem about?
    a. Revolutionary War   b. Civil War
    c. Boston Tea Party   d. Battle of Gettysburg
2. What was the purpose of the rider, Paul Revere?
3. In the second stanza, what was the signal to tell whether the British were arriving by land or by sea?
4. In the fifth and seventh stanzas, where was the signal given?

Continued on next page. >>>

5. According to the poem, what are the names of the towns that Paul Revere rode through?
6. What happened as a result of Paul Revere's warning?
7. Does the poem "Paul Revere's Ride" use sound devices?
8. Which sound devices are used?
9. Look at the eighth stanza. What are some examples of alliteration?
10. What are some examples of repetition?
11. Look at the second stanza. What are some examples of rhyme?
12. The poem uses figurative language to create images in order to compare one thing to another. Which figurative language is used?
    Look at the sixth stanza. How is personification used?
    Look at the tenth stanza. How is personification used?
    Look at the eleventh stanza. How is personification used?
    Look at the third stanza. How is simile used?
    Look at the sixth stanza. How is simile used?
13. What does this poem mean to you?

Learn It: DIAMANTE AND LIMERICK POEMS

Reference 213 **Diamante and Limerick Poems**

A **diamante** (*dee-ah-mahn-tay*) poem is a diamond-shaped poem that tells about opposites. First, select two opposite nouns to describe. Then, follow the directions below to write each line.

Line 1. Write the first noun.
Line 2. Write two adjectives describing the first noun.
Line 3. Write three *ing* words that describe the first noun.
Line 4. Write two synonyms for the first noun.
    Write two synonyms for the second (*opposite*) noun.
Line 5. Write three *ing* words describing the second noun.
Line 6. Write two adjectives describing the second noun.
Line 7. Write the second (*opposite*) noun.

Ocean
peaceful and clean
moving, raging, living
sea, water, sand, heat
dying, wandering, drying
empty and lonely
Desert

The **limerick** is a popular type of rhymed poem consisting of five lines. The poet Ogden Nash popularized it in the United States. The intent of the *limerick* is to evoke a smile or chuckle in the reader. Almost all *limericks* are humorous and are fun to write. The rules are simple. The first, second, and fifth lines contain three strong beats, or accents, and rhyme with each other. The third and fourth lines contain two strong beats, or accents, and rhyme with each other.

THE NEST
Two birds built a nest in my hat,
And I couldn't do much about that.
So, I just wore it to church
And let the birds perch,
While I listened to the sermon and sat.

Writing Time

Write It: **WRITING ASSIGNMENT 42**

Writing Assignment 42

Choose one of the options below about which to write your poem.

1. The poem "Paul Revere's Ride" is a narrative poem in which the poet tells a story with emphasis on action and details. This poem is based on an event in early American history. Some of the details of the poem differ from what actually happened. Look up Paul Revere in an encyclopedia or on the Internet to find out the differences in the poem and what really happened. Write a short poem or paragraph about the similarities and differences.

2. Choose another historical event, or make up a story of your own. Write the historical event or story in narrative poem style.

3. Write a diamante poem.

4. Write a limerick. Think of words that will make it funny.

5. Make up a poem of your own.

Activity:

Look up poems by poets Walter de La Mare and Robert Frost. Pick out the poem you like the best. Why do you like this poem? What is your interpretation of the poem? Read and discuss it with a partner. What does your partner think about the poem?

Special Instructions:

1. Type this assignment on the computer or write it neatly on notebook paper.

2. Illustrate your poem with your own artwork, clip art, or magazine pictures.

3. Read your poem to a family member or a friend.

4. Give the finished poem to your teacher in the next lesson.

Write It: **HOME WRITING ASSIGNMENT 43**

Home Writing Assignment 43

Purpose: To inform
Type of Writing: Expository paragraph or essay
Audience: Classmates
Writing Topic: Henry Wadsworth Longfellow

Special Instructions:

1. You have been studying a poem by Henry Wadsworth Longfellow. Look up more information about him, using the Internet, a poetry reference, and/or an encyclopedia.

2. Write a paragraph or essay that includes the following information.
Introduction: Tell who Henry Wadsworth Longfellow was and what he did.
Body: Tell one or more important or unusual facts about Henry Wadsworth Longfellow's early life. Tell one or more important or unusual facts about Henry Wadsworth Longfellow's later life. Mention one or more important works written by Henry Wadsworth Longfellow.
Conclusion: Give a summation, or wrap-up, of what the paragraph/essay is about.

3. Type your paragraph or essay on the computer or write it neatly on notebook paper. Everyone's report will be compiled into a classroom booklet.

4. Use standard, time-order, or transition writing form.
See Reference 70 on page 107.

5. Write in third person. See Reference 71 on page 108.

START LESSON 8

Lesson 8

You will
- share reports and poems.
- do Across the Curriculum activity.

Literature Time

Discuss It: **WRITING ASSIGNMENT 43**

What did you learn about Henry Wadsworth Longfellow in your writing assignment?

Did you discover anything about Henry Wadsworth Longfellow's life that could have influenced him to write "Paul Revere's Ride"?

Give your report about Henry Wadsworth Longfellow to your teacher to be placed in a class booklet. This booklet will be available to you for checkout so you may enjoy the research that was done.

Share It: **WRITING ASSIGNMENT 42**

You have several ways of sharing your poem.

1. You may share your poem aloud.
2. You may have your poem put in the class poetry booklet for everyone to read.
3. You may give your poem to your teacher.

If you do not want to display your poem in the class booklet, you must write "return" in the lower right corner of your paper. It will be returned in a few days. The poems in the class booklet will be returned before the end of the school year. This will give everyone a chance to read and enjoy the poems.

Across the Curriculum

Science/Math/Social Studies/Poetry/Music Connection:

1. Get into small groups. Each group will select a paragraph in a science, math, or social studies book that contains several facts. Using the facts, write a poem. Use rhyme and rhythm in your poem. You can also use a musical tune from a song you know to help you write your poem. Recite, rap, or sing the poem for the other groups.

2. Create a "Live Poets Society" to write and share future poems.

Writing Time

Learn It: RESEARCH REPORT WRITING

Today, you will learn how to write a research report, using a five-paragraph format. There are certain steps you need to follow in order to make writing a report easy and interesting. In this chapter, you will learn the steps of writing a report. First, you will study references that cover the basic guidelines for each step. These are the same steps you will use when you write an independent report in the next chapter.

✏ Reference 214	Steps for Writing a Research Report

When you are assigned a report, you will gather information about your topic. This search for information is called **research**. In doing this research, you will learn facts and details about a specific subject that you did not know before.

Then, you will organize these facts and details into a clear, well-written report. By writing a report, you are sharing with others the information you have learned.

There are twelve steps you will follow in order to research a topic and write a report.

Step 1: Select and narrow a topic.

Step 2: Select the main points.

Step 3: Select sources by skimming.

Step 4: Make a bibliography card for each source selected.

Step 5: Take notes on note cards.

Step 6: Organize note cards.

Step 7: Write an outline from the information on note cards.

Step 8: Write a rough draft, using the outline.

Step 9: Revise and edit the rough draft.

Step 10: Write the final outline.

Step 11: Write the final report from the revised and edited rough draft.

Step 12: Put the final report and all related research work in the correct order.

(**Note:** Write everything in pencil except your final outline and report.)

Lesson 1

You will

- read and discuss research report writing.
- read and discuss The Topic Guide.
- read and discuss Steps 1–2 in a research report:
  — Select and narrow a topic.
  — Select main points.

Learn It: THE TOPIC GUIDE

 Reference 215 | **The Topic Guide**

When you choose a topic, visualizing different topic areas can help. The Topic Guide provides different topic categories with main-point ideas for each one. It will help you choose and narrow a topic, select main points about a topic, and organize the information gathered about a topic.

For the body of your report, you may choose three different main points, or you may choose one point and expand it into three or more main points.

TOPIC CATEGORY FOR PEOPLE
Introduction: First paragraph
Body: Choose three or more main points
1. Childhood
2. Adult life
3. People or events that influenced his/her life
4. Accomplishments
5. Characteristics
6. Unusual/interesting facts
7. Think of your own main point to fit the topic.
Conclusion: Last paragraph

TOPIC CATEGORY FOR ANIMALS
Introduction: First paragraph
Body: Choose three or more main points
1. Habitat (where it lives)
2. Physical characteristics (what it looks like)
3. Usual and/or unusual behaviors
4. What it eats and how it gets its food
5. Enemies
6. Interesting or little known facts
7. Think of your own main point to fit the topic.
Conclusion: Last paragraph

TOPIC CATEGORY FOR THINGS
Introduction: First paragraph
Body: Choose three or more main points
1. Physical appearance, makeup, or identification (size, shape, looks, texture, weight, color, etc.)
2. Can it be classified into different groups?
3. Important characteristics or uses
4. Unusual and interesting facts
5. Does it change with time?
6. Think of your own main point to fit the topic.
Conclusion: Last paragraph

TOPIC CATEGORY FOR PLACES
Introduction: First paragraph
   Include the location. Is it real or imaginary?
Body: Choose three or more main points
1. Famous landmarks
2. Physical characteristics and climate
3. History or interesting facts
4. People and/or animals that live there
5. Major industries, products, and services
6. Think of your own main point to fit the topic.
Conclusion: Last paragraph

TOPIC CATEGORY FOR A PROCESS
A process is how something is done or made.
Introduction: First paragraph
   Identify the process.
   Identify why the process is necessary.
Body: Choose the main points
   List the steps you must take in order to complete the process in the most logical order.
Conclusion: Last paragraph

TOPIC CATEGORY FOR AN EVENT
Introduction: First paragraph
   What was the event?
   When and where did the event occur?
   Who or what was involved in the event?
Body: Choose three or more main points
1. Reasons why the event occurred
2. What was the effect of the event?
3. Widespread importance of the event
4. Think of your own main point to fit the topic.
Conclusion: Last paragraph

TOPIC CATEGORY FOR OPINIONS
To write an opinion research report, follow the five-paragraph-persuasive-essay outline.
Introduction: First paragraph
Body: Main points
1. First point and supporting sentences
2. Second point and supporting sentences
3. Third point and supporting sentences
Conclusion: Last paragraph

TOPIC CATEGORY FOR IDEAS
Introduction: First paragraph
   Include facts and definitions.
Body: Main points
1. Reasons
2. Examples
3. Think of your own main point to fit the topic.
Conclusion: Last paragraph

Learn It: **STEP 1: SELECT AND NARROW A TOPIC**

 Reference 216 ## (Step 1) Select and Narrow a Topic

In order to choose a topic, look over the topic categories in your Topic Guide in Reference 215. The topic categories are people, things, animals, places, processes, events, opinions, and ideas. Then, choose the topic category that you want to explore. As you can see, each topic category covers a large amount of information. This means the topics are too broad. When a topic is too broad, you need to narrow it. To narrow the topic means to reduce or limit it. No matter which topic category you choose, it must be narrowed. The scenario below shows one way a topic was narrowed.

First, the writer looked at all the topic categories in the Topic Guide and chose the category **Animals** for his broad writing topic. The writer knew the topic category he chose had to be narrowed. He thought about all the different kinds of animals and decided that he wanted to know more about wild animals. However, he knew that the narrowed topic, **Wild Animals**, was still too broad because there were too many wild animals to write about. So, he chose one group of wild animals, **Wolves**, as his further narrowed topic. Now that the topic was narrowed to a specific animal, the writer needed to narrow the topic one last time because the topic, Wolves, was still too broad. Before the writer could select a final narrowed topic, he returned to the Topic Guide and chose the three main points he wanted to present in his report. The selection of these points helped the writer finalize his narrowed topic, **The Ways of Wolves**.

Topic Category: Animals

Narrowed Topic: Wild Animals

Further Narrowed Topic: Wolves

Final Narrowed Topic: The Ways of Wolves

Learn It: **STEP 2: SELECT THE MAIN POINTS**

 Reference 217 ## (Step 2) Select the Main Points

To select the main points, look at the choices listed under the category selected in the Topic Guide. Choose three separate points, or choose one point and expand it into three points. The scenario below shows one way the main points were selected.

First, the writer looked at the seven main points listed in the Topic Guide under the category for **Animals**. Each point listed a specific area about animals. The writer could either choose three separate points, or he could choose only one and expand it into three points. The writer decided to choose three separate points. The writer then made his final choice for a narrowed topic: **The Ways of Wolves**.

Main Points:

1. **Living Areas of Wolves**
2. **Physical Characteristics of Wolves**
3. **Social Behavior of Wolves**

The writer now has a final narrowed topic and has selected three main points for his report. His next step will be to look up information about the Living Areas of Wolves, the Physical Characteristics of Wolves, and Social Behavior of Wolves so he can determine if these points are the ones he wants to develop and support in the body of his report.

Your topic choices may go through many changes as you determine the direction of your report. If you cannot find enough interesting information about your final narrowed topic, go back to the Topic Guide and choose other points to write about. If you change your points, you must remember to change your final narrowed topic.

START LESSON 2

Lesson 2

You will

- read and discuss main sources used to research a topic.
- read and discuss Steps 3-4 in a research report:
  — Select sources by skimming.
  — Make bibliography cards.
- write in your journal.

Writing Time

Learn It: **MAIN SOURCES USED TO RESEARCH A TOPIC**

There are four main sources that you have available when you research a topic for a report. They are encyclopedias, the Internet, books, and magazines.

📖 Reference 218	**Main Sources Used to Research a Topic**

AN ENCYCLOPEDIA SOURCE

Encyclopedias are always good sources for reports because they give you a general introduction to your topic, along with specific details. Encyclopedia articles on your narrowed topic are usually easy to find because they are listed alphabetically. However, if you cannot find your narrowed topic in an encyclopedia, you may need to look under a broader topic.

> **Example: Narrowed topic:** Wolves; **Broader topic:** Wild Animals

Before you leave your first encyclopedia article, check the end of that article for a list of related encyclopedia articles that also match your topic. This list will be helpful whether you use the first article or not. Always check the publication date when using an encyclopedia. Depending on the nature of the topic, material in an older encyclopedia could be outdated. Most current encyclopedias are also available in CD-ROM format in public libraries.

THE INTERNET AS A SOURCE

Most libraries provide access to the Internet through computers. Computers provide an excellent way for you to search for different types of information. If you have a computer and access to the Internet, you can do on-line searches to find information about a specific topic. To find information through an on-line search engine, type in a key word, phrase, or topic. If a key word is too general, it may provide a list of articles that is too broad for your topic. Check Internet sources carefully to make sure they are reliable. *(For example, is the site or author associated with a college, university, or other credible organization? Does the site include links to other reliable documents?)* As you find information you can use, write down the source of that information just as you would for a book. If possible, print the information. It is also a good idea to write the date on which you found the information since information on the Internet can change daily.

A BOOK SOURCE

Books can give details about your narrowed topic. Use the card catalog in the library to find books related to your topic. Then, use the book's index and table of contents to find the information you need. Review the table of contents to get an overall picture of what the book is about. If you see any chapter titles that relate to your topic, skim the pages in those chapters. Also, look in the index for information related to your topic. Then, look on the specific pages listed in the index to see if the information can be used. It is usually not necessary to read the whole book in order to locate specific information about your topic.

Continued on next page. >>>

Reference 218 continued from previous page.

A MAGAZINE SOURCE

Magazine articles can also give you details about your topic. Use the *Readers' Guide to Periodical Literature* to find magazine articles related to your topic. Magazine articles are listed alphabetically by topic and by author. Some entries have cross-references (marked See or See also) that will help you find related articles. Since periodical materials cannot be checked out, you may need to ask the librarian for assistance.

For more information about using an encyclopedia, the Internet, books, and magazines as sources for a report, see the Resource Tools Section on pages 524–528, 532.

Learn It: **STEP 3: SELECT SOURCES BY SKIMMING**

Reference 219   (Step 3) Select Sources by Skimming

1. **Skimming** is reading only the key parts of a source to determine quickly if that source has information that will fit the narrowed topic and main points you have selected from the Topic Guide.

2. Skim key parts, such as titles, topic headings in boldface type, first sentences of paragraphs, underlining, captions under pictures, text outlined by boxes, questions, and summaries.

3. The best way to skim several paragraphs in a longer article is to read all of the first paragraph because it usually contains a brief summary of the article. Then, read only the first sentence of each paragraph in the body of the article. This will give you a brief summary of each paragraph. Finally, read all of the last paragraph because it restates the most important points.

4. As you skim an article, consider these things: Does this information contain enough facts about your narrowed topic and main points? Is the information interesting enough to use in your report? Is the information presented clearly, and is it easy to understand?

5. Skimming a source will quickly help you decide if the source can be used. If the source has enough information about your narrowed topic and main points, then it **can be used**. If the source does not have enough information about your narrowed topic and main points, then it **should not be used**. If, after skimming several sources, you cannot find enough information about the final narrowed topic and main points, you need to go back to the Topic Guide and choose new main points. Be aware that this could change your final narrowed topic. If you still cannot find enough information, you may need to choose a different topic and select three or more main points for the new topic.

Learn It: **STEP 4: MAKE BIBLIOGRAPHY CARDS**

Reference 220   (Step 4) Make a Bibliography Card for Each Source Selected

As soon as you decide to use an article in an encyclopedia, a book, the Internet, or a magazine, immediately make a bibliography card that records specific, detailed information about that source. You will later use your bibliography cards to make a bibliography page for your report.

The **bibliography** page gives credit to the sources actually used in your report and tells others where they can find information on your subject. This is done even if you have only one source. The directions below tell you how to record bibliographic information from each of the four types of sources. The examples show you how each card is arranged and punctuated.

- **Book:** To record a book source on your bibliography card, write the name of the author(s), the title of the book, the city where the book is published, the publisher, and the date of publication.

Continued on next page. >>>

Reference 220 continued from previous page.

- **Encyclopedia:** To record an encyclopedia source on your bibliography card, write the name of the author(s) (if given), the title of the article, the name of the encyclopedia, and the edition date of the encyclopedia.
- **Internet:** To record an Internet source on your bibliography card, write the name of the author(s) (if given), the title of the page or article, the name of the web site, the date posted/revised, and the name of the organization associated with the web site. Next, include the day, month, and year you looked up the information. Finally, write the electronic address.
- **Magazine:** To record a magazine source on your bibliography card, write the name of the author(s); the title of the article; the name of the magazine; the day, the month, and the year of publication; and the page number(s).

Bibliography Card (Book)	Bibliography Card (Internet)
The Complete Book of Animals. Grand Rapids, Michigan: American Education Publishing, 2004.	"Just the Facts." wolf.org. 1995/2006. International Wolf Center. Jan. 2001. http://www.wolf.org/wolves/learn/justkids/kids.asp

Bibliography Card (Encyclopedia)	Bibliography Card (Magazine)
"Wolves." Encyclopedia Britannica Ultimate Reference Suite CD-ROM. 2004 ed.	Line, Les. "Watching Wolves On a Wild Ride." National Wildlife Dec/Jan 2001: 10-18.

>>>>>>>>>>>>>>>>>>>>>> **Student Tip...**

JOURNAL WRITING 48

Write an entry in your journal. Use Reference 9 on page 12 for ideas.

1. Use colored index cards to record your bibliography sources. This makes it easy to distinguish them from the white note cards you will make in the next lesson.

2. For a review of the library, computer terminology, and the Internet, refer to the Resource Tools Section on pages 524–525, 532–535.

English Made Easy

Writing Time

Learn It: **STEP 5: TAKE NOTES**

Lesson 3

You will
- read and discuss Steps 5–6 in a research report:
  — Take notes.
  — Organize note cards.
- write in your journal.

✎* **Reference 221** **(Step 5) Take Notes**

Notes are recorded information that is written in your own words by using words and phrases. Write your notes on note cards and use a different note card for each set of facts you record. Later, when you get to the outlining step of your report, it will be easier to shuffle and rearrange the order of your information by shifting the order of the cards. The directions below will guide you as you take notes.

1. INTRODUCTION

Write the word *Introduction-1* at the top of a note card. On the first **introduction** note card, write words or phrases that tell what your report is about. Write the word *Introduction-2* at the top of another note card. On the second **introduction** note card, list extra information or a definition that tells more about the topic.

2. BODY

Write a 1st and the first **main-point heading** at the top of several note cards. Write words or phrases that support your first main point on each of these cards. Write only one or two notes on each card.

Write a 2nd and the second **main-point heading** at the top of several note cards. Write words or phrases that support your second main point on each of these cards. Write only one or two notes on each card.

Write a 3rd and the third **main-point heading** at the top of several note cards. Write words or phrases that support your third main point on each of these cards. Write only one or two notes on each card.

3. CONCLUSION

Write the word *Conclusion-1* at the top of a note card. On the first **conclusion** note card, write words or phrases that describe your topic again. Write the word *Conclusion-2* at the top of another note card. On the second *Conclusion-2* note card, write supporting facts, opinions, or quotations that help you summarize the conclusions that you have drawn from your research.

Writing Notes

- As you take your notes, start at the beginning of the article and work to the end. If the information you are reading does not support a main point, keep moving through the source.

- Put the information you write on your note cards *in your own words*. Put only one note from a source on a note card.

- Write your notes in **phrases**, not complete sentences. A good way to do this is to read the information, set your source aside, and then write the information on your note cards as you remember it.

- At the bottom of every note card, write the author's last name and the page number where the information is found. You will use this information in the body of your report as you acknowledge your sources. If no author is given, write the name of the source and the page number.

📖 **Reference 222**   **Sample Note Cards**

Introduction-1   1

member of dog family
Known for intelligence and courage
appears in many stories,
symbols of strength and courage

Encyclopedia Britannica, p. 1

Introduction-2   2

carnivores - eat other animals
earned bad reputation as hunters
hunt in packs

A Complete Book of Animals, p. 38

1st Main Point - Living Areas   3

home called a lair or den
usually a cave, hollow, fallen tree
trunk, group of rocks

Encyclopedia Britannica, p. 1

1st Main Point - Living Areas   4

United States: western, southwestern
region
Great Lakes area
Alaska

Encyclopedia Britannica, p. 1

1st Main Point - Living Areas   5

Other: Canada, Balkans, Russia,
Scandinavia, and
Southern Europe

Encyclopedia Britannica, p. 1

2nd Main Point - Physical Features   6

Looks: large feet, narrow chest,
broad head
similar to dog but longer legs
and bigger paws powerfully built
Soft, very thick, long fur
to keep warm

Encyclopedia Britannica, p. 1

2nd Main Point - Physical Features   7

Size: height - 32 inches at shoulder
weight - 44 to 175 pounds for males
length - 6½ feet long

Encyclopedia Britannica, p. 1

2nd Main Point - Physical Features   8

senses of smell, hearing, and eyesight
very good hears sounds 10 miles away

A Complete Book of Animals, p. 35

3rd Main Point - Social Behavior   9

live in family group called a pack
6-20 wolves
purpose of pack is to hunt together
and raise pups
protective and loyal

A Complete Book of Animals, p. 36

3rd Main Point - Social Behavior   10

pack has male and female adult
parents called alpha pair

Encyclopedia Britannica, p. 2

3rd Main Point - Social Behavior   11

pack also has offspring of alpha pair
litter of pups usually 6-7
older offspring that stay as "helpers"

Encyclopedia Britannica, p. 2

3rd Main Point - Social Behavior   12

hunting for food
territory of 40 to 400 square miles
eat large and small animals deer, moose,
caribou, squirrels, rabbits, some plants

Encyclopedia Britannica, p. 2

3rd Main Point - Social Behavior   13

hunting for food done as a group
at night

Encyclopedia Britannica, p. 2

3rd Main Point - Social Behavior   14

hunting for food
chase prey at speeds up to
40 miles per hour
surround prey when its tired

A Complete Book of Animals, p. 38

3rd Main Point - Social Behavior   15

rearing of young
newborn pups nurse milk from
mother, mother fed by pack
3+ week old pups fed regurgitated
meat from pack adults

Encyclopedia Britannica, p. 2

3rd Main Point - Social Behavior   16

rearing of young
trained to hunt by pack
some leave lair when young adult
some choose to stay and be
"helpers"

Encyclopedia Britannica, p. 2

Conclusion-1   17

attack livestock, such as cattle,
sheep, and goats so many killed by
humans, almost extinct efforts made
in last several decades to protect

Encyclopedia Britannica, p. 2

Conclusion-2   18

curious, intelligent, loyal animals
loving toward their pack

A Complete Book of Animals, p. 36

English Made Easy

Learn It: **STEP 6: ORGANIZE NOTE CARDS**

Reference 223 — (Step 6) Organize Note Cards

Once you have finished your reading and note-taking, the next step is to organize the note cards. Follow the directions below to help you.

1. Since you have written the introduction, main points, and conclusion at the top of your note cards, most of your information is already organized.

2. Now, sort your note cards into piles according to the titles at the top of the note cards. You should have five piles: introduction, first main point, second main point, third main point, and conclusion.

3. Arrange the introduction note cards in the correct order for your report. Then, write **Paragraph 1** on the back of each card.

4. Next, decide if you want to keep the order of the main points that you have written on your note cards. Renumber and rearrange the cards, if necessary.

5. Arrange the note cards within each main point in a logical order for your report.

6. On the note cards for each main point, write **Paragraph 2** on the back of the first main-point cards, **Paragraph 3** on the back of the second main-point cards, and **Paragraph 4** on the back of the third main-point cards.

7. Arrange the conclusion note cards in the correct order for your report. Then, write **Paragraph 5** on the back of each card.

8. Finally, number all your note cards (1, 2, 3, 4, etc.) in the upper right hand corner to prevent them from getting out of order. Put the bibliography card(s) at the end.

9. Store all note cards in a plastic zip bag. You will use these note cards to complete **Step 7, Write an Outline**. You will hand in your note cards with your final report.

JOURNAL WRITING 49

Write an entry in your journal. Use Reference 9 on page 12 for ideas.

START LESSON 4

Lesson 4

You will

- read and discuss Step 7 in a research report:
  — Write an outline.

⏱ Writing Time

Learn It: **STEP 7: WRITE AN OUTLINE**

Once you have organized your note cards, you are ready to make an outline. Remember that an outline is your road map. You must constantly check your outline to make adjustments and to make sure you keep focused on the narrowed topic of your report.

Reference 224   **(Step 7) Write an Outline**

An **outline** is a concisely written list of the information on your note cards in the order it will be presented in your report. To make an outline for your report, you must use the note cards that you have already organized. You will put your notes from the note cards into correct outline form. Keep in mind that you may not use all of your notes as you make your outline. *(See References 202–203 on pages 442–443 for outline examples.)*

Use the information below to guide you as you make your outline.

1. **Title.** Write your outline title on the top line of your paper. It should be the same or similar to your narrowed topic.

2. **Details for the introduction.** Look at the notes on the note cards titled Introduction. Using these notes, write at least three phrases for the introductory paragraph. The first phrase will tell what your report is about. The other phrases will give extra information or a definition that tells more about the topic.

3. **Main Points.** Next, find the note cards titled *1st (main point), 2nd (main point),* and *3rd (main point).* Write the main points in parallel form on your outline. Put a Roman numeral beside each main point, capitalize the first word, and skip several lines after each main point to give you room to write the rest of your outline.

4. **Subtopics or details for the first main point.** Look at the note cards titled *1st (main point).* Write the notes that support the first main topic as subtopics A., B., C., etc. Under each subtopic, list any details from your notes that support it as 1., 2., 3. Write the subtopics (A., B., C.) and details (1., 2., 3.) in parallel form.

5. **Subtopics or details for the second main point.** Look at the note cards titled *2nd (main point).* Write the notes that support the second main topic as subtopics A., B., C., etc. Under each subtopic, list any details from your notes that support it as 1., 2., 3. Write the subtopics (A., B., C.) and details (1., 2., 3.) in parallel form.

6. **Subtopics or details for the third main point.** Look at the note cards titled *3rd (main point).* Write the notes that support the third main topic as subtopics A., B., C., etc. Under each subtopic, list any details from your notes that support it as 1., 2., 3. Write the subtopics (A., B., C.) and details (1., 2., 3.) in parallel form.

7. **Details for the conclusion.** Look at the notes on the note cards titled Conclusion. Using these notes, write at least two phrases for the concluding paragraph. The first phrase restates or supports the information in the introduction. The other phrases give supporting facts, opinions, or quotations to help summarize the conclusions you have drawn from your research.

Discuss It:

Sometimes, there is too much information on the note cards to include in your report. When that happens, you must decide which information you want to use and which you should discard. When you get ready to write your rough draft, you will write from your outline, not from your note cards.

Now, look at Reference 225. This is the report outline that was made from the notes about wolves. Some of the information on some of the note cards was left out when the outline was made. The information left out of the outline will not be used in the report. For example, none of the information on two cards was used. Can you find the two cards that were not used at all?

Also, on three of the note cards, only part of the information was left out of the outline. What detail was left out on note card 6? What detail was left out on note card 7? What detail was left out on note card 15? Since none of this information was put in the outline, it will not be mentioned in the report.

Continued on next page. >>>

Also, notice how the topics and subtopics on the outline have been lined up and how they have been made parallel. This is the standard outline form that you should follow every time you make an outline.

Reference 225 — Example of an Outline

The Ways of Wolves
Introduction
    Are intelligent members of the dog family
    Are carnivorous, hunt in packs, and earn bad reputation by killing livestock
    Portrayed as strong and courageous
    Have definite living areas, physical characteristics, and social behavior

I. Living areas of wolves
  A. Location
    1. United States (western and southwestern regions, Alaska, Great Lakes area)
    2. Other (Canada, Balkans, Russia, Scandinavia, southern Europe)
  B. Home
    1. Lair or den
    2. Caves, fallen tree trunks, holes in ground, or rocks
II. Physical characteristics of wolves
  A. Looks
    1. Similar to dog but larger paws and longer legs
    2. Long, thick fur to keep warm
  B. Size
    1. Height—32 inches at shoulder
    2. Weight—44 to 175 pounds for males
III. Social behavior of wolves
  A. Living in a pack (family group of 6–20 wolves)
    1. Male and female parents (alpha pair)
    2. Offspring of varying ages (litter of 6–7 pups, plus older "helpers")
    3. Purpose of pack (hunt together and raise pups)
  B. Hunting for food
    1. Territory range of 40 to 400 square miles
    2. Large and small animals (deer, moose, caribou, rabbits, squirrels)
  C. Rearing young
    1. Fed meat and trained to hunt
    2. May leave pack when young adult

Conclusion
    Threatened with extinction because people kill them to protect livestock
    Developed understanding of their living areas, physical characteristics, and social behaviors
    Protected by laws and are flourishing

START LESSON 5

Lesson 5

You will

- read and discuss Step 8 in a research report:
  — Write a rough draft.

Writing Time

Write It: **STEP 8: WRITE A ROUGH DRAFT**

📝 **Reference 226** **(Step 8) Write a Rough Draft**

With your outline before you, you are ready to write your rough draft. There are several things you need to do to write the rough draft of your research report.

- Follow the order of your outline.
- If you decide to include another main topic or eliminate a main topic, stop and use your note cards to reorganize the outline.
- Remember, your outline is the "visual map" of your report. It will keep you going in the right direction. Keep it up-to-date.
- You should **use your own words in your report** as you present facts and give examples. This will make your paper special because no one writes quite like you.

1. Your report will be a five-paragraph report. You will have an introductory paragraph, three paragraphs in the body (a paragraph for each of the main points), and a concluding paragraph. Use a pencil and skip every other line on your notebook paper.

2. **Paragraph 1: Introduction.** Look at the introduction on your outline and write at least three sentences for the introductory paragraph. The first sentence is a topic sentence that tells what your report is about. Remember to indent this sentence because it is the first sentence of the paragraph. The next sentences give extra information, a definition, or a quotation that tells more about the topic.

3. **Paragraph 2: 1st Main Point.** Look at the first main point on your outline (Roman numeral I.) Write a topic sentence that states the first main point and that tells what the paragraph is about. Remember to indent this sentence because it is the first sentence of the paragraph. Then, using the subtopics and details in the outline, write complete sentences that support this main point. Make sure these sentences are arranged in the same order as they appear in the outline.

4. **Paragraph 3: 2nd Main Point.** Look at the second main point on your outline (Roman numeral II.) Write a topic sentence that states the second main point and that tells what the paragraph is about. Remember to indent this sentence because it is the first sentence of the paragraph. Then, using the subtopics and details in the outline, write complete sentences that support this main point. Make sure these sentences are arranged in the same order as they appear in the outline.

5. **Paragraph 4: 3rd Main Point.** Look at the third main point on your outline (Roman numeral III.) Write a topic sentence that states the third main point and that tells what the paragraph is about. Remember to indent this sentence because it is the first sentence of the paragraph. Then, using the subtopics and details in the outline, write complete sentences that support this main point. Make sure these sentences are arranged in the same order as they appear in the outline.

6. **Paragraph 5: Conclusion.** Look at the conclusion on your outline and write at least two sentences for the concluding paragraph. The first sentence is a concluding general statement that restates or supports the information in the introduction. Remember to indent this sentence because it is the first sentence of the paragraph. The next sentence or sentences use facts, opinions or quotations to summarize the conclusions that you have drawn from your research.

Continued on next page. >>>

Reference 226 continued from previous page.

7. **Title Page.** The title page will be the **first page** of your report. Make a title page, using the following information: Write neatly in ink. Skip three lines from the top line. On the fourth line, center and write the title of your report. Skip three more lines. Then, on the next line, center and write **By** *(your name)*. Skip three more lines, and on the next line, center and write **For** *(your teacher's name)*. On the next line, under the teacher's name, write the date the report is due.

8. **Bibliography Page or Works Cited Page.** At the end of your report, you will use your bibliography cards to list all the encyclopedias, books, articles, and Internet sources **that you actually used** to write your report. The bibliography will be the **last page** of your report. Write neatly in ink. On the top line, center and write **Bibliography**, skip two lines, then copy the information from your bibliography cards to your notebook paper.

   These entries should be listed in alphabetical order, according to the last name of the author. *(Note: In the example below, the article from the encyclopedia does not have an author listed. In this case, you should use the first word of the article title.)*

   Do not number the sources on the bibliography page. Use a "hanging indent" when an entry's information wraps to a second line. "Hanging indent" means to indent the information on the second and additional lines five to seven spaces.

9. **Citations Within Your Report.** Within the text of your report, you must acknowledge any paraphrased idea or quotation that you have borrowed from someone else. Even if you have summarized the information in your own words, you are still using another person's idea and must include a citation. The only information that does not have to be cited is your own personal opinion, or original ideas, or well-known facts.

   To cite a source, place the author's last name and the page number where the information was found in parentheses at the end of each sentence. If several sentences in a row contain information from the same source, acknowledgement need only appear at the end of the last sentence.

   Example: (Britannica 1).

Example of a Bibliography Page

BIBLIOGRAPHY

The Complete Book of Animals. Grand Rapids, Michigan: American
    Education Publishing, 2004.

"Wolves." Encyclopedia Britannica Ultimate Reference Suite CD-ROM.
    2004 ed.

START LESSON 6

Lesson 6

You will

- read and discuss Steps 9–12 in a research report:
  - Revise and edit your rough draft.
  - Write final outline.
  - Write the final report.
  - Put final report and all related research work in the correct order.
- write in your journal.

Writing Time

Write It: **STEP 9: REVISE AND EDIT THE ROUGH DRAFT**

Reference 227   **(Step 9) Revise & Edit the Rough Draft**

Revision and editing are part of the writing process. During the revision and editing, use References 51 and 53 on pages 69, 71. As you revise and edit your paper, make sure you check for good organization, for clear and logical development of ideas, and for general statements supported by details and examples. After you revise and edit your rough draft, ask at least one more person to edit it. The final responsibility for revision and editing, however, is yours. A quick review is provided below to help you do a final proofreading of your report.

1. Is the first line of each paragraph indented?
2. Does your paper have an introduction, a body, and a conclusion?
3. Does each supporting sentence develop the main idea in each of the main-point paragraphs?
4. Do your main points and supporting sentences follow the order of your outline?
5. Have you capitalized and punctuated your sentences correctly?
6. Have you spelled each word correctly?
7. Have you read your report orally to see how it sounds?
8. Have you checked for sentence fragments and run-on sentences?
9. Are your sentences varied to avoid monotony?
10. Have you completed a title page, an outline, and a bibliography?

Learn It: **STEP 10: WRITE THE FINAL OUTLINE**

Reference 228   **(Step 10) Write the Final Outline**

Check over your first outline to see if there are any revisions necessary after writing and editing the rough draft of your report. Make any necessary changes. Then, write your final outline neatly in ink. Both outlines will be handed in with your final report.

Learn It: **STEP 11: WRITE THE FINAL REPORT**

Reference 229   **(Step 11) Write the Final Report**

Before you recopy your edited rough draft for your final paper, reread your report and make any necessary changes. Also, decide if you want to include illustrations or visual aids with your final report. If so, they must be completed at this time. Then, write your final report neatly. Finally, proofread your final paper again.

Discuss It:

Reference 230 | **Example of a Final Report**

The Ways of Wolves

Wolves are highly intelligent and courageous members of the dog family (Britannica 1). Because they are carnivorous, or meat-eaters, and hunt in packs, they have sometimes had a bad reputation with humans because packs would attack and kill livestock (A Complete Book 36). However, many stories have been written that portray the wolf as loyal and intelligent family members (Britannica 1). The more we learn about wolves, the better we can appreciate their ways.

Wolves live in many areas around the world. In the United States, wolves are found in the forests of the western and southwestern regions, in the Great Lakes area, and in Alaska. Wolves are also found in Canada, the Balkans, Russia, Scandinavia, and southern Europe. A wolf home is called a lair, or den. It can be made from a cave, a fallen tree trunk, a large hole dug in the ground, or a group of rocks (Britannica 1).

The physical characteristics of wolves are very similar to those of dogs. Wolves have bigger paws and longer legs than dogs. They also have thicker and longer fur to keep them warm. Wolves can be 32 inches tall at the shoulder, and males can weigh 44 to 175 pounds (Britannica 1).

The social behavior of wolves is probably their most interesting characteristic. Wolves live in a family group called a pack. A pack can have from 6 to 20 wolves in it (A Complete Book 36). The male and female parents, called the alpha pair, and their offspring make up the pack. The offspring are various ages, ranging from pups to older "helpers" (Britannica 2). The purpose of the pack is to hunt together and to raise the pups. When wolves hunt, they have a territory of 40 to 400 square miles. They hunt large and small animals, such as deer, moose, caribou, rabbits, and squirrels. All adults in the pack are responsible for raising the young litter. Adults bring the young pups meat and train them to hunt as they get older. Stronger, more independent adult wolves usually choose to leave home to form their own pack (Britannica 2).

Wolves around the world have been threatened with extinction because people kill them to protect their livestock. As we learn more about the unique ways of wolves, we have developed an understanding of their living areas, and social behaviors. In the past fifty years, laws have been passed to protect wolves from extinction (Britannica 2). Now, wolves are once again living and flourishing in forests around the world.

Learn It: **STEP 12: PUT THE FINAL REPORT AND ALL RELATED RESEARCH WORK IN THE CORRECT ORDER.**

Reference 231 | **(Step 12) Put the Final Report and All Related Research Papers in the Correct Order**

1. Title page (in ink or typed)
2. Final report (in ink or typed)
3. Illustrations and visual aids (optional)
4. Bibliography page (in ink or typed)
5. Final outline (in ink or typed)
6. Rough draft (in pencil)
7. First outline (in pencil)
8. Note cards and bibliography cards (Put all cards in a plastic zip bag.)
9. Hand in final report and all related papers when your teacher calls for them.

JOURNAL WRITING 50

Write an entry in your journal. Use Reference 9 on page 12 for ideas.

START LESSON 7

Lesson 7

You will

- review Steps 1-12 in writing a research report.
- write an evaluation essay for WA 44.

Writing Time

Write It: EVALUATING THE STEPS IN A RESEARCH REPORT

Write an evaluation of the steps used in writing a report. Look at Writing Assignment 44. The writing prompt tells you the points to include in your evaluation.

Writing Assignment [44]

Purpose: To evaluate the steps used in writing a research report

Type of Writing: Evaluation essay

Audience: Classmates or teacher

Writing Prompt:

Use at least three of the questions below to help you write your evaluation of the steps in a report.

1. Which steps did you find most useful and why?

2. Which steps did you find most difficult and why?

3. Would you add, delete, or change the order of any of the steps? Explain your reasoning.

4. Do you think you can write a report by following these steps? Why or why not?

Special Instructions:

1. Write in first person. See Reference 71 on page 108.
   (First-person pronouns are I, me, my, mine, we, us, our, and ours.)

2. Write in complete sentences.

3. Write your evaluation in paragraph form.

Note: Reference 214 on page 475 gives the steps for writing a research report.

English Made Easy

Writing Time

Learn It: **SCHEDULE FOR AN INDEPENDENT RESEARCH REPORT**

Today, you will begin working on your independent research report. Look at Reference 232. This reference gives you the schedule you will follow as you work on your report.

This is Day 1, and you will do Steps 1–3. First, you must select and narrow a topic. Your topic choices are listed in Writing Assignment 45.

✐* **Reference 232**	**Schedule for an Independent Research Report**

DAY 1 Use References 214-219 on pages 475-479.

Step 1: Select and narrow a topic.

Step 2: Select the main points.

Step 3: Select sources by skimming.

DAY 2 Use Reference 220 on page 479.

Step 4: Make a bibliography card for each source selected.

DAY 3 Use References 221-222 on pages 481-482.

Step 5: Take notes.

DAY 4 Use References 223-225 on pages 483-485.

Step 6: Organize note cards.

Step 7: Write a first-draft outline.

DAY 5 Use Reference 226 on page 486.

Step 8: Write a rough draft.

DAY 6 Use References 227-228 on page 488.

Step 9: Revise and edit the rough draft.

Step 10: Write the final outline.

DAY 7 Use References 229-231 on pages 488-489.

Step 11: Write the final report.

Step 12: Put the final report and all related research work in the correct order.

(**Note:** Make sure you write everything, except your final outline and report, in pencil.)

DAY 8 Share and Evaluate

DAY 9 Share and Evaluate

Lesson 1

You will

- read and discuss the schedule for writing an independent research report.
- apply Steps 1-3 for research report (WA 45):
  — Select and narrow a topic.
  — Select main points.
  — Select sources by skimming.

Write It: INDEPENDENT REPORT WRITING 45

Writing Assignment 45

Purpose: To inform

Type of Writing: Independent report

Audience: Classmates

Choose and narrow one of the report topics below.

1. A city, state, or country
2. A famous person (scientist, inventor, entertainer, etc.)
3. A musical instrument (woodwind, brass, percussion, string, etc.)
4. An interesting or unusual animal
5. A famous American
6. A sport (a team sport or an individual sport)
7. A current event or issue

Special Instructions:

1. Use References 214–232 on pages 475–491 to help you write your independent report.
2. Use standard, time-order, or transition writing form.
   See Reference 70 on page 107.
3. Write in third person. See Reference 71 on page 108.
   (Third-person pronouns: *he, his, him, she, her, hers, it, its, they, their, theirs, and them.*)

End of Lesson 1

START LESSON 2

Lesson 2

You will

- apply Step 4 for research report (WA 45):
  - Make a bibliography card for each source.

End of Lesson 2

Write It: INDEPENDENT RESEARCH REPORT WRITING 45

Use the schedule in Reference 232 on page 491 as you continue working on your independent report. This is Day 2, and you will do do Step 4.

START LESSON 3

Lesson 3

You will

- apply Step 5 for research report (WA 45):
  - Take notes.

Write It: INDEPENDENT RESEARCH REPORT WRITING 45

Use the schedule in Reference 232 on page 491 as you continue working on your independent report. This is Day 3, and you will do Step 5.

End of Lesson 3

Writing Time

Write It: **INDEPENDENT RESEARCH REPORT WRITING 45**

Use the schedule in Reference 232 on page 491 as you continue working on your independent report. This is Day 4, and you will do Steps 6–7.

Lesson 4

You will

- apply Steps 6-7 for research report (WA 45):
  - Organize note cards.
  - Write a first-draft outline.

End of Lesson 4

Writing Time

Write It: **INDEPENDENT RESEARCH REPORT WRITING 45**

Use the schedule in Reference 232 on page 491 as you continue working on your independent report. This is Day 5, and you will do Step 8.

Lesson 5

You will

- apply Step 8 for research report (WA 45):
  - Write a rough draft.

End of Lesson 5

Writing Time

Write It: **INDEPENDENT RESEARCH REPORT WRITING 45**

Use the schedule in Reference 232 on page 491 as you continue working on your independent report. This is Day 6, and you will do Steps 9–10.

Lesson 6

You will

- apply Steps 9-10 for research report (WA 45):
  - Revise and edit the rough draft.
  - Write the final outline.

End of Lesson 6

Writing Time

Write It: **INDEPENDENT RESEARCH REPORT WRITING 45**

Use the schedule in Reference 232 on page 491 as you continue working on your independent report. This is Day 7, and you will do Steps 11–12.

Lesson 7

You will

- apply Steps 11-12 for research report (WA 45):
  - Write the final report.
  - Put the final report and all related research work in the correct order.

Plan It:

Your teacher will give you a presentation schedule to follow as you share your research report with your class in the next two lessons. If you are in Group 1, you will share in Lesson 8. If you are in Group 2, you will share in Lesson 9.

End of Lesson 7

START LESSON 8

Lesson 8

You will

- begin publishing WA 45 by sharing independent research reports.
- write an evaluation of a classmate's presentation for WA 46.
- write an evaluation of your own report presentation for WA 47.

Writing Time

Write It: **WRITING ASSIGNMENTS 46 AND 47**

Writing Assignment [46]

You will choose a classmate's report for a commentary that you will write in your journal. A commentary is an essay that tells what you think about a person's work or presentation. At the top of a new journal page, write the date and title of your favorite presentation from today. Write a commentary that includes an introduction, a paragraph that tells why you liked the report, a paragraph that tells what you learned from it, and a conclusion.

Writing Assignment [47]

Do this part only on the day you give your report. For your own report, write a commentary in your journal that includes the reasons why you liked your topic, some of the most interesting things you learned during your research, and an evaluation of your presentation.

Publishing Time

Publish It: **SHARE INDEPENDENT RESEARCH REPORTS**

Now, you will share your research report with your classmates. Students in Group 1 will share today, and students in Group 2 will share during the next lesson. Use the Share Time Guidelines as reports are shared.

| **Reference 68** | **Share Time Guidelines** |

Speaker Presentation

1. Have your paper ready to read when called upon.
2. Tell the title of your writing selection.
3. Tell the purpose and type of writing used.

PRESENTATION TIPS:

4. Stand with your feet flat on the floor and your shoulders straight. Do not shift your weight as you stand.
5. Hold your paper about chin high to help you project your voice to your audience.
6. Make sure you do not read too fast.
7. Read in a clear voice that can be heard so that your audience does not have to strain to hear you.
8. Change your voice tone for different characters or for different parts of the writing selection.

Audience Response

1. Look at the speaker.
2. Turn your body toward the speaker.
3. Listen attentively. Do not let your thoughts wander.
4. Do not make distracting noises as you listen.
5. Do not make distracting motions as you listen.
6. Show interest in what the speaker is saying.
7. Silently summarize what the speaker is saying. Take notes if necessary.
8. Ask questions about anything that is not clear.
9. Show appreciation by clapping after the speaker has finished.

English Made Easy

Writing Time

Write It: **WRITING ASSIGNMENTS 47 AND 48**

Lesson 9

You will

- finish publishing WA 45 by sharing independent research reports.
- write an evaluation of your own report presentation for WA 47.
- write an evaluation of a different classmate's report presentation for WA 48.

Writing Assignment [47]

Do this part only on the day you give your report. For your own report, write a commentary in your journal that includes the reasons why you liked your topic, some of the most interesting things you learned during your research, and an evaluation of your presentation.

Writing Assignment [48]

You will choose another classmate's report for a commentary that you will write in your journal. A commentary is an essay that tells what you think about a person's work or presentation. At the top of a new journal page, write the date and title of your favorite presentation from today. Write a commentary that includes an introduction, a paragraph that tells why you liked the report, a paragraph that tells what you learned from it, and a conclusion.

Publishing Time

Publish It: **SHARE INDEPENDENT RESEARCH REPORTS**

If you are in Group 2, you will share your research report with your classmates today. Use the Share Time Guidelines as reports are shared.

Jingle Time

SHURLEY ENGLISH

Student Textbook

Level 5

♪ Jingle 1 — The Study Skills Jingle

Un-Quigley, Un-Quigley,
What are you going to do?
You've got a frown on your face,
And you're singing the blues!
You're not organized, Quigley;
You are not prepared.
You're not listening,
And your mind's not there.
You don't have plans, and you don't have goals.
Your homework's unfinished,
And you've been told.
You need to get your act together
'Cause you don't have a clue.
You've got the Study Skills Blues!

O-Quigley, O-Quigley,
Now, you see what to do.
You've got a smile on your face,
And you're lookin' cool!
You're so organized, Quigley;
You are so prepared.
You're listening carefully,
And your mind is there.
You've got plans, and you've got goals.
Your homework is finished;
You don't have to be told.
You've got your act together, Quigley,
'Cause you followed the clues.
And you're not singing the Study Skills Blues!

♪ Jingle 2 — The Sentence Jingle

A sentence, sentence, sentence
Is complete, complete, complete
When five simple rules
It meets, meets, meets.

It has a subject, subject, subject
And a verb, verb, verb.
And it makes sense, sense, sense
With every word, word, word.

Add a capital letter
And a punctuation mark.
And now our sentence has all its parts!

But REMEMBER—
Subject and **verb** and **complete sense**,
With a **capital letter** and an **end mark**, too.
Our sentence is complete,
And now we're through!

English Made Easy

The Noun Jingle

This is a noun jingle, my friend,
A noun jingle, my friend.
You can shake it to the left
And shake it to the right.
Find yourself a noun,
And then recite:

A noun names a person.
A noun names a thing.
A noun names a person,
Place, or thing,
And sometimes an idea.

Person, place, thing, idea!
Person, place, thing, idea!
So, shake it to the left,
And shake it to the right.
Find yourself a noun,
And feel just right!

The Verb Jingle

A verb, a verb.
What is a verb?
Haven't you heard?
There are two kinds of verbs:
The **action verb**
And the **linking verb**.

The action verb
Shows a state of action,
Like **stand** and **sit** and **smile**.
The action verb is always in motion
Because it tells what the subject does.
*We **stand**! We **sit**! We **smile**!*

The linking verb shows a state of being,
Like **am**, **is**, **are**, **was**, and **were**,
Looks, **becomes**, **grows**, and **feels**.
The linking verb shows no action
Because it tells what the subject is.
*He **is** a clown. He **looks** funny.*

The Adverb Jingle

An adverb modifies a verb, adjective, or another adverb.
An adverb asks, "HOW? WHEN? WHERE?"
To find an adverb: **Go,** *(snap)* **Ask,** *(snap)* **Get.** *(snap)*
But where do I **go**? *To a verb, adjective, or another adverb.*
What do I **ask**? HOW? WHEN? WHERE?
What do I **get**? An adverb, man. Cool!

The Adjective Jingle

An adjective modifies a noun or a pronoun.
An adjective asks, "WHAT KIND?"
An adjective asks, "WHICH ONE?"
An adjective asks, "HOW MANY?"
To identify an adjective: **Go!** *(stomp, stomp)* **Ask!** *(clap, clap)* **Get!** *(snap)*
Where do I **go**? *(stomp, stomp)* To a noun or a pronoun.
What do I **ask**? *(clap, clap)* WHAT KIND? WHICH ONE? or HOW MANY?
What do I **get**? *(snap, snap)* An Adjective!

The Article Adjective Jingle

We are the article adjectives,
Teeny, tiny adjectives.
A, AN, THE — A, AN, THE

We are called article adjectives and noun markers.
We are memorized and used every day.
So, if you spot us, you can mark us
With a capital A.

We are the article adjectives,
Teeny, tiny adjectives.
A, AN, THE — A, AN, THE

SHURLEY ENGLISH

♪ Jingle 8 — The Preposition Jingle

A prep, prep, preposition
Is an extra-special word

That connects a
Noun, noun, noun

Or a pro, pro, pronoun
To the rest of the sentence.

♪ Jingle 9 — The Object of the Preposition Jingle

An object of the preposition
Is a NOUN or PRONOUN.
An object of the preposition
Is a NOUN or PRONOUN

After the prep, prep, prep
After the prep, prep, prep
After the prep, prep, prep
That answers **WHAT** or **WHOM**.

♪ Jingle 10 — The Prepositional Phrase Jingle

I've been working with prepositions
'Til I can work no more.
They're connecting their objects
To the rest of the sentence before.

When I put them all together,
The prep and its noun or pro,
I get a prepositional phrase
That could cause my mind to blow!

♪ Jingle 11 — The Preposition Flow Jingle

1. Preposition, Preposition,
   Starting with an **A**:
   **aboard, about, above,
   across, after, against,
   along, among, around, as, at!**

2. Preposition, Preposition,
   Starting with a **B**:
   **before, behind, below,
   beneath, beside, between,
   beyond, but,** and **by!**

3. Preposition, Preposition,
   Starting with a **D**:
   **despite, down, during
   despite, down, during!**

4. Oh, Preposition,
   Please, don't go away.
   Go to the middle of the alphabet,
   And see just what we say.
   E and **F** and **I** and **L**
   And **N** and **O** and **P**:
   **except, for, from,
   in, inside, into, like,
   near, of, off, on, out,
   outside, over, past!**

5. Preposition, Preposition,
   Almost through.
   Start with **S** and end with **W**:
   **since, through,
   throughout, to, toward,
   under, underneath,
   until, up, upon,
   with, within, without!**

6. Preposition, Preposition,
   Easy as can be.
   We just recited
   All **fifty-one** of these!

♪ | Jingle 12 | **The Transition Words Jingle**

Aw, listen, comrades, and you shall hear
About transition words
That make your writing smooth and clear.

Transition words are connecting words.
You add them to the beginning
Of sentences and paragraphs
To keep your ideas spinning and give your writing flow.

These words can clarify, summarize, or emphasize,
Compare or contrast, inform or show time.
Learn them now, and your writing will shine!

Transition, Transition,
For words that **SHOW TIME:**
first, second, third, before, during, after,
next, then, and *finally.*

Transition, Transition,
For words that **INFORM:**
for example, for instance, in addition, as well,
also, next, another, along with, and *besides.*

Transition, Transition,
For words that **CONTRAST:**
although, even though, but, yet, still,
otherwise, however, and *on the other hand.*

Transition, Transition,
For words that **COMPARE:**
as, also, like, and *likewise.*

Transition, Transition,
For words that **CLARIFY:**
for example, for instance, and *in other words.*

Transition, Transition,
For words that **EMPHASIZE:**
truly, again, for this reason, and *in fact.*

Transition, Transition,
For words that **SUMMARIZE:**
therefore, in conclusion, in summary, and *finally,*
to sum it up, all in all, as a result, and *last.*

TRANSITION WORD

♪ | Jingle 13 | **The Pronoun Jingle**

These little pronouns,
Hangin' around,
Can take the place
Of any of the nouns.

With a smile and a nod
And a twinkle of the eye,
Give those pronouns
A big high five! Yeah!

♪ Jingle 14 — The Subject Pronoun Jingle

There are seven subject pronouns
That are easy as can be.
SUBJECT PRONOUNS!
I and **We**,
He and **She**,
It and **They** and **You**.
Those are the subject pronouns!

♪ Jingle 15 — The Possessive Pronoun Jingle

There are seven possessive pronouns
That are easy as can be.
POSSESSIVE PRONOUNS!
My and **Our**,
His and **Her**,
Its and **Their** and **Your**.
Those are possessive pronouns!

♪ Jingle 16 — The Conjunction Sound-Off Jingle

Conjunctions are a part of speech.
Conjunctions are a part of speech.
They join words or sentences; it's quite a feat!
They join words or sentences; it's quite a feat!
Sound off! Conjunctions! Sound off! AND, OR, BUT!
There are many conjunctions, but three stand out.
There are many conjunctions, but three stand out.
Put your hands together and give a shout!
Put your hands together and give a shout!
Sound off! Conjunctions! Sound off! AND, OR, BUT!
Sound off! Conjunctions! Sound off! AND, OR, BUT!

♪ Jingle 17 — The 23 Helping Verbs of the Mean, Lean, Verb Machine Jingle

These twenty-three helping verbs
will be on my test.
I've gotta remember them so I can do my best.
I'll start out with eight and finish with fifteen.
Just call me the mean, lean, verb machine.

There are the eight **be** verbs
that are easy as can be.
am, is, are   was and **were**
am, is, are   was and **were**
am, is, are   was and **were**
be, being, and **been**

All together now, the eight **be** verbs:
am, is, are   was and **were   be, being,** and **been**
am, is, are   was and **were   be, being,** and **been**
am, is, are   was and **were   be, being,** and **been**

There are twenty-three helping verbs,
and I've recited eight.
That leaves fifteen more that I must relate.
Knowing all these verbs will save my grade.
The mean, lean, verb machine is here to stay.
has, have, and **had   do, does,** and **did**
has, have, and **had   do, does,** and **did**
might, must, and **may**
might, must, and **may**
can and **could   would** and **should**
can and **could   would** and **should**
shall and **will   shall** and **will**
has, have, and **had   do, does,** and **did**
might, must, and **may**
can and **could, would** and **should**
shall and **will**
In record time, I did this drill.
I'm the mean, lean, verb machine—STILL!

♪ Jingle 18 — The Interjection Jingle

Oh, Interjection, Interjection, Interjection, who are you?
I'm a part of speech through and through.
Well, Interjection, Interjection, Interjection, what do you do?
I show strong or mild emotion; need a review?
Oh, Interjection, Interjection, I still don't have a clue.
I show strong emotion, like Wow! Great! or Yahoo!
I show mild emotion, like Oh, Yes, Fine, or Toodle-oo.
Well, Interjection, Interjection, you really know how to groove!
That's because I'm a part of speech through and through!

♪ Jingle 19 — The Possessive Noun Jingle

A possessive noun just can't be beat.
It shows ownership, and that is neat.
Add an apostrophe to show possession.
This is a great ownership lesson.
Adjective is its part of speech.
Ask **WHOSE** to find it as you speak.
Whose house? Tommy's house.
Possessive Noun Adjective!

♪ Jingle 20 — The Eight Parts of Speech Jingle

Want to know how to write?
Use the eight parts of speech.
They're dynamite!

Nouns, **V**erbs, and **P**ronouns.
They rule!
They're called the **NVP's**, and they're really cool!
The **Double A's** are on the move.
Adjectives and **A**dverbs help you to groove.
Next come the **PIC's**, and then we're done.
They're **P**reposition, **I**nterjection, and **C**onjunction!

All together now.
The eight parts of speech, abbreviations, please.
NVP—AA—and—PIC!

♪ Jingle 21 — The Direct Object Jingle

A **direct object** is a NOUN or a PRO,
Is a noun or a pro, is a noun or a pro.
A **direct object** completes the meaning,
Completes the meaning of the sentence.
A **direct object** follows the verb,
Follows the **verb-transitive**.
To find a direct object,
Ask **WHAT** or **WHOM**
Ask **WHAT** or **WHOM**
After the verb.

♪ Jingle 22 — The Object Pronoun Jingle

There are seven object pronouns
That are easy as can be.
OBJECT PRONOUNS!

Me and **Us**,
Him and **Her**,
It and **Them** and **You**.
Those are the object pronouns.

♪ Jingle 23 — The Indirect Object Jingle

Indirect, oh, indirect, oh, indirect object.
Give me that indirect, oh, indirect, oh, indirect object.

An indirect object is a NOUN or a PRONOUN
That receives what the direct, the direct object names.
An indirect object is found between the verb, **verb-transitive**,
And the direct object.
To find the indirect object,   *(sha-bop)*
Ask **TO WHOM** or **FOR WHOM**   *(sha-bop)*
After the direct object.   *(sha-bop)*

An indirect, indirect, indirect, indirect, yeah!
An indirect object!
Just give me that indirect, oh, indirect, oh, indirect object.
Give me that indirect, oh, indirect, oh, indirect object.
Give me that object, oh, indirect, oh, indirect object.
An INDIRECT OBJECT!

♪ Jingle 24 — The Predicate Noun Jingle

A predicate, predicate noun
Is a special, special noun
In the predicate, predicate, predicate
That means the **same as the subject**,
The simple, simple subject.

A predicate, predicate noun
Follows after a linking verb.
To locate a predicate noun,
Ask **WHAT** or **WHO** after the verb
And verify the answer.
Verify that the noun in the predicate
Means the **same thing as the subject**,
The simple, simple subject.

♪ Jingle 25 — The Noun Job Jingle

Nouns will give you a run for your money.
They do so many jobs
That it's not even funny.
A noun—person, place, thing, or idea—
is very appealing!
But it's the noun job (noun job)
That is so revealing!

To find the nouns in a sentence,
Go to their jobs (go to their jobs)
Nouns can do objective jobs (objective jobs)
They're the **IO** (IO), **DO** (DO), and **OP** jobs (OP jobs).
And nouns can do subjective jobs (subjective jobs).
They're the **SN** (SN) and **PrN** jobs (PrN jobs).
Jobs. Jobs. Noun Jobs! Yeah!

♪ Jingle 26 — The Predicate Adjective Jingle

A predicate, predicate, predicate adjective
Is a special, special adjective
In the predicate, predicate, predicate
That modifies, modifies, **modifies**
The simple, simple **subject**.

A predicate, predicate, predicate adjective
Follows after a linking verb.
To find a predicate adjective,
Ask **WHAT KIND** of subject and verify the answer.
Verify that the adjective in the predicate
Modifies, modifies, modifies
The simple, simple subject.

Level 5   Student Textbook

Resource Tools

SHURLEY ENGLISH

SHURLEY ENGLISH

Resource Tool: Level 5 References

The following list provides a quick reference to the Reference Boxes used in Shurley English.

English Made Easy

English Made Easy

Resource Tool: Space for DISCOVERY TIME

Discovery Time provides an opportunity for you to investigate the theme from Level 5, which is space. During Discovery Time, you will learn interesting facts about space-related topics. After reviewing these facts, you may look for more information at the library, at home, or on the Internet. Reports written on any of these topics may be shared with classmates during Discovery Share Time. Use the information below to guide your exploration.

Page	Chapter	Lesson	Date	Space Topic
91	3	3		Sun
95	3	4	1473-1543	Nicolaus Copernicus
122	4	3		Mercury
125	4	4	1564-1642	Galileo Galilei
153	5	3		Venus
156	5	4	1656-1742	Edmund Halley
183	6	3		Earth
186	6	4	1930-Present	Neil Armstrong
215	7	3		Mars
218	7	4	1889-1953	Edwin Powell Hubble
245	8	3		Jupiter
248	8	4	1957	Sputnik I
274	9	3		Saturn
277	9	4	1934-1968	Yury Gagarin
277	9	4	1923-1998	Alan B. Shepard, Jr
301	10	3		Uranus
304	10	4	1738-1822	Sir William Herschel
328	11	3		Neptune
333	11	4	1958	NASA
360	12	3		Aurora
363	12	4	1973	Skylab
380	13	3		Moon
382	13	4	1966	Luna 9
402	14	2		Constellations
406	14	3		Asteroids, Comets, and Meteors

Resource Tool: Abbreviations Used in Shurley English

The following list provides a quick reference of the most commonly used abbreviations in Shurley English.

Abbreviation	Description
N	Noun
SN	Subject Noun
CSN	Compound Subject Noun
Pro	Pronoun
SP	Subject Pronoun
CSP	Compound Subject Pronoun
V	Verb
HV	Helping Verb
CV	Compound Verb
V-t	Verb-transitive
CV-t	Compound Verb-transitive
LV	Linking Verb
CLV	Compound Linking Verb
A	Article Adjective
Adj	Adjective
CAdj	Compound Adjective
Adv	Adverb
CAdv	Compound Adverb
P	Preposition
OP	Object of the Preposition
COP	Compound Object of the Preposition
PPA	Possessive Pronoun Adjective
PNA	Possessive Noun Adjective

Abbreviation	Description
C	Conjunction
I	Interjection
DO	Direct Object
CDO	Compound Direct Object
IO	Indirect Object
CIO	Compound Indirect Object
PrN	Predicate Noun
CPrN	Compound Predicate Noun
PA	Predicate Adjective
CPA	Compound Predicate Adjective

Sentences	
D	Declarative Sentence
E	Exclamatory Sentence
Int	Interrogative Sentence
Imp	Imperative Sentence
S	Simple Sentence
F	Fragment
SCS	Simple Sentence Compound Subject
SCV	Simple Sentence Compound Verb
CD	Compound Sentence
CX	Complex Sentence

Level 5 Patterns	
SN V P1	Subject Noun Verb Pattern 1
SN V-t DO P2	Subject Noun Verb-transitive Direct Object Pattern 2
SN V-t IO DO P3	Subject Noun Verb-transitive Indirect Object Direct Object Pattern 3
SN LV PrN P4	Subject Noun Linking Verb Predicate Noun Pattern 4
SN LV PA P5	Subject Noun Linking Verb Predicate Adjective Pattern 5

Resource Tool: Vocabulary

Prefixes

A **prefix** is a word part added to the beginning of a base word to change its meaning. Prefixes have meanings of their own. If you know the meanings of the prefix part and the base word, you can usually figure out the meaning of the new word that is made from combining the two parts. Some common prefixes are listed below to help you learn their meanings.

Prefix	Meaning	Examples
bi	two, twice	bilingual; bimonthly
dis, non, un	not, opposite of, without	distrust; nonfat; unhappy
im, in	not, in, into	impatient; incapable
inter	between, among	interstate; interact
mis	wrong, wrongly, badly	misbehave; mistake
post	after	posttest
pre	before	pretest
re	again, back	repay; return
sub	beneath, under	submarine; subway

Suffixes

A suffix is a word part added to the end of a base word to change its meaning. Suffixes have meanings of their own, too. If you know the meanings of the suffix part and the base word, you can usually figure out the meaning of the new word that is made from the two parts. Some common suffixes are listed below to help you learn their meanings.

Suffix	Meaning	Examples
able, ible	able to, likely to	usable, sensible
er, or	one who, that which	teacher, actor
ful	full of	joyful
ize	to make	vocalize, finalize
less	without	homeless
ly	in the manner of	quietly
ment, ion, tion	the act of, result of, condition	contentment, action, invention
ness	state of, quality of	happiness
ous	full of, filled with	glorious
ward	moving, direction	forward, upward

Suffix Spelling Check

The following spelling rules will help you when you add suffixes to words. Since there are several exceptions to these rules, always check the dictionary if you are in doubt about the spelling of a word.

1. To add a suffix to a word that ends in a **silent** -e, ***drop the final -e*** if the suffix begins with a **vowel**.
   close / closure   sense / sensible   come / coming   **Exception:** noticeable

2. To add a suffix to a word that ends in a **silent** -e, ***keep the final -e*** if the suffix begins with a **consonant**.
   hope / hopeful   home / homeless   advance / advancement   **Exception:** true / truly

3. To add a suffix to a word ending in a **consonant** plus -y, ***change the -y to i*** unless the suffix begins with i-.
   cry / cries / crying   try / tries / trying   copy / copied / copying

4. To add a suffix to a word ending in a **vowel** plus -y, ***do not change the -y to i***.
   play / played   joy / joyful

5. To add a suffix to a short word that ends with one vowel and one consonant, ***double*** the final consonant.
   skip / skipping   flat / flatter   clap / clapping   hot / hottest   **Exception:** job / jobless

Resource Tool: LISTENING AND SPEAKING

Following Written Directions

It is important that you learn to follow written directions. Sometimes, you must read directions several times in order to understand what to do. Written directions are used for many reasons. Some of the ways you will follow written directions include following recipes, filling out forms, taking tests, and following "how to" instructions. You can see from the following examples why following directions is important.

Directions are especially important when you write a process, or "how to," essay. Notice the use of time-order words in the following "how to" essay.

Directions from Sammy's Snack Shack to Cinema One Theater

From the front exit of Sammy's Snack Shack, turn right onto Elm. Go straight on Elm for about one mile. You will pass through two stoplights. At the third light, turn right on Bailey Street. Go three blocks. At the intersection of Bailey and Ashton, turn left onto Ashton. There will be a library on the right. The Cinema One movie theater will be on the left.

How to Play Dots and Boxes

The game, Dots and Boxes, is sometimes called Capture. After you read these instructions, you will know why. To play this game, you will need two players, pencils, and a sheet of paper.

First, draw a grid of dots in even rows on a sheet of paper. Next, one player draws a line to connect two of the dots. The other player then draws a line to connect two of the dots. Players take turns drawing a line to connect two dots. Each player tries to connect dots that complete a square, thereby "capturing" the box. When a player captures a box, he puts his initials inside it. If his line completes more than one square, he captures those boxes, too. The winner of the game is the player who captures the most boxes.

Dots and Boxes is a fun game to play in the car or in places that require you to be still and reasonably quiet. Grownups also like to play this game, so you might ask a parent or relative to play. It just takes pencil, paper, and another player to "capture" a fun time!

HANDS-ON ACTIVITIES

1. **Writing Connection:** Create a set of written directions for a student partner to follow. Observe as the partner follows your written directions. At the end of this activity, you and your partner will evaluate how easy the directions were to follow and how correctly the partner followed them. Analyze what went wrong if mistakes were made.

2. **Listening/Writing Connection:** Create different versions of "Simon Says" and see if your instructions for each version are clear and complete.

3. **Science Connection:** In small groups, find an interesting science experiment in a science book. Describe the importance of following the instructions for the experiment. Predict the outcome of the experiment. Discuss how the results would be different if the instructions were not followed. Discuss the usefulness of the experiment. Write directions for an experiment of your own.

Following Oral Directions

Also important is training yourself to listen to oral directions well enough to follow them correctly. Oral directions are spoken directions. When you do not listen carefully, you waste time and make careless mistakes.

To find out how well you can listen and follow oral directions, select a partner and do the activity below. First, each of you will select a number 1 or a number 2. Then, for the activity, the person with number 1 will read the directions while his partner follows them. Use a large book to separate the partners so that the reader cannot see the finished picture. Then, the roles will be reversed. The person with number 2 will now read the directions for the activity while his partner follows them. Compare the two pictures after both of you have completed the activity. Was it easier or harder for the first reader to follow the directions? Why? Do you prefer oral directions or written directions? Report the findings to your teacher.

STUDENT INSTRUCTIONS: Read these directions orally to your partner:

1. Today, you will follow oral directions to draw a penguin. I will read each step two times. You will have a short working time between each step.

2. Get out one sheet of notebook paper, a pencil, a black crayon, and an orange crayon.

3. First, draw a medium-sized oval in the middle of your page to make the body.

4. Draw a small circle sitting on top of the oval to make the head.

5. Starting on the left side of the head, divide the head in half with a line that dips in the middle.

6. Draw one round eye in the middle of the top half of the head with your black crayon.

7. Color the top half of the head black and the bottom half of the head orange.

8. Draw a beak on the right side of the head. Start it slightly on the inside of the head. Color it black.

9. Draw long, thin penguin wings on each side of the body. Each wing will look like a long pointed nose close to the body. Color them black.

10. Draw two small webbed feet at the bottom of your penguin. Each webbed foot looks like an umbrella without the handle. Color the feet black.

11. Draw a black line underneath the feet.

12. Lightly draw eight small v's all over the body with the black crayon.

HANDS-ON ACTIVITY

Social Studies Connection: Use the map below to write detailed directions from Point A to Point B. Select your Point A and Point B from places on the map, such as the library, the post office, the gas station, etc. Now, read your directions to a friend to see if he can follow them.

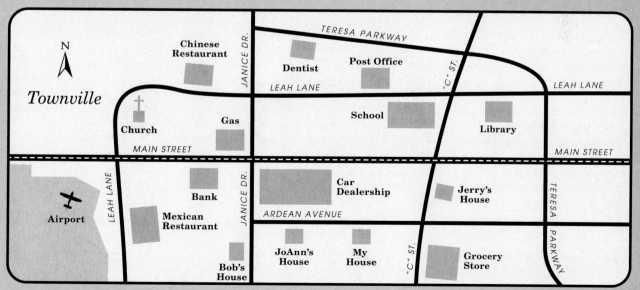

Resource Tool: LISTENING AND SPEAKING

Interviews

You conduct an interview when you ask a knowledgeable person a series of questions in order to get information about a particular subject. The information that is gathered from an interview is most often used for reports or articles. Family interviews can be used to document and preserve events rooted in family history. Community interviews serve the same purpose as they preserve the history of local events.

The type of interview you are conducting will determine the questions you ask. However, it is helpful to have a few general guidelines to help you conduct a successful interview. Use the suggestions below to help you plan an interview.

Guidelines for Conducting Interviews

1. Call the person you want to interview, explain the purpose of the interview, and make an appointment. Be courteous and be on time for the interview.

2. Write down the questions that you will ask during the interview. Make sure the questions are designed to get the information you need. Avoid asking yes-no questions because they do not give you enough information. The who, what, when, why, and where questions are always good to ask because they will provide plenty of details. (Examples: How do you feel about…, What do you think about…, Why did you…, What are the results of…, When do you expect…, What motivated you to…, etc.) Make sure your questions stay on the subject and are in good taste.

3. Take notes or use a tape recorder. If you take notes, leave plenty of space to write the answer to each question. If you use a tape recorder, ask permission first.

4. Make sure your notes accurately reflect what the person said. If you quote a person, be sure to place the exact words in quotation marks. If you are in doubt about any answers, repeat them to the person being interviewed to make sure your information is correct. This is especially important when recording dates or numbers.

5. Thank the person for the interview. Follow this up with a thank-you note expressing your appreciation for his time.

6. Write the article as soon as possible after the interview while the details are fresh in your mind.

7. If possible, give a copy of the article to the person you interviewed as a courtesy before it is published.

HANDS-ON ACTIVITIES

1. **Social Studies Connection:** Create a list of questions for an imaginary interview with a person of your choice from your family, school, or community. Make sure the topic of the interview is interesting and in good taste. With your teacher's approval, you can try to set up a real interview.

2. **Science Connection:** Each student will research an assigned or a selected science topic. Half the class will be designated as the interviewers, and the other half as the "experts" who are being interviewed. All the experts' names are put in a basket. Each interviewer will draw an expert's name from the basket to interview. The expert and the interviewer will work together to develop a set of questions specifically designed for the expert's topic. Then, the interview begins, with the interviewer taking notes. Finally, reverse the two groups and repeat the process.

3. **Media Connection:** Interview a reporter from a local newspaper, magazine, or TV station. Include these questions in your interview: How do you find the person to interview? How do you know what questions to ask? Do you use a tape recorder or take notes? What determines how long you interview a person? How long does it take to write the article? What do you do to get the article ready for publication?

Resource Tool: LISTENING AND SPEAKING

Video Presentations

Making video presentations is a fun way to publish any writing, including tall tales, poetry, and book reviews. Some general guidelines that will help video presentations go smoothly are listed below.

Student Guidelines for Making Video Presentations

1. Check the posted schedule so you will know when it is your turn to present.

2. Stay seated until the current presenter has finished and the video camera is no longer recording.

3. When it is your turn, go to the designated area. Make all preparations necessary for your presentation before the camera begins recording.

4. When you are ready, look at the camera operator and wait for the signal to begin.

5. Introduce yourself and your presentation. Be sure to say your first and last name. Here are two examples.

   • Say, "Hello, my name is (*your first and last name*). The title of my story is (*the title of your story*)."
   • Say, "(*the title of your story*) by (*your first and last name*)."

6. Read clearly, slowly, and loudly enough for everyone to hear and for the equipment to record your voice. Read with expression. Do not be afraid to raise your voice and read with feeling. Even though you are reading from your paper, make an effort to look directly into the camera from time to time.

7. Do not make fast movements. If you move, give the camera operator time to follow you. If you make a mistake, correct it and keep going. Most people do not notice minor mistakes if the speaker recovers quickly and smoothly. It takes practice to become a calm and fluent speaker.

8. After you have finished, look at the camera operator and wait for the signal that the camera is no longer recording.

9. You are part of the audience when you are not presenting. The camera may also zoom over the audience from time to time. As a member of the audience, you must be as quiet as possible because the recording equipment will pick up classroom sounds and movements.

Teacher Guidelines for Pre-Filming

1. Set the equipment up and test it before the presentations begin.

2. Make sure a responsible adult is present to help with setting up the presentation area.

3. Rope or tape an area around the recording equipment and the person operating the camera. Only authorized persons should be in this area!

4. Tape down any cords or loose wires around the equipment so no one will trip over them.

5. Make sure you have a blank video. Keep an extra one on hand just in case something happens to the first one.

6. Place tape marks on the floor where you want the presenters to stand while they give their presentations.

7. If possible, do a test run. Film the area where the students will be presenting. Is the lighting good? Is there a glare from the sunlight or indoor lights? Is the background appropriate? Do you have plenty of space for the presenter? Do you have everything close by that the presenter might need without being in the camera's view?

8. Be relaxed so you can encourage and reassure your students. Presentations in front of a camera will provide students with invaluable experience and will develop poise and confidence.

9. Have a prior schedule posted so everyone will know when it is his turn to present.

SCENE: Tall Tale
TAKE: 3
DIRECTOR: Quigley

Resource Tool: LISTENING AND SPEAKING

Guidelines for Evaluating Video Presentations

At the top of a sheet of paper, write the date and title of your presentation. Next, choose the evaluation prompt according to the way you made your presentation. For example, if you portrayed a character, use the evaluation section under Character Portrayal. For each number, write your answers and comments in complete sentences. Try to be as objective as possible. This self-evaluation will help you improve your next video presentation.

Character Portrayal	Illustration	Reading Dramatization
1. Explain why you made the choice to do a character portrayal.	1. Explain why you made the choice to use illustrations for your presentation.	1. Explain why you made the choice to do a dramatic reading of your story.
2. Which character did you choose to portray? Explain how you made your choice.	2. How did you illustrate your story? Did you use paint, markers, chalk, crayons, pencils, or other media? Were your illustrations easy for the audience to see? Did you use them effectively?	2. Were you aware of nonverbal cues in your presentation? Did you hold your paper so that your face could be seen? Did you look at the audience from time to time? Did you use facial expressions and body gestures effectively? Did you move around or did you stand still?
3. How did you look? (Describe your hair, face, and costume or outfit.)		
4. Did you use any other props? If so, what were they? Did they add to your presentation? Did they distract from it?	3. Did you use any other props? If so, what were they? Did they add to your presentation? Did they distract from it?	
5. Were you aware of nonverbal cues in your presentation? Did you hold your paper so that your face could be seen? Did you look at the audience from time to time? Did you use facial expressions and body gestures effectively? Did you move around or did you stand still?	4. Were you aware of nonverbal cues in your presentation? Did you hold your paper so that your face could be seen? Did you look at the audience from time to time? Did you use facial expressions and body gestures effectively? Did you move around or did you stand still?	3. Did you speak clearly and loudly enough to be heard? Did you use inflections in your voice to make the characters come alive?
6. Did you speak clearly and loudly enough to be heard? Did you use inflections in your voice to make the characters come alive?	5. Did you speak clearly and loudly enough to be heard? Did you use inflections in your voice to make the characters come alive?	4. How could you enhance your presentation? What would you change and what would you not change?
7. How could you enhance your presentation? What would you change and what would you not change?	6. How could you enhance your presentation? What would you change and what would you not change?	5. What is your honest opinion of your presentation? What were the strong points, and what areas needed improvement?
8. What is your honest opinion of your presentation? What were the strong points, and what areas needed improvement?	7. What is your honest opinion of your presentation? What were the strong points and what areas needed improvement?	

Resource Tool: Writing Invitations

Invitations

With all the commercial cards available today, the art of writing personal, unique, and individual invitations is almost obsolete. However, learning to write invitations is an important skill. An invitation should follow the same form as a friendly letter: heading, greeting, body, closing, and signature.

Before you begin writing an invitation, it helps to make an outline that includes specific information (what, who, where, when) in any logical order. Study the example of the outline and the invitation below.

An invitation will sometimes contain an RSVP. This is an acronym for a French expression that means "please respond," and a reply is needed. If a phone number is included, reply by phone. Otherwise, a written reply is expected.

Invitation Outline

1. What . . . . Tell what the event or special occasion is. A graduation party
2. Who . . . . Tell whom the event is for. . . . . For J. D. Graham
3. Where . . . . Tell where the event will take place. . . . . At Foxdale Country Club
4. When . . . . Tell the date and time of the event. . . . . On Friday, August 16, at 6:00
5. Whipped Cream . . . . A polite statement written to make the person feel welcome. . . . . . We hope to see you there!

Sample Invitation

> 13 Ross Circle
> Cabot, Arkansas 72023
> August 6, 20—
>
> Dear Kristen,
>
> You are invited to a graduation party for J. D. Graham. He will be graduating from UCLA. The party will be at the Foxdale Country Club at 65 Foxdale Road in Jacksonville on Friday, August 16, at 6:00 p.m. There will be lots of food and a live band. We hope to see you there!
>
> Your friend,
> Sharon Miller

Check Your Understanding

Why do you send an invitation? _____

HANDS-ON ACTIVITIES

1. **Literature Connection:** Create an invitation to ask your friends or family to attend a book fair or to participate in a book swapping event.
2. **Science Connection:** Create an invitation to encourage your parents, relatives, and friends to visit a science fair your school is sponsoring.
3. **Social Studies Connection:** Study another culture to find out how the people use written invitations for special events. Create an invitation from another culture.
4. **Writing Connection:** Pretend you are giving your little sister a birthday party. Create an invitation for her special event.

Resource Tool: STUDY SKILLS

Test-Taking

Preparing for Tests

1. Keep up with daily work to develop an understanding of the material.

2. Pay attention during the class review. The teacher will usually highlight important information to study.

3. Ask questions about things you do not understand before the test.

4. Find out what testing format will be used (essay, true/false, multiple choice, fill-in-the-blank, etc.).

5. Begin studying several days before the test so you do not have to cram.

6. Use notes, worksheets, review sheets, etc., to help you. Reread your notes and look over references.

7. Create acronyms to memorize a series of items, using the first letters of each word.

8. If your teacher permits, tape-record lectures and/or notes. You can play them back as many times as necessary to help you learn the information.

9. Have a study-buddy. Find a classmate who takes his studies as seriously as you do. You can design a sample test for each other. Or, you can have oral reviews of the content to be covered on the next test.

10. You can design a lecture on the material to be covered on the next test. Then, you can "teach" a couple of your peers. Remember, you know it if you can teach it.

Taking the Test

1. Stay calm and do your best.

2. Read all directions carefully before you begin marking answers. Identify key words in the directions.

3. Go through your test and answer the ones you are sure about first.

4. Pace yourself. If you do not know an answer right away, come back to it later.

5. Utilize all your test time. Double-check your answers after you have finished.

6. Know how the test is scored. If you are penalized for wrong answers, answer only questions you are sure you know. If no points are deducted for wrong answers, make sure you've answered all the questions.

Test-taking Tips for True-False Tests

1. Read true-false questions carefully.

2. If a statement is <u>always</u> true, mark true. If it is only true sometimes, mark false.

3. Watch for tricky phrases such as: *it seems, I think, always, never,* and *maybe.*

Test-taking Tips for Fill-in-the-Blank Tests

1. Read and reread each question carefully.

2. If an answer bank is provided, check off answers as you use them.

3. Do not scratch answers out because you may need to read them again later.

4. Copy answers in the blanks correctly. Pay attention to correct spelling.

5. Write or print all answers as neatly as possible. Make sure each answer is legible.

6. If an answer bank is not provided, make sure you know whether to study for spelling as well as facts.

Test-taking Tips for Multiple-Choice Tests

1. Read and reread each question and any sample sentence or paragraph carefully.

2. Read all the answer choices carefully before choosing an answer.

3. Eliminate choices you know are wrong.

4. If more than one answer on a multiple choice test looks correct, mark the one that makes the strongest impression.

5. Write or print all letters as neatly as possible. Make sure each answer is legible.

6. If the test requires shading ovals, make sure each oval is filled in fully.

Test-taking Tips for Essay Tests

1. Read and reread each question or writing prompt carefully. Understand what kind of response is expected from the question or writing prompt.

2. Think about your purpose and audience.

3. Plan how you will organize your writing by jotting down ideas on a separate piece of paper. Use your favorite style of graphic organizer to organize your ideas.

4. Make sure the main idea is stated clearly in the topic sentence.

5. Use only details that support each of your main points.

6. If you have time, write a rough draft on another sheet of paper so you can revise and edit it.

7. Write the final essay as neatly as possible. Make sure every word is legible.

8. Reread the essay. Check one last time for correct punctuation, capitalization, and spelling.

Resource Tool: STUDY SKILLS

Handwriting Tips

There are two different kinds of handwriting: **manuscript** and **cursive**. When you first learn to write the letters of the alphabet, you print them in manuscript form. **Manuscript writing** means that each letter in a word is written separately. Sometimes, manuscript writing is called printing. After you have learned and practiced manuscript writing, you are taught cursive writing. **Cursive writing** means that you connect the letters within a word.

Whether you use manuscript or cursive writing, you should make your writing legible. **Legible** means writing that is neat and easy to read. Sloppy handwriting not only creates a negative impression, it often prevents clear communication.

Tips to Make Your Writing Legible

1. Make all similar letters uniform in height.
2. Use the correct slant and keep slant uniform.
3. Space letters and words correctly.
4. Connect the letters correctly.
5. Recognize unacceptable standards and redo the paper.

Other Handwriting Tips

1. **Use good writing posture.** Sit up straight with your feet flat on the floor. Your wrists should rest on the desk, but they should not support the weight of your body. Don't slouch.
2. **Hold your pencil correctly.** Place your pencil between the tip of your thumb and your index finger. The pencil will rest on your middle finger. Grip your pencil at the end of the painted wood, right above where the sharpened part begins.
3. **Position your paper correctly.** Place your paper in front of you, slightly slanted, and parallel with your writing arm.
4. **Anchor your paper so it doesn't slide.** If you are right-handed, put your left hand lightly on the top left corner of the paper to keep it from moving. If you are left-handed, use your right hand on the top right corner. Make sure your hand stays flat and relaxed.
5. **Continue to check your writing posture and your paper placement.** As you near the bottom of your paper, slide your paper up so your arms don't hang off your desk. Your elbows should always remain under your shoulders.

HANDS-ON ACTIVITY

In order to evaluate your writing posture, have someone videotape you as you are writing an essay. As you view the video, check how well you accomplished each of the areas under "Other Handwriting Tips."

1. Did you use good writing posture?
2. Did you hold your pencil correctly?
3. Did you position your paper correctly?
4. Did you anchor your paper?
5. Did you continue to check your writing posture and your paper placement?
6. Did you see any areas that needed improvement?
7. Did this evaluation help you make improvements?

Resource Tool: STUDY SKILLS

Guide for Cursive Handwriting Standards

In the samples below, the small **x** shows you where to start, and the arrows guide your starting direction.

Group 1 Letters: a, c, e, i, m, n, o, r, s, u, v, w, x
- All characters rest on the baseline and have an x-height that stops at the waist line.

Group 2 Letters: b, h, k, l
- All characters rest on the baseline and have a tall thin loop that ascends to the cap line.

Group 3 Letters: d, t
- Both characters rest on the baseline and have a single line that ascends to the cap line.

Group 4 Letters: g, j, q, y, z
- All characters rest on the baseline, have an x-height that stops at the waist line, and have a looping tail.

Group 5 Letters: f, p
- **f**—The character has a tall thin loop that ascends to the cap line, descends below the baseline, and has a looping tail.
- **p**—The character rests on the baseline, has an x-height that stops at the waist line, and has a single-line tail that descends below the baseline.

Capital Letters: A, B, C, D, E, F, G, H, I, J, K, L, M, N, O, P, Q, R, S, T, U, V, W, X, Y, Z
- All characters rest on the baseline and ascend to the cap line.
- The letters **J, Y, Z** have looping tails that descend below the baseline.
- Care should be taken to connect to lower case letters correctly.

Resource Tool: STUDY SKILLS

The Dictionary / Thesaurus

Sometimes, studying involves looking words up in a dictionary. You may need to see if you have spelled a word correctly, or you may want to check a word's meaning. A **dictionary** gives you correct spellings, pronunciations, meanings, usage, and history of words.

A **thesaurus** is a type of dictionary that contains synonyms and antonyms for different words. Most writers use a thesaurus to find synonyms and antonyms that will make their writing clearer and more appealing.

Alphabetical order is important to know because words in a dictionary and a thesaurus are arranged in alphabetical order. There are two rules that help you put words in alphabetical order.

Rule 1: If the first letters of the words are different, use only the first letters to put the words in alphabetical order.

Rule 2: If the first letters of the words are the same, use the second letters to put the words in alphabetical order. If the second letters are the same, use the third to put the words in alphabetical order, etc.

Guide words are the two words listed at the top of each dictionary page. Guide words tell the first and last words on the page. If the word you are looking up can be put alphabetically between the two guide words, then the word is located on that page. As you look up a word in the dictionary, you will use the first letter of the word to find the section you need. After you have found that section in the dictionary, you can use *guide words* to keep you from looking at every word on every page.

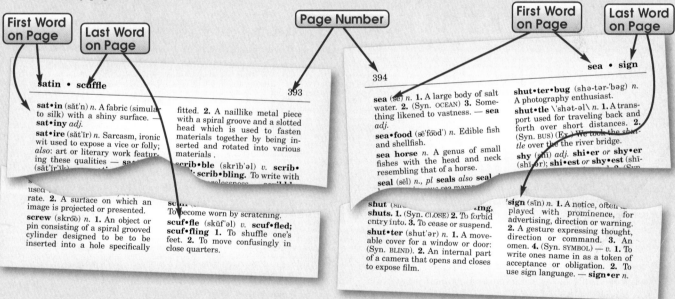

Entry words in a dictionary are the words in bold type that are listed in alphabetical order and defined. A dictionary provides many kinds of information about an entry word.

- pronunciation – tells how to pronounce a word. It is usually in parentheses at the beginning.
- part of speech – shows small *n.* for noun, small *v.* for verb, *adj.* for adjective, etc.
- meaning – gives numbered definitions of the word according to its parts of speech.
- example – gives sentences that use the entry word to explain a meaning. Shown as (Ex.)
- synonym – lists words that have similar meanings to the entry word. Shown as (Syn.)
- origins – tells when and where the word was originally used. Shown as [1350–1400 ME]. The date tells when the word was first used in its present form, and the initials tell the language origin. (ME stands for Middle English, Gr stands for Greek, Fr stands for French, L stands for Latin, Sp stands for Spanish, G stands for German, OE stands for Old English, etc.)

Some entries are slang words. The dictionary identifies slang words as nonstandard or informal. Slang words are not suitable for formal writing or speaking but may be used in casual speech.

Sample Entry Word

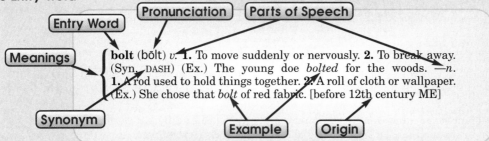

Entry Word → Pronunciation → Parts of Speech

Meanings →

bolt (bōlt) *v.* **1.** To move suddenly or nervously. **2.** To break away. (Syn. DASH) (Ex.) The young doe *bolted* for the woods. —*n.* **1.** A rod used to hold things together. **2.** A roll of cloth or wallpaper. (Ex.) She chose that *bolt* of red fabric. [before 12th century ME]

Synonym → Example ← Origin

Check Your Understanding

1. How are words listed in a dictionary? _____

2. What are guide words in a dictionary? _____

_____

3. What kind of information does the dictionary give for each entry word?

_____

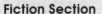

Resource Tool: STUDY SKILLS

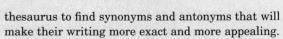

The Library

When you visit a library, you need to know how the books are arranged. Most libraries have three main sections for books: fiction, nonfiction, and reference.

Fiction Section

Fiction books contain stories about people, places, or things that are not true even though the writer, or author, may use ideas based on real people or events. Fiction books are arranged on the shelves in alphabetical order according to the authors' last names.

Nonfiction Section

Nonfiction books contain information and stories that are true. You can find a nonfiction book on just about any subject. Nonfiction books are grouped together in numerical order, according to a call number. A call number is the number found on the spine of all nonfiction books.

Reference Section

The Reference Section is designed to help you find information on many topics. The Reference Section contains many different kinds of reference books and materials. Some of these references are listed below.

1. **Dictionary.** The dictionary gives the definition, spelling, and pronunciation of words and tells briefly about famous people and places. Words in a dictionary are listed in alphabetical order.

2. **Thesaurus.** The thesaurus is actually a dictionary of synonyms and antonyms. Words in a thesaurus are listed in alphabetical order. Most writers use a thesaurus to find synonyms and antonyms that will make their writing more exact and more appealing.

3. **Encyclopedia.** The encyclopedia gives concise, factual information about persons, places, and events of world-wide interest. Topics are arranged in alphabetical order in books called volumes. Each volume has a letter or letters on the spine that indicates the range of topics in that volume.

4. **Atlas.** The atlas is primarily a book of maps, but it often contains facts about oceans, lakes, mountains, areas, population, products, and climates in every part of the world.

5. **Almanac.** An almanac is a book that is published once a year and contains brief, up-to-date, factual information on important people, places, events, and a variety of other topics.

6. **Periodical.** Periodicals are magazines. The *Readers' Guide to Periodical Literature* is an index of magazine articles. It is a monthly booklet that lists the titles of articles, stories, and poems published in all leading magazines. These titles are listed under topics that are arranged alphabetically. The monthly issues of *the Readers' Guide to Periodical Literature* are bound together in a single volume once a year and are filed in the library. By using the *Readers' Guide*, a person researching a topic can know which back issues of magazines might be helpful.

Card Catalog

The card catalog is an index to the books in a library. A book is listed in a card catalog in three ways—by author, by title, and by subject. An electronic index or traditional card catalog can help you find any book in the library. All three kinds of cards are arranged alphabetically by the word or words on the top line. The main difference in the cards is how the information is arranged.

Author Card	Title Card	Subject Card
745.3 **Author: Pinnington, Andrea** **Title:** 10 Minute Activities: Paper Pictures by Richard Brown St. Martin's Press, New York (c2001) 24p.	745.3 **Title: 10 Minute Activities: Paper** **Author:** Pinnington, Andrea Pictures by Richard Brown St. Martin's Press, New York (c2001) 24p.	745.3 **Subject: Science Projects** **Author:** Pinnington, Andrea **Title:** 10 Minute Activities: Paper Pictures by Richard Brown St. Martin's Press, New York (c2001) 24p.

Check your understanding

1. What is a card catalog? _____

2. What are the names of the three kinds of cards in a card catalog? _____

3. What are the three main book sections in the library? _____

4. How are fiction books arranged on the shelves? _____

5. How are nonfiction books arranged on the shelves? _____

6. What is a call number? _____

HANDS-ON ACTIVITIES

1. **Art Connection:** Pretend you are an illustrator. You have been asked to design a book cover for a famous author. Create the book cover and write an article about the new book. Tell why your book cover will invite people to read the book. Share your book cover and article with family and friends.
2. **Drama Connection:** Choose a scene from your favorite book or play and act it out with several of your classmates.
3. **History Connection:** What interesting facts can you find about your school or community library?
4. **Literature Connection:** Research the history of the Newberry and Caldecott books. Look up the Newberry and Caldecott winners. Make a list of the Newberry and Caldecott books you have read and the ones you would like to read.
5. **Writing Connection:** Choose a book in the library. Read a few pages from the middle of the book. Write a prediction of what you think happened at the beginning and end of the book. Then, read the book. Write how your predictions were similar and different from the original version.

Resource Tool: STUDY SKILLS

Parts of a Book

Do you know the parts of a nonfiction book? Actually, a book can be divided into three sections: the front, the body, and the back. Knowing the parts of a book will help you make full use of the special features that are frequently found in nonfiction books. The front includes these parts: title page, copyright page, preface, and table of contents. The body is the main section, or text, of the book. The back includes these parts: appendix, glossary, bibliography, and index. *(Note: For a more detailed description of the parts of a book, see Chapter 11, Lesson 6.)*

HANDS-ON ACTIVITY

Use the parts of a book to complete the puzzle below. Then, use your vocabulary words, science words, social studies words, or spelling words to make your own crossword puzzle or word-search puzzle.

```
A  B  G  E  F  G  J  K  L  M  N  T  P
Z  Y  L  R  X  W  V  U  S  T  R  A  Q
A  D  O  E  G  I  K  N  O  Q  R  H  S
B  C  S  A  P  P  E  N  D  I  X  O  T
D  S  S  F  H  J  L  M  K  P  V  L  U
C  T  A  B  A  Z  Y  C  X  W  B  D  T
E  N  R  G  I  K  A  H  L  I  I  E  I
F  E  Y  D  O  B  P  O  M  N  B  A  T
P  T  Q  S  W  Y  V  U  T  R  L  S  L
R  N  F  R  O  N  T  X  Z  A  I  Y  E
E  O  B  D  F  K  N  R  U  C  O  Y  P
F  C  H  I  P  Y  G  M  E  E  G  L  A
A  F  L  W  A  D  I  O  R  J  R  F  G
C  O  P  Y  R  I  G  H  T  P  A  G  E
E  E  K  I  T  N  O  N  E  M  P  P  Q
G  L  A  D  E  D  E  A  R  S  H  B  V
O  B  O  L  D  E  A  S  Y  L  Y  A  Z
T  A  H  O  A  X  R  A  Y  S  Q  J  B
X  T  C  A  N  D  Y  J  A  B  P  Y  F
```

Parts of a Book

1. Contains meanings of important words in a book.

2. Tells the reason the book was written.

3. Is the first section of a book.

4. Tells the publisher's name and city where the book was published. (2 words)

5. Is the second section of a book that contains the text of a book.

6. Is the third section of a book.

7. Contains titles of units and chapters. (3 words)

8. Gives exact page numbers for a particular topic.

9. Has the copyright date and ISBN. (2 words)

10. Contains extra maps in a book.

11. Is a list of sources used by the author as references.

Check Your Understanding

1. What parts of a book are located in the front matter? _____

   _____

2. What parts of a book are located in the back matter? _____

   _____

3. What is the text of a book called? _____

Resource Tool: STUDY SKILLS

The Table of Contents

Make your study time count by learning to use the shortcuts already available in a book. When you are looking for general information in a book, you can use a table of contents to help you find information quickly. A table of contents tells you four things.

1. What the book is about.
2. How many chapters are in a book.
3. The title of each chapter.
4. The first page of each chapter.

The main heading is *Contents*. The title of the first chapter is *"Selecting a Breed."* By reading over the rest of the chapter titles, you can tell that this book is about cats.

The chapter numbers are the numbers on the left under the heading *Chapter*. There are eight chapters in the book. The beginning page numbers are the numbers on the right under the heading *Page*. The page number listed to the right of each title tells the **first** page of the chapter. Chapter 1 begins on page 2. To find the last page of Chapter 1, go to the page where Chapter 2 begins and back up one page number. Chapter 2 begins on page 18. Back up one number, and you will be on page 17. So, Chapter 1 ends on page 17.

Contents

Check Your Understanding

1. A table of contents tells you four things. What are they? _____

2. What is the title of the chapter that would tell you how often to feed your cat?

   _____

3. What is the number of the chapter? _____

4. On which page does Chapter 3 begin? _____

5. On which page does Chapter 3 end? _____

HANDS-ON ACTIVITIES

1. Choose a nonfiction book that has a table of contents. Before you study the book's table of contents, make up an original table of contents, using the information you think will be in the book. Compare your table of contents to the one in the book. Analyze the similarities and differences. Evaluate why a table of contents is important in finding information about a book.

Resource Tool: STUDY SKILLS

The Index

Do you know why an index of a book is important and how to use it? When you are looking for information about a specific topic in a book, you can use the index to help you find the information quickly. The index is located in the back of the book. It has an alphabetical listing of specific topics and tells on which page that information can be found. It is similar to the table of contents, but it is much more detailed. There are three main reasons to use an index:

1. When you want to find an answer quickly.
2. When you want to know the answer to a specific question.
3. When you want to know more about a subject.

There are **six features of an index** that you should know:

1. An index is located at the back of the book.
2. An index lists information alphabetically.
3. When an index lists key ideas in a book, they are called topics.
4. When an index lists specific information under a topic, it is called a subtopic.
5. The numbers following topics and subtopics tell on which pages the information is found.
6. Punctuation of page numbers appears in subtopics.
   - When you see a **dash** between numbers, say "**through**." (23–25 *means page 23 through page 25*)
   - When you see a **comma** between numbers, say "**and**." (23–25, 44 *means page 23 through page 25 and page 44*)
   - When you see a **semicolon**, it means stop. Go no further for pages on this subtopic.

Sample Index

Index

Allergies, 23–25, 44	**Behavior,**	**Tail,** 37
	communicative, 23–24, 43;	**Teeth,** 49–53
	mothering, 45–48;	**Tongue,** *see* Grooming.
	newborn kittens, 49–53;	
	nocturnal, 25–26;	
	social, 23–25, 44;	
	territorial, 23–24	

The index topic under the letter *B* is *Behavior*. Notice that *Behavior* is the only word that is capitalized and the subtopics under it are indented. Each subtopic tells about the main topic *Behavior*.

Page numbers are listed after each subtopic. The page numbers listed after the subtopic *communicative* are *23–24, 43*. The **dash** between the 23 and 24 is read as *23 through 24*. The **comma** between 24 and 43 is read as *and*. Together, it would mean that information about <u>communicative</u> behavior is found on pages 23 <u>through</u> 24 <u>and</u> on page 43.

Check Your Understanding

How is information in an index listed? _____

HANDS-ON ACTIVITY

Choose two or three nonfiction books with indexes. Compare how the indexes are alike and how they are different. Exchange ideas with a partner. Write a paragraph to evaluate what you have learned about the value of the index.

Resource Tool: STUDY SKILLS

Reading Maps, Charts, and Graphs

Maps

Being able to read a map is an art unto itself. The more detailed the map, the greater the skill needed to interpret it. Virtually all maps have a legend for interpreting them. The legend includes such things as a distance scale, a set of symbols, and a collection of demographic information. The distance scale enables one to approximate the number of miles between two points. In addition to the distance scale, there is a set of symbols, which shows, among other things, types of roads, rest areas, medical facilities, historic markers, and airports. Finally, the demographic information contains the names of capital cities, populations, and land areas. A weather map has a legend that includes precipitation, highs and lows, fronts, and temperatures. Map information will vary, depending on the purpose of the map.

Trails at Canyon Ridge Resort

Behind the Guest Lodge at Canyon Ridge Resort, trails wind through woods and open fields to various points of interest.

Task:
1. The only trail that leads to the Cedar Mill is what?
   _____

2. How many trails cross Silver Creek?
   _____

3. Which trail provides the most direct route to Sampson Cemetery? _____

4. Which trail runs mostly east and west? _____

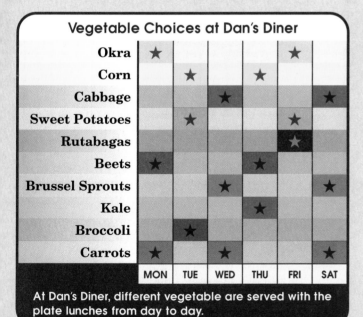

Vegetable Choices at Dan's Diner

	MON	TUE	WED	THU	FRI	SAT
Okra	★				★	
Corn		★		★		
Cabbage			★			★
Sweet Potatoes		★			★	
Rutabagas					★	
Beets	★			★		
Brussel Sprouts			★			★
Kale				★		
Broccoli		★				
Carrots	★		★			★

At Dan's Diner, different vegetable are served with the plate lunches from day to day.

Charts

There are many different types of charts. Among others, there are meteorological charts (having to do with weather), navigational charts (having to do with air and/or water travel), and general information charts (having to do with facts and figures about some particular subject matter). Information in charts is usually easy to read and to understand because the facts and figures are arranged in columns and headings. Some charts contain directions for interpreting them. Other less technical charts are designed in such a way that interpreting them is self-explanatory.

Task:
1. Which vegetables are served only once a week?
   _____

2. What vegetable is served on Mondays and Thursdays only?
   _____

3. What vegetable is served most frequently during the week?
   _____

4. How many vegetables are served at Dan's Diner? _____

Graphs

Graphs reveal a wealth of information without making it necessary to read a series of paragraphs. A graph compares facts and figures in an easy-to-read format that can be read at a glance. Usually, a graph is accompanied by a legend that enables the reader to interpret it. Ordinarily, the purpose of a bar graph is to make a comparison between something past and present whereas the purpose of a pie graph is to show and compare the component parts that make up a whole. Sometimes, as in the case of a line graph, the intent is to show progression over a period of time.

Line Graph

Task: 1. In the past decade, Bluff City's tax revenues were lowest during what year?

_____

2. What were the town's tax revenues in 1996?

_____

3. How did the town's tax revenues compare in 1994 and 2001?

_____

4. In which years were the revenues at or above $4,000?

_____

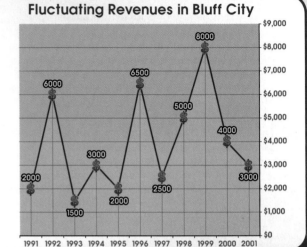

The Mayor of Bluff City is having considerable difficulty putting together a budget for the coming year. The town's tax revenues over the past decade have ranged from one extreme to the other. As the graph indicates, the last ten years have been a financial roller coaster ride.

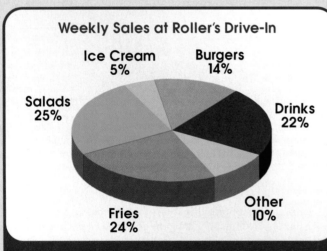

The weekly percentage of food sales at Roller's Drive-In helped the company determine its marketing strategy.

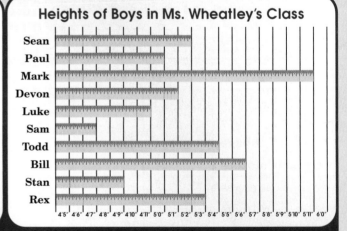

The boys in Ms. Wheatley's seventh-grade class range in height from 4'7" to 5'11".

Pie Graph

Task: 1. Where do burger sales rank in relation to the other food items? _____

2. Are the sales of burgers and ice cream more or less than the sales of drinks?

_____

3. Which item is sold the most? _____

4. What is the percentage of fries and salad sold? _____

Bar Graph

Task: 1. How tall is Luke? _____

2. The second shortest boy in Ms. Wheatley's class is who? _____

3. How many boys in the class are over five feet tall? _____

4. Which boy is five feet tall? _____

HANDS-ON ACTIVITIES

1. **Math, Science, and Social Studies Connections:** Look at the local or national weather report in a newspaper or on the Internet. Find and cut out examples of a weather map, a bar graph, a line graph, and a chart. Mount these examples on poster board. Identify them by labeling each kind, and, then, write one or two sentences explaining each one. Evaluate what you have learned about the value of maps, graphs, and charts.

2. **Math, Science, and Social Studies Connections:** Make your own map, graph, or chart. Choose a topic that you can look up information about and display in a map, graph, or chart. You can put the map, graph, or chart that you make on construction paper or poster board. Make sure you organize and label the information so that it is easy to read. Share your project with others. Evaluate what you have learned about maps, graphs, and charts.

 **STUDY SKILLS**

Cause and Effect

A cause-effect relationship exists in everyday events and situations. If you think about these events and situations carefully, you can learn why or how one thing (**cause**) makes another thing (**effect**) happen. Practically every event in life is either the **cause of** or the **result of** some other event.

In other words, a cause is the reason something happens. An effect is the event that happens as a result of the cause. For example, a storm was the **cause** of the damage. The damage was the result, or **effect**, of a storm. When cause-effect or effect-cause sentences are combined, the words *because* or *since* are commonly used to connect them. Sometimes, sentences do not show a cause-effect relationship.

Example of the cause listed first: Because of the tornado, there was great damage. (CE)

Example of the effect listed first: There was great damage because of the tornado. (EC)

Example of no cause-effect relationship: She ate dinner. Then, she read a book.

Comprehension Activities

1. List two possible results (effects) that might result from the cause listed below.
   Cause—She ate the whole pie by herself.

2. Complete the missing part of the effect-cause and cause-effect relationships below.
   I couldn't sleep last night because
   Because my grades were bad,

3. Find an example of cause and effect in a book. Share your findings in cooperative learning groups.

4. Look for an article in the newspaper that shows cause and effect. Bring the news article to school. Explain the cause and effect relationship of the news article in a report to the class.

5. Make two effect-cause sentences and two cause-effect sentences.

_____

_____

_____

_____

Resource Tool: Technology

On-line Searches

Using the Internet for obtaining information is quick and effective. Many search engines exist on the Internet, and which one to use is a personal choice. For an example, assume you want more information about the doctor who was killed at the Alamo in the Texas Revolution. First, you need keywords for the search engine to use. In this case, "Texas" and "Alamo doctor" may be good first choices. Too many words limit the results; too few words result in too many "hits." Use quotation marks around any phrase that you want used as a group and not as independent words.

Go to your favorite search engine website on the Internet and enter your keywords in the appropriate line. Click "Search" or hit the "Enter" key. A list of websites, usually with the most appropriate ones first, will appear on your screen. Click on any website link that seems to meet your needs. A new page will appear from that website. If this is not the information you need, click the "Back" option on the tool bar to return to the search results and try a different site.

If you decide to use the information, you may choose to print it in order to retain a hard copy of the information. This printout will usually also have the web address, or URL (Universal Resource Locator), of the site in case you wish to return to the site at a later time for more information. One website will usually link, or connect, to other websites that have additional information. It is very easy to get distracted by irrelevant information, so remain focused on the topic.

Once you have found all the information you need from one website, return to the search result page and try additional websites. You may need to refine your search criteria. If you use the information in a report, make sure you document your source. If you use someone else's work without giving them appropriate credit, it is called plagiarism. Plagiarism is not only unethical, but it is illegal as well.

Be aware that all information on the Internet is not necessarily true. Most information is true and valuable, but a significant amount is completely or partially false. You should take the responsibility of verifying whether the information you obtain is valid before using it.

Privacy and the Internet

Since the Internet connects you to people all over the world, you must protect your privacy when using the Internet. Because you do not know if you can trust everyone who is connected to the Internet, some precautions are necessary.

1. All computers connected to the Internet should have a good software program for virus protection installed. It should be upgraded regularly.
2. Never enter ANY personal information about yourself or your family on ANY website. This includes names, addresses, phone numbers, and social security numbers.
3. Never agree to a personal meeting with anyone you meet on the computer. All safety rules designed to protect you from strangers apply when using the Internet.
4. Never go to websites that you know you should not see or that you are forbidden to use. If in doubt, don't go there.
5. Keep your parents informed. Tell your parents, guardian, or another responsible adult if something on the Internet makes you uncomfortable. Make sure a responsible adult has your password so that he/she can help keep you safe. Do not give out your password to anyone else.
6. Never use a web camera without permission.
7. Go to www.cybercrime.gov/rules for additional tips on how to use the Internet safely.

E-mail

E-mail, or electronic mail, is a great means for communicating with people across town or on the other side of the world. However, e-mail is different than regular mail. The guidelines below will help you use e-mail correctly.

1. Type an appropriate message title in the Subject line.
2. Keep your e-mail paragraphs short and to the point.
3. Try not to use special type fonts because some computers may not display them properly.
4. Put space between paragraphs by skipping a line.
5. Use appropriate spelling, capitalization, and punctuation.
6. Do not get in the habit of forwarding messages to everyone in your address book. Only forward appropriate messages to a minimum number of people.
7. Do not reply to the "to be removed from our mailing list" messages. This only verifies your e-mail address is valid and will result in even more SPAM, or unwanted e-mail.
8. Tell an adult immediately if you get an e-mail that scares you or upsets you.
9. If it is going to require some time to respond to an e-mail, you may wish to go offline, compose your message, and then "paste" it into your e-mail. This will minimize your connection time to the Internet.

Computer Terms

Whether you use a computer at home or at school, you will need to have a working knowledge of the most commonly used technology terms. Becoming familiar with computer terms and what they mean will be helpful as you learn more about computers. The definitions for the technology and computer terms below will guide you as you gain knowledge of how computers work.

Computer Files to Organize Writing

Think of your computer as a file cabinet that organizes and stores your writing in electronic folders. The number of folders you can create is almost unlimited. You can create separate folders for every type of writing that you do: stories, poems, reports, letters, and unfinished pieces. You can put these writing folders on your hard drive or copy your files onto other electronic storage devices. It is easy for you to add new documents or files throughout the year.

Bit	the smallest unit of measurement for information (This is sometimes referred to as binary code, which has two positions. It can be thought of as a computational quantity that takes on one of two values such as "0/1", "on/off" or "yes/no.")
Byte	a sequence of eight bits processed as a single unit of alphanumeric data that represents one character of information
Megabyte Gigabyte Terabyte	Megabyte (MB) is a unit of information equal to one million bytes. Gigabyte (GB) is a unit of information equal to one billion bytes or one million megabytes. Terabyte (TB) is a unit of information equal to a trillion bytes or one million gigabytes. Most computer memory and storage are referred to as megabyte, gigabyte, or terabyte.
CD-ROM	a portable storage medium for computers (It consists of a plastic-like, round disk upon which data or music has been burned by a laser. CD-ROM's typically hold approximately 700 megabytes of data.)
CPU	Central Processing Unit; the main brain of a computer system that contains the electrical parts that interpret and execute the commands necessary for data processing
cursor	a mechanism, usually a square or bar, blinking on a computer screen (The cursor indicates where the next character typed will appear or where the next command issued will be performed.)
data	pieces of information before they are formatted and organized into usable facts
disk drive	an internal computer component for accessing data stored on a floppy disk or a hard drive (The term "disk drive" is sometimes used to refer to a hard drive.)
document	an electronic file typically associated with a word-processing program
DVD	Digital Video Disc; a DVD is a computer-storage medium, similar in size to a CD-ROM, but holding approximately 4700 megabytes (4.7 GB) of data. (A single DVD is typically used to hold a full-length motion picture.)
floppy disk	a rectangular plastic portable storage medium used to store data for computers, holding approximately 1.44 megabytes of data (Early versions were flexible, hence the name "floppy disks," but current ones are rigid.)
font	a set of typeface glyphs, or letters and numbers (Fonts vary in size and artistic representation and can be used by word-processing applications on computers.)
hard copy	any electronic computer data file that has been printed on paper
hard drive	a storage medium for storing large amounts of data on a computer system (Typical hard disks now store thousands of megabytes, or gigabytes, of data.)
hardware	any part of a computer, or its accessories, that is physical, such as the keyboard, mouse, monitor, CPU, and printer
keyboard	an accessory for a computer. (It consists of typewriter-style keys, usually arranged in the standard keyboard arrangement, which is sometimes identified as QWERTY.)
menu	a list of options or commands shown on a monitor screen that is available to a user and allows the user to execute any command of choice

Continued on next page. >>>

Continued from previous page.

monitor	that part of a computer system that displays information on a screen and allows the user to interact with the system
mouse	a small input device used to position a cursor on a document and execute commands
printer	a computer accessory that prints hard copies of electronic documents
RAM	Random Access Memory; the most common computer memory used by programs to perform necessary tasks while the computer is on (This integrated circuit memory chip allows information to be stored or accessed in any order, and all storage locations are equally accessible.)
ROM	Read Only Memory; the contents of a memory chip that can be accessed and read but cannot be changed, also known as fixed storage (This chip allows the computer to start the system when it is turned on.)
software	programs that tell computers what tasks to accomplish, also referred to as Applications (Software programs are nonphysical components of a computer system and are written by human programmers.)

Word Processing Terms

Computer users must have a working knowledge of the terminology and commands used in word processing. These commands can be executed from a menu on the screen or by typing a series of keys on the keyboard.

close	a command that allows you to exit a document
copy	a command that puts a selected (highlighted) object or text into a computer's memory for pasting into another location
cut	a command that removes highlighted text and places it into a storage area for later use
delete	a key or a command that removes highlighted text (Deleted text is not saved for later use.)
find	a command that locates specified letters, words, or phrases in a document
font	a menu item that allows you to choose a typestyle (Times New Roman, Courier, etc.)
new	a command that creates a new document
open	a command that brings up and displays a document from existing files
page break	a command that ends a page wherever you want it to end and creates a new page
paste	a command that allows copied or cut text to be inserted at a different location in the current document or in another document
print	a command that produces a printout (hardcopy) of the current document
exit/quit	a command that exits/quits the current application
return	an "enter" key that sends the cursor to the next line
save	a command that keeps all changes in a document for later use
select	a command to highlight chosen text
shift	a key that allows capital letters to be typed (It is also used for various other commands.)
spelling	a command that checks the spelling of the words in a document
tab	a command or key that moves the cursor to the right at specified intervals

Internet Terms

Internet users must have a working knowledge of the terminology and commands used in searching the web or using e-mail. A list of common terms relating to the Internet is provided below.

address book	a list of e-mail addresses and other important information most frequently used by an individual
browser	an application to view web pages such as Netscape, Internet Explorer, etc.
chat room	a place for an interactive conversation through the Internet by using the keyboard
cookies	software technology that collects (gathers) information of all users that visit a particular website
download	a process used to copy a file from the Internet to a user's computer
DSL	Digital Subscriber Line; a fast method of connection to the Internet
dial-up	a slower method to connect to the Internet
e-mail (mail)	electronic mail messages sent through the Internet
e-mail address	an electronic mail address for an individual computer user
forward mail	a process to send a copy of an e-mail message to another computer user
home page	the web page that appears when a web browser is started
IP address	a number assigned to a user's computer by a web server for the purpose of tracking the user's use or habits of what sites are visited
Internet	a world-wide collection of computers networked together
junk mail	unwanted e-mail, usually soliciting money (also called SPAM)
instant messaging	real-time, person-to-person interaction through the Internet
modem	a computer accessory that enables a computer to connect to other computers, such as the Internet, through a connection, using a standard telephone line or cable wire
news groups	an Internet group of users sharing an interest in a common topic
password	a series of unique characters that must be entered to access some websites, personal or company accounts, some files or directories, etc.
SSL	Secure Sockets Layers; a way to protect private information between web servers
search engine	an application used to find appropriate websites by entering in "keywords" of a subject
send	button (or option) that sends an e-mail into the Internet
SPAM	unwanted junk e-mail messages sent in large quantities
surfing	exploring the Internet
URL	Universal or Uniform Resource Locator; unique address used to identify a document, file, web page, web site, etc.
upload	a process of sending a file to another user's computer
virus	a disguised program that inserts itself into programs of other computers to perform a malicious action such as destroying data or an entire hard drive
www	World Wide Web; refers to the network of computers that make up the Internet
web address	*see **URL***; characters keyed in a web browser to get to a particular website
web cam	an electronic camera device used to send images over the Internet

Glossary

A

Action verb: a verb that shows a state of action and tells what the subject does. (*Sara **runs** home.*)

Adjective: a word that describes, or modifies, a noun or pronoun; one of the eight parts of speech. (***That black** dog jumped on the bed.*)

Adverb: a word that describes, or modifies, a verb, adjective, or another adverb; one of the eight parts of speech. (*The employees worked **feverishly**.*)

Alliteration: the repetition of consonant sounds at the beginning of words; used mostly in poetry. (***Five fine feathered fowls***)

Analogy: a kind of reasoning based on comparing one pair of words with another pair of words that are related in the same way. (*hand : glove :: sock : foot*) (*purpose or use relationship*)

Antecedent: the noun to which a pronoun refers. (*The **cat** devoured **its** food.*)

Antonyms: words that have opposite meanings. (*black, white*)

Apostrophe: a punctuation mark (') used in contractions and possessive nouns. (*Harvey **won't** work on Saturday. **Mary's** car was parked in the street.*)

Appositive: a word, phrase, title, or degree used directly after a noun to rename it. (*Sally, **my best friend**, helped me with the decorations.*)

Article adjectives: specific adjectives (**a, an, the**) that come before a noun. (***A** bee stung me. I ate **an** orange at lunch. **The** paper was not delivered on time.*)

Assonance: the repetition of vowel sounds within words; used mostly in poetry. (*low moan*)

Audience: person or people that read, listen, or watch something.

Autobiography: nonfiction writing in which the author tells about his own life.

Auxiliary verb: *See* helping verb.

B

Biography: a nonfiction writing in which the author tells about another person's life.

Brainstorm: to develop, broaden, or elaborate ideas.

C

Capitalization: the use of capital letters in certain grammatical situations, such as to denote a proper noun or the beginning of a sentence.

Case: the position of nouns and pronouns in a sentence that shows whether they are used as subjects (*nominative or subjective case*), objects (*objective case*), or possessive words (*possessive case*).

Classification: the grouping of items into categories based on their similarities.

Clause: a group of words that has a subject and a verb. A clause that expresses a complete thought is an independent clause. A clause that does not express a complete thought is a dependent clause.

Colon: a punctuation mark (:) used to separate a sentence from a list of words or hours from minutes or words in an analogy.

Comma: a punctuation mark (,) used to separate items in a series, appositives, cities from states, dates, compound sentences, complex sentences, and in a variety of other grammatical situations.

Comma splice: a punctuation error in which two independent clauses are joined by a comma only. (*The doorbell rang, Jane answered the door.*)

Common noun: a noun referring to any person, place, or thing rather than to a specific person, place, or thing. (*desk, boys, playground*)

Comparative form: the form of an adjective or adverb that compares two people, places, or things. To make comparative forms, add -er, -ly, -ful or more to the simple form. (*slower, more generous*)

Comparison/contrast: a type of writing in which the author's purpose is to tell how things are alike and how things are different.

Complete predicate: the main verb and all the words that modify the verb in a sentence. (*That red car raced down our street.*)

Glossary

Complete subject: the subject noun or pronoun and all the words that modify it. (*That red car raced down our street.*)

Complex sentence: a sentence made by joining two clauses together: an independent clause and a subordinate clause. (*The windows lock **when the store is closed.***)

Compound sentence: a sentence containing two independent clauses and no dependent clauses. (*The girls rode the motorcycles, **and** the boys rode the four-wheelers.*)

Compound subject: two or more subjects in a sentence that are joined by the words and, or, or but. (***Michael** and **Judy** worked on a project in science class.*)

Compound verb: two or more verbs that are joined by the words and, or, or but. (*Michelle **sang** and **danced** in the talent contest.*)

Conjunction: a word used to connect other words, phrases, clauses, or sentences. The three most common conjunctions are **and**, **or**, **but**; one of the eight parts of speech. (*Sally **and** David played the violin in the recital.*)

Contraction: a word formed by combining two words and adding an apostrophe to replace the letter or letters that have been left out. (*did not / didn't*)

Coordinate conjunction: a word that connects words, phrases, or sentences of equal importance. The three most common coordinate conjunctions are **and**, **or**, **but**. (*The weather was sunny, **but** the wind made it cool.*)

Creative writing: a type of writing in which the author's purpose is to entertain through stories, poems, plays, etc.

D

Declarative sentence: a sentence that makes a statement. (*I went to work with my dad.*)

Degree of comparison: adding er, est, more, most or making a word change to an adjective or adverb so that it shows a comparison to something else. (*big, bigger, biggest / beautiful, more beautiful, most beautiful / bad, worse, worst*)

Descriptive writing: a type of writing in which the author's purpose is to describe.

Direct object: a noun or pronoun that receives the action of the verb in a sentence. A direct object tells what or whom after the verb. (*Amy took her **books** to the library.*)

Double negative: a grammatical error involving the use of two negative words in the same sentence. (*The plumber **can't** find **nothing** wrong with our sink.*)

E

Editing: the fourth step in the writing process. Editing involves checking and correcting mistakes in spelling, grammar, usage, capitalization, and punctuation.

Exclamatory sentence: a sentence that expresses strong feeling. (*My car is on fire!*)

Expository: a type of writing in which the author's purpose is to explain or inform.

F

Fact: a specific statement that can be looked up, measured, counted, or otherwise proven. (*John is six feet tall.*)

Fiction: stories about people, places, or things that are not true even though the author may use ideas based on real people or events.

Figurative language: *See* Figure of speech.

Figure of speech: a poetic device, sometimes called figurative language, that uses words to create images that compare one thing to another. Three figures of speech are simile, metaphor, and personification.

First person point of view: the writer writes as though he is personally involved in what is happening. The writer uses the personal pronouns I, we, me, us, my, our, mine, and ours. (***We** will leave for **our** vacation.*)

Fragment: an incomplete sentence. A fragment is missing one or more of the core parts: a subject, a verb, or a complete thought. (*After the game.*)

Future tense: the form of a verb that refers to a future action or future state of being. (*She **will ride** the bus home after school today. She **will be** a good teacher.*)

Glossary

G

Genre: a category that identifies what type of writing a piece of literature is. (*essays, poems, short stories, plays, etc.*)

H

Helping verb: a verb or verbs that combine with a main verb. Helping verbs are also called auxiliary verbs. (*He **did** not help his brother with his homework.*)

Homographs: words that are spelled alike but have different meanings and/or different pronunciations. (*You have the **right** answer. Turn into the **right** lane.*) (*He will **lead** us to a safe place. The metal pipe contained **lead**.*)

Homonyms: words that sound alike but have different meanings and spellings. Homonyms can be a combination of homographs and homophones.

Homophones: words that sound alike but have different meanings and spellings. (*write, right*)

I

Imperative sentence: a sentence that gives a command and has an understood subject. (*Wash the dishes.*)

Indefinite pronoun: a pronoun that does not refer to a definite person, place, thing, or idea. (*anybody, everything*)

Indirect object: a noun or pronoun that receives what the direct object names. An indirect object tells to whom or for whom after the direct object. (*I gave **you** the invitation.*)

Interjection: a word or short phrase that expresses strong or mild feeling; one of the eight parts of speech. (*No! Oh my! Wow! No way! Great!*)

Internet: an international network of computers.

Intransitive verb: a verb in a sentence that does not have an object to receive the action. (*He **laughed**.*)

Inverted order: an adverb, prepositional phrase, or helping verb that is located at the beginning of the complete subject and modifies the predicate. (*Today, we / went to school. During the play, Jan / sang a song. Did he / write that song?*)

I

Irregular verb: a verb that forms the past tense by having a vowel change or by not changing at all. (*I **know** his name. / I **knew** his name. Today, I **let** my dog eat a treat. Yesterday, I **let** my dog eat a treat.*)

J

Jargon: the language of a special group or profession.

Journal: a written record of personal thoughts and feelings.

L

Linking verb: a verb that connects the subject of a sentence with a word that renames or describes the subject. (*That man **is** a clown. That dress **was** beautiful.*)

M

Main idea: the most important idea in a paragraph or an essay.

Metaphor: a figure of speech that compares things by stating that one thing is something else. Metaphors use linking verbs such as am, is, are, was, and were. (*The **fog was a curtain** during the morning hours.*)

Modify: to describe another word. Adjectives and adverbs are words that describe, or modify, other words in a sentence.

N

Narrative: a type of writing in which the author's purpose is to tell a story.

Natural order: a sentence with all the subject parts located before the verb and the predicate parts located after the verb. (*We / went to the school play yesterday.*)

Nonfiction: information and stories that are true. Autobiographies, biographies, and reference books are nonfiction.

Noun: a word that names a person, place, thing, or idea; one of the eight parts of speech. (*Mother, desk, Alaska*)

O

Object of the preposition: the noun or pronoun after a preposition in a sentence. (*She rode down the **elevator** with her **friend**.*)

Glossary

Object pronoun: a pronoun that functions as an object of the preposition, a direct object, or an indirect object in a sentence. (Common object pronouns: **me**, **us**, **him**, **her**, **it**, **them**, **you**.) (*He gave **me** the ball. He went with **us** to town.*)

Opinion: a personal belief, judgment, or feeling held by one or more persons that cannot be checked or proven. (*John is a considerate young man.*)

P

Paragraph: a group of sentences that is written about one particular subject, or topic.

Parallel form: the wording of topics, subtopics, and details within sections of an outline so that they begin in the same way: as nouns, verbs, noun phrases, verb phrases, prepositional phrases, etc.

Part of speech: one of eight categories of words that have different functions within a sentence. The eight parts of speech are noun, verb, adverb, adjective, pronoun, preposition, conjunction, and interjection.

Past tense: a verb form that shows that something has happened in the past. (*The cars **raced**. The children **sang**.*)

Period: a punctuation mark (**.**) used at the end of a declarative or imperative sentence to signify the end of a complete thought. A period is also used at the end of abbreviations, initials, and after Roman numerals, Arabic numbers, and letters of the alphabet in an outline.

Personal pronoun: pronouns like *I*, *we*, *me*, *he*, *she*, *it*, *they*, and *you* that refer either to a person, people, or things.

Personification: a figure of speech used to compare things by giving human qualities to something nonhuman. (*The door eyed the visitor with contempt and refused to open.*)

Persuasive: a type of writing in which the author's purpose is to convince someone to agree with his/her opinion.

Plural noun: more than one person, place, thing, or idea. (*cats, glasses, children, women*)

Poetry: one of the oldest and most artistic forms of literature. Poetry is both visual and auditory and may include rhyme, rhythm, and various figures of speech.

Point of view: the writer's use of personal pronouns to show who is telling a story. First-person point of view uses the pronouns: *I*, *we*, *me*, *us*, *my*, *our*, *mine*, and *ours*. Second-person point of view uses the pronouns: *you*, *your*, and *yours*. Third-person point of view uses the pronouns: *he*, *his*, *him*, *she*, *her*, *hers*, *it*, *its*, *they*, *their*, *theirs*, and *them*.

Possessive noun: the name of a person, place, or thing that owns something. The possessive noun will have either an apostrophe before the s (**'s**) or an apostrophe after the s (**s'**). The apostrophe makes a noun show ownership. (Kim's car)

Possessive pronoun: a pronoun that shows ownership and takes the place of a possessive noun. (Common possessive pronouns: **my**, **our**, **his**, **her**, **its**, **their**, **your**.)

Predicate adjective: an adjective in the predicate of a sentence that modifies the simple subject. It tells what kind of subject. (*Her new dress is absolutely **gorgeous**!*)

Predicate nominative: another name for a predicate noun or a predicate pronoun.

Predicate noun: a noun located in the predicate of a sentence that means the same thing as the simple subject. (*Dad is an excellent **carpenter**.*)

Prefix: a word part added to the beginning of a base word to change its meaning. (***bi**monthly, **inter**state, **un**happy*)

Preposition: a word that shows the relationship of its object to other words in the sentence; one of the eight parts of speech. (*The little boy walked **beside** his mother.*) (*The Preposition Flow Jingle gives a list of common prepositions.*)

Prepositional phrase: a group of words that starts with a preposition, ends with a noun or pronoun object, and includes any modifiers of that object. (*The little boy walked **beside his mother**.*)

Present tense: a verb form that shows that something is happening in the present. (*The cars **race**. The children **run**.*)

Prewriting: the first step in the writing process. The planning and organization for writing is done during this stage.

Pronoun: a word that can take the place of a person, place, thing, or idea in a sentence; one of the eight parts of speech.

Glossary

Proofreading: part of the fourth step in the writing process. Proofreading involves checking sentences or paragraphs for mistakes in spelling, grammar, usage, capitalization, and punctuation.

Propaganda: an organized effort to spread ideas or information in an attempt to change the opinions and actions of a group of people. Propaganda usually contains some accurate facts along with exaggerations and untruths.

Proper adjective: an adjective that is formed from a proper noun. Proper adjectives are always capitalized no matter where they are located in the sentence. (*Mexican food, English language, French bread, Japanese maple*)

Proper noun: a noun that names a specific, or particular, person, place, or thing. Proper nouns are always capitalized no matter where they are located in the sentence. (*Charles is my dad. We are moving to Peru.*)

Publishing: the sixth step in the writing process. Publishing is sharing the final copy of a writing with others.

Purpose of writing: the author's reason for writing. The purpose of writing determines the organization of a piece of writing.

Q

Question and Answer Flow: an oral set of questions and answers used to find the function of each word in a sentence.

Quotations: the exact words spoken by someone in a piece of writing. Quotation marks (" ") are used to indicate a direct quotation. Quotations are also called dialogue in narrative writing.

R

Regular verb: a verb that is made past tense by adding an **–ed**, **–d**, or **–t** ending. (*want, wanted; race, raced; mean, meant*)

Repetition: saying or doing something again and again.

Revision: the third step in the writing process. Revising is the process of improving the content and meaning of a sentence or paragraph.

Rhyme: the sound-alike quality of words, regardless of their spellings (*do/few, made/paid*). Rhyme may be of two types: end rhymes and internal rhymes. Rhyme is often used in poetry.

Rough draft: the second step in the writing process. A rough draft is a first attempt at putting all prewriting ideas from a Prewriting Map into sentences and paragraphs.

Run-on sentence: a grammatical error that occurs when two or more sentences are written continuously without the required punctuation.

S

Second-person point of view: used in giving directions. The writer uses the pronouns you, your, or yours almost exclusively to name the person or thing being addressed. (*You may leave now.*)

Semicolon: a punctuation mark (;) used to join two independent clauses in a compound sentence.

Simile: a figure of speech that compares things by using the words like or as. (*Jeff is as tall as a giraffe. My brother jumps like a frog.*)

Simple form: the form of an adjective or adverb that is used when no comparison is made. (*pretty, fast, good*)

Simple predicate: another name for the verb in a sentence. (*Our soccer team played well yesterday.*)

Simple sentence: a sentence having three core parts: a subject, a verb, and a complete thought.

Simple subject: another name for the subject noun or subject pronoun in a sentence. (*Our soccer team played well.*)

Simple tense: the present, past, and future tense of verbs. (*walk, walked, will walk*)

Singular noun: only one person, place, thing, or idea. (*cat, glass, child, woman*)

Slang: informal language used in everyday conversation. It is not considered appropriate in formal writing. (*dude, cool*)

Stanza: divisions of a rhyming poem.

Strophe: divisions of a poem that does not rhyme.

Subject noun: a noun that tells who or what a sentence is about.

540

Subject pronoun: a pronoun that tells who or what a sentence is about. (Common subject pronouns: **I, we, he, she, it, they, you.**)

Subordinate clause: a clause having a subject and a verb but not expressing a complete thought. (*When the bell rang for class.*)

Subordinate conjunction: a connecting word that introduces a subordinate clause. (*after, before, since, etc.*)

Suffix: a word part added to the end of a base word to change its meaning. (*care**less**, advance**ment**, joy**ful**, hugg**able**.*)

Superlative form: an adjective or adverb that compares three or more people, places, or things. To make the superlative form, add –est or most to the simple form. (*fast**est**, **most** nervous*)

Synonym: words that have similar, or almost the same, meanings. (*guess, surmise*)

T

Tall tale: a humorous story that makes use of exaggeration, but it also includes believable events and situations.

Tenses: the forms of a verb that show when an action takes place. (*present tense, past tense, future tense.*)

Third-person point of view: the writer writes as though he is watching the events take place. The writer uses the pronouns he, his, him, she, her, hers, it, its, they, their, theirs, and them. (*He bought **his** new car today.*)

Topic: a word or group of words that tells what something is about.

Topic sentence: a sentence that states the main idea of a paragraph or essay.

Transition word: a word or phrase that shows a link between sentences and paragraphs. (*The Transition Words Jingle gives a list of common transition words.*)

Transitive verb: a verb that transfers action to a direct object in a sentence.

U

Underlining: a form of punctuation appropriate for the titles of books, magazines, works of art, ships, newspapers, motion pictures, etc.

V

Verb: a word in a sentence that expresses action (*see* action verb) or a state of being (*see* linking verb); one of the eight parts of speech.

Voice: the aspect of writing in which the writers' thoughts and personal viewpoints are clearly and genuinely revealed.

W

World Wide Web: a network of computers that makes up the Internet.

Writing process: the steps it takes to plan, write, rewrite and publish a final paper. Steps in the writing process include pre-writing, writing a rough draft, revising, editing, writing a final paper, and publishing.

Index

Linking verbs. *See* Verbs, linking

Listening,

as a response to poetry, 457, 461, 462, 465, 471,472

during share time,103, 391,454

in study skills, 5

in a discussion, 28, 78, 112, 142, 178, 204, 235, 261, 293, 319, 352, 373, 396, 413, 429, 449, 457, 461–462, 465, 471–472

to book review, 365,391

to discovery-time reports, 131, 163, 193, 225, 255, 284, 314, 344, 368, 390, 409

to follow instructions, 5

to oral presentations, 391, 392, 393

to oral review questions, 28, 78, 112, 142, 178, 204, 235, 261, 293, 319, 352, 373, 396, 413, 429, 449

to research reports, 493, 494

Literary terms, 456–474, 536–541

Literature, 456–474

M

Magazines, 479–480

Main idea, 58, 436–437, 538

Main topic in outlines, 441–442

Main verbs. *See* Verbs, main

Maps, 529

Mechanics.

See Capitalization; Punctuation

Media, 433, 516

Metaphor, 256, 456, 538

Modifiers, *See* Adjectives; Adverbs

N

Narratives. See Writing, narratives

Negatives, 387

News media, 433

Nonfiction, 309, 338, 339, 340, 525, 526, 527, 538

Non-supporting sentences.

See Sentences, non-supporting

Note-taking, 481, 482, 483

Noun jobs, 86, 331, 499

Nouns, 30, 50, 297, 324, 499, 504, 505, 512, 538

O

Objects, 80, 104, 206, 237, 263, 327, 500, 501, 504

Opinions, 430, 431, 539

Oral language. *See* speaking

Oral review questions, 28, 78, 112, 142, 173, 204, 235, 261, 293, 319, 352, 373, 396, 413, 429, 449

Outlines, 62, 136, 167, 198, 441, 442, 488

P

Paragraphs.

See Writing Parts of speech,

Adjective, 34, 36, 37, 40, 50, 374, 376, 499, 505, 536

Adverb, 34, 35, 37, 50, 81, 144, 146, 147, 164, 499, 536

Conjunction, 116, 117, 132, 146, 178, 502, 537

Interjection, 174, 175, 194, 503, 538

Noun, 29, 30, 37, 50, 538

Preposition, 79, 80, 81, 104, 500

Pronoun, 113, 114, 115, 132

Verb, 29, 30, 209

Patterns, 31, 206, 263, 321, 375

Periodicals, 479, 524

Periods, 17, 539

Persuasive writing.

See Writing, persuasive

Plot, 288, 315

Plural nouns, 84, 297, 539

Poetry, 456–474

Points of view, 109, 539

Possessive nouns, 175, 176, 324, 539

Possessive pronouns.

See Pronouns, possessive

Practice sentence, 32, 36, 48, 50, 104, 132, 164, 194, 226, 344, 386

Predicate

Complete, 45, 85

Simple, 86

Predicate adjectives, 374, 375, 539

Predicate noun, 321, 539

Prefixes, 513, 539

Prepositions, 79, 80, 81, 88, 104, 500, 539

Prewriting.

See Writing process, prewriting

Pronouns

Antecedents, 354

Cases, 327

Indefinite, 356, 357

Object, 79, 80, 81, 236, 237

Possessive, 113, 115, 132

Subject, 113, 132

understood subject, 113, 114

Propaganda techniques, 430, 431, 433

Proper nouns, 84, 540

Publishing.

See Writing process, publishing

Punctuation, 17, 18, 19, 20

Purpose for writing, 540

Q

Question mark, 17

Quotation marks, 19

Quotations

Beginning, 267, 560

End, 268, 560

Other, 273, 560

Split, 269, 560

R

Reasons for reading, 436, 437

Research reports, 475, 478, 479, 480, 481, 489, 491

Revised sentence, 50, 104, 132, 164, 194, 226, 344, 386

Revising. *See* Writing process, revising

Rhyme, 456, 540

Rhythm, 456

Rough draft.

See Writing process, rough draft

Run-on. *See* Sentences, run-on

S

Sentences

complete, 31

compound, 147, 148, 180, 537

compound parts, 117, 118

complex, 179, 180, 537

declarative, 44–45, 512, 537

exclamatory, 44–45, 512, 537

imperative, 44–45, 114, 512, 538

interrogative, 44–45, 512

jingle, 22, 498

non-supporting, 53

pattern. *See* Pattern sentences

run-on, 148, 540

supporting, 53, 136, 167, 198

Setting, 288–289, 315–316

Sharing, 102–103, 131, 162, 163, 192, 193, 224, 225, 254, 255, 283, 284, 313, 314, 343, 344, 365, 367, 368, 390, 391, 393, 409, 460, 464, 469, 474, 494, 495

Simile, 456–474, 540

Simple predicate, 86, 540

Simple subject, 86, 540

Singular nouns, 84, 324, 540

Sources, 338, 433, 478–480

Speaking

discovery share time, 131, 163, 193, 225, 255, 284, 314, 344, 368, 390, 409

discussions, 4–8, 28, 35–36, 41, 58, 61, 63, 66, 69–73, 78, 112, 117, 131, 142, 163, 173, 193, 204, 207, 225, 235, 255, 258, 261, 264, 284, 292, 314, 319, 322, 324, 344, 352, 368, 373, 375, 390, 396, 409, 413, 429, 437–439, 449, 457–458, 460, 461–462, 464, 465, 469, 471–472, 474, 484–485

giving instructions, 514–515

guidelines for dramatic presentations, 390

guidelines for share time, 103, 131

interviews, 516

sharing book reviews, 365